Studies in Church History

60

(2024)

THE CHURCH, HYPOCRISY AND DISSIMULATION

THE CHURCH, HYPOCRISY AND DISSIMULATION

EDITED BY

CATHERINE CUBITT
CHARLOTTE METHUEN
ANDREW SPICER

PUBLISHED FOR
THE ECCLESIASTICAL HISTORY SOCIETY
BY
CAMBRIDGE UNIVERSITY PRESS
2024

Published by Cambridge University Press & Assessment
on behalf of the Ecclesiastical History Society
University Printing House, Cambridge CB2 8BS, United Kingdom

First published 2024

ISBN 9781009567176

ISSN 0424–2084

SUBSCRIPTIONS: *Studies in Church History* is an annual subscription journal (ISSN 0424–2084). The 2024 subscription price (excluding VAT), which includes print and electronic access, is £144 (US $230 in the USA, Canada and Mexico) for institutions and £79 (US $127 in the USA, Canada and Mexico) for individuals ordering direct from the Press and certifying that the volume is for their personal use. An electronic-only subscription is also available to institutions at £87 (US $139 in the USA, Canada and Mexico). Special arrangements exist for members of the Ecclesiastical History Society.

Previous volumes are available online at www.cambridge.org/StudCH

Printed in Great Britain by Henry Ling Limited, The Dorset Press, Dorchester, DT1 1HD

A catalogue record for this publication is available from the British Library

Contents

Preface

Studies in Church History 60 collects papers presented at the Summer Conference held at the University of York in July 2022 and the Winter Meeting held online in January 2023, under the presidency of Professor Catherine Cubitt. The Summer Conference was seriously affected by falling on the hottest days ever recorded in the UK, which caused significant travel disruption. The president and editors are grateful to those who managed to attend nonetheless, and also to those who could not attend but gave their papers online.

The articles in this volume provide a range of fascinating insights into the understudied question of the role of hypocrisy in the Church. We are grateful to Professor Cubitt for proposing the theme. We also wish to thank the Society's Conference Secretary, Professor Elizabeth Tingle, for her meticulous and careful planning of both the Summer Conference and Winter Meeting, and to the Society's Secretary and Treasurer, Dr Jacqueline Rose and Simon Jenkins, for their invaluable contributions to the Society's work. Dr Rose stepped down as Secretary while this volume was in preparation.

The editors also wish to express their gratitude to all who offered contributions and submitted papers for consideration, and to those who peer reviewed the contributions. The volume has benefitted from Dr Alice Soulieux-Evans' careful work as assistant editor, and the editors are very grateful to the Society for funding her post. Studies in Church History 60 is the final volume to be co-edited by Professor Andrew Spicer. On behalf of the EHS Committee, we wish to express our thanks to him for his contribution not only to Studies in Church History as co-editor for volumes 51 to 60, but also for his introduction of a rigorous peer review system, his role in liaising with Cambridge University Press, but also for his vision for the Society as a whole through the reconceiving of the Winter Meeting and the initiation of the EHS book prize. We are very grateful to Professor Spicer for his inspirational contribution as co-editor.

The Ecclesiastical History Society is pleased to award the Kennedy Prize, for the best contribution by a postgraduate student, to Alice

Kinghorn for her fascinating article 'The Rev. John Stainsby and the "diffusion of Gospel truth" in Early Nineteenth-Century Jamaica.' The President's Prize, for the best article by an early career scholar, is awarded to Paula Tutty for her thought-provoking study '"In Defiance of his Cloth": Monastic (Im)piety in Late Antique Egypt.'

Charlotte Methuen
University of Glasgow

Andrew Spicer
Oxford Brookes University

Contributors

Emily Baylor
Postgraduate student, University of Edinburgh

Mark D. Chapman
Professor of the History of Modern Theology, University of Oxford

Catherine Cubitt
Professor Emerita of Medieval History, University of East Anglia

Dennis C. Dickerson
Reverend James Lawson Chair in History, Vanderbilt University

David Fletcher
Honorary Research Fellow, University of Warwick

Konstantinos Gravanis
Postdoctoral researcher, National and Kapodistrian University of Athens, Greece

Alice Kinghorn
Lecturer in British History, University of Gloucester

Sophie Lunn-Rockliffe
Associate Professor in Patristics, University of Cambridge

Simone Maghenzani
Dame Marilyn Strathern Associate Professor of History, Fellow and Director of Studies, Girton College, University of Cambridge

Edward G. Manger
Independent scholar and licensure candidate with the Associate Reformed Presbyterian Church

Charlotte Methuen
Professor of Ecclesiastical History, University of Glasgow

Adam Morton
Senior Lecturer in British History, Newcastle University

Iveta Nakládalová
Assistant Professor, Palacký University Olomouc, Czech Republic

David Parry
Lecturer in English, University of Exeter

Anna Pravdica
Postgraduate student, Department of History, University of Warwick

John Sabapathy
Professor of History, University College London

Ethan H. Shagan
Professor of History, University of California, Berkeley

Mark Smith
Associate Professor in History, University of Oxford

Paula Tutty
Freelance researcher, Liverpool

Christy Wang
JSPS Postdoctoral Fellow, The University of Tokyo

Peter Webster
Independent scholar, Chichester

William Whyte
Professor of Social and Architectural History, St John's College, Oxford

Abbreviations

ACW	J. Quasten and J. C. Plumpe, eds, Ancient Christian Writers
AV	Authorized [King James] Version
BIA	Borthwick Institute for Archives
BN	Bibliothèque nationale de France
Bodl.	Bodleian Library
CathHR	*Catholic Historical Review* (1915–)
CChr.CM	Corpus Christianorum, continuatio medievalis (1966–)
CChr.SL	Corpus Christianorum, series Latina (1953–)
ChH	*Church History* (1932–)
CRL	Cadbury Research Library, University of Birmingham
CSEL	Corpus Scriptorum Ecclesiasticorum Latinorum (Vienna, 1866–)
DOP	*Dumbarton Oaks Papers* (1941–)
DWL	Dr Williams's Library
EETS	Early English Text Society
EHR	*English Historical Review* (1886–)
ELH	*English Literary History* (1934–)
EME	*Early Medieval Europe* (1992–)
ESV	English Standard Version
ET	English translation
GCS	Die Griechischen Christlichen Schriftsteller
HC Deb.	House of Commons Debates
HistJ	*Historical Journal* (1958–)
HL Deb.	House of Lords Debates
HR	*Historical Research* (1986–)
HThR	*Harvard Theological Review* (1908–)
JBS	*Journal of British Studies* (1961–)
JECS	*Journal of Early Christian Studies* (1993–)
JEH	*Journal of Ecclesiastical History* (1950–)
JRH	*Journal of Religious History* (1960–)
JRS	*Journal of Roman Studies* (1911–)
JThS	*Journal of Theological Studies* (1899–)
LCL	Loeb Classical Library
LMA	London Metropolitan Archive
LPL	Lambeth Palace Library

LW	J. Pelikan and H. Lehmann, eds, *Luther's Works*, 55 vols (St Louis, MO, 1955–75)
n.d.	no date
NET	New English Translation
n.pl.	no place
NRSV	New Revised Standard Version
NRSVUE	New Revised Standard Version Updated Edition
OED	*Oxford English Dictionary*
P&P	*Past and Present* (1952–)
PH	*Parliamentary History* (1982–)
PL	J.-P. Migne, ed., Patrologia Latina, 217 vols + 4 index vols (Paris, 1844–65)
RTAM	*Recherches de théologie ancienne et médiévale* (1929–97)
SC	Sources Chrétiennes (Paris, 1941–)
SCH	Studies in Church History (1964–)
SCH Sub	Studies in Church History Subsidia, 14 vols (1978–2012)
SCJ	Sixteenth Century Journal (1970–2006)
s.v.	*sub verbo* ('under the word')
TNA	The National Archives (Kew)
TRHS	*Transactions of the Royal Historical Society* (1871–)
WA	J. K. F. Knaake et al., eds, *D. Martin Luthers Werke: Kritische Gesamtausgabe* (Weimar, 1883–)
TTH	Translated Texts for Historians

Introduction

> There are many different kinds of hypocrites, but the religious hypocrite is the first and most enduring of all.[1]

This collection of articles is the product of the Ecclesiastical History Society's Summer 2022 and Winter 2023 conferences on the theme of 'The Church, Hypocrisy and Dissimulation'. In the tradition of Studies in Church History, it brings together a varied set of discussions on a broad theme, approaching that subject from the perspective of different periods and places. The format is an ideal one for exploring concepts and phenomena across time and space. The contributions in this volume range from Sophie Lunn Rockliffe's article on early Christian and late antique teaching on the devil as deceiver, to those by William Whyte and Mark Chapman on debates about sexuality in the twentieth-century Church of England; and geographically takes in North Africa (Lunn-Rockliffe), Egypt (Tutty), France, Germany and Italy (Sabapathy, Methuen, Maghenzani, Cubitt), China and Japan (Nakladalova), Jamaica and the United States of America (Kinghorn, Wang, Manger and Dickinson) and England (Cubitt, Shagan, Pravdica, Fletcher, Morton, Parry, Smith, Baylor, Chapman, Webster, Whyte). The topics discussed in this volume embrace the diverse types of hypocritical and dissimulating behaviour which arise from the distance, at times the chasm, between Christian teaching and ecclesiastical action or, indeed, inaction. This includes the church's promotion and toleration of racism (Dickerson), and of fascism and Nazism (raised by Sabapathy); its support for and institutional failure to condemn and prohibit the inhumanity of slavery (Kinghorn, Dickerson); its failings over sexual abuse, particularly of minors (raised again by Sabapathy); and its intolerance of different sexual identities and its fostering of double standards (Whyte, Chapman).

The pithy observation by Judith Shklar which prefaces this introduction raises the question of whether the church is a special case, an institution peculiarly prone to hypocrisy. The theoretical modelling and deliberations of the organizational scientist, Nils Brunsson, on

[1] Judith Shklar, *Ordinary Vices* (Cambridge, MA, 1984), 47.

Studies in Church History 60 (2024), 1–16
doi: 10.1017/stc.2024.26

secular organizations and businesses may indicate as much, since the church possesses many features which he singles out as conducive to institutional hypocrisy. It has, for example, always been faced by competing pressures and demands by individuals and groups within it, seeking different things. It is, as Brunsson puts it, 'squeezed between ideology and practice'.[2] As an ancient institution, it has been and is subject to shifting demands. The institutional hypocrisy of the church is an issue addressed by a number of articles in this volume.

Foremost amongst the institutional hypocrisies of the church must be its support for, and toleration of, racism and slavery. Dennis Dickerson's 'Hypocrisy Defined, Hypocrisy Defied' both shines a fierce spotlight on the institutional church's hypocrisy and describes how black activists found a way to be true to the gospel in embracing non-violent protest. In the United States, the unification of the Methodist Church in 1939 combined two white churches and excluded the black, forcing it into a separate Central Jurisdiction, segregating black ministers and parishes. Black intellectuals found inspiration in Gandhi's campaign of non-violent opposition to British imperial colonialism in India. They opposed white racial violence with peaceful protest and action, and reclaimed Jesus's own lowly social status in a land colonized by the Romans as a model. Embracing non-violence enabled them to maintain their own Christian integrity while opposing white hypocrisy.

While institutional hypocrisy is an ancient feature of the church, there are historical questions about how and when discourses denouncing hypocrisy emerge. John Sabapathy's exploration of a series of fourteenth-century case studies uncovers the emergence of critical appraisals of institutional authority in the church's failure to live up to its moral claims. The case of Pope Boniface VIII, posthumously vilified by his enemies for his debauchery and atheism, laid bare the chasm between his conduct and his ambitions to elevate his position as pope, for example. Such unflinching critiques of ecclesiastical behaviour nurtured criticism of political double-dealing, such as that of Phillip IV of France and his regime which had brutally extinguished the Templars for their moral failings.

In the seventeenth century, the Congregation of Bishops and Regulars, a division of the papal Curia, actively impeded the

[2] Nils Brunsson, 'Organized Hypocrisy', in idem, *The Consequences of Decision-Making* (Oxford, 2007), 111–34, at 114.

implementation of the pastoral reforms of the Council of Trent by suppressing cases of clerical transgression and failing to support bishops in their diocesan disciplinary oversight to avoid scandal. Simone Maghenzani argues that this policy was justified by the defence of the honour of the church, a priority which could override Tridentine reforms and was seen as the operation of prudence, in line with Christ's exhortation to his disciples to be 'as wise as serpents' in their work of evangelization in a hostile world. The institutional hypocrisy described in Emily Baylor's article on the bitter controversies over the 1844 Brothel Suppression Act concerns the income generated for the dean and chapter of Westminster on rents from London properties occupied by brothels. This embarrassing fact was used by the first Earl Fitzhardinge to fatally undermine a bill sponsored by the bishop of Exeter designed to prevent the sexual exploitation of women, particularly minors. Baylor also highlights the hypocrisy embedded in the protection of property owners' rights and that of the powerful by the House of Lords: Fitzhardinge himself was a landowner and notorious rake.

As Baylor's account of the failure of the 1844 Brothel Suppression Act shows, institutional hypocrisy often combined with individual hypocrisy. The Rev. John Stainsby, the subject of Alice Kinghorn's article, was a missionary in early nineteenth-century Jamaica, a prominent advocate for the amelioration of slave conditions and for their education and conversion. His mission to disseminate the gospel to the slave population necessitated careful footwork with the plantocracy to ensure their toleration and facilitation of the mission. He, and other missionaries, needed the financial support and assistance of plantation owners to reach the enslaved. Stainsby thus worked within an institutional framework of hypocrisy, but this was conjoined to his personal hypocrisy in his ownership of thirty-six slaves. The distance between Christian teaching and slavery is glaringly indicated by the production of a 'Slave Bible' for use amongst the enslaved, in which roughly ninety per cent of the Old Testament and fifty per cent of the New was omitted to avoid passages which might inspire rebellion. Stainsby was a representative of the Church of England's work in promoting a pro-slavery form of Christianity.

The issue of hypocrisy within the church, both institutional and individual, is an important one. In other fields, hypocrisy may be tolerated or even regarded as a necessary and, indeed, useful tool. The question of whether hypocrisy was necessarily a bad thing was foregrounded by Judith Shklar's brilliant anatomy of hypocrisy and anti-hypocrisy in her *Ordinary Vices* (1984), in which she explores 'the mentality of those who put hypocrisy first' and concludes that such a mindset can impede compromise and undermine pluralism. It can, Shklar warns, lead to an obsession with conscience as the ultimate moral arbiter, with sincerity becoming a form of aggressive hypocrisy.[3] 'To put hypocrisy first entangles us in too much moral cruelty, exposes us too easily to misanthropy, and unbalances our politics.'[4] Students of politics and political thought have debated Shklar's defence of the utility of hypocrisy, refining her ideas. David Runciman, for example, distinguishes between different types of hypocrisy to explore its role in politics, while Dennis Thompson argues that the consequences of institutional hypocrisy are much graver than those of individual hypocrisy.[5] The dispassionate debate amongst political scientists has not been replicated within the church, where the allowability and utility of hypocrisy and dissimulation have been the subject of intense and divisive discussion and controversy. As Runciman observes: 'because hypocrisy always involves an element of pretence, it might be said that all forms of hypocrisy are a kind of lie.'[6] For Augustine of Hippo, lying, whether with good intentions or bad, could never be tolerated.[7] Augustine composed two treatises on the subject, *On Lying* and *Against Lying*, and pursued a ferocious argument with Jerome over the interpretation of Paul's rebuke of Peter in Galatians 2: 11–14 for his ceasing to eat with gentiles to avoid giving offence to Jewish Christians, despite believing that Jewish food restrictions were not applicable in the Christian faith.[8] Peter was therefore dissembling, observing Jewish laws without believing in their legitimacy. Similar issues were raised in the Reformation debates over adiaphora. The Bible could be mined for

[3] Shklar, *Ordinary Vices*, 45–86. See also the article by John Sabapathy in this volume.
[4] Shklar, *Ordinary Vices*, 86.
[5] David Runciman, *Political Hypocrisy: The Mask of Power from Hobbes to Orwell and Beyond* (Princeton, NJ, 2008); Dennis F. Thompson, *Restoring Responsibility Ethics in Government, Business and Healthcare* (Cambridge, 2004), 209–26; Brunsson, 'Organized Hypocrisy'.
[6] Runciman, *Political Hypocrisy*, 9.
[7] Paul J. Griffiths, *Lying: An Augustinian Theology of Duplicity* (Grand Rapids, MI, 2004).
[8] On this, see Perez Zagorin, *Ways of Lying: Dissimulation, Persecution, and Conformity in Early Modern Europe* (Cambridge, MA, 1990), 15–20; Frederic Amory, 'Whited Sepulchres: The Semantic History of Hypocrisy to the High Middle Ages', *Recherches de théologie ancienne et médiévale* 53 (1986), 5–39.

examples of hypocrisy and dissimulation by holy men and women: Paul, although he rebuked Peter, had himself stated: 'To the Jews I became as a Jew' (1 Corinthians 9: 20) [ESV]. In the Old Testament, for example, King Jehu pretended to be a pagan in order to assemble the priests of Baal and slaughter them (2 Kings 10: 18–28); while in the New Testament, Christ on the road to Emmaus feigned that he was going beyond the town to which the disciples were travelling (Luke 24: 28). On the other hand, other parts of Scripture were unequivocal in condemning hypocritical conduct, particularly the condemnations of the Pharisees in the New Testament for their false religion and pride. In Matthew 23: 27, Jesus compared the Pharisees to whited sepulchres, beautiful on the outside but full of filth within.

Scriptural teaching and the interpretation of the devil as the arch-deceiver, 'the father of lies' (John 8: 44) [ESV], was a powerful element in the Christian condemnation of, and anxiety over, deceit and lying. It was the snake's lie to Eve in the Garden of Eden which led to Adam's disobedience. Sophie Lunn-Rockliffe shows how such passages and their exegesis were used in denunciations of those thought to be heretics or schismatics to portray them as deceivers, diabolically possessed or inspired. Their demonic character was the product, not of their adherence to false teaching, but of their deceit in leading others into error. They were characterized as deceivers seducing others into heresy, not simply instruments of the devil, but his progeny. The discourse of demonic deceit could be deployed by both sides in conflicts over heresy and correct teaching, as Lunn-Rockliffe's case study of the Donatist controversy in fourth and fifth centuries demonstrates.

The continual danger of the deceiving devil, on the prowl to ensnare the faithful, was a sharp fear for Pope Gregory the Great, which was intensified by his sense of living in the last days of the world. The Bible taught that the Antichrist, whose advent preceded the last judgment, would lead the faithful into damnation by his false teaching. Furthermore, the period before his coming would be marked by an intensification of evil, when his forerunners, deceivers like him, would lead believers to their ruin. I argue in my own article that, for Gregory, false teaching encompassed not only heretical doctrine but a fake Christianity in which the external façade of piety masked interior sinfulness. Hypocrites, whose pride was disguised by the show of humility, undermined the church. Hypocrisy was the hallmark of the approaching end and of the Antichrist, the 'head of all hypocrites'.

The depictions of the *Sermon and Deeds of the Antichrist* in Luca Signorelli's fresco cycle (1499–1504) in the Cappella Nuova of Orvieto Cathedral were exceptionally innovative in their visual imagery. They show Antichrist occupied in preaching, the poison of his error fed into his ear by the devil himself, standing behind him. Konstantinos Gravanis emphasizes how this new iconography of the Antichrist was fuelled by contemporary eschatological anxieties, and argues that the image of debating friars in the Antichrist's audience and a discarded sketch of four demons as learned scholars may have been inspired by current criticism of clerical hypocrisy.

Biblical counter-examples of dissimulation and misleading behaviour, as well as the first half of Jesus's exhortation to his disciples to be 'as wise as serpents and innocent as doves' (Matthew 10: 16) [ESV], could be exploited to justify Christian deceptions. The question of whether and in what circumstances it was acceptable to dissemble was particularly pressing in the contexts of persecution and religious conflict and their aftermath. It is ironic that Augustine denounced the Donatists for purportedly advising their converts to deny their baptism in order to gain a second, Donatist one, given the rigorist stance of the Donatists in condemning Christians who had survived the Diocletian persecutions by making accommodations to Roman demands.[9] The embittered religious controversies of the Reformation in the sixteenth and seventeenth centuries raised the question with fresh urgency, with Nicodemism – the outward conforming to Roman Catholicism practised by some Protestants – stimulating extensive discussions over the issue of dissimulation, as well as Calvin's condemnation.[10] Iveta Nakládalová anatomizes the different forms of dissimulation which Roman Catholic missionaries to Japan and China were forced to adopt. These went beyond accommodations to local beliefs and customs to concealing the practice of faith, sometimes extending to opposition to the commands of the Congregation for the Propagation of the Faith, which required converts to make an oath of obedience, on the grounds that it would lead

[9] See the article by Sophie Lunn-Rockliffe in this volume.

[10] See the article by David Parry in this volume for a Dissenting critique of the hypocrisy induced by persecution and forced religious conformity. Compare also Zagorin, *Ways of Lying*; and Diarmaid MacCulloch, *Silence: A Christian History* (London, 2013), 163–84.

to their discovery and to persecution of the mission by the Chinese emperor. Most remarkably, Ferdinand Verbiest (1623–88), a leading member of the Jesuit Apostolate in China, envisaged the conversion of the Chinese Middle Kingdom by stealth, 'the secret and silent conversion' which would proceed unnoticed until Christianity was suddenly revealed to have prevailed.

Nakládalová highlights the forced circumstances of the Asian missions which could be seen to justify secret evangelization. Justifications of hypocrisy and dissimulation could be grounded in ideology and principles. Maghenzani situates the face-saving, obstructionist tactic of the Roman Curia within contemporary seventeenth-century understandings of politics, where hypocrisy could be regarded as a 'virtue of statesmanship'.[11] Christy Wang argues that a discourse of providentialism was used to legitimate and justify an egregious fraud carried out by John Davenport (d. 1670), a leading Congregationalist minister in New England. While Congregationalism required a pastor obtain permission from his existing church to move to another – a ruling which Davenport ostensibly advocated – he nonetheless practised forgery in order to take up a position in the First Church of Boston. The minister not only tampered with a letter from the New Haven church, converting it from a refusal to dismiss him into a permission, but also lied about this authorization. Davenport's blatant fraud was defended by him and his supporters on the grounds of providentialism, that his move to Boston was God's will. 'Providential pragmatism' enabled Congregationalists to 'navigate the ecclesiological ambiguity in a way that most benefitted themselves.'[12]

Such justifications of double standards and hypocrisy attracted the scorn of satirists: David Fletcher's survey of portrayals of religious hypocrisy in Restoration drama in England bristles with parodic casuistry. In Thomas Ashenden's play, *The Cheats* (1663), the character Scruple reasons his way into taking the oath of conformity so that he can accept a lucrative living, declaring: 'I have found an Expedient … . The Swearer is not bound to the meaning of the Prescriber of the Oath, or his own meaning'. 'I will Conform, Reform, Transform, Perform, Deform, Inform, any Form: —Form—Form— 'Tis but one syllable, and has no very ill sound—It may be swallowed.'[13]

11 See the article by Simone Maghenzani in this volume.
12 See the article by Christy Wang in this volume.
13 See the article by David Fletcher in this volume.

The casuistical justification of hypocrisy is also exploited as a trigger for humour in the joke books analyzed by Ethan Shagan.[14] These include jokes which satirize the excuses which could be made for impious behaviour. Other jokes home in on the distance between ideal Christian conduct and the messy realities of worldly life, such as the indifference of bored and deaf parishioners to the pompous preaching of priests, or the desire of parishioners for a Sunday lie-in on the day of rest. The tension between ideal and reality, and the accommodations made by the devout to the demands of everyday life, are highlighted in the studies by Paula Tutty and Mark Smith, which focus on the disparity between the lived actuality of holy men or revered figures, and their idealization. Tutty uses the letters of Apa John, a fourth-century holy man in Egypt, to examine the complexities of his social role, assisting and perhaps exploiting the difficulties of those who petitioned him for help. In contrast to hagiographical depictions of the holy man in late antique local society, which formed the source material for Peter Brown's seminal account, Apa John's correspondence shows the holy man berated for his lack of success and possibly also illicitly profiting from his petitioners. Mark Smith's comparison of the biography of William Wilberforce authored by his sons, Robert and Samuel, with the diaries kept by Wilberforce himself, casts a spotlight on the discrepancy between their idealization of their father and the everyday struggles and reality of his actual life. Robert and Samuel Wilberforce tailored their presentation of their father to fit the social and religious mores of their own day, downplaying his sympathy for Dissent, ironing out the mundane misery of flea-ridden accommodation, omitting his addiction to opium, and avoiding the hard-drinking reality of Georgian political culture. The literary construction of holy men and Christian heroes presented exemplars of the Christian life, a long tradition which surely exacerbated the pressures on individuals to align their inner and outer lives with unattainable ideals.

Peter Webster takes a different type of literary representation, the novels of Iris Murdoch, to explore how Murdoch explored the tensions between the ministry and lives of churchmen, and their place in a secularized, increasingly unbelieving society. Her novels depict the predicament of priests inwardly experiencing a loss of faith while still outwardly performing their pastoral office, and the

[14] See the article by Ethan Shagan in this volume on the parson's excuse for kneeling.

rejection of clerical authority and ministry by a laity increasingly distrustful of priestly spiritual counsel. The intervention of a priest at moments of personal crisis is depicted not as compassionate but as complacent, an intrusion into intimate matters which serves the priestly ego rather than the individual in need. These priests are subtly drawn versions of the predatory hypocrites beloved of the seventeenth-century plays described by Fletcher.

The tensions generated by the distance between the messy and sometimes brutal realities of everyday life and the ideals of Christian teaching are reflected in preoccupations with hypocrisy. Anxieties over hypocrisy coincide with the prominence of sincerity and authenticity in Christian piety: they form two sides of the same spiritual coin. William Whyte's account of the outing of bishops thought to be gay in the 1990s demonstrates the importance of this connection. He argues that the campaigns by OutRage! and other movements to name gay clergymen and to unmask their dissimulation arose through a conjunction of the rise of gay activism and the 'expressive revolution' which 'placed a premium on self-discovery and self-realization'.[15]

The primacy of sincerity and authentic faith fostered disciplines of self-examination and personal doubt. In his *Being Protestant in Reformation Britain* (2013), Alec Ryrie analyzes the spiritual and emotional aspects of sixteenth- and seventeenth-century Protestant culture, with its emphasis on prayer, penitence and self-scrutiny. Believers were worried about being stone-hearted and prized deep religious feeling: the perils of antinomianism, self-righteousness and over-confidence in one's salvation were widespread fears. An emphasis on outward fervour led to accusations of hypocrisy by others and also to inner anxieties about false piety. Hypocrisy was identified not only in those who strived to deceive others, but in those who deceived themselves.[16] In seventeenth-century New England puritan communities, the importance of grace and an authentic conversion experience led to advocacy of intensive self-scrutiny and, with it, an obsession with uncovering hypocrisy within the heart. This

[15] See the article by William Whyte in this volume.

[16] Alec Ryrie, *Being Protestant in Reformation Britain* (Oxford, 2013), 27–62, 104–5, 461–2. See also Andy Dorsey, 'A Rhetoric of American Experience: Thomas Shepard's Cambridge Confessions and the Discourse of Spiritual Hypocrisy', *Early American Literature* 49 (2014), 629–62.

seventeenth-century puritan formulation of hypocrisy curiously echoes the meditations of Pope Gregory the Great in his *Moralia* in which hypocrites are not only those who feign piety but also those whose inner life is empty, who deceive themselves in their parade of virtue. They lack the constant inner vigilance essential to faith and do not practice *discretio*, the discernment of good and evil.[17] The discipline of self-scrutiny required by Gregory is not so very distant from the continual self-monitoring displayed in William Wilberforce's diaries, which facilitated his sons' biography of him and enabled Mark Smith's detection of their editorial trickery. Wilberforce critically recorded his habits of sociability and consumption, assessing them against his desired self-regulation, for example, chastising himself for laughing 'improperly at something rather profane Pitt said', a confession which today seems amusing but was clearly heartfelt.[18]

Given the prominence of sincerity in Protestant, and particularly puritan, spirituality, it is not surprising that advice on how to nurture sincerity was offered by preachers.[19] Anna Pravdica takes four figures from seventeenth-century England – Nicholas Lockyer, a Cromwellian Independent; the Welsh Presbyterian Christopher Love, who was executed for his part in a monarchist plot; James Oldfield, a Church of England minister in Norfolk; and John Tillottson, the latitudinarian archbishop of Canterbury – and explores the differences and similarities in their spiritual counsel. All placed sincerity at the heart of their teaching. but differed as to what this meant and how Christians should manifest their sincerity. For Oldfield preaching to his rural parishioners, they should concern themselves with the battle against sin rather than judging the hypocrisy of others; while Archbishop Tillotson advocated moderation and toleration, criticizing the hypocrisy of those who felt their godliness entitled them to censure others. Lockyer, on the other hand, argued that the sincere should oppose the hypocrisy they saw around them. His version of sincerity was effectively the hypocrisy decried by Oldfield and Tillotson.

17 See the article by Catherine Cubitt in this volume.

18 See the article by Mark Smith in this volume.

19 See also Lionel Trilling, *Sincerity and Authenticity* (Cambridge, MA, 1971); David Parry, '"A Divine Kind of Rhetoric": Rhetorical Strategy and Spirit-Wrought Sincerity in English Puritan Writing', *Christianity and Literature* 67 (2017), 113–38.

The body of seventeenth- and eighteenth-century sermons preached in Exeter which David Parry considers provides fertile ground for his exploration of the integral bond between hypocrisy and sincerity amongst Dissenters. The imperative of absolute inward sincerity resulted in urgent questions about the outward signs of inner faith, ritual and Christian conduct, and whether behaviour and the practice of piety could really be an indicator of internal conversion and grace. The fearful deceits of the devil were such that even those who earnestly sought salvation could be seduced into a counterfeit of sincere faith through a demonic imitation of the effects of divine grace, which could only be detected and opposed by rigorous self-examination. Hypocrisy was ubiquitous, manifest in the overt performance of false religion, but also in the deceits of the human heart. The devil could imitate the effect of divine grace, leading the pious into sinful hypocrisy and his deceptions encompassed the practice of vice dressed up as virtue, such as covetousness passed off as thrift.

The early modern era, with the turmoil of the Reformation, is the period when hypocrisy and dissimulation became major religious preoccupations.[20] The articles by Pravdica, Parry and Wang, as has already been seen, all emphasize how the central place of sincerity in Protestant piety created doubts, not only about the faith of those outside their denominational groups but also, disquietingly, that of those within. Religious intolerance and persecution resulted in passionate debates about the justification or illegitimacy of dissimulation. False piety was detected on all sides of the denominational divide, with religious ritual and ceremony decried as sham performances, the moral integrity of religious leaders called into question, and puritanical rigour denounced as a deception. Hypocrisy was a significant theme in religious debate and developed as a particularly powerful and virulent polemical discourse. Charlotte Methuen shows how accusations of hypocrisy could be a key component of anti-clerical discourse in Reformation Germany.[21] Her analysis focusses on a vehement critique in the form of a letter written

[20] See, for example, Zagorin, *Ways of Lying*; Trilling, *Sincerity and Authenticity*; Miriam Eliav-Feldon and Tamar Herzog, eds, *Dissimulation and Deceit in Early Modern Europe* (Basingstoke, 2015).

[21] For earlier manifestations of hypocrisy and anticlericalism and antifraternalism, see the articles by Sabapathy and Konstantinos Gravanis in this volume.

(supposedly) by an anonymous laywoman in sixteenth-century Germany to her sister, a member of a religious order. She excoriates the clergy for their parading of piety, their greed, spiritual ignorance and false ministry, and attacks the female religious for their spiritual complacency and pride. Her accusations conform to the polemical discourse of anticlericalism found in the early writings of the German reformers Luther and Karlstadt, but she shows herself to be immersed in Scripture, drawing not only on Jesus's castigation of the Pharisees but on a wider and more unusual set of texts.

Accusations of hypocrisy in anticlericalism and anti-monasticism both had precedents reaching back into the Middle Ages, as Sabapathy and Gravanis show, and a long, long future. Their fertile manifestations in sixteenth- and seventeenth-century England form the subject of papers by David Fletcher and Adam Morton. Fletcher's parade of religious hypocrites in English Restoration theatre includes hypocritical clergy and monks whose sordid lives betray their calling; casuists whose ingenuity can justify any moral transgression, both their own and those of others; and predatory hypocrites whose dissembling enables them to take advantage of others. Religious hypocrites in Restoration drama are not confined to a single denomination: the dramatists lampooned Roman Catholics, conformists and nonconformists alike, and stressed the congruence between Roman Catholic and puritan fervour, incorporating characters such as a 'Puritanical Jesuit' and a 'Jesuitical Puritan'. As Fletcher argues, the use of such religious stereotypes enabled playwrights to launch an anti-clerical attack on religion.[22]

Adam Morton takes a visual image of hypocrisy, *The Turncoats* (1711), a print satirically commenting on the readiness of Dissenting ministers to adapt their calling to the new, more stringent demands of the Tory government for conformity to the established church, by depicting two Dissenting ministers at a tailor's, commissioning the transformation of their Dissenting garb into 'Anglican' robes. Morton argues that this ridicule reflected the anxieties arising from the new toleration of religious dissent, and from the ability of Dissenters to mask their real identities by 'occasional conformity' following the 1689 Toleration Act. Tory high churchmen warned that the church was being undermined from within by the hypocrisy of insincere conforming Dissenters, and of those churchmen who

[22] See the article by Fletcher in this volume.

tolerated them. The print draws upon long-established anti-clerical stereotypes, the figure of the Vicar of Bray and accusations of priestcraft.

As Judith Shklar observed, accusations of hypocrisy are an easy way of undermining the views of opponents.[23] They can be made particularly potent by the use of humour, exploiting the amusement gained from the discrepancy between outward action and inner belief, or between espoused views and covert behaviour, as the articles by Morton and Baylor show, and frequently, as in the case of the conflicts between the North and South in the American Civil War, draw upon old stereotypes, particularly of puritan hypocrisy.[24] Ethan Shagan explores jokes targeting religious hypocrisy in jestbooks published between the sixteenth and eighteenth centuries. These provide a rich and complex resource, repositories of recycled and topical jokes which, in Shagan's analysis, can be used to reveal shifts in religious mentalities. They ridicule a range of hypocrisies, from the tergiversations of those who shifted religious allegiance in response to political and religious pressure, to the excuses made by those who indulged in fleshly pleasures against the teaching of their faith. They often target the casuistical justifications of hypocritical behaviour. Humour can be a flexible and multifaceted tool. Just as Morton stressed the dual purposes of the print *The Turncoats* in mocking not only the ease and speed with which Dissenters took on 'Anglican' respectability but also religious hypocrisy more widely, so does Shagan report a number of jokes that laugh both at and with the impious behaviour described, representing a certain robust scepticism about religious behaviour and particularly about the piety of the professional religious, a type of joke which becomes more common over time. The 'gleeful irreverence' expressed in these jokes reflected a shift in mentalities from the Reformation onwards towards a kind of profane Protestantism, which took the form of an anxiety about the meaning and value of ordinary Christianity.[25] Shagan's analysis shows how these humorous depictions of hypocritical behaviour act as an illuminating guide to changing religious attitudes.

This raises the question of why the concepts of hypocrisy and dissimulation are more prominent in religious and public discourse at

[23] Shklar, *Ordinary Vices*, 48.
[24] See the article by Edward G. Manger in this volume.
[25] See the article by Shagan in this volume.

some historical periods than at others. Denunciations of hypocrisy were generative and could lead to something of a fashion in polemic. The fact that accusations of hypocrisy breed counter-accusations, 'reactive hypocrisy', is amply demonstrated by a number of contributions in this volume.[26] The phenomenon can be seen in the political and religious turmoil generated by the 1689 Toleration Act, as described by Morton, and in Edward Manger's account of the polemical war between North and South in the American Civil War. Whyte notes that the campaign by the group OutRage! to out bishops who were believed to be gay opened up the group itself to charges of hypocrisy in victimizing fellow gays, and showed the double-standards of the press in condemning their tactic while simultaneously publishing their revelations.

Nevertheless, the currency and popularity of accusations of hypocrisy are more than a passing rhetorical fad. The sixteenth and seventeenth centuries represent a period of intense debate and discussion about hypocrisy and about the possible justification of dissimulation. The Reformation and its aftermath were times of profound religious conflict which bred persecution and oppression. It was also, some have argued, a period in which deceits and deceptions, particularly involving fake identities and false religious conversions, abounded in Europe.[27] Accusations of hypocrisy were deployed by both Roman Catholics and Protestants, and the rights and wrongs of religious dissimulation were keenly debated. The obsession with hypocrisy evolved as new ideas and modes of behaviour developed, for example, with the rise of a culture of politeness.[28] The early Middle Ages were a barren period for hypocritical discourse: the survey of Latin text references carried out by Sita Steckel and reproduced by John Sabapathy demonstrates its rarity until the twelfth and thirteenth centuries when, for example, it became a feature of the hostilities between the religious orders and mendicants, penetrating, as Sabapathy shows, critiques of secular power by the fourteenth century.[29] The early development of hypocrisy in anticlericalism can

[26] Shklar, *Ordinary Vices*, 62.

[27] Eliav-Feldon and Herzog, eds, *Dissimulation and Deceit*.

[28] This is highlighted by Ethan Shagan, Anna Pravdica and Adam Morton in this volume.

[29] See the article by Sabapathy in this volume; Sita Steckel, 'Hypocrites! Critiques of Religious Movements and Criticism of the Church, 1050–1300', in Jennifer Kolpacoff Deane and Anne E. Lester, eds, *Between Orders and Heresy* (Toronto, 2022), 79–126, at 108–11; Courtney Booker, 'Hypocrisy, Performativity, and the Carolingian Pursuit

be detected in the controversies between the secular clergy and mendicant orders.[30] Scriptural and exegetical teachings about Antichrist as the arch-deceiver and -hypocrite, and the prevalence of evil and deceit in the last days, also raised its prominence at moments of eschatological anticipation, although it is not clear how far the detection of contemporary hypocrisy fuelled apocalyptic anxiety or was fostered by it.[31]

The emergence of hypocrisy as a major vice in and after 1100 may be linked, as Nicholas Watson has argued, to the tensions between centralization in the church and greater diversity within it. Sabapathy too highlights increasing institutional complexity in both secular and religious bodies, with an increase in reformist rhetoric in both and a critical questioning of their conduct. The charge of outward feigning is, of course, intimately connected to questions of interiority and authenticity. It is a moot question whether the experience of interiority in the earlier Middle Ages was different in quality and intensity.[32] Certainly, as Whyte demonstrates, the importance attached to the authentic self in the 1990s fostered accusations of hypocrisy against the Church of England. It is notable that while the concealment of gay sexual identities in the modern church could be regarded as a form of dissimulation akin to early modern Nicodemism, as Diarmaid MacCulloch has argued, the controversies of the 1990s do not seem to have used this language or exploited such ideas.[33]

The shifting prominence of debates over hypocrisy and dissimulation is an area ripe for further exploration. This collection of articles also highlights some historiographical gaps, such as the place of hypocrisy in early German Reformation debates and teaching, as noted by Methuen. The question of the gendering of depictions of hypocrisy is raised by Fletcher, whose survey of hypocrites in

of Truth', *Early Medieval Europe* 26 (2018), 174–202. See also Nicholas Watson, 'Whited Sepulchres: Towards a History of Hypocrisy, 1100–1400', unpublished paper to the Medieval Academy (2010), which highlights the emergence of hypocrisy as a public vice in the thirteenth century. I am very grateful to Professor Watson for sharing this with me. Compare Amory, 'Whited Sepulchres: The Semantic History', 5–39.

30 Steckel, 'Hypocrites!', 79–126.

31 Watson, 'Whited Sepulchres'.

32 See, for example, Catherine Cubitt, *Sin and Society* (Cambridge, forthcoming).

33 MacCulloch, *Silence*, 184–90.

English Restoration theatre reveals the prevalence of men in these satires, in part a reflection of the anti-clerical nature of accusations of hypocrisy. Hypocrisy accusations, such as those levelled at Pope Boniface VIII, frequently addressed the disparity between the ideals of public office and the inner lives of those who held it; the near complete exclusion of women throughout much of Western history from such positions inevitably leads to a gender imbalance. It is telling that in Fletcher's overview, one of the notable exceptions is the supposed female pope, Joan. Women were not immune from accusations of hypocrisy (the sixteenth-century anonymous German female writer accuses the women's religious orders of it in writing to her sister, a religious). The gendering of depictions of hypocrisy and dissimulation is a rich field for further study.

The articles in this rich and diverse volume thus offer much food for thought, both to their individual specialized areas and to the larger field of study on the discourses of hypocrisy and dissimulation.

Catherine Cubitt

The Devil as 'Father of Lies': Ideas of Diabolical Deceit in the Donatist Controversy

Sophie Lunn-Rockliffe*
University of Cambridge

This article examines the connections in late antique Christian thought between the ideas that heretics were inspired by the devil, and that the devil was a liar. It begins by showing that the association of the devil with lies was founded on scriptural exegesis, and that Scripture was regularly deployed in heresiologies to cement the links between the devil as 'father of lies', and heretics and schismatics as liars in Satan's image. It then offers a detailed case study of when, where and how accusations of direct and indirect diabolical dissimulation were made by the opposing parties of the 'Donatist controversy' in polemical texts produced primarily for their own side. The final part considers how these accusations were modulated in invented textual dialogues and in oral debates between the two sides, showing how direct accusations of diabolical activity made against opponents were often eschewed for more subtle insinuations of diabolical association.

In a sermon on Psalm 39, preached in North Africa in the second decade of the fifth century, Augustine warned his congregation about the devil's ability to switch from the open violence of persecution to the more insidious deceit entailed by heresy.[1] He used bestial

* E-mail: sjl39@cam.ac.uk.

[1] Augustine, *Enarrationes in Psalmos* 39 (transl. adapted from Maria Boulding, *New City Press Works of St Augustine* III/16 [Hyde Park, NY, 2000], 194–238; Latin text: PL 36: 431–52). As Possidius explains in a catalogue of Augustine's works attached to his *Life*, the *Enarrationes in Psalmos* contain a number of different kinds of texts, and he classifies *En. Ps.* 39 as a 'sermon preached to the people': *Indiculus* 10.4.3. Seraphim Zarb, 'Chronologia Enarrationum S. Augustini in Psalmos', *Angelicum* 15.3 (1938), 382–408, at 402–5, analyzes internal references to urban topography and festivals in this sermon and concludes that it was preached at Carthage between 411 and 413. By contrast, Henri Rondet, 'Essais sur la chronologie des 'Enarrationes in Psalmos' de saint Augustin (suite)', *Bulletin de littérature ecclésiastique* 65 (1964), 110–36, at 131–4, places it in Hippo, between 405 and 415, perhaps more specifically between 411 and 415.

Studies in Church History 60 (2024), 17–42
doi: 10.1017/stc.2024.1

metaphors drawn from Scripture to show that where Satan had previously been a lion 'savaging openly' (*aperte saeviebat*), he was now a snake 'lying hidden in ambush' (*occulte insidiatur*),[2] and pithily summarized the devil's shift in tactics thus: 'In former days he used to force [*cogebat*] Christians to deny Christ; nowadays he teaches [*docet*] them to deny Christ'.[3] He then imagined an encounter between a heretic and a Christian in vivid metaphorical terms:

> But the slippery snake approaches unseen, a serpent with silent, gliding motion, drawing his length along softly as he creeps in, craftily whispering, and he does not say, 'Deny Christ'. … What he does say is, 'be a Christian'. The hearer is struck by this remarkable saying. If the poison has not yet penetrated, he replies, 'I am a Christian, that's obvious.' But if he is swayed and captivated by the serpent's tooth, he replies, 'Why do you say to me, be a Christian? How can you say that? Am I not a Christian already?' The snake answers, 'No'. 'I'm not?' 'No.' 'Well, make me then a Christian then, if I'm not one.' 'Come along then. But when the bishop begins to question you about what you are, do not say, I am a Christian, or I am a believer, but say you are not. If you follow this advice, you may become one.'[4]

In this passage, it emerges that the diabolical snake is a so-called 'Donatist', a member of a rigorist Christian community in North Africa stigmatized by bishops and emperors as schismatic and heretical.[5] The Donatist 'snake' is trying to inveigle a Christian to be re-baptized, a practice which had been repeatedly condemned by anti-Donatist bishops and emperors in the later fourth and early fifth centuries.[6] In Augustine's imagined scenario, a Christian who

[2] Augustine, *En. Ps.* 39.3 (transl. Boulding, 195). Central scriptural passages interpreted by early Christians as evidence for the connection between the snake, the lion and the devil, are found at Gen. 3; Ps. 90 (91): 13 (itself cited by Augustine in *En. Ps.* 39.1); Rev. 12: 9 and 20: 2; 1 Pet. 5: 8.

[3] Augustine *En. Ps.* 39.3 (transl. Boulding, 195).

[4] Ibid.

[5] On the problems of using the labels of 'Donatist' versus 'catholic' to describe the two opposing parties, see Brent Shaw, *Sacred Violence: African Christians and Sectarian Hatred in the Age of Augustine* (Cambridge, 2011), 5–6. In this article, I use 'Donatist' throughout as a label of convenience and prefer 'anti-Donatist' to describe their opponents, since members of both groups considered themselves to be 'catholic'.

[6] Seven imperial edicts which forbid or otherwise stigmatize re-baptism are preserved in title 16.6 of the *Theodosian Code*, 'Holy baptism shall not be repeated': transl. Clyde Pharr, *Theodosian Code* (Princeton, NJ, 1952), 463. See Noel Lenski, 'Imperial

had already been baptized would be coached knowingly to tell a lie ('do not say, "I am a Christian" … but say you are not') during the process of scrutiny early in catechesis, in order to receive a second, Donatist, baptism.[7]

Augustine's dramatic sketch builds on two long-established traditions of early Christian polemic: that the Christian experience of persecution and heresy here on earth is not merely a human conflict, but reflects a broader reality of cosmic combat between God and the spiritual forces of wickedness; and more specifically, that one of the devil's key techniques for attacking humans is to spread lies among them, using heretics and schismatics to disseminate bad doctrine, bad exegesis and bad ethics.[8] While scholars have noted that accusations of heresy in late antiquity were regularly yoked to the devil, and that deceit was one of his main tactics, little sustained attention has been paid to the relationship between these notions, nor to how opposing parties deployed such accusations in a range of textual and oral contexts.[9] In the first part of this article, I seek to bridge these gaps by demonstrating that the association of the devil with lies was underpinned by the exegesis of Scripture, and that scriptural passages about diabolical deceit were in turn frequently deployed in a range of heresiological works to cement the link between the devil as 'father of lies', and heretics and schismatics as liars in Satan's image. In the second part, I move to a detailed case study of when, where and how accusations of direct and indirect diabolical dissimulation were made by the opposing parties of the 'Donatist controversy' in

Legislation and the Donatist Controversy: From Constantine to Honorius', in Richard Miles, ed., *The Donatist Schism: Controversy and Contexts* (Liverpool, 2016), 166–219, with a useful appendix of imperial communications on Donatism at 196–219.

7 On the rite of 'scrutiny' during Lenten catechesis in Augustine's Hippo, see William Harmless, *Augustine and the Catechumenate*, revised edition by Allan Fitzgerald (Collegeville, MI, 2014), 219–25.

8 On the working out of this idea in ecclesiastical histories, see Sophie Lunn-Rockliffe, 'Diabolical Motivations: The Devil in Ecclesiastical Histories from Eusebius to Evagrius', in Geoffrey Greatrex, Hugh Elton and Lucas McMahon, eds, *Shifting Genres in Late Antiquity* (Farnham, 2015), 119–31.

9 On the devil as first liar, see Dallas Denery II, *The Devil Wins: A History of Lying from the Garden of Eden to the Enlightenment* (Princeton, NJ, 2015), 21–61. On the demonization of heretics, see Elaine Pagels, *The Origin of Satan* (New York, 1995), 149–78. On Satan the heretic, see Neil Forsyth, *The Old Enemy* (Princeton, NJ, 1987), 309–17. On the rhetoric of polarization, see David Gwynn, *The Eusebians: The Polemic of Athanasius of Alexandria and the Construction of the 'Arian Controversy'* (Oxford, 2007), 171–7.

polemical texts produced for consumption mainly by their own side. In the final part, I consider how these accusations were modulated both in invented textual dialogues and in oral debates between the two sides, showing how direct accusations of diabolical activity made against opponents were often eschewed for more subtle, often scripturally derived, insinuations of diabolical association.

The Donatist controversy is ripe for analysis because it is attested through a rich array of records and a range of different kinds of rhetoric: the eloquent instruments of imperial letters, designed to deliver words from one end of the empire to the other; clerical treatises addressed both to and against their opponents; transcripts of sermons preached to insiders; polemical treatises engaging in selective quotation and then refutation of their opponents' arguments; and stenographic records of the real-time exchanges of church councils and conferences.[10] Sermons and conciliar proceedings in particular give us some sense of spoken language, with the caveat that they have often been tidied up for dissemination.[11] Furthermore, the evidential trail represents both sides of the debate, albeit often unevenly, allowing us to see something of how the notion of diabolical inspiration for heretical deceit was deployed by opposing parties. This is relatively unusual, since many theologies and communities stigmatized as heresies or schisms in late antiquity leave very little trace of themselves in textual terms. For example, there are few remaining texts representing the views of so-called 'Arians', another early fourth-century theological grouping that was stigmatized by emperors and bishops alike as diabolical,[12] and the demonization of the 'Messalians' was in part a constructive process of making a heresy out of a scattering of

[10] The evidence for the Donatist controversy has been systematically mined in Brent Shaw's *Sacred Violence*. He notes the linking of heretics with Satan as 'Father of lies' but suggests that 'for the Africans' [i.e. 'Donatists'], 'the Antichrist was an even more powerful figure': Shaw, *Sacred Violence*, 323–4.

[11] On the variety of stages of editorial polish of sermons, see Nikolai Lipatov-Chicherin, 'Preaching as the Audience heard it: Unedited Transcripts of Patristic Homilies', *Studia Patristica* 64 (2013), 277–98. On the problems with stenographic transcripts of councils, see Tommaso Mari, 'Working on the Minutes of Late Antique Church Councils: A Methodological Framework', *Journal for Late Antique Religion and Culture* 13 (2019), 42–59.

[12] On the demonization of Arianism by Athanasius, see Gwynn, *Eusebians*, 171–7. For a discussion of the difficulties of reconstructing the Arian *Thalia*, see Rowan Williams, *Arius: Heresy and Tradition*, 2nd edn (London, 2001; first publ. 1987), 62–6 and 98–107.

individuals who leave almost no independent trace of their teachings and practices.[13]

The Devil as 'Father of Lies' in Exegesis and Heresiology

There was widespread agreement among early Christians that the devil's defining character traits were violence and deception, and these were chiefly established through the exegesis of scriptural stories in which Satan played a part. In his first fall from angelic favour and proximity to God, Satan was held to have lied in likening himself to God.[14] The snake in Eden lied to the first humans, seducing Eve to persuade Adam to disobey God's command, and the devil also provided a model of deception and betrayal for subsequent humans, such as Judas, to imitate.[15] Influential characterizations of the devil as a liar were also found in, or read into, sayings of Jesus and his followers. Paul famously compared 'false apostles' 'disguising themselves as apostles of Christ' with Satan who 'disguises himself as an angel of light' (2 Corinthians 11: 13–14).[16] Jesus's parables contain vivid allegorical figures of the wolf in sheep's clothing (Matthew 7: 15), and the enemy sowing tares among the wheat (Matthew 13: 24–30). Perhaps most important of all was the passage in the Gospel of John in which Jesus inveighed against the Jews in Jerusalem in blisteringly cosmic terms: 'you are from your father the devil, and you choose to do your father's desires; he was a murderer from the beginning and does not stand in the truth because there is no truth in him; when he lies, he speaks according to his own nature, for he is a liar and the father of lies' (John 8: 44).

[13] On the lack of 'Messalian' texts, see Columba Stewart, '*Working the Earth of the Heart*': *The Messalian Controversy in History, Texts and Language to AD 431* (Oxford, 1991), 4–11. On the demonization of Messalianism, see Sophie Lunn-Rockliffe, 'The Invention and Demonization of a "Messalian" Heresiarch: Philoxenus of Mabbug on Adelphius', *JEH* 68 (2017), 1–19.

[14] On debates about Satan's own fall, including the idea that it circled round deceit, see Sophie Lunn-Rockliffe, 'The Diabolical Problem of Satan's First Sin: Self-Moved Pride or a Response to the Goads of Envy?', *Studia Patristica* 63 (2013), 121–40.

[15] On the devil suggesting sin to Eve and others in Scripture, see Sophie Lunn-Rockliffe, 'Augustine on the Diabolical Suggestion of Sin', in James Aitken, Hector Patmore and Ishay Rosen-Zvi, eds, *The Evil Inclination in Early Judaism and Christianity* (Cambridge, 2021), 212–31.

[16] Biblical quotations are taken from the NRSVUE.

Interpretation of John 8: 44 became a crucial point of debate between theological parties, with some apparently reading the ambiguous Greek grammar of the first clause of this verse to mean that the devil himself had a father or grandfather, who could be identified with God.[17] Such interpretations were resisted by Origen in his *Commentary on John* of the 240s,[18] and by Epiphanius in his *Panarion,* a massive anti-heretical treatise of the 370s.[19] In unpacking the sinful genealogy of this verse, both writers constructed moral relationships of 'fatherhood', which relied on notions of imitation and participation, rather than biological descent and nature, to explain the relationship between the devil and his human offspring. Thus for Origen, drawing on 1 John 3: 8–12, 'each person who sins is generically a child of the devil … but in addition, more specifically, he is a child as well either of Cain or Cham or Chanaan or Pharaoh or Nabuchodonosor, or some other impious person.'[20] Furthermore, he held the devil uniquely responsible for the generation of lies: 'And the reason why truth is not in him [the devil] is that he has been deceived and accepts lies, and he has himself been deceived by himself. On this basis he is reckoned to be worse than the rest of these who are deceived, since they are deceived by him, but he creates his own deception himself.'[21]

[17] See David Litwa, '"The Father of the Devil" (John 8: 44): A Christian Exegetical Inspiration for the Evil Creator', *Vigiliae Christianae* 74 (2020), 540–65.

[18] 'The text is ambiguous. One meaning suggested by it is that the devil has a father, and, so far as the literal meaning is concerned, those addressed by this word appear to be derived from this father. There is another [possible meaning] however, which is preferable, namely, "You are of this father, concerning whom the title 'devil' is predicated."' Origen, *Commentary on the Gospel of John* 20.171 (transl. Ronald Heine, *Fathers of the Church* 89 [Washington, DC, 2006], 241–2). Heine explains: 'The text of John could possibly be read "You are of the father of the devil." This takes the second genitive phrase to express relationship, rather than being in apposition with the first genitive phrase.' Heine, *Commentary on John,* 241 n. 182. On the dating of Origen's commentary, see ibid. 4–18.

[19] '… the other sects allege that the devil is the father of the Jews, and that he has a different father, and his father in turn has a father. … They are tracing the devil's ancestry to the Lord of all, the God of the Jews, the Christians, and all men, by saying that he is the father of the devil's father…': Epiphanius, *Panarion* 38.4.3–4 (transl. Frank Williams, *The* Panarion *of Epiphanius of Salamis: Book 1 (Sects 1–46),* 2nd edn [Leiden, 2009; first publ. 1987], 272–3).

[20] Origen, *Commentary on John* 20.78 (transl. Heine, 222–3) and 20.99-113 (transl. Heine, 227–30).

[21] Origen, *Commentary on John* 20.244 (transl. Heine, 257).

Epiphanius condemned the so-called 'Cainites' for honouring Cain, explaining that Jesus meant Judas when he told the Jews their father was the devil, and then elaborated a genealogy by which Judas had as his father Cain, whom he imitated in lying and killing, and Cain in turn had the devil as his father, whom he imitated in 'fratricide, hatred and falsehood'.[22] In a gospel commentary of the 420s, Cyril of Alexandria read the final clause of John 8: 44 not as 'he is a liar and the father of lies', but as 'he is a liar just like his father', and asked in mock puzzlement: 'Who would we reasonably suppose is the devil's father? Who else fell before him to whom the later one may be compared in classification and behaviour?'[23] He solved the conundrum in a similar manner to Epiphanius, arguing that the father of the Jews was in fact Cain, and that Cain's father was in turn the devil, whose primal rebellion against God was followed by deceit and eventually murder.[24]

Moving west, we find that Augustine also foregrounded notions of imitation in his tractate on John 8: 44 (delivered as a sermon in the period 411–16), asking: 'How, then, were the Jews the children of the devil?'; and answering: 'by imitation, not by birth [*imitando, non nascendo*]'.[25] Augustine then offered an excursus on the nature of lying

[22] Epiphanius, *Panarion* 38.4.3–5.2 (transl. Williams, 272–3).

[23] Cyril of Alexandria, *Commentary on the Gospel of John* 6.94 (transl. Joel Elowsky, *Ancient Christian Texts* 2 [Downers Grove, IL, 2015], 1). On the dating of this text to 425–8, see Elowsky, *Commentary on John*, xvi–xvii. It is not clear if Cyril of Alexandria knew Epiphanius, although it is plausible that he would have done so: see Matthew Crawford, *Cyril of Alexandria's Trinitarian Theology of Scripture* (Oxford, 2014), 81.

[24] 'Since we have said that Cain was listed as the father of the Jews and Satan as the father of Cain himself, come let us go through our own words and clearly demonstrate that Satan was the first to rear his head against God's correction, that he then went on to lie and deceive, and that he finally committed murder because of envy. Then we will show that Cain has the same behaviour and mindset as him. And third, we will bring home the argument to the Jews, who possess the image of his wickedness in its entirety.' Cyril of Alexandria, *Commentary on John* 6.97 (transl. Elowsky, 3). John Byron outlines a longer Jewish tradition in which Cain was biologically descended from Satan: John Byron, *Cain and Abel in Text and Tradition: Jewish and Christian Interpretations of the First Sibling Rivalry* (Leiden, 2011), 16–20.

[25] Augustine, *Tractate on the Gospel of John* 42.10.4 (transl. John Rettig, *Fathers of the Church* 88 [Washington, DC, 1993], 156). Seraphim Zarb identifies this as one of the sermons delivered to Augustine's congregation at Hippo in the period between 411 and 416: Seraphim Zarb, 'Chronologia Tractatum S. Augustini in Evangelium primamque Epistulam Ioannis Apostoli', *Angelicum* 10 (1933), 50–110. Rettig surveys the complex history of dating the tractates more generally: Rettig, *Tractate on John*, 23–31. On Augustine's diabolization of the Jews, see Shaw, *Sacred Violence*, 299.

which explained why the devil was more to blame for his lying than his subsequent human imitators, in an argument which resembles Origen's:[26]

> For not everyone who lies is the father of his lying. For if you received the lie from another and told it, you indeed lied by making known the lie; but you are not the father of the lie itself because you received the lie from another. But the devil is a liar on his own [*diabolus autem a seipso mendax fuit*]; he himself begot [*genuit*] his own lying, he heard it from no-one. As God the Father begot [*genuit*] his son, truth, so the devil after his fall begot a son, so to speak, lying [*genuit quasi filium mendacium*].[27]

Augustine productively repeated the theological language of 'begetting', applying it in the first half of the sentence to the relationship between Father and Son, and in the second half to the relationship between the devil and lying. This underlined the generative quality of the devil as 'father of falsehood', and offered a parodic inversion of the truthfulness of Christ.

While some Christian teachers applied Jesus's words in John 8: 44 to condemn Jews in their own day,[28] others applied the label of 'children of the devil' – as well as other archetypal scriptural passages about diabolical dissimulation – to heretics and schismatics who were deemed to be related to 'the father of the lies' in their refusal to accept 'orthodox' doctrine. This phenomenon can be seen in heresiologies from the second century onwards, which worked to catalogue and stigmatize as 'heretics' and 'schismatics' groups whose beliefs and/or practices were determined to be errant.[29] Heresiologies had an insistent genealogical logic, adopting the notion of 'successions'

[26] On this relationship more generally, see György Heidl, *The Influence of Origen on the Young Augustine: A Chapter of the History of Origenism* (Piscataway, NJ, 2009). On Augustine and lying more generally, see Paul Griffiths, *Lying: An Augustine Theology of Duplicity* (Eugene, OR, 2004), esp. 23–110.

[27] Augustine, *Tractate on John* 42.13 (transl. Rettig, 159). A similar emphasis on the devil's self-generated sin can be found in the earlier Latin exegesis of Ambrosiaster, *Quaestiones* 90 and 98, ed. Alexnder Souter, CSEL 50 (Vienna, 1908), 150–1 and 187–9.

[28] See John Chrysostom, *Discourse Against Judaizing Christians* 8.8.4-6 (transl. Paul Harkins, *Fathers of the Church* 68 [Washington, DC, 1979], 235–7), where John 8: 44 is used to justify the prohibition on seeking amulets and healings from Jews at Antioch.

[29] The classic account of the construction of heresy is Walter Bauer, *Orthodoxy and Heresy in Earliest Christianity*, transl. Paul Achtemeier (Philadelphia, PA, 1979), more recently

(*diadochai*) of teachers found in classical philosophical schools.[30] In some cases, heresiologists traced the ultimate origin of heresy back through generations of human heretics to their ultimate instigator, the devil.[31]

In his massive treatise *Against Heresies* of the late second century, Irenaeus of Lyons regularly assumed that particular heretics were under various forms of diabolical or demonic influence, and his references to other texts and writers who shared this idea demonstrates that it was a broader worldview. He reported the verse attack of a contemporary, perhaps Polycarp, against Marcus, which accused him of tricking and deceiving his followers using miracles facilitated by Satan, 'your father' (a nod to John 8: 44).[32] He described the followers of Carpocrates as 'being sent forth by Satan to the pagans to malign the holy name of the church', and convincing people to turn away from the truth.[33] Of Marcion, Irenaeus claimed that he spoke 'with the devil's mouth', 'uttering all things contrary to the truth'; indeed, as the serpent spoke to Eve, so it was the 'serpent which was in Marcion' who spoke.[34] Tertullian's treatise *On the Prescription of Heretics,* written *c.*200, shows less interest than Irenaeus in the devil's intervention in precise moments of human history, but he used Jesus's parable of the wheat and the tares (Matthew 13: 24–30) to suggest that heresy had been introduced by the devil, and he contrasted the 'priority of truth' with 'the comparative lateness of falsehood'.[35] In his exhaustive catalogue of and invective against

contested by essays in Paul Hartog, ed., *Orthodoxy and Heresy in Early Christian Contexts: Reconsidering the Bauer Thesis* (Eugene, OR, 2015).

[30] On the notion of a *diadochē* ('succession') of teachers underpinning both philosophical and heretical successions, see Allen Brent, 'Diogenes Laertius and the Apostolic Succession', *JEH* 44 (1993), 367–89; Geoffrey Smith, *Guilt by Association: Heresy Catalogues in Early Christianity* (Oxford, 2014), 10, notes the importance of 'demonic error' to heresy catalogues.

[31] On the relationship between heresy and Satan, see Pagels, *Origin of Satan,* 149–78; Todd Berzon, *Classifying Christians: Ethnography, Heresiology and the Limits of Knowledge in Late Antiquity* (Oakland, CA, 2016), 150–3 (on Theodoret and Epiphanius).

[32] Irenaeus, *Against Heresies* 1.15.6 (transl. Dominic Unger, revised edition by John Dillon, ACW 65 [Mahwah, NJ, 1992], 68).

[33] Ibid. 1.25.3 (transl. Unger, 88).

[34] Ibid. 1.27.3 (transl. Unger, 92).

[35] Tertullian, *On the Prescription of Heretics* 31 (ed. and transl. R. Refoulé and Pierre Labriolle, SC 46 [Paris, 1957], 130).

heresies, the *Panarion,* Epiphanius suggested relationships of influence between the devil and particular heretics in a range of scriptural images. For example, he deployed the gospel accounts of Satan entering into Judas's heart to describe Satan's possession of the heretic Nicolaus: 'Later, however, the devil slipped into him and deceived his heart …'.[36] He described the teachings and scriptures of heretics like the Gnostics as 'a devil's sowing', evoking Jesus's parable of the weeds and the tares, and accused heretics of wearing sheep's fleeces to disguise the inner ravening wolf.[37]

So far, we have seen that the scripturally derived understanding of the devil as an archetypal liar regularly shaped the hostile depiction of heretics as diabolical liars, although our exegetes and controversialists were keen to stress that much heretical deceit was derivative and imitative, and only the devil himself had no predecessors in lying, uniquely begat the first lies, and was thus the ultimate 'father of lies'. In the remainder of this article, I will demonstrate that both Donatists and anti-Donatists, battling in words and sometimes violent deeds, regularly made accusations of diabolical inspiration or possession against their opponents, which in turn frequently evoked deceit as a defining diabolical characteristic. I will also argue that the varying modulations of those accusations, themselves often alluding to scriptural images and phrases, imply different levels of moral responsibility for the humans so possessed, but were also shaped by contemporary norms which set different limits to polemical rhetoric in given contexts.

Diabolical Dissimulation in Donatist and Anti-Donatist Polemic

Some dozen and a half of the emperor Constantine's surviving letters deal with Donatism, mostly in correspondence with bishops.[38] Scholars generally agree that the distinctive and consistent rhetorical

[36] Epiphanius, *Panarion* 25.1.3 (transl. Williams, 84), evoking the Satanic deception of Judas described at Luke 22: 3, John 13: 2 and John 13: 27.

[37] Epiphanius, *Panarion* 26.3.2 (transl. Williams, 92) on tares; and 40.1.4 and 46.2.1 (transl. Williams, 283 and 377) on sheep and wolves.

[38] Many of Constantine's letters are preserved in Eusebius's *Life of Constantine* (in Greek translation) and in Optatus's *Appendix* (in Latin). See the texts assembled by Jean-Louis Maier, *Le dossier du donatisme,* 1: *des origines à la mort de Constance II (303–61)* (Berlin, 1987), 137–254, and the catalogue in Lenski, 'Imperial Legislation', 197–207.

tone of those letters reflect Constantine's own perspective and preoccupations, even though they were probably drafted by his chancery.[39] The letters contain a fair amount of generalizing invective against schismatics – including accusations of deceit – which did not often accuse them of being diabolical, instead drawing on older Roman traditions critiquing religious deviants for their anger, madness and obstinacy.[40] Thus, for example, in a letter to the vicar of Africa, Aelafius, of 314, Constantine condemned the Donatists for their 'rabid anger' (*vesano furore*) and for acting 'in a stubborn and pertinacious manner' (*obnixe ac pertinaciter*); and in a letter to Celsus of 315, he denounced Maenalius as gripped by 'insanity' (*insania*) and those who have 'departed from truth and given themselves most basely [*praevissimo*] to error'.[41] In the single surviving letter to a group of bishops of the Donatist party, dated to about 315, Constantine criticized them as 'troublemakers' (*turbulentos*), 'obstinate in mind' and of 'excessive obstinacy' (*obstinato animo* and *nimia … obstinatione*), who did not respect 'the spirit of upright truth', but, perhaps diplomatically, made no mention of Satan.[42]

By contrast, in two separate letters to groups of anti-Donatist bishops, Constantine explicitly and repeatedly identified the devil's influence in their opponents. In a letter of 314 addressed to 'catholic' bishops who had been at the council of Arles earlier that year, Constantine characterized the Donatists as those 'whom the wickedness of the devil [*malignitas diaboli*] seemed to have diverted by his contemptible persuasion', and referred to their 'repudiating truth', being 'wicked men' who are 'officers of the devil' (*maligni homines officia … diaboli*), and 'unspeakable deceivers of religion' (*infandos*

[39] On the distinctive rhetoric of Constantine's correspondence, see Averil Cameron and Stuart Hall, *Life of Constantine* (Oxford, 1999), 240; Andrew Pottenger, *Power and Rhetoric in the Ecclesiastical Correspondence of Constantine the Great* (London, 2022), 4–5; Shaw, *Sacred Violence*, 491.

[40] Pottenger sketches the longer background of metaphors of madness and reason, and of sickness and healing, used by Constantine in his correspondence: Pottenger, *Power and Rhetoric*, 97–128. It has also been shown that heresy was prosecuted using existing legal categories: see Caroline Humfress, *Orthodoxy and the Courts in Late Antiquity* (Oxford, 2007), 217–42.

[41] Constantine, Letter to Aelafius (Maier, *Dossier*, 153–8; transl. Mark Edwards in Optatus, *Against the Donatists* [Liverpool, 1997], 181–4); Letter to Celsus (Maier, *Dossier*, 194–6; transl. Edwards, 193–4).

[42] Constantine, Letter to the African bishops (Maier, *Dossier*, 192–3; transl. Edwards, 192).

deceptores religionis).[43] The double use of *malignus* and cognates here, the first time related explicitly to the devil, tallies with broader fourth-century Latin usage, where they are words strongly associated with Satan.[44]

In 330, Constantine made an even more programmatic and sustained account of the devil's work in Donatism in a letter to a group of named Numidian bishops.[45] He indicated subtly that he was withdrawing his intervention in the affair and commended the bishops for abstaining from quarrels with the schismatics. The letter strikes a florid rhetorical tone and is especially rich in scriptural allusions, perhaps to distract from his withdrawal from direct intervention.[46] It starts with an overarching characterization of diabolical motivation which is familiar from heresiologies and later recapped by Eusebius:

> there is no doubt that heresy and schism proceeds from the devil, who is the fount of evil [*caput est malitiae*], and thus there is no doubting that whatever is done by heretics occurs at the instigation of him [*eius instinctu*] who has possessed their sense and reason [*qui eorum sensus mentes cogitationesque possedit*].'[47]

A schismatic is condemned as one 'who runs with headlong error to the devil's party' (*ad diaboli partem*). Constantine repeated the idea

43 Constantine, Letter to the 'catholic' bishops (Maier, *Dossier,* 167–71; transl. Edwards, 189–91).

44 Augustine, *Homily* 5 on 1 John quotes a Latin text of 1 John 3: 12 which renders *ponēros* ('the evil one') as *malignus* ('the wicked one'). Elsewhere, Augustine collocates *malignitas diaboli* ('the wickedness of the devil') at least twice: *Letter* 78.2 and *On the Grace of Christ* 2.40.46.

45 Constantine, Letter to the Numidian bishops (Maier, *Dossier*, 246–52; transl. Edwards, 198–201). This text overlaps with the edited version of a law to the governor of Numidia in the *Theodosian Code* 16.2.7 (transl. Pharr, 441–2), both of which were issued at Serdica on 5 February 330. Shaw compares the 'neatly trimmed and edited version of the law that appears in the law code' with 'the original words that were *heard* by the Africans' (emphasis original): Shaw, *Sacred Violence,* 540. Lenski identifies a petition, three letters and one mandate produced on this date: Lenski, 'Legislation', 206–7.

46 Scriptural references in this letter include allusions to 2 Tim. 3: 1–5; Matt. 12: 38, John 8: 44, Deut. 32: 55 and Rom. 12: 19. Shaw suggests that the 'heavy language' is designed to 'distract attention from the little that he was actually going to do or from the unexpected course that he was going to take': Shaw, *Sacred Violence,* 541.

47 Maier suggests that Eusebius had seen this letter, presumably on the basis of similar comments on the devil's instigation of Donatism in his *Life of Constantine* 1.45 (transl. Cameron and Hall, 88): Maier, *Dossier*, 247 n. 3.

that heretics were diabolically possessed, stating that 'those who are possessed by the devil [*qui a diabolo possessi sunt*] follow his falsehood and iniquity', and went on to evoke John 8: 44, noting that heretics and schismatics 'are agreed to adhere to the devil who is their father [*diabolo quo eorum pater est*]'.[48] Overall, there is some negotiation in this letter between the notions that heretics are possessed, not in their right mind, and thus not in control of their actions and, on the other hand, that they are culpable in seeking to do the devil's work, and in remaining obstinately in their error.[49]

The intensity of Constantine's epistolary attacks on the Donatists may, of course, have been designed to replace actual action. However, whether or not they were 'all bark and no bite', it is notable that in both these letters, Constantine was writing in the first place to those who shared his hostile attitude to the Donatists.[50] This might explain the confidence with which he asserted their relationship with Satan. Of course, in practice, the actual audience for these letters – as for all letters, especially imperial letters, in antiquity – was potentially much larger than their immediate addressees. We know that Constantine's letters were circulated more widely, both from Eusebius's references to receiving them and making translations of them into Greek, and from looser allusions to their contents in his summary of the Donatist affair in the *Life of Constantine.*[51] That is, the assumption of an intimate anti-Donatist solidarity is in part a literary pose. The Donatists would surely also have had access to Constantine's letters, adding to their conviction that imperial authorities of different religious stripes were hostile to their 'pure church', and were themselves diabolically inspired.

Let us now switch perspective to explore how the Donatists deployed similar accusations against their opponents. There survive a number of texts which were either authored by, or edited by, those with Donatist sympathies, and which celebrate both those who died under persecuting 'pagan' authorities rather than hand

[48] Constantine, Letter to the Numidian bishops (Maier, *Dossier*, 248; transl. Edwards, 199).

[49] On the moral implications of sins being externally stimulated by demons or Satan, see Lunn-Rockliffe, 'On the Diabolical Suggestion of Sins', 223–8.

[50] For the suggestion that the 'rhetoric is no sure guide to the government's behaviour', see Shaw, *Sacred Violence*, 491–3.

[51] On the sources and deployment of imperial documents (including letters) in Eusebius's *Life of Constantine*, see Cameron and Hall, 16–21.

over scriptures or renounce their faith, and those who died under Christian emperors hostile to Donatism, from Constantine onwards.[52] Scholars have shown that Donatist identity revolved around their being the church of 'the pure' and 'the martyrs' involved in an apocalyptic struggle between good and evil, and that these notions were scripturally inflected.[53] While the longer tradition of martyr acts beyond the Donatist sphere sometimes invoked the devil and demons, Donatist martyrology had a much more ingrained and sustained diabolical inflection.[54]

Here, I will focus on three 'Donatist' texts. The earlier two texts, which both bear hallmarks of being delivered in liturgical contexts, narrate the stories of 'Donatists' executed during the reigns of Christian emperors: the homiletic *Passion of Donatus and Avocatus*, set in the reign of Constantine;[55] and the *Passion of Maximian and Isaac,* apparently set during the reign of Constans after his promulgation of an edict of unity in 347.[56] The third is a Donatist version of *The Acts of the Abitinian Martyrs* which recounts the suffering of a group of Christians under the pagan emperors Diocletian and Maximian in 304; the text was either first authored or redacted by

[52] On 'Donatist' texts, see Alan Dearn, 'Donatist Martyrs, Stories and Attitudes', in Miles, ed., *The Donatist Schism,* 70–100; Richard Miles, 'Textual Communities and the Donatist Controversy', in Miles, ed., *The Donatist Schism*, 249–83.

[53] See Maureen Tilley, *The Bible in Christian North Africa: The Donatist World* (Minneapolis, MI, 1997), 93–129; Jesse Hoover, *The Donatist Church in an Apocalyptic Age* (Oxford, 2018).

[54] Nicole Hartmann suggests that demons are notably absent from martyrology, and are only introduced and 'escalate' after the end of persecution; nonetheless, her discussion includes some examples of pre-Constantinian martyrologies invoking Satan: Nicole Hartmann, 'On Demons in Early Martyrology', in Eva Elm and Nicole Hartmann, eds, *Demons in Late Antiquity: Their Perception and Transformation in Different Literary Genres* (Berlin, 2019), 61–80.

[55] *Passion of Donatus and Avocatus* (Maier, *Dossier*, 198–211; transl. Maureen Tilley, *Donatist Martyr Stories: The Church in Conflict in Roman North Africa* [Liverpool, 1996], 51–60). See Dearn, 'Donatist Martyrs, Stories and Attitudes', 93–6, on this text, leaving open its possible date of delivery at some point at or after the 320s. Its liturgical function can be seen from the introduction (transl. Tilley, 52): 'on this annual solemnity we read the [acts] not unadvisedly in honour of the martyrs and for the edification of believers …'.

[56] *Passion of Maximian and Isaac* (Maier, *Dossier*, 256–75; transl. Tilley, *Donatist Martyr Stories,* 61–75). On this text, see Dearn, 'Donatist Martyrs', 81–4, including at 81 the argument that its liturgical use can be inferred from the *inscriptio* in manuscripts which gives the date of martyrdom, leaving open the date of composition to either the 340s or 360s.

Donatists to present these martyrs as emblematic of the faith, not just of Christians under 'pagan' attack, but of Donatists under Christian imperial attack, and in its current state seems to reflect fifth-century values.[57]

This trio of texts share some fundamental smear strategies. Their framing narratives regularly present events as unfolding as part of a grand diabolical plan. The *Passion of Donatus* starts by setting the scene using an adjusted dating formula: 'when Caecilian Eudinepisus was there, and Leontius had been appointed *comes*, Ursatius was *dux*, Marcellinus tribune, and the devil appeared as counsellor for all of them [*diabolo tamen omnium istorum consiliatore exsistente*]'.[58] *The Passion of Maximian and Isaac* presents the persecution of Donatists in North Africa as the revival of diabolical persecution: 'At that time the devil, enraged for a second time, kindled the dying embers of fury into torture and aroused the insane arms of violence.'[59] The *Acts of the Abitinian Martyrs* begins by stating bluntly: 'the devil waged war against the Christians … [*bellum diabolus christianis indixit* …]. This battle was to be fought not so much against human beings as against the devil [*non tam contra homines quam contra diabolum pugnaturus*].'[60]

Secondly, framing narratives also directly present imperial policies and activities as the work of the devil, sometimes cast as the chief actor and grammatical agent. The *Passion of Donatus* indicts Constantine's policy of handing out cash to anti-Donatists and then segues into a parody of the kind of lofty rhetoric that emperors from Constantine onwards used against Donatists and indeed 'heretics' more generally: 'The enemy of salvation [*salutis inimicus*] concocted a more subtle argument to violate the purity of faith.

[57] *Acts of the Abitinian Martyrs* (Maier, *Dossier*, 57–92; transl. Tilley, *Donatist Martyr Stories*, 25–49). Tilley argues that the acts were written between 304 and 311/312: Tilley, *Donatist Martyr Stories*, 26. For the view that this text was redacted by 'Donatists', see Maier, *Dossier*, 67–8. For the view that it was in fact first authored by Donatists and should be seen as a text of the fifth century, see Alan Dearn, 'The Abitinian Martyrs and the Outbreak of the Donatist Schism', *JEH* 55 (2004), 1–18.

[58] *Passion of Donatus* 2 (Maier, *Dossier*, 202; transl. Tilley, *Donatist Martyr Stories*, 53).

[59] *Passion of Maximian* 3 (Maier, *Dossier*, 262; transl. Tilley, *Donatist Martyr Stories*, 65).

[60] *Abitinian Martyrs* 2 (Maier, *Dossier*, 61; transl. Tilley, *Donatist Martyr Stories*, 28). There is almost certainly an allusion here to the earlier, famous story of Perpetua's martyrdom: Perpetua realizes after a dream 'that I was going to fight with the devil and not with the beasts' (*me non ad bestias sed contra diabolum esse pugnaturam*): *The Passion of Perpetua and Felicity* 10.14, ed. and transl. Thomas Heffernan (New York, 2012), 130.

"Christ", he said, "is the lover of unity. Therefore, let there be unity [*unitas igitur fiat*]."'[61] This casts Constantine's oft-stated commitment to unity as itself a diabolical tactic.[62] In the same vein, the *Passion of Maximian* provides a hostile account of the anti-Donatist legislation of the emperor Constans: 'he immediately ordered a treaty of sacrilegious unity to be solemnly enacted with tortures and sanctions.'[63] Maximian is then praised for the provocative act of tearing up and scattering pieces of Constans's edict of unity 'as if he were tearing the devil limb from limb' (*tamquam diaboli ibi membra discerperet*).[64]

Thirdly, these texts use scriptural phrases and allusions to implicate the devil in events. The *Passion of Donatus* describes the devil as the 'old dragon' (*inveteratus draco*), echoing Revelation 12: 9,[65] and played on the idea of the serpent's cunning, stressed in Genesis 3: 1: 'By cunning deception [*callida fraude*], he strove to lay hold of those he could not conquer by direct persuasion. The author of deception lay hidden so that his deception might proceed more easily [*ut eo facilius deceptio proderet quo deceptionis auctor latuisset*].'[66] The *Acts of the Abitinian Martyrs* applies the same phrase in a passage condemning the clerics Mensurius and Caecilian of Carthage for being part of a diabolical conspiracy:

> There was lacking neither cunning deception [*callidissimam fraudem*] on the part of all those traitors nor the conspiracy of the noxious remainder of those whose faith had been shipwrecked. These were brought together by diabolical art [*diabolica arte*] which, under the guise of religion [*sub praetextu religionis*], attacked faith, overturned law and disturbed divine authority.[67]

61 *Passion of Donatus* 3 (Maier, *Dossier*, 204; transl. Tilley, *Donatist Martyr Stories*, 54).
62 On Constantine's commitment to ecclesiastical unity, see Pottenger, *Power and Rhetoric*, 97–128.
63 *Passion of Maximian* 3 (Maier, *Dossier*, 261; transl. Tilley, *Donatist Martyr Stories*, 659).
64 *Passion of Maximian* 5 (Maier, *Dossier*, 263; transl. Tilley, *Donatist Martyr Stories*, 66). Shaw notes that this incident replays a foundational martyr story from the era of Diocletian: Shaw, *Sacred Violence*, 174–8.
65 This phrase conflates two ideas from Rev. 12: 9 (of the great dragon and the old serpent); one manuscript (K) of the *Vetus Latina* renders this as *ille draco magnus ille serpens antiquus*. See Roger Gryson, *Die Reste der altlateinischen Bibel*, 26/2: *Apocalypsus Johannis* (Freiburg, 2002), 465.
66 *Passion of Donatus* 2 (Maier, *Dossier*, 202; transl. Tilley, *Donatist Martyr Stories*, 53).
67 *Abitinian Martyrs* 20 (Maier, *Dossier*, 86; transl. Tilley, *Donatist Martyr Stories*, 45, adjusted).

Of course, scriptural references were sometimes fleeting or elusive, as when the narrator of *The Passion of Donatus* asks a rhetorical question which quotes John 8: 44 only in passing: 'Who denies that such deeds [the conversion of a basilica by anti-Donatists] have the children of the devil [*filiis diaboli*] as their authors?'[68]

Fourthly, these martyr texts accused persecuting humans of being variously ministers of the devil, diabolically possessed, or 'the devil' himself. This was sometimes found in the authors' or editors' framing narrative, as for example in the *Passion of Maximian* where the martyr's experience of torture is cast as a war waged between 'a soldier of Christ and soldiers of the devil' (*milites diaboli*);[69] or in the *Acts of the Abitinian martyrs*, where the narrator states that 'the devil' speaks 'through the judge' (*per iudicem*),[70] and twice refers to the proconsul as 'the devil'.[71] On other occasions, the charge of diabolical inspiration or possession was made directly by Donatist martyrs to Roman officials, testing the limits of *parrhēsia* (free speech).[72] In the *Acts of the Abitinian Martyrs*, the narrator claimed that the martyrs' words were directly reported, perhaps deriving from a contemporary stenographic transcript.[73] They contain portions of direct speech in which the martyr Dativus addresses the prosecutor Pompeianus directly: 'What are you doing in this place, you devil? [*quid agis hoc in loco, diabole?*]'[74] Later in the same text, the martyr Felix addresses the tyrannical proconsul Anulinus as 'O Satan'.[75]

So far, I have looked at texts addressed in the first instance to insiders, which assumed that their readers or listeners had a shared target of hostility in a devil who animated their opponents in both violence and deceit. In the final part of this article, I will explore another

68 *Passion of Donatus* 4 (Maier, *Dossier*, 205; transl. Tilley, *Donatist Martyr Stories*, 55).

69 *Passion of Maximian* 5 (Maier, *Dossier*, 264; transl. Tilley, *Donatist Martyr Stories*, 66).

70 *Abitinian Martyrs* 6 (Maier, *Dossier*, 68; transl. Tilley, *Donatist Martyr Stories,* 32).

71 *Abitinian Martyrs* 10 (Maier, *Dossier*, 72; transl. Tilley, *Donatist Martyr Stories,* 35) and 15 (Maier, *Dossier*, 79; transl. Tilley, *Donatist Martyr Stories,* 40).

72 See Irene van Renswoude, 'The Steadfast Martyr', in eadem, *The Rhetoric of Free Speech in Late Antiquity and the Early Middle Ages* (Cambridge, 2019), 21–40.

73 'I begin to write using public records [*ex actis publicis*] …': *Abitinian Martyrs* 1 (Maier, *Dossier*, 60; transl. Tilley, *Donatist Martyr Stories,* 28). 'When it comes to the struggles of their battles, I shall not proceed so much in my own words as in those of the martyrs [*non tam meis exsequar quam martyrum dictis*] …': *Abitinian Martyrs* 4 (Maier, *Dossier*, 65; transl. Tilley, *Donatist Martyr Stories,* 30).

74 *Abitinian Martyrs* 9 (Maier, *Dossier*, 71; transl. Tilley, *Donatist Martyr Stories,* 34).

75 *Abitinian Martyrs* 13 (Maier, *Dossier*, 77; transl. Tilley, *Donatist Martyr Stories,* 38).

group of texts from the late fourth and early fifth centuries of the Donatist controversy, which either construct themselves as, or are direct records of, dialogues or debates between the opposing parties. In these debates, real and fictitious, accusations of diabolical deceit vary significantly in intensity.

Diabolical Deceit in Donatist and Anti-Donatist Dialogues

In the 380s, several decades after a violent crackdown on Donatism in the 340s by Roman officials under Constans, Optatus of Milevis wrote a lengthy rebuttal of a (now lost) treatise by the Donatist Parmenian.[76] Optatus addressed Parmenian in the second person as if he were speaking to his face, but of course this text was addressed to a much wider audience, and participated in the broader rhetorical habit in late antiquity of constructing an apparent dialogue in which one party nonetheless maintains complete control of both sides.[77] It is not possible to know how accurately Optatus represented his opponent's argument; in the main, tellingly, he tended to paraphrase rather than to quote Parmenian.

In his framing historical narrative, Optatus claims that the devil was grieved by the unification and pacification of the church under Constantine, and that under the (pagan) emperor Julian's restoration of privileges to Donatists in the early 360s, 'it was almost at the same instant that your [i.e. the Donatists'] madness returned to Africa, and the devil was released from his imprisonment.'[78] This resembles a common strategy of both the Donatists and their opponents to frame events in cosmic terms: whether Eusebius, explaining that schism in Africa during the reign of Constantine was provoked by 'some evil demon apparently resenting the unstinted present prosperity';[79] or the narrator of the Donatist *Passion of Maximian and Isaac*, explaining that after a wave of persecution had died down, the devil

[76] Optatus of Milevis, *Against the Donatists* (ed. and transl. Mireille Labrousse, SC 412–13 [Paris, 1995–6]; transl. Mark Edwards [Liverpool, 1997]). Edwards includes detailed discussion of dating at xvi–xviii.

[77] On the '"cut-and-paste" technique which creates the impression … [of] verbal debate', see Caroline Humfress, 'Controversialist: Augustine in Combat', in Mark Vessey, ed., *A Companion to Augustine* (Chichester, 2012), 323–35, at 329–30.

[78] Optatus, *Against the Donatists* 2.15 and 17 (transl. Edwards, 43, 44).

[79] Eusebius, *Life of Constantine* 1.45.2 (transl. Cameron and Hall, 88).

'enraged for a second time, kindled the dying embers of fury into torture.'[80]

Thereafter, Optatus tends to insinuate that Parmenian and his party were diabolical through scriptural allusions, rather than direct accusations. Early in Book I, Optatus writes that the Donatists 'conspire with that thief who robs God',[81] an elliptical reference to a notion of diabolical robbery that he reprises later in an attack on the Donatist practice of re-baptism, when he states that 'the devil who like a thief wished to rob something [John 10: 10], helped by your actions, sees the person made entirely his own from whom he wished to steal a little.'[82] That is, the Donatist practice of re-baptism is presented as having the unwanted effect of banishing the Holy Spirit from the candidate, thereby allowing the devil access. Optatus accuses Parmenian of deception and seduction in his teaching: 'you have acted subtly for the purpose of seducing and deceiving the minds of your audience …'.[83] He cites Ezekiel 13: 10 on the whitewashed wall to point the finger at the Donatists as 'false prophets who seduce'.[84] At times, particular phrases or metaphors subtly allude to a diabolical referent, for example in references to the heretics' 'pernicious doctrine' and the 'subtle seduction of their words' corrupting the 'health of the faithful with creeping disease'.[85] In complaints that his opponent's party 'have been able to seduce by factious or devious talk', Optatus even evokes an important scriptural passage for diabolical dissimulation which we encountered earlier, claiming that those the Donatists have deceived, 'once sheep', 'have suddenly become wolves' (Matthew 7: 15).[86]

A more direct brand of diabolical accusation can be found in invective from the turn of the fourth and fifth centuries by a Donatist bishop of Cirta, Petilian, who wrote a letter to his clergy trashing his opponents using familiar forms of diabolical attack.[87] Augustine

80 *Passion of Maximian* 3 (Maier, 260; transl. Tilley, *Donatist Martyr Stories,* 64).
81 Ibid. 1.3 (transl. Edwards, 3).
82 Ibid. 4.6 (transl. Edwards, 91).
83 Ibid. 1.9 (transl. Edwards, 7).
84 Ibid 3.10–11 (transl. Edwards, 7).
85 Ibid. 4.5 (transl. Edwards, 88–9).
86 Ibid. 6.8 (transl. Edwards, 125).
87 Augustine, *Answer to Petilian* (ed. Petschenig, CSEL 52 [Vienna, 1909], 3–277; transl. Maureen Tilley and Boniface Ramsey, *New City Press Works of St Augustine* 21 [Hyde Park, NY, 2019], 47–264). See Alexander Evers, '*Contra litteras Petiliani*', in Karla

first of all received and rebutted a portion of this letter in *c.*400, preserved as Book I of his *Answer to Petilian;* a year later, when he had acquired access to the entirety of Petilian's letter, he produced a lengthier refutation of it, preserved as Book II of the same work. In this more detailed refutation, Augustine quoted directly and extensively from Petilian's work, allowing us to see something of the Donatist's writing.[88] The impression produced by Book II of his *Answer* that this was a genuine in-person dialogue between two parties is certainly illusory, since Augustine was very much in control, openly admitting that he was in fact manufacturing the appearance of a stenographically transcribed dialogue: 'I shall cite passages from [Petilian's] letter under his name, and I shall give my response under my name, as though we were debating and being recorded by secretaries [*tamquam, cum ageremus, a notariis excepta sint*].'[89]

If we assume that Petilian's invective against his opponents was accurately reported in Book II of Augustine's *Answer*, it turns out to contain some well-established themes. They include the biting deployment of John 8: 44 in diatribes against a bishop whose precise identity is unclear:

> Yes, yes, wicked persecutor, with whatever cloak of benevolence you cover yourself, under whichever word for peace you wage war with your kisses, with whichever term of unity [*quolibet unitatis vocabulo*] you lead astray the race of men, you who even now are lying and deceiving are truly the devil's son, showing your father by your character [*vere diaboli filius es, dum moribus indicas patrem*].[90]

This condemnation of his opponent's stated goal of unity as a diabolical trick reminds us of the representation of Constans's edict of unity

Pollmann and Willemien Otten, eds, *The Oxford Guide to the Historical Reception of Augustine*, 3 vols (Oxford, 2013), 1: 213–15.

[88] The fact that Augustine quoted (and sometimes criticized) his opponents' biblical texts when they differed from his own texts demonstrates that, in this respect at least, his quotations were accurate: cf. Hugh Houghton, *Augustine's Text of John: Patristic Citations and Latin Gospel Manuscripts* (Oxford, 2008), 81–5.

[89] Augustine, *Answer to Petilian,* 2.1 (transl. Tilley and Ramsey, 75). On Augustine's techniques of quotation and ventriloquization, see Humfress, 'Controversialist', 330; on Augustine creating an impression of dialogue with the Donatists, see Jennifer Ebbeler, *Disciplining Christians: Correction and Community in Augustine's Letters* (New York, 2012), 151–90.

[90] Augustine, *Answer to Petilian* 2.17.38 (transl. Tilley and Ramsey, 91, adapted).

in the *Passion of Donatus* as a cunning ruse of Satan, and the reference to waging war with kisses evokes Judas's traitorous kiss.[91] Augustine replies that Petilian's opponents had made the very same charges against the Donatists. He then quoted Petilian's long list of scriptural proof texts which Petilian had adduced to demonstrate that his opponent had taken on the title of bishop falsely:

> Petilian said: 'It is not so surprising that you unlawfully take on the title of bishop for yourself. This is the devil's true way of acting [*haec est vera diaboli consuetudo*], to deceive precisely by claiming for himself the title of sanctity, as the apostle proclaims: "It is not surprising", he says, "if Satan transforms himself as though into an angel of light, and his ministers as though into ministers of righteousness." [2 Corinthians 11: 13–14]. Neither is it surprising, therefore, that you falsely call yourself a bishop…'.[92]

Augustine responds tartly that all Petilian has proved is that there were false bishops, something on which they agreed. Petilian subsequently composed what was apparently an abusive response to Augustine's second book, to which Augustine responded with a final, third book, but, in this instance, he provided almost no direct quotations of Petilian's accusations, deliberately refusing to engage with the personal attacks made against him.[93]

Not quite ten years after Augustine had staged this debate with Petilian in literary terms, the two bishops encountered each other in person for the first time at the so-called Conference of Carthage in June 411. This quasi-judicial meeting between two massed groups of several hundred Donatist and anti-Donatist bishops was summoned and adjudicated over by imperial officials, and was designed to find, once and for all, in favour of the anti-Donatists.[94] The spoken words of all the participants were stenographically transcribed by a large team of secular and ecclesiastical notaries, and that record was

[91] *Passion of Donatus* 3 (Maier, *Dossier*, 204; transl. Tilley, *Donatist Martyr Stories*, 54–5), discussed above in section two. On the idea of a 'war of kisses', see Shaw, *Sacred Violence*, 546; he also cites Prov. 27: 6 as a possible source for this passage of Petilian.

[92] Augustine, *Answer to Petilian* 2.18.40 (transl. Tilley and Ramsey, 91).

[93] Augustine, *Answer to Petilian* 3.1.1–2 (transl. Tilley and Ramsey, 342–3).

[94] On the Conference of Carthage, see Shaw, *Sacred Violence*, 544–86. For a modification of the view that its end was pre-determined, see Neil McLynn, 'The Conference of Carthage Reconsidered', in Miles, ed., *The Donatist Schism*, 220–48.

then meticulously authenticated, line by line, by its participants.[95] It is notable that in the surviving record of the three days of debate, much of which was procedural, there are barely any accusations of specifically diabolical inspiration or assistance made by the episcopal participants. The relatively restrained tone for the conference seems to have been set by the convening officers, among whose lengthy preambles can be found only muted allusions to diabolical machinations. Thus the notary and tribune Marcellinus, acting as judge in the proceedings, referred obliquely in his opening words to the devil : 'God desires to see the error of the old enemy [*antiqui hostis*] amended, so that the true religion does not long give the pagans the spectacle of its dissensions …'.[96] One of the notaries, Martialis, before laying out the elaborate ground rules about the process of transcribing the debate, explained why this was necessary using language which also loosely evoked the diabolical serpent of Scripture: 'to prevent the slightest slanderous suspicion [*aliquatenus calumniosa suspicio*] from creeping [*inserpat*] into this examination intended to draw out the truth'.[97]

The opening process was designed to authenticate the presence of every single attending bishop, Donatist and anti-Donatist, who filed in one by one while their identities were checked. During this process, bishops from both sides accused each other of underhand tactics and even of lying, but not directly of devilish behaviour.[98] The Donatist Petilian exclaimed that it was possible that his opponents had included under their lists of bishops those of a lower clerical order and fictitiously granted them a higher status, as a way of swelling their numbers; his indictment included the passing accusation that his opponents lied, earning a swift rebuke from Marcellinus that it was not fitting for a bishop to make a false accusation against

[95] On the creation of records at the Conference of Carthage, see Thomas Graumann, *The Acts of the Early Church Councils: Production and Character* (Oxford, 2021), 32–40.

[96] *Acts of the Council of Carthage* 1.3 (ed. and transl. Serge Lancel, SC 195 [Paris, 1972], 562–3). In expounding Leviathan in Ps. 103: 29, Augustine glosses the phrase *antiquus hostis* ('the old enemy') as 'the devil' in combination with *draco* ('dragon'), perhaps a loose allusion to Rev. 12: 9: *En. Ps.* 103.7 (transl. Boulding, *New City Press Works of St Augustine* III/19 [Hyde Park, NY, 2003] 172).

[97] *Acts of the Council of Carthage* 1.10.70 (ed. and transl. Lancel, 582–3).

[98] Erica Hermanowicz, *Possidius of Calama: A Study of the North African Episcopate in the Age of Augustine* (Oxford, 2008), 214 and n. 81, cites 'at least seven occasions during the conference when the Donatists accuse the Catholics of lying', but her stated examples do not encompass those discussed here.

one of his colleagues.[99] Other bishops clashed about who had real authority in any particular town: Victor, an anti-Donatist, and Januarius, a Donatist, both claimed to be bishop of the town of Libertina (south-west of Carthage): 'Januarius: "The diocese is mine"; Victor: "Since he has no-one there, neither church nor anyone from his communion, it is in vain that he lies that it is his diocese [*frustra mentitur quod sit eius dioecesis*]."'[100] Another accusation of lying was made by Severianus, an anti-Donatist bishop, who objected to the claim of the Donatist Adeodatus that the people of Ceramussa (near Milevis) were 'his', but that his opponents' violence had chased away all his clerics. Severianus responded: 'He lies, as God is my witness [*mentitur, teste Deo*].' Marcellinus reminded Adeodatus to keep it short: 'Will your Sanctity please just say if there is currently a bishop of your party in this community?' When Adeodatus made another rather rambling claim, Severianus again retorted, curtly, 'He lies [*mentitur*].'[101]

Testy accusations of falsehood and fraud there were, then, but almost no accusations of diabolical influence. Indeed, it appears that the only time such accusations were made was in the third session of the debate, the complete stenographic record of which has frustratingly been lost and for which only abbreviated accounts survive in Marcellus's chapter headings and in Augustine's *Breviculus*, a retrospective and partisan summary.[102] Here, it seems that the anti-Donatists had accused the Donatists, in ripping out the eyes of their opponents, of surpassing the devil, probably referring here to a tactic associated with the so-called circumcellions, Donatist shock-troops associated with committing acts of shocking violence including blinding.[103] The Donatists' riposte was that the catholics took the part of the devil. It is striking that it was only in the context of overt violence, rather than more insidious deceit, that the accusation of diabolical involvement was levelled, taking us back to our

[99] *Acts of the Council of Carthage* 1.61-62 (ed. and transl. Lancel, 674–5).

[100] Ibid. 1.116 (ed. and transl. Lancel, 706–9).

[101] Ibid. 1.134 (ed. and transl. Lancel, 772–3).

[102] See Sara Matteoli, '*Breviculus collationis cum Donatistis*', in Pollmann and Otten, eds, *The Oxford Guide to the Historical Reception of Augustine*, 1: 164–6.

[103] *Capitula* of the *Acts of the Council of Carthage* 3.298–9 (ed. and transl. Serge Lancel, SC 224 [Paris, 1975], 504–5); Augustine, *Breviculus* 3.11.2§–2 (ed. Serge Lancel, CChr.SL 149A [Turnholt, 1974], 287–8). On accusations of violence made against the circumcellions that include blinding, see Shaw, *Sacred Violence*, 675–720.

starting point of Augustine's sermon, and his stress on Satan's tactical flexibility.

Another way in which the Donatists introduced the possibility of diabolical activity at Carthage was at one remove, through the reading of other texts adduced as evidence. Again at the point where the stenographic transcript no longer survives, and events are only attested to by Marcellus's chapter headings and Augustine's summary, we learn that the Donatists produced a set of martyr acts to be read aloud as part of their argument against the authenticity of the 'protocol of Cirta'.[104] From various internal clues, this text was most probably some version of the *Acts of the Abitinian Martyrs* (discussed above in section two) which was replete with lurid accusations of the diabolical inspiration of imperial officials, both in one of the early framing dating passages ('In the times of Diocletian and Maximian, the devil waged war against the Christians ...') and in subsequent accusations made by the martyrs against their pagan persecutors.[105]

Overall, a great deal of effort went into the careful management of the encounter at Carthage between hostile communities who had a history of violent encounters, and this probably constrained exchanges of the kind of invective we find in Augustine's invented dialogue with Petilian.[106] The solemnity of the occasion – presided over by imperial officials and conducted according to the elaborate rules of politesse demanded by late antique ceremonial – seems to have tamped down the trading of direct diabolical insults, demonstrating the importance of context and convention in regulating the extremes of invective.

Conclusion

We have seen that the accusation of diabolical dissimulation was made regularly by both Donatists and their opponents in a range of written and spoken words. There were distinctive variations in

[104] *Capitula* of the *Acts of the Council of Carthage* 3.433, 446–7 (ed. and transl. Lancel, 528–31); Augustine, *Breviculus* 3.17.32–3 (ed. Lancel, 296–8). On the date and contents of the 'protocol of Cirta', see Shaw, *Sacred Violence*, 816–18.

[105] On the identification of this set of martyr acts with the *Acts of the Abitinian Martyrs*, see discussion by Lancel, SC 194, 95–6. On the possible deployment of this text at the Conference of Carthage, see Dearn, 'Abitinian Martyrs', 9–11.

[106] On the necessity of stage managing the encounter, see Shaw, *Sacred Violence*, 564–9.

the ways in which those accusations were made, which included a kind of direct name-calling, where martyrs addressed their persecutors as 'devil'; general statements that one's opponents were animated or possessed by the father of lies; and the deployment of metaphorical language which evoked scriptural templates of diabolical deceit without making the accusation directly. Of course, the varying tone and register of those accusations was in part shaped by conventions about what kinds of polemical rhetoric were appropriate in different contexts. The audiences, genres and contexts of such invective shaped what was polite or possible to say. Unsurprisingly, it was easier to accuse opponents of diabolical dissimulation to an insider audience, than to do so directly to their faces. More broadly, we have seen that in Christian letters, sermons and treatises of late antiquity, especially those addressed to 'insiders' sharing a point of view, accusations of lying made against opponents were rife, and went in both directions.

Augustine defined lying not by the contents of the lie, but by its direction; not so much as saying things that are not true, but rather, saying things with the intention to deceive.[107] In this context, those stigmatized as heretics and schismatics like the Donatists were considered diabolical, not only because their ecclesiology or sacramental theology was false, but because in trying to disseminate their ideas, they were – like Augustine's wily serpentine Donatist with whom I started – deceiving and poisoning others. In two separate treatises and a letter on the topic, Augustine reiterated that all lying was sinful, but his views were developed in part against contemporary Christian arguments that lying could sometimes be permissible and that Jesus himself had lied.[108] That some Christians thought lying itself was not problematic if well intended can be seen further from the development of a theological argument that Christ's incarnation was itself a form of deception, cunningly designed to displace Satan from his mastery over humans.[109] Indeed, a variety of Christian emperors,

[107] For Augustine's ideas about lying, see Griffiths, *Lying*, 25–39.

[108] See Augustine, *On Lying* (transl. Muldowney, *Fathers of the Church* 16 [Washington, DC, 1952], 53–110). His letter refuting Oceanus's charge that Jesus's denial of knowledge about the timing of the end of the world was a 'useful lie': *Letter* 180.3–5 (transl. Teske, *New City Press Works of St Augustine* II/3 [Hyde Park, NY, 2003], 159–60); and *Against Lying* (transl. Jaffee, *Fathers of the Church* 16 [Washington, DC, 1952], 125–79).

[109] See, for instance, the case study by John Egan, 'The Deceit of the Devil According to Gregory Nazianzen', *Studia Patristica* 22 (1989), 8–13.

clerics and laypersons admitted to or counselled practising dissimulation in practical situations where the ends justified the means. For example, Augustine's treatise *Against Lying* denounced both the so-called Priscillianists who argued that the presence of lies in Scripture sanctioned the very practice of lying, and the Priscillianists' opponents, who had taken to lying to infiltrate the group. Returning to the Donatist controversy, we find an imperial sanctioning of similarly deceitful tactics. In 315, the emperor Constantine wrote to Celsus, *vicarius* of Africa, commanding that he 'accept the necessity of dissimulation' (*dissimulandum … cognoscas*) in treating schismatic Donatists decently, while waiting for the emperor to visit and give judgment; the pretence of hospitality was presumably designed not to alert the Donatists to Constantine's menacing promise to 'destroy and scatter' (*perdam atque discutiam*) once he arrived.[110] We have come full circle. The Christian Roman emperor who, like the anti-Donatist clerics of North Africa, decried the violence and deceit of the Donatists as diabolical, was recommending precisely this combination of tactics to overcome them.

[110] Constantine, Letter to Celsus (Maier, *Dossier,* 194–6, transl. Edwards, 193–4).

‘In Defiance of his Cloth’: Monastic (Im)Piety in Late Antique Egypt

Paula Tutty*

Liverpool

Hagiographical writing promotes a vision of Egyptian monasticism in which pious ascetic figures are isolated from the world. Peter Brown highlighted the role of the holy man as patron, but nonetheless reinforced a traditional view of Egyptian monasticism based on his readings of works such as the sixth-century Aphothegmata Patrum. *Surviving monastic correspondence, in contrast, demonstrates that there was a highly individualized approach to the monastic vocation. In this article, I turn to documentary material to consider the complexities of the early development of the movement. As a case study, I use the Greek and Coptic correspondence of a fourth-century monk called Apa John. My conclusion is that activities and behaviours described in the texts do not always accord with any known typology or ideal, but they are invaluable for exploring aspects of the early monastic impulse and the role played by the movement in wider society.*

Introduction

Over the centuries, literary descriptions of the lives of the earliest Egyptian monks have acted as an inspiration to Christian thinkers, who tended to perceive the monks’ ascetic lifestyle as standing in stark contrast to the excesses of their own generations. During the Middle Ages, the inclusion of tales of the desert fathers in Jacobus de Varagine’s very popular *Golden Legend* (composed in Genoa *c.*1260) boosted this reputation.[1] In addition, the inception of the medieval Observant Reform Movement (*observantia regulae*), with its burning desire to return to the simplicity of the earliest days, owed much to the reading of the monastic biographies found in

* E-mail: paula.tutty@gmail.com.

[1] See Pia Palladino, ‘Pilgrims and the Desert Fathers: Dominican Spirituality and the Holy Land’, in Laurence Kanter and Pia Palladino, eds, *Fra Angelico* (New Haven, CT, 2005), 27–39, at 32–4.

Studies in Church History 60 (2024), 43–63
doi: 10.1017/stc.2024.2

the works of St Jerome, Cassian and Augustine.[2] Renaissance writers and artists were similarly moved to create a new vision of the early monastic landscape.[3] Later audiences, imbued with the teachings of the Enlightenment, were less well disposed: some, upon encountering descriptions of ascetic excess, considered the behaviours of the monks as frankly fanatical and abhorrent. Edward Gibbon, the famed eighteenth-century historian, put in writing a commonly felt sentiment of the period when he wrote: 'These unhappy exiles from social life were impelled by the dark and implacable genius of superstition.'[4]

The reputation of early ascetics was not entirely lost, however, and they continued to attract many admirers, but there was an increasing tendency to regard their renunciative practices, at least as described in hagiographical literature, as unhealthily extreme. Peter Brown's 1971 article, 'The Rise and Function of the Holy Man', did much to mediate against this when he placed the ascetic ideal centre stage in his discussion of the growth of early Christianity.[5] Using evidence largely collated from Syrian hagiographical writing, Brown presented the relationships between the monks and the rural populations in which they resided as following a patron-client pattern. He considered the holy man to be a liminal figure, who operated outside the social structure and who had the capability to effect great change due to his charisma and strong mindedness. At the time that Brown wrote his seminal work, contemporary Egyptian documentary materials, particularly those written in Coptic, were relatively inaccessible to non-specialists, and Brown was thus heavily reliant on literary descriptions of Egyptian monasticism that emphasized the ascetic impulse as it was imagined within a harsh desert landscape.

[2] Bert Roest, 'Observant Reform in Religious Orders', in Miri Rubin and Walter Simons, eds, *Christianity in Western Europe* c.*1100*–c.*1500*, 7: *Reform and Renewal* (Cambridge, 2010), 446–57.

[3] Ann Leader, 'The Church and Desert Fathers in Early Renaissance Florence: Further Thoughts on a "New" Thebaid', in John Garton and Diane Wolfthal, eds, *New Studies on Old Masters: Essays in Renaissance Art in Honour of Colin Eisler*, Essays and Studies 26 (Toronto, 2011), 221–34.

[4] Edward Gibbon, *History of the Decline and Fall of the Roman Empire*, 6 vols (London, 1846), 3: 346. On Gibbon and monasticism, see Mark Sheridan, 'The Modern Historiography of Early Egyptian Monasticism', in Mark Sheridan, ed., *From the Nile to the Rhone and Beyond: Studies in Early Monastic Literature and Scriptural Interpretation*, Studia Anselmiana 12 (Rome, 2012), 159–62.

[5] Peter Brown, 'The Rise and Function of the Holy Man in Late Antiquity', *JRS* 61 (1971), 80–101.

This gave rise to his suggestion that, due to geographical limitations, Egyptian holy men were unable to interact with local society in the way that the monks of Syria, Asia Minor and Palestine did:

> The links between the holy man and society constantly yielded to the pressure of this great fact. To survive at all in the hostile environment of such a desert, the Egyptian had to transplant into it the tenacious and all-absorbing routines of the villages of the οἰκουμένη. To live at all, a man had to remain in one place, earning his living from manual labour, from pottery and reed-weaving.[6]

In 1988, Brown returned to this theme in *The Body and Society: Men, Women, and Sexual Renunciation in Early Christianity*, in which Egyptian ascetics were described as surviving on a meagre diet gained by way of the manual labour they performed as hired hands in the local villages.[7]

Brown's writings may have radically changed perceptions of ascetic holy men and their place in history, but they did little to enhance the reputation of Egyptian monks. Brown himself, when reflecting on his earlier work, wrote: 'Looking back at what I would now have to abandon and modify in my previous picture of the holy man, I think that the greatest single feature of my portrayal of the holy man in need of revision would be his "splendid isolation".'[8] Averil Cameron took this a step further by arguing that the concept of the holy man as described by Brown was a literary construction rather than a social reality.[9] Such conclusions accord with Jacob Ashkenazi's 2014 article on monasticism in the late antique Levant.[10] He revises Brown's model by arguing that we need to distinguish between 'the Holy Man' as a product of hagiographic literature, and the socially established role of monk which was an integral feature of the local countryside. He concludes that many monks, rather than being revered as

[6] Ibid. 83.

[7] Peter Brown, *The Body and Society: Men, Women, and Sexual Renunciation in Early Christianity* (New York, 1988), 218–20.

[8] Peter Brown, 'The Saint as Exemplar in Late Antiquity', *Representations* 2 (1983), 1–25, at 11.

[9] Averil Cameron, 'On Defining the Holy Man', in James Howard-Johnston and Paul Antony Hayward, eds, *The Cult of Saints in Late Antiquity and the Middle Ages: Essays on the Contribution of Peter Brown* (Oxford, 1999), 27–44.

[10] Jacob Ashkenazi, 'Holy Man versus Monk—Village and Monastery in the Late Antique Levant: Between Hagiography and Archaeology', *Journal of the Economic and Social History of the Orient* 57 (2014), 745–65.

patrons, were established members of local communities, living and working alongside their fellow villagers.[11] The monks of the Levant may have ideologically renounced the world, but they retained familial, economic and social ties that bound them to the society in which they dwelt.

In recent times, Brown's theories regarding Egyptian monks have undergone further modification. Claudia Rapp, in her use of monastic letter collections, was able to demonstrate that Egyptian monks, rather than focusing inwards, were often called upon to act as intercessory figures for the local community through the use of prayer as intervention.[12] In particular, she made use of letters written to the fourth-century hermit Paphnutius, whose petitions were deemed particularly potent by his correspondents.[13] The model of monk as a form of spiritual patron is well evidenced in the letters of Paphnutius, who was clearly venerated by the writers of these surviving letters. However, monks were not just 'patrons' in the sense described by Brown: other letters quoted by Rapp, such as the fourth-century Nepheros collection, provide evidence for involvement in very different activities, as Rapp herself acknowledges. The letters of Nepheros are those of a person fulfilling a difficult managerial role within a busy monastic federation, and a significant portion of his correspondence describes the problems faced by his secular agent Paul in the sale of monastic produce and the procurement of scarce items. There are few demands for prayers of the type that fill the letters of Paphnutius.[14] This preoccupation with financial and practical matters is a common theme in other surviving monastic letters of the period, such as those discovered inside the binding of the Nag Hammadi Codices.[15] Additionally, recent research by scholars such as Eva Wipszycka and James Goehring has demonstrated that fourth- and fifth-century monasticism was a phenomenon that

[11] Ibid. 764–5.

[12] Claudia Rapp, '"For next to God, you are my salvation": Reflections on the Rise of the Holy Man in Late Antiquity', in Howard-Johnston and Hayward, eds, *The Cult of Saints*, 63–82.

[13] Rapp, '"For next to God, you are my salvation"', 69–71. See also Tim Vivian, 'Holy Men and Businessmen: Monks as Intercessors in Fourth-Century Egypt as Illustrated by the Papyri and Ostraca', *Cistercian Studies Quarterly* 39 (2004), 235–69.

[14] Rapp, '"For next to God, you are my salvation"', 71–2.

[15] Published in John W. B. Barns, Gerald M. Browne and John C. Shelton, eds, *Nag Hammadi Codices: Greek and Coptic Papyri from the Cartonnage of the Covers*, Nag Hammadi Series 16 (Leiden, 1981).

developed as much within the towns and villages of Egypt as it did in the barren regions that lay alongside the river Nile.[16]

Whilst the ideal of Egyptian monasticism promoted by Brown has been revised, its underlying message, with its emphasis on the holy man living in solitude safe from the temptations of the secular world, continues to dominate descriptions of Egyptian monastic life. In this article, I turn to contemporary documentation in order to discuss the extent to which the activities related therein compare with the monastic ideal as promoted by hagiographical literature. As we shall see, when the behaviours and activities described in the documentation are placed alongside the accounts of early Egyptian monasticism found in works such as *The Life of Antony* as described by Athanasius, or Jerome's *Life of Paul of Thebes*, the situations and attitudes prove so very different it can create a marked sense of dissonance within the reader. An individual case study, here using the letters of a fourth-century monk from Middle Egypt called Apa John, further emphasizes this point. The segment of John's correspondence that has survived gives us a lively first-hand account of aspects of his involvement in local affairs and his interactions with a wide range of petitioners. The result is that, rather than acting as archetypal 'holy men' living far removed from society, the surviving evidence suggests that many Egyptian monks were heavily engaged in the world, with all its demands and vicissitudes. Not all monks were models of piety but, rather, displayed their human frailties in a way that finds its echo throughout history.

The Development of a Monastic Code in Late Antique Egypt

The origins of monasticism in Egypt are obscure, but the terms 'monks' and 'nuns' appear in the papyrological record from around 324 CE, a time when St Antony was still active in his mission.[17] The evidence for the development of a monastic code is sparse and

[16] Ewa Wipszycka, 'Le monachisme égyptien et les villes', *Travaux et mémoires* 12 (1994), 1–10; James E. Goehring, 'The World Engaged: The Social and Economic World of Early Egyptian Monasticism', in James E. Goehring et al., eds, *Gnosticism and the Early Christian World: Essays in Honor of James M. Robinson* (Sonoma, CA, 1990), 134–44.

[17] The first datable example of the term 'monk' is found in a petition to the Praepositus Pagi for Karanis: *P.Col.* VII 171. See Edwin A. Judge, 'The Earliest Use of Monachos for "Monk" (P.Coll. Youtie 77) and the Origins of Monasticism', *Jahrbuch für Antike und Christentum* 20 (1977), 72–89.

difficult to determine, since widely accepted ground rules did not initially exist for the regulation of the movement we now call monasticism. The most popular, and still commonly quoted, descriptions of early Egyptian monastic ideals are those found in the sixth-century *Apophthegmata Patrum*. Here we discover a multitude of pithy stories in which older monks guide novices towards an understanding of the proper way to conduct an ascetic lifestyle. These vignettes have an immediate appeal, but they have proven themselves to be highly problematic as a source material. One major issue is their disputed origin for, as Columba Stewart reminds us, the sayings found within the *Apophthegmata Patrum* 'are not time capsules from fourth-century and early fifth-century Egypt, but carefully curated selections chosen in Palestine at least a century after they were supposedly uttered.'[18] Valuable as paideia (the educational training that was deemed necessary for the inculcation of cultural ideals) to be used in the formation of novices, they cannot be considered reliable sources for the period they claim to represent, although it is possible that they do contain some distilled essence of historical detail in regard to certain aspects of ascetic life.

More reliable are the contemporary eyewitness accounts that evolved from religious tourism. Men and women from across the Roman empire eagerly made their way to Egypt in search of the ascetic experience. Their output includes the *Historia Monachorum in Aegypto* (*Enquiry about the Monks in Egypt*), which contains the recollections of a Christian traveller in the winter of 395/6 CE, Palladius's *Historia Lausiaca* (*Lausiac Histories*) and Egeria's *Itinerarium Egeriae* (*Travels of Egeria*). These writings also have their limitations: the motivation for their creation was to inspire fellow Christians, rather than act as accurate portrayals of all aspects of monastic life. Even so, they contain invaluable information about the living situation of the hermits who dwelt in the barren terrain of Scetis and Nitria, far from the settled communities located along the banks of the Nile, and about the organization of the early *coenobia* (formalized monastic communities), such as those founded by Pachomius in Upper Egypt. Other literary sources of note include

[18] Columba Stewart, 'Rethinking the History of Monasticism East and West: A Modest Tour d'Horizon', in Santha Bhattacharji, Rowan Williams and Dominic Mattos, eds, *Prayer and Thought in Monastic Tradition: Essays in Honour of Benedicta Ward SLG* (New York, 2014), 3–16, at 6.

biographies of the foremost holy men and women, such as the universally popular *Life of Antony*, reputedly written by Bishop Athanasius in around 360 CE and generally considered the ultimate exemplar of its genre, establishing the idealized prototype of the ascetic monk.[19] Athanasius's careful construction creates a vision of an obedient and unworldly ascetic who lives in a way that conforms to standards laid out by Athanasius himself.[20] Gregory of Nazianzus was even moved to suggest that the *Life of Antony* had been composed as a rule for the monastic life in narrative form.[21] Such writings enable us to understand the type of characteristics considered worthy of emulation by the mainstream church. What they cannot tell us is how monasticism was experienced as an everyday phenomenon and how it positioned itself within local communities and secular society in general.

In the papyrological records, monks and nuns start to appear with increasing frequency from the mid-fourth century. The evidence demonstrates that would-be monks dressed distinctively, thus creating a conscious badge of identity which soon became associated with an embryonic moral code. In a mid-fourth-century letter from the archive of Nepheros (*P.Neph.* 7), for example, a monk accused of deceitfulness and of failure to pay his debts is said to have had no shame for his 'cloth' (σχῆμα), suggesting that, even at this early date, wearing a monastic habit already carried with it certain social obligations.[22] The letters of St Antony make several references to those who knowingly donned the habit, yet continued to act sinfully.[23] A petition from a woman called Aurelia Nonna living in Spania, a village close to Oxyrhynchus, provides contemporary evidence on this matter. Her nephew, whom she describes as a monk, had physically attacked her over a disputed marriage proposal for her daughter.[24] Furthermore, he had torn her clothes in the process, adding a hint of sexual scandal to his impropriety. As Aurelia Nonna

[19] William Harmless, *Desert Christians: An Introduction to the Literature of Early Monasticism* (Oxford, 2004), 57–114.

[20] David Brakke, *Athanasius and Asceticism* (Baltimore, MD, 1995), 205.

[21] Gregory of Nazianzus, *Orationes theologicae* 21.5.

[22] Bärbel Kramer, John C. Shelton and Gerald M. Browne, *Das Archiv des Nepheros und verwandte Texte*, Aegyptiaca Treverensia 4 (Mainz, 1987), 54–6.

[23] Anthony the Great, *Epistolae* 2.34; 3.33; 5.29; 7.47.

[24] London, BL, Papyrus 2217. Harold Idris Bell, 'Episcopalis Audientia in Byzantine Egypt', *Byzantion* 1 (1924), 139–44.

pointedly remarks, the nephew's behaviour was 'in defiance of his cloth.'[25] Hostile witnesses, such as the pagan Libanius, complain about those 'that accompany their drinking with the singing of hymns, who hide these excesses under an artificially contrived pallor'.[26] Libanius may stand accused of bias, but state authorities clearly had concerns. The Roman emperor Valens took action and Jerome, writing in 375, records: 'Valens made a law that monks must do military service, and ordered that any who did not want to should be beaten to death with their own staves [*fustis*].'[27] Jerome further reports that: 'many of the monks at Nitria were slaughtered by the tribunes and the soldiers.'[28] Other accounts would seem to accord with this: the monk Piamun, for example, wrote to John Cassian recounting that he had travelled with monks from Egypt and the Thebaid who had been exiled to the mines of Pontus and Armenia under Valens in the 370s.[29] The Roman emperor Marcian wrote in 452 CE, telling Alexandrian monks to 'keep your own selves also from unspeakable canons and contrary assemblies, lest in addition to the loss of your souls you should be subjected to legal punishments.'[30] This was closely followed by another prescript against heretical assemblies only three years later.[31] Even as late as the sixth century, non-aligned monks remained a problem in Egypt, as two sixth-century Coptic letters concerning an imprisoned ϲαρακωτε (sarabaites) monk demonstrate.[32] Such wandering monks not only

[25] 'συνάπτεσθαι, π[αρὰ] ṭὸ σχῆμ[α]': BL, Papyrus 2217.9–10.

[26] Libanius, *Orationes* 30, 'pro Templis' (*c*.385–7 CE), written in protest at the actions of monks in the city of Antioch. *Libanius: Selected Orations*, transl. Albert F. Norman, 3 vols, LCL 451–2 (Cambridge, MA, 1969), 2: 113.

[27] 'Valens lege data ut monachi militarent, nolentes fustibus iussit interfici': transl. Noel Lenski, 'Valens and the Monks: Cudgeling and Conscription as a Means of Social Control', *DOP* 58 (2004), 93–117, at 93. See Rudolf Helm and Ursula Treu, *Eusebius Werke*, 7: *Die Chronik des Hieronymus. Hieronymi Chronicon*, GCS 47 (Berlin, 1984), 248. It should be noted, however, that Jerome is the only witness for this allegation.

[28] 'Multi monachorum Nitriae per tribunos et milites caesi': transl. Lenski, 'Valens and the Monks', 97.

[29] Cassian, *Collationes* 18.7; transl. Lenski, 'Valens and the Monks', 98.

[30] *Marcian* 7.481–4; transl. Paul R. Coleman-Norton, *Roman State and Christian Church: A Collection of Legal Documents to A.D. 535*, 2 vols (London, 1966), 2: 827–8.

[31] Andrea Sterk, *Renouncing the World yet Leading the Church: The Monk-Bishop in Late Antiquity* (Cambridge, MA, 2004), 166.

[32] *P.Cair.S.R.* 3733.5bis and 6bis. Loreleï Vanderheyden, 'Les lettres coptes des archives de Dioscore d'Aphrodité', in Paul Schubert, ed., *Actes du 26e Congrès international de papyrologie. Genève 16-21 août 2010* (Geneva, 2012), 793–800.

flouted societal norms, but were seen as a direct threat to public order. They were repeatedly condemned by church authorities, including Augustine who referred to them as hypocrites and pseudo-monks.[33] Instead, monks were urged to remain secluded, submissive to their elders and engaged in spiritual reflection and honest manual labour.

In the late fourth century, Cassian and Jerome outlined neat, threefold typologies of different kinds of monk. Alongside the anchorites, who lived out their lives in solitary spaces, and coenobites, dwelling in organized communities, there was a third group: Cassian's 'Sarabaites' and Jerome's 'Remnuoth'. According to Cassian, this category of monk could be found living in various situations, including secluded within their own homes or in loosely governed communities, but their main hallmark was their lack of obedience to authority.[34] The documentary evidence for the period is less clear-cut and definitive labels are hard to ascribe. For example, we read of two nuns, Theodora and Tauris, who lived in their own home, but rented out a portion of their dwelling place to a Jew.[35] Also, unusually, a Pachomian monk, a member of a community that demanded its members to forfeit all possessions, is recorded as paying tax on privately owned lands.[36] Such evidence would indicate that, in the fourth century, even in what might be considered highly regulated coenobitic communities, the rules for permitted activities had yet to be firmly established.[37] In the monastic letters, there is a

[33] Daniel Caner, *Wandering, Begging Monks*, The Transformation of the Classical Heritage 33 (Berkeley, CA, 2002), 158–62.

[34] Cassian, *Collations* 18.7 and 18.10. In *Theodosian Code* 16.3.1, 'de monachis' (390 CE), wandering monks were banned from the towns and cities. Clyde Pharr, *The Theodosian Code and Novels, and the Sirmondian Constitutions*, Corpus of Roman Law 1 (Princeton, NJ, 1952), 449. See also Lenski, 'Valens and the Monks', 93–117.

[35] Michael W. Haslam, 'P.Oxy. 3203', *Oxyrhynchus Papyri* 44 (1976), 182–4. See also James E. Goehring, 'Through a Glass Darkly: Diverse Images of the "apotaktikoi(ai)" of Early Egyptian Monasticism', *Semeia* 58 (1992), 25–45.

[36] Ewa Wipszycka, 'Les terres de la congrégation pachômienne dans une liste des payements pour les apora', in Jean Bingen, Guy Cambier and Georges Nachtergael, eds, *Le monde grec. Pensée, littérature, histoire, documents. Hommages à Claire Préaux* (Brussels, 1975), 625–36. For the suggestion that the tax was paid on behalf of the local villagers, see Malcolm Choat, 'Property Ownership and Tax Payment', in Anne Boud'hors and Petra Sijpesteijn, eds, *Monastic Estates in Late Antique and Early Islamic Egypt: Ostraca, Papyri, and Essays in Memory of Sarah Clackson*, American Society of Papyrologists 46 (Cincinnati, OH, 2009), 129–40, at 130–3.

[37] On the establishment of authority and tradition in the Pachomian Federations, see James E. Goehring, 'New Frontiers in Pachomian Studies', in Birger A. Pearson and

similar lack of exactitude. Apa John is variously named as an ἀποτακτικός (village ascetic)[38] and ἀναχώρητης (anchorite).[39] Despite the use of these titles, it is clear that Apa John did not live as a lone hermit, but dwelt in some form of community, as attested by letters addressed to him and 'all the (monastic) brothers', with lists of their names.[40] These small glimpses into everyday life remind us that the fourth century was a time of innovation and change as people who called themselves by the term 'monk' could draw together in a variety of permutations.

Andrea Sterk notes how the establishment of monasteries closely aligned to church and state powers played a large part in taming Egyptian monasticism and improving its reputation for waywardness.[41] In itself, however, this did not dampen down accusations of impiety against monks. Instead, the issue was focused within the confines of the *coenobium*, rather than appearing in the guise of a wider urban problem. The problem and challenge of deviant behaviour is a constant theme in the writing of the foremost Egyptian monastic leader of the late fourth to mid-fifth century, Apa Shenoute of the White Monastery Federation in Atripe, Upper Egypt. A large proportion of his flock consisted of families who had joined en masse as an escape from grinding poverty. Shenoute's letters are filled with descriptions of the resultant problems, including accusations of food theft, favouritism and attempts to thwart clandestine family meetings. Shenoute struggled to maintain control over his flock and his letters detail the frequent interpersonal conflicts that took place within the confines of the monastery walls.[42] Sexual pollution was an obvious area of concern, but other accusations include

James E. Goehring, eds, *The Roots of Egyptian Christianity* (Philadelphia, PA, 1986), 236–57, at 240–7.

38 *P.Herm.* 9.

39 *P.Herm.* 7.10 (Greek) and *P.Lond. Copt.* I 1123 (Coptic). The term is relatively rare in the records. See Wipszycka, 'ἀναχώρητης, ἐρημίτης, ἔγκλειστος, ἀποτακτικός: sur la terminologie monastique en Égypte', *Journal of Juristic Papyrology* 31 (2001), 147–68, at 11–12.

40 *P.Herm.* 8, ll. 21–2; *P.Ryl. Copt.* 269, 273, 276.

41 Sterk, *Renouncing the World*, 164–5.

42 Bentley Layton, 'Rules, Patterns, and the Exercise of Power in Shenoute's Monastery: The Problem of World Replacement and Identity Maintenance', *JECS* 15 (2007), 45–73. For further examples, see Caroline T. Schroeder, *Monastic Bodies: Discipline and Salvation in Shenoute of Atripe* (Philadelphia, PA, 2013), 1–24.

deceitful or defiant behaviours that are taken by Shenoute to indicate a lack of respect for his position as leader of the monastery.[43] The consequence was that monks and nuns were regularly punished, including beatings on the soles of the feet for women.[44] Shenoute himself faced accusations of impiety, and in one instance a monk died at his hands as the result of a severe flogging.[45] Shenoute defended himself vigorously, calling it an act of God, but he is clearly aware that his actions were not universally viewed in a favourable light. In the fourth- to fifth-century Pachomian literature, monks are also repeatedly depicted as rejecting the required standards of monastic behaviour, or of failing to live up to them. Pachomius and his senior monks responded by using public humiliation as an organic form of social control. The Pachomian annals describe how one 'bad' monk who had recently died was ritually dishonoured when his garments were burnt in the centre of the monastic compound before the entire community.[46] As might be expected, some people opted out of the system entirely, such as the 'former monk Proous' mentioned in a letter of Apa Paieous dated to 334.[47]

A common theme in works such as the *Aphothegmata Patrum* is that of the errant monk who succumbs to temptation in a whole range of ways. Such tales may have acted as a warning to young novices but, for all their focus on the sinful temptations of the flesh, they do not really engage with the harsh realities of life as they were experienced by the vast majority of Egypt's inhabitants. Ensuring personal survival in the late Roman Empire was never easy, particularly for those who lacked wealth or status. The ideal of the monk making a living through weaving reeds into baskets, as proposed by Brown and many others, was scarcely feasible in a society in which most families possessed the capacity to weave their own items for free.[48] Monks without personal wealth needed a regular income, no matter how

[43] David Brakke, *Demons and the Making of the Monk: Spiritual Combat in Early Christianity* (Harvard, MA, 2006) 100–13.

[44] Schroeder, *Monastic Bodies*, 24–53; Rebecca Krawiec, *Shenoute and the Women of the White Monastery* (Oxford, 2004), 40–6.

[45] Krawiec, *Shenoute and the Women of the White Monastery*, 43–64.

[46] *First Greek Life of Pachomius* G^1, 103; transl. Armand Veilleux, *Pachomian Koinonia*, 1: *The Life of Saint Pachomius*, Cistercian Studies Series 45 (Kalamzoo, MI, 1980), 368.

[47] For example, the 'former monk Proous' in *P.Lond.* 1913.10.

[48] Ewa Wipszycka, *Moines et communautés monastiques en Égypte (IVe–VIIIe siècles)*, Journal of Juristic Papyrology Supplements 11 (Warsaw, 2009), 472–9, 532–45.

ascetic their practices, and they would work on the land if necessity commanded. The monk who renounces his inheritance may be lauded in saintly literature, but this type of behaviour clashed with societal norms to such a degree that it was commonly accepted that only the most extraordinary saint could or would perform such an act.[49] Surviving records reveal that monks and nuns retained property and other forms of personal wealth.[50] One famous example is that of Melania the Elder who, whilst having officially renounced her wealth, was evidently still in control of sizable resources, which she spent in pursuit of her religious ideals.[51] In the documentation, the monk Ammonius is recorded as inheriting property from a certain Gemellus.[52] Another, Macarius, is described as owning sixteen arouras of land in the Hermopolite nome.[53] The continued appearance in documentation of monks and monasteries as landowners throughout the following centuries acts as further confirmation that it was considered an acceptable social norm for monks, not merely to own property, but also to benefit from that ownership through the collection of rents and other incomes.[54] Evidence from later centuries further demonstrates that monks and clergy regularly performed work for pay, with the copying and illustrating of books being a popular source of revenue.[55] Some monks, and monasteries, even lent out money at interest.[56] Banding together was one way to gain economic

[49] Jaclyn L. Maxwell, *Simplicity and Humility in Late Antique Christian Thought: Elites and the Challenge of Apostolic Life* (Cambridge, 2021), 1–12.

[50] Roger S. Bagnall, 'Monks and Property: Rhetoric, Law, and Patronage in the *Apophthegmata Patrum* and the Papyri', *Greek, Roman and Byzantine Studies* 42 (2001), 7–24.

[51] Peter Brown, *Through the Eye of a Needle: Wealth, the Fall of Rome, and the Making of Christianity in the West, 350–550 AD* (Princeton, NJ, 2012), 291–300.

[52] *P.Oxy*. XL VI 3311; Bagnall, 'Monks and Property', 12.

[53] *P.Herm. Landl.* G505/F722; Judge, 'The Earliest Use of Monachos for "Monk"', 169.

[54] James E. Goehring, '"Through a Glass Darkly": Diverse Images of the ἀποτακτικόι(αι) in Early Egyptian Monasticism', in James E. Goehring, ed., *Ascetics, Society, and the Desert: Studies in Early Egyptian Monasticism* (Harrisburg, PA, 1999), 60–8; Jean Gascou, 'Monasteries, Economic Activities of', in Aziz S. Atiya, ed., *The Coptic Encyclopedia* (New York, 1991), 1639–40.

[55] Anastasia Maravela, 'Monastic Book Production in Christian Egypt', in Harald Froschauer and Cornelia Römer, eds, *Spätantike Bibliotheken. Leben und Lesen in den frühen Klöstern Ägyptens* (Vienna, 2008), 25–37.

[56] Tomasz Markiewicz, 'The Church, Clerics, Monks and Credit in the Papyri', in Anne Boud'hors, ed., *Monastic Estates in Late Antique and Early Islamic Egypt: Ostraca, Papyri, and Studies in Honour of Sarah Clackson* (Cincinnati, OH, 2008), 178–204; Amin

security, perhaps by forming a semi-eremitical laura – a community consisting of a cluster of cells based around communal facilities – or as members of a coenobitic community. Hermits could be connected to more formalized monastic communities, perhaps withdrawing on a temporary basis before returning to the monastery. It is against this diverse, and sometimes contradictory, background that we turn to look at the letters of Apa John.

An Individual Case History – Apa John

It is unfortunate that a comprehensive edition of the Apa John archive has yet to be published, as the contents are highly illuminating of the daily activities of this well-connected monk. The total number of letters belonging to the archive is still in doubt, but the main core consists of four letters in Greek and nine in Coptic.[57] Their origin is obscure: the collection was discovered early in the twentieth century by persons unknown, before being sold off to a dealer in Cairo. Several museums and private collectors then competed to buy the individual letters and information about their place of origin was lost.[58] Palaeographical and internal features indicate that the letters were written sometime in the mid- to late fourth century, perhaps in or near the city of Hermopolis in Middle Egypt.[59] The Apa John of the letters was evidently well connected socially, leading many scholars to speculate that this is none other than the famous John of Lycopolis, a notable holy man, active at the time these letters were presumed to have been dictated, who was particularly famed for his gift of clairvoyance and the ability to effect healings from

Benaissa, 'A Usurious Monk from the Apa Apollo Monastery in Bawit', *Chronique d'Égypte* 85 (2010), 374–81.

[57] Malcolm Choat, 'Monastic Letters on Papyrus from Late Antique Egypt', in idem and Mariachiara Giorda, eds, *Writing and Communication in Early Egyptian Monasticism*, Texts and Studies in Early Christianity 9 (Leiden, 2017), 37–40.

[58] Malcolm Choat, 'The Archive of Apa Johannes: Notes on a Proposed New Edition', in Jaakko Frösén and Suomen Tiedeseura, eds, *Proceedings of the 24th International Congress of Papyrologists: Helsinki, 1–7 August 2004*, Commentationes Humanarum Litterarum 122 (Helsinki, 2007), 175–83.

[59] A reference to military recruitment practices in *P.Herm.* 7 suggests a post-381 CE date. See Constantine Zuckerman, 'The Hapless Recruit Psois and the Mighty Anchorite, Apa John', *Bulletin of the American Society of Papyrologists* 32 (1995), 183–94, at 183–8.

afar.[60] Palladius's vivid description portrays John as an uneducated Egyptian monoglot, dwelling in a cell on the mountain of Lyco and communicating with his illustrious visitors through a small window at the weekend.[61] John of Lycopolis features prominently in the work of several authors, including John Cassian, Jerome and Augustine of Hippo.[62] The John of the letters is certainly addressed with a fulsome civility, as would become any respected holy man. One example begins:

> Therefore I greet your reverence by this letter, begging you to remember myself who greets you, and my entire house, in the prayers which you send up every day to the Lord our Saviour. For I trust that through your most pious prayers, I may be relieved also from the trouble in which we are and return to you. Therefore master, truly a man of God, be so good as to hold us in your memory.[63]

There is sparse remaining evidence for identifying the author of this small collection of letters, and the surviving clues do not always align with John's known characteristics. The social engagements and hints at communal living seem at odds with the traditional descriptions of the immured hermit. The letters never contain requests for healing, John of Lycopolis's forte; instead, they beg for practical help in cases of dire need. Furthermore, the letters of Apa John are written in both Coptic and Greek, an unlikely choice for those corresponding with a man who famously did not speak a word of the latter language.

The petitioners usually live in wretched circumstances: some have fallen foul of the military authorities or other secular powers, and several are widows. Some of the letters mention threatened or actual

60 Zuckerman, 'The Hapless Recruit Psois and the Mighty Anchorite, Apa John', 191–4. See also Wipszycka, *Moines et communautés monastiques en Égypte*, 83–5.

61 Mark Sheridan, 'John of Lycopolis', in Gawdat Gabra and Hany Takla, eds, *Christianity and Monasticism in Middle Egypt: Al-Minya and Asyut* (Cairo, 2015), 123–32.

62 Palladius, *Historia Lausiaca* 35.

63 'προσαγορεύω σου τοιγαροῦν τὴν εὐλάβειάν{σου} δ̣ι̣ὰ τούτων μου τ̣[ῶν γ]ραμμάτων, παρα̣κ̣α̣λῶν ὅπως μνημονεύῃς καὶ καμοῦ τοῦ σε προσκυνοῦντος καὶ π̣αντὸς τοῦ οἴκου μου ἐ̣ν̣ α̣ἷ̣ ἀναπέμπει̣ς [ἀεὶ] πέποιθα γὰρ ὡς διὰ τ̣ῶν ἁγιοτάτων καὶ μεθ' ἡμέραν εὐχαῖς τ̣ῷ κυρίῳ σωτῆρει ἡμῶν. πέποιθα γὰρ ὡς διὰ τ̣ῶν ἁγιοτάτων σου εὐχῶν καὶ τ̣ο̣ῦ̣ κ̣[α]μάτου τούτου ἐν ᾧ̣ ἐσμὲ̣ν̣ ἐλ̣ε̣υ̣θ̣ερωθῆναι καὶ ἐπανελθεῖν πρὸς [ὑ]μᾶς. λ̣οιπόν, δ̣έ̣σποτα, ἀληθῶς Θεοῦ̣ ἄνθρωπε, καταξίωσον ἐ̣[ν] μνήμαι̣ς ἔχειν ἡμᾶς': *P.Herm.* 8.12–20. Author's translation.

prison sentences.[64] For example, we find a letter written in Greek sent by an unknown person asking that Apa John write to his gaoler, a certain Apollonius, commanding him to release him.[65] Similarly, in a badly damaged Coptic letter, surviving details include the mention of an imprisoned old man whose affairs are connected in some way with the local magistrate, (Ni?)lammon.[66] The economic affairs of the local community also receive a mention. In one letter, John is asked to help resolve a land dispute that has relevance to the tax collector.[67] The correspondent writes: 'Now then, the matter is about some fields where the water has carried off the returns (?) of the tax collector … They said, "appeal to the Hegemon".'[68] It could be considered quite significant that the local dux is mentioned here, a point often used to support an identification with John of Lycopolis. Scribbled above one of the lines in this letter, however, is the insertion, 'make haste and write to Apa John the priest', which might seem an odd appellation for a solitary hermit.[69]

Whether this John should be identified with John of Lycopolis or not, these examples demonstrate how monks such as John were viewed by their fellow citizens as potential ombudsmen.[70] The letters from widows are particularly poignant. One widow of twelve years' standing writes that she has a male relative who is in debt.[71] Her letter implies that her children have been seized as sureties. Faced with problems of this immensity, it is hardly surprising that the widow in question writes: 'I have neither eaten nor

[64] *P.Ryl. Copt.* 272, 310, 311; and *P.Herm.* 7, in James G. Keenan, Joseph G. Manning and Uri Yiftach-Firanko, eds, *Law and Legal Practice in Egypt from Alexander to the Arab Conquest: A Selection of Papyrological Sources in Translation, with Introductions and Commentary* (Cambridge, 2014), 536–8.

[65] *P.Misc. inv.* II 70.

[66] *P.Ryl. Copt.* 272.

[67] *P.Ryl. Copt.* 273.

[68] 'ⲁⲉⲓⲧⲛⲟⲟⲩϥ̣ ϣⲁⲣⲟⲕ ϫⲉⲁⲛⲁ̣ⲣⲭⲱⲛ ϫⲟⲟⲥ ⲛⲁⲓ ϫⲉϥϩⲏϣ̣ ⲉⲧⲃⲉⲟⲩ ⲡⲣⲁⲕⲙⲁ ⲟⲩ̣ⲁⲛⲁⲅⲅⲉⲟⲛ̣ ⲛ̄ⲣⲱⲙⲉⲡⲉ ⲕⲁⲧⲁ ⲧⲥⲩⲛⲧⲉⲥⲓⲥ ⲁⲗ̣ⲗⲁ ⲟⲩϭⲱⲃ ⲕⲁⲧⲁ ⲯⲱⲙⲁ ⲧⲉⲛⲟⲩϭⲉ ⲡ̇ⲉⲡⲣⲁⲅⲙⲁ ⲛ̄ϩⲉⲛⲉⲓⲱϩⲉⲡⲉ ⲉⲁⲡⲙⲟⲟⲩ ϥⲓⲧⲟⲩ ⲉⲛⲁⲯⲁ ⲛⲉⲕⲥⲁⲕⲧⲱⲣⲛⲉ . . . ⲁⲩϫⲟⲟⲥ ⲛⲁϥ ϫⲉⲥⲙⲙⲉ ⲛ̄ⲫⲏⲅⲉⲙⲟⲛ': *P.Ryl. Copt.* 272.14–15. Author's translation.

[69] 'ϫⲉⲁⲣⲓ ⲟⲩⲥⲡⲟⲩⲇⲏ ⲛⲅⲥ̣ϩⲁ̣ⲓ ⲛⲁ[ⲡ]ⲁ ⲓⲟⲁⲛⲏⲥ ⲡ̣ⲡⲣⲉ̣ⲥ̣…': *P.Ryl. Copt.* 273.12. Author's translation.

[70] On the role of monks as ombudsmen, see Peter Van Minnen, 'The Roots of Egyptian Christianity', *Zeitschrift für Papyrologie und Epigraphik* 40 [hereafter: *ZPE*] (1996), 71–86, at 80.

[71] *P.Ryl. Copt.* 310.

drunk'.[72] She also reports that she had been sent to the *hypographeus* (public notary) of Antinoe.[73] This is significant, as such an official would be expected to act as an amanuensis, rather than merely as a scribe.[74] Another widow, Leuchis, implores John's assistance in helping her to rid the house of certain unwanted people. She notes that a particular tribune, a man called 'Gunthus', is the person who has the power to remove them. It has been hypothesized that the 'them' in question are soldiers, although the form here is feminine and may possibly refer to women who had some association with the activities of the local military. Leuchis's desperation in this case is clear: she, or at least the scribe she had commissioned, finished her letter in a plaintive tone, beseeching: 'My Lord, do it for God's sake!'[75] Unfortunately, Apa John's reply, if there ever was one, has not survived and we cannot know what aid, if any, he may have provided in this case, or what his relationship was with the tribune in question. Other letters written in a similar vein include cases such as a young man in trouble and a sick woman in need of help.[76]

On reading these missives, one is impressed by the extent to which John appears to be at the heart of the social mission of the church. However, John's clients sometimes expressed an impatience that suggests a lack of satisfaction with his efforts. A fragmentary letter written in Coptic from a certain Porphyra is a case in point.[77] The letter begins with Porphyra offering fulsome praise and pleading with John to help him. He then mentions an ongoing dispute between himself and some men, who he claims were involved in taking items stored in sacks, perhaps foodstuffs. Porphyra is ostensibly seeking help, but he then becomes accusatory towards John, complaining: 'You did not give account of me about … that the men have ta(ken) … sacks. You did not give account of me before

[72] 'ⲟⲩⲇⲉ ⲙⲡⲓⲟⲩⲱⲙ ⲛ[ϩⲏ]ⲧⲟⲩ ⲙⲡⲓⲥⲱ ⲛϩⲏⲧⲟⲩ': *P.Ryl. Copt.* 310.20–2. Author's translation.

[73] 'ⲁϥⲧⲁⲁϥ ⲛⲧⲛⲡϩⲩⲡⲁⲣⲏⲥ ⲛⲁⲛⲧⲓⲛⲟⲟⲩ': *P.Ryl. Copt.* 310.15–16. Author's translation.

[74] Herbert C. Youtie, 'ὑπογραφεύς: The Social Impact of Illiteracy in Graeco-Roman Egypt', *ZPE* 17 (1975), 201–21.

[75] 'κύριέ μου, διὰ των Θεὼν πύει': *P.Herm.* 17.6. Author's translation.

[76] *P.Ryl. Copt.* 268 and 313.

[77] *P.Ryl. Copt.* 270.

the military unit(?).'[78] Why does Porphyra take this tone with someone whose help he apparently needs desperately? Did he feel that John had an obligation to act based on some form of transactional arrangement, perhaps one involving payment? Porphyra then moves on to request that John write yet another letter but, unfortunately, there is a lacuna at this point, and we cannot know to whom John was supposed to write or why.

A second letter is similarly interesting in that it could be interpreted in a way that puts John in a rather poor light.[79] The letter, written in wildly ungrammatical Greek, has been sent by a man called Psois, who, rather confusingly, comments on the actions of another man by the same name. This second Psois, a former military tribune, has promised to aid the release of the first Psois from military service. In the fourth century, conscription was common but unpopular, as evidenced by references to draft dodgers and deserters in the *Codex Theodosianus* (7.18).[80] It is worth quoting the letter in some detail for what it reveals about the case. Psois says:

> Write a letter to Psois from Taeto, the ex-tribune, to have me released, if I haven't yet been released. Psios' son already has seven gold solidi and his assistant has another gold solidi. Because you took money from me for my release but I have not been released. I ask God that you either release me or hand over the eight gold solidi. I am Psois son of Kyllos from the village of Pocheos in the Antaeopolite nome. Do not neglect this master, for God's sake, for you have already given my children as security to the moneylender because of the gold.[81]

The Greek is very confused here and the main sense of the letter has possibly been lost, but what does seem clear is that, despite having laid out money, Psois is still being held captive. It also rather

[78] '[м]пртⲓ ⲱп ⲛⲉⲙⲁⲓ ⲕⲁ[т]ⲁ ⲛ[. . . .] ϫⲉⲛⲧⲁⲛⲣⲱⲙⲉ ⲧⲁ [. . .]ⲥⲟⲟⲕ ⲙⲡⲉϯ ⲱп ⲛⲉⲙⲁⲓ ϩⲛⲃⲟⲗ ⲛⲡⲁⲣⲙ̣ⲁ̣ⲧ̣ⲁ̣ⲩ': *P.Ryl. Copt.* 270.5–9. Author's translation.

[79] *P.Herm.* 7.

[80] John Bagnall, *Egypt in Late Antiquity* (Princeton, NJ, 1993), 178.

[81] 'γράψοṿ εις ἐπιστολη πρὸς Ψοις ἀπὸ Ταετῷ ἀπὸ τριβουνου, ἵνα ἀπολύομαι ἐαν μὴ ἀπ̣ο̣-λ̣υθήσο̣μαι. ἤδη γὰρ ὁ υἱὸς Ψοῖς ἀπαίτησε̣ μαι χρυσ(οῦ) νομ(ισμάτια) ζ καὶ τοῦ βοηθὸς ἄλλα̣ χρυ̣ς̣(οῦ) νομ(ισμάτιον) α̣· ἔλαβες γὰρ παρ' ἐμοῦ ἵνα ἀπολ̣ύ̣ω̣μαι καὶ οὐκ ἀπόλυσόν μαι. ἀξιῶ τὸν Θεὸν ἵνα ἢ ἀπόλυσόν μαι ἢ παραδοτε μ̣οι το χρυσ (οῦ) νομ(ισμάτια) η. ἐγὼ γάρ εἰμι Ψόϊς Κυλλός ἀπὸ κώμης [Π]ώχεως το̣ῦ̣ Ἀνταιουπολείτου ν̣ο̣μοῦ. νῦν οὖν μὴ ἀ̣μελήσῃς, δέσ̣πο̣τα̣, διὰ̣ το̣ν̣ [Θ]εό̣[ν]. ἤδη γὰρ τὰ τ̣έκνα μου ἔδωκας ὑποθήκ̣α̣ς [τ]ῷ̣ δανι̣[στ]ῃς διὰ τὸ̣ χ̣ρ̣υσάφι̣ν̣': *P.Herm.* 7. Author's translation.

remarkably implies that John has put Psois's children into bondage with a moneylender to act as a form of surety, the type of situation previously mentioned in relation to the widow in letter *P.Ryl. Copt.* 310.[82] Whilst there is much evidence to show that parents did place their children into servitude in the fourth century, such an act was illegal according to Roman law and it was generally considered to be morally reprehensible for a moneylender to accept children as pledges.[83] Faced with the contents of this letter, scholars who support John's identification with John of Lycopolis are in a conundrum: how could a renowned saint willingly collude in the seizure of children as a payment for debt? One suggestion is to amend the term ἔδωκας, 'you gave', to ἔδωκα, 'I gave', on the grounds of the poor syntax, to produce the reading: 'I have already given my children as security.'[84] This is certainly plausible, but some caution is needed here as we are in danger of accepting an emendation of the text merely on the grounds that it is essential to preserve the sanctity of the saint, leaving the hapless Psois to stand condemned for his poor parenting as a consequence. If the letter is taken at face value, then we are faced with needing to acknowledge that John was an accessory to a deed that was considered repugnant, even by the standards of the Roman authorities. Another possibility is that the 'you' in question here is not John, but Psois the ex-tribune. Alas, no further evidence is available to assist us in our choice of meaning.

Another fourth-century letter describing a similar situation is that written to Apa Paieous (*P.Lond.* VI 1915), a predecessor of the monk Nepheros who dwelt in the monastery of Hathor. He was asked to intervene on behalf of an indebted wine salesman called Pamonthis who had had all his possessions seized, including his two children. Paieous was required to act as an intermediary in this instance, indicating that such situations were not uncommon in the caseloads of monks who acted as ombusdmen.

[82] See also the letters to Apa Paieous on the same topic: *P.Lond.* VI 1915 and *P.Lond.* VI 1916.

[83] Ville Vuolanto, 'Selling a Freeborn Child: Rhetoric and Social Realities in the Late Roman World', *Ancient Society* 33 (2003), 178–97.

[84] Erwin Seidl, 'Juristische Papyruskunde. 16. Bericht (Neuerscheinungen vom September 1964 bis September 1967)', *Studia et documenta historiae et iuris* 33 (1967), 503–79, at 513; Luc Fournet, *The Rise of Coptic: Egyptian Versus Greek in Late Antiquity* (Princeton, NJ, 2020), 50–7. Cf. Zuckerman, 'The Hapless Recruit Psois and the Mighty Anchorite, Apa John', 183.

The letters of John, like those of his fellow monks, certainly indicate that monks who had the abilities and prestige regularly became enmeshed in the social and political life of their local communities. There are surviving examples of this type of engagement in Egyptian religious literature. The *vita* of the fourth- or fifth-century Aaron for example, a famously ascetic figure, also praises the work he regularly undertook as a legal adviser for people in the locality.[85] This Coptic text, like so many, has only recently been edited and translated, meaning that his biography has been relatively unknown to earlier religious historians.[86] This type of work adds support to the evidence found in the letters written to Apa John for the close social engagement by monks. What is particularly interesting in the case of the Apa John letters is the tone taken by some of his supplicants. Of course, the seeming impatience of the writers may be taken as a form of rhetoric. It is not unusual to find accusations of neglect or of a failure to act in letters of the period, particularly in those sent to close family members and friends, including monastic brethren. However, such accusations are unusual in a client-patron context. It might be imagined that John lacked the time necessary for performing all the tasks demanded of him by his spiritual flock. The lack of legal services prompted many church figures to take on the roles of public officials. Augustine, for example, begged his congregation not to expect him, as their bishop, to have the ability to carry out all the functions of the local magistrate.[87] Part of the puzzle is that we do not know how these letters to John survived: are these the last cases John was working on at the time of his death, or did these letters form part of an archive that covers decades of activity? If these were indeed remnants of a collection treasured by John, and perhaps even members of a community who preserved them after his death, then it would infer that John, or his followers, thought they contained nothing that was unexceptional. If so, then they indicate that relationships between influential monks like John and his clients might be expected to be fraught at times as not all their problems were negotiable or easy to untangle.

[85] Nicholas Browder Venable, 'Legal Authority and Monastic Institutions in Late Monastic Egypt' (PhD thesis, University of Chicago, 2018), 32–5.

[86] Jacques van der Vliet and Jitse Dijkstra, *The Coptic Life of Aaron: Critical Edition, Translation and Commentary*, Vigiliae Christianae Suppl. 155 (Leiden, 2019).

[87] Leonard A. Curchin, 'The End of Local Magistrates in the Roman Empire', *Gerión* 32 (2014), 271–87, at 282.

Conclusion

For many centuries, the reliance on literary accounts of early Egyptian monasticism led to the creation of an idealized image of eremitic monasticism. Monks were popularly viewed as pious, often illiterate ascetics and their descriptions were invoked to encourage the Christian reader to engage in a form of religious *aemulatio*. This has tended to overshadow the historical reality and an exploration of surviving documentation from the period acts as a welcome counterbalance, revealing, as it does, that the lives of the earliest monks and nuns were as complex and entangled with the everyday as that of their present-day counterparts. What becomes clear from examining the contemporary sources is that those who, in the first few decades after its inception, sought to self-designate using the term 'monk' had a variety of expectations about what constituted the monastic vocation and their motivations for taking on the habit differed considerably. As a result, their lifestyles reflected their circumstances and opportunities, with the result that a sizable proportion of monks remained within an urban setting, taking up occupations that suited their vocation. The Christian community very quickly engaged with the concept of 'monasticism' and the role of monk, and all that it entailed, and it rapidly became an established and regulated part of the Christian movement. One consequence was the promotion of the coenobitic movement by the church authorities. Alexandrian patriarchs such as Athanasius and Cyril actively promoted an ideal in which monks were held in check through rigorous discipline and religious education. Their descriptions of movements such as the Pachomians for example, provided inspiration to newly formed monastic communities who emulated their predecessors in their structure and formation. In reality, the early coenobitic movement went through a complex and sometimes difficult foundational period, as evidenced by the writings of Shenoute of Atripe, for example, where personal conflict and power struggles are highly evident.

The letters of Apa John are noteworthy in that they were written during the formative period of the monastic movement, and he can rightfully be considered a model 'patron' in that his correspondents considered him a useful intermediary. However, when examined in more detail, John's lifestyle seems very different from that of the famous John of Lycopolis, with whom he is often associated, or the liminal figures described in Brown's 1971 article. The saintly monks of the hagiographies may wield an almost limitless authority in their dealings with the ruling elite but, in real life, monks such as John were quite evidently constrained in what they could do and the time it took to do it. Other letters, such as those of Nepheros, further demonstrate that holy men faced much more mundane daily challenges than those of their literary counterparts. Lower down the social scale were the large majority of monks and nuns, often subject to superiors and regularly participating in manual labour. Although closely bound by society's rules, there were those who created scandal through their misdemeanours or scandalous lifestyles – a point even the hagiographies acknowledge with their tales of sinful and remorseful monks. An acknowledgement of the pragmatic entanglement of monks within society takes us away from the static image of the eremitic saint, as painted in the hagiographies, towards an acknowledgment that monasticism was a dynamic and fluid movement. From its inception, far from being merely a movement of saintly ascetics, it remained entangled with the world in a manner that elicited a very human response from its practitioners and the society in which they lived.

Ostriches, Spiders' Webs and Antichrist: Hypocrisy in Writings of Pope Gregory the Great and Archbishop Wulfstan II of York

Catherine Cubitt*
University of East Anglia

This article examines the use of the concepts of hypocrisy and the hypocrite in the writings of Pope Gregory the Great (590–604) and Archbishop Wulfstan of York (1002–23). Although separated by many centuries, these two treatments are connected through Wulfstan's debt to Gregory's ideas on the evil of hypocrisy, and particularly in his depiction of Antichrist as the chief of all hypocrites. Both use the idea of hypocrisy to critique their contemporary situation: for Gregory, the pride of the Patriarch John IV of Constantinople in adopting the title 'Ecumenical Patriarch'; and for Wulfstan, the court politics in the turbulent final years of the reign of Æthelred the Unready.

In her seminal treatment of hypocrisy in her book, *Ordinary Vices*, Judith Shklar claimed: 'Every age, every form of literature, and every public stage has held [the hypocrite] up for contempt and ridicule.'[1] However, unlike some of the other vices discussed in her book – cruelty, betrayal and misanthropy – the figure of the hypocrite and conceptions of hypocrisy are not constant themes in Christian discourse, but their prominence fluctuates over time. In the early Middle Ages, their profile is low.[2] My own interest in this subject was provoked by a long denunciation of hypocrisy in a sermon by the early eleventh-century archbishop of York, Wulfstan, which I shall argue was aimed at the court of the English king, Æthelred II

* I would like to thank the editors, Charlotte Methuen and Andrew Spicer, for their work, and the anonymous readers for their helpful comments. E-mail: katy.cubitt@uea.ac.uk.

[1] Judith Shklar, *Ordinary Vices* (Cambridge, MA, 1984), 45.

[2] Courtney Booker, 'Hypocrisy, Performativity, and the Carolingian Pursuit of Truth', *EME* 26 (2018), 174–202.

Studies in Church History 60 (2024), 64–90
doi: 10.1017/stc.2024.3

'the Unready' (978–1016). I was struck by how unusual this accusation was in my period – the early Middle Ages – and this stimulated my interest in exploring this topic further. My investigations so far have tended to confirm the comparative lack of a polemic about hypocrites in the early Middle Ages, but have also led me to the sixth-century pope, Gregory the Great, in whose writings hypocrites occupy a very significant place. This article will therefore take two case studies from the early Middle Ages: the writings of Gregory (590–604) and Wulfstan (d. 1023). Five hundred years apart, these two treatments of hypocrisy are intimately linked by the pope's influence on the archbishop, but they provide contrasting treatments: Gregory's detailed expositions of the hypocrite, as opposed to Wulfstan's polemical usage.

Gregory the Great

Hypocrisy is a significant preoccupation for Gregory the Great, who was a towering figure in the Middle Ages, revered as a pope, saintly monk and church father.[3] Gregory is not only unusual in the extensive treatment he devotes to the evils of hypocrites, but he is also one of the few figures in this period who actually levels an accusation of hypocrisy against a contemporary, no less a person than the patriarch of Constantinople. Gregory's reflections on hypocrisy have merited some scholarly attention through his description of Antichrist as *caput omnium hypocritarum*, 'the head of all hypocrites', but scholars have failed to do justice to the complexity and importance of hypocrisy in his thinking.[4]

The Bible was a powerful inspiration in Gregory's discussion of hypocrites, particularly the Book of Job to which he devoted his longest work, the *Moralia in Job*.[5] This was initially composed by Gregory when he was serving as papal envoy, *apocrisiarius*, at the court of the Byzantine emperor in Constantinople from 579 to 585/6. It started life as a series of sermons and was revised by

[3] On Gregory, see Bronwen Neil and Matthew J. Dal Santo, eds, *A Companion to Gregory the Great* (Leiden, 2013); Robert Markus, *Gregory the Great and his World* (Cambridge, 1997).

[4] The best account of Gregory's treatment of hypocrisy is Carole Straw, 'Gregory, Cassian, and the Cardinal Vices', in Richard Newhauser, ed., *In the Garden of Evil: The Vices and Culture in the Middle Ages* (Toronto, 2005), 35–58, at 49–58.

[5] Gregory the Great, *Moralia in Iob*, ed. Marcus Adriaen, 3 vols, CChr.SL 143, 143A, 143B (Turnhout, 1979).

Gregory when he returned to Rome in 586, but only released for wider dissemination in 596.[6] It is a lengthy and capacious text, numbering thirty-five books, and has been described by Carole Straw as both 'a loose, baggy monster' as well as 'an "all-you-need-to-know" manual for Christian life, folded within the exegesis of Job'. The *Moralia* also bears the imprint of Gregory's own personal circumstances, and especially the tension he felt between his monastic vocation and the demands of high ecclesiastical office.[7] It is not surprising that the Book of Job stimulated him to ponder the issue of hypocrisy: Job's friends or comforters were seen as hypocrites because of their self-righteous reproaches and upbraiding of Job. In fact, seven out of the ten references to hypocrisy in the Old Testament are located in this book.[8] The pope's musings on hypocrisy, however, go far beyond the exegetical demands of individual passages and, cumulatively, they construct a substantial set of ideas.

Gregory on Hypocrites

Gregory's understanding of hypocrisy is grounded in Scripture, informed not only by the text of Job but also by his own immersion in the Bible as a whole.[9] The following passage, for example, weaves into its explication of Job 20 on the hypocrisy of Job's friend, Zophar, an echo of and allusion to Matthew 23: 5:

> Often the hypocrite passes himself off as holy, without a fear of letting himself appear wicked, he is honoured by everyone, and the glory of holiness is awarded to him, by those who perceive the outside, and are not able to look into the interior of things. And so it happens, that he rejoices in having the first seat, is overjoyed in getting the first couch, filled with pride at receiving the first invitation, elevated at the respectful address of his followers, swollen in the pride of his heart at the servitude of his dependents, just it is said by the voice of Truth Himself concerning such people. *But all their works they do for to be seen of men: they make broad their phylacteries, and enlarge the borders*

[6] Carole Straw, 'Job's Sin in the *Moralia* of Gregory the Great', in Franklin Harkins and Aaron Canty, eds, *A Companion to Job in the Middle Ages* (Leiden, 2016), 71–100, at 76.

[7] Straw, 'Job's Sin', quotation from 73.

[8] Booker, 'Hypocrisy', 182.

[9] On Gregory's thought see, Carole Straw, *Gregory the Great: Perfection in Imperfection* (Berkeley, CA, 1988).

of their garments, and love the uppermost rooms at feasts, and the chief seats in the synagogues, and greetings in the markets, and to be called of men, Rabbi.[10]

The discourse of hypocrisy in the *Moralia* is immensely rich, fed by Gregory's astonishingly fertile imagination. Hypocrites are likened *inter alia* to ostriches, tigers and spiders' webs. Why is an ostrich like a hypocrite? Because it has wings but cannot fly.[11] Unlike the heron and hawk, ostriches are unable to rise up to heaven but creep along the ground, weighed down by earthly cares despite their appearance of piety. A tiger's coat is variegated, making manifest the terrible sins of the hypocrite underneath his virtues.[12] The works of the hypocrite are like spiders' webs because, after the spider's great effort of spinning, they are fragile and destroyed by 'the wind of mortal life', in the same way that the glory sought by hypocrites is transient and earthly.[13]

These examples illustrate something of the creativity of Gregory's thinking and its variety. His concept of hypocrisy is more multidimensional than the simple feigning of virtue. To be sure, deceit is crucial: Gregory distinguishes between those who manage the appearance of virtue but fall into sin because of their infirmity, and those hypocrites whose wrongdoing is the sin of malice. He sees

[10] 'Saepe hypocrita dum sanctum se simulat, et iniquum exhibere minime formidat, ab omnibus honoratur eique sanctitatis gloria defertur ab iis qui exteriora cernunt, sed interiora perspicere nequeunt. Vnde fit ut gaudeat in prima sessione, hilarescat in primo recubitu, infletur in prima salutatione, eleuetur in reuerenti uoce obsequentium; et superba cogitatione tumeat in famulatu subditorum, sicut uoce quoque Veritatis de talibus dicitur: *Omnia uero opera sua faciunt, ut uideantur ab hominibus. Dilatant enim phylacteria sua et magnificant fimbrias suas. Amant enim primos recubitus in cenis, et primas cathedras in synagogis, et salutationes in foro, uocari ab hominibus: Rabbi.*' *Moralia* 15.3.4 (CChr.SL 143, 143A and 143B, 143A: 750–1). Italics for biblical quotations, as in the CChr.SL edition. English translations in this article (with some modifications) are from *Morals on the Book of Job by St. Gregory the Great*, transl. John Henry Parker (London, 1844), online at: <http://www.lectionarycentral.com/GregoryMoraliaIndex.html>, accessed 22 November 2023.

[11] *Moralia* 7.27.36; 20.39.75; 31.8.11; *Moralia* 15.3.4; and see 31.9.14; 31.10.15; 31.11.16; 31.12.17; also 31.13.25; 31.15.27, 28, 29; 31.20.36; 31.22.38–9; 31.33.42. For a comparison with rushes, see ibid. 8.42.65–9; 8.43.70. René-Jean Hesbert, 'Le bestiaire de Grégoire', in Jacques Fontaine, Robert Gillet and Stan Pellistrandi, eds, *Grégoire le Grand. Chantilly, centre culturel Les Fontaines 15–19 septembre 1982* (Paris, 1986), 454–66, at 458–9; Straw, *Gregory the Great*, 51–2.

[12] *Moralia* 5.20.39.

[13] 'Uentus uitae mortalis': *Moralia* 8.44.72 (CChr.SL 143: 437).

hypocrites as agents of destruction who hide their own evil to destroy others.[14]

For Gregory, hypocrisy is essentially a manifestation of the cardinal sin of pride.[15] Pride is in turn essentially impiety against God, it is being exalted by false glory.[16] It is the pre-eminent sin, because it alone can destroy all other virtues; it poses therefore the greatest threat to the salvation of the soul.[17] It hardens the soul against perceiving its sinfulness and spawns a whole series of lesser sins – vainglory, envy, anger, melancholy, avarice, gluttony and lust – and these, in turn, nurture a further brood of evils, which each have 'their army against us.' 'For from vain glory there arise disobedience, boasting, hypocrisy, contentions, obstinacies, discords, and the presumptions of novelties'.[18]

In Gregory's mind, vainglory leads to hypocrisy because the hypocrite seeks earthly praise and admiration, rather than seeking to please God. The hypocrite is the superficial master of Christian virtues and qualities, but he desires only to win human applause and lacks the interior love and fear of God.[19] He imagines that God will – like the hypocrite's fellows – only judge him on his exterior, but he will find at the last judgement that he is condemned:

> Such are the minds of hypocrites: while they do one thing, they exhibit another to men. They win applause by the show of holy living itself; they are set before many better people in the esteem of men, and while within themselves in their silent thoughts they are proud, on the outside they exhibit themselves as humble. And whereas they are excessively praised by men; they imagine that in the eyes of God also they are that which they delight to present themselves to be to their fellow-creatures.[20]

[14] *Moralia* 5.17.34; 5.20.43; 7.31.46; 15.28.34; and see 15.15.19. Straw, *Gregory the Great*, 233. On the sin of deficient Christians, see *Moralia* 29.7.14.

[15] Straw, 'Gregory, Cassian', 49–50.

[16] *Moralia* 32.9.11 and see 29.8.18.

[17] *Moralia* 31.45.87–8; 32.9.11. Straw, 'Job's Sin', 77; eadem, 'Gregory, Cassian', 46–7, 49–50.

[18] *Moralia* 15.53.60; 31.45.87–8. 'Sed habent contra nos haec singula exercitum suum. Nam de inani gloria, inoboedentia, iactantia, hypocrisis, contentiones, pertinaciae, discordiae, et nouitatum praesumptiones oriuntur': ibid. 31.45.88 (CChr.SL 143B: 1610). See also Straw, *Gregory the Great*, 241–2.

[19] *Moralia* 8.42.69, 8.44.72, 73, 8.45.75, 8.48.81; Straw, 'Gregory, Cassian', 54–5.

[20] 'Sic hypocritarum mentes dum aliud est quod agunt, atque aliud quod hominibus ostendunt, laudes de ipsa sanctitatis ostentatione recipiunt, in aestimatione hominum

Hypocrites are puffed up by praise and feel themselves to be superior to others. Gregory says: 'every hypocrite, by counterfeiting the life of justice, claims himself the praise that belongs to the just'.[21] Beneath their façade of virtue, they conceal overweening pride.

Gregory's negative depictions of the hypocrite in the *Moralia* are inverse descriptions of the necessary spiritual resources and conduct of a Christian. His hypocrites are characterized by the essentially hollow nature of their spiritual lives.[22] They are, in other words, Christians on the cheap, who fail to practise the interior rigours of the religious life and possess only its simulacra. Their façade of piety may deceive, but to Gregory the real failings are the consequences of pride: spiritual blindness, lack of self-knowledge and of self-examination, and a failure to endure worldly and spiritual afflictions.[23] In Gregorian thought, the Christian life is a perpetual battle: the faithful must be ever vigilant against sin, constantly active in self-examination to discern its beginnings.[24] They must exercise the faculty of discernment, *discretio*, to maintain consciousness of their sinfulness and of God's goodness and grace.[25] This constant watchfulness leads to penitence, vital for spiritual wellbeing, the purging force which can atone for humanity's perpetual sinfulness and enable the faithful to turn to God and to 're-connect' with him.[26] The faithful must also learn to bear both prosperity and adversity as the operation of divine will.[27] Both are sent by God

multis melioribus praeferuntur, et cum intus apud se tacita cogitatione superbiant, foris se humiles demonstrant. Cumque ab hominibus immoderate laudantur, tales esse se quoque apud Deum existimant quales se gaudent hominibus innotuisse.' *Moralia* 15.6.7 (CChr.SL 143A: 752–3). See also ibid. 8.72; 15.3.

21 'Omnis autem hypocrita quia uitam iustitiae simulans, iustorum sibi laudem arripit': *Moralia* 5.20.39 (CChr.SL 143A: 245).

22 *Moralia* 8.42.66 (comparison with rushes).

23 *Moralia* 5.10.16; 5.22.44; 7.20.39; 7.35.36; 8.47.77.

24 For example, *Moralia* 8.6.9–10; 32.1.1; Straw, 'Gregory, Cassian', 55–6.

25 On *discretio*, see Straw, *Gregory the Great*, 73, 99, 217–18, 227–8, 231–4, 252–3; eadem, 'Gregory the Great's Moral Theology: Divine Providence and Human Responsibility', in Neil and Dal Santo, eds, *A Companion to Gregory*, 177–204, at 198–200; eadem, 'Job's Sin', 72–3; eadem, 'Gregory, Cassian', 42–7.

26 Straw, *Gregory the Great*, 175–9, 200, 213, 236; eadem, 'Gregory's Moral Theology', 200–4. For fear of death leading to self-examination and penitence, see eadem, 'Purity and Death', in John C. Cavadini, ed., *Gregory the Great: A Symposium* (Notre Dame, IN, 1995), 16–37.

27 See, for instance, *Moralia* 5.16.33; 31.28.55; Straw, *Gregory the Great*, 236; eadem, 'Job's Sin', 85; eadem, '"*Adversitas*" et "*prosperitas*". Une illustration du motif structurel de la complémentarité', in Fontaine, Gillet and Pellistrandi, eds, *Grégoire le Grand*, 277–88.

and can be sources of spiritual growth or of sin. The faithful must not be puffed up by earthly or spiritual prosperity and tempted into pride; nor should they be overwhelmed when things go wrong, but should see adversity as a form of spiritual training, sent by God, to discipline their souls and share in earthly chastisement for sin.[28]

Gregory's hypocrites do none of these things: they love human applause and are gratified by earthly honours and praise.[29] They are inflated with self-congratulation at their earthly successes. Their virtues are like the exterior of a house but are absent within, as the hypocrite only seeks worldly reputation.[30] They are blinded to the true state of their souls and imagine themselves to be holy in God's sight, when they lack humility and penitence. Their spiritual blindness means that they no longer exercise discernment and can neither perceive their own sinfulness nor the forbearance of God.[31] They fail to do penance.[32] Lacking the tough discipline which Gregory requires of the holy, the inner strength of self-scrutiny and fear of God, they flourish like untended vines, which bear luxuriant fruit on the ground where it quickly perishes.[33]

The wealth of denunciations of hypocrites in the *Moralia* has an urgent purpose: the dangers of hypocrisy lie all around the faithful, especially those who lead in the church. The temptation to pride is ever-present, even for good teachers. Gregory describes with great acuity – and feeling – how spiritual gifts can easily provoke their opposite vices and turn to sin. For example, an outstanding knowledge of divine law can become a source of pride. Hypocrisy is a particular threat to spiritual leadership. Hypocrites are false shepherds who love themselves more than God or their spiritual charges. Lacking real spiritual growth, they cannot nurture their followers in Christian virtue.[34] In contrast to holy men whose spiritual self-discipline enables them to discern the secret faults of others, hypocrites do not practise self-examination and are unable to correct others: 'Hypocrites therefore do not gather together the thoughts of their

[28] *Moralia* 29.30.62; Straw, '"*Adversitas*" et "*prosperitas*"'.
[29] *Moralia* 8.47.80; 15.13.15.
[30] *Moralia* 8.45.74–5.
[31] *Moralia* 8.42.67–9; 8.43.70–1; 8.44.72; 31.15.28.
[32] *Moralia* 8.47.77; 15.12.14.
[33] *Moralia* 8.43.70.
[34] *Moralia* 31.9.14 (pursuing the metaphor of ostriches who lay their eggs in the ground and supposedly do not look after them), and 8.43.66.

mind, … when do they, who are ignorant of their own faults, detect the faults of those committed to them?'[35] Their ignorance of God means that they do not understand the inner meaning of Scripture and descend into heresy.[36] This passage illustrates how hypocrisy not only endangers the soul of the individual hypocrite, but imperils the entire church.

Hypocrisy, the Devil and Antichrist

The centrality of pride in Gregory's conceptualization of hypocrisy, and the hypocrite's desire to be unworthily set above others, leads to an intimate connection to Lucifer and his demonic pride. The devil – and man – fell because 'they desired to be like God, not by righteousness, but by power.' Lucifer was set by God above the angels, but chose to overreach himself and assert his equality with God.[37] This web of sinful kinship leads inevitably to Antichrist, whose reign would be preceded, according to New Testament prophecy, by false prophets and false Christs, Antichrist's harbingers. Antichrist himself would claim to be God, exalted in pride; his reign would unleash a terrible time when many of the faithful would be seduced by his counterfeiting of sanctity, his fake miracles and signs, while those who resisted would be subject to terrible persecution.[38]

Antichrist was for Gregory the arch-hypocrite, the *caput omnium hypocritarum*, because he claimed to be God.[39] More terrifying still are his followers, because Antichrist is the inverse image of Christ:

[35] 'Hypocritae igitur, quia cogitationes mentis non colligunt … Et qui sua nesciunt, commissorum sibi quando delicta deprehendunt?' *Moralia* 31.12.20 (CChr.SL 143B: 1565).

[36] *Moralia* 15.13.16.

[37] 'Idcirco ergo uterque cecidit, quia esse Deo similis non per iustitiam, sed per potentiam concupuit.' *Moralia* 29.8.18 (CChr.SL 143B: 1446).

[38] *Moralia* 29.6.10; 29.7.15; 29.7.17; 29.8.18; Frederic Amory, 'Whited Sepulchres: The Semantic History of Hypocrisy to the High Middle Ages', *Recherches de théologie ancienne et médiévale* 53 (1986), 5–39, at 10; Hervé Savon, 'L'Antéchrist dans l'œuvre de Grégoire le Grand', in Fontaine, Gillet and Pellistrandi, eds, *Grégoire le Grand*, 389–405; Jane Baun, 'Gregory's Eschatology', in Neil and Dal Santo, eds, *Companion to Gregory*, 157–76, esp. 171–3. For biblical and early Christian views, see now Mateusz Kusio, *The Antichrist Tradition in Antiquity: Antimessianism in Second Temple and Early Christian Literature* (Tübingen, 2020); Cristian Badilita, *Métamorphoses de l'antichrist chez les pères de l'église* (Paris, 2005).

[39] Straw, 'Gregory, Cassian', 49–50.

like Christ he is the head of a body of the faithful, his own Church, whose members carried out his work. Commenting on Job 34: 30, 'Who maketh a man that is a hypocrite to reign for the sins of the people' [Douay-Rheims], Gregory saw this as an allusion to Antichrist:

> Antichrist, the very chief of all hypocrites. For that seducer pretends to sanctity that he may draw men away in iniquity … . Although most them have not beheld his sovereign power and yet they are enslaved to it, by the condition in which their sins have placed them … . Are they not his very members, who seek by a show of affected sanctity to seem what they are not?[40]

By their sinfulness, the godless in the present time are enslaved to Antichrist and are his members. Hypocrites therefore are a type of fifth column in the church, working its destruction from within.[41] Gregory's conceptualization of the characteristics of hypocrites thus works on two levels: an individual level, in which hypocritical Christians endanger their own salvation; and a collective level, where hypocrites, even unknowingly, are agents of demonic subversion, undermining the church.

Antichrist was no abstract figure for Gregory but an imminent threat, for he believed that he was living in the last days, in the time prophesied by Christ when false prophets would arise, nations would be at war with one another, and there would be earthquakes and famines. Gregory believed that these signs had been fulfilled. In the period between the inception of the *Moralia* in Constantinople in 579 and its wider distribution in 596, the pope had witnessed warfare in the form of the Lombard attacks, devastations of towns and settlements, plagues and natural catastrophes, and heard report of earthquakes. Not all the signs had been fulfilled, but enough to convince him that the end was imminent. His anxieties about

[40] 'Potest ipsum omnium hypocritarum caput antichristus designatur. Seductor quippe ille tunc sanctitatem simulat, ut ad iniquitatem trahat … quamuis plerique et principatum illius non uiderunt, et tamen eius principatui peccatorum suorum conditione deseruiunt, … An non eius membra sunt, qui per affectatatc sanctitatis speciem appetunt uideri quod non sunt?' *Moralia* 25.16.34 (CChr.SL 143B: 1259). On Gregory's innovative thinking concerning the Antichrist as the head of a body of followers, see Savon, 'L'Antéchrist'; Claude Dagens, 'La fin du temps et l'église selon Grégoire le Grand', *Recherches de science religieuse* 58 (1970), 273–88.

[41] *Moralia* 29.7.15, 17; 29.8.18.

Antichrist and the endemic presence of his members were keen and urgent. Having suffered persecution under the pagan empire, the church was now under threat from internal enemies: heretics and hypocrites, false shepherds.[42]

Gregory's letters reveal in a remarkable fashion how he saw these dangers realized in his own times.[43] The pope's apocalyptic sensibilities were particularly acute around 595 with increased pressure from the Lombards and the failure, as he perceived it, of imperial protection for the Italian provinces, especially Rome. His fears were exacerbated by what he saw as the overweening pride of John IV, patriarch of Constantinople, in his use of the title 'Ecumenical Patriarch'. In his letters of protest, Gregory denounces John IV's action as an act of hypocrisy.[44]

The dispute over John's adoption of the title had arisen during the pontificate of Gregory's predecessor, Pope Pelagius II, who had protested at its ascription to John in the acts of a council in Constantinople sent to him.[45] While the title had much earlier origins, it had been used as an honorific for bishops with wide jurisdictions. The papacy, however, eschewed it. In the sixth century, it was deployed frequently for the patriarch of Constantinople; however, John's adoption of the title was remarkable, as he had applied it to himself.[46] The meaning and implications of the title are obscure: Siméon Vailhé suggested that it could signify 'Universal' without indicating ambitions to universal authority. However, he considered that once the term came to be used more sparingly, its significance

[42] Baun, 'Gregory's Eschatology'; Markus, *Gregory*, 51–67; idem, 'Gregory the Great's Europe', *Transactions of the Royal Historical Society* 5th series 31 (1981), 21–36.

[43] Gregory the Great, *S. Gregorii Magni Registrum epistolarum*, ed. Dag Norberg, 2 vols, CChr.SL 140, 140a (Turnhout, 1982); idem, *The Letters of Gregory the Great,* transl. John R. C. Martyn, 3 vols (Toronto, 2004).

[44] *S. Gregorii Magni Registrum* 5.39, 5.45 (CChr.SL 140: 314–15, 337).

[45] George E. Demacopoulos, 'Gregory the Great and the Sixth-Century Dispute over the Ecumenical Title', *Theological Studies* 70 (2009), 600–21, is a useful reference point but does not supersede the important articles by Siméon Vailhé: 'Le titre patriarche œcuménique avant Grégoire le Grand', *Échos d'Orient* 11 (1908), 65–9, and 'Saint Grégoire le Grand et le titre patriarche œcuménique', *Échos d'Orient* 11 (1908), 161–71. See also Markus, *Gregory*, 91–6; Erich Caspar, *Geschichte des Papsttums von den Anfängen bis zur Höhe der Weltherrschaft,* 2 vols (Tübingen, 1933), 2: 449–65; André Tuilier, 'Grégoire le Grand et le titre de patriarche œcuménique', in Fontaine, Gillet and Pellistrandi, eds, *Grégoire le Grand,* 69–80, George E. Demacopoulos, *The Invention of St Peter* (Philadelphia, PA, 2013), 152–7; Barbara Müller, *Führung im Denken und Handeln Gregors des Grossen* (Tübingen, 2009), 324–9.

[46] Vailhé, 'Le titre patriarche œcuménique avant Grégoire le Grand', 65–9.

shifted to a statement of superior authority.[47] The precise meaning of the title for John and for the other patriarchs is not clear and has been subject to different scholarly interpretations. It may have indicated the sovereignty of the patriarch within his jurisdiction.[48] Gregory's objection to John's use of the title was grounded in his view that this use represented an act of pride, a claim to a status above that of other bishops, which deprived all other bishops of their full authority.[49] The title was not simply an arrogant assertion of superior status, but one which fundamentally challenged the church, both by denying the authority of other bishops and by ascribing authority uniquely to the patriarch of Constantinople.

Gregory argued that the title was against Scripture and canon law. His consternation at John IV's behaviour was compounded by the fact that he also believed that in a synod of Constantinople, John had unjustly condemned a monk and a priest as heretics.[50] It was the receipt of the acts of this synod – in which John had repeatedly used the title – which provoked Gregory to write a string of protest letters in June 595 to the emperor, the empress, to John himself and the patriarchs of Alexandria and Antioch, and to the papal envoy in Constantinople, Sabinian.[51] In these letters, Gregory sets out how John's adoption of the title is a mark of pride, an usurpation of the authority of other bishops. He also warns of the imminence of the advent of Antichrist: John IV's act of pride is a harbinger of his coming.[52]

[47] Ibid. 68–9.

[48] See Demacopoulos, 'Gregory the Great', 616–19, for a summary of the range of opinions. For tensions between Rome and Constantinople concerning their ecclesiastical status, see Philippe Blaudeau, *Le siège de Rome et l'orient (448–536). Étude géo-ecclésiologique* (Rome, 2012); idem, 'Between Petrine Ideology and Realpolitik: The See of Constantinople in Roman Geo-Ecclesiology (449–536)', in Lucy Grig and Gavin Kelly, eds, *Two Romes: Rome and Constantinople in Late Antiquity* (Oxford, 2012), 364–84; Judith Herrin, 'The Quinisext Council (692) as a Continuation of Chalcedon', in Richard Price and Mary Whitby, eds, *Chalcedon in Context: Church Councils 400–700* (Liverpool, 2009), 148–68.

[49] See the helpful formulation by Markus, *Gregory*, 94: 'To use the title "universal", on whichever bishop it was bestowed, was to undercut the legitimate standing of each and every bishop in his own church: if any particular bishop was "universal", no bishop anywhere else could be in possession of full episcopal status'.

[50] *S. Gregorii Magni Registrum* 3.52 (CChr.SL 140: 197–9).

[51] *S. Gregorii Magni Registrum* 5.37, 5.39, 5.41, 5.44, 5.45 (CChr.SL 140: 308–11, 314–18, 320–5, 329–37, 337–8).

[52] *S. Gregorii Magni Registrum* 5.39, 5.45 (CChr.SL 140: 314–18, 337–8).

Nonetheless, Gregory is not using the accusation of hypocrisy as an empty polemic. In fact, he generally avoids explicit accusations of hypocrisy and only uses the word in two letters, both, I think, to close associates. However, if the criticisms in his letters of John IV are mapped against the *Moralia*'s description of hypocrites, they are revealed as virtually textbook applications of it. To John himself, he writes:

> that most holy friend of mine, Lord John, a man of such great abstinence and humility, after being seduced by friendly tongues, has resorted to such great arrogance, that in his appetite for a perverse title, he tries to be like him who, while arrogantly wanting to be like God, even lost the grace of the likeness given to him. And because he sought false glory, he threw away true blessedness.[53]

He also warns John against the counsels of those who flatter him, and against seeking an elevated position, quoting from Jesus's denunciation of the Pharisees in Matthew 23: 8–9, although Gregory does not here cite the passages which call them hypocrites.[54]

Gregory is explicit about his view of John's hypocrisy only in a letter to Sabinian, the Roman envoy in Constantinople and his trusted deacon, writing: 'I hope in Almighty God that our celestial Majesty is destroying that man's hypocrisy'.[55] To the Empress Constantina, Gregory is rather more oblique, saying: 'I still ask that you allow nobody's hypocrisy to prevail against the truth'.[56] In what follows this rather muddy statement, Gregory gives an implicit account of John as a hypocrite but in generalized terms without naming him:

> I still ask that you allow nobody's hypocrisy to prevail against the truth, because there are some who, in accordance with the words of the

53 'Quod ille noster sanctissimus domnus Iohannes, tantae abstinentiae atque humilitatis uir, familiarium seductione linguarum ad tantam superbiam erupit, ut in appetitu peruersi nominis illi esse conetur similis, qui, dum superbe esse Deo similis uoluit, etiam donatae similitudinis gratiam amisit et ideo ueram beatitudinem perdidit, quia falsam gloriam quaesiuit.' *S. Gregorii Magni Registrum* 5.44 (CChr.SL 140: 332). Translation from *Letters,* transl. Martyn, 2: 367.

54 *S. Gregorii Magni Registrum* 5.44 (CChr.SL 140: 335).

55 'Spero in omnipotentem Deum quia hypocrisin illius superna maiestas soluit': *S. Gregorii Magni Registrum* 5.45 (CChr.SL 140: 337). Translation from *Letters,* transl. Martyn, 2: 371.

56 'Vnde adhuc peto ut nullius praeualere contra ueritatem hypocrisin permittas … .' *S. Gregorii Magni Registrum* 5.39 (CChr.SL 140: 314). Translation from *Letters,* transl. Martyn, 2: 356.

> egregious preacher, 'by good words and fair speeches deceive the hearts of the simple.' They have certainly been despised for their clothing, but they are proud in their hearts, and they seem to despise everything in this world, and yet at the same time seek to obtain all those worldly things. They confess to all men that they are unworthy, but cannot be content with private titles, because they seek out ways to appear more worthy than all others.[57]

These criticisms echo Gregory's depiction of hypocrites. It is no surprise, therefore, that later in this letter, Gregory asserts that John is imitating Antichrist.[58]

This attack on the patriarch is particularly interesting, because John IV was renowned for his asceticism and was given the epithet 'the Faster'. He is praised in seventh-century Byzantine sources for his fasting, vigils, prayers, personal poverty and his almsgiving to the poor.[59] His reputation as an ascetic had even reached the West: Isidore of Seville (*c.*560–636) includes him in his *De viris illustribus*, noting his inestimable abstinence and great generosity to the poor of Constantinople.[60] Gregory knew John personally from his time in Constantinople and alludes in his letters to John's exceptional self-

[57] 'Vnde adhuc peto ut nullius praeualere contra ueritatem hypocrisin permittas, quia sunt quidam qui iuxta egregii praedicatores uocem *per dulces sermones et benedictiones seducunt corda innocentium*; qui ueste quidem despecti sunt sed corde tumente et quasi in hoc mundo cuncta despiciunt sed tamen ea quae mundi sunt cuncta simul adipisci quaerunt; qui indignos se omnibus hominibus fatentur sed priuatis uocabulis contenti esse non possunt, quia illud appetunt unde omnibus digniores esse uideantur.' *S. Gregorii Magni Registrum* 5.39 (CChr.SL 140: 314–15). Italics in CChr.SL edition. Translation from *Letters,* transl. Martyn, 2: 356.

[58] *S. Gregorii Magni Registrum* 5.39 (CChr.SL 140: 316). See also ibid. 7.30, where, to the emperor, he draws a comparison between the title as a 'frivolity' and the work of Antichrist. In 5.28, to the new Patriarch Cyriacus, he alludes to the coming of Antichrist.

[59] *The History of Theophylact Simocatta: An English Translation with Introduction and Notes*, ed. Michael and Mary Whitby (Oxford, 1986), 1.1.1–4 (p. 19), 1.10.1–3 (pp. 32–3), 1.11.14–20 (pp. 36–7), 7.6.1–5 (p. 186). On John IV, see the biographical entry by Daniel Stiernon, *Dictionaire de spiritualité ascétique et mystique. Doctrine et histoire*, 17 vols in 21 (Paris, 1932–95), 8: 586–9; Müller, *Führung*, 84–7. On the patriarchs of Constantinople, see Claudia Rapp, 'The Early Patriarchate (325–726)', in Christian Gastgeber et al., eds, *A Companion to the Patriarchate of Constantinople* (Leiden, 2021), 1–23; Hans-Georg Beck, *Kirche und theologische Literatur im byzantinischen Reich* (Munich, 1959), 214, 423–4, 775. I am most grateful to Claudia Rapp and Phil Booth for help with John and with the Byzantine church.

[60] *El «De Viris Illustribus» de Isidoro de Sevilla Estudio y Edicion Critica*, ed. Carmen Cordoner Merino (Salamanca, 1964), 146–7: 'inaestimabilis abstinentiae et elemosynis … largissimus'.

denial, both expressing admiration for it and using it as a weapon against him. Indeed, the contrast between John's ascetic practices and the claim which the pope saw in his adoption of the title of ecumenical patriarch is integral to much of Gregory's denunciation of John. For example, in his letters concerning the ecumenical title to the Patriarchs Anastasius of Antioch and Eulogius of Alexandria, he describes John's excellence in prayers, fasting and almsgiving, but continues by denouncing his pretence at humility which, according to Gregory, masks his pride in claiming a title superior to that of other bishops.[61] Other aspects of John's conduct and life match Gregory's critique of hypocrisy: like the hypocrites in the *Moralia*, John was also learned in Scripture, having written a treatise on baptism. The patriarch's wrongful condemnation of the two men for heresy demonstrated his lack of discernment and his unfitness for office. Gregory knew John well and was quick to note the disparity between his apparent sanctity and his – in Gregory's view – proud and sinful behaviour.

John, then, is a false pastor who fails his flock. Just like the hypocrites of the *Moralia*, he claims to be what he is not; he holds high office in the church. There can be no doubt of the severity of the danger which Gregory saw in the hypocrisy of John and his supporters. At a time when the advent of Antichrist was imminent, John was the breach in the citadel of the church which allowed the devil to penetrate. He was destroying the unity of the church and leaving it exposed to satanic attack.[62] Implicit in Gregory's portrayal of John as a hypocrite is the notion that he is therefore a member of Antichrist's body and his agent. Gregory, unsurprisingly, does not go so far as to say this explicitly, but it would surely have been clear to anyone, like Sabinian, who knew his *Moralia*.

Gregory's protests fell on deaf ears: the emperor Maurice rebuked him, declaring the title not to be a serious matter.[63] John IV's successor, Cyriacus, continued to use it, leading to further, more muted

[61] *S. Gregorii Magni Registrum* 5.41 (CChr.SL 140: 324). See also ibid. 5.37 for the same accusation. Compare also *S. Gregorii Magni Registrum* 3.52 (CChr.SL 140: 198), where, in a preliminary phase of the controversy, Gregory accuses John of lying and states that it is a greater sin to use the mouth to lie than to eat meat.

[62] Charlotte Kingston, 'The Devil in the Writings and Thought of Pope Gregory the Great (590–604)' (DPhil thesis, University of York, 2011), 198–219.

[63] *S. Gregorii Magni Registrum* 7.30 (CChr.SL 140: 491), Gregory's letter concerning Cyriacus, June 597.

objections on Gregory's part.[64] The pope's letters to Patriarchs Eulogius of Alexandria and Anastasius of Antioch failed to win him their support.[65] Anastasius apparently also described the title as not important.[66] Initially, Eulogius did not reply and when he did, failed so badly to understand the nature of Gregory's objections that he applied the title to Gregory himself, much to the pope's consternation.[67] Some scholars suggest that latterly, faced with this incomprehension and hostility, Gregory may have softened his stance and accepted the title, but this is by no means certain.[68]

Despite the central place that the hypocrite occupies in the nexus of Gregory's thought, he has received scarcely any attention.[69] Yet this figure of duplicity was the bearer of a spiritual message of the greatest significance: the dangers of pride and of secular acclaim for Christians, especially religious leaders. Gregory's hypocrite is not a failing Christian, one whose way of life is flawed, but a believer whose commitment to the faith is essentially shallow, one unable to withstand the rigours and demands of the faith. These men are a danger to the whole church because they are in thrall to the devil and do the work of Antichrist in anticipation of his reign. Scholarly neglect of the importance of the hypocrite has meant that the real import of Gregory's letters to John IV over the ecumenical title has been missed and the significance of this conflict underplayed, at least by some scholars.[70] Gregory saw the empire as a providential institution, and the emperor as divinely appointed. His letters address the emperor with traditional deference and recognize and appeal to his authority in the protection of the church in the empire.[71] While

[64] *S. Gregorii Magni Registrum* 7.24, .30 (CChr.SL 140: 478–80, 490–1), to Cyriacus and Maurice; 9.157 (CChr.SL 140A: 714–16), to the Illyrian bishops, May 599.

[65] *S. Gregorii Magni Registrum* 5.41 (CChr.SL 140: 320–5); 7.24 (CChr.SL 140: 478–80), to Anastasius, June 597; 7.31 (CChr.SL 140: 492–5).

[66] *S. Gregorii Magni Registrum* 7.24 (CChr.SL 140: 479), June 597.

[67] *S. Gregorii Magni Registrum* 6.61 (CChr.SL 140: 434–5), July 596; 8.29 (CChr.SL 140A: 550–3), July 598.

[68] Markus, *Gregory*, 94; Demacopoulos, 'Gregory the Great', 613.

[69] With the exception of Straw, 'Gregory, Cassian'.

[70] See, for instance, Matthew Dal Santo, 'Gregory the Great, the Empire, and the Emperor', in Neil and Dal Santo, eds, *Companion to Gregory*, 57–81, at 71, who only briefly mentions the conflict, describing it as 'a squabble', albeit a grave one because it threatened the unity of the church. Savon, 'L'Antéchrist', 404 n. 112, notes the significant implications of Gregory's writings on hypocrisy, Antichrist and John the Faster.

[71] Markus, 'Gregory the Great's Europe'; Dal Santo, 'Gregory the Great', 57–81. See also Phil Booth, 'Gregory and the Greek East', in Neil and Dal Santo, eds, *Companion to*

Gregory continued to affirm the place of the emperor in the divinely-ordained empire, he could be critical of imperial actions. The contemporary situation in Italy, where Byzantine power was limited and unable to provide sufficient defence against the Lombard attacks led to conflicts.[72] Relations with the emperor and with the patriarch in Constantinople could be tense; it is clear from his letters concerning the ecumenical title that he had profound anxieties about the patriarch and his leadership of the church of Constantinople. It is no small matter that Gregory considered the emperor's foremost church leader and spiritual adviser as an agent of Antichrist.

Gregory's criticism of John IV as a hypocrite is revealing with regard to his composition of the *Moralia*, the work of Gregory where hypocrites and hypocrisy feature most prominently. It is intriguing to note that Gregory was composing this work as an *apocrisiarius* in Constantinople, at the time when he came to know John. Claudia Rapp has shown that asceticism was a vital component of episcopal status: a reputation for ascetic sanctity demonstrated the gift of the Holy Spirit to the bishop, and could serve as a fundamental element in legitimizing his authority.[73] This therefore raises a question about the extent to which Gregory's reflections on hypocrites in the *Moralia* were prompted by his reservations concerning the public performance of ascetic holiness by church leaders such as John.

Gregory's writings were hugely influential, and the *Moralia* was widely circulated and read. It survived in countless medieval manuscripts and was excerpted and abbreviated by a number of authors.[74]

Gregory, 109–31, esp. 113–17; Carole Straw, 'Gregory's Politics: Theory and Practice', in *Gregorio magno e il suo tempo. XIX Incontro di Studiosi dell'Antichità Cristiana, Roma, 9–12 maggio 1990*, 2 vols, Studia Ephemeridis Augustianum 33–4 (Rome, 1991), 1: 47–63. See also Claude Dagens, 'Grégoire le Grand et le monde oriental', *Rivista di storia e letteratura religiosa* 17 (1981), 243–52 ; Lellia Cracco Ruggini, 'Grégoire le Grand et le monde byzantin', in Fontaine, Gillet and Pellistrandi, eds, *Grégoire le Grand*, 83–94.

72 Rosamond McKitterick, *Rome and the Invention of the Papacy: The* Liber pontificalis (Cambridge, 2020), 17–23; eadem, 'The Papacy and Byzantium in the Seventh- and Early Eighth-Century Sections of the *Liber pontificalis*', *Papers of the British School at Rome* 84 (2016), 241–73.

73 Claudia Rapp, *Holy Bishops in Late Antiquity* (London, 2005), esp. 100–55.

74 René Wasselynck, 'Les compilations des "Moralia in Job" du VIIe au XIIe siècles', *Recherches de théologie ancienne et médiévale* 29 (1962), 5–32; idem, 'Les "Moralia in Job" dans les ouvrages de morale du haut moyen âge latin', *Recherches de théologie ancienne et médiévale* 31 (1964), 5–31; and idem, 'L'influence de l'éxegèse de S. Grégoire le Grand sur les commentaires bibliques médiévaux (VIIe–XIIe s.)', *Recherches de théologie ancienne*

In the tenth century, for example, John of Gorze read the *Moralia* so frequently that he knew it almost by heart, while Odo of Cluny made an abridgement of the work at the request of the canons of St Martin of Tours.[75] The Gregorian hypocrite, however, did not really take off as a significant theme in early medieval discourse, neither as a polemical figure, nor as part of the burgeoning field of apocalyptic thought.[76] For example, one of the most popular and influential texts on the Apocalypse, the tenth-century biography of Antichrist by the Frankish monk Adso, the *De Ortu et Tempore Antichristi*, makes no mention whatsoever of hypocrisy or simulation.[77] Nonetheless, Gregory's exposition of the apocalyptic nature of hypocrisy in the present, his depiction of the essential connection between the arch-hypocrite Antichrist, and those whose Christianity was a façade maintained by deception, was still a powerful one with rich potential for exploitation. Gregory's exposition of the role of Antichrist and his army of hypocrites at the end of time did attract the attention of at least one figure: the eleventh-century archbishop, Wulfstan of York, who, in a lengthy denunciation of hypocrisy, describes Antichrist as 'the arch-hypocrite', in Old English 'se Þeodlicetere'. Wulfstan knew Gregory's *Moralia* and drew upon it in his eschatological sermons.[78] Given that Gregory's

et médiévale 32 (1965), 157–204. See also Gabriella Braga, '*Moralia in Iob*. Epitomi dei secoli VII–X e loro evoluzione', in Fontaine, Gillet and Pellistrandi, eds, *Grégoire le Grand*, 561–8. My thanks to Tessa Webber for advice on the circulation of the *Moralia*.

75 Jean de Saint-Arnoul, *La Vie de Jean, abbé de Gorze*, ed. and transl. Michel Parisse (Paris, 1999), cap. 83, pp. 110–11; John of Salerno, *Life of Odo of Cluny* 1.20 (PL 133: 43–86, at 52); English translation in *St Odo of Cluny*, ed. and transl. Gerard Sitwell (London, 1958), 1–87, at 22–3. On Odo's *Epitome Moralium in Job*, see Isabelle Rosé, *Construire une société seugneuriale* (Turnhout, 2008), 107–9.

76 See Savon, 'L'Antéchrist', for the influence of Gregory's vision of Antichrist and his church and the work of his members in the present. Compare also Adriaan Bredero, 'The Announcement of the Coming of Antichrist and the Medieval Concept of Time', in Michael Wilks, ed., *Prophecy and Eschatology*, SCH Sub 10 (Oxford, 1994), 3–13.

77 Adso Devensis, *De ortu et tempore Antechristi, necnon et tractatus qui ab eo dependunt*, ed. Daniel Verhelst, CChr.CM 45 (Turnhout, 1976). On the identity of Adso, see Simon MacLean, 'Reform, Queenship and the End of the World in Tenth-Century France: Adso's "Letter on the Origin and Time of Antichrist" reconsidered', *Revue belge de philologie et histoire* 86 (2008), 645–75.

78 For Wulfstan's use of Gregory, see *The Homilies of Wulfstan*, ed. Dorothy Bethurum (Oxford, 1957), 61, 96–7, 281–4, 289, 350; Joyce Lionarons, *The Homiletic Writings of Archbishop Wulfstan* (Woodbridge, 2010), 55, 57, 100, 111, 166. Source-hunting suggests that Wulfstan knew Gregory's dialogues, Gospel homilies and homilies of Ezekiel,

designation of Antichrist as the chief hypocrite is not taken up by other early medieval authors (as far as I can tell), he must surely have derived this description from the *Moralia*.[79]

Gregory's *Moralia* was well known to and widely read amongst the English monastic reformers of the tenth and eleventh centuries. Although the evidence for its manuscript transmission in England at this time is very sparse and, literally, fragmentary, quotations from and allusions to it can be found in both Old English and Latin writings. Two manuscript witnesses to the work survive from England in this period.[80] Oxford, Bodleian Library, Ms 310 is a ninth-century continental manuscript, possibly from the Rhineland, of Books XI–XVI. Rosamond McKitterick finds that this had reached England by the tenth century.[81] Two binding fragments – Oxford, Bodleian Library, Ms G. 1. 7 Med and G 1. 9 Med – were copied in England in the early eleventh century.[82] The *Moralia* is a sizeable text, which attracted more compact redactions: the epitome made by Laidcenn Mac Baith in the seventh century, the *Ecloga de Moralibus in Iob*, also circulated in pre-Conquest England.[83] A tenth-century manuscript of this, possibly of continental origin,

as well as the *Moralia*. For a wider context, see also Andy Orchard, 'The Library of Wulfstan of York', in Richard Gameson, ed., *The Cambridge History of the Book in Britain*, 1: c.*400–1100* (Cambridge, 2012), 694–700, although this does not discuss Wulfstan's debt to Gregory.

[79] Searches of the Library of Latin Texts database does not reveal the use of this phrase in other authors. For the *Moralia* in Anglo-Saxon England, see Michael Lapidge, *The Anglo-Saxon Library* (Oxford, 2006), 305–6.

[80] Helmut Gneuss and Michael Lapidge, *Anglo-Saxon Manuscripts: A Bibliographical Handlist of Manuscripts and Manuscript Fragments written or owned in England up to 1100* (Toronto, 2014), nos 166e, 188.8e, 241e, 453.6, 469.3, 564e, 668.5f, 677.3f, 691e, 704, 7736e, 773.7e, 840.5e, 858f, 865.5f, 946.5e. Four of these are early copies from the eighth and ninth centuries. Nos 840.5e, 865.5f and 946.5e have a continental provenance, while 865.5f (New York, Pierpont Morgan Library, Ms G 30) was copied at Wearmouth Jarrow.

[81] Gneuss and Lapidge, *Anglo-Saxon Manuscripts*, no. 564e; Rosamond McKitterick, 'Exchanges between England and the Continent', in Gameson, ed., *Cambridge History of the Book in Britain,* 1: 330; Lapidge, *Anglo-Saxon Library*, 171, 306.

[82] Gneuss and Lapidge, *Anglo-Saxon Manuscripts*, no. 668.5; see also Lapidge, *Anglo-Saxon Library*, 306.

[83] *Egloga, quam scripsit Lathcen filius Baith de Moralibus Iob quas Gregorius fecit*, ed. Marcus Adriaen, CChr.SL 145 (Turnhout, 1969); Gneuss and Lapidge, *Anglo-Saxon Manuscripts*, nos 135, 818.6f, another eighth- or ninth-century fragment with a continental provenance.

was at St Augustine's Abbey, Canterbury, by the second half of the century.[84] This meagre haul of manuscript evidence must be set against the knowledge of the text demonstrated by authors associated with English monastic reform: in addition to Wulfstan, the *Moralia* was known to Ælfric of Eynsham (*c.*950–*c.*1010), Byrhtferth of Ramsey (*fl. c.*986–*c.*1016) and Lantfred of Winchester (*fl.* 974–84).[85] Ælfric drew upon his knowledge of the *Moralia* in a number of homilies, particularly his homily for the first Sunday in September, when he dedicated an entire homily to the story of Job.[86] Lantfred, a monk at Old Minster, Winchester, came to England from Fleury so may have derived his knowledge of it from his earlier education; but Byrhtferth, whose writings draw upon phrases and sentences from numerous places in Gregory's *Moralia*, was a Benedictine monk at Ramsey.[87]

Wulfstan was a major figure at the English court, who drafted law codes for both King Æthelred and his successor, the conquering king, Cnut. He was most likely a monk and achieved high office, first as bishop of London in 996, and subsequently as bishop of Worcester

[84] Gneuss and Lapidge, *Anglo-Saxon Manuscripts*, no. 135, and see Lucia Castaldi, 'La trasmissione e rielaborazione dell'esegesi patristica nella lettatura ibernica delle origini', *Settimane* 57 (2010), 393–428, at 400.

[85] Lapidge, *Anglo-Saxon Library*, 305, for a list of *Moralia* MSS in England; *Fontes Anglo-Saxonici*, online at: <https://www.st-andrews.ac.uk/~cr30/Mercian/Fontes>, accessed 22 November 2023. Lantfred came from Fleury and may have encountered the text there, rather than in England.

[86] For Ælfric and the *Moralia*, see Lawrence L. Besserman, 'A Note on the Source of Aelfric's Homily on the Book of Job', *English Language Notes* 10 (1973), 248–52; Malcolm Godden, *Ælfric's Catholic Homilies: Introduction, Commentary and Glossary*, EETS s.s. 18 (Oxford, 2000), 592–60; Martin Chase, 'The Book of Job and the Figure of Job in Old English Literature', in Harkins and Canty, eds, *Companion to Job in the Middle Ages*, 354–91; Lapidge, *Anglo-Saxon Library*, 259; and *Fontes Anglo-Saxonici*, online at: <https://www.st-andrews.ac.uk/~cr30/Mercian/Fontes>, accessed 22 November 2023, with reference to the commentary in Godden's *Ælfric's Catholic Homilies*, with a fuller discussion of Ælfric's sources indicating some citations as parallels, rather than direct quotations or allusions.

[87] Mechthild Gretsch, *Ælfric and the Cult of the Saints in Late Anglo-Saxon England* (Cambridge, 2006), 46–9; Lapidge, *Anglo-Saxon Library*, 241, 270. Chase, 'The Book of Job', 377–8, identifies the *Moralia* as a source for the Old English homily: *Wulfstan. Sammlung der ihm zugeschriebenen Homilien nebst Untersuchungen über ihre Echtheit*, ed. Arthur Napier (Dublin and Zurich, 1883; repr. Cambridge, 1967), 249 (homily 48). However, this homily is an extract from the postscript to Byrhtferth's *Encheiridion*. See the edition by Peter S. Baker and Michael Lapidge, *Byrhtferth's Enchiridion*, EETS s.s. 15 (Oxford, 1995), cxxiii, 242–7, 370–1, who identify Isidore's *Sententiae* as the source for the comments on the sins of pride and lust which Chase traces to the *Moralia*.

and archbishop of York, two sees which he initially held together. These ecclesiastical offices gave him a powerful position at court. He has achieved literary renown for his vernacular sermons, a number of which address the crises of his day, and some of which were delivered to the royal council.[88]

Like Gregory, Wulfstan believed that he lived in the last age of the world, in the time of tribulation immediately preceding the coming of Antichrist. Also like Gregory, he found himself providing spiritual leadership at a time of great political turmoil and uncertainty. These two strands came together for Wulfstan: the English kingdom was under external threat from Viking campaigns, which resulted in conquest in 1016 and the replacement of the West Saxon dynasty by the Danish ruler, Cnut. This series of devastating attacks placed the kingdom under enormous pressure and loyalties fractured. The royal court of King Æthelred was factionalized, uncertain how best to defend itself against the Vikings and riven by accusations of treachery.[89] Wulfstan saw treachery and godlessness all around him. In 1014, Æthelred was driven into temporary exile in Normandy and the archbishop denounced the sinfulness of the English which had led to God's wrath. Around the year 1000, as the Viking attacks escalated, Wulfstan's anxiety about the advent of Antichrist intensified; the collapse of moral and political order in his kingdom signified to him the fulfilment of St Paul's prophecy about the intensification of evil in the days before the reign of Antichrist.[90]

[88] On Wulfstan, see Patrick Wormald, 'Wulfstan [Lupus] (d. 1023)', *ODNB,* online edn (2004), at: <https://doi.org/10.1093/ref:odnb/30098>, accessed 22 November 2023; Andrew Rabin, *The Political Writings of Archbishop Wulfstan of York* (Manchester, 2015); Joyce Lionarons, *The Homiletic Writings of Archbishop Wulfstan* (Woodbridge, 2010); Patrick Wormald, 'Archbishop Wulfstan: Eleventh-Century State-Builder', in Matthew Townend, ed., *Wulfstan, Archbishop of York* (Turnhout, 2004), 9–27; Catherine Cubitt, '"Now what I want is Facts": Deconstructing and Reconstructing the Career of Archbishop Wulfstan II of York', *Quaestio insularis* (forthcoming).

[89] Pauline Stafford, 'The Reign of Æthelred II: A Study in the Limitations on Royal Policy and Action', in David Hill, ed., *Ethelred the Unready*, British Archaeological Reports British Series 59 (Oxford, 1978), 15–46; Catherine Cubitt, 'Reassessing the Reign of King Æthelred the Unready', *Anglo-Norman Studies* 42 (2020), 1–28; Simon Keynes, *The Diplomas of King Æthelred the Unready 978–1016* (Cambridge, 1980); Ann Williams, *Æthelred the Unready: The Ill-Counselled King* (London, 2003); Levi Roach, *Æthelred the Unready* (New Haven, CT, 2016); Ryan Lavelle, *Æthelred II King of the English 978–1016* (Stroud, 2002).

[90] Catherine Cubitt, 'On Living in the Time of Tribulation: Archbishop Wulfstan's *Sermo Lupi ad Anglos* in its Eschatological Context', in Rory Naismith and David

Wulfstan's most interesting denunciation of hypocrisy is found in a sermon on the seven gifts of the Holy Spirit and their opposing vices, a sermon which superficially is neither eschatological nor ostensibly political, but which is exceptionally revealing.[91] It shows not only that Wulfstan translated Gregory's vision of apocalyptic hypocrisy into a critique of contemporary life, but also how he deployed it as a polemic aimed, most likely, at the royal court itself. The sermon itself is a revised and extended treatment by the archbishop of a base text written by his contemporary, the homilist Ælfric, perhaps commissioned by Wulfstan himself.[92] This original sermon is, however, little more than a catalogue of virtues and vices which follows an earlier tradition in noting that the opposing vices simulate the virtues they replace. In Ælfric's sermon, the element of hypocrisy and simulation is lightly sketched, but Wulfstan builds on this to denounce full-blown hypocrisy. He turns what is essentially a spiritual tract on the gifts of the Spirit and their opposing vices, into a critique of contemporary evils, directly connecting the deliberate, deceitful simulation of virtue with the reign of the arch-hypocrite, Antichrist, and the hypocritical work of his members in the present.[93]

Wulfstan does this in two ways, firstly by rewriting the original text to emphasize the deceit of hypocrisy, heightening the verbal register of the tract by additional words designating lying, deceit and hypocrisy, and by adding a substantial conclusion concerning Antichrist and his work in the present.[94] One example of his verbal elaboration will have to suffice:

A. Woodman, eds, *Writing, Kingship and Power in Anglo-Saxon England* (Cambridge, 2018), 202–33; eadem, 'Apocalyptic and Eschatological Thought in England around the Year 1000', *TRHS* 25 (2015), 27–52; Levi Roach, 'Apocalypse and Atonement in the Politics of Later Æthelredian England', *English Studies* 95 (2014), 733–57.

91 *The Homilies of Wulfstan*, ed. Dorothy Bethurum (Oxford, 1957), 185–91 (homily 9). See also Sherif Abdelkarim, 'The Terms of Hypocrisy in Early English Law and Literature: Ælfric and Wulfstan', in Anya Adair and Andrew Rabin, eds, *Law, Literature, and Social Regulation in Early Medieval England* (Woodbridge, 2023), 236–258, esp. 246.

92 *Ælfrician Homilies and Varia Editions, Translations and Commentary*, ed. Aaron J. Kleist and Robert K. Upchurch, 2 vols (Woodbridge, 2022), 2: 787–801, 803–26 (no. 16), which updates Loredana Teresi, 'A Possible Source for the *seofonfealdan Godes gifa*', *Leeds Studies in English* 37 (2006), 101–10.

93 On the *Moralia* in pre-Conquest England, see n. 87 above.

94 Angus McIntosh, 'Wulfstan's Prose', *Proceedings of the British Academy* 35 (1949), 109–42; Andy Orchard, 'Crying Wolf: Oral Style and the *Sermones Lupi*', *Anglo-Saxon England* 21 (1992), 239–64, esp. 243–47, 259–64.

> [Ælfric:] Wisdom is holy, a gift of the Holy Spirit, and the devil gives foolishness in opposition [to it] so that [the person] neither pays heed to wisdom nor lives wisely, and yet it is more despicable that he considers himself to be wise and so has pretended to be wise.[95]

> [Wulfstan:] Wisdom is, as we have already said, is the gift of the holy spirit and the devil sows in opposition unwisdom and deception, and he does so that the unblessed man does not desire wisdom nor does he order his life wisely, and he does what is more wicked, that he considers the while himself cautious and wise and he will also, as a hypocrite, feign that he is wise, although he considers more about deception/treachery than wisdom.[96]

The treatise concludes with the final gift, fear of God, the lack of which causes foolish behaviour, recklessness and the pretence of virtue. Wulfstan uses Ælfric's conclusion on those who lack the fear of God as a bridge into a treatment of Antichrist, by warning that the devil can cause those who lack the fear of God to become feigning hypocrites, completely filled with evil in their inner thoughts. Wulfstan's added conclusion is a text of over forty lines, effectively a rant against the arch-hypocrite, Antichrist, and those who follow him in the present, feigning virtue and wisdom. It opens with these words: 'There is no worse evil nor one more hateful to God than the hypocritical evil because the devil himself guides and forms it'.[97] Antichrist's reign of deception will cause many to join him and speak or appear other than they think. The deceptions of the arch-hypocrite will defeat the defences of the faithful because 'there will never be anyone in the world more worldly-wise nor more fluent in words nor worse in heart and more deceptively

[95] 'Se wisdo<m> is halig, þæs Halgan Gastes gifu, and se deofol forgifð þærtogeanes dysig þæt he wisdomes ne gyme ne wislice ne libbe, and gyt þæt forcuþre is þæt he telle hine wisne and bið swa gehiwod swylce he wis sy': *Ælfrician Homilies*, ed. Kleist and Upchurch, 2: 810–13 (translation from this edition).

[96] 'Se wisdom is, swa we ær cwædon, þæs halgan gastes gifu, 7 deofol sæwð þærtogeanes unwisdom 7 swicdom 7 gedeð swa þurh þæt unsælig man wisdomes ne gymeð ne wislice his lif ne fadað, 7 gyt eac gedeð þæt forcuðre is, þæt he talað þeh hwilum hine sylfne wærne 7 wisne, 7 bið eac for oft swa gehiwod licetere swylce he wis sy, byð þeah smeagende oftor ymbe swicdom ðonne ymb wisdom.' *Homilies*, ed. Bethurum, 187 (no. 9). See also Orchard, 'Crying Wolf', 262–3.

[97] 'Nis næfre nan wyrse yfel ne Gode laðre þonne þæt gehiwode yfel, forðan deofol sylf hit gefadað 7 gehywað to þam … .' *Homilies*, ed. Bethurum, 189.

deceitful than he is'.[98] If Antichrist is the arch-hypocrite, his followers are 'downright hypocrites' who do his work:

> There are now, he says, too many men in this deceitful world who speak or think something completely different in this way through feigning. They conduct themselves as if cautious so that they are able to deceive treacherously; and all this comes from the devil, although they do not believe this, and they both injure with such clever deeds first themselves and then too many … . Traitors who in this way deceitfully deceive very often through evil … .[99]

These are deceitful traitors who do terrible harm and, although they do not realize it, 'they are forerunners and thralls of Antichrist who prepare his way'.[100]

This diatribe against Antichrist and his deceitful followers connects therefore with the earlier account of the devil's counter-vices, with Wulfstan's words recalling here his previous condemnation of those who make a pretence of wisdom. He concludes the sermon by warning against those who deceive by pretending to teach true doctrine but who advocate false teaching by approving the earthly satisfaction of bodily pleasures, specifically sexual ones. These are pleasing Antichrist by their wickedness and promote his reign.

Why did Wulfstan pen this invective against the wickedness of hypocrites of his own day? It seems to me that this polemic is at least partly aimed at the royal council, which Wulfstan later denounced for exactly such deceit and treachery. Looking back on the reign of Æthelred at the inception of Cnut's reign, Wulfstan wrote:

> Indeed, formerly treachery was everywhere greater than wisdom, and at that time he was considered wisest who was most devious and who

[98] 'Forðam ne weorþeð on worulde ænig woruldsnotera ne on wordum getingra ne on heortan wyrsa 7 lytelice swicolra þonne he wyrðeþ.' *Homilies*, ed. Bethurum, 189.

[99] 'And to fela manna eac is nu on ðissere swicelan worulde þe ealswa to swyðe þurh hiwunge eal oðer specað oþer hy þencað 7 lætað þæt to wærscype þæt hy oðre specað oþer hy þencað 7 lætað þæt to wærscype þæt hy oðre magan swa swicollice pæcan; ac eal þæt cymð of deofle, ðeah hy swa ne wenan, 7 ægðer hy deriað mid swa gerædan dædan ge ærest him sylfum gesyððan to manegan… And swa gerade manswican þe on ða wisan swæslice swiciað oftost on unriht 7 ðurh þæt deriað for Gode 7 for worulde, þæt syndan forbodan 7 Antecristes þrælas þe his weg rymað, þeah hy swa ne wenan.' *Homilies*, ed. Bethurum, 189–90.

[100] *Homilies*, ed. Bethurum, 189–90 (original text in previous footnote).

understood most cunningly how to profess falsely that lies were truth and the unjust how to judge others to their detriment; but woe to them for their cunning and all of their pride.'[101]

The dating of Wulfstan's composition of the sermon of the seven gifts of the Spirit is complicated. It has been dated to 1002 x 1008. Malcolm Godden, however, argued that Wulfstan may have derived all his Ælfric-based sermon material from a collection put together after 1006, and therefore these texts have to be dated to 1006–12 or later.[102] The first two decades of the eleventh century were a particularly troubled period, with an intensification of the Viking onslaught. There are signs within the English elite of distrust and anxieties concerning allegiance and treachery. In 1002, Æthelred ordered the massacre of Danes living in England (probably those who had settled relatively recently as mercenaries), whom a contemporary charter describes in an apocalyptic reference as 'cockles amongst the wheat'.[103] 1005–6 saw a court revolution of a particularly vicious kind: in addition to the retirement of a number of longstanding court members, one was forced out by accusations of treachery, while another, Ealdorman Ælfhelm, was murdered, allegedly having been lured to his death by an invitation to a feast by another prominent court member. Ælfhelm's sons, also court members, were then blinded on the orders of the king.[104] This episode appears to suggest Æthelred's collusion in this political assassination. The purge was therefore a bloody one which was marked by

[101] Rabin, *Political Writings*, 147. 'forþam ær þysan wæs gehwar swicdom swyðra, þonne wisdom, and þuhte hwilum wisast, se þe wæs swicolost ans se þe lytelicost cuðe leaslice hiwjan unsoð to soðe and undom deman oðrum to hynde. ac wa heom þæs wærscipes and ealles þæs weorðscipes.' *Wulfstan Sammlung*, ed. Napier, 268 (homily 50). On the theme of fair speaking and deceit in Old English, see Jonathan T. Randle, 'The "Homiletics" of the Vercelli Book Poems: The Case of *Homiletic Fragment* I', in Samantha Zacher and Andy Orchard, eds, *New Readings in the Vercelli Book* (Toronto, 2009), 185–224.

[102] Malcolm Godden, 'The Relations of Wulfstan and Ælfric: A Reassessment', in Townend, ed., *Wulfstan, Archbishop of York*, 353–74, at 366–72; see also Sara M. Pons-Sanz, *Norse-Derived Vocabulary in the Late Old English Texts* (Odense, 2007), 25; and Wormald, 'Archbishop Wulfstan', 26.

[103] Simon Keynes, 'The Massacre of St Brice's Day (13 November 1002)', in Niels Lund, ed., *Beretning fra seksogtyvende tværfaglife vikingesymposium* (Aarhus, 2007), 32–66; Roach, *Æthelred*, 187–200; idem, 'Apocalypse and Atonement in the Politics of Æthelredian England', *English Studies* 95 (2014), 733–57. See also Jon Wilcox, 'St Brice's Day Massacre and Archbishop Wulfstan', in Diane Wolfthal, ed., *Peace and Negotiation Strategies for Co-existence in the Middle Ages and Renaissance* (Turnhout, 2000), 79–91.

[104] Keynes, *Diplomas of King Æthelred the Unready*, 208–11.

allegations of treason and double-dealing. Moreover, previously high-ranking and respected court members were disgraced and removed through accusations of sinful behaviour and abuse of office. Wulfstan's allegiances probably lay with those who were forced out, as these seem to have been men with a track record of supporting church reform, while many of those who remained important members of the king's council were notorious for their treachery and duplicity.[105] This is evidenced by such witnesses as the Anglo-Saxon Chronicle, the annals of which are a catalogue of allegations of cowardice, deceit and disloyalty on the part of the elite; while the homilist Ælfric, a tart commentator on contemporary politics, also denounced the deceitful practices in judgements of the king's council.[106] The palace coup of 1005–6 seems to have expunged the court of those who saw the current disasters as the product of the abuse of the church and its property, and brought about their replacement by men of a more secular turn of mind. Perhaps Wulfstan's words on the dangerous evil of hypocrisy and the work of Antichrist were aimed at the political elite, urging them to reflect on their own behaviours and that of other council members at a time of great political stress.

Conclusion

Wulfstan was deeply influenced by Gregory's account of the hypocrisy of Antichrist and the wicked work of his forerunners. The connection made by the pope between the false Christians of his own time, the hypocrites and the apocalyptic scenario of the last days was a powerful one which intensified the evil of hypocrisy. It held great appeal for Wulfstan. He translated the pope's essentially spiritual interpretation of hypocrisy into an immediate political polemic, weaponizing his ideas to attack his fellow councillors at court in a

[105] On a reform party at court, see Keynes, *Æthelred*, 154–231; Roach, *Æthelred*, 133–85; Catherine Cubitt, 'The Politics of Remorse: Penance and Royal Piety in the Reign of Æthelred the Unready', *HR* 85 (2012), 179–92.

[106] 'Annals 978–1016 (CD)', in *The Anglo-Saxon Chronicle*, in *English Historical Documents,* c.*500–1042*, ed. Dorothy Whitelock, 2nd edn (London, 1996; first publ. 1955); *The Anglo-Saxon Chronicle: A Collaborative Edition 5 Ms C*, ed. Katherine O'Brien O'Keefe (Woodbridge, 2001), 84–103; *Homilies of Ælfric: A Supplementary Collection*, ed. John C. Pope, 2 vols, EETS 259–60 (Oxford, 1967–8), 2: 497–510 (no. 13).

deeply-factionalized and highly charged situation. It was a powerful tool: as Judith Shklar has observed, 'it is … easier to dispose of an opponent's character by exposing his hypocrisy than to show that his political convictions are wrong'.[107] At the same time, Wulfstan's denunciation of those at court who mask their real thoughts and views is more, I think, than political manoeuvring. Wulfstan really did believe that Antichrist's reign was imminent. The kingdom was in turmoil, on the brink of disastrous defeat. Political, military and spiritual solutions had all been attempted, but to no avail. Where in this uncertain world did truth lie? Who could discern how best to please God and assuage his wrath? Wulfstan took from Gregory the association between hypocrisy and the end time, and the role of hypocrites as the unwitting forerunners of Antichrist who do his work. The archbishop does not articulate in his writings any of the depth of Gregory's thought: Wulfstan's hypocrites are characterized by their deception, their simulation of virtue and their association with Antichrist, not by pride or by a desire for human applause. While Wulfstan's understanding of hypocrisy must rest upon his reading of the *Moralia*, his expression of it is a polemic one.

Gregory's deployment of the idea of hypocrisy in his letters to the Empress Constantina and to his deacon, Sabinian, is very different. Here it stands as not as invective, but as something less overt, a signal, a signpost to his recipients of his deepest fears and anxieties about the contemporary condition of the world, a warning, but a careful one. His psychologically complex, spiritual interpretation of hypocrisy informed his reading of current events. Gregory's hypocrite is a vessel for his anxieties about authentic Christianity and about the state of the contemporary church. The hypocrite is an antitype of the true Christian, a useful device for articulating what Christians should not be.

But why was it the hypocrite who occupied this central place? I think that there was something in the ambiguity of the hypocrite which made him a profoundly unsettling figure. A hypocrite is not what he seems. He is a type of category confusion like the ostrich, a flightless bird. For Gregory, the ascetic monk, the hypocrite also encapsulated his deepest fears about the dangers of ecclesiastical office, the pull of worldly affairs, the ever-present peril of pride.

[107] Shklar, *Ordinary Vices*, 48.

His conception of hypocrisy was in part a critique of spiritual leadership which reminded his audience that they too could fall into the trap of pride and become lazy about their faith. His anxieties were intensified by the imminence of the reign of Antichrist, which made the detection and denunciation of his hypocritical agents all the more urgent and necessary.

Contrary to Judith Shklar, hypocrisy in the early Middle Ages was no ordinary vice. Gregory's and Wulfstan's hypocrites are terrifying figures, diabolical agents whose simulations endanger both their own salvation and the safety of the church. Gregory's and Wulfstan's understanding of hypocrisy is rooted in their own experience of the present, but their hypocrites transcend the contemporary world and occupy a place in the spiritual order, in eschatological expectations. Wulfstan's treatment of hypocrites is derived from Gregory's, but is deployed in a different way and to a different end. The examples of Gregory and Wulfstan demonstrate not only the historically embedded nature of interpretations of hypocrisy, but also its enduring appeal.

Cannibal, Scorpion, Horse, Owl: Institutional Hypocrites and the Early Fourteenth-Century Church

John Sabapathy*
University College London

The status of hypocrisy as a vice has varied historically, but analysis has tended to stress the issue in relation to individuals, rather than institutions. Taking Judith Shklar and Boccaccio as points of departure, this article explores how and why hypocrisy mattered in the context of the early fourteenth-century church. Analysing charges of hypocrisy made by and against Pope Boniface VIII at the papal Curia; Angelo Clareno within the Franciscan Order; and the later Capetian court in relation to the Roman de Fauvel *allows us to see how anxiety about hypocrisy became especially acute across a range of early fourteenth institutions. Contemporaries questioned what their institutions meant and increasingly put their claims to the test, often in heightened apocalyptic terms. In and around the early fourteenth-century church, worry about institutional hypocrisy shows how responsibility was increasingly on trial.*

Does hypocrisy matter? Here is a story that helps to answer the question.[1]

* I want to thank Katy Cubitt and the EHS for the invitation to think about this topic; the conference audience for comments; and discussants at a seminar on conscience and the sources of moral authority organized by Emily Corran and Christophe Grellard at the École pratique des hautes études / L'Institut d'études avancées: Marie Dejoux, Arnaud Fossier, John Arnold, Nicolette Zeeman, Frédérique Lachaud and Ian Forrest. My thanks to SCH's readers for their careful and encouraging suggestions, as well as to Peggy Brown, David d'Avray and Kate Sabapathy for generous readings and discussion. An especial *mille mercis* to Jane Gilbert for grooming my *Fauvel* translations with enormous thoughtfulness. None bear responsibility for the views here. I finally wish to thank the Board of the British Library and the Bibliothèque nationale de France for permission to reproduce the two images. University College London, Gower Street, London, WC1E 6BT. E-mail: j.sabapathy@ucl.ac.uk.

[1] On the usefulness of starting with stories for political theory, see Judith Shklar's comments in *Ordinary Vices* (Cambridge, MA, 1984), 228–30.

Studies in Church History 60 (2024), 91–120
doi: 10.1017/stc.2024.4

Once upon a time, in thirteenth-century Paris, there was an upstanding Jewish merchant called Abraham whose gentile friend, Jehannot, yearned for him to convert to Christianity.[2] Finally submitting to his friend's entreaties, Abraham decided to visit Rome to find out about this religion for himself. Hearing this, Jehannot was desperate to dissuade him, knowing just what depravity he would find there. Indeed, at Rome, Abraham found the papal court riddled with the worst sodomitical, simoniacal, gluttonous slave traders you could possibly imagine. On his return to Paris, Jehannot visited Abraham with low expectations, which he confirmed by dark tales. Yet, Abraham said, this horrendous curial behaviour was at such odds with the growing popularity and grandeur of Christianity that he could only deduce that the Holy Ghost, rather than the depraved papacy, was at the root of this splendid religion: he was persuaded to convert. And so they went to Notre Dame, where Abraham was converted, living in Paris happily and prosperously ever after.

This story, the second to be told in Giovanni Boccaccio's *Decameron* (1349–51, rev. 1370–2), offers an apparently clear answer to the question of whether hypocrisy mattered for the fourteenth-century church: it did not.[3] Boccaccio stresses Abraham's perceptiveness. In Rome, he sees through the ecclesiastical jargon used to veil vice: 'procurations' for simony, 'sustentation' (*substentazioni*) for gluttony. He is not taken in by the depraved hypocrisy of the Curia, yet converts even so. Further, Abraham insists on drawing a striking distinction between the church's revolting human leaders, and the underlying, healthy, metaphysical and physical institution.[4] The result is a palpable win for a fallible church. Does Abraham's response show great maturity, or great stupidity? Should we laugh at him, the church, both – or neither?[5]

In favour of reading Abraham as a mature discerner of institutions might be analysts such as David Runciman who criticize the

[2] I am guessing about the thirteenth century, but the story assumes the Curia is at Rome.

[3] Giovanni Boccaccio, *Decameron*, ed. Vittore Branca, 9th edn (Milan, 2008; first publ. 1951–2), 47–51.

[4] I take institutions broadly as social practices, though my focus here is ecclesiastical organizational forms. For discussion, see Antonia Fitzpatrick and John Sabapathy, 'Introduction: Individuals and Institutions in Medieval Scholasticism', in idem, eds, *Individuals and Institutions in Medieval Scholasticism* (London, 2020), 1–50.

[5] Giuseppe Mazzotta's *The World at Play in Boccaccio's Decameron* (Princeton, NJ, 1986) is a classic exploration.

contemporary world's permanent sirens denouncing the latest hypocrisy, since 'there is no way of breaking out from the hypocrisy of political life, and all attempts to find such an escape route are a delusion.'[6] Abraham's refusal to throw the good religion out with the filthy pope might then look like the discrimination of someone who does not discard the person behind a mask simply because the one does not reflect the other (to use Isidore of Seville's definition of the hypocrite).[7] The management theorist Nils Brunsson would probably endorse Abraham's acceptance of the church's hypocrisy since institutions face multiple conflicting demands, meaning that hypocrisy is both functional and unavoidable.[8] Judith Shklar might note that Abraham, counter-intuitively perhaps, eschews what she called the tempting 'psychic annihilation … of opponents by exposing their hypocrisy', which in fact simply generates an infinite death loop of hypocritical charge and countercharge.[9] Shklar argues rather that charges of hypocrisy are a shared tactical language for public critique where fundamental disagreements about substance mean that antagonists, lacking common ground, 'cannot reach them directly'.[10] Alleging hypocrisy is how we argue around what we cannot argue about.

For Shklar, the cultural dominance of hypocrisy as a vice stems from European religious disputes and an elevation of moral over

[6] David Runciman, *Political Hypocrisy: The Mask of Power from Hobbes to Orwell and Beyond*, rev. edn (Princeton, NJ, 2018; first publ. 2008), 196.

[7] 'Hypocrite (*hypocrita*) from the Greek (i.e., ὑποκριτής "play-actor, dissembler") is translated into Latin as "dissembler" (*simulator*). Such a one outwardly appears as good, while he is evil within, for ὑπο- means "false" and κριτής means "judgment." … The sense of this theatrical hypocritical appearance has been transferred to those who proceed with a false face and pretend to be what they are not. They cannot be called hypocrites from the moment they reveal themselves outwardly.' Isidore of Seville, *The Etymologies of Isidore of Seville*, ed. and transl. Stephen A. Barney et al. (Cambridge, 2006), 220 (X. H. 118–20). On the inside/outside division which recurs below, see Delphine Carron, '*Intus Nero Foris Cato*. Une sémiologie de l'hypocrisie', in Manuel Guay, Marie-Pascale Halary and Patrick Moran, eds, *Intus et Foris. Une catégorie de la pensée médiévale?* (Paris, 2013), 171–83. See also Frederic Amory, 'Whited Sepulchres: The Semantic History of Hypocrisy to the High Middle Ages', *RTAM* 53 (1986), 5–39.

[8] Nils Brunsson, 'Organized Hypocrisy', in idem, *The Consequences of Decision-Making* (Oxford, 2007), 111–34.

[9] Shklar, *Ordinary Vices*, 66–7; also 50, 82 and chapter 2 generally (45–86). For recent evaluations of Shklar, see Samantha Ashenden and Andreas Hess, eds, *Between Utopia and Realism: The Political Thought of Judith N. Shklar* (Philadelphia, PA, 2019).

[10] Shklar, *Ordinary Vices*, 79, also 48.

physical cruelty which owes much to organized religion.[11] (It is notable that Abraham, converting despite Christian hypocrisy, is Jewish, when the Pharisees' hypocritical piety in condemning Christ was proverbial amongst Christians.[12]) Putting cruelty first instead, as Shklar recommends, comes with a stress on crimes against humans rather than against God, and her broad account of how this shift happened in the West is also a modernizing and secularizing narrative.[13] That makes the theme of hypocrisy especially interesting given the ecclesiastical focus of this volume, which is plainly also an institutional focus.

Any response to the suggestion in *Decameron* I.2 that hypocrisy does not matter may well depend a good deal on our judgement about the central claims of the institution at its centre, the Roman Catholic Church and its officers. It was in this context that the writer Tim Parks recently invoked Boccaccio's story when discussing the highly controversial responses of Pope Pius XII (r. 1939–58) to the Holocaust during the Second World War. 'In my forty years in Italy,' Parks reflected, 'I have never had any inkling that the Vatican's miserable war record, its proven financial corruption, or its coverups of widespread sexual abuse make any dent in the commitment of its supporters.'[14]

The case of Pius XII raises stark questions about institutional hypocrisies and the cruelties they can produce: cruelty and hypocrisy may both come first, here if not always.[15] Perhaps hypocrisy is more corrosive than some modern liberal democratic theorists suggest,

[11] Ibid. 48, 42.

[12] See, for instance, Dante Alighieri, *Commedia*, 1: *Inferno*, ed. Anna M. Chiavacci Leonardi (Milan, 1991), canto 23, ll. 91–123.

[13] Shklar, *Ordinary Vices*, 239–41.

[14] Tim Parks, 'The Pope's Many Silences', *New York Review of Books*, 20 October 2022, reviewing David I. Kertzer's *The Pope at War: The Secret History of Pius XII, Mussolini, and Hitler* (Oxford, 2022) and Michael Hesemann, *The Pope and the Holocaust: Pius XII and the Vatican Secret Archives* (San Francisco, CA, 2022), online at: <https://www.nybooks.com/articles/2022/10/20/the-popes-many-silences-tim-parks/>, accessed 1 March 2023. A letter exchange followed: Michael Hesemann and Tim Parks, 'The Silence of Pius XII: An Exchange', *New York Review of Books*, 24 November 2022, online at: <https://www.nybooks.com/articles/2022/11/24/the-silence-of-pius-xii-an-exchange/>, accessed 1 March 2023.

[15] See Kertzer, *Pope at War*, 478–9 on Pius's goal to protect the church institutionally. Kertzer's theme of prudent silence (esp. 472–80) recurs below, as does its opposite, verbosity.

notwithstanding the 'maze-like inescapability' it produces.[16] Parks himself is puzzled, not blithe, about the indifference to ecclesiastical hypocrisy which he perceives. Institutional hypocrisy may need different, or more attentive, handling apart from the individual hypocrisy which is so often the focus of analysis, as the political theorist Dennis Thompson has argued.[17] Even so, some institutional analysts, like Brunsson, endorse the functional value of hypocrisy to groups: organizations saying they are going to do something which they will not, is a way of deferring, possibly avoiding, conflicting demands coming to a head.[18] How adequate an account of Pius XII's response to fascism that produces, I cannot address.

Given the scale effects of institutions, it is worth asking whether, how and where they can be hypocritical. Since institutional hypocrisy involves multiple individuals and elements that are read as a social whole, it poses analytical challenges different from personal hypocrisy (as with questions of institutional racism, sexism, and so on).[19] Thompson suggests that institutional hypocrisy comprises 'a disparity between the publicly avowed purposes of an institution and its actual performance or function. This disparity often develops over time as an institution comes to serve purposes other than those for which it was established.'[20] This, however, raises more questions than it resolves. Are institutions strapped to a doctrinaire originalism? If not, who decides what is legitimate institutional change?[21] What if institutional purposes turn out to be contradictory? And how do we ascertain what those purposes were? Hypocrisy revolves around inconsistencies, between claims, motives and, often, actions. Affirming hypocrisy then entails converting actions into words since the inconsistency which fuels hypocrisy charges can only exist

[16] Shklar, *Ordinary Vices*, 66.

[17] Dennis F. Thompson, 'Hypocrisy and Democracy', in idem, *Restoring Responsibility: Ethics in Government, Business, and Healthcare* (Cambridge, 2004), 209–26.

[18] Brunsson, 'Organized Hypocrisy', 115–16, 118. Cf. Richard J. Evans's discussion of Kertzer and Pius XII: 'Why Did He Not Speak Out?', *London Review of Books*, 19 October 2023, online at: <https://www.lrb.co.uk/the-paper/v45/n20/richard-j.-evans/why-did-he-not-speak-out>, accessed 12 October 2023.

[19] Cf. Brunsson, 'Organized Hypocrisy', 124, 125.

[20] Thompson, 'Hypocrisy and Democracy', 212.

[21] See David Runciman's discussion, 'Institutional Hypocrisy', *London Review of Books*, 21 April 2005, online at: <https://www.lrb.co.uk/the-paper/v27/n08/david-runciman/institutional-hypocrisy>, accessed 1 March 2023.

between logical propositions, not actions.[22] Judging hypocrisy therefore often entails framing actions as statements: 'for the acts argue for the words' as one text, discussed below, says about the Sanhedrim's 'hypocritical' condemnation of Christ.[23] For institutions, this raises the fundamental question of whose action-words count when we want to locate institutional hypocrisy. Finally, are there particular historical moments when institutional hypocrisy becomes a heightened concern, or indeed matters more for a society?

A provisional assessment of attention to hypocrisy between the fifth and thirteenth centuries has been provided by Sita Steckel in an analysis of Latin texts (Table 1). The usual qualifications should be made that her data is drawn from a particular set of texts, focuses on a particular semantic form, and cannot specify contexts nor terms of use. Even so, the increased attention to hypocrisy in the thirteenth century is striking. Steckel argues that concern about hypocrisy increased following the Gregorian 'reform' associated with Pope Gregory VII (1073–85). For her, the 'formation of a polemical society' occurred as more religious elites competed in a battle for authenticity: 'institutional renewal and institutional diversity generated and popularized diagnoses of decay', expressed via hypocrisy.[24]

Steckel focused on ecclesiastical discourses. Thomas Bisson gives an interesting analysis of what he has called clerical critics' 'learned moralising' about lay institutions around 1200, which he suggests was limited both by their conceptual framework and by the pretensions of the institutions themselves.[25] By 1300, certainly, it does not

Table 1. Occurrence of 'hypocri*' in the Library of Latin Texts Series A and B

Century	5th	6th	7th	8th	9th	10th	11th	12th	13th
Occurrences	266	263	95	75	213	13	21	513	959

[22] Raymond Geuss, 'Moralism and *Realpolitik*', in idem, *Politics and the Imagination* (Princeton, NJ, 2009), 31–42, at 36–7.

[23] *Le Roman de Fauvel*, ed. Armand Strubel (Paris, 2012), 670, ll. 5878–96, at 5892 [hereafter: *Fauvel*]. I give page and line numbers (the edition's continuous and separate line numberings require page references).

[24] Sita Steckel, 'Hypocrites! Critiques of Religious Movements and Criticism of the Church, 1050–1300', in Jennifer Kolpacoff Deane and Anne E. Lester, eds, *Between Orders and Heresy: Rethinking Medieval Religious Movements* (Toronto, 2022), 79–126, at 108–11. Table 1 reproduces Steckel's data in ibid. 113 n. 16.

[25] Thomas N. Bisson, *The Crisis of the Twelfth Century: Power, Lordship, and the Origins of European Government* (Princeton, NJ, 2009), 445–56, 489–99.

seem necessary to restrict European 'hypocrisy worry' solely to religious institutions, as will be seen. Rather, a broader concern is apparent regarding whether various institutions' internal substance had become dislocated from their external claims. The most explosive proof would be the systematic immolation of the Templars (1307–12) for alleged institutional perversions and hypocrisies.[26] Here, I explore these questions through the fourteenth-century church and the motley collection of creatures of my title. An ecclesiastical cannibal and scorpions lead the way; a lay horse and owl bring up the rear, pointing to wider conclusions.[27] The analysis begins with the alleged cannibal, Pope Boniface VIII (1294–1303).

I. Cannibal

After the infamous attack on Boniface VIII in his hometown of Anagni on 7 September 1303 by the Capetian and Colonna hit squad of Guillaume de Nogaret and Sciarra Colonna, the pope escaped to Rome shaken and sick, dying in the night of 11–12 October.[28] An account of that last night offers a frightening picture of the controversial *Bonifacius* unveiled as *malefacius*: Boniface confesses to having demonic familiars whose orders he follows. Terrible storms and flocks of black birds appear over the house 'of that tyrant'. Boniface denounces the evil spirit encased in his magic ring. His closest companions urge him to confess, but when the eucharist is brought, he is 'extraordinarily indignant, convulsed by the demon, growling and baring his teeth at the man bearing the body of the lord, as if he wanted to devour that priest'. Boniface reddens like the diabolic lion of 1 Peter 5: 8 against whom one should guard.

[26] From a vast literature, I cite Malcolm Barber, *The Trial of the Templars*, 2nd edn (Cambridge, 2006; first publ. 1978) and Julien Théry, 'A Heresy of State: Philip the Fair, the Trial of the "Perfidious Templars" and the Pontificalization of the French Monarchy', *Journal of Medieval Religious Cultures* 39 (2013), 117–48.

[27] Quite deliberately, this article does not contrast 'secular' and 'ecclesiastical' regimes. Religious concerns animated all forms of rule in this period and I have preferred to speak of 'lay'/'princely' rule.

[28] See Henry G. J. Beck, 'William Hundleby's Account of the Anagni Outrage', *CathHR* 32 (1946), 190–220; Agostino Paravicini Bagliani, *Boniface VIII. Un pape hérétique?* (Paris, 2003), 388–90, 393–6. Despite its notoriety, many European responses were interestingly indifferent: Robert Fawtier, 'L'Attentat d'Anagni', *Mélanges de l'école française de Rome* 60 (1948), 153–79; Teofilo F. Ruiz, 'Reaction to Anagni', *CathHR* 65 (1979), 385–401.

His companions flee, 'rightly thinking him insane, or more truly a devil'. They return, bringing a favoured boy to relieve him 'who he used to hold for his pleasure before and carry in his arms', but 'when he saw the said infant, he went straight for him and seemed to want to devour him, and if he had not been taken away, he would have torn off the child's nose with his teeth'. Soon afterwards, Boniface dies, unconfessed, to the sound of thunderclaps, tempests and dragons vomiting fire over the city.[29]

This image of Boniface as a thwarted cannibal, hungrier for his catamite than for Christ's body, is a malevolence, probably Pietro Colonna's in 1309, during the campaign to condemn Boniface posthumously as a heretic (1306–12).[30] The text provides an exceptionally bad death, the papal hypocrite unmasking himself in his terminal throes. This pope is obviously not what he should be. Because of their partisan hostility, these and the many other accusations are of unresolvable value in determining Boniface's actual actions.[31] They are, however, very useful at revealing the strategy of attack, and the role of hypocrisy within it.

Plainly Boniface's many crimes were crimes per se: heresy, homicide, demonolatry, sodomy. Boniface was accused of straightforward hypocrisy as false piety, but we can say more interesting things than this.[32] The crimes' public resonance came from the wedge they sought to drive between the form of Boniface's office as pope, and his unworthiness as a person,

[29] For this account, see document DS3 in *Boniface VIII en procès. Articles d'accusation et dépositions des témoins (1303–1311)*, ed. Jean Coste (Rome, 1995), 872–5 [hereafter: *BeP*]. I cite document references alone, unless a specific page range is needed. For *Bonifacius-malefacius*, see ibid. 113 n. 1; Paravicini Bagliani, *Boniface*, 95–7; Peter Herde, *Bonifaz VIII. (1294–1303)*, erster Halbband: *Benedikt Caetani* (Stuttgart, 2015), 247–8.

[30] *BeP*, 870–1; Paravicini Bagliani, *Boniface*, 349–66.

[31] See Jeffrey Denton, 'The Attempted Trial of Boniface VIII for Heresy', in Maureen Mulholland and Brian Pullan, eds, *Judicial Tribunals in England and Europe, 1200–1700*, 1: *The Trial in History* (Manchester, 2003), 117–28; Paravicini Bagliani, *Boniface*, 349–66; *BeP*, 895–908. For a superb cameo of Boniface, see Robert Brentano, *Rome before Avignon: A Social History of Thirteenth-century Rome* (London, 1974), 155–64.

[32] Nogaret accused Boniface of doing good works 'hypocritically without love, as is clearly proved by many other evil works, as many other false prophets have done': Pierre Dupuy, *Histoire du différend d'entre le Pape Boniface VIII. et Philippes le Bel Roy de France* (Paris, 1655), 378 and further 380 (the latter also in Coste, *Boniface… en procès*, 481).

invalidating his claim to the office, and justifying his posthumous condemnation.[33]

Hypocritical deceit was pervasive in the accusations as they became increasingly focused. The initial 1297 written denunciations of Boniface (by Cardinals Giacomo and Pietro Colonna) disputed his legitimate election following Celestine V's forced abdication.[34] Although in their earlier attacks on Boniface the Colonna family had characterized him as a *pseudopresul* or *pseudoprefectus* (third Colonna accusation, 1297),[35] it was with Nogaret's denunciation at the Louvre before King Philip IV on 12 March 1303 that mendacity and falseness became emphatic aspects of the attack. Nogaret's preamble makes much of 2 Peter 2, where Peter's description of how 'there were pseudo-prophets amongst the people' becomes a prediction regarding his contemporary successor, 'which today our eyes perceive to the letter'.[36] 'For,' says Nogaret, 'the prince of perfidy (*mendaciorum magister*) sits on the throne of the blessed Peter, having himself called a do-gooder (*Bonifacium*) when he is in every way an evil-doer (*maleficus*), and thus he takes a false name for himself....'[37] Accusing the pope of being illegitimately elected, a heretic, simoniac and wholly subversive of the 'state of the church', Nogaret petitioned Philip to press for a general council, arguing that his faith, his royalty and his oath to defend the church obliged him to do so.[38] The absence of the word hypocrisy does not mask its dominance.

A paradox remains, however, around the allegations of papal hypocrisy. Many of Boniface's imputed crimes concerned what he said he believed. Amongst many more, the June 1303 accusations by Guillaume de Plaisans at the Louvre included the accusation that Boniface says he does not believe in the eternal soul, in eternal life, in the eucharist as a sacrament, in sex as more sinful than rubbing your hands together, or in anything Christ or St Peter would say if they came down to earth.[39] There are obviously tensions, to say

[33] On papal office and persons, see Walter Ullmann, 'Leo I and the Theme of Papal Primacy', *JThS* 11 (1960), 25–51, esp. 33–4, 41–4, 47–8, 50.

[34] *BeP*, PR1 (10 May 1297) and PR2 (11–16 May). PR3 (15 June) begins to open out a wider front.

[35] Ibid. 52, 57 (PR3).

[36] Ibid. 112 (A).

[37] Ibid. 112–13 (A): the first extant example of the *Bonifacius malefacius* dyad.

[38] Ibid. 116–20 (A).

[39] Ibid. B8, B9, B11, B13, B20.

the least, between such statements and Boniface's papal office, opening him to the charge of double-speaking (*bilinguum*).[40] This is more incompatibility than inconsistency. Further, we know these things because Boniface was supposed to have said them in conversation. The Louvre allegations (for instance) did not try to assert that Boniface was secretive about his beliefs: their entire thrust was that they permeated 'public opinion and belief' (*publica vox et fama*).[41] From this standpoint, if Boniface believed what his accusers alleged, then he was telling the truth, not speaking with a forked tongue, still less with false piety. Ironically, partly by virtue of his accusers' desire to hang him high on the bar of public opinion with words out of his own mouth, the one thing Boniface arguably cannot be accused of is hypocrisy, if 'they cannot be called hypocrites from the moment they reveal themselves outwardly'.[42]

The most fitting illustration of this is when witnesses make Boniface himself repeatedly accuse someone else of hypocrisy: Christ.[43] This occurs within two later hearings before Clement V, informally during spring 1310, and then formally in late summer, at Avignon. The accusations come first from friends of Giacomo da Pisa, the banker whose son was allegedly brought to comfort Boniface in his final agonies. We are told that in 1297 Boniface had had an argument with a friend's wife at St Peter's about the decency of the pope playing dice with her. Boniface retorted:

> 'You animal, man has to get whatever good out of this world that he can, since there's no other world than this, and no other life than this.' And then the lady Cola replied and said to him, 'You will die damned and have to account for yourself to Christ and the Virgin Mary.' And Boniface himself replied, in the witness's presence and hearing, 'Christ wasn't [her] son, he was just some clever guy and some hypocrite [*quidam sagax homo et quidam ypocrita*].'[44]

[40] On *bilinguum*, see Gabriella I. Baika, *The Rose and Geryon: The Poetics of Fraud and Violence in Jean de Meun and Dante* (Washington, DC, 2014), 21, 40.

[41] See, for example, *BeP*, B10, B13, B17, B18, B19. There are accusations which Boniface is said to have made publicly (B14 about the French, B19 about simony, B20 about St Peter, B22 about the French as heretics etc.).

[42] *Etymologies of Isidore*, ed. Barney et al., 220 (X. H. 120).

[43] See *BeP*, Q71, Q77, Q88, V116, V315, V335, V354, V378, V403.

[44] Ibid. 533 (Q77), also Q71. This witness, Guglielmo di Pietro da Caltagirone, repeats the argument about Christ just being a clever speaker and no God under formal questioning, but does not use the word hypocrite then (V315).

Other witnesses repeat the hypocrisy charge later in the summer, when asked formally about Nogaret's allegations that Boniface had mocked and flouted fasting rules, as well as cursing the 'she-ass' Virgin Mary who 'had never been the son of God's mother'.[45] Witnesses from a Tuscan embassy from November 1300 remember a conversation which ended with the non-existence of the immaterial world, the triviality of sexual pleasure, and the Bolognese ambassador, Antonio Gallucci, deducing from the pope's lesson that 'we should just enjoy ourselves then'. Gallucci's conclusion followed a discussion of what the pope meant when he said 'the world has ceased' for a dead Campanian soldier mentioned by a visiting chaplain. The hapless chaplain had suggested that Christ still held the man's soul. Boniface set him straight:

> Idiot—who are you commending his soul to, when Christ couldn't even help himself, how could he help anyone else when he wasn't God, but one clever guy and a great hypocrite [*unus sapiens homo et magnus hypocrita*]?[46]

The attacks on Boniface focused on his individual actions as a pseudo-prelate. Indeed, Boniface, infamous for his statues of himself and his assertions of papal power, worked more than any other thirteenth-century pope against the longstanding project to 'disassociate the transient (physical) person of the pope and the eternal (papal) function', according to Agostino Paravicini Bagliani.[47] It nevertheless remained impossible to avoid hitting the papacy when targeting this pope.

Implications for institutional hypocrisy follow in this article's conclusions. Now I turn from one arguably hypocritical, alleged cannibal at the top of the church's hierarchy to the nest of hypocritical scorpions tormenting a contemporary of Boniface's at that hierarchy's base (at least in terms of formal power): the sometime Franciscan Angelo Clareno.

II. Scorpion

Scorpions plague devout Franciscans in Angelo Clareno's apocalyptic history of his Order, written in the 1320s.[48] Quoting the pseudo-

[45] For Nogaret's articles of accusation, see *BeP*, U1, U2, U3.

[46] Ibid. 715 (V354), elaborated at 705 (V315). See also V335.

[47] Agostino Paravicini Bagliani, *Il corpo del papa* (Turin, 1994), 340–3 (quotation at 341).

[48] I use *Liber Chronicarum, sive tribulationum ordinis minorum di Frate Angelo Clareno*, ed. Giovanni Boccali (Santa Maria degli Angeli, 1999) with Angelo Clareno, *A Chronicle*

Joachite *Oraculum Cyrilli* (after 1294), Angelo recounts how that oracle describes the enemies of the great Franciscan radical Peter John Olivi (d. 1298) as:

> 'scorpion-like', born and propagated of scorpions, imitators of scorpions. For hypocrites are compared with scorpions because they put on charming faces, say all the right things, and pretend to act out of pure love, so that they can gain human praise and favour and carry out their malign intentions. They sting with their tails and inject poison, corrupting those who hear them through the depravity of their words and actions, tainting those who follow them with hypocritical filth and defilement.[49]

Who were these scorpions?

Angelo was born Pietro da Fossombrone in the Marches of Ancona, perhaps in 1255, and entered the Franciscan Order perhaps in 1270; he died in 1337.[50] In Ancona, debate about whether the Franciscans were sliding away from the substance of Franciscan life was then becoming intense; Angelo would later identify the Second

---

or History of the Seven Tribulations of the Order of Brothers Minor, transl. David Burr and E. Randolph Daniel (St Bonaventure, NY, 2005). Page references are to Burr and Daniel's translation with Boccali's section references in brackets. There is no satisfactory edition: see Roberto Paciocco, 'Le tribolazioni di Angelo Clareno (in margine alle recenti edizioni)', *Collectanea franciscana* 71 (2001), 493–519. Gian Luca Potestà, 'La duplice redazione della *Historia septem tribulationum*', *Rivista di storia e letteratura religiosa* 38 (2002), 1–38, argued for a twofold recension but against this, see Felice Accrocca, '*Filii carnis—filii spiritus*: Il *Liber chronicarum sive tribulationum ordinis minorum*', in *Angelo Clareno Francescano: Atti Del XXXIV Convegno Internazionale, Assisi, 5-7 Ottobre 2006* (Spoleto, 2007), 49–90.

[49] Clareno, *Chronicle*, 132 (§5.43–6). The *Oraculum Cyrilli* is edited by Paul Piur, in *Briefwechsel des Cola di Rienzo*, ed. Konrad Burdach, *Vom Mittelalter zur Reformation*, 5 vols (Berlin, 1912–29), 2: 220–327.

[50] For this and what follows, see Gian Luca Potestà, *Angelo Clareno. Dai poveri eremiti ai fraticelli* (Rome, 1990); David Burr, 'History as Prophecy: Angelo Clareno's Chronicle as a Spiritual Franciscan Apocalypse', in Michael F. Cusato and Guy Geltner, eds, *Defenders and Critics of Franciscan Life: Essays in Honor of John V. Fleming* (Leiden, 2009), 119–38; idem, *The Spiritual Franciscans: From Protest to Persecution in the Century after Saint Francis* (University Park, PA, 2001), 43–6, 95–6, 279–301; idem, 'John XXII and the Spirituals: Is Angelo Clareno Telling the Truth?', *Franciscan Studies* 63 (2005), 271–87; Sylvain Piron, 'An Institution Made of Individuals: Peter John Olivi and Angelo Clareno on the Franciscan Experience', in Fitzpatrick and Sabapathy, eds, *Individuals and Institutions*, 157–76; idem, 'Extraits de l'*Histoire des sept tribulations de l'Ordre des Mineurs*. Introduction', in Jacques Dalarun, ed., *François d'Assise. Écrits, vies, témoignages*, 2 vols (Paris, 2010), 2: 2565–75.

Council of Lyons (1274) as a particular pivot.[51] The controversy prompted consideration of whether friars should or could leave the Order if constrained to practise what they thought incompatible with it, such as owning property.[52] Around 1279, the Order imprisoned friars, including Angelo, who argued that current practices already abrogated Francis's template. They were released a decade later by a new minister general, Raymond Geoffroi, who encouraged them to proselytize in Armenia. By 1294, they were back in Italy where Geoffroi encouraged them to petition the ageing monk-pope Celestine V so that they could observe the rule 'without harassment and interference from others … who had fallen from that faithful and pure observance' of Francis. Celestine instead 'absolved' them from 'all obedience to the brothers', instructing that 'to protect the peace and honour of the Friars Minor and the Order they should not call themselves Friars Minor but rather his [i.e. Celestine's] friars and poor hermits'.[53] Strikingly, it was at this point, when this Franciscan was no longer a Franciscan, that he changed his name to reflect his Franciscan commitment, from Pietro to Angelo Clareno, probably after one of Francis's earliest companions, Angelo Tancredi.

Angelo's life thereafter was one of flight and evasion. Celestine's successor-cum-gaoler Boniface VIII rescinded all his decrees, prompting the Poor Hermits to flee to Greece. Angelo returned west only in 1309, where he was protected at Avignon by Boniface's antagonist Giacomo Colonna, following the collapse of Clement V's attempt to find some rapprochement between the Franciscans' extremes. Clement's successor, John XXII (1316–34), pushed Angelo towards another group when he directed him towards Celestine's eponymous Benedictine congregation of 'Celestines'. Angelo avoided this by seeking refuge in 1318 at Benedict's ancient foundation at Subiaco (Lazio), where he wrote both his history and a commentary on the Franciscan rule. Whilst there, he carefully avoided outright disobedience of the leadership while producing a profound critique of the Franciscans' past in his *History*. Renewed papal concern about

[51] Clareno, *Chronicle*, 133, 148–9 (§5.50, §5.270–80). It begins his fifth tribulation (up to Celestine's pontificate and Olivi's persecutions *c.*1294).

[52] For this and what follows, see ibid. 148–58; David Burr, *Olivi and Franciscan Poverty: The Origins of the Usus Pauper Controversy* (Philadelphia, PA, 1989), 28–9; idem, *Spiritual Franciscans*, 43–6.

[53] Clareno, *Chronicle*, 155–6 (§5.384–5, §5.393–8).

Angelo's group prompted a final flight in 1334 to Naples, where he died at the hermitage of Santa Maria dell'Aspro.

Angelo's *History* is preoccupied by several themes: the problem of recognizing those who are truly Christ-inspired within the Franciscan Order; the failure of many in its leadership to do so; their worldly prudence, elevating nominal faithfulness to Francis's practice over actual adherence to it; and, consequently, a deceitful religiosity which Angelo describes as hypocrisy at key points. All of these generate the apocalyptical momentum of the seven successive tribulations which overwhelm the Order, but whose watershed Angelo thinks he can see coming in 1331. The result is a sharp polarity opposing the (generally powerless) true Franciscans who recognize the real Francis against those (generally powerful) fake Franciscans who do not, but instead persecute practitioners such as Angelo. There are few in-between figures.[54]

Dangerous, fleshly, prudential reason is central to the Order's inversion (cf. Romans 8: 5–8).[55] Angelo's prologue provides 'speeches' from the Order's early days by Christ, Francis, and the seraph who appeared to Francis on La Verna. In one, Francis predicts that:

> the hostile man will try to sow darnel [Matt. 13: 25 – tares] in the religion [*in religione*, i.e. the Order]. Many will enter the religion who will begin to live not for Christ but for themselves and who will follow carnal prudence more than obedience to the faith and to the rule.[56]

He itemizes how this will become apparent (receipt of money, pursuit of formal learning, etc.):

> They will despise as insane [*insanos*] those brothers who desire to adhere to humility and who strive to get to heaven by pure observance of their promises [*observantiam promissorum*]. They will look down on the holy brothers as useless and as of no importance. Instead they will praise those who probe lofty mysteries and those whom they will esteem and consider as wise, and they will laud their prudence.[57]

[54] Bonaventure is one, but even his depiction is pretty brutal: ibid. 119 20 (§4.204–6).

[55] Caesarius of Speyer makes a similar criticism in his *Sacrum commercium*, where worldly *providentia* is the issue. According to Angelo, Caesarius died at the hands of his Franciscan jailors: ibid. 78–9 (§2.93–114).

[56] Ibid. 14 (prologue, §195–7).

[57] Ibid. 15 (prologue, §217–19).

Such inversions slide effortlessly into false piety and hypocrisy, Angelo says.[58] Hypocrisy in the forms of false humility and piety is the product. The sixth tribulation running from Celestine's resignation (1294), the end of Raymond Geoffroi's tenure as minister general (1296) and Olivi's death (1298), will be characterized by hypocrisy and its perversions. Angelo opens his description of that tribulation with a high denunciation:

> Hypocrisy produces blindness of the mind and heart [Deuteuronomy 28: 28], and deceit is conjoined with vanity. When a hypocrite seeks human favour and praise, envy seeps into his bones, corroding and devouring his insides just as rust does iron, or a moth, clothing [Matthew 6: 19]. In fact those who reveal the truth through their hypocrisy are doubly destroyed. Recognized for what they are, they nevertheless spread their venom like a generation of vipers [Matthew 23: 33; Luke 3: 7].[59]

Unveiling hypocrites comes too late: the damage is already done. The Order is stuffed with such friars, indifferent to Francis's original *vita* yet desirous of its status.[60] An 'anti-Christian fraud' (*antichristiane fraudis*) is the result.[61] During the fifth tribulation, Angelo indeed compares the Anconan spirituals' treatment by their Franciscan brethren as worse or equivalent to the laws and cruelties of Muslims or Mongols (as well as being Pharisaical).[62] More troubling still, these symptoms have clear apocalyptic implications. Such inversions belong to Antichrist. The spirituals' judges:

> make a show of assuming the incorruptible mantle of justice fit for those who offer the eternal sacrifice [Daniel 8: 11–13], so that through malice and depravity they can gain a reputation for holiness and justice. For to establish lies in the place of the truth [*Mendacium enim pro veritate statuere*], to replace zeal for divine praise with zeal for praise of oneself, to make laws based on the caprices and considerations of one's own heart, supporting them with improperly interpreted authorities, is to place the likeness of Antichrist in God's temple even before he

[58] Ibid. 21 (prologue, §299–300).
[59] Ibid. 179, adapted (§6.1–4).
[60] Ibid. 179–80 (§6.16–17).
[61] Ibid. 180 (§6.19).
[62] Ibid. 150, 151, 152 (§5.303, §5.319–21, §5.326).

> comes [cf. 1 John 2: 18; Daniel 9: 27], introduce his sect before he preaches, and do battle for him before he draws near.[63]

This is not simply hypocrisy as pseudo-religiosity but a transcendental inversion of the ties between things and their names. This is an institution, Angelo says, that hypocrisy has turned inside out, trailing Antichrist in its wake.

Yet it is striking that Angelo, who places institutional false prudence and hypocrisy at the centre of his diagnosis of Franciscan error, is also the friar so fiercely committed to the Franciscan ideal that he cycles through no less than three religious groups in order to adhere to it: the Franciscans, the Celestines (courtesy of Celestine V), and then the Benedictine abbey of Subiaco. In short, is Angelo not the hypocrite?

He seems quite clear on the binding nature of the vow in his commentary on the Franciscan rule: 'it is no small sin to promise the highest life and then, after vowing it, live indifferently and seek that which is imperfect'.[64] Indeed, 'it is illicit for those who profess this religion [*religione*] to leave it or transfer to another [*transire*] on the pretext of seeking a more perfect life, for no one who puts his hand to the plough and then looks backward is worthy of the kingdom.'[65] Likewise,

> since there is nothing more perfect than the evangelical life and rule of Christ, the rule announces to all promising it that it will be absolutely forbidden to them to leave this life [*de ista religione exire*] once that promise has been made, for the rectitude, justice, and sanctity which the evangelical life establishes and imposes represents the ultimate and optimum state [*habet in suppremo et optimo statu*] in regard to action and contemplation, permanence, and perpetual firmness.[66]

This is more ambiguous than it seems, however, since Angelo's weight rests on the adherence to the practice (*religio*) more than the

[63] Ibid, 152 (§5.328-333).

[64] David Burr, ed., *Early Commentaries of the Rule of the Friars Minor*, 3: *Angelo Clareno* (Bonaventure, NY, 2015), 27; Livario Oliger, ed., *Expositio Regulae Fratrum Minorum auctore Fr. Angelo Clareno* (Florence, 1912), 33.

[65] Burr, *Early Commentaries … Angelo Clareno*, 23; Oliger, *Expositio … Angelo Clareno*, 28. Angelo is referring to the second chapter of the *regula bullata*: *Fontes Franciscani*, ed. Enrico Menestò et al. (Assisi, 1995), 173.

[66] Burr, *Early Commentaries … Angelo Clareno*, 58; Oliger, *Expositio … Angelo Clareno*, 63.

institutional carapace where it is expressed.[67] Wherever he is, Angelo is a Franciscan. His pithiest assertion of this is the *History*'s account of his exchange with John XXII when summoned in 1317 to explain what his group was up to:

> When brother Angelo had come before him, the pope asked whether he was a Franciscan [*an ipse esset friar minor*], and he replied that he was [*quod sic*]. And the pope asked him, 'Why have you then left them?' [*Quare recessit ab eis*?] Brother Angelo replied, 'Holy Father, I have not left them. Ask them why they have rejected me'. [*ego non recessi ab eis, sed interrogate eos quare ipsi repulerunt me.*] And the pope was silent.[68]

Such silences were only temporary however, and if Angelo thought his position self-evident many others did not. In an extended debate during the 1330s, the Galician Franciscan Alvaro Pais (1275/80–1349/50) demanded that Angelo explain how his position could be reconciled with claims to obedience.[69] A stinging illustration of how Angelo's casuistry could be disastrously understood came from less learned southern French beguins, predisposed *towards* the spirituals.[70] Peire Tort was captured by inquisitors at Cintegabelle in April 1322. Interrogated, he said that 'Some say that Antichrist will be an apostate Franciscan … and that it will be Brother Angelo, who is an apostate of the Order of Friars Minor'.[71] To some, Angelo looked like the scorpion.

III. Horse

Boniface and Angelo might appear to be extravagant religious contortionists, unindicative of anything beyond their own extreme

[67] On *religio*, see Peter Biller, 'Words and the Medieval Notion of "Religion"', *JEH* 36 (1985), 351–69.

[68] Clareno, *Chronicle*, 204–5, adapted (§6.356–62).

[69] I lack the space to describe this satisfactorily. See Victorin Doucet, 'Angelus Clarinus, *Apologia pro vita sua*', *Archivum franciscanum historicum* 39 (1946), 63–200; *Scritti inediti di Fra Álvaro Pais*, ed. Vittorino Meneghin (Lisbon, 1969), 54–92, as well as numerous letters in *Angeli Clareni Opera*, 1: *Epistole*, ed. Lydia von Auw, Fonti per la storia d'Italia pubblicate dall'Istituto storico italiano per il Medio Evo 103 (Rome, 1980).

[70] Southern beguins should be distinguished from northern ones: see Louisa A. Burnham, *So Great a Light, So Great a Smoke: The Beguin Heretics of Languedoc* (Ithaca, NY, 2008), 2–3.

[71] Philippus van Limborch, 'Liber sententiarum', in *Historia inquisitionis* (Amsterdam, 1692), 330. See Burr, *Spiritual Franciscans*, 221–8, 250–1; Burnham, *So Great a Light*, 69–70, 169.

positions. It is clear, however, that they reflected wider institutional uncertainties.

First, the pursuit of Boniface comprised an attack on the recognized leader of the church by both its own elite (the Colonna family, including cardinals) and a historical lay ally (the Capetian court). It risked discrediting the church and establishing competing power poles undermining the singularity of papal authority. The Colonna were well aware of all this. Anticipating counter-attacks to their July 1297 manifesto against Boniface, they conceded the problem:

> there is nothing worse than to call inquisitors after the truth [i.e. us, the Colonna] schismatics or deem them heretics. For if those seeking truth [i.e. us, the Colonna] are rightly called schismatics, or heretics, clearly truth is rightly called schism or heresy. But this is impossible.[72]

It was indeed truly impossible, but the general point is that in such situations it becomes very difficult for observers to determine who is truth-seeker and who is schismatic, since the right to decide is the issue at stake. How do the faithful decide who is who?

Second, the problems posed by Angelo (in every sense) had wider consequences for the Order. As with the Colonna and Boniface, the issue was where the real Franciscans were. Michael Cusato has shown that it was following *Dudum ad apostolatus* – Clement V's favourable 1310 judgement protecting the spirituals and exempting their leaders from ministers' discipline – that 'the community' emerged as a term for the Order: 'it is a term applied to the Order not by its detractors nor even by the papacy but by the Franciscan leadership itself … the use of the [civil] term *communitas* is a declaration that *they* are the Order', in contrast to those now beyond its jurisdiction.[73] Critiques such as Angelo's changed how the Order talked about itself.

Beyond this we can see that there were broader worries about hypocrisy beyond the church *c.*1300. We pass, then, from cannibal and scorpion, to first my horse, then my owl.

The *Roman de Fauvel* is a satire in which the kingdom of France is revealed to have been turned upside down by everyone's adoration of

[72] *BeP*, 63 (PR3).

[73] Michael F. Cusato, 'Whence "the Community"?', *Franciscan Studies* 60 (2002), 39–92, at 65. Emphasis original.

Figure 1. Paris, BN, MS français 146, fol. 1r detail, 'de torcher Fauvel doucement | Trop i a grant assemblement' (ll. 33–4). Reproduced by permission of the Bibliothèque nationale de France.

Fauvel, the 'king of deceit', a jumped-up 'fawn' horse that all want to groom (*torcher*), who wants to consolidate his rule by marrying Fortune, and whose name expresses his corruption (Figure 1):[74]

[74] *Fauvel*, 224 l. 855 ('le roy de fallace'), 128 l. 1 ('torcher'). See generally Jean-Claude Mühlethaler, *Fauvel au pouvoir. Lire la satire médiévale* (Paris, 1994). The MS is digitized online at: <https://gallica.bnf.fr/ark:/12148/btv1b8454675g>, accessed 1 March 2023.

Fauvel is made of 'false' and 'veil',
for his whole Spiel lies
in well-veiled falsity,
and honey-sweet trickery …
From FAUVEL first springs **F**lattery,
who lords it over all the world,
and then **A**varice appears—
she'll groom Fauvel, never fear—
then **U**npredictability, **V**illainy,
and last not least, **E**nvy and **L**ily
Liver. These six ladies, there they are,
are what is meant, by him, Fauvel.[75]

A first book dates from 1310, with the second originating in 1314, the year after Nogaret's death. 1314 was a convulsive year, seeing the burning of Templar leaders Jacques de Molay and Geoffroi de Charney, more torture and executions linked to the adulteries of Philip IV's daughters-in-law, Philip's own death, and the start of his son Louis X's short reign (1314–16), which included the hanging of Philip's chamberlain Enguerrand de Marigny on charges of sorcery and fraud, followed closely by Louis's son John's even shorter reign (1316) and John's succession by Louis's brother Philip V in 1317, the year the enhanced *Fauvel* was completed. Its origins are impossible to isolate absolutely, but a critique of Philip IV, Louis X and Philip V is generally agreed on, with some encouragement generally attributed to Philip IV's brother, Charles of Valois.[76] The expanded *Fauvel* in the

[75] 'Fauvel est de FAUS et de VEL | Compost, car il a son revel | Assis sus fausete voilee | Et sus tricherie mielee …. De Fauvel descent **F**laterie, | Qui du monde a la seigneurie, | Et puis en descent **A**varice, | Qui de torcher Fauvel n'est nice, | **V**ilanie et **V**arieté, | Et puis **E**nvie et **L**aschete. | Ces.vj. Dames que j'ai nommées | Sont par Fauvel senefiées.' *Fauvel*, 154 ll. 229–42, 245–52. My free translation, here and below, is indebted to Jane Gilbert's expert dressage. The letters in bold (emphasis added) spell out Fauvel's name. For a poet's riff, see Ian Duhig, *The Speed of Dark* (London, 2007).

[76] For these complexities, see Andrew Wathey, 'Gervès du Bus, the Roman de Fauvel, and the Politics of the Later Capetian Court', in Margaret Bent and Andrew Wathey, eds, *Fauvel Studies: Allegory, Chronicle, Music, and Image in Paris, Bibliothèque Nationale de France, MS français 146* (Oxford, 1998), 599–613; Elizabeth A. R. Brown, '*Rex Ioians, Ionnes, Iolis*: Louis X, Philip V, and the *Livres de Fauvel*', in ibid. 53–72; eadem, 'Philip the Fair of France and his Family's Disgrace: The Adultery Scandal of 1314 Revealed, Recounted, Reimagined, and Redated', *Mediaevistik* 32 (2019), 71–103; Jean Favier, *Un conseiller de Philippe le Bel. Enguerran de Marigny*,

unique BNF MS français 146, with its visual, musical and poetical additions, is not only a satire of upstarts such as Marigny, but a critique of all powers and organizations undoing themselves, and France, by fawning over Fauvel, thus ushering in the apocalypse:

> Since every king's a liar
> and the rich just flatter,
> prelates burst with vain coquetry
> and fine folk detest the church …
> So I deduce, with all good reason,
> that round the corner comes the season
> when the world must terminate,
> now all sick things pullulate …[77]

Every institution has turned itself inside out. This swingeing critique of a France ruined by deceit, sycophancy and lies came from the deepest Capetian circles.[78] Book II was ostensibly written by Marigny's former chaplain, Gervès du Bus, and continued by a Chaillou de Pesstain. MS 146's script is a bastard chancery, unusual outside that context, its artist (the 'Fauvel Master') also the illuminator of a mirror for princes (*Le somme le roi*) and two royal registers completed under Louis X.[79] *Fauvel* does not worry at hypocrisy simply as false piety run riot. 'Ypocrisie' appears, indeed, as one of Vainglory's daughters, but such personifications do not exhaust this poem's concern with deceit, falsehood, misrepresentation and duplicity. This is plural and pervasive. It reaches its apogee in Fauvel's extended

---

Mémoires et documents publiés par la Société de l'École des Chartes 16 (Paris, 1963), 193–200.

[77] 'Puisque les rois sont menteeurs | Et riches hommes flateeurs, | Prelas plains de vainne cointise, | Et gentilz gens heent l'Eglise | … Je conclu par droite raison | Que pres sommes de la saison | En quoi doit defenir le monde, | Car toute malice y redonde …': *Fauvel*, 250 ll. 1137–40, 252 ll. 1169–72.

[78] For fauveline France, see *Fauvel*, 156–7, 534–8, 646, 654–6, 660–2, 664, 674, 678–80.

[79] See Armand Strubel, 'Le *Roman de Fauvel.* Une satire du gouvernement royal de Philippe le Bel et de ses ministres', in Bernard Moreau and Julien Théry, eds, *La royauté capétienne et le Midi au temps de Guillaume de Nogaret. Actes du colloque de Montpellier et de Nîmes, 29 et 30 Novembre 2013* (Nîmes, 2015), 157–72. For the 'Fauvel Master', see Richard H. Rouse and Mary A. Rouse, 'Geoffrey de St-Léger & Son, Gérard De Montaigu, and the "Roman de Fauvel"', in idem, *Illiterati et Uxorati: Manuscripts and Their Makers. Commercial Book Producers in Medieval Paris, 1200–1500* (London, 2000), 203–33 (but underplaying *Fauvel*'s bite at 233).

mimicry of a courtly love complaint, when protesting against Fortune's rejection of his marriage plea. She retorts that he is 'a sack full of shit'.[80] Hypocrisy, as elsewhere, can be a very thick ethical concept.[81]

Fauvel, then, focuses on the deformations and disorientations arising from mistaking one thing or person for another, because of sycophancy or insecurity:

> [Fauvel] does everything by inversion [*par antifrasin*],
> That's to say, by sheer perversion.
> Everyone needs to steer well clear,
> since in him and in his visage
> you'll see the perfect image
> of all falsity, flattery,
> as well as total idolatry.
> All take lessons at this school
> To render Fauvel their false idol.[82]

Antiphrasis – saying one thing to mean another – runs through *Fauvel*, including its very form as a beast satire.

The 'politics' of *Fauvel* are hard to extrapolate. Philip IV's action against the Templars is praised, yet any wider elevation of kings over popes is critiqued. At the same time, the pope fawns equally over Fauvel. Excavating all this would require another article.[83] What matters here is that *Fauvel* builds on a tradition of critiquing religious institutions for hypocrisy, but transfers and extends this worry to royal and lay spaces:

[80] *Fauvel*, 282–4 ll. 36–43 ('Ypocrisie'); 423–86, 502–13 (the 'complainte de Fauvel'); 492 l. 3851 ('sac tout plain de merde'). See also, for example, 134–5 ll. 1–9 (on hypocritical prelates); 244 l. 1044 (on 'faus semblant' and 'desloiauté'); 270 ll. 1315, 1324 (on Barat, 'faussetè', guille and 'Ypocrisie'); 306 ll. 1611–34 ('Ypocrisie' as false humility); 276–8 (the description of Fauvel's palace); 400–10 ll. 26–30, 43–59 (the reused lay of Philip the Chancellor); 538 l. 4219 ('Ypocrisie' at Fauvel's marriage); 671 ll. 5878–96 (Jews as hypocrites in betraying Christ).

[81] I.e. joining fact and value: Bernard Williams, *Ethics and the Limits of Philosophy*, new edn (London, 2006; first publ. 1985), 129–30, 140–5.

[82] 'Mainne tout par antifrasin | C'est a dire par le contraire. | Chascun s'en devroit bien retraire | Car en lui et en son viaire | Veons figurer et pourtraire | Touz faus et toute flaterie, Et general ydolatrie; | Touz suivent auy jour d'ui l'escole | De conreer Fauvel l'ydole …': *Fauvel*, 254 ll. 1190–8.

[83] See especially Strubel, '*Roman de Fauvel*', 165–70.

Alas, France! Into great ruin
your beauty now tumbles today
because of that Fauveline dynasty
that pleasures in acting evilly!
They've struck the fleur de lis so hard,
Fauvel and Vain Glory joined,
that it totters, so I'd say.[84]

This implies serious expectations about the pretensions of royal institutions as sites of political and moral claims: claims which are therefore vulnerable to charges of hypocrisy.[85] It seems then uncoincidental that hypocrisy figures prominently (verbally and visually) in *Le somme le roi*, that Dominican royal 'mirror' written for Philip III, a version of which the 'Fauvel Master' illustrated for Louis of Bourbon. Philip IV's own 1295 copy exemplifies 'the connections of [its] illuminator 'Honoré' with the French royal crown'.[86] Here, mendicants, hypocrisy and apocalypse again join hands. Its treaty on vices opens with the beast of the apocalypse crushing a saint while a very different Jew from Boccaccio's Abraham genuflects: 'this beast vanquishes the saints and the hypocrites [i.e. the Jews] adore it' (Figure 2).[87] The period indeed appears to be an 'apocalyptic age of hypocrisy', and not only in ecclesiastical contexts.[88]

[84] 'Hé! Las! France, com ta beauté | Vet au jour d'ui en grant ruine | Par la mesnie fauveline | Qui en tout mal met ses deliz! | Hurtee ont si la fleur de lis | Fauvel et Vainne Gloire ensemble, | Qu'elle chancele, ce me semble.': *Fauvel*, 660–2 ll. 5812–18.

[85] See the comments on Bisson's *Crisis of the Twelfth Century* at p. 96 above.

[86] Laurent d'Orléans, *La somme le roi*, ed. Édith Brayer and Anne-Françoise Leurquin Labie, Société des anciens textes français (Paris, 2008), 124–5, 153–4, 178, 287, 325–6; for manuscripts, see ibid. 23–7, 33–42. Milan, Biblioteca Ambrosiana, MS H 106 supra, was Louis's; London, BL, MS Additional 54180, was Philip's. See Richard H. Rouse and Mary A. Rouse, 'Honoré and the Papeleu Master: The Dissemination of the Illustrated "Somme Le Roi"', in idem, *Illiterati Et Uxorati,* 145–71 (quote at 145).

[87] The image is digitized online at: <https://www.bl.uk/manuscripts/Viewer.aspx?ref=add_ms_54180_fs001r>, accessed 1 March 2023. See also fol. 5^v^ in the same manuscript. BL, MS Additional 54180, fol. 14^v^, is reproduced courtesy of the British Library Board.

[88] Stressing the ecclesiastical, Richard Kenneth Emmerson and Ronald B. Herzman, 'The Apocalyptic Age of Hypocrisy: *Faus Semblant* and *Amant* in the *Roman de la rose*', *Speculum* 62 (1987), 612–34.

Figure 2. The Beast of the Apocalypse, London, BL, MS Additional 54180, fol 14ᵛ, 'Ceste beste senefie le deable'. Reproduced courtesy of the British Library Board.

IV. Owl

Hypocrisy needs words.[89] Fauvel and Angelo obliged with their persistent self-justifications. As for Boniface, his mere death could not prevent his enemies ventriloquizing even a pope beyond the grave. Inquisitions were machines for verbalizing unorthodoxy or un-orthopraxy, manifesting hypocrisy in cases where public personae were at odds with personal conduct.[90] Almost anyone could be made to speak. Consequently, the ability to withhold speech, and not incriminate oneself hypocritically, was an enormous power. To illustrate this, I close with a figure who knew this, and was central to much of this article's hypocrisy talk, a man whom historians have endlessly ceased to get to the bottom of, precisely because 'he left us neither a single line, nor a single word whereby one could say with certitude what was his and his alone': Philip IV of France (1285–1314).[91] Contemporaries were similarly perplexed, including Philip's enemies, such as Bishop Bernard Saisset of Pamiers. According to one witness during the inquisitions (naturally) into Saisset's misdeeds in May 1301:

> The Bishop of Pamiers said to the witness [Bonetus de Binis] himself,
>
> 'The birds of antiquity made a king, so the stories say, and they made as king a certain large bird called "Duc" [an eagle owl], bigger and more beautiful than other birds, and of absolutely no value, indeed it is the vilest bird there is.' And he said, 'Once the magpie complained about the hawk to the Duc, the said king of birds, and he gave absolutely no reply, but just broke wind [*flavit*].'
>
> And the said Bishop said that our King of France was just like that—he was a very beautiful man of the world, but he didn't know how to do anything, except to look at people.[92]

[89] See n. 22 above.
[90] On the excess of inquisitorial testimony, see John H. Arnold, *Inquisition and Power: Catharism and the Confessing Subject in Medieval Languedoc* (Philadelphia, PA, 2001), 12–13, 75–6, 86, 114–15, 119–23, 224–25, 228.
[91] Robert Fawtier, *L'Europe occidentale de 1270 à 1380* (Paris, 1940), 298. On Philip's speech and silence, see Elizabeth A. R. Brown, '*Persona et Gesta*: The Image and Deeds of the Thirteenth-Century Capetians, 3: The Case of Philip the Fair', *Viator* 19 (1988), 219–46, esp. 219–20, 228–9, 230–1, 233, 236.
[92] Dupuy, *Histoire du différend*, 643–4. See further Joseph R. Strayer, *The Reign of Philip the Fair* (Princeton, NJ, 1980), 262–74.

The problem of Philip's silences has long preoccupied historians, who have resorted to ingenious lengths to match his actions with the policies and choices of his regime so as to gauge the king's responsibility for, and involvement in them.[93] Arguably, Philip's silences were both tactical and principled. While Boniface's loquacity implies a sense of impunity, Philip's taciturnity guaranteed his majesty, which 'is always surrounded by silence. It accuses silently and therefore is that which guarantees the true'.[94] Like inquisitors trying to correlate external actions with beliefs, historians have therefore tried to triangulate Philip's actions, his avowed intent and his regime's justifications in order to locate the motives – hypocritical or otherwise – behind Capetian responses to challenges such as Boniface VIII or the Templars.[95] The search for 'real' motives certainly risks an infinite historiographical game of whack-a-mole (as Julien Théry has suggested), but in aiming at it we are striking at a real medieval worry, given *Fauvel*'s plain anxieties about hypocrisy at the highest levels of the Capetian regime in Philip IV's wake.[96] If, then, we can see parallel concerns about institutional hypocrisy in distinct princely, mendicant and papal contexts around 1300, it remains to be asked in conclusion what wider explanations might be offered to explain the pattern.

V. Hypocrisy Worry and its Meanings

'Styles in guile change', argued Judith Shklar, and it is predicable that hypocrisy worry should reflect the changing institutional contexts

[93] Most famously in Robert-Henri Bautier's use of diplomatic to argue for Philip's lack of interest in politics in his 'Diplomatique et histoire politique. Ce que la critique diplomatique nous apprend sur la personnalité de Philippe le Bel', *Revue historique* 259 (1978), 3–27.

[94] Jacques Chiffoleau, 'Dire l'indicible. Remarques sur la catégorie du *nefandum* du XIIe au XVe siècle', *Annales. Histoire, sciences sociales* 45 (1990), 289–324, at 309, citing Kantorowicz but without reference. The allusion is perhaps to Ernst H. Kantorowicz, 'Mysteries of State: An Absolutist Concept and its Late Mediaeval Origins', *HThR* 48 (1955), 65–91, at 69.

[95] For the importance of actions as signalling beliefs and inquisitorial thinking about this, see Peter Biller, '"Deep Is the Heart of Man, and Inscrutable": Signs of Heresy in Medieval Languedoc', in Helen Barr and Ann M. Hutchinson, eds, *Text and Controversy from Wyclif to Bale: Essays in Honour of Anne Hudson* (Turnhout, 2005), 267–80.

[96] See Théry, 'Heresy of State', esp. 143 n. 63, for the arguably futile nature of historians' hypocrisy diagnoses. At the same time, he is concerned to discern Philip's motives: ibid. 118, 127.

which produced evolving practices of deceit.[97] I close with the following arguments, suggesting a wider context for my analysis.

First, a 'reformist' rise in the examination of conscience, intention and casuistry with the pastoral care 'revolution', pivoting around the 1215 Fourth Lateran Council, was a notable feature of the thirteenth century, notwithstanding earlier roots.[98] This generated much energy amongst elites worrying at questions of private and public conduct across a wide range of contexts, from taxation to heresy.[99] Inquisitions into beliefs and motivations raised the prominence of consistent conduct further.[100] An important corollary was that institutions 'pushing conscience', for instance through confession and preaching, consequently themselves came under increased scrutiny. It is hardly accidental that mendicants, especially Franciscans, appear prominently at the centre of thirteenth-century hypocrisy worry.[101]

Second, by 1300, reform projects were not the monopoly of ecclesiastical regimes alone. Princely regimes were making such salvific claims for themselves, and likewise articulated 'rational' inquisitorial techniques for securing them.[102] Channelling Ernst Kantorowicz,

[97] Shklar, *Ordinary Vices*, 71.

[98] For chronology, see Alexander Murray, *Conscience and Authority in the Medieval Church* (Oxford, 2015), 5–16; for reform, see, for example, canons 7, 12, 14, 33 of Lateran IV, and more widely Julia Barrow, 'Ideas and Applications of Reform', in Thomas F. X. Noble and Julia M. H. Smith, eds, *The Cambridge History of Christianity: Early Medieval Christianities, c.600-c.1100* (Cambridge, 2008), 345–62.

[99] As discussed above at pp. 96–7, 113. See, for example, Bisson, *Crisis*, 445–56, 489–99; John W. Baldwin, *Masters, Princes, and Merchants: The Social Views of Peter the Chanter and His Circle*, 2 vols (Princeton, NJ, 1970); Emily Corran, *Lying and Perjury in Medieval Practical Thought: A Study in the History of Casuistry* (Oxford, 2018); Biller, 'Deep Is the Heart'; John Sabapathy, 'Robert of Courson's Systematic Thinking About Early Thirteenth-Century Institutions', in Fitzpatrick and Sabapathy, eds, *Individuals and Institutions*, 199–216.

[100] John Sabapathy, 'Some Difficulties in Forming Persecuting Societies before Lateran IV Canon 8: Robert of Courson Thinks about Communities and Inquisition', in Gert Melville and Johannes Helmrath, eds, *The Fourth Lateran Council: Institutional Reform and Spiritual Renewal* (Affalterbach, 2017), 175–200.

[101] See, for instance, William of Saint-Amour, *De periculis novissimorum temporum*, ed. Guy Geltner (Paris, 2008); *The Opuscula of William of Saint-Amour: The Minor Works of 1255–1256*, ed. Andrew G. Traver, Beiträge zur Geschichte der Philosophie und Theologie des Mittelalters Neue Folge 63 (Münster, 2003), 155–78; Rutebeuf, *Œuvres completes*, ed. Michel Zink (Paris, 2001), 'D'hypocrisie', 136–42; 'La complainte de Maître Guillaume de Saint-Amour', 154–64 ; 'Le dit des règles', 168–78; 'Le dit de mensonge', 218–30; 'La leçon d'Hypocrisie et d'Humilité', 296–315.

[102] For princely imitation of ecclesiastical 'reform', see Marie Dejoux, 'À la recherche de la *reformatio regni* dans les royaumes de France et d'Angleterre au XIIIe siècle', in eadem,

Théry has argued that, in France specifically, this produced a Capetian 'pontificalization' of the crown, aping papal claims and behaviours.[103] Even analysts more sympathetic to Philip IV have argued that he was 'a dogmatic fanatic about French kings' supreme authority'.[104] By the time of the confrontation between Boniface and Philip, others have suggested, 'fragments of a theory of the church' were sparking against 'fragments of a theory of the state'.[105] Distinct institutional powers were locked into a transcendent arms race.

Third, these transcendent claims seem directly connected to apocalyptic charges of hypocrisy. Hypocrisy worry was frequently married to eschatology worry as a function of the claims that institutions were making. Worrying about institutional hypocrisy was a consequence of believing in the integrity of given institutions, precisely because of their claims to transcendent significance.[106] Thus, Bernard McGinn argued that it was essential to grasp that belief in both positive angel popes or negative papal Antichrists was itself 'an act of faith in the ultimate *religious* value of the papacy'.[107] Transcendent claims flowed into an apocalyptic throbbing in both papal and Franciscan cases.[108] McGinn's argument that by about 1300 belief in institutions'

ed., *Reformatio? Les mots pour dire la réforme à la fin du Moyen Âge* (Paris, 2023), 101–23, and on English Montfortian pretensions and controversies, see David Carpenter, *Henry III: Reform, Rebellion, Civil War, Settlement, 1259–1372* (New Haven, CT, 2023), 357–8, 371, 398–415, and John Sabapathy, 'Gui Foucois, la "réforme", le Midi et l'Angleterre', *Gui Foucois, Pape Clément IV, et le Midi. Cahiers de Fanjeaux* 57 (2023), 299–333, esp. 318–21. For inquisitorial techniques across different sites, see John Sabapathy, 'Making Public Knowledge—Making Knowledge Public: The Territorial, Reparative, Heretical, and Canonization Inquiries of Gui Foucois (ca. 1200–1268)', *Journal for the History of Knowledge* 1 (2020), 1–21.

[103] Théry, 'Heresy of State', 130–1; idem, 'The Pioneer of Royal Theocracy: Guillaume de Nogaret and the Conflicts between Philip the Fair and the Papacy', in William Chester Jordan and Jenna Rebecca Phillips, eds, *The Capetian Century, 1214–1314* (Turnhout, 2017), 219–59, and earlier Kantorowicz, 'Mysteries of State', at (for instance) 67.

[104] Fawtier, *Europe occidentale*, 301.

[105] Gabriel Le Bras, 'Boniface VIII. Symphoniste et modérateur', in Charles-Edmond Perrin, ed., *Mélanges d'histoire du Moyen Âge dédiés à la memoire de Louis Halphen* (Paris, 1951), 383–94, at 394.

[106] How far such comments could be made of contemporary rulership might perhaps challenge Shklar's contention that 'we' inhabit 'an ex-Christian mental universe': *Ordinary Vices*, 240.

[107] Bernard McGinn, 'Angel Pope and Papal Antichrist', *ChH* 47 (1978), 155–73, at 173. Emphasis mine.

[108] See, for instance, ibid. and Burr, *Spiritual Franciscans*, *s.v.* 'apocalyptic expectations'.

immanent claims was producing apocalyptic projections is worth pausing at. Since lay institutions had also claimed reform agendas well before 1300, McGinn's argument that increasing frustration with reform after Lateran IV fed into the papacy's heightened eschatological profile *c.*1300 might also help to explain apocalypticism around princely regimes.[109] The parallel growth of more generalized apocalyptic worry alongside administrative government may not be coincidental.[110]

As we have seen, *Fauvel* also fretted about apocalypse by fretting about hypocrisy in a princely context which was busy pumping administrative iron. So it was (fourth), entirely in keeping with the pattern of increased ecclesiastical worry about clerical hypocrisy that lay regimes behaving like them should worry about their own institutional good faith. This is what Elizabeth Brown's studies of uneasy Capetian consciences imply.[111] It is what I have suggested *Fauvel* shows. The appearance of *Fauvel* immediately following the Capetian court's monomaniacal pursuit of Boniface and the Templars (moralistic prosecutions of the cloudiest motivations!) is notable, to say the least.

So finally (and fifth), worry about institutional hypocrisy signalled that the credibility of institutions' claims was under wider pressure. Responsibility itself was increasingly on trial.[112] This was so, whether criticism ultimately focused on individual rather than institutional culpability (as with attacks on Boniface), was extended to group criticism (as with Angelo on his own Order), or oscillated in focus (as

[109] McGinn, 'Angel Pope', 157.

[110] Cf. James Given, 'Chasing Phantoms: Philip IV and the Fantastic', in Michael Frassetto, ed., *Heresy and the Persecuting Society in the Middle Ages: Essays on the Work of R. I. Moore*, Studies in the History of Christian Traditions 129 (Leiden, 2005), 271–89, contrasting, but not connecting, the two at 289.

[111] Elizabeth A. R. Brown, 'The Faith of Guillaume de Nogaret, his Excommunication, and the Fall of the Knights Templar', in Laura Andreani and Agostino Paravicini Bagliani, eds, *Cristo e il potere. Teologia, antropologia e politica* (Florence, 2017), 157–82; eadem, '*Veritas* à la cour de Philippe le Bel de France. Pierre Dubois, Guillaume de Nogaret et Marguerite Porete', in Jean-Philippe Genêt, ed., *La vérité. Vérité et crédibilité: Construire la verité dans le système de communication de L'Occident (XIIIe–XVIIe siècle)* (Paris, 2015), 425–45; eadem, 'Philip the Fair and his Ministers: Guillaume de Nogaret and Enguerran de Marigny', in Jordan and Phillips, eds, *Capetian Century*, 185–218; eadem, 'Réflexions sur Philippe Le Bel', *Annuaire-Bulletin de la Société de l'histoire de France* 555 (2014), 7–24; eadem, 'Moral Imperatives and Conundrums of Conscience: Reflections on Philip the Fair of France', *Speculum* 87 (2012), 1–36.

[112] For the argument in an English context, see Sabapathy, 'Gui Foucois', 321–3.

with critiques of the Capetian court).[113] It is interesting, perhaps surprising, that the least 'institutional' hypocrisy charges of those analyzed here were those clustering around Boniface VIII himself. We could circle back to Boccaccio here. His Jehannot preferred an institutional reading of curial corruption. One reading of the lesson of *Decameron* I.2 would argue that its apparent demonstration of the church's sacrality, despite its hypocrisy, instead underlines the ridiculousness of Abraham 'deducing' this. By implying that Abraham's logic is risible, Boccaccio also queries whether the church's immanent claims really are institutionally insulated from contamination by its own leaders' culpable conduct. Does the fish rot from the head down, or is the prince misled by bad advisers? Different critics placed the blame for institutional failings at different doors, sometimes personal, sometimes collective. Certainly, the medieval tendency to personify institutions poses interesting challenges for analysts of these institutions. Contemporary critics were well aware that different levels of critique were possible. Either way, hypocrisy did matter.

Hypocrisy worry both relieved and inflamed the itch of institutional credibility in this period. Strictly speaking, Boniface seems guiltless of hypocrisy, given the frankness of his opinions. Yet the allegations levelled at him were deliberately intended to demonstrate the unreconcilable chasm between what he was and what he was supposed to be, to the point that his status at the apex of his institution was indefensible. The plain thrust of those charges was that Boniface was an arch-hypocrite. Even if his accusers, with their forgeries, witness manipulation and embroideries, were the bigger hypocrites, it is hard to see how belief in the institutional church could not be damaged by the scandal of Boniface. At the opposite end of the spectrum, Angelo Clareno was a principled hypocrite who rejected the institutional shell which should house his Franciscan identity in order to better express it inside other religious orders, which Francis himself had rejected. Again, institutionally, it was impossible that this position would not corrode wider confidence in what the Franciscan Order meant, or even where it was. As for Fauvel, he seems the itch run riot. Anxiety about hypocrisy was a thick, red thread tangling up numerous institutions in early fourteenth-century Europe. It is instructive for historians to unravel it.

113 On the Capetian side, see, for instance, Tilmann Schmidt, 'La condamnation de Pierre Flote par le pape Boniface VIII', *Mélanges de l'école française de Rome. Moyen Âge* 118 (2006), 109–21, and the works by Brown given in n. 112 above.

False Religion and Hypocrisy in Signorelli's *Antichrist*

Konstantinos Gravanis*
National and Kapodistrian University of Athens

This article discusses the iconography of Luca Signorelli's Sermon and Deeds of the Antichrist *(c.1502–3) in the Cappella Nuova at the cathedral of Orvieto. A combined investigation of the Antichrist's subject matter, Signorelli's literary and visual sources, as well as his discarded drawings for the entire fresco decoration of the Cappella Nuova, brings fresh insights to the thematic intentions of the artist and his advisers. Signorelli's entire view of eschatology marked a renewed interest of Italian artists in the apocalyptic sublime. It also signified a revival of the medieval tradition of the Antichrist as the arch-hypocrite, and his reign as an apocalyptic age of hypocrisy. At the same time, the artist's treatment of the subject matter indicates an ambiguous stance toward religious hypocrisy characterized by a suppression of the anti-clerical and millenarian aspects of the Antichrist myth.*

The End of the World by Luca Signorelli

The closing decades of the fifteenth century were a period of general anxiety in Italy, marked by a revival of fatalistic worldviews and prophetic systems of belief.[1] The approaching of the chiliastic year 1500 also coincided with a deep and multi-faceted crisis that emerged following the French invasion of the Italian peninsula in 1494. In this turbulent period of unceasing conflict and recurrent epidemics, visual

* I would like to thank the anonymous reviewers whose thoughtful comments and suggestions improved the quality of this article. Many thanks also go to Tom Henry, Laurence Kanter and Claire van Cleave for their valuable insights. The publication of the article in OA mode was financially supported by HEAL-Link. E-mail: kgravani@arch.uoa.gr.

[1] For the socio-religious climate in Italy during the 1480s and 1490s, see André Chastel, 'L'Antéchrist à la Renaissance', in Enrico Castelli, ed., *L'Umanesimo e il demoniaco nell' arte. Atti del II Congresso Internazionale di Studi Umanistici Roma 1952* (Rome, 1953), 177–86; Marjorie Reeves, *The Influence of Prophecy in the Later Middle Ages: A Study in Joachimism* (New York, 1969), 430–40.

Studies in Church History 60 (2024), 121–147
doi: 10.1017/stc.2024.6

culture and the decorative arts served as expressive vehicles of a preoccupation with apocalyptic visions of the end of the world, millennial anticipations of a new age and a resurgence of medieval prophecies for the coming of Antichrist.[2]

The most significant Italian artwork dealing with these concerns was Luca Signorelli's fresco cycle (1499–1504) of the last judgement in the Cappella Nuova (today often known as the San Brizio Chapel) in Orvieto Cathedral, a milestone of visual eschatology and a crowning achievement of Renaissance art. Commissioned by the Opera del Duomo of Orvieto in April 1499, the Cappella Nuova frescoes depict the court of heaven in the vault, and episodes from the end of the world and the last judgement on the walls. Some of the ceiling compartments had already been painted in 1447 by the Dominican friar Fra Angelico (*c.*1395–1455), with images of biblical prophets and Christ sitting in judgement. The majority of the extant frescoes were executed by the Umbrian painter Luca Signorelli (*c.*1450–1523), who found the opportunity to demonstrate his expressive power and creative genius, predominantly in his masterful depictions of the anatomy of the human body.[3] No artist before him had taken on the challenge of inventing such an immense variety of nude figures, an accomplishment of unprecedented scale and great influence on later artists, most notably the Old Testament ceiling frescoes (1508–12) and the *Last Judgement* (1535–41) by Michelangelo (1475–1564) in the Sistine Chapel.[4]

Signorelli's ceiling paintings in the Cappella Nuova represent angels, apostles, church fathers, Patriarchs, virgins and martyrs, a

[2] The apocalyptic culture of the day found expression in paintings such as Sandro Botticelli (1445–1510), *Mystic Nativity* (*c.*1500–1); on which, see Rab Hatfield, 'Botticelli's "Mystic Nativity", Savonarola and the Millenium', *Journal of the Warburg and Courtauld Institutes* 58 (1995), 88–114. One of the most famous eschatological artworks created north of the Alps was Albrecht Dürer (1471–1528), *Apocalypse* (1498), a widely diffused series of fifteen woodcuts based on the Book of Revelation.

[3] For Signorelli's mastery of the nude, see Giorgio Vasari, *Le Vite de' più eccellenti pittori scultori e architettori nelle redazioni del 1550 e 1568*, ed. Paola Barocchi and Rosanna Bettarini, 6 vols (Florence, 1966–87), 3: 633 and 640. For his creative genius and inventiveness, exalted by fellow artists and patrons, see Tom Henry, 'Luca de ingegno et spirito pelegrino', in Davide Gasparotto and Serena Magnani, eds, *Matteo di Giovanni e la pala d'altare nel senese e nell'aretino 1450–1500. Atti del Convegno Internazionale di Studi, Sansepolcro, 9–10 Ottobre 1998* (Sansepolcro, 2002), 175–83.

[4] On the influence of this work on Michelangelo's *Last Judgement*, see Vasari, *Le Vite*, 3: 637.

scheme that had already been devised by Fra Angelico half a century earlier.[5] The major wall frescoes depict the *Sermon and Deeds of the Antichrist*, the *Signs of the End of the World*, the *Resurrection of the Dead*, the *Crowning of the Elect*, the *Elect Being Called to Paradise*, the *Damned Being Plunged into Hell*, and the *Torments of the Damned*; monumental subjects that complemented the effect of liturgical ceremonies by arousing feelings of awe and terror in the congregation.[6] This profoundly symbolic cycle of eschatology was not invented by Signorelli alone. According to the minutes of the Opera's board meeting of 25 November 1499, a proposal by Gian Ludovico Benincasa that the decoration in the chapel should be 'advised orally by the venerable masters in theology of this city … provided that it may not depart from the theme of the Last Judgement' found unanimous approval.[7] The identity of Signorelli's advisers remains a subject of speculation, but they most likely belonged to the predominant religious order in Orvieto, the Dominicans.[8]

[5] Fra Angelico had left drawings of the last judgement for the remaining compartments of the south vault. It is generally agreed that the completion of the vault by Signorelli followed his design: see Edwin Hall and Horst Uhr, 'Patrons and Painter in Quest of an Iconographic Program: The Case of the Signorelli Frescoes in Orvieto', *Zeitschrift für Kunstgeschichte* 55 (1992), 35–56, at 39; Jonathan B. Riess, *The Renaissance Antichrist: Luca Signorelli's Orvieto Frescoes* (Princeton, NJ, 1995), 16–7. For the importance of Fra Angelico's role in the formation of the chapel's iconographic programme, see Creighton Gilbert, *How Fra Angelico and Signorelli Saw the End of the World* (University Park, PA, 2003), 23–59.

[6] For the liturgical function and meaning of Signorelli's frescoes in the ritualistic space of the Cappella Nuova, see Sara Nair James, *Signorelli and Fra Angelico at Orvieto: Liturgy, Poetry and a Vision of the End-time* (Burlington, VT, 2003).

[7] The document was first published by Luigi Fumi, *Il Duomo di Orvieto e i suoi restauri* (Rome, 1891), 408 (doc. 158). This report seems to refer to the decoration of the second half of the chapel's ceiling and probably also its walls. For a transcription of this document, see the *Italian Renaissance Document Site*, online at: <https://irds-project.org/doc/516/441/>, accessed 15 October 2023. For the translation of the original text used here, see Hall and Uhr, 'The Signorelli Frescoes in Orvieto', 40 n. 19.

[8] On possible candidates for the role of Signorelli's iconographic adviser, see Tom Henry, *The Life and Art of Luca Signorelli* (New Haven, CT, 2012), 197–8. For a convincing case that the esteemed theologians of Orvieto ('venerabiles magistros sacre pagine huius Civitatis') who reportedly advised Signorelli were largely Dominicans, see James, *Signorelli and Fra Angelico*, 48–51, 137–46; Alison Wright, 'Authority and Vision: The Painter's Position in the Cappella Nova at Orvieto', *Renaissance Studies* 21 (2007), 20–43, at 31–2. For the predominance of the Dominican Order in Orvieto and the representation of Dominican friars in Signorelli's *Antichrist*, including the painter Fra Angelico, see Riess, *The Renaissance Antichrist*, 14–6, 18, 56–7.

A different individual must have collaborated with Signorelli on the iconography of the chapel's lower walls. These areas were decorated with naturalistic busts of six celebrated poets, including Dante and Virgil, framed by grotesque ornamental motifs.[9] Their portraits are surrounded by monochrome roundels with underworld episodes from the works of these authors, such as *Purgatorio* and the *Aeneid*, representing mythological voyages made to Hades by Hercules, Orpheus, Aeneas and Dante. Situated at eye level and intended for close examination, these classical episodes demonstrate a wide imaginative scope and literary power, which in turn indicates the involvement of a learned iconographic adviser.[10]

The Innovation of the *Antichrist*

The narrative sequence of the Orvieto cycle begins on the north side of the chapel's eastern wall with the *Sermon and Deeds of the Antichrist* (Figure 1), one of the most provocative topics in the history of the Christian faith. The protagonist is the arch-deceiver and false prophet of the medieval tradition, the Antichrist,[11] a long-haired man who superficially resembles Christ both in his looks and actions. The central story in the right foreground presents the greatest of hypocrites seducing his audience through preaching. Immediately behind him

[9] The identity of the other authors remains a subject of speculation. For an iconographic examination of the author portraits and the illustrations of the surrounding *tondi*, see Stanley Meltzoff, *Botticelli, Signorelli and Savonarola: 'Theologia Poetica' and Painting from Boccaccio to Poliziano* (Florence, 1987), 316–41; Rose Marie San Juan, 'The Illustrious Poets in Signorelli's Frescoes for the Cappella Nuova of Orvieto Cathedral', *Journal of the Warburg and Courtauld Institutes* 52 (1989), 71–84; Dugald McLellan, 'Luca Signorelli's Last Judgement Fresco Cycle at Orvieto: An Interpretation of the Fears and Hopes of the Commune and People of Orvieto at a Time of Reckoning' (PhD thesis, University of Melbourne, 1992), 313–57; Gilbert, *Fra Angelico and Signorelli*, 91–116.

[10] On the question of Signorelli's adviser for the socle decorations with classical episodes and portraits of their authors, see Dugald McLellan, *Antonio Mancinelli ad Orvieto. Maestro comunale, pubblico intellettuale e interprete delle Muse* (Rome, 2014), 33, 61–3.

[11] As André Chastel noted, the myth of the Antichrist, rather formless in Christian Scripture, became clearer in the Middle Ages: see Chastel, 'L'Apocalypse en 1500. La fresque de l'Antéchrist à la chapelle Saint-Brice d'Orvieto', *Bibliothèque d'Humanisme et Renaissance* 14 (Mélanges Augustin Renaudet) (1952), 124–40, at 125. For the New Testament's references to false Christs, false prophets and false apostles, see Mark 13: 22; Matt. 7: 15–20; 24: 23–4; 2 Cor. 11: 13–15; 1 John 4: 1; Rev. 19: 20; 20: 10. For specific references to an 'Antichrist', see 1 John 2: 18–22; 4: 3; and 2 John 1: 7.

Figure 1. Luca Signorelli, *Sermon and Deeds of the Antichrist*, *c.*1502–4, fresco, San Brizio Chapel, Orvieto Cathedral, Orvieto. Image in the Public Domain on Wikimedia Commons, online at: <https://commons.wikimedia.org/wiki/File:Luca_Signorelli_-_Sermon_and_Deeds_of_the_Antichrist_-_WGA21202.jpg>, accessed 21 December 2022.

stands the devil himself, a symbolically left-handed demon,[12] who is literally manipulating the actions of the Antichrist and whispers evil instructions to his ear. The people attending the sermon, one of which is Dante Alighieri, are of different ages, time periods and social classes.[13] Some of these figures are portraits of famous men of

[12] The Latin word *sinister* originally meant 'left', as it still does, but it soon came to be associated with bad omens and the power of evil, a superstition deriving from ancient Greek methods of north-facing divination, that identified 'east' with 'right' and 'west' with 'left'. It is noteworthy that Signorelli painted the *Elect* on the right-hand side of Christ, that is on the east wall, and the *Damned* on the left-hand side of Christ, on the west wall. The arrangement was apparently anticipated by Fra Angelico's ceiling representation of Christ the Judge.

[13] With the sole exception of Dante's likeness, the identification of several of these figures with historical personalities such as Alexander the Great, Christoper Columbus and Cesare Borgia has proved problematic: see Tom Henry, 'Review of "The Renaissance

Signorelli's time,[14] an indication of a narrative that is both urgently contemporary and timeless, but also a stern reminder that the Antichrist's preaching could deceive even the most excellent individuals.

In the composition's background, Signorelli depicted a variety of smaller groups representing the actions of the Antichrist and their disastrous consequences: he conducts false miracles in imitation of Christ, such as the pseudo-healing of a sick man (or perhaps the pseudo-resurrection of a dead man) who is seen rising from his bed; with the pretense of justice, he orders the beheading of two virtuous old men, namely the two witnesses of the last days who would be murdered by the beast (Revelation 11: 3–14);[15] his distribution of seductive bribes and gifts spreads corruption and greed, a condition personified by the stereotypical figure of a Jewish moneylender surrounded by avaricious men and women;[16] his hypocritical preaching captivates learned audiences and causes confusion among theologians and churchmen; his wrathful intentions cause outbreaks of violence, especially against those who refuse to worship him; finally, he has ordered the construction of a centrally planned church – conceived by Signorelli in the High Renaissance style – dedicated to his false religion and guarded by violent soldiers, a spectacular, yet structurally disturbing, temple in Jerusalem that creates a purposeful effect of asymmetry.[17] The dramatic ending of the story takes place in the

Antichrist: Luca Signorelli's Orvieto Frescoes" by Jonathan B. Riess', *The Burlington Magazine* 137 (1995), 755–6.

[14] Vasari, *Le Vite*, 3: 637.

[15] Early Christian writers and medieval exegetes identified the two witnesses with the prophets Enoch and Elias. Medieval tradition held that these two prophets would be executed by order of the Antichrist. For the interpretation of Signorelli's scene as the beheading of Enoch and Elias, first made in the eighteenth century, see Hall and Uhr, 'The Signorelli Frescoes in Orvieto', 47 and 47 n. 55.

[16] The prominent foreground figure of a Jewish moneylender or merchant reflects the anti-Judaic rhetoric in fifteenth-century Orvieto, as well as the traditional conception of the Antichrist's Jewish origin or his cooperation with Jews: see Riess, *The Renaissance Antichrist*, 52, 115–21; Ingrid D. Rowland, 'When the Antichrist came to Orvieto', *The New York Review*, 7 May 2010; Debra Higgs Strickland, 'Antichrist and the Jews in Medieval Art and Protestant Propaganda', *Studies in Iconography* 32 (2011), 1–50.

[17] Most theologians of the late fifteenth century, including Girolamo Savonarola, believed that the Antichrist would appear in Jerusalem and persecute the faithful: see Hatfield, 'Savonarola and the Millenium', 103. Emmerson and Herzman saw Signorelli's architectural reference as symbolic of the old expectation that the Antichrist

upper lefthand section of the composition: at the peak of his pride, the Antichrist has attempted a pseudo-Ascension into heaven from the Mount of Olives. There, he is confronted by the Archangel Michael who smites him to the ground along with his crushed followers.

Context, Sources and Meaning

The *Antichrist* has generally been praised as the most singular innovation in the Cappella Nuova, and sometimes also as the central story of the entire cycle.[18] Signorelli's sense of pride in this masterpiece is testified by his inclusion of a full-body self-portrait in the far lefthand corner of the picture. More than an authorship signature, the imposing figure of the dignified, black-clothed painter stands next to the dying and dead bodies of the victims of violence and murdered martyrs. His gaze is fixed directly on the viewer, acting as both an Albertian narrator and a contemporary prophet who visualized the end times with tremendous vividness.[19] The man who stands beside him, dressed as a Dominican monk, is most probably Fra Angelico, the friar who had painted the chapel's vault half a century earlier. By looking and pointing outside the pictorial frame toward the chapel's altar, Fra Angelico leads the spectator's gaze toward the centre of devotion. The faithful presence and testimony of the two artists

---

would take possession of the Temple of Jerusalem, proclaiming himself to be God: see Richard Kenneth Emmerson and Ronald B. Herzman, 'Antichrist, Simon Magus, and Dante's "Inferno" XIX', *Traditio* 36 (1980), 373–98, at 374. Most authors believe that Signorelli's building is the Temple of Solomon, but some have plausibly noted that this is in fact a temple constructed by the Antichrist: see Riess, *The Renaissance Antichrist*, 167 n. 38.

[18] See Chastel, 'L'Apocalypse en 1500', 124–40; Riess, *The Renaissance Antichrist*, 23–65. However, compare also Kanter who pointed to stylistic and physical evidence suggesting that Signorelli's *Antichrist* was not an integral part of the chapel's decoration, but rather an afterthought or a result of programme modification around 1502–3: Laurence Kanter, 'Review of "The Renaissance Antichrist: Luca Signorelli's Orvieto Frescoes" by Jonathan B. Riess', *Renaissance Quarterly* 50 (1997), 1260–1, at 1260.

[19] According to the fifteenth-century art theorist Leon Battista Alberti, painters should consider adding to their compositions a mediating figure which introduces the painting's story and explains its meaning to the audience: see Leon Battista Alberti, *On Painting*, transl. Cecil Grayson (London, 1991), book 2, 42. Countless pictorial narratives of the Italian Renaissance were based upon this crucial agent, whose telling expression, gaze or gesture was meant to engage the spectator and lead the eye toward the composition's important parts.

thus creates a meaningful contrast with the false doctrines of the Antichrist.[20]

Signorelli's subject derived largely from the medieval iconography of the Antichrist and the traditional understanding of his life as an outward imitation of Christ's life.[21] It is therefore all the more surprising that the Orvieto Antichrist was an entirely novel subject with no iconographic precedents or successors in the visual art of Italy.[22] Its general meaning can be contextualized within a climate of socio-economic hardship, public health crisis and revived eschatology in late fifteenth-century Orvieto. In addition to its civic history of heresy and strife,[23] the fortress town had been under siege by French troops, who bombarded it in 1497. Its population had also been severely affected by the first known epidemic of syphilis,[24] which appeared in Naples in 1495 and spread almost immediately throughout Europe. The completion of a 1,500-year period after the Saviour's birth was further marked by terrifying signs, such as a sublime celestial event witnessed in Gubbio on 29 September 1499 and interpreted by the Orvietan notary and chronicler Tommaso di Silvestro as a monstrous omen and a cause for despair.[25]

[20] The double portrait of Signorelli and Fra Angelico has been seen as a symbolic parallelism to the two witnesses of the Apocalypse (Rev. 11: 3–14), but also as enacting the roles of Dante and Virgil in the *Divina Commedia*: see Dugald McLellan, *Signorelli's Orvieto Frescoes: A Guide to the Cappella Nuova* (Orvieto, 1998), 25; James, *Signorelli and Fra Angelico*, 69; Wright, 'Authority and Vision', 34–5.

[21] Richard Kenneth Emmerson, *Antichrist in the Middle Ages: A Study of Medieval Apocalypticism, Art, and Literature* (Seattle, WA, 1981), 125, 225.

[22] Chastel, 'L'Apocalypse en 1500', 126. For European imagery of the Antichrist in illustrated manuscripts and block-books of medieval and Renaissance apocalypticism, see John Barnes, 'Transformations of the Renaissance Iconography of Antichrist', 2 vols (PhD thesis, Birmingham City University, 2008), 2: plates 1–30.

[23] For a connection between the town's legacy of heresy and the iconographic programme of the Cappella Nuova, see Dugald McLellan, 'Tra culto e ruolo civico. Una lettura degli affreschi di Luca Signorelli nel Duomo di Orvieto', *Bollettino dell'Istituto Storico Artistico Orvietano* 50–7 (1994–2001), 347–73.

[24] McLellan notes that, in the summer of 1496 alone, 600 people died in Orvieto because of the plague: see Dugald McLellan, 'The Cappella Nuova at Orvieto before Signorelli: Perugino and the Opera del Duomo. A Question of Commitment', *Studi di Storia dell' Arte* 7 (1996), 307–32, at 312 n. 79. The Orvietan notary Tommaso di Silvestro described the severe symptoms of the 'French disease', which he contracted in 1496 and then again in 1498: see Tommaso di Silvestro, 'Diario, 1482–1514', in Luigi Fumi, ed., *Ephemerides Urbevetanae; Rerum Italicarum Scriptores* 15/5, 2 vols (Castello, 1902–20), 2: 1–531, at 88.

[25] Di Silvestro, 'Diario', 126. For a translation and discussion of the diarist's entry (7 November 1499), see Riess, *The Renaissance Antichrist*, 9–15.

A subject that has not yet been fully resolved concerns the literary and visual sources used by Signorelli. A common proposal refers to the *Golden Legend* (*c.*1265), a highly influential late medieval book of hagiographies compiled by the Dominican archbishop, Jacobus de Voragine, which described the disastrous acts of the Antichrist, ending with his annihilation by the Archangel Michael in a manner similar to Signorelli's visual narrative.[26] Other scholars have drawn attention to the *Liber chronicarum*,[27] a famous illustrated encyclopedic text by the German humanist Hartmann Schedel with accounts of world history, including the reign of the Antichrist and the end of the world. Published in Nuremberg in Latin and German editions in 1493, the chronicle enjoyed wide distribution across Europe, and it is highly likely that Signorelli or some local theologian in Orvieto was aware of its content. The similarities between the Orvieto fresco and the chronicle are indeed compelling: the latter's story of the Antichrist (fol. 262^{v}), illustrated by Michael Wohlgemut (Figure 2), represents the exalted protagonist in the act of preaching, while the bestial devil behind him is whispering instructions to his ear, a unique pictorial motif repeated by Signorelli a few years later. Furthermore, the chronicle's Antichrist is defeated by the Archangel Michael in an aerial battle which produces a rain of fire and brimstone, another invention that was strikingly similar to the Orvieto scene.

An alternative interpretation was offered by André Chastel, who saw Signorelli's *Antichrist* as a veiled condemnation of the short-lived puritanical regime of Florence (1494–8) under the 'demonic' influence of the Dominican friar Girolamo Savonarola (1452–98).[28] The key text for comprehending Signorelli's fresco, Chastel argued, is a letter by the humanist Marsilio Ficino addressed to the Roman Curia, with an introduction entitled: 'Apology of Marsilio Ficino on Behalf of the Many Florentines Deceived by the Antichrist, Girolamo of Ferrara,

[26] See Giusi Testa, Raffaele Davanzo and Luciano Marchetti, *La Cappella Nova o di San Brizio* (Viterbo, 1997), 22–3; McLellan, *Signorelli's Orvieto Frescoes*, 33; Gilbert, *Fra Angelio and Signorelli*, 130–2.

[27] See Pietro Scarpellini, *Luca Signorelli* (Florence, 1964), 41, 133; Emmerson and Herzman, 'Antichrist, Simon Magus, and Dante's "Inferno" XIX', 378; Antonio Paolucci, *Luca Signorelli* (Florence, 1990), 44; and especially Hall and Uhr, 'The Signorelli Frescoes in Orvieto', 46–51.

[28] Chastel, 'L'Apocalypse en 1500', 124–40. For a cautious support of Chastel's intriguing hypothesis, see Emmerson and Herzman, 'Antichrist, Simon Magus, and Dante's "Inferno" XIX', 376. For a full endorsement of it, see Meltzoff, *Botticelli, Signorelli and Savonarola*, 287–356.

Figure 2. Michael Wohlgemut, 'Sermon of the Antichrist', in Hartmann Schedel, *Liber chronicarum* (Nuremberg, 1493), fol. 262v, woodcut, Cambridge University Library, Inc.0.A.7.2[888]. Reproduced by permission of the Syndics of Cambridge University Library.

the Greatest of Hypocrites, to the College of the Cardinals'.[29] The date of this letter, the authenticity of which is now widely accepted, falls between Savonarola's execution in May 1498 and Ficino's death in early October 1499. Its apologetic content identified the recently-executed Dominican with the long-anticipated Antichrist as a pseudo-prophet whose diabolic enterprise had deceived even the most virtuous Florentines with the power of his hypocrisy.[30]

The hypothesis that Signorelli was aware of Ficino's letter is apparently purely speculative. One might still argue that the artist was personally motivated to denounce the fraudulent attitude of Savonarola. Both men had enjoyed the patronal support of the Medici family in Florence during the late 1480s. However, whereas Signorelli had reportedly risked his own life for Medici causes,[31] Savonarola would eventually turn against them. It could be further assumed that the posthumous demonization of Savonarola might have been particularly important to the religious authorities of Orvieto, a town with close ties to the papacy. Savonarola's accusations of clerical corruption and papal hypocrisy had led to his excommunication by Pope Alexander VI (r. 1492–1503) in May 1497. It is therefore not entirely implausible that Signorelli's patrons, ever faithful to Rome, decided to denounce the friar.[32] Nonetheless, the problematic aspects

[29] 'Apologia Marsilij Ficini pro multis florentinis ab antichristo Hieronimo Ferrariense, hypocritar[um] summo deceptis: ad collegiu[m] Cardinalium': Dallas, Bridwell Library, MS 34; published by Luigi Passerini, 'Apologia de Marsilio Ficino contro Savonarola,' *Giornale storico degli archivi toscani che si pubblica dalla soprintendenza generale agli archivi toscani* 3 (1859), 113–5; and Paul Oscar Kristeller, *Supplementum Ficinianum*, 2 vols (Florence, 1937), 1: cxli; 2: 76–9. For the English translation of the letter's introduction used here, see Jeremy Bentham, ed., *Selected Writings of Girolamo Savonarola* (New Haven, CT, 2006), 355–9.

[30] Chastel suggests, interestingly, that Signorelli's otherwise inexplicable placing of Dante among the listeners of the Antichrist may have alluded to the city of Florence and its *literati* who had been seduced by Savonarola's sermons: see Chastel, 'L'Apocalypse en 1500', 129.

[31] For a discussion of Signorelli's claim, in an exchange with Michelangelo in 1513, that he 'almost had his head cut off for love of the house of Medici', see Henry, *Luca Signorelli*, 80 n. 83. A document dated 25 September 1512 reports that Signorelli was sent as an ambassador from Cortona to Florence to congratulate the Medici on their return: see the *Italian Renaissance Document Site*, online at: <https://irds-project.org/doc/691/765/>, accessed 3 October 2023. For two of Signorelli's paintings commissioned by the Medici family around 1490, see Vasari, *Le Vite*, 3: 636.

[32] For counter-arguments to Chastel's hypothesis that Alexander VI retained his hostility to Savonarola, even after the friar's death, see Romeo de Maio, 'Savonarola, Alessandro VI, e il mito dell'Anticristo', *Rivista storica italiana* 82 (1970), 533–59.

of Chastel's hypothesis are many and can only be summarized here in brief. Signorelli's Antichrist neither resembles the known likeness of Savonarola,[33] nor is he dressed in contemporary clerical clothing. More importantly, the notorious case of Savonarola would not only have been a sensitive issue for the primarily Dominican theologians who were consulted on the subject matter of the Cappella Nuova,[34] but would also have been irrelevant to the local concerns of the town's politico-ecclesiastical authorities.[35]

The Medieval Antichrist as the Arch-Hypocrite

Notwithstanding the general dismissal of Chastel's interpretation, his unintended association of Signorelli's preaching Antichrist with the intellectual perversion of hypocrisy (and its successful effect in current society) deserves exploration. The vivid theatricality of Signorelli's scene was plausibly related by Jonathan Riess to the theatrical tradition of the Antichrist myth, arguing that the painter may have seen or read a mystery play about the Antichrist and the end of the world. We know, for example, of a play about Antichrist that was staged in the cathedral of Orvieto in 1508, although there is no evidence that a similar drama had been staged in the town before the execution of Signorelli's fresco around 1503.[36]

Riess also saw a similarity between the surviving stage directions of the medieval German drama *Ludus de Antichristo* ('The Play about the Antichrist') and Signorelli's composition, namely in the spatial relation of the spectators to the Temple of Jerusalem.[37] Surviving in a single manuscript from the Benedictine monastery of Tegernsee in Bavaria (*c.*1160),[38] the *Ludus de Antichristo* is the earliest

33 As noted by Hall and Uhr, 'The Signorelli Frescoes in Orvieto', 54 n. 57.

34 See n. 8 above.

35 Most Signorelli scholars have now rejected Chastel's argument, mainly because it overlooked the Orvietan context of Signorelli's commission for the sake of Florentine politics and interests: see Riess, *The Renaissance Antichrist*, 135–8; Hall and Uhr, *Signorelli Frescoes in Orvieto*, 53–4.

36 See Robert Vischer, *Luca Signorelli und die italienische Renaissance* (Leipzig, 1879), 183; Riess, *The Renaissance Antichrist*, 75–81. This mystery play was probably inspired by Signorelli's fresco, rather than the reverse: see ibid. 75. Its content was outlined by the Orvietan diarist, Tommaso di Silvestro, in 1508: see Di Silvestro, *Diario*, 372.

37 Riess, *The Renaissance Antichrist*, 78.

38 Munich, Bayerische Staatsbibliothek, *Codex latinus monacensis*, 19411.

and the most impressive of the known medieval Antichrist plays. Its protagonist is described as accompanied by 'Hypocrisy' on the right, and 'Heresy' on the left, both escorted by choruses. The false humility of the former enables the Antichrist to win the favour and support of the laity, while the latter helps him to demolish the teaching of the clergy. In a dramatic climax, the Antichrist approaches the throne of the king of Jerusalem, sings to the hypocrites that he was born within the church, and then reveals his true intentions. The hypocrites lay down their outer garments before their master; they depose the king of Jerusalem – who had been deceived by their good appearances – and crown the Antichrist.[39]

With its demonstration of hypocrisy as an apocalyptic sign of the last days and a key feature of the Antichrist, the *Ludus de Antichristo* essentially revived the long-forgotten Gregorian image of the Antichrist as the absolute master of hypocrisy (*omnium hypocritarum caput*) and the head of an 'ecclesiastic' body of hypocrites (*Moralia* 25.16.34).[40] The sixth-century portrayal of the Antichrist by Saint Gregory as an exemplar of hypocrisy appears not to be found in the religious thought of fifteenth-century Italy, but some aspects of it would have survived in the theatrical tradition of the Antichrist, not least because of the intrinsic relationship of the theatrical medium to the very notion of hypocrisy.[41] It is surely difficult to tell whether Signorelli or his advisers were aware either of the *Ludus de Antichristo* or of the Gregorian portrayal of the Antichrist as the arch-hypocrite. Yet their iconographic emphasis on theatrical notions of oratorical performance and deception makes it plausible to assume that the reign of the Orvieto Antichrist was conceived as an apocalyptic age of hypocrisy.

[39] For an English translation of the play, see Bernard McGinn, *Visions of the End: Apocalyptic Traditions in the Middle Ages* (New York, 1979), 119–21. The most recent publication on the topic, including a Latin edition with a new English verse translation, is Kyle A. Thomas and Carol Symes, *The Play about the Antichrist (Ludus de Antichristo)* (Kalamazoo, MI, 2023).

[40] Frederic Amory, 'Whited Sepulchres: The Semantic History of Hypocrisy to the High Middle Ages', *Recherches de théologie ancienne et médiévale* 53 (1986), 5–39, at 11, 33–7. For the Antichrist as the master of hypocrisy in Gregory, see Catherine Cubitt's article in this volume.

[41] The original meaning of the Greek word 'hypocrites' ('υποκριτής') was stage player or actor. The word's literal etymology ('an interpreter from underneath') probably referred to the actor's role-play under a large figurative mask.

The Iconography of Hypocrisy

Regardless of humanistic worldviews and millenarian trends, references to clerical hypocrisy in the art of Signorelli's time are scarce. Essentially, they are confined to illustrations of the *Divina Commedia*, such as Sandro Botticelli's graphic representation of monk-like hypocrites (*Inferno*, Canto XVIII), bowed down by the weight of their leaden cloaks.[42] Even a prominent critic of ecclesiastical hypocrisy such as Leonardo da Vinci (1452–1519) was seemingly uninterested or perhaps reluctant to use his art to criticize the church. In one of his polemical writings, Leonardo epitomized the timelessness of clerical hypocrisy with the aphorism: 'Pharisees – that is to say, friars';[43] while in another, he compared the clergymen who criticized painters for working on feast days to the Pharisees who had rebuked Jesus and his disciples for healing people and gathering food on the Sabbath.[44] These anti-clerical sentiments are not visible in Leonardo's artistic production, apart perhaps from his portrait of Judas in the *Last Supper* fresco (*c.*1495–8), which was allegedly based on the likeness of an importunate prior of Santa Maria della Grazie (Milan).[45]

The rarity of visual references to hypocrisy is surprising, given the rich iconographic tradition found in Italy and other regions during

[42] Berlin, Staatliche Museen, Kupferstichkabinett, inv. Botticelli, Inferno 23; for a reproduction, see online at: <https://id.smb.museum/object/943079>, accessed 28 September 2023.

[43] 'Farisei: frati santi vol dire': see Leonardo da Vinci, *The Notebooks of Leonardo da Vinci*, ed. Jean Paul Richter, 2 vols (New York, 2015), 2: 302 (no. 1209).

[44] 'Of those who blame him who designs on feast days and investigates the works of God. Among the number of fools there is a certain sect, called hypocrites, who continually endeavour to deceive themselves and others, but others more than themselves. Yet in truth they deceive themselves more than they do others. And they blame painters who, on feast days, study such things as pertain to the true understanding of all the forms of nature's works, and solicitously contrive to acquire an understanding of those forms so far as is possible. But let such censors be still, for this is the way to understand the Creator of so many admirable things, and this is the way to love such a great Inventor. In truth, great love is born of great knowledge of the thing that is loved, and if you do not know it, you can love it little or not at all'. See Leonardo da Vinci, *Treatise on Painting: Codex Urbinas Latinus 1270*, transl. and annotated by Amos Philip McMahon, 2 vols (Princeton, NJ, 1956), 1: 53 (no. 80).

[45] See Vasari, *Le Vite*, 4: 26. A physiognomic study of five caricature heads by a follower of Leonardo (after 1490), now in Venice, Gallerie dell'Accademia (inv. 227), was based on a drawing by the master. It could be conjectured that two of these heads might mock ecclesiastical vices.

the fourteenth and early fifteenth century.[46] Two common examples are the French type of a nun with a rosary faking the acts of devotional reading and prayer (*Papelardie*);[47] and the animal allegory of a fox in priest's garb preaching to a flock of geese, a warning against the rhetorical brilliance of hypocritical preachers seducing naïve flocks.[48] The Italian tradition of that period relied heavily on Dante's *Inferno*,[49] particularly on the placement of hypocritical clergymen amongst the fraudulent of the second lowest circle of hell (Canto XXIII).[50] The depiction of hypocrites in large wall paintings often came with a satire on their sanctimonious religiosity, including invented scenes from the last judgement, narrating the unsuccessful attempts of hypocrite friars to secretly put themselves amongst the good.[51] It therefore seems that Signorelli's eschatology signified the reignited interest of Italian artists in the visualization of nearly every aspect of the apocalyptic sublime: the medieval iconography of the Antichrist, the cruelty of his hypocritical regime leading the world to its end, the satirical horrors of the final judgement and hellish visions of the afterlife.

[46] Satire of church and state in fifteenth-century Italian frescoes representing hell, including the satire of clerical hypocrisy, was much reduced compared with that found in the fourteenth century: see Eugene Paul Nassar, 'The Iconography of Hell: From the Baptistery Mosaic to the Michelangelo Fresco', *Dante Studies, with the Annual Report of the Dante Society* 111 (1993), 53–105, at 97. Criticism of religious hypocrisy in the visual arts of the fourteenth century was largely inspired by its criticism in the literary arts, most notably in Dante's *Inferno* (Canto XXIII) and Boccaccio's *Decameron* (I.6).

[47] This type, found in numerous French illuminated manuscripts, originated from the *Roman de la rose* (mid-thirteenth century).

[48] Deriving from the famous late medieval cycle of Reynard the Fox, this allegory became particularly popular in England where it was utilized by the church to resource propaganda against the preaching of the Lollards, a proto-Protestant movement of the mid-fourteenth century: see Janetta Rebold Benton, *Holy Terrors: Gargoyles on Medieval Buildings* (New York, 1997), 83.

[49] See Nassar, *The Iconography of Hell*, 75, 86, 97. One of the most famous late medieval artists who illustrated the *Divina Commedia* was Andrea Orcagna (*c.*1308–68), whom Vasari described as an ardent student of Dante: see Vasari, *Le Vite*, 2: 218 ('nell'altra faccia fece l'Inferno, con le bolge, cerchî et altre cose descritte da Dante, del quale fu Andrea studiosissimo').

[50] The named hypocrites of *Inferno* are the Jewish high priest Caiaphas who condemned Jesus (John 18), and Catalano de' Malavolti and Loderingo degli Andalo, prominent members of a medieval religious group that was sarcastically called the 'Jolly Friars' due to their luxurious lifestyle.

[51] See Vasari, *Le Vite*, 2: 221: 'E poco di sopra, cioè nel mezzo, è un frate ipocrito, che uscito d'una sepoltura si vuole furtivamente mettere fra i buoni, mentre un Angelo lo scuopre e lo spigne [fra i dannati]'.

Millenarian Aspects of the Antichrist Myth

A question that is worth asking is whether Signorelli's portrayal of the Antichrist as a preaching hypocrite came with a subtle criticism of clerical hypocrisy. His revival of the Antichrist tradition arguably emphasized the ever-looming danger of false teachers and heretics in a manner that was not devoid of ambiguity. It has been suggested, for example, that the story's warning signs of doomsday do not refer to contemporary ideas of millenarian theology and church reform.[52] However, the imposing temple of Signorelli's fresco alludes to the unholy church of the Antichrist, a concept used by millenarian theorists from as early as the twelfth and thirteenth centuries.[53] The contradictions of Signorelli's message are even more visible in his treatment of eschatological prophecy and preaching. Even a critic of Chastel's hypothesis such as Riess stressed that the *Antichrist* functioned as a condemnation of uncontrolled apocalyptic exhortation of contemporary doomsday preachers, who prophesied that the current church was in its last days, and whose false miracles and lies had been emboldened by the greatly influential sermons of Savonarola.[54] Some reasonable questions are, therefore: how could a religious narrative persuade audiences of the closeness of the end of the world by outrightly denouncing all those who prophesied about it; and how could the artist negotiate the anti-clerical connotations of the Antichrist myth?

The entire notion of an Antichrist presented serious threats to the Church, which was one reason why accounts of Antichrist had been traditionally relegated to the sphere of the legendary and non-orthodox.[55] The unpopularity of the story amongst ecclesiastical patrons of art in Italy was apparently owed to its malefic and provocative aspects, but

[52] To quote Jonathan Riess, 'the *Antichrist* can be regarded as a counter-blast on the part of ecclesiastical authorities against those reformers and apocalyptic preachers who in the last years of the fifteenth and in the first years of the sixteenth centuries were finding the Church a chief fount of earthly corruption': Riess, *The Renaissance Antichrist*, 6. For millenarian worldviews and the problem of church reform in Renaissance Italy, see Sharon Leftley, 'The Millennium in Renaissance Italy: A Persecuted Belief?,' *Renaissance Studies* 13 (1999), 117–29.

[53] See Norman Cohn, *The Pursuit of the Millenium: Revolutionary Millenarians and Mystical Anarchists of the Middle Ages*, rev. and exp. edn (New York, 1970), 84–5.

[54] Riess, *The Renaissance Antichrist*, 135–6. Action against doomsday preachers was taken by Pope Leo X (r. 1513–21) in 1516 through a decree of the Fifth Lateran Council (*Supernae majestatis praesidio*) which forbade unauthorized and unreviewed prophecies and preachments.

[55] Riess, *The Renaissance Antichrist*, 7.

perhaps also to its anti-clerical allusions. The appearance of the Antichrist, even on a fictional or symbolic level, presupposed a time of major crisis and discord for both church and state. The prophesied pseudo-Christs of the New Testament would be 'disguising themselves as apostles of Christ' (2 Corinthians 11: 13), having the appearance and attitude, not of a bestial demon, but of a seeming saint, a Christ-like man who 'takes his seat in the temple of God, proclaiming himself to be God' (2 Thessalonians 2: 4).[56] The Antichrist would inevitably appear within the Church, in the form of heresy, as a wolf in sheep's clothing, which explains, for example, why the *Liber chronicarum*, which, as discussed above, was the most likely source for Signorelli's fresco, depicted the Antichrist in contemporary clerical clothing (a choice not followed by Signorelli).

An answer to the question of whether or not Signorelli's narrative came with millenarian hints could be found in the assembly of debating friars of different orders, who are seen standing right behind the Antichrist and the devil. For some commentators, these learned clergymen stand as the sole pillar of faith and resistance against the evil one and his heresy,[57] whereas others have read them as disputing, and confused by, or converted to, his false teachings.[58] Apart from a white-clothed friar who is pointing toward the heavens, the rest of the group engages in futile disputes or consults the scriptures. These signs may well indicate confusion and discord within the Church of God, typical symptoms of the age of the Antichrist. However, this particular assembly may have been invented by Signorelli at a later stage in the design, in order to replace an initial group of debating demons who are inspecting a book, as has been recently proposed.[59] The latter construct has survived in a magnificent black-chalk drawing by Signorelli (*c.*1500–3), now in the Morgan Library and Museum

[56] Translation of both passages is taken from the ESV.

[57] See Riess, *The Renaissance Antichrist*, 55–6; Wright, 'Authority and Vision', 31. A similar explanation is that these men are experts on the Antichrist, calculating the end of the world, warning for its signs and consulting the scriptures: see Raffaele Davanzo, *La Capella di San Brizio in Orvieto. Visita ai contenuti pittorici, storici e letterari* (Foligno, 2021), 86.

[58] See Hall and Uhr, 'The Signorelli Frescoes in Orvieto', 49; McLellan, *Signorelli's Orvieto Frescoes*, 36; Rhoda Eitel-Porter, Catalogue entry for Signorelli's 'Four Demons Inspecting a Book', in eadem and John Marciari, eds, *Italian Renaissance Drawings at the Morgan Library and Museum* (New York, 2019), 131–3 (no. 23).

[59] See Eitel-Porter, 'Four Demons Inspecting a Book', 131–3 (no. 23).

(Figure 5),[60] the enigmatic purpose of which deserves elaboration. Indeed, the entire graphic production of Signorelli for the Cappella Nuova frescoes requires close study in the attempt to shed light on the artist's original intentions for the *Antichrist.*

Invention and Design – the Influences of Dante

The *Antichrist*'s novelty differentiates it from every other narrative in the Cappella Nuova, apart perhaps from the equally innovative *End of the World.* Despite being the first episode in chronological order of the events of the Apocalypse, technical and stylistic evidence show that the *Antichrist* was executed in the later stages of decoration (*c.*1503),[61] possibly after thematic modifications. The surviving contracts for the overall commission clarify that the iconography was developed with theological advisers within the specific context of the last judgement;[62] unusually restrictive terms which suggest that Signorelli may have sought leeway for originality from the outset of his project. His artistic profile and previous experience with complex iconographies reveal, indeed, a highly inventive draftsman and painter who would not have unquestionably complied with iconographic prescriptions.[63] The ambitious nature of his project would have inspired him to try out novel ideas and explore different solutions, at least on drawing paper. Besides, for such large-scale narrative paintings there was plenty of creative space for all the agents involved (patrons, advisers and artist), although the degree of dialogue and flexibility allowed by the commissioners is not easy to assess.[64]

[60] See ibid. See also New York, Morgan Library and Museum, inv. 1965.15, black chalk on paper, 35.5 x 28.4 cm; for a reproduction, see online at: <https://www.themorgan.org/drawings/item/142689>, accessed 22 February 2023.

[61] Kanter, 'Review of "The Renaissance Antichrist"', 1260.

[62] See nn. 7 and 8 above. Compare also Hall and Uhr, 'The Signorelli Frescoes in Orvieto', 39–47.

[63] One of the Orvieto contracts (27 April 1500) referred to Signorelli as 'ingenioso pictori magistro Luce Egidii de Cortonio': see the *Italian Renaissance Document Site*, online at: <https://irds-project.org/doc/518/446/>, accessed 15 February 2023. In his eulogy of the greatest painters of his time, Giovanni Santi (*c.*1440–94), a court painter in Urbino and the father of Raphael (1483–1520), praised Signorelli as an extraordinarily inventive talent and an unusual intellect: see Henry, 'Luca de ingegno', 175–6. For the artist's creative talents and literary interests, see ibid. 175–83.

[64] For a discussion of the artist's level of initiative and participation in the formation of the iconographic programme, see Henry, *Luca Signorelli*, 197–8.

Signorelli's primary model of inspiration was the *Divina Commedia*.[65] His study of Dante's masterpiece is attested by the eleven episodes from *Purgatorio* (Cantos I–XI) painted on the chapel's lower walls; by the depiction of the damned entering hell *(Antinferno*, Canto III) on the altar wall;[66] as well as by the two portraits of Dante in the socle area and in the *Antichrist*. Signorelli's entire view of eschatology was heavily inspired by Dante: both produced a universal yet deeply personal vision of the contemporary world and the eternal afterlife. It has even been suggested that the aims and methods of the two artists are so analogous that 'a knowledge of the *Commedia* helps one to understand Signorelli's frescoes better ...[and] an understanding of the frescoes can also help us to understand the *Commedia*, even though the painter worked a century and a half after the poet'.[67]

A crucial aspect of Dante's worldview was the sharp distinction between true faith and institutional religion, for which reason the simoniac popes of his time, along with countless sinful cardinals and bishops, were condemned to the eternal punishments of hell. While this anti-clerical aspect of the *Commedia* is not observed in Signorelli's frescoes, a study of his extant drawings indicates that some of his boldest ideas remained unexecuted, perhaps owing to his patrons' disapproval. Among his surviving studies on paper, about ten have been related to the last judgement cycle, none of which is a compositional drawing.[68] Of these, only two correspond clearly to executed figures, namely the avaricious moneylender in

[65] See Adolfo Venturi, *Luca Signorelli interprete di Dante* (Florence, 1922); Leopold Dussler, *Signorelli, des Meisters Gemälde* (Stuttgart, 1927), xxxii–xxxvii; Scarpellini, *Luca Signorelli*, 40–5; Enzo Carli, *Il Duomo di Orvieto* (Rome, 1965), 106–11; Corrado Gizzi, ed., *Signorelli e Dante* (Milan, 1991); James, *Signorelli and Fra Angelico*, 91–105, 141–4; Silvia Maddalo, 'Poesia in Figura. Dante e Luca Signorelli', in Gaetano Platania, ed., "*Pot Purri*". *Studi in onore di Silvana Ferreri* (Viterbo, 2016), 337–52.

[66] Signorelli's pictorial source for the *Damned Being Plunged into Hell* may have been the illustration of the same canto by Nardo di Cione (active *c.*1343–66 in Florence) in the Strozzi Chapel, Santa Maria Novella, Florence: see Nassar, 'The Iconography of Hell', 75.

[67] Emmerson and Herzman, 'Antichrist, Simon Magus, and Dante's "Inferno" XIX', 373.

[68] For studies of Signorelli's last judgement drawings, see Andrew Martindale, 'Luca Signorelli and the Drawings Connected with the Orvieto Frescoes', *The Burlington Magazine* 103 (1961), 216–20; McLellan, 'Signorelli's Last Judgement', 194–228; Claire van Cleave, 'I disegni preparatori', in Giusi Testa, ed., *La Cappella Nova o di San Brizio nel Duomo di Orvieto* (Milan, 1996), 241–51.

the foreground of the *Antichrist*,[69] and a demon throttling a nude man in the *Torments of the Damned*.[70] A couple of studies are seemingly related to the monochrome roundels, and most of the others represent helpless nude men and women who are being captured, carried or beaten by demons. Judging from the content of these stories, including their fictive illumination from the left side, they were intended for the *Torments of the Damned*.[71] The absence of drawings connected to the actual paintings is due not only to an accident of survival, but also to the experimental character of a design process that was remarkably fluid and lengthy. As an absolute master in the anatomical design of the human body, Signorelli would have prepared hundreds of drawings, trying out and eventually discarding numerous ideas before reaching successful solutions for the vigorous body postures and actions of his figures.

Discarded Novelties

One of the most captivating drawings relating to the Orvieto cycle represents a scene from Dante's *Inferno* (Cantos XXXII.124–39; XXXIII.1–90): in the second region of the lowest circle of hell – the icy Antenora – Dante and Virgil encounter two wicked men in the circle of traitors: Count Ugolino and Archbishop Ruggieri (Figure 3).[72] Ugolino, the less evil of these two men is narrating his

[69] Paris, Louvre Museum, Département des arts graphiques, inv. 1796, black and red chalk, heightened with white, pricked for transfer to square paper, 46.5 x 25.5 cm; for a reproduction, see online at: <https://collections.louvre.fr/en/ark:/53355/cl020002502>, accessed 15 February 2023.

[70] London, British Museum, Department of Prints and Drawings, inv. 1895,0915.601, brush drawing in brown ink, over black chalk, 35.7 x 23.3 cm; for a reproduction, see online at: <https://www.britishmuseum.org/collection/object/P_1895-0915-601>, accessed 14 November 2023. This drawing is a faithful copy after a Signorelli drawing for the *Torments of the Damned*.

[71] The locations of the drawings are: British Museum, Department of Prints and Drawings, inv. 1946,0713.10 (see online at: <https://www.britishmuseum.org/collection/object/P_1946-0713-10>, accessed 22 February 2023); Florence, Galleria degli Uffizi, Gabinetto dei Disegni e delle Stampe, inv. 1246 E (see online at: <https://euploos.uffizi.it/scheda-catalogo.php?invn=1246+E>, accessed 15 February 2023); and Louvre Museum, Département des arts graphiques, inv. 1801r (see online at: <https://collections.louvre.fr/en/ark:/53355/cl020002507>, accessed 22 February 2023).

[72] British Museum, Department of Prints and Drawings, inv. 1885,0509.41, black chalk, 31.2 x 25.6 cm; for a reproduction, see online at: <https://www.britishmuseum.org/collection/object/P_1885-0509-41>, accessed 15 February 2023. For a discussion of

Figure 3. Luca Signorelli, *The Encounter of Dante and Virgil with Count Ugolino and Archbishop Ruggieri*, *c.*1500–3, drawing, black chalk on paper, 31.2 x 25.6 cm, British Museum, London, Department of Prints and Drawings, inv. 1885,0509.41. Reproduced by permission of the Trustees of the British Museum, London.

betrayal by the archbishop of Pisa, who had him and his innocent children imprisoned and starved to death. While narrating, Ugolino is holding down Ruggieri by the neck and is about to

this drawing, see Arthur E. Popham and Philip Pouncey, *Italian Drawings in the Department of Prints and Drawings in the British Museum: The Fourteenth and Fifteenth Centuries*, 2 vols (London, 1950), 1: 149–50.

continue gnawing his already deformed skull. The latter, whose hands are tied behind his back, is silently enduring the horrific punishment of being cannibalized, one of the most disturbing scenes in the entire *Inferno*.[73] The particular subject and circular format of this composition leave no doubt that it was intended for the decoration of the Cappella Nuova's lower walls with monochrome roundels. Its infernal subject and fictive illumination from the left side further indicate that it was intended for the socle zone beneath the *Torments of the Damned* (Figure 4).[74] For reasons which are not clear, the scene was discarded. A possible justification for this decision is that the infernal punishment of a highly placed cleric may have been judged by Signorelli's advisers or patrons as an inappropriate image for worshippers.[75] An entire series from *Inferno* may actually have been planned at an early stage, but later abandoned due to its controversial character.[76] Two possible relics of this hypothetical programme have been traced to below the altar wall's *Antinferno*: the partial figure of an avaricious sinner lying on the ground and biting his hand, revealed during the restoration of the altar wall's pictures in the mid-1990s, may have been inspired by the *Inferno*'s region of Caina; and a rectangular episode with the scourging of women and the flaying of men by demons might be a variation on two different stories from the *Inferno*, the punishment of lust (Canto XVIII) and politico-ecclesiastical discord (Canto XXVIII), respectively.[77]

[73] Ugolino, who is the more sympathetic sinner, appeals to Dante for judging which of the two is the greatest offender. The narrator is not moved since the count had been involved in the remorseless slaying of Gano degli Scornigiani: see *Purgatorio*, Canto VI.18.
[74] The possibility that this episode was originally painted in the socle zone of the altar wall, but was either destroyed or concealed by the insertion of a late Baroque altar created by Bernardino Cametti (*c.*1712–15) is unlikely, because the drawn scene is illuminated from the left side. All monochromes in the altar wall, as well as the monochrome episodes from *Purgatorio*, are lit from the right, therefore the *Inferno* drawing almost certainly belonged to a set of unexecuted stories that were planned to be placed beneath the *Torments of the Damned.*
[75] An alternative proposal by Dugald McLellan is that given the history of internecine strife in Orvieto, an episode highlighting the evil of treachery against one's own country or faction may have been a subject too sensitive for Signorelli's patrons: see McLellan, 'Signorelli's Last Judgement', 211 n. 71.
[76] See Laurence Kanter, 'The Late Works of Luca Signorelli and His Followers, 1498–1559' (PhD thesis, New York University, 1989), 39–40; McLellan, 'Signorelli's Last Judgement', 210–11.
[77] See Meltzoff, *Signorelli and Savonarola*, 334–6; for a reproduction, see Riess, *The Renaissance Antichrist*, figure 60.

Figure 4. Luca Signorelli, *Torments of the Damned*, *c.*1500–3, fresco, San Brizio Chapel, Orvieto Cathedral, Orvieto. Image in the Public Domain on Wikimedia Commons, online at: <https://commons.wikimedia.org/wiki/File:Luca_Signorelli_-_The_Damned_-_WGA21220.jpg>, accessed 21 December 2022.

Another discarded invention, and one of the most impressive drawings of Signorelli's entire graphic oeuvre, is the previously mentioned study of four bat-winged demons acting as learned scholars (Figure 5).[78] The demon with the largest horns on the right is holding up an open book in the manner of prophesying or preaching a heretical doctrine. The other three are viewing the book's content, and one of them, the farthest, makes use of pince-nez spectacles, an ingenious mocking of false erudition, or false prophecy and heresy. Art historians have generally agreed that this drawing was intended for

[78] See n. 60 above.

Figure 5. Luca Signorelli, *Four Demons Inspecting a Book*, *c.*1500–3, drawing, black chalk on paper, 35.5 x 28.4 cm, The Morgan Library and Museum, New York, inv. 1965.15. Photographic credit: The Morgan Library and Museum, New York.

the Orvieto cycle; however, no consensus has been reached about its purpose and meaning.

A close investigation of the chapel's paintings shows that the western frescoes receive fictive light from the left, and the eastern frescoes from the right: their notional sources of illumination were therefore the southern windows behind and above the altar. This pattern of painted light had a double function: it reflected the direction of real sunlight coming inside the chapel, but it also symbolized the spiritual light of divine grace radiating, as it were, from the altar. Given that the Morgan drawing is lit from the right, it must have been associated either with the *Antichrist*, the *Signs of the End of the World*, the *Crowning of the Elect* or the monochrome roundels in the dados. The *Crowning* can be safely excluded on thematic grounds, while the idea for an abandoned monochrome is highly unlikely because of the drawing's ambitious scale and content.[79] The attitudes and postures of the four demons resemble some of the prophesying figures in the right foreground of the *Signs of the End of the World* (Figure 6) as some authors have already proposed;[80] although the former's pseudo-scholarly subject has little to do with the latter's scenes of physical disaster and chaos.

On balance, the Morgan study seems to fit in better with the *Sermon and Deeds of the Antichrist* in its early stages of design, due to their common emphasis on hypocritical preaching, devilish sophistry, and what the *Golden Legend* described as 'the Antichrist's false explanation of the Scriptures'.[81] In any event, the crucial question is why an invention of such skill and wit was eventually abandoned? To assume that Signorelli merely experimented with this idea without intending to use it would unconvincingly relegate a sheet that demonstrates all the artist's virtues at once into a purposeless study. In fact, the mastery of its black-chalk technique, the volume of its figures, and the specificity of its narrative, point to a carefully planned thought that was meant to convey a certain message related to the pretensions of devilish heretics and false prophets. A possible explanation for its omission is that the scene came under scrutiny by Signorelli's advisers who eventually disapproved of it. The sarcastic conception of demons acting as learned scholars (or theologians) could have been perceived as reminiscent of millenarian accounts and satires of demonic clergymen acting as the devil's instruments. The revival of the millenarian movement during the last decades of

[79] McLellan rightly noted that the Morgan drawing cannot have been intended for the socle zone, since it lacks both the violent action of the roundel episodes and the figures of Dante and Virgil. However, the author's connection of the study to the *Torments of the Damned* overlooked the latter's fictive illumination from the left side: see McLellan, 'Signorelli's Last Judgement', 215 n. 81.

[80] See Cara D. Denison and Helen B. Mules, eds, *European Drawings 1375–1825* (New York, 1981), no. 4; Van Cleave, 'I disegni preparatori', 249–50.

[81] It is perhaps worth noting that the opening scene of the previously mentioned play about Antichrist in Orvieto (1508) involved twelve naked devils – an antithesis to the twelve apostles – entering to worship the Antichrist: see Riess, *The Renaissance Antichrist*, 76. See n. 36 above.

Figure 6. Luca Signorelli, *Signs of the End of the World*, *c.*1502–4, fresco, San Brizio Chapel, Orvieto Cathedral, Orvieto. Image in the Public Domain on Wikimedia Commons, online at: <https://en.m.wikipedia.org/wiki/File:Luca_signorelli,_cappella_di_san_brizio,_apocalisse_01.jpg>, accessed 21 December 2022.

the fifteenth century had come with the revived conception of corrupt clergy as a demonic, bestial fraternity that belonged to the hordes of the Antichrist.[82] The Orvietan authorities, ever faithful to the papacy,

[82] For the millenarian movement in Savonarola's Florence, see Donald Weinstein, 'Savonarola, Florence, and the Millenarial Tradition', *ChH* 27 (1958), 291–305. The demonization of the clergy was a commonplace in millenarian thought. To quote Norman Cohn: 'Martin Luther was not (as is often supposed) the first to hit upon the idea that the Antichrist who sets up his throne in the Temple can be no other than the Pope at Rome and that the Church of Rome is therefore the Church of Satan. Amongst the eschatologically minded in the later Middle Ages the idea was already a commonplace. Even such a champion of the Church as St Bernard could come to believe, in his tense expectation of the final drama, that many of the clergy belonged to the hosts of Antichrist … every millenarian movement was in fact almost compelled by the situation in which it found itself to see the clergy as a demonic fraternity … the clergy as the Beast of the Apocalypse: what image could be more convincing to enthusiastic millenarians in whose eyes the life of the clergy was indeed nothing but bestiality, the *vita animalis*, an existence utterly given over to the World and the Flesh?' See Cohn, *The Pursuit of the Millenium*, 80–4.

may have exerted tight control over Signorelli's most ambiguous inventions.[83] Hence, instead of the four naked demons, the less controversial group of disputing theologians with books was eventually depicted right behind the devil, in order to express the confusion in ecclesiastic circles caused by the discourses of the Antichrist.

In conclusion, the available evidence regarding the execution of the Cappella Nuova cycle points toward a prolonged process of design characterized by stimulating oral discussions and programme modifications. The commission of such an artistically promising, yet controversial, project resulted in astonishing novelties, but perhaps also in abandonments of potentially offensive ideas. The idea that Signorelli's cycle of the last judgement may have initially included millenarian hints cannot be argued with certainty, not least because it would project post-Reformation views on to an artist of the late Quattrocento. Yet the discarding of Signorelli's controversial inventions, the overall absence of episodes from the *Inferno*, as well as the suppression of anti-clerical aspects of both the *Commedia* of Dante and the Antichrist myth, indicate a politically correct iconographic approach and reassurance to contemporary viewers that the church and its clergy could not be blamed for the socio-political decay and hypocrisy of the last days.

[83] Some of the harshest critics of bold artistic inventions in the Italian Renaissance were Observant Dominicans: see Alexander Nagel, *The Controversy of Renaissance Art* (Chicago, IL, 2011), 23 and 290 n. 35.

'God really hated the hypocrites': Hypocrisy and Anti-clerical Rhetoric in the Early Lutheran Reformation

Charlotte Methuen*

University of Glasgow

In 1524, two anonymous pamphlets were published, both professing to be letters written by a married woman to her sister, a nun. Both draw on a range of New Testament texts to express criticism of 'the hypocrites', a term the anonymous author uses to refer particularly to clergy and religious. This article examines how the author of these pamphlets constructed and characterized the category of the hypocrite. Drawing on the work of Hans-Christoph Rublack, the article shows that her critique is coherent with anti-clerical rhetoric found in a wide range of early Reformation pamphlets. It then compares her strictures on hypocrisy with references to hypocrisy and hypocrites in the early German writings of Martin Luther and Andreas Bodenstein von Karlstadt to explore the extent to which accusations of hypocrisy were entwined with anti-clerical and anti-monastic rhetoric in the early Lutheran Reformation. It concludes that while accusations against clergy and religious were often couched in terms of their hypocrisy, Luther's use of the term hypocrite was much broader, extending to all those whom he viewed as presenting themselves as 'holier than thou', while Karlstadt made less use of the term.

In 1524, two anonymous pamphlets were published, both claiming to be written by a married woman in response to her sister, a nun. The shorter (at seventeen printed pages), and apparently earlier of the two, *Ayn bezwungene antwort vber eynen Sendbrieff eyner Closter nunnen, an jr schwester im̄ Eelichē standt zugeschickt / darin̄ sy vil vergebner vnnützer sorg fürhelt vn̄ jre gaistliche weißhait vn̄ gemalte hayligkait zů menschlichem gesicht auffmutzet* ['A necessary answer to an

* Theology and Religious Studies, No 4 The Square, University of Glasgow, G12 8QQ. E-mail: charlotte.methuen@glasgow.ac.uk.

Studies in Church History 60 (2024), 148–175
doi: 10.1017/stc.2024.7

open letter sent by a cloistered woman to her married sister in which she presents many unnecessary and useless concerns and presents to the world an embellished image of her spiritual wisdom and apparent holiness'], was probably published in Nuremberg. The longer (twenty-five printed pages), and probably later work, *Ain Sendtbrieff von Ainer erbern frawen im Eelichen stand / an ain Klosterfrawen / gethon über berümung ettlicher haylicher geschrifft in Sermon begriffen / so die Klosterfrauw verbrent / und darauf ein lange vngesaltzne geschrifft zu ursach erzelt hat &c.* ['An open letter from a respectable married woman to a nun, written in praise of all the parts of Holy Scripture included in a sermon that the nun burnt, afterwards presenting her reasons in a long tasteless letter &c.'] was printed in Augsburg.[1] The title of the first of these letters indicates one of the key themes of both: the anonymous author's concern that her sister's outward trappings of faith did not match the inner reality of her relationship to God. This is developed by the unknown author – here referred to as Anonyma – into an impassioned, scripturally founded critique of the hypocrisy of the clergy, and more generally of those who had taken religious vows. It is Anonyma's intertwining of hypocrisy and anticlericalism – including anti-monasticism – which forms the subject of this article. After a brief consideration of the relationship between hypocrisy and anticlericalism in

[1] All English translations from these letters and from other texts are by the author, Charlotte Methuen, unless an English translation is specified in the footnotes. Dorothee Kommer is of the opinion that the two letters were written by the same author and that they represent published versions of actual letters: Dorothee Kommer, *Reformatorische Flugschriften von Frauen. Flugschriftenautorinnen der frühen Reformationszeit und ihre Sicht von Geistlichkeit* (Leipzig, 2013), 117–29. Miriam Usher Chrisman treats the pamphlets as having been written by different authors, a 'converted sister' (based on a mistranslation of the title as 'A Convert Answers a Letter sent by a Convent Nun to her Married Sister') and an 'honorable woman': Miriam Usher Chrisman, *Conflicting Visions of Reform: German Lay Propaganda Pamphlets, 1519–1530*, Studies in German Histories 7 (Atlantic Highlands, NJ, 1996), 140, 145. Kommer's assertion is based largely on the coherence in the use of the Bible in the two pamphlets, a position which is supported and strengthened by the argument in Charlotte Methuen, '"dañ got vnd die haylig geschrifft leerent dich so̊llichs nit": Autorinnenschaft und Bibelverwendung in zwei anonymen reformatorischen Flugschriften', in eadem, Gury Schneider-Ludorff and Lothar Vogel, eds, *Reformatorische Bewegung im 16. und 17. Jh.*, Die Bibel und die Frauen 7.1 (Stuttgart, 2024), 173–94. ET: eadem, '"God and Holy Scripture do not teach you such things": Female Authorship and the Use of The Bible in two Anonymous Reformation Pamphlets,' in eadem, Gury Schneider-Ludorff and Lothar Vogel, eds, *Reformation Movements in the Sixteenth and Seventeenth Centuries*, Bible and Women 7.1 (Atlanta, GA, forthcoming 2024).

the scholarly literature relating to the early German Reformation, this article explores how Anonyma's construction of hypocrisy and her characterization of hypocrites inform her anti-clerical and anti-monastic rhetoric. Anonyma's use of Scripture to buttress her argument reveals an excellent knowledge of relevant biblical texts, not all of which were commonly used by other authors of this period. Drawing on a useful taxonomy of anticlericalism in German pamphlets proposed by Hans-Christoph Rublack, the article shows that the arguments presented in Anonyma's letters are coherent with – and indeed typical of – popular rhetoric in this period of the Lutheran Reformation. Reading Rublack's taxonomy through the lens of Anonyma's writings, however, also indicates that the accusation of hypocrisy underlies most of the categories of anticlericalism which he identifies. In a final step, Anonyma's criticisms of the clergy and religious are brought into conversation with accusations of hypocrisy in the early German works of the reformers Andreas Bodenstein von Karlstadt and Martin Luther, both of whom have been identified as influences on Anonyma,[2] to explore the extent to which hypocrisy for Karlstadt and Luther was associated with anticlericalism. It concludes that while both often couched criticisms of clergy and religious in terms of their hypocrisy, Luther's use of the term hypocrite was broader, extending to all those whom he viewed as succumbing to the temptation of presenting themselves as 'holier than thou'. Anonyma's use of hypocrisy to focus her anti-clerical discourse thus emerges as a distinctive characteristic of her writings, but one which is coherent with early Reformation polemic.

Anticlericalism has long been identified as a motivating factor in the German Reformation.[3] As Andrew Weeks observes, 'hostility to

[2] See Kommer, *Reformatorische Flugschriften von Frauen*, 129, 141; compare also Stefania Salvadori, 'Frauen und Bibel bei Andreas Bodenstein von Karlstadt: zwischen dem Ruf nach der Freiheit des Evangeliums und der Mahnung zur sozialen Bindung', in Methuen, Schneider-Ludorff and Vogel, eds, *Reformatorische Bewegung*, 153–72, at 170–2; ET: eadem, 'Women and the Bible in the Writings of Andreas Bodenstein von Karlstadt: Freedom to read Scripture whilst conforming to Social Norms', in eadem, Gury Schneider-Ludorff and Lothar Vogel, eds, *Reformation Movements in the Sixteenth and Seventeenth Centuries*.

[3] See, for instance, R. W. Scribner, 'Anticlericalism and the Reformation in Germany', in idem, *Popular Culture and Popular Movements in Reformation Germany* (London, 1987), 243–56; idem, *For the Sake of Simple Folk: Popular Propaganda for the German Reformation* (Oxford, 1994); Peter A. Dykema and Heiko A. Oberman, eds, *Anticlericalism in Late Medieval and Early Modern Europe* (Leiden, 1994); Hans-Jürgen Goertz,

priests, monks, nuns, bishops, popes, ceremonies, ecclesiastical fees and corruption' is recognized by historians 'as a driving force of the Reformation as a popular movement.'[4] Such critique predates the Reformation. Although, as Kaspar Elm and Hans-Jürgen Goertz point out, the term 'anticlericalism' first emerged in the nineteenth century,[5] clerical behaviour was criticized throughout the medieval period. Across Europe, clergy and religious faced 'serious accusations, expressed in derisive verse and lampoons, in satirical images and sketches, relating to their morals, the (non-)observance of their vows, their privileges and unjustified wealth, their ignorance and negligence of their duties.'[6] Rublack similarly notes that 'accusations of avarice, negligence and depravity directed against individual clerics, the clergy as a whole, and the church as an institution, in addition to the exploitation of laymen by ecclesiastical recourse to secular power, are recurrent themes in the medieval apocalyptic tradition.'[7] These were also common themes in medieval German literature, as Albrecht Classen illustrates.[8] Elm argues that while accusations that clergy and religious failed to live according to their vows had long been widespread, by the fifteenth century, these criticisms were

Antiklerikalismus und Reformation. Sozialgeschichtliche Untersuchungen (Göttingen, 1995); Geoffrey Dipple, *Antifraternalism and Anticlericalism in the German Reformation: Johann Eberlin von Günzburg and the Campaign Against the Friars* (Aldershot, 1996); Albrecht Classen, 'Anticlericalism and Criticism of Clerics in Medieval and Early-Modern German Literature', *Amsterdamer Beiträge zur älteren Germanistik* 72 (2014), 283–306; Andrew Weeks, 'Die antiklerikale Reformation und ihr Feindbild, der "Dr. Theologiae" Faustus', *Neophilologus* 102 (2018), 217–40.

4 Weeks, 'Die antiklerikale Reformation', 220.

5 Kaspar Elm, 'Antiklerikalismus im Deutschen Mittelalter', in Dykema and Oberman, eds, *Anticlericalism in Late Medieval and Early Modern Europe*, 3–18, at 3–4; Goertz, *Antiklerikalismus und Reformation*, 11–12. The first use of the English noun 'anticlericalism' is given by the *Oxford English Dictionary* as 1867, although the adjective 'anticlerical' was already in use by 1651: see the OED lemmas 'anticlericalism' and 'anticlerical', *OED*, online at: <https://www.oed.com/view/Entry/103709986> and <https://www.oed.com/view/Entry/8568> respectively, accessed 21 December 2023.

6 Elm, 'Antiklerikalismus im Deutschen Mittelalter', 5.

7 Hans-Christoph Rublack, 'Anticlericalism in German Reformation Pamphlets', in Dykema and Oberman, eds, *Anticlericalism in Late Medieval and Early Modern Europe*, 461–89, at 462.

8 Classen points out that 'Medieval literature knows countless examples where clerics become the butt of the joke, or where severe criticism is voiced against the representatives of the Church because of their hypocrisy': Classen, 'Anticlericalism and Criticism of Clerics', 286. The specific examples from medieval literature Classen discusses are drawn from Walther von der Vogelweide, the Stricker, Mæren, and Schwänke.

being 'directed not only at the episcopate and the local clergy, at monks, canons and mendicants, but also, increasingly turned against the Pope and the Roman Curia.'[9] Scribner sees such anticlericalism in Germany as primarily a response to abuses of clerical power, whether 'political, economic, legal, social, sexual [or] sacred.'[10] Such anti-clerical language helped to shape the swingeing critiques of the papal church which characterized the early Reformation.

In contrast, there seems to have been no study on the role of hypocrisy in the German Reformation or its relationship to anti-clericalism. This is odd, not least because a standard early modern High German dictionary defines the term *Gleisnerei* as 'falsehood as a characteristic of individuals or as the customary behaviour attributed to certain groups, above all the clergy …; associated with the self-promotion of their own piety, honesty, knowledge and skills.'[11] Goertz points out that late medieval and early modern anticlericalism was not seeking to eradicate clerical influence from public life; rather 'the clergy were ridiculed and insulted, threatened and even attacked, because they had neglected their official duties and committed one moral offence after another.'[12] Late medieval anticlericalism clearly included aspects which amount to accusations of hypocrisy, but Elm (for instance) does not use the term hypocrisy in his article at all (which is to say that he does not refer to the terms *Heuchelei*, *Gleisnerei* or *Scheinheiligkeit*, the three German nouns most usually translated into English as hypocrisy, or to *Gleisner*, hypocrite).[13] In

[9] Elm, 'Antiklerikalismus im Deutschen Mittelalter', 8.

[10] Scribner, 'Anticlericalism and the Reformation', 244. See also idem, 'Anticlericalism and the Cities', in Dykema and Oberman, eds, *Anticlericalism in Late Medieval and Early Modern Europe*, 147–66, at 151 [repr. in idem, *Religion and Culture in Germany (1400–1800)*, ed. Lyndal Roper (Leiden, 2001), 149–71].

[11] Lemma 'gleichsnerei', *Frühneuhochdeutsches Wörterbuch*, online at: <https://fwb-online.de/lemma/gleichsnerei.s.1f?q=Glei%C3%9Fnerei&page=1>, accessed 21 December 2023. Common variant spellings include *gleichsnerei*, *gleyßnerei*, *Gleiszerei* and *Gleisnerei*.

[12] Goertz, *Antiklerikalismus und Reformation*, 11–12.

[13] *Heuchelei* and *Gleisnerei* (the older form) are synonyms, both used to translate *simulatio* and *hypocrisis*. *Scheinheiligkeit* literally means pretended or seeming holiness. All three terms refer to 'the act or state of pretending to be better than one is or to have feelings or beliefs which one does not actually have': see *Cambridge Dictionary*, online at: <https://dictionary.cambridge.org/dictionary/german-english/heuchelei>, accessed 21 December 2023. Compare also the lemmas 'Heuchelei', 'Heucheln', 'Gleiszerei' and 'Scheinheiligkeit', *Deutsches Wörterbuch von Jacob Grimm und Wilhelm Grimm*, online at: <http://woerterbuchnetz.de/DWB/>, accessed 21 December 2023.

his survey of critiques of the clergy in over four hundred German Reformation pamphlets, Rublack identifies the condemnation of clergy as hypocrites as one of nine categories of accusations levelled against them.[14] Scribner and Classen both mention hypocrisy in their discussions of anticlericalism, but neither of them explore the way in which hypocrisy informs anticlericalism.[15]

At the same time, the relationship between hypocrisy and false religion, and the appeal to biblical texts in the definition of hypocrisy, have been recognized as central to medieval and early modern hypocrisy in the English context. Introducing the essay collection, *Forms of Hypocrisy in Early Modern England*, Lucia Nigri and Naya Tsentourou remark that the association of hypocrisy and false religion frequently draws on 'the biblical precedent of the archetypal hypocrites: the Pharisees.'[16] They identify several key scriptural texts relating hypocrisy and false religion: the parable of the Pharisee and the tax collector (Luke 18: 9–14); the condemnation of the Pharisees as hypocrites (Matthew 23: 13–36); and Jesus's introduction to the Lord's Prayer (Matthew 6: 5–6), in which he commands: 'whenever you pray, do not be like the hypocrites; for they love to stand and pray in the synagogues and at the street corners, so that they may be seen by others' [NRSV].[17] In her consideration of hypocrisy in drama, Nigri further remarks that early modern portrayals of hypocrites drew on a medieval tradition 'associating hypocrisy with the Roman Catholic religion'[18] and, more particularly, on a tradition of anti-clerical polemic.[19] Indeed, Michael D. Bailey points out that 'Augustine and other Church Fathers … thought about falsity in terms of *hypocrisis* or *ironia* … or *simulatio*,' and that hypocrisy 'became increasingly associated with false religion or godlessness,' with the Pharisees seen as 'the archetypical hypocrites in the

[14] Rublack, 'Anticlericalism in German Reformation Pamphlets', 468–78.

[15] Scribner, 'Anticlericalism and the Reformation', 246, 253. See also idem, 'Anticlericalism and the Cities', 153, 156–7; Classen, 'Anticlericalism and Criticism of Clerics', 286, 289–90, 296–8, 300.

[16] Lucia Nigri and Naya Tsentourou, 'Introduction', in eaedem, eds, *Forms of Hypocrisy in Early Modern England* (Abingdon, 2018), 1–14, at 4.

[17] Ibid. 4–5.

[18] Lucia Nigri, 'Religious Hypocrisy in Performance: Roman Catholicism and the London Stage', in eadem and Tsentourou, eds, *Forms of Hypocrisy in Early Modern England*, 57–71, at 57.

[19] Ibid. 57–9.

Gospels.'[20] Nigri offers Chaucer's Pardoner as an example of the association between hypocrisy and anticlericalism. In all these studies, hypocrisy is recognized as fundamental to critiques of religion such as those articulated in early modern German anticlericalism. It therefore seems fruitful, in a volume considering the church and hypocrisy, to probe the relationship between hypocrisy and anticlericalism in the German Reformation.

Exploring the nature of hypocrisy as presented in Anonyma's texts provides what seems likely to have been a lay perspective emerging from – and speaking into – the heated debates about evangelical theology and practice that were taking place in both Augsburg and Nuremberg in the early 1520s, with their consequences for the reassessment of religious identity and priorities.[21] Anonyma's position in these debates was clearly supportive of evangelical challenges to traditional church life. Indeed, her letters testify to a wider conflict between members of religious orders and their evangelically-influenced relatives, of which other examples can be found in both Augsburg and Nuremberg.[22] Applying Rublack's taxonomy of anticlericalism to these texts shows that Anonyma's critique of clergy and members of religious orders is typical of the anti-clerical and anti-monastic polemic of the time: as will be seen, her letters include examples of all but one of the categories which Rublack identifies.[23]

[20] Michael D. Bailey, 'Superstition and Dissimulation: Discerning False Religion in the Fifteenth Century', in Miriam Eliav-Feldon and Tamar Herzig, eds, *Dissimulation and Deceit in Early Modern Europe* (Basingstoke, 2015), 9–26, at 10.

[21] For Augsburg at this period, see, for instance, Michele Zelinsky Hanson, *Religious Identity in an Early Reformation Community: Augsburg, 1517–1555*, Studies in Central European Histories 45 (Leiden, 2009); for Nuremberg, see Gottfried Seebass, 'The Importance of the Imperial City of Nuremberg in the Reformation', in James Kirk, ed., *Humanism and Reform: The Church in Europe, England, and Scotland, 1400–1643*, SCH Sub 8 (Oxford, 1991), 113–27.

[22] See Kommer, *Reformatorische Flugschriften von Frauen*, 126–7. Compare also Ulrike Strasser, 'Brides of Christ, Daughters of Men: Nuremberg Poor Clares in Defense of Their Identity (1524–1529)', *Magistra: A Journal of Women's Spirituality in History* 1 (1995), 193–248; Marjorie Elizabeth Plummer, *Stripping the Veil: Convent Reform, Protestant Nuns, and Female Devotional Life in Sixteenth Century Germany* (Oxford, 2022), esp. 19–29.

[23] Anonyma does not offer any critique which fits closely with Rublack's first category, that of the impoverished priest at the bottom of the ecclesiastical hierarchy who, as a 'poor ass', distorts religious truth, and whose attention is focused on securing his own comfort through exploitation of the congregation. This is perhaps because her primary critique of the clergy focuses on bishops. For this category, see Rublack, 'Anticlericalism in German Reformation Pamphlets', 468–9.

Moreover, although Rublack only explicitly associates the second of his nine categories of anti-clerical discourse with hypocrisy, reading his taxonomy through the lens of Anonyma's letters reveals that all nine of the categories he identifies represent a mismatch between the expectations of clergy and the reality of their lives, and thus equate to accusations of hypocrisy. For Anonyma, at least, concerns about clerical hypocrisy were a fundamental driver of her anti-clerical polemic.

Dorothee Kommer is one of the few scholars to have explored Anonyma's letters in any depth, as part of her study of German Reformation pamphlets authored by women.[24] She remarks that Anonyma's criticism of her sister, to whom the letters are ostensibly addressed, is 'inseparably connected to her critique of convent life and of the religious in general, extending to general anticlericalism.'[25] Anonyma expresses this critique through explicit and implied charges of hypocrisy. As already noted, one of the key points of criticism raised by Anonyma in both her letters is the disconnect between the outward trappings of faith and inner spiritual reality. However, although this theme is named in the title of the earlier letter, it is much more developed in the longer second letter, which therefore forms the basis of the discussion that follows. In it, Anonyma argues for the importance of true faith held with integrity. Christ's miracles, she says, were done 'to increase [his disciples'] faith in him, and that was necessary because God really hated the hypocrites [*dañ got hat die gleyßner gantz seer gehasszt*].'[26] She cites the parable of the Pharisee and the tax collector as a key example of the problematic incongruence between outward faith and inner reality:

> Look what we find in Luke 18 about the hypocrite [*gleyßner*] who said in the temple: 'Lord I thank you that I am not like other people; I give a tenth of my income; I fast two days every week; I do not commit adultery. In particular I am not like this man, who sins publicly &c.' This hypocrite was still unclean when he went home. The poor public sinner, who sat slumped over in his regret, and said, 'God have mercy on

[24] Kommer, *Reformatorische Flugschriften von Frauen*, 115–44. The pamphlets are considered more briefly by Chrisman, *Conflicting Visions of Reform*, 140, 144, 145–8.
[25] Ibid. 136.
[26] Anonyma, *Ain Sendbrieff von Ainer erbern frawen im Eelichen stand / an ain Klosterfrawen / gethon über berümung ettlicher haylicher geschrifft in Sermon begriffen / so die Klosterfrauw verbrent / und darauf ein lange vngesaltzne geschrifft zu ursach erzelt hat &c.* (Augsburg, 1524) [hereafter: *Ain Sendbrieff*], fol. C^{r}.

> me, a poor sinner', went home whole: the one who had confessed himself to be sick and was healed. The other called himself healthy but was left without any medicine.[27]

This sets the tone for Anonyma's critique. In an approach which Martin Jung has described as typical of the writing style of pamphlet authors who did not have a university education, Anonyma cites a plethora of biblical texts to stress the importance of ensuring coherence between the internal and the external, using them to highlight her criticisms of hypocritical behaviour.[28]

Anonyma accuses clergy (particularly bishops) and religious not only of being hypocrites, but of ministering 'for the sake of financial gain'.[29] This combined criticism fits with Rublack's second category of anti-clerical discourse, which characterizes the priest as a trader in masses (*Messkrämer*) and 'from a scriptural viewpoint, a hypocrite[e] (*Gleisner*), whose pretence at piety cannot conceal his concern to secure and expand his living.'[30] Anonyma is particularly concerned about those whose learning does not lead them to the truth:

> What does Paul say to Timothy, in the second epistle, chapter 3? They look as though they have a spiritual life and do nothing but learn, but they never come to the truth; rather, they oppose the truth &c.[31]

This echoes Rublack's third category: clergy who are ignorant of Scripture, so that their sermons and teaching represent, at best, the blind leading the blind and, at worse, make them preachers of lies (*Lugenprediger*).[32] Anonyma also finds that most priests have either

[27] *Ain Sendbrieff*, fol. C[r], referring to Luke 18: 10–14.

[28] Martin Jung identifies the 'Häufung von Bibelzitaten' ('the amassing of biblical quotations') as characteristic of such pamphlets: Martin Jung, 'Katharina Zell geb. Schütz (1497/98–1562). Eine "Laientheologin" der Reformationszeit?', *Zeitschrift für Kirchengeschichte* 107 (1996), 145–78 [repr. in idem, *Nonnen, Prophetinnen, Kirchenmütter. Kirchen- und frömmigkeitsgeschichtliche Studien zu Frauen der Reformationszeit* (Leipzig, 2002), 121–68].

[29] *Ain Sendbrieff*, fol. Aiii[v].

[30] Rublack, 'Anticlericalism in German Reformation Pamphlets', 469–71.

[31] *Ain Sendbrieff*, fol. [Biv][v], referring to 2 Tim. 3: 1–8. See also Anonyma, *Ayn bezwungene antwort vber eynen Sendbrieff eyner Closter nunnen, an jr schwester im̄ Eelichē standt zugeschickt / darin̄ sy vil vergebner vnnützer sorg fürhelt vn̄ jre gaistliche weißhait vn̄ gemalte hayligkait zů menschlichem gesicht auffmutzet* (Nuremberg, 1524) [hereafter: *Ayn bezwungene antwort*], fol. Cii[r].

[32] Rublack, 'Anticlericalism in German Reformation Pamphlets', 471–2.

'fat bellies or fat purses',[33] a concern that coheres with both Rublack's fourth category, the critique of clergy as greedy and gluttonous folk (*Fressvolk*), for whom 'their belly is their God' (*Bauchprediger*);[34] and with his fifth, with clergy as 'avaricious bucks' or 'fishers of pennies (*Pfennigfischer*)', rather than fishers of souls.[35] Rublack sees this critique of clerical greed and gluttony as associated with a view of the cleric as sexually incontinent, a '"mating horse" (*brünstiges Pferd*) or "lewd bull" (*geiler Stier*)',[36] but this association is not present in Anonyma's text.

Anonyma warns of the deceptiveness of clergy, in language which is consistent with Rublack's sixth category, which castigates priests as robbers or thieves, characterized by the biblical image of 'the wolf in sheep's clothing' or even as the 'murderer of souls (*Seelmörder*)'.[37] Again, Anonyma articulates the less extreme criticism:

> What does it say in Matthew 7? Be cautious: beware of those who come to you in sheep's clothing, when inwardly they are ravening wolves. From their fruits you should recognise them &c.[38]

She is also concerned about clergy whose primary interest is in emphasizing and buttressing their own position, comparing them to the Levites:

> What does Matthew 23 say? They do all their works before the Levites so that they will be seen by others; they make the fringes on their clothes especially long and want people to call them Rabbi. That is, those who are carved from prelatical wood want to be called honourable sir, or honourable lady.[39]

This should be a concern not only for prelates and clergy, but for all Christians, as Anonyma makes clear through an appeal to Luke 22 and the teaching of Christ that, 'Whoever amongst you will be the

[33] *Ain Sendbrieff*, fol. Diii^{v}: 'ich sieh wol das sy der meertayl fayßt seyndt / Es sey am bauch oder am beüttel'.
[34] Rublack, 'Anticlericalism in German Reformation Pamphlets', 472–3.
[35] Ibid. 473–4.
[36] Ibid. 472.
[37] Ibid. 474–5.
[38] *Ain Sendbrieff*, fol. [Biv]^{v}, referring to Matt. 7: 15–16a. See also *Ayn bezwungene antwort*, fol. Cii^{r}.
[39] *Ain Sendbrieff*, fol. [Biv]^{v}, referring to Matt. 23: 5–7.

greatest, he should be a servant to all the others.'[40] Nonetheless, there are parallels here to Rublack's seventh category, the ecclesiastical lord or *Kirchenjunker* as a tyrant or 'a devilish lord (*teuflischer Herr*)', implying 'a perverted usurpation of God's lordship, and a life style directly contrary to Christ's commandment'.[41] Here too, Anonyma's language is not as extreme as that found in some of the pamphlets discussed by Rublack, but the content of the critique is very similar.

Rublack's eighth category, which he sees as 'the most severe comparison', is the association of the clergy with the Pharisees.[42] This is a central theme for Anonyma. In her view, the Gospel of Matthew gives clear instructions as to how those who are truly holy should conduct their lives, as she draws out in both letters. Referring to Matthew 23, she cites Christ's criticisms of the Pharisees:

> What did Christ the Lord say in Matthew chapter 23: They will lay heavy burdens on people's shoulders and will not lift a little finger to help them? … Read the eight woes [*die acht wee*] where he reproaches them and explains the meaning of Moses' seat in which they are supposed to be sitting.[43]

The 'eight woes' – seven in modern translations – refer to the repeated words of Jesus, 'Woe to you, scribes and Pharisees, hypocrites! …' (Matthew 23: 13–36) in his condemnation of the outward holiness but internal depravity of the Pharisees. It is apparent that, for Anonyma, the comparison between the clergy and the Pharisees is integrally bound up with the hypocrisy of the Pharisees, and by extension, that of the clergy.

For Anonyma, the need for the outward practices of faith to be congruent with inner spiritual reality relates also to the necessity of distinguishing between true and false prophets. She refers indirectly to the danger of false prophets, exhorting her sister, or her readers, to

[40] *Ain Sendbrieff*, fol. [Biv]^{v}, referring to Luke 22: 24–6. See also *Ayn bezwungene antwort*, fol. Cii^{v}. Biblical texts in Anonyma's letters are translated from her own words, since she is not using an identifiable biblical translation. For a detailed discussion of the German Bible translations available to Anonyma and their relation to her biblical quotations, see also Methuen, 'dan got vnd die haylig geschrifft'.

[41] Rublack, 'Anticlericalism in German Reformation Pamphlets', 476–7.

[42] Ibid. 477.

[43] *Ain Sendbrieff*, fol. Aiii^{v}, referring to Matt. 23: 4 and 13–36. See also *Ayn bezwungene antwort*, fol. Cii^{r}.

'Read John's first canonical epistle, chapter 4, where he says, first test the spirit to see whether it is from God, etc.'[44] She is probably thinking here of 1 John 4: 1, 'Beloved, do not believe every spirit, but test the spirits to see whether they are from God; for many false prophets have gone out into the world' [NRSV]. This resonates with Rublack's ninth and final category of anti-clerical discourse, which sees the clergy as false prophets, sometimes extended to present them as '"Baal's prophets," the apostles and disciples of the Antichrist'.[45] Again, Anonyma articulates the milder form. Elsewhere she insists that she herself is able to test the spirits, arguing:

> If a prophet stands up and speaks inspired by his own dreams or good ideas, and does not speak my word, then put him to death or stone him. Do you think that we are bound to Luther or others like him? No! We are bound to the word, and not to human laws and teachings.[46]

Human ideas, affirms Anonyma, 'are not certain, but God's Scripture is certain.'[47] It is following Scripture that leads to true faith, and to love of neighbour: 'offering help in [Christ's] name to our neighbours, the most needy and the least amongst us' is 'what to do if with God's help you want to do good, and please God'.[48] It is this that makes it possible to avoid hypocrisy.

It is apparent from this that Anonyma's critique of the clergy is entirely coherent with anti-clerical discourse expressed in the other German pamphlets of this period studied by Rublack. However, it is also apparent that Anonyma's critique of the clergy is expressed in terms of concerns about their hypocrisy. This emerges also in her discussion of Christ's instructions about prayer. In the shorter exhortation in *Ayn bezwungene antwort*, she focuses on the way that hypocrites pray:

> When you pray you should not behave like the hypocrites [*die heüchler*] who stand there and pray in the schools of the congregations and on the corners of the streets so that they will be seen and heard by the people.[49]

[44] *Ain Sendbrieff*, fol. Aii^{v}; compare also ibid. fols Biii^{r-v}.
[45] Rublack, 'Anticlericalism in German Reformation Pamphlets', 478.
[46] *Ain Sendbrieff*, fol. B^{v}. See also *Ayn bezwungene antwort*, fol. Aiii^{v}.
[47] *Ain Sendbrieff*, fol. B^{v}.
[48] *Ain Sendbrieff*, fol. C^{r}.
[49] *Ayn bezwungene antwort*, fol. Bii^{v}, referring to Matt. 6: 5.

This passage leads into a summary of the Lord's Prayer.[50] In *Ain Sendbrieff*, she cites Matthew 6 more extensively, emphasizing even more strongly the instruction to pray privately and not hypocritically:

> He says, do not give alms before other people, and never do so because you want to be seen; otherwise you will have no reward from your father. Do not make a big show of yourselves, or blow your own trumpets, like the hypocrites [*die heüchler*] in the streets. When you want to pray, do not do so publicly in the synagogues, that is, in the congregations, or on the street corners or in the streets, which might be seen by other people as hypocritical [*gleyßnerisch*]. Rather go secretly into your chamber and shut the door and pray to your father in private.[51]

Anonyma reiterates (with a sideswipe at members of religious orders) that these instructions do not pertain only to the liturgy, but are also about ensuring that a Christian's whole life is lived without hypocrisy:

> This is not only about Maundy Thursday ... when the stinking feet of the monks and nuns are washed. You should do these things to honour God and help your neighbours throughout the year, at all times, not for appearances or profit, and with no outward hypocrisy [*on allen scheyn vnnd gbreng thůn / mit kainem eusserlichen anzaygend gleyßnerey*].[52]

Anonyma's critique of the clergy is, therefore, fundamentally a critique of their hypocritical behaviour.

Anonyma's critique of hypocrisy is aimed not only at various groups within the church, but at the traditions of the church per se. She compares the teaching of the gospel with the teachings of the church as defined in the decretals:

> The gospel reveals only poverty, patience, humility and physical work, along with a strong faith and trust in Christ. In contrast, the decretals show great pomp and much arrogance, greed and laziness, income from many benefices and a luxurious life. This is a new law on top of the other law, a burden for Christ's flock. It has many human laws and teachings, none of which are founded in God's Scripture.[53]

[50] *Ayn bezwungene antwort*, fols Bii^{v}–C^{r}.
[51] *Ain Sendbrieff*, fol. C^{r}, referring to Matt. 6: 1–8.
[52] *Ain Sendbrieff*, fol. [Biv]^{v}.
[53] *Ain Sendbrieff*, fols [Aiv]^{v}–B^{r}, referring to Matt. 15: 8–9, 13. Decretals are papal decrees concerning points of doctrine or (more often) canon law.

Similarly, the church fathers have also 'darkened and defiled the Holy Scripture with their human fabrications and turns of phrase.'[54] Indeed, down the centuries, the teachers of the church, she argues, 'have written so much that disagreed with the evangelists and the twelve apostles.'[55] For Anonyma, Scripture must be the only measure of true faith: 'If one of today's teachers wants to teach us something different, whether it is Luther or Cunz or B[r]enz, or if they have learned something different than the pure unadulterated word of God, why would we want to follow him?'[56] She relates this point to the necessity of distinguishing between true and false prophets and the importance of following divine, rather than human, teaching.[57] The very tradition of the church itself, therefore, is in Anonyma's view vulnerable to the criticism of hypocrisy due to the failure of the tradition and its teachers to respect the teachings of Scripture.

Within the church and its structures, Anonyma views certain groups of people as more vulnerable to the charge of hypocrisy. Priests are often hypocrites: her sister has argued that 'they have always been God's anointed,' a claim about which Anonyma is deeply sceptical:

> I do not enquire whether they have been anointed, or just smeared with oil. I can see that most of them have fat bellies or fat purses. But that blessedness can be attained through them is has long been very doubtful, if it is possible at all, on account of what I have heard about their sermons. For the Holy Scripture calls no-one a priest unless they reveal the word of God according to the pure text.[58]

Similarly, Anonyma finds that the bishops have failed in their responsibility to teach and preach the gospel: 'amongst all those posturing mitred bishops robed in purple, I know none who teaches me well. I have never heard one preach.'[59] The hypocritical behaviour of the bishops, however, goes far beyond this failure to preach and teach

[54] *Ain Sendbrieff*, fol. B^{r}.
[55] *Ain Sendbrieff*, fol. B^{r}.
[56] *Ain Sendbrieff*, fol. B^{v}, referring to Deut. 13: 1–5a. See also *Ayn bezwungene antwort*, fol. Aiii^{v}.
[57] See the passage cited above, at pp. 158–9.
[58] *Ain Sendbrieff*, fol. Dii^{v}.
[59] *Ain Sendbrieff*, fol. [Aiv]^{v}.

the gospel to encompass their luxurious lifestyles and their encouragement of hypocritical behaviour amongst the clergy:

> Did [Christ] say to the apostles, stay at home, keep lavish courts, play cards, live a good life, make sure that all your treasure chests and coffers are full, burden your poor people with many tolls and taxes, teach sinfulness by your example, ride through the town with great pomp, rape the virgins, bully the wives? Did he say, cheat the world with your pretentious power, tear people's consciences apart and make them afraid? Did he say, tell them about the strict law of Moses and say nothing about Christ's mercy or how he delivers them from sin through his death? Did he say, invent many things about purgatory and offer high praise for indulgences, which are of this world, and for a church that behaves as if it were a royal court? Did he say, be sure to forbid the parsons to have wives, but allow them to live in sin with women, and charge them a hefty fine when they do?[60]

Although she also criticizes the clergy more widely, it appears that Anonyma is particularly concerned about the behaviour of bishops.

The final group she regards as hypocritical is made up of convent women and female religious, including her own sister. Anonyma provides a swingeing and strikingly well-informed critique of the role of worldly values and status within convents:

> Now I know that you convent women would like to pretend that this is not your problem, as if you believed yourselves not to be in the world any more. But this will not help you. You believe that as long as you are enclosed within the convent walls you lack no aspect of holiness, but your bliss will deceive you. Amongst you there are still many ugly aspects of the world. For instance, one sister asserts that she was born of nobler parents than the others, and she is given an office and more freedom.[61]

Anonyma's critique of female religious offers a strong reminder that late medieval and early modern anticlericalism was directed against all members of the religious hierarchy, including members of religious orders. Reflecting on the nativity, she comments that Christ was not visited in the crib by 'Herod, Annas, Caiaphas, bishops or cardinals, monks or parsons [*Bischoff / oder Cardinaͤl / Münchē / oder*

60 *Ain Sendbrieff*, fol. Aiii^{r}.
61 *Ain Sendbrieff*, fol. Cii^{v}.

Nolhart],' but by the shepherds: here she clearly associates both clergy and religious with Caiaphas and Annas, the high priests, and the shepherds with the laypeople of her own day.[62] Geoffrey Dipple has chosen for this reason to refer to 'antifraternalism' as well as 'anti-clericalism'.[63] However, Anonyma's letters demonstrate that such criticisms were not only directed against friars, but also against monks and nuns.[64]

In sum, Anonyma believes that those whose hypocritical behaviour she criticizes have abandoned the truth in ways that are similar to those against which the apostle Paul warned:

> Show me also Paul's first letter to Timothy, chapter 4. There he says that many people abandon the faith and follow the spirit of error and the teachings of the devil. Their consciences are wounded; they refuse to marry and forbid the food that God created to be enjoyed by believers at all times, giving thanks for his grace &c.[65]

However, Paul also offers guidance as to the behaviour expected of Christians:

> Look at what Paul says to the Romans in chapter 12: dear brothers, be diligent, patient, mild, gentle, and lead a good life setting a good

[62] *Ayn bezwungene antwort*, fol. Aiii^{v}.

[63] As in the title of his PhD thesis: Geoffrey L. Dipple, '"Woe unto you, Stomachpreachers, Cheesbeggars and Hypocrites": Antifraternalism and Reformation Anticlericalism' (PhD thesis, Queens University, Kingston, 1991), published as idem, *Antifraternalism and Anticlericalism in the German Reformation: Johann Eberlin von Günzburg and the Campaign against the Friars* (Aldershot, 1996).

[64] Hans-Jürgen Goertz, by contrast, remarks that anti-clerical criticism might be directed towards 'the pope, the bishops, canons and prelates (the higher clergy) or secular priests, nuns and monks (the "ordinary priesthood"),' thus counting members of religious orders as clergy: see Hans-Jürgen Goertz, '"What a tangled and tenuous mess the clergy is!": Clerical Anticlericalism in the Reformation Period', in Dykema and Oberman, eds, *Anticlericalism in Late Medieval and Early Modern Europe*, 499–519, at 503. I have preferred, in this article, to distinguish between clergy and religious by referring to anti-monasticism. In his critique of monastic vows, Martin Luther sometimes refers in German to 'Klosterleute' or 'Klostervolk' (which in *LW* is generally rendered 'monks'); thus 'Bapst, Bischoff, Priester, Kloster volck' becomes 'pope, bishop, priests, and monks': *WA* 6: 407; *LW* 44: 127. Luther's works are cited according to the *Weimarer Ausgabe* (*WA*); English translations from *Luther's Works* (*LW*) are given where they exist.

[65] *Ain Sendbrieff*, fol. Aiii^{v}, referring to 1 Tim. 4: 1–3 (the text here actually specifies 2 Tim., but the passage is clearly from 1 Tim.). See also *Ayn bezwungene antwort*, fol. B^{v} (here the reference is to 'Paul. zů Timo. iiii,' not specifying which letter to Timothy is meant, but the text again clearly alludes to 1 Tim.).

example, not only before God but also especially before other people. You should not compare yourself with this world, &c.[66]

For Anonyma, Scripture provides the measure by which all believers, including clergy, religious and laypeople, should seek to live.

Anonyma's critiques of the hypocrisy of the clergy and members of religious orders are explicitly rooted in Scripture, and both letters are replete with scriptural references and allusions.[67] As observed above, Jung sees the proliferation of scriptural citations as characteristic of lay pamphlets in this period. However, Anonyma's choice of Scripture is distinctive. Comparing Reformation pamphlets authored by women, Kommer finds that although some of the texts cited by Anonyma are also referred to in other pamphlets, a good number are used only by Anonyma in her letters.[68] These include Anonyma's use of Deuteronomy 13,[69] Matthew 6: 1–8[70] and Matthew 23: 5–7, 8–9, as well as her description of Matthew 23: 13–36 as the 'eight woes',[71] all of which are texts which Anonyma uses to highlight the hypocritical behaviour of clergy and religious. Moreover, Kommer's comparative table shows that Anonyma's reference to the parable of the Pharisee (or, to use her language, hypocrite) and the publican (Luke 18: 10–14) is also unique in this sample of texts.[72] It is striking that Luke 18, Matthew 6 and Matthew 23 are the three key texts which Nigri and Tsentourou found to underlie biblically-founded accusations of hypocrisy.[73] The extent of Anonyma's references to Luke 22: 24–6, Romans 12 and 2 Timothy 3: 2–8 is also unusual, with other authors discussed by Kommer referring only to Luke 22: 24, to single verses in Romans 12, and to 2 Timothy 3: 1–5 or 3: 5.[74] In comparison, texts such as Matthew 7: 15–16a, Matthew 15:

[66] *Ain Sendbrieff*, fol. Aiii^{v}, referring to Rom. 12: 11–12, 2.

[67] See also Methuen, 'dañ got vnd die haylig geschrifft'.

[68] Kommer, *Reformatorische Flugschriften von Frauen*, 122–3, and compare also her comparative index of scriptural texts used or referred to in the pamphlets she considers: ibid. 378–420.

[69] Ibid. 123 and compare 379.

[70] Ibid. 123 and compare 392.

[71] Ibid. 123. Kommer notes that specific verses in this passage are referred to by other authors, including Katharina Schütz Zell and Ursula Weyda, and in other anonymous texts: see ibid. 397.

[72] Ibid. 401.

[73] Nigri and Tsentourou, 'Introduction', 4–5, and see above, p. 153.

[74] Kommer, *Reformatorische Flugschriften von Frauen*, 401 (Luke 22), 410–11 (Rom. 12), 417 (2 Tim. 3).

8–9, 13, Matthew 23: 4, 1 Timothy 4: 1–3 and 1 John 4: 1 are also referred to by other female authors, such as Argula von Grumbach, Ursula von Münsterberg, Katharina Schütz Zell and Ursula Weyda, and in other anonymous pamphlets with apparently female authors.[75] Anonyma's strong emphasis on the hypocrisy of members of the clergy and religious orders thus emerges as potentially distinctive, even though, as the comparison with Rublack's categories has shown, her anti-clerical and anti-monastic critique can be seen as typifying that found in other lay writings of the period.

From this exploration of Anonyma's argument, a question arises: was her appeal to hypocrisy as an (anti-clerical) lens through which to assess the church, its clergy and its religious more typical of her time than the literature on anticlericalism might suggest? The final part of this article will consider references to hypocrisy by Luther and Karlstadt in their early (mostly German) works and (in Luther's case) German sermons. This exploration suggests that, while Karlstadt rarely made explicit accusations of hypocrisy, his use of the term in his polemical works was often anti-clerical or anti-papal in tone, but he also applied the concept of hypocrisy more widely, criticizing hypocritical behaviour as in opposition to what he regarded as the 'supreme virtue' of *Gelassenheit*, not always using the term hypocrite.[76] Luther uses the term hypocrite rather more frequently: while he too accused clergy and religious of hypocrisy, his main focus is also more general, using the accusation of hypocrisy to call out all aspects of false religion. Thus neither Karlstadt nor Luther use the term exclusively to buttress their criticism of the clergy, although that use is more prominent in polemical works, especially those by Karlstadt.[77]

[75] Ibid. 393 (Matt. 7), 395 (Matt. 15), 397 (Matt. 23), 417 (1 Tim. 4), 419 (1 John 4).

[76] The term *Gelassenheit* derives from the German mystical tradition, where it means a surrender of the self and union with God; it is notoriously difficult to translate into English. On the English translation of *Gelassenheit*, see Ulrich Bubenheimer, 'Gelassenheit und Ablösung', *Zeitschrift für Kirchengeschichte* 92 (1981), 250–68; ET: idem, '*Gelassenheit* and Detachment: A psycho-historical Study of Andreas Bodenstein of Karlstadt – and his Conflict with Martin Luther', online at: <https://karlstadt-edition.org/wp-content/uploads/2020/12/Gelassenheit-and-Detachment.pdf>, note 1, accessed 21 December 2023. On Karlstadt's understanding of *Gelassenheit*, see Vincent Evener, 'Andreas Bodenstein von Karlstadt', in Ronald K. Rittgers and Vincent Evener, eds, *Protestants and Mysticism in Reformation Europe* (Leiden, 2019), 78–99, esp. 79, 82–6, 87–8, 91.

[77] I would like to express my deep thanks to Stefania Salvadori for her invaluable comments on the Karlstadt section of this article.

Karlstadt seldom uses the term 'hypocrite' (*gleyßner/gleszner*, *heuchler*), and although many of his early uses of it are associated with polemic against the papacy or the clergy, he also sees hypocritical behaviour as a more general issue.[78] Writing in 1520 on 'the supreme virtue of *Gelassenheit*', he asserts that Christ is found in the temple of the believer who is 'serene' or 'detached' (*gelassen mensch*) and not with 'the pharisees and hypocrites, the pope and his coxcombs' (*die Phariseyer und gleyßner / der Babst und seyn Gecken*).[79] Hypocrisy here emerges as the counterpoint to *Gelassenheit* which is not specific to clergy and religious. At the same time, Karlstadt describes the high priests Annas and Caiaphas as 'hypocrites, who do not pay much attention to what gives [God's] law and word its content and makes it useful,' associating them also with 'the pope and all the cardinals and bishops' (*der Bapst etzliche Cardinalen und etzliche Bischoffen*).[80] Later that year, in *Welche Bücher biblisch sind* (*Which Books are Biblical*; 1520), he accuses the pope of 'letting his hellish decretals be called canons', although (in Karlstadt's view) these are 'not the rules of the Christian faithful but of the hypocrites.'[81] Karlstadt expounds on the hypocrisy of the pope at some length in *Von Päpstlicher Heiligkeit* (*On Papal Holiness*; 1520): the words of 'the pope and his hypocrites' (*des Bapsts und seiner heuchler*) have failed to recognize that 'scripture is more holy than any unliving

[78] This has been ascertained by a search on 'gle*' in the online edition of the *Kritische Gesamtausgabe der Schriften und Briefe Andreas Bodensteins von Karlstadt* [hereafter: KGK], which currently extends to December 1521: see KGK, online at: <http://dev2.hab.de/apps/edoc/view.html?id=kgk_edition>, accessed 21 December 2023. I am grateful to Stefania Salvadori for giving me early access to the recently published KGK 6. References to the edition are given in the form: KGK (no. [letter number]) [volume number]: [page number].[line number(s)]. A link to the online text is given where one exists.

[79] Andreas Bodenstein von Karlstadt, *Missive von der allerhöchsten Tugend Gelassenheit*, fol. B2r, KGK (no. 166) 3: 404.8–13, online at: <http://dev2.hab.de/apps/edoc/view.html?id=kgk_166_transcript>, accessed 21 December 2023.

[80] Ibid., fol. A2r, KGK (no. 166) 3: 392.17–19.

[81] Karlstadt says of the pope that 'er sein hellische Decretalen lasset Canones nennen / dan sie seint nicht regel der christglaubigen / sunder der gleyszner': Andreas Bodenstein von Karlstadt, *Welche Bücher biblisch sind*, fol. C4r, KGK (no. 171), 3: 546.17–19, online at: <http://dev2.hab.de/apps/edoc/view.html?id=kgk_171_transcript>, accessed 21 December 2023. There is a striking parallel here to Anonyma's strictures on the decretals (see text at note 52 above). However, Luther also comments that 'papal decretals occasionally are erroneous and militate against Holy Scriptures and Christian love': Martin Luther, 'Acta Augustana' ['Proceedings at Augsburg'], *WA* 2: 10; *LW* 31: 265.

temple, chalice, altar, monstrance and so on,' have equated papal law with divine law, and have denied imperial dignity.[82] In *Verba Dei* (1520), Johannes Eck, Karlstadt's opponent at the 1519 Leipzig Disputation, is the *hypocrita*, 'feigning theological discourse to the disciples in God's temple' (*simulans theologicum ad discipulos in dei templo sermonem*).[83] More expansively, in the full title of *Von Gelübden Unterrichtung* (*Teachings on Monastic Vows*; 1521), a treatise of which, Kommer argues, Anonyma was aware,[84] he explains that he will show the 'hypocritical life' (*gleyßneriſch leebenn*) of 'priests, monks and nuns' (*Pfaffen / Monchē / vn̄ Nonnen*).[85] Here he expresses many criticisms of the religious life similar to those offered by Anonyma, although he does not explicitly mention hypocrisy until the end of the treatise, where he draws on Matthew 6 to emphasize the importance of praying privately rather than 'openly like the hypocrites', and criticizes the 'long prayers of the hypocrites', identifying those hypocrites with 'vicars, monks and nuns.'[86] Their behaviour is to be contrasted with God's desire for 'mercy not sacrifice', which Karlstadt, referring to Hosea 6: 6 and Matthew 9: 13, interprets to mean 'mercy not vows'.[87] Similarly, in *Das Reich Gottes leidet Gewalt* (*The Kingdom of God suffers Violence*; 1521), Karlstadt accuses the 'Pharisees, hypocrites and scribes' (or, elsewhere, the 'hypocrites, scribes and pharisees') of blocking the way to God's word and of being 'born to crush and to rob the kingdom of God'; here too he identifies them with 'priests and monks' (*Pfaffen / und*

[82] Andreas Bodenstein von Karlstadt, *Von Bepstlicher heylickeit*, quotations at fols C3^{r}, E4^{v}; KGK (no. 167) 3: esp. 430–1, 442–5, 455, 465; quotations at 443.23 and 463.3–7, online at: <http://dev2.hab.de/apps/edoc/view.html?id=kgk_167_transcript>, accessed 21 December 2023.

[83] Andreas Bodenstein von Karlstadt, *Verba Dei*, fols C3^{r}, G1^{r}; KGK (no. 146) 3: 50.14–15; 93.25–8, online at: <http://dev2.hab.de/apps/edoc/view.html?id=kgk_146_transcript>, accessed 21 December 2023.

[84] Kommer, *Reformatorische Flugschriften von Frauen*, 129.

[85] Andreas Bodenstein von Karlstadt, *Von Gelübden Unterrichtung*, title page; KGK (no. 203) 4: 509–10, online at: <http://dev2.hab.de/apps/edoc/view.html?id=kgk_203_transcript>, accessed 21 December 2023.

[86] Ibid., fols F1^{r}, F3^{v}; KGK (no. 203) 4: 566.18–19; 572.10–13.

[87] Ibid., fols G3^{v}–G4^{r}; KGK (no. 203) 4: 581.5–12. He argues similarly in his Latin treatise *Super coelibatu, monachatu et viduitate axiomata*, KGK (no. 190) 4: 191–255, online at: <http://dev2.hab.de/apps/edoc/view.html?id=kgk_190_transcript>, accessed 21 December 2023. Compare also Salvadori, 'Frauen und Bibel bei Andreas Bodenstein von Karlstadt', 163 nn. 31 and 32.

Monnichen).[88] He also, at times, associates hypocrisy with criticism of the clergy by implication, for instance when he criticizes 'the apparently spiritual people' (*die vermeyndte geistliche leüte*) who have made of the Lord's Supper 'a sacrifice or mass' and sold it for money, a crticism which, by its nature, must refer primarily to clergy.[89]

However, Karlstadt also refers to hypocrites in a more general way. It has already been observed that he understands hypocrisy as the counterpoint to *Gelassenheit*, and this emerges as a fundamental understanding of hypocrisy in Karlstadt's theology. In her introduction to *Von Mannigfaltigkeit des einfältigen, einigen Willens Gottes. Was Sünde sei* (*Of the Multiplicity of the Simple, unified Will of God. And what Sin is*; 1523), Stefania Salvadori observes that Karlstadt contrasts tax collectors and prostitutes, who have been able to recognize and confess their sin, with 'hypocrites and monks', who – convinced of their piety and good works – are much slower to recognize their sin.[90] However, Karlstadt is also aware that it is not only monks and clergy who are hypocrites. Vincent Evener observes that 'Karlstadt equates "hypocrisy" with *Annehmlichkeit* (finding something pleasing; here, the self), which claims good for the self in work or suffering and flows from the assertion of human ego.'[91] Referring in 1519 to Job (presumably 13: 16), he emphasizes that 'no hypocrite persists before God' (*kein gleiszner bestet vor got*), because the hypocrite is unable to confess their sins: a true believer can say 'I confess my impurity; that is my purity' (*Ich erken mein unreinigkeit / das ist mein reinigkeit*).[92] In 1521, he uses the same verse from Job to define as hypocrites all those who seek to use the

[88] Andreas Bodenstein von Karlstadt, *Das Reich Gottes leidet Gewalt*, fols B4^{v}–C1^{r}, C2^{r}; KGK (no. 191) 4: 284.11–18; 287.14–18, online at: <http://dev2.hab.de/apps/edoc/view.html?id=kgk_191_transcript>, accessed 21 December 2023.

[89] Andrews Bodenstein von Karlstadt, *Ob man mit heyliger schrifft erweysen müge / das Christus mit leyb / blůt vnd sele / im Sacrament sey* (Basel, 1524), fol. B^{r}.

[90] Stefania Salvadori, 'Einleitung', KGK (no. 239) 6: 13–26, at 24, referring to Karlstadt's argument in *Von Mannigfaltigkeit des einfältigen, einigen Willens Gottes. Was Sünde sei*, fols G1$^{r–v}$; KGK (no. 239) 6: 69.11–70.11.

[91] Evener, 'Andreas Bodenstein von Karlstadt', 88.

[92] Andreas Bodenstein von Karlstadt, *Auszlegung unnd Leuterung etzlicher heyligenn geschrifften … kurtzlich berurth und angetzeichent in den figurn und schrifften der wagen*, fol. C4^{r}; KGK (no. 124) 2: 238.11–18, quotations at lines 14 and 17–18, online at: <http://dev2.hab.de/apps/edoc/view.html?id=kgk_124_transcript>, accessed 21 December 2023. Job 13: 16 reads in the Vulgate: 'Et ipse erit salvator meus: non enim veniet in conspectu ejus omnis hypocrita' (AV: 'He also shall be my salvation: for an hypocrite shall not come before him').

sacraments, other forms of piety and good works to show themselves worthy: 'All those who come with works and piety are hypocrites' (*Gleyszner seyndt alle und jede / so mit wercken und frumekeit kummen*).[93] Similarly, when condemning indulgences, Karlstadt applies Christ's criticism of the hypocrites for 'giving a tenth of your spices ... but neglecting the most important matters of the law' (Matthew 23: 23) to all penitents (*bußwircker*).[94] Indeed, as he makes clear in *De legis litera sive carne et spiritu enarratio* (*An account of the letter of the law, or flesh and spirit*; 1521), anyone who believes only according to the letter of the law 'resembles the Jews, Pharisees and hypocrites' (*Iudaeos, Pharisaeos, et Hypocritas*), who do not believe in God, but in human laws and regulations.[95]

Although for Karlstaadt, hypocritical behaviour is the counterpart to *Gelassenheit*, he does not always use the term hypocrisy when condemning the behaviour. In a discussion of the difference between *Gelassenheit* and *Ungelassenheit*, he associates the latter with those who 'surely recognise or even love the letter but do not know God' (*den bůchstaben erkent ainer wol / oder hat lust in ime / aber gott erkennet er nit*), precisely those whom elsewhere he has labelled hypocrites.[96] Similarly, in a consideration of the origins of 'unfaith' (*unglauben*), which, he says, 'comes from lies and from a liar', namely Satan, he presents faith as being 'of the light', and unfaith as 'of the darkness'.[97] Again, the behaviour he describes equates to that of those he has elsewhere termed hypocrites. Although he makes sparing use of the term hypocrisy outside his polemical writings, hypocrites and

[93] Andreas Bodenstein von Karlstadt, *Von den Empfängern, Zeichen und Zusagen des heiligen Sakraments des Fleischs und Bluts Christi*, fol. B3r; KGK (no. 183) 4: 110.10–14, online at: <http://dev2.hab.de/apps/edoc/view.html?id=kgk_183_transcript>, accessed 21 December 2021.

[94] Andreas Bodenstein von Karlstadt, *Von Vermögen des Ablass*, fol. B3v; KGK (no 161) 3: 229.14–18, online at: <http://dev2.hab.de/apps/edoc/view.html?id=kgk_161_transcript>, accessed 21 December 2021.

[95] Andreas Bodenstein von Karlstadt, *De Legis litera sive carne, et spiritu*, fol. A3r; KGK (no. 197) 4: 412.14–26, online at: <http://dev2.hab.de/apps/edoc/view.html?id=kgk_197_transcript>, accessed 21 December 2021.

[96] Andreas Bodenstein von Karlstadt, *Was gesagt ist: Sich gelassen. Was das Wort Gelassenheit bedeutet und wo es in Heiliger Schrift erscheint*, fols B1v–B2v; KGK (no. 241), 6: 113–15, esp. 113.23–114.3.

[97] Andreas Bodenstein von Karlstadt, *Wje sich der gelaub vnd vnglaub gegen dem liecht vnd finsternus, gegen warheit vn[d] lügen, gegen got vnd dem teufel halten* (Basel, 1524), fols [Civ]r, [Div]v.

their hypocritical behaviour provide an important counterpoint in Karlstadt's theology of *Gelassenheit.*

Like Karlstadt, Luther was deeply concerned with apparent holiness. His concern for the dangerous paradox posed by those who like to appear holy, although in reality they are not, was already articulated in his lectures on the Psalms (1513–15). He regards 'good counsel for an evil purpose' to be 'truly hypocrisy, sham, and deceit [*prope hypocrisis, simulatio et dolus*] – as when a person uses good means, for example, praying, fasting, and all that is good, to do something to the glow of the world or for gain or some other vanity.'[98] The 'nature of hypocrisy [*natura Hypocrisis*] … is a righteous performance in the eyes of men on earth, but is evil in the heart.'[99] In these early lectures, Luther associates hypocrisy with heresy, asserting: 'Such are all heretics, all pretenders who create an appearance in public to which their heart does not correspond.'[100] In his defence of the Ninety-Five Theses (1518), Luther draws on Matthew 6: 6 to identify 'the most arrogant hypocrites [*superbissimi hypocritae*]' as those who pervert true repentance 'by distorting their faces in fasts and by praying in streets and heralding their giving of alms.'[101] When penance is not sincere, it is to be understood 'as hypocritical [*hypocritarum est*] and not that which Christ teaches.'[102] Similarly, commenting on the Lord's Prayer for 'simple folk' in 1519, Luther sees the world as full of 'sinful ungodly spirits' (*frevelen ungottfürtigenn geyster*), whom he compares with 'the hypocrite in the gospel' (*dem glysner ym Evangelio*).[103] When Luther preached on the parable of the Pharisee (or hypocrite) and the tax collector in 1522, he criticized the Pharisee, who 'misleads the whole world with his glittering hypocritical life' (*verfurt die gantzen welt mit seinem scheinenden gleissenden leben*), to argue for the need to judge people 'with spiritual eyes' (*mit geistlichen augen*).[104] Here Luther's focus when condemning

[98] Martin Luther, *Dictata super Psalterium* [*First Lectures on the Psalms*], *WA* 3: 27; *LW* 10: 28.

[99] Ibid., *WA* 3: 323; *LW* 10: 268.

[100] Ibid.

[101] Martin Luther, *Resolutiones disputationum de indulgentiarum virtute* [*Explanations of the Ninety-Five Theses*], *WA* 1: 531; *LW* 31: 84.

[102] Ibid., *WA* 1: 531; *LW* 31: 85.

[103] Martin Luther, *Auslegung deutsch des Vater unnser fuer dye einfeltigen leyen* [*A German Interpretation of the Our Father for Simple Lay People*], *WA* 2: 80–130, at 90.

[104] Martin Luther, *Ein Sermon von dem Gleißner und offenbaren Sünder* [*A Sermon on the Hypocrite and Public Sinner*], *WA* 10/3: 293–303, esp. 302–3.

hypocrisy is not exclusively on the clergy and religious, but on all who offer a deceitful appearance of piety.

However, Luther does at times associate hypocrisy specifically with the spiritual estate. Thus, in *An den Christlichen Adel deutscher Nation von des christlichen Standes Besserung* (*To the Christian Nobility of the German Nation*; 1520), he condemns the distinction between the spiritual and temporal estates as 'pure invention' (*man hats erfunden*), and 'indeed a piece of deceit and hypocrisy' (*wilchs gar ein feyn Comment und gleyssen ist*).[105] In the Latin version of *Tractatus de libertate christiana* (*The Freedom of a Christian*; 1520), Luther argues:

> It does not help the soul if the body is adorned with the sacred robes of priests or dwells in sacred places or is occupied with sacred duties or prays, fasts, abstains from certain kinds of food, or does any work that can be done by the body and in the body. The righteousness and the freedom of the soul require something far different since the things which have been mentioned could be done by any wicked person. Such works produce nothing but hypocrites [*nec his studiis alii quam hypocritae evadant*]. On the other hand, it will not harm the soul if the body is clothed in secular dress, dwells in unconsecrated places, eats and drinks as others do, does not pray aloud, and neglects to do all the above-mentioned things which hypocrites can do.[106]

Moreover, Luther condemns many of the differences between Christian groups as intrinsically hypocritical: 'The world has been filled with fakes and hypocrites [*gleyssner und heuchler*] and with so many sects, orders, and divisions of the one people of Christ that almost every city is divided into ten parties or even more.' Such sects and individuals 'wrangle about their self-contrived ways and methods like fools and madmen'; the result is 'the destruction of Christian love and unity'.[107]

Again, in *Von den guten Werken* (*On Good Works*; also written in 1520), Luther identifies the 'holy hypocrites [*heilige gleissener*]' as those who 'consider themselves pious, and … let others regard

[105] Martin Luther, *An den Christlichen Adel deutscher Nation von des christlichen Standes Besserung* [*To the Christian Nobility of the German Nation*], *WA* 6: 407; *LW* 44: 127.

[106] Martin Luther, *Tractatus de libertate christiana* [*The Freedom of a Christian*], *WA* 7: 50 [Latin]; *LW* 31: 345. This passage is much shorter in the German edition, and although its import is the same, the German text does not mention hypocrites (*WA* 7: 21).

[107] Martin Luther, *Eyn sermon von dem newen Testament, das ist von der heyligen Messe* [*A Treatise on the New Testament, that is, the Holy Mass*], *WA* 6: 356; *LW* 35: 80.

them as such,'[108] expanding on this in the 1523 edition to explain that the honouring of God's name through worship with 'the lips, bending of the knees, kissing, and other postures,' if it is 'not done in the heart by faith, in confident trust in God's grace,' is in reality 'nothing more than a hypocritical semblance and pretense [*nichts dan ein schein und farb der gleissenerey*].'[109] In his *Judgment on Monastic Vows* (1521), Luther reflects that 'the holier a thing is the more it is assailed by the perverted copying of blasphemous hypocrites [*imo quo sanctior res est, hoc magis peititur impiorum et hypocritarum perversa aemulatione*].'[110] Vows, and particularly vows of chastity – which the gospel teaches should be 'a matter of free choice'[111] – have been perverted by the papacy. Luther concludes that 'the pope is resisting the Holy Spirit and that his teaching is devilish, erroneous, and pure hypocrisy [*doctrinam suam esse daemoniorum et erroneam et meram hypocrisin*],'[112] and that monastic vows are 'declared illusory, satanic, and hypocritical teaching by the divine judgment of the Spirit [*pronuncientur esse doctrinae erroneae er daemoniacae et hypocriticae*].'[113] In *The Misuse of the Mass* (1521), Luther even goes so far as to suggest 'that those who pray the seven hours without sincere desire and joy in God sin much more in his sight than those who neglect to pray them at all'; they are, he says, 'vain hypocrites [*eyttel gleyßner*], who pretend to pray and speak to God.'[114] In his *Sermon … for the Instruction of Consciences* (1521), he accuses clergy of setting a bad example for lay people, misleading them into believing 'that all they have to do is to keep their fasts and feasts.'[115] Here Luther draws on the 'woes' in Matthew 23 to express his disapproval of this position and those who teach it:

[108] Martin Luther, *Von den guten Werken* [*Treatise on Good Works*], *WA* 6: 210; *LW* 44: 31.
[109] Ibid., *WA* 6: 218; *LW* 44: 40.
[110] Martin Luther, *De votis monasticis Martini Lutheri iudicium* [*The Judgment of Martin Luther on Monastic Vows*], *WA* 8: 577; *LW* 44: 252.
[111] Ibid., *WA* 8: 579; *LW* 44: 255.
[112] Ibid., *WA* 8: 597–8; *LW* 44: 284.
[113] Ibid., *WA* 8: 598; *LW* 44: 285.
[114] Martin Luther, *Vom Mißbrauch der Messe* [*The Misuse of the Mass*], *WA* 8: 534; *LW* 36: 194.
[115] Martin Luther, *Ein Sermon von dreierlei gutem Leben, das Gewißen zu unterrichten* [*A Sermon on the three Kinds of Good Life for the Instruction of Consciences*], *WA* 7: 797; *LW* 44: 237.

> As if our God were bothered in the slightest whether you drink beer or water, whether you eat fish or meat, whether you keep the feasts or fasts! It was of people like this that Christ spoke in Matthew 23[: 23–24], 'Woe to you, scribes and Pharisees, hypocrites [*We euch schrift-gelhrten, geistlichen und allen gleisnern*]! For you tithe mint and dill and cumin, and have neglected the weightier matters of the law, justice and mercy and faith.'[116]

Preaching in 1522 in a series of sermons which Robert J. Bast has identified as key to understanding his developing anticlericalism, Luther complains that those who claim to make up the spiritual estate 'know nothing about either the smallest or the greatest of Christ's commandments. The more spiritual and more hypocritical they are, the blinder they are. And yet they still pride themselves on being the most spiritual and the most pious.'[117] In this line of argument, Luther is clearly associating hypocrisy with a swingeing critique of the clergy.

He is clear, however, that there is a true church which is not hypocritical. By 1521, in his defence of his teachings against the papal bull, Luther had begun to distinguish between 'the counterfeit and hypocritical church or church leadership [*der geferbeten unnd gleyssender kirchen oder geystlichkeytt*], and the true, basically sound church.'[118] The true church, he protested, has long been 'hidden … beneath sacred vestments, ritual, works, and similar outward pretensions and man-made laws', which had taught people 'that [they] can be saved through the contribution of money rather than through faith.'[119] Hypocrisy, he argued in his 1523 lectures on

[116] Ibid.

[117] Martin Luther, *Predigt in der Schloßkirche zu Weimar* [*Sermon in the Castle Church in Weimar*], 19 October 1522, *WA* 10/3: 344: 'die selben menschen wissen wider vom cleinsten noch grösten gebott Cristi. Also ie geistlicher und gleisnern, ie blinder. Aber dennoch rümen sie sich die geistlichen die frümsten zu sein.' Compare Robert J. Bast, 'Je Geistlicher … Je Blinder: Anticlericalism, the Law, and Social Ethics in Luther's Sermons on Matthew 22: 34–41', in Dykema and Oberman, eds, *Anticlericalism in Late Medieval and Early Modern Europe*, 367–78, at 372. Curiously, Bast makes no reference to Luther's use of *gleisner*.

[118] Martin Luther, *Grund und Ursach aller Artikel D. Martin Luthers, so durch römische Bulle unrechtlich verdammt sind* [*Defense and Explanation of All the Articles of Dr. Martin Luther which were Unjustly Condemned by the Roman Bull*], *WA* 7: 308 (and cf. 309); *LW* 32: 7.

[119] Ibid. The distinction between the 'hypocritical and bloodthirsty church' and the true church 'which is without influence, forsaken, and exposed to suffering and the cross, and

Deuteronomy, was associated with living under the law whilst members of the true church lived under the gospel.[120] Luther's anticlericalism needs to be understood in the context of his efforts, in this period, to define the shape of the true church and the behaviour of its members. His criticism of the clergy, while often as emotionally charged as that offered by Anonyma, is offered in the context of an attempt to provide a model for true Christian living. His pastoral awareness of the spiritual deficiencies, not only of clergy but also of laypeople, surely underlies his accusations of (or concerns about) the existence of hypocrisy amongst believers more generally.

It is scarcely surprising that Anonyma does not argue with the same theological sophistication as Luther or Karlstadt. Karlstadt's mentions of hypocrites in his polemical works are closer in tone to Anonyma's strictures against the clergy, although Anonyma's anticlerical polemic is much more explicitly rooted in accusations of hypocrisy and her choice of biblical texts does much to substantiate this association. It is also striking that although Luther's concern with hypocrisy is much wider, often focusing on *Scheinheiligkeit* (pretended holiness or false piety), hypocrisy nonetheless offers a useful

which before the world and in the sight of that hypocritical church is … vanity and nothing,' would emerge as an important theme in Luther's 1535 lectures on Genesis, and particularly his exegesis of the stories of Cain and Abel and of Jacob and Esau. Cain and Esau become for Luther the types of the hypocrite. The Genesis lectures also show Luther's deepening understanding that hypocrisy may express itself as excessive asceticism as well as gluttony: 'the gloomy hypocrites … consider it piety and saintliness to abstain from gold, silver, food, clothing, or the like. [They]… imagine that they are showing deference to God if they abstain. Thus neither hypocrites nor gluttons have a correct understanding of Scripture. There is a time for feasting, fasting, mourning, and rejoicing.' See Martin Luther, *Lectures on Genesis*, *LW* 1–8; quotations at *WA* 42: 187; *LW* 1: 252 and *WA* 43: 333, 334; *LW* 4: 276, 277. Luther's discussion of hypocrisy in the Genesis lectures and other later writings bear some striking similarities to the themes identified by Sophie Lunn-Rockliffe in her article in this volume, and would bear further investigation; however, such an investigation is beyond the scope of this article.

[120] Martin Luther, *Deuteronomion Mosi cum annotationibus* [*Lectures on Deuteronomy*], *WA* 14: 654; *LW* 9: 141: 'For the Law first forces to works and when taken in the fleshly sense produces brilliant hypocrites [*speciosos hypocritas*], who imagine themselves to be the first of all, and to whom everything is due.' See also ibid., *WA* 14: 723–4; *LW* 9: 260: 'if you look at the external show of works, there are many who fulfil the Law at least in many respects; and so they do not seem to be under the curse, as the hypocrites are. If, however, you look at the spirit which loves the Law, there are none who fulfil one jot or tittle. And so all are under the curse, and especially those who do outward works without the inward spirit'.

lens through which to understand his anticlericalism and his critiques of monasticism. Both Luther and Karlstadt were exponents of 'clerical anticlericalism', the critique of clergy and religious articulated by those who were themselves priests (and, in Luther's case, also a member of a religious order),[121] although they did not restrict their critiques of hypocrisy to the clergy and religious. Anonyma, by contrast, presents her anti-clerical and anti-monastic rhetoric as one who was not (and, as a woman, could not be) ordained; nor had she taken religious vows. She may offer a more specifically lay perspective, since she was not in a position to preach amendment of life from the pulpit, as both Luther and Karlstadt could and did.

Starting from the close relationship between hypocrisy and anticlericalism found in Anonyma's letters, this article has argued that the nexus of these critical tropes formed a leitmotif in the early Reformation, albeit expressed more explicitly by this lay author than by either Karlstadt or Luther, whose theological interests were undoubtedly wider. Hypocrisy, particularly in the form of false claims to piety and godliness, emerges as an important – and understudied – theme which underlies much Reformation rhetoric. As the ecclesiastical landscape became more confessional, concern about false piety seems to have given way to a focus on the distinction between hypocrisy and dissimulation, particularly in relation to the range of behaviours that constituted religious conformity.[122] In this early period of the Reformation, however, as in much of the medieval period, the evidence of Anonyma's letters and Karlstadt's and Luther's writings suggests that hypocrisy and anticlericalism, hypocrisy and antimonasticism, were closely – indeed intrinsically – intertwined.

[121] For a discussion of this phenomenon, see Susan C. Karant-Nunn, 'Clerical Anticlericalism in the Early German Reformation: An Oxymoron?', in Dykema and Oberman, eds, *Anticlericalism in Late Medieval and Early Modern Europe*, 521–34. Elm argues that in the later medieval period, it was primarily the laity who identified the negative consequences of clerical misbehaviour, and they often sought to restore the condition of the church through fraternities and other forms of semi-religious community. By contrast, clergy who internalized similar critiques were seeking to renew the order to which they belonged: Elm, 'Antiklerikalismus im Deutschen Mittelalter', 11–12.

[122] See, for instance, Perez Zagorin, *Ways of Lying: Dissimulation, Persecution, and Conformity in Early Modern Europe* (Cambridge, MA, 1990); Jon Balserak, 'Geneva's Use of Lies, Deceit, and Simulation in their Efforts to Reform France, 1536–1563', *Harvard Theological Review* 112 (2019), 76–100.

Hypocrisy and Humour in the English Reformation

Ethan H. Shagan*
University of California, Berkeley

This article examines jokes about religion, particularly religious hypocrisy, in early modern English jestbooks, from the 1520s to the 1740s. It argues that over the course of England's Long Reformation, we find more and more jokes in which the solution, or alternative, to hypocrisy is not a more robust faith, making the inward heart correspond to one's outward show of religion, but rather a more profane Christianity, making one's outward face correspond to an all-too-human and worldly heart. Jokes about religious hypocrisy thus betray both a deep anxiety about piety, and the emergence of a profane species of Protestantism.

The word 'hypocrisy' comes from a Greek term for stage actors, considered untrustworthy because so adept at impersonation.[1] The early church actually forbade actors, along with prostitutes and gladiators, from becoming Christians unless they abandoned their profession.[2] More than a thousand years later, as the Christian West fractured into hostile religious factions, putting on a false face came to be seen as the characteristic danger of the early modern age. Accusations of hypocrisy were an intrinsic part of Reformation controversy, not only because the interior condition of the Christian took on a radically new spiritual significance, but because hiding one's true beliefs really did find eloquent new advocates, under the guise of Tacitean 'prudence' or the virtue of

* Department of History, University of California, Berkeley, 3229 Dwinelle Hall, Berkeley, CA 94720, USA. E-mail: shagan@berkeley.edu.

[1] The *Oxford English Dictionary*'s entry under 'hypocrisy' says: 'Greek ὑπόκρισις, the acting of a part on the stage, feigning, pretence'; and under 'hypocrite': 'Greek ὑποκριτής an actor on the stage, pretender, dissembler': 'Hypocrisy, noun' and 'Hypocrite, noun', *OED*, online at: <https://www.oed.com/dictionary/hypocrisy_n?tab=etymology#1051130 >, accessed 12 January 2024.

[2] Augustine, *St. Augustine on Faith and Works*, transl. Gregory Lombardo (New York, 1988), 18.33, p. 41; *The Apostolic Tradition of Hippolytus* 16, online at: <https://www.gutenberg.org/files/61614/61614-h/61614-h.htm>, accessed 12 January 2024.

Studies in Church History 60 (2024), 176–196 Published by Cambridge University Press on behalf of the Ecclesiastical History Society.
doi: 10.1017/stc.2024.5

'politeness'.[3] Protestants accused Roman Catholics and the seething mass of unregenerate humanity of being, in fact, Christians in name only, while they in turn accused Protestants of demanding a purity in others which they failed to exercise themselves.

This is the typical context in which Reformation historians write about hypocrisy;[4] it is not the subject of this article. At best, it forms the intellectual backdrop for another subject which is of equal significance for understanding religion in the early modern era, but which historians rarely talk about: humour, particularly the ways that hypocrisy was an occasion for wit and parody, rather than polemic. Humour has always served as a vehicle for interrogating the uncomfortable gap between people's words and deeds, from the plays of Aristophanes and the satires of Juvenal, to Geoffrey Chaucer's 'Pardoner' trafficking in fake relics, to Martin Marprelate's scurrilous attacks on English bishops. Like all comedy, humour lampooning hypocrisy sometimes served a serious purpose. But religious humour was not simply divinity in drag, and we should not read it for doctrine, as if we were reading a treatise or a sermon. Theologians might use humour, of course. But just as plausibly, humourists might use theology, and their projects were not necessarily the same.

This is therefore a serious article about jokes. The jestbook, a new genre developed in the Italian Renaissance (although with classical and medieval antecedents), achieved great heights of popularity in early modern England.[5] Scholars have rarely noticed that, second

[3] See, for instance, Gerhard Oestreich, *Neostoicism and the Early Modern State*, transl. David McLintock (Cambridge, 1982); Jenny Davidson, *Hypocrisy and the Politics of Politeness: Manners and Morals from Locke to Austen* (Cambridge, 2004).

[4] On early modern England in particular, where 'puritan' was often imagined as synonymous with 'hypocrite', see, for example, Lucia Nigri and Naya Tsentourou, eds, *Forms of Hypocrisy in Early Modern England* (New York, 2018); Carys Brown, *Friends, Neighbours, Sinners: Religious Difference and English Society, 1689–1750* (Cambridge, 2022), esp. ch. 3 (109–50); Alec Ryrie, *Being Protestant in Reformation Britain* (Oxford, 2013). For an excellent recent account of the broader Reformation scene, see Ulinka Rublack, *Reformation Europe*, 2nd edn (Cambridge, 2017; first publ. 2005).

[5] Jestbooks have been studied by many literary scholars but few historians: see, for instance, Mark Knights and Adam Morton, eds, *The Power of Laughter and Satire in Early Modern Britain: Political and Religious Culture, 1500–1820* (Woodbridge, 2017); Pamela Brown, *Better a Shrew than a Sheep: Women and the Culture of Jest in Early Modern England* (Ithaca, NY, 2003); Chris Holcomb, *Mirth Making: The Rhetorical Discourse on Jesting in Early Modern England* (Columbia, SC, 2001); George Minois, *Histoire du rire et de la dérision* (Paris, 2000); Don Nilsen, *Humor in Eighteenth- and Nineteenth-Century British Literature: A Reference Guide* (Westport, CT, 1998); idem,

only to sex, religion saturated early modern jokes, forming a rich mine of sources for the history of religion that lies almost wholly unexcavated. Within this motherlode, one important vein of jokes about religion lampooned hypocrisy: jesters wagged their fingers at supposedly devout and pious Christians who turned out to be worldly and sinful. This is not surprising. But what perhaps is surprising is that, over the course of England's Long Reformation, we find more and more jokes in which the solution, or alternative, to hypocrisy is not a more robust faith, in which the inward heart corresponds to one's outward show of religion, but rather a more profane Christianity, where one's outward face is made to correspond to an all-too-human and worldly heart.

We should not, however, imagine these jokes as prescriptive. People who told jokes about blasphemy did not necessarily want to live in a blasphemous world, any more than men who told endless jokes about cuckoldry approved of their wives' infidelity. If there is anything universal about jokes, it is that they consist in transgression. Nonetheless, in the same way that feminist scholars have used cuckold jokes to explore the contours of male anxiety, an analysis of religious jokes can tell us a great deal about the gathering clouds of religious apprehension.[6] In at least some jokes about religious hypocrisy, we can observe the lengthening shadows of worries that could not easily be expressed in the kinds of prescriptive sources which ecclesiastical historians typically read: not only that the pious were not as saintly as they claimed, but that piety itself might be something less than what it was cracked up to be. By telling jokes about religious hypocrisy, at least some early modern subjects found ways to accept and accommodate their own profanity, even if that meant laughing at themselves.

Humor in British Literature from the Middle Ages to the Restoration: A Reference Guide (Westport, CT, 1997); Jan Bremmer and Herman Roodenburg, eds, *A Cultural History of Humour: From Antiquity to the Present Day* (Cambridge, MA, 1997), especially the article by Derek Brewer, 'Prose Jest-Books Mainly in the Sixteenth to Eighteenth Centuries in England', 90–111; Raymond Anselment, *'Betwixt Jest and Earnest': Marprelate, Milton, Marvell, Swift & the Decorum of Religious Ridicule* (Toronto, 1979); Keith Thomas, 'The Place of Laughter in Tudor and Stuart England', *The Times Literary Supplement* 21 (1977), 77–81.

[6] See, for example, Claire McEachern, 'Why do Cuckolds Have Horns?', *Huntington Library Quarterly* 71 (2008), 607–31.

I.

Before proceeding, a few brief introductory comments will help to set the scene. The revived classical genre of the jestbook percolated outwards from Italy with the rest of Renaissance humanism around the end of the fifteenth century. Its most important early exemplar was Poggio Bracciolini's toweringly smutty *Facetiae* (*c.*1470). The first English jestbook, called *A Hundred Merry Tales*, was published in 1526 and proved popular enough to be mentioned by Shakespeare in *Much Ado about Nothing*, where Beatrice is accused of having acquired her splendid wit 'out of the hundred merry tales'.[7] A second English jestbook was published soon thereafter in 1532, followed by a long hiatus during the mid-sixteenth century, before returning in the later Elizabethan period. Throughout Europe, and in England too, jestbooks gradually evolved, riding the market for print more broadly, from demonstrations of humanist wit to genuinely popular works aimed at a broad audience.[8]

Jestbooks are only one aspect of a mountain of humorous sources from early modern England, many of which, like Samuel Butler's anti-puritan masterpiece *Hudibras* (first published 1663), made hypocrisy their cornerstone. But jestbooks were, even more so than most early modern humour, generally boorish and obscene. Despite occasional efforts to wrap bawdy jokes in moralizing clothes, there was simply no getting around their indecent content. In *A Hundred Merry Tales*, for instance, we hear of a pubescent gentleman who has grown hair only on his lip but not yet on his chin. A gentlewoman says to him: 'Sir, ye have a beard above and none beneath'; to which he replies, 'Mistress, ye have a beard beneath and none above.' 'Marry, quod she, then set the one against the other. Which answer made the gentleman so abashed that he had not one word to answer.'[9] Despite Robert Darnton's famous dictum that the key to unlocking past mentalities is in what they found funny but we do not, with these

[7] Ian Munro, 'Shakespeare's Jestbook: Wit, Print, Performance', *ELH* 71 (2004), 89–113, at 89.

[8] As late as the middle of the seventeenth century, there is evidence of gentlemen making their own manuscript jestbooks, compiling material they had read and heard in order to demonstrate their wit. See, for instance, the manuscript jestbook of Sir Nicholas Le Strange (1603–55), published in a modern edition as Nicholas Le Strange, *'Merry Passages and Jeasts': A Manuscript Jestbbook*, ed. H. F. Lippincott (Salzburg, 1974).

[9] *A C Mery Talys* (London, 1526), fol. 8[v].

jokes there is generally no need: despite obsolete topicality and archaic expression, most of this material, for good or ill, is familiar rather than alien, still funny if you are the kind of person who finds that kind of thing funny.[10]

We should not underestimate the complexity and difficulty of using jestbooks as historical sources. One obvious problem is their lack of originality, and hence historical specificity: these books sometimes read like vast accretions of plagiarism held together by thin tissues of novelty. Jokes were recycled from generation to generation, an expanding hoard, rather than a series of discreet cultural moments. Many jokes had classical or continental sources, meaning they only obliquely reflect English conditions. For instance, *Wits Fittes and Fancies* (1595), by the English Roman Catholic poet Anthony Copley, is partially compiled from *La Floresta Espagñola* (1574), whose Spanish jokes then passed into common English usage in dozens of other jestbooks.[11] Compounding the problem of provenance is the fact that many jokes were packaged and marketed under the names of famous, but safely dead celebrities, such as Queen Elizabeth's clown Richard Tarleton (sometimes identified as the model for Shakespeare's Yorick, that fellow of infinite jest), or Archy Armstrong, jester to James VI/I and then Charles I, until an ill-timed jibe at Archbishop Laud about the Scottish National Covenant saw him banished from court.[12] In the eighteenth century, so many jestbooks purported to contain jokes by the actor Joe Miller – friend to the artist William Hogarth, famous for his portrayal of Hamlet's gravedigger – that jokes themselves became known as 'Millerisms', even though it appears unlikely that Miller wrote virtually any of them.

Jokes, therefore, do not make a simple source for historians: they speak in no distinct voice and reflect no distinct opinions. Yet few good sources are simple, and while recycling undoubtedly occurred, its impact should not be overestimated. Novelty sold jestbooks, as did topicality, and a systematic reading of these books from the early sixteenth century to the early eighteenth reveals a process of

[10] Robert Darnton, 'Workers Revolt: The Great Cat Massacre of the Rue Saint-Séverin', in idem, *The Great Cat Massacre and Other Episodes in French Cultural History* (New York, 1985), 75–104.

[11] Anthony Copley, *Wits Fittes and Fancies* (London, 1595).

[12] See Andrea Shannon, '"Uncouth Language to a Princes Ears": Archibald Armstrong, Court Jester, and Early Stuart Politics', *SCJ* 42 (2011), 99–112.

transformation. Individual authors curated their works, increasingly appealing to a popular market. New jokes were constantly added. Some were successful and thus entered the repertoire; others failed and were never heard of again; still others were topical, living short, glorious lives before their relevance waned. Over the course of centuries, old jokes were tweaked, or sometimes boldly recast, to remain popular. Hence, while we cannot simply pick up a jestbook and assume that its contents reflect the conditions of its date of publication, in the aggregate, we can track trends and notice novelty arising out of convention.

These preliminaries established, we can now jump into the jestbooks themselves. If we begin synchronically, taking early modern jokes as a whole, we can broadly organize jokes about religion into three undoubtedly overlapping, but conceptually distinct categories. First, there are jokes that poke fun at ignorance and irreligion, at all those ostensible Christians who have not the slightest inkling of Christianity, and therefore unintentionally say or do funny things. Sometimes, these jokes take as their stock character the ignorant priest, the country yokel or the foppish gentleman. Sometimes, they employ the misogynist trope of the ignorant peasant woman. To give a few examples, there is an oft-repeated joke about two gentlemen who do not know which holiday they are celebrating, but decide it is probably the day of our blessed lady's circumcision.[13] In a joke with many variants, a minister asks an old man if he knows 'who made him', but the old man cannot answer. The minister tells him it is shameful he should be so ignorant, when a young child knows the answer. The man replies: 'He is but newly made, and may well remember it, but four score years are past since I was made.'[14] In another joke:

> An ignorant old woman in the country, hearing a minister preach on the passion of Christ, of the cruel and barbarous death that the Jews put him to, wept grievously. And when the minister had done, she came to him and asked him how long ago it was since this sad thing was done? The minister told her it was sixteen hundred years since. *O then*, says

[13] Anon., *A Banquet of Jests: Or, a Collection of Court, Camp, Colledge, Citie, Country Iests, In Two Bookes. The Sixth Edition, much enlarged for the delight of the reader* (London, 1640), 54.

[14] A. S. Gent. [Robert Chamberlain?], 'The Two Last Centuries of Bulls, Iests and Lies', in *The Booke of Bvlls* (London, 1636), 11.

the woman, being a little revived, *if it be so long ago, I hope in God it may not be true.*[15]

A second category consists of jokes that make fun of doctrinal or confessional opponents. One joke, introduced just before the English Civil War, mocked the absurdity of puritanism. 'Some Cambridge scholars reasoning together, one of them would have the word "mass" never once named.' That is, instead of Christmas, there would be Christ-tide; instead of Michaelmas, there would be Michael-tide, and so forth. But one of the company objected: 'For, said he, my name is Thomas, so is many an honest man's more, and why, for what reason, should we be called Tom-tides?'[16] Sometimes, these jokes could be clever and sophisticated. In one jestbook, written by an English Roman Catholic, a country parson preaches to his parishioners that we are saved not by Peter or Paul, 'but by God's blood only'. The parishioners respond by telling him not to swear. He repeats: 'Nay, by God's death then you are all to be saved and no[t] otherwise'; and again they answer: 'O swear not.' This dynamic repeats itself several more times, making comedy of the fact that phrases such as 'by God's blood' and 'by God's death' are pious pronouncements in the mouth of a Protestant preacher, but in the ears of his parishioners are the impious oaths which he had forbidden them from uttering.[17] Less subtly, a 1638 joke described a Jesuit administering the sacrament to a sick Roman Catholic, saying: 'Take, eat, this is Christ's body'; the sick man 'answered him that it stood against his conscience to eat flesh on a Friday'.[18] Another joke from 1674 finds a Protestant and a Roman Catholic in Paris, arguing about the pope's infallibility: 'The priest said that the pope may err as a man but not as a pope; I would fain know (said the gentleman) why the pope doth not instruct or reform the man?'[19]

Most of these jokes were surprisingly gentle. Jestbooks were not polemical and tended to take a light touch when it came to confessional differences. Of course, we should not forget that words carry weight, and that even the softest jokes at the expense of persecuted

15 Humphrey Crouch, *England's Jests Refin'd and Improv'd* (London, 1693), 52–3 (no. 102). Italics original.

16 Anon., *A Banquet of Jests*, 126–7.

17 Copley, *Wits Fittes and Fancies*, 156.

18 H. L. Oxon., Gratiae Ludentes: *Iests, from the Universitie* (London, 1638), 52–3.

19 Anon., *The Complaisant Companion, or New Jests* (London, 1674), 19.

minorities still land blows. But given the reality of so much hatred and violence in the early modern era, many of these jokes were almost friendly by comparison, and might possibly have released tension rather than adding to it. In this context, it is noteworthy that many anti-Catholic jokes in English jestbooks were actually adapted from continental Renaissance antecedents: these were actually pre-Reformation jokes in which Roman Catholics had made fun of one another, now tweaked by Protestants, but not invented by them.

A third category consists of jokes making fun of hypocrisy. Naturally, these jokes focused on the sins of the supposedly devout, especially puritans and Roman Catholics, but sometimes of simple people in general. Since sex is always the most common subject of humour, these jokes tended to harp on sexual sins. Thus a man 'who had lain with his female servant', the next day catechized her as usual, asking her how many commandments there were. 'She answered nine. Thou Fool, quoth he, hast thou lived to this age, and knowest no better? There are ten. *I know*, says she, *very well, there were ten yesterday; but you and I broke one of them the last night, so that there are but nine of them left*.'[20] In another joke, a man sees the married 'Mistress Temperance' – obviously a puritan by her name – and swears he will lie with her. She acts offended, but then says: 'but that I am tender of oaths, and would be loath to have you break yours, for the oath's sake I am willing to consent to you at present'.[21] The 1677 book that included this joke, *Coffee House Jests*, by the former Royalist William Hicks, was filled with mockery of puritan hypocrisy in particular. For instance, 'A fanatic did lately extremely exclaim against the surplice in the church, but a little after he was catch'd a-bed with one of his holy sisters; and in the same place where he would not have a surplice worn, he poor heart was forc'd there to wear a sheet' (that is, the white cloth worn for public penance).[22]

Sex was far from the only arena in which words and deeds might diverge. Consider the following joke:

> A priest in an abbey being a fisherman's son, was used every meal to have a net laid on the table instead of a tablecloth in token of humility,

[20] Crouch, *England's Jests Refin'd and Improv'd*, 66 (no. 128). Italics original.

[21] [William Hicks], *Coffee-House Jests: By the Author of the Oxford-Jests* (London, 1677), 42 (no. 71).

[22] [Hicks], *Coffee-House Jests*, 45 (no. 77).

> and to remember from whence he came; but the abbot dying, for his pretended humility's sake he was elected abbot, and then the net was not laid on the table as before, and being asked the reason, told 'em, *I have that which I fished for, I have no need of the net now.*[23]

A joke printed in 1679, offers a satire of conformity:

> An old doctor, which had been a Protestant in King Edward's days, a papist in Queen Mary's days, and a Protestant again in Queen Elizabeth's, seeing a lady dance a galliard, commended her dance very much. To which she answered, that *She knew she danced well enough, only she could not turn so well as he.*[24]

Or consider a joke called 'Of a puritan's kneeling to the king's health', from a 1636 jestbook entitled the *Book of Bulls*: 'A certain major at his table began the king's health on his knee, on purpose to fetch a puritan alderman down to his.' That is, he was trying to trap the puritan in disloyalty to the king, since puritans sometimes considered kneeling a form of idolatry. 'The puritan, contrary to all men's expectation, pledged it on both knees, and the major demanding the reason why he kneeled down on both knees, he answered, that he kneeled on one in honor of the king, and on the other to ask God forgiveness for so doing.'[25] Another joke in the same book finds a 'distracted schismatical fellow', in other words a puritan, in Rome. When he sees the pope ride by, he shouts at him: 'Thou art the antichrist!' Naturally, he is arrested, convicted of heresy and brought to the stake to be burned. At which point, inevitably, he makes a complete retraction, saying 'that he was resolved to die till he saw the fire, which much terrified him; for, said he, I came into the world a poor raw thing, and would be loath to go out roasted.'[26]

Taking these three different categories of jokes together, the first thing to note is that we can describe them all as conventionally pious. That is, they criticize things that ought to be criticized, according to orthodox religious authorities of one stripe or another. Those

[23] William Hicks, *Oxford Jests, Refined and Enlarged: Being a Collection of Witty Jests, Merry Tales, Pleasant Joques* (London, 1671), 162 (no. 550). Italics original.

[24] Democritus Junior, *Versatile Ingenium, the Wittie Companion, or Jests of All Sorts* (London, 1679), 39 (no. 13). Italics original.

[25] A. S. Gent. [Robert Chamberlain?], *The Booke of Bvlls, Baited with two Centuries of Bold Jests, and nimble-lies* (London, 1636), part 2, 69–70.

[26] Ibid. 59–61.

authorities might not necessarily appreciate the medium of criticism, since humour itself had a complex theological history. One strain of Christianity, running from John Chrysostom through Benedict of Nursia, and on to some of the English puritans, condemned laughter almost without exception. This was the strain so memorably fictionalized in Umberto Eco's *The Name of the Rose*. But for most Christians, it was unproblematic that ignorance, error and hypocrisy might be laughed at; hence jokes which made fun of ignorance, error and hypocrisy could proudly wear the mantle of orthodoxy.

The second thing to note is that the third category, those jokes which make fun of hypocrisy in particular, were not as conventionally pious as they at first glance appear. In principle, in order to make fun of hypocrites, you yourself have to be sincere, with your heart and words aligning, in the same way that, in order to make fun of error, you yourself have to be orthodox. But in fact, the superficial piety of these jokes about hypocrisy is overtly, gloriously insincere, because they are found in jestbooks which also, almost without exception, traffic in indecency, gleefully offending the morals of pious readers.

Take the joke about the 'Nine Commandments', which ostensibly condemns a gentleman for the hypocrisy of catechizing his servant about God's law the morning after he has slept with her. This joke is found in Humphrey Crouch's *England's Jests Refined and Improved* (published with slight variations in 1687 and 1693) which insisted in its preface that its jokes were harmless entertainment, which 'do not interfere with religion or good manners'.[27] That claim was not easy to square with a joke such as the following:

> A gentleman riding on the road, overtook a young brisk country lass, who after some time travelling together, consented to his amours; the man being conscious of what he had done, and how prejudicial it might prove to the maid, told her, if anything came of their endeavours, she should hear of him at a certain place in London. *'Tis no matter Sir,* said she, *I am to be married on Monday.*[28]

Or take the *Oxford Jests* (1671) from which is drawn the joke about the false humility of the priest who used fishing nets as tablecloths, as well as the joke about Mistress Temperance being tender of oaths.

[27] Crouch, *England's Jests Refin'd and Improv'd*, preface, sig. A3^{v}.

[28] Ibid. 52 (no. 101). Italics original.

Oxford Jests also included a joke about 'some naked boys at Norton', who 'clapped some clay upon the hole of every boy's bum; a wench being among them, being to be clapped upon her bum also; one said, Hey ding! Here's a boy has two holes, give me two pieces of dirt'.[29] Surely no pious Christians in the seventeenth century would have approved of the transgressive profanity of these jokes.

Virtually all jokes about religious hypocrisy were thus themselves hypocritical. With a wink and a nod to readers, jestbooks knowingly adopted a holier-than-thou attitude in order to poke fun at the holier-than-thou, all the while positively revelling in the fact that they were not holy at all, and that the mere act of reading them subverted the supposed piety that authorized jokes about religious hypocrisy in the first place. This was less a matter of authorial or editorial intent, than a generic feature of the jestbooks themselves, where ostensibly religious material mingled with content that ranged from merely irreverent to blatantly smutty.

This is why it is crucially important that we not read religious jokes as polemic by other means, and that we not abstract these jokes from their literary context. In the form of their production and consumption, jokes which mocked religious hypocrisy were double-edged and rhetorically ambiguous, hiding a kind of obstreperous insubordination within the folds of their seeming piety.

II.

Having identified this strain of meta-hypocrisy as a generic feature of jestbooks, we can notice another feature: crossover jokes which might be placed in more than one of our notional categories. Of course, some jokes were both about doctrinal difference and about hypocrisy; while others were about the ignorance of confessional opponents. But most importantly, there was a variant of jokes from the first category – making fun of ignorant or irreligious people – which also raised the spectre of hypocrisy. In this variant, ignorant or irreligious people are made objects of ridicule, but in the process, those ignorant or irreligious people call out and expose overblown, sanctimonious or hypocritical holiness in others. In other words, the satire of these jokes falls, like rain, on both the just and the unjust. We are asked not only to

[29] Hicks, *Oxford Jests*, 44 (no. 174).

laugh *at* impiety, but also to laugh *with* impiety, because at least that impiety is honest and sincere.

Perhaps the earliest joke that fits this description comes from the 1532 *Tales and Quicke Answers*, the second jestbook to be printed in England. In this joke, a friar announces in his sermon what an honourable charge St Christopher had, to bear our saviour in his arms; this was a reference to the legend that St Christopher had carried a child across a river, who turned out to be Jesus, which is why Christopher became the patron saint of travellers. 'Was there ever any like him in grace?', the friar asks rhetorically. To which a 'homely, blunt fellow' responds that, yes, there was: 'the ass that bore both him and his mother.'[30] Notice the productive ambiguity in this joke. If you wanted to, you could interpret it as mocking the 'homely, blunt fellow' and yokels like him, who misinterpret religion by taking it carnally, rather than spiritually. But just as easily, you could interpret it as mocking the pompous friar's insincerity or ridiculousness. These two interpretations are not mutually exclusive: it is the possibility of the first meaning that authorizes the joke and renders it orthodox, thereby making the second meaning available to readers, who are clearly meant to identify, not with the friar, but with the 'homely, blunt fellow' and to find wisdom in his worldliness. We could also dig more deeply into the theology of this joke. For instance, its mocking of saints' legends is reminiscent of Erasmus, and there are other jokes in the same jestbook borrowed from Erasmus, Poggio Bracciolini and other humanist sources. We could thus choose to imagine this joke as a contribution to the *philosophia Christi*, Erasmus's conception of faith-centred piety. But we do not have to. By mocking the friar's piety without offering any clearly pious alternative, the joke might be taken to relegate piety itself to the sidelines. That is the kind of joke we must now consider.

It is hard to make chronological arguments about jestbooks because of their constant recycling. Nonetheless, while it would be difficult to prove systematically, there is no doubt that, broadly, while there were occasional early examples, this type of joke became increasingly common over the course of this period, as jestbooks themselves became genuinely mass media, written less as humanist rhetorical exercises and more for an increasingly popular audience.

[30] Anon., *Tales and quicke answeres, very mery, and pleasant to rede* (London, 1532), sig. A1^{r} (no. 2).

By the late seventeenth and early eighteenth centuries, we find more and more jokes about religion which seem ready to embrace a kind of honest worldliness, asking us to laugh alongside the kinds of inveterate yokels who feature as figures of opprobrium in so many puritan attacks on popular culture. In *A Choice Banquet of Witty Jests* (1660), we find the first iteration of a joke about the Christian legend of St George, 'how he killed the dragon that would else have devoured the maid'. A man who heard the story wondered aloud that men would devise such lies, for 'it is held by most men, that there was never such a man as St. George, nor such a creature as a dragon'. His companion answered that, on the contrary, it was easy to believe in both the saint and the dragon, but whether there was really a maid was another matter.[31] In the same book, we learn that 'certain country clowns' are too familiar with their ministers, not calling them by their proper titles. One of these bumpkins is told by 'one of the more knowing amongst them' that he ought to address his minister as 'Pastor … because, saith he, Pastor is as much as shepherd, or the head of sheep'. Thereafter, the bumpkin addresses his minister as 'Master Sheep's head'.[32]

In one joke from the 1671 *Oxford Jests*, a priest tells a condemned felon about to be executed 'that though his dinner was sharp and harsh, yet he should find a joyful supper in heaven'. This is the traditional language of early modern piety; Charles I had said something similar before walking to the scaffold. 'Ah, says he, 'twill do me no good, for I never eat any suppers.'[33] In another example, a woman confesses to a friar that her chief sin is lying with men. 'Well, says the friar, whoredom is a thing which doth much displease God. Faith, says she, I am sorry for that, for I am sure it pleased me.'[34] In these jokes, it is not clear whether the priests are mocked for their pomposity in general, or for their hypocrisy in particular; we shall return to this question below. As in the joke about St Christopher, the point is that sinners give the pious their comeuppance, even though those sinners are ostensibly the ones being mocked.

31 Anon., *A Choice Banquet of Witty Jests* (London, 1660), 15 (no. 46).
32 Ibid. 137 (no. 374).
33 Hicks, *Oxford Jests*, 14 (no. 60).
34 Ibid. 63 (no. 237).

More examples can be found in *The Complaisant Companion* (1674), published anonymously, but probably written by Richard Head. In one joke, 'A country parson having bitterly inveighed against the vices of his parishioners in his sermon, a silly woman that was present went to his mother … to complain of him, saying that her son had threatened them all with hell and damnation if they did not speedily amend.' 'O, said his mother, he was a liar from his cradle, I never whipped him but for telling an untruth, and you are mad if you believe him now.'[35]

The culmination of this trend came in a series of jestbooks published in the 1720s and 1730s. One good example is *Polly Peachum's Jests* from 1728, among the most popular new jestbooks of the eighteenth century, which shamelessly stole its title from one of the characters in John Gay's recently-released smash hit *The Beggar's Opera*. In one of Polly Peachum's jokes, 'A melting sermon being preached in a country church, all fell a weeping but one man; who being asked why he did not weep with the rest: O! said he, I belong to another parish.'[36] This is a perfect example of the kind of joke we are considering. It remains ostensibly orthodox, because its target can be taken to be the man from another parish who cares not a fig for sermons; yet at the same time, the author is rolling his eyes at the absurdity of these pious churchgoers and their minister who claim, literally in this case, to be holier-than-thou. Another joke describes a servant to the chaplain on a naval ship, who asks a servant on another ship how often he went to prayers. The other servant answers, 'in case of a storm or danger'. 'Ah, said the first, there's some sense in that, but my master makes us pray when there is no more occasion for it than for my leaping overboard.'[37] There is another example concerning 'a certain reverend drone in the country' – that is, a pious preacher – who complains to another 'that it was a great fatigue to preach twice a day'. 'Oh, said the other, I preach twice every Sunday and *make nothing of it*.' Or yet another on 'A parson preaching a tiresome sermon on happiness or bliss; when he had done a gentleman told him he had forgot one sort of happiness, *Happy are they that did not hear your sermon*.'[38] No kind of religion

[35] Anon., *Complaisant Companion*, 77.
[36] Anon., *Polly Peachum's Jests* (London, 1728), 41 (no. 110).
[37] Ibid. 20 (no. 49).
[38] Ibid. 3 (no. 6) and 30 (no. 78). Italics original.

can escape these mockeries, because the 'reverend drones' and their holier-than-thou followers are no more or less objects of mirth than the irreverent wits who mock them.

Let us consider another jestbook called *England's Genius: Or, Wit Triumphant* (1734). A 'country wench', jostling through the aisle of St Clement's Church to get closer to the pulpit, accidentally pushes an elderly woman. The girl apologizes, saying she only wanted to get near enough to hear. 'To hear?', replies the old woman incredulously, 'Why, thou bold baggage, I have sat here these thirty years and never heard a word the parson said in all that time.'[39] Who is being laughed at here, the irreligious woman, the pious girl or the preacher who is never heard? Surely all of them at once. Or for another example: 'A drunken rake, that made it his constant practice to lie in bed every Sunday, was sharply reprimanded for it by a clergyman.' He answered, 'that he was sorry a person of the sacred function understood the scriptures no better, when the Sabbath was appointed for a day of rest'.[40]

It is worth pausing here for a moment to consider the ecclesio-political orientation of these jokes. We must be cautions in making this assessment, because the editorial slant of jestbooks is always muddy, and looking for consistency is a fool's errand. Nonetheless, rough sensibilities can often be gleaned, and in general, unsurprisingly, we find these jokes predominantly in jestbooks that were broadly anti-puritan. One jestbook that specialized in this kind of joke was the 1671 *Oxford Jests* by William Hicks, a proud purveyor of lowbrow humour ('Oxford' for the town, not the gown), known as Captain Hicks for his royalism during the English Civil War. Another example is *The Complaisant Companion* (1674), probably written by Richard Head, author of *The English Rogue* (1665) among other, sometimes indecent, adventures. *A Choice Banquet of Witty Jests* (1660) was one of several jestbooks in which famous Parliamentarians from the Civil War, such as the army chaplain Hugh Peters, appeared as clowns like the stock figures of *commedia dell'arte*.[41]

[39] Anon., *England's Genius: Or, Wit Triumphant* (London, 1734), 21.

[40] Ibid. 35.

[41] This is a fascinating phenomenon. Elsewhere, Peters is demoted to 'a kind of buffoon jester to Oliver Cromwell': [J. S.], *England's Merry Jester: or, Court, City and Country Jests* (London, 1693), 13 (no. 16). Whole jestbooks, *The Tales and Jests of Mr Hugh Peters* (London, 1660) and *Hugh Peters Figaries* (London, 1660), used Peters as a comic

It seems, then, that jokes which mocked the pious and impious together are most often found in jestbooks which were broadly anti-puritan. This observation, however, is not actually very helpful and, analytically, it does not get us very far. In one sense, it is simply trivial, because, Martin Marprelate notwithstanding, there was no such thing as a puritan jestbook: of course indecent humour was anti-puritan. But it is also a red herring for another reason: even if they were against puritans, it is not clear what ecclesio-political 'side' these jokes were supposed to be for. There was no pro-impiety party in early modern England, no 'Church of Staying Home in Bed'. The appreciation shown in these jestbooks for blunt goodfellows might have made them in some sense culturally 'Anglican' (as we may start to call a certain kind of Church of England sensibility in the decades after 1660), but they were plainly as offensive to Church of England and especially to high church religious ideals as they were to puritan ones. Again, we must resist the urge to imagine jokes about religion as somehow practising divinity without a licence; instead of asserting a stark religious position, the assertion of stark religious positions was part of what they were laughing at. Or, to put it differently, it is not the case that there was somehow a market for Anglican jokes; instead there was a Church of England market for jokes which were broadly impious.

With that observation, we can now return to the issue of hypocrisy, which is analytically helpful and gets us much further. In some of the jokes making fun of the pious and impious together, hypocrisy is very obviously at stake. But in others, hypocrisy is left implicit and has to be assumed or deduced by the reader. It is implicit rather than absent, because the honest simplicity of the impious sinner is clearly highlighted: what had been derided earlier as ignorance now feels more like plain-dealing authenticity, and that authenticity is presumably being contrasted with something. Readers might reasonably connect the dots and imagine that the antithesis of honest authenticity is hypocrisy, which would explain, in a theologically palatable way, why the pious deserve to be laughed at just as much as the blunt goodfellow. On the other hand, it is also possible that the pious are simply pious, and that in these jokes it is no

character. For more on this, see Arnold Hunt, *Protestant Bodies: Gesture in the English Reformation* (Cambridge, forthcoming 2024), which I was privileged to read in draft.

more or less than their piety which is being laughed at. The minister who complains about the drunk sleeping in on Sundays is a blowhard, and we are invited to laugh at him. But is he a blowhard because he is no less a sinner than his hungover parishioner, or is he a blowhard because he should just mind his own business? The jestbook does not answer this question and, again, we must appreciate what a productive ambiguity this is. By hinting that seemingly pious men and women are hypocrites, these jokes preserve for themselves a kind of orthodoxy: the assumption that it is always allowable to laugh at hypocrites. But they also open up the more subversive possibility that all piety is in some sense hypocritical, or even worse, that piety is *ipso facto* ridiculous, whether sincere or not.

This movement finds its epitome in a joke in the 1742 *Ecclesiastical Transactions: Or, a Collection of Reverend Jokes*, a weird and derivative hybrid, but nonetheless the first and perhaps only English jestbook wholly focused on religion. There, a gentleman (the judge and MP Joseph Jekyll, safely dead by 1742) worriedly tells his secretary, described as 'an honest, inoffensive, though not an over-religious man', that he never sees him in church. 'No, replied the other, I seldom go; not that I think there is any harm in it neither.'[42] The existence of this joke, looked at from an early modern perspective, is downright shocking. By 1742, it was evidently possible to imagine that going to church, as much as not going to church, was laughable. One possible reason why, overtly if quietly signalled, is hypocrisy: it is the 'honest' man who does not go, and the joke implies that there is something dishonest about being 'over-religious'. But another possibility, left wide open, is that churchgoing is simply a waste of time. The joke dances on the edge of this freethinking anti-Christianity, but retreats back into a plausibly Christian critique of hypocrisy with two centuries of respectable pedigree behind it.

III.

To understand what was at stake in this emerging deployment of hypocrisy, let us turn to one final anecdote, this time not from a jestbook, but from a conventionally pious cleric. In 1530, a monk of Syon Abbey named Richard Whitford, England's bestselling

[42] Anon., *Ecclesiastical Transactions: Or, a Collection of Reverend Jokes* (London, 1742), 8.

devotional author, warned his readers that piety would look ridiculous in the eyes of the world. When he recommended intensive daily devotions for all his readers, Whitford noted: 'Some of you will say, "Sir, this work is good for religious persons … [but] if we should use these things in presence of our fellows, some would laugh us to scorn and mock us."'[43] Whitford's point was not that piety would be laughed at because it was somehow misguided or wrong. There is no hint of heterodoxy or freethinking here; Whitford's imaginary goodfellows are no less Christian than he is. Instead, the rabble laugh at piety because it is so alien to the world, allowable for monks, but outrageous in the laity.

This suggestion corresponds to the views of the philosopher John Morreal, whose 1983 book, *Taking Laughter Seriously*, delineated three principal theories of laughter.[44] First is the superiority theory, where humour is a kind of aggression to establish dominance; this is what Robert Burton, in his *Anatomy of Melancholy* (1621), called 'bitter jests'.[45] Second is the relief theory, in which laughter eases tensions and avoids catastrophes that might result from more serious responses; this is the safety-valve principle, made famous to early modernists by Mikhail Baktin in his classic *Rabelais and His World*.[46] Third is the incongruity theory, where laughter results from an irruption of the unexpected, illogical or inappropriate; as Blaise Pascal put it: 'nothing produces laughter more than a surprising disproportion between that which one expects and that which one sees.'[47] Studies of religion, to the extent that they take laughter seriously, have generally privileged the first and the second versions: 'relief' paradigmatically describes the long tradition of carnivalesque inversion, while 'superiority' describes the more savage satire of Reformation controversy. Early modern jokes about religion, however, increasingly drew their humour from 'incongruity': the failure of religion to fit into the social world.

This failure was obviously not new; saints had been laughed at in antiquity as well. But it intensified with the great new movements of

[43] Richard Whitford, *A Werk for Housholders* (London, 1530), sig. B1^{v}. I owe this reference to Peter Marshall: see also his *Heretics and Believers: A History of the English Reformation* (New Haven, CT, 2017), 60.

[44] John Morreall, *Taking Laughter Seriously* (Albany, NY, 1983).

[45] Democritus Junior [Robert Burton], *The Anatomy of Melancholy* (Oxford, 1621), 196.

[46] Mikhail Baktin, *Rabelais and His World* (Cambridge, MA, 1968).

[47] Cited in Morreall, *Taking Laughter Seriously*, 16.

lay piety that characterized the later Middle Ages. After all, the oddity which generated laughter in Whitford's anecdote was the fact that laypeople were now supposed to act like monks, breaking down the division of labour (and piety) that had usually prevented religion from spilling into the profane world. It exploded into prominence with the Reformation, which shattered the partition wall dividing the monastery from the world and attempted to sanctify virtually every aspect of social life. In this environment, a new world of jokes about religion unfolded, in which the quintessential anti-hypocrites were not pious professors who lived a life of self-examination and repentance, but the punters in the pews, straight shooters who did not pretend to be any more or less than ordinary people.

But there was a problem. Having determined that deeply pious and otherworldly religion was funny because of its incongruity with mundane social reality, one was left instead with a religion that was not deeply pious or otherworldly. This, however, was precisely the kind of religion that had been lampooned for centuries as humorous because of its failure to live up to Christian ideals. Nothing was left over; there was no third possibility. Once it was conceded that religion was ludicrous, whether it succeeded or failed, then the line between a religious joke and an irreligious joke started to disappear: there was no religious position left to inhabit that was not rightfully the object of humour. The accusation of religious hypocrisy therefore became a kind of safety valve of its own, a way for these jesters to maintain an authentically Christian position, even while expanding the realm of the laughable to include wide swathes of conventional Christianity. We are all hypocrites when we practise religion, these jokes seem to say; whether we choose to put on a face and practise it nonetheless, or whether we choose to sleep in on Sundays, the important thing is that we are able to laugh at ourselves.

This gleeful irreverence was still, in its own way, an expression of Christianity, operating in a different register, and employing the concept of hypocrisy very differently than we would ever find expressed in formal Reformation controversy. To emphasize the incongruity between religion and the world was, on the one hand, wholly orthodox. To admit that we are all hypocrites, going through the motions of religion in the hope that grace will catch us in the act and make our pantomime real, was orthodox as well. Both positions were broadly Augustinian and very Protestant, albeit Protestant in a rough-and-ready, non-evangelical sort of way. But the difference between the view from the pulpit and the view from the jestbooks was the difference between apologizing for this incongruity between religion and the world, and laughing at it. To the limited extent that there was a kind of unrefined *lumpen* theology at stake in these jokes, it allowed for religion without repentance, leaving the hard part to God. This position was never quite celebrated as a good idea; after all, it is the butt of these jokes. Yet nor was it any worse than hypocritically believing one's self capable of sainthood. The result was a kind of profane Protestantism, authentic but always a bit ridiculous.

This is why it is so important for historians of religion to read jokes. Profane Protestantism, if I may coin an oxymoronic expression, is certainly known to historians. It is the subject of a great deal of scholarship on festive popular culture: maypoles, church ales, Sunday sports, and the like.[48] One particularly important work in this tradition is Christopher Haigh's *The Plainman's Pathways to Heaven: Kinds of Christianity in Post-Reformation England* (2007), which rather brilliantly analyzes the subject-positions inhabited by unlearned rustics and boisterous delinquents in the face of pressure from the emerging ecclesiastical state, showing how attitudes which puritans attacked as atheism were subjectively their own brands of religion.[49] However, this scholarship tends to paint profane Protestantism as an ecclesiastical position, a proto-denomination, an alternative but parallel set of religious beliefs and practices constructed out of the same stuff as Lutheranism or Calvinism.[50] Jokes about religious hypocrisy, by contrast, allow us to see how different profane Protestantism was, because from within this subject-position, the opposite of hypocrisy was not always or necessarily an alternative piety. They suggest how painfully difficult it must have been for the producers and consumers of these jokes to resolve themselves into a self-conscious and confident ecclesiastical position. These jokes reveal a real precarity, an anxiety inherent in profane Protestantism, an awareness of being on the outside of English Christianity looking

[48] See, for instance, Ronald Hutton, *The Rise and Fall of Merry England: The Ritual Year, 1400–1700* (Oxford, 1994); Eamon Duffy, *The Stripping of the Altars: Traditional Religion in England, 1400–1580* (New Haven, CT, 1992); Christopher Marsh, *Popular Religion in Sixteenth-Century England* (New York, 1998).

[49] Christopher Haigh, *The Plain Man's Pathways to Heaven: Kinds of Christianity in Post-Reformation England 1570–1640* (Oxford, 2007).

[50] See especially Judith Maltby, *Prayer Book and People in Elizabethan and Early Stuart England* (Cambridge, 1998).

in. In works of 'Anglican' divinity, there is a bold attempt to paint traditionalism as the authentic Christianity of the people; but the jokes reveal a more fraught world where the authentic Christianity of the people is not so very Christian after all, even if it is embraced anyway.

To put this slightly differently, scholarship which has taken profane Protestantism in England seriously has tended to see it as a step on the path to modern Anglicanism. The evidence from jokes suggests that we might do better to see it as part of a long process whereby the confessional divisions of the Long Reformation lost their hold on the imaginations of English people and gradually ceased to organize their mental worlds. The concept of 'secularization' is intensely fraught in the historiography; even among historians willing to use the term, it has been located everywhere from the Reformation to the late twentieth century.[51] The evidence presented here has not been sufficient to the task of re-evaluating this important concept. But minimally, jokes about the hypocrisy of piety reflect the emergence of new ways of thinking about humanity's relationship to the sacred which earlier generations would not have recognized as religious at all. Perhaps the joke was on them.

[51] See C. John Sommerville, *The Secularization of Early Modern England: From Religious Culture to Religious Faith* (New York, 1992); Callum Brown, *The Death of Christian Britain: Understanding Secularisation 1800–2000* (New York, 2001).

Prudentes sicut serpentes: Dissimulation and Concealment in Japanese and Chinese Missions in the Seventeenth Century

Iveta Nakládalová*
Palacky University Olomouc, Czech Republic

This volume aims to explore the concepts of hypocrisy and dissimulation, conceived in the framework of the 'tensions at the heart of Christian teaching and experience'. This tension primarily points towards a conflict between ideal and lived practice; however, in certain circumstances, dissimulation and deceit might be understood as legitimate responses to a given situation. This article examines significant aspects of dissimulation in the specific case of early modern missions in China and Japan at the end of the sixteenth and throughout the seventeenth century, where missionaries often had to resort to disguise and concealment. Many of them had to overcome immense difficulties just to enter the country; some had to evangelize in secret, living in constant fear and facing ongoing persecution. In these territories, the 'policy of deceit' therefore became a relevant part of the proselytizing enterprise. I examine these practices of dissimulation with regard to evangelization strategies, and relate them to the sincerity and the confession of the faith, two of the central problems of the Christian credo. I argue that dissimulation was perceived, by the missionaries, as a legitimate and tactical response to the challenging and complex circumstances of the Japanese and Chinese missions in this period.

---

* The present article is part of the project 'Early Modern Evangelization of China: The Franciscan Mission and its Theory', which received funding from the European Union's Horizon 2020 research and innovation programme under the Marie Skłodowska-Curie grant agreement No. 892795, and which was carried out at Palacký University Olomouc. Křížkovského 511/8, 779 00 Olomouc, Czech Republic. E-mail: iveta.nakladalova@upol.cz.

Studies in Church History 60 (2024), 197–215
doi: 10.1017/stc.2024.10

Introduction

'Dissimulation' is an extremely rich and multifaceted notion, one which has played a vital role in Western philosophical, political and theological thought. Its conceptual genealogy is very complex, and its polysemous nature is overwhelming, since it associates a range of meanings which are related, but at the same time quite different. In one sense, dissimulation refers to disguise, camouflage or concealment; in another, it points towards falsehood, imposition or lying. I would like to emphasize the ambivalence between secrecy or hiding (in itself morally neutral) and, in contrast, the ethically questionable acts of fraud, hypocrisy and lying. This dichotomy embodies essential concerns about human conscience and conduct,[1] and fundamental dilemmas of truth, authenticity and fallacy. This is a particular issue in religious settings and in matters of faith and the Apostolate, where this antagonism has been described in terms of tension and conflict between, on the one side, sincerity of faith and ideal practice and, on the other, lived experience and the practical demands of society and evangelization.

In this article, I explore this topic in the context of early modern evangelization, because the missionary experience seems to exemplify, with particular clarity, multiple facets of dissimulation and hypocrisy in religious practice. Early modern missionaries were often working in environments hostile to the Christian faith, facing persecution and danger. Dissimulation, therefore, became a vital part of their experience, especially in those territories where evangelization was not part of an imperial or colonial enterprise. That is the case with both the Chinese and Japanese empires, which deliberately practised a policy of seclusion and suspicion towards foreigners that did not allow for any direct military or political support for the Apostolate on behalf of European rulers. From this point of view, the framework of early modern missions in Asia provides a useful insight into the complexity and richness of dissimulation, deceit and hypocrisy in religious and evangelization practice.

This volume of Studies in Church History is focused on hypocrisy and, particularly, on the moral implication of two-facedness. In my article, I will show how, in the context of evangelization, the terms

[1] For the genealogy of dissimulation and lying in European thought, see Perez Zagorin, *Ways of Lying: Dissimulation, Persecution and Conformity in Early Modern Europe* (Cambridge, MA, 1990), 5.

'hypocrisy' and 'dissimulation' themselves become problematic, because they often refer to disguise and concealment which are, in the given situation, inevitable. My first aim, therefore, is to provide a glimpse into the casuistry of duplicity and deceit in the mission field, which shows that early modern missionaries did not understand them as ethically questionable. I do so by presenting several contexts in which missionaries came to consider dissimulation as unavoidable. I also link some of these cases to the theological problem of the confession of faith, that is, the public statement or acknowledgment of Christian belief. Secondly, I demonstrate that this pragmatic understanding of dissimulation – particularly the aspect which I call 'smuggling the faith' – has profound implications, not only for evangelization strategies, but also for the early modern notion of conversion and the very idea of the truthfulness of the faith. My aim is not to offer a systematic treatment of dissimulation in the wider context of premodern evangelization, but to provide a case study analyzing a collection of significant testimonies which show that dissimulation was perceived by missionaries as a legitimate and pragmatical response to the complex circumstances of the early modern Japanese and Chinese mission. This approach represents only one facet of dissimulation in the context of the early modern Apostolate, not a universal missiological principle, but it sheds light on the relevant challenges and dilemmas of the evangelization enterprise.

Dissimulation in Recent Scholarship

In order to provide appropriate contextualization, I begin by offering a brief review of the relevant academic literature on the topic of dissimulation, which recent scholarship views as 'historically and … hermeneutically central to the political, religious, and literary culture of Early Modern Europe'.[2] It is even described as the 'central axis of the discussion on the religious freedom, the law, intimacy and the delicate relationship between the morals and the politics' in Europe after 1500.[3]

[2] Stefania Tutino, 'Jesuit Accommodation, Dissimulation, Mental Reservation', in Ines G. Županov, ed., *The Oxford Handbook of the Jesuits* (Oxford, 2019), 216–40, at 216.
[3] Diego Rubio, 'Di/simulación y fronteras religiosas en la temprana modernidad', in José Luis Betrán, Bernat Hernández and Doris Moreno, eds, *Identidades culturales en el mundo ibérico de la Edad Moderna* (Bellaterra, 2016), 39–50, at 39.

This religiously motivated dissimulation has been explored particularly in the context of doctrinal dissent, and specifically in relation to Nicodemism. However, Nicodemism applies mainly to European Protestant environments and, therefore, cannot be extrapolated without concessions to the overseas evangelization enterprise.[4] Several recent studies focus on specific practices of dissimulation, such as mental reservation and equivocation,[5] developed especially in the framework of the Reformation and Counter-Reformation in reaction to religious persecution, intolerance and increasing doctrinal imposition.[6] This was a period when 'the phenomenon of dissimulation became a focus of increased attention of dispute'[7] and it was widely discussed among Protestants.[8] Most significantly for this study, dissimulation has also been explored in relation to the tension between the 'inner space of conscience' or inner experience, on the one hand, and outward appearance and action, and the obligation to conform to political, social and religious standards, on the other.[9] All this scholarship is relevant for this study, although it is important to bear in mind that it explores dissimulation strategies in relation to religious dissent within Christianity. This differs significantly from the context of the overseas Apostolate, where similar strategies are applied in confrontation with peoples who were completely unfamiliar with the Christian faith. Dissimulation in the missionary context is still relatively

[4] See, for instance, Delio Cantimori, *Eretici italiani del Cinquecento e altri scritti*, ed. Adriano Prosperi (Turin, 1992; first publ. 1939); Carlo Ginzburg, *Il Nicodemismo. Simulazione e dissimulazione nell'Europa del '500* (Turin, 1970).

[5] See, for example, Perez Zagorin, 'The Historical Significance of Lying and Dissimulation', *Social Research* 63 (1996), 863–912; Zagorin, *Ways of Lying*, esp. 153–85.

[6] See, for instance, Albano Biondi, 'La giustificazione della simulazione del Cinquecento', in idem et al., eds, *Eresia e Riforma nell'Italia del Cinquecento. Miscellanea I* (Florence, 1974), 7–68.

[7] Zagorin, 'The Historical Significance of Lying and Dissimulation', 885.

[8] Ibid. 894.

[9] See, for example, Jean-Pierre Cavaillé, *Dis/simulations. Jules-César Vanini, François La Mothe Le Vayer, Gabriel Naudé, Louis Machon et Torquato Accetto. Religion, morale et politique au XVIIe siècle* (Paris, 2002). A further important strand of recent scholarship on dissimulation focuses on *ars dissimulandi*, that is, on the dissimulation related specifically to early modern courtly culture and political life, on the hiding of true thoughts and feelings, on the displays of etiquette and conversations skills. See Jon R. Snyder, *Dissimulation and the Culture of Secrecy in Early Modern Europe* (Berkeley, CA, 2009). Compare also Rosario Villari, *L'elogio della dissimulazione. La lotta politica nel Seicento* (Bari, 1987). For case studies of early modern dissimulation, lying and deceit, see Miriam Eliav-Feldon and Tamar Herzig, eds, *Dissimulation and Deceit in Early Modern Europe* (London, 2015).

unexplored territory, with only a few studies devoted specifically to missionary documents and experience.[10]

However, some scholars, such as Stefania Tutino, study the well-known strategy of missionary *accommodatio* in terms of dissimulation.[11] Accommodation is inherent to the approach taken by the Society of Jesus in its Apostolate in Japan and China, and the scholarship on this topic is extensive.[12] I would argue, however, that even though *accommodatio* did imply an adaptation to local societal and political norms, it lacked the element of secrecy and disguise which is an essential aspect of dissimulation. Furthermore, contemporary Jesuit perceptions of accommodation saw it, not in terms of

[10] See Tutino, 'Jesuit Accommodation, Dissimulation, Mental Reservation'. There is also a growing number of studies on missionary habit and clothing customs, especially in relation to missionary social identity, the strategy of accommodation and the discrepant attitudes of different orders towards evangelization. See Eugenio Menegon, '"The habit that hides the monk": Missionary Fashion Strategies in Late Imperial Chinese Society and Court Culture', in Nadine Amsler et al., eds, *Catholic Missionaries in Early Modern Asia: Patterns of Localization* (London, 2020), 30–49; Nadine Amsler, *Jesuits and Matriarchs: Domestic Worship in Early Modern China* (Seattle, WA, 2018), esp. 13–31 (ch. 1, '"Clothes make the man": The Jesuits' Adoption of Literati Masculinity'); Marina Torres Trimállez, 'Finding Norms for the Chinese Mission: The Hat Controversy in the Canton Conference of 1667/1668', in Manuel Bastias Saavedra, ed., *Norms beyond Empire: Law-Making and Local Normativities in Iberian Asia, 1500–1800* (Leiden, 2022), 285–328; and Rômulo da Silva Ehalt, 'Theology in the Dark: The Missionary Casuistry of Japan Jesuits and Dominicans during the Tokugawa Persecution (1616–1622)', in Bastias Saavedra, ed., *Norms beyond Empire*, 249–84. Ehalt quotes the letter of the Dominican Angel Ferrer Orsucci to his brother, in which he states that the priests in Japan 'used to dress like Spaniards', with a sword tied to the waist, long beards but no tonsure—a style that would later earn them the moniker 'barbones' or 'big beards' (ibid. 250). He adds, however, that in 'Japan Jesuits met severe criticism, both internal and external, when they decided to imitate Buddhist monks and wear their robes' (ibid. 251 n. 10).

[11] See, for example, Tutino, 'Jesuit Accommodation, Dissimulation, Mental Reservation'.

[12] For a general introduction to the topic of missionary accommodation and religious syncretism, see James S. Cummins, *Christianity and Missions, 1450–1800* (London, 1997); David E. Mungello, *Curious Land: Jesuit Accommodation and the Origins of Sinology* (Stuttgart, 1985); Anthony C. Clarke, *A Voluntary Exile: Chinese Christianity and Cultural Confluence since 1552* (Bethlehem, 2013); Joan-Pau Rubiés, 'The Concept of Cultural Dialogue and the Jesuit Method of Accommodation: Between Idolatry and Civilization', *Archivium Historicum Societatis Iesu* 74 (2005), 237–80; Andrés I. Prieto, 'The Perils of Accommodation: Jesuit Missionary Strategies in the Early Modern World', *Journal of Jesuit Studies* 4 (2017), 395–414; Ana Carolina Hosne, 'The Tricky Concepts of "Hispanicization" in Peru and "Accommodation" in China', in eadem, *The Jesuit Missions to China and Peru, 1570–1610: Expectations and Appraisals of Expansionism* (New York, 2013), 71–96.

deceit,[13] but rather in terms of extremely pragmatic adaptation to circumstances. In its utilitarianism, *accommodatio* is undoubtedly related to dissimulation; however, the dissimulation I want to explore here does not imply turning a blind eye to controversial dilemmas and to the lack of doctrinal purity in favour of a syncretical blending of the Christian faith with local customs, which is the central focus in the study of Jesuit *accommodatio* in their overseas missions.[14]

Historical Context: Early Modern Missions in China and Japan, and their Sources

In the early modern period, the Society of Jesus was the first order to arrive in the East Indies. Although the founder of the mission, Francis Xavier, never actually reached mainland China, he nonetheless laid the foundation of the Jesuit Japanese mission after his arrival in Japan in 1549. The Franciscans started their evangelization activities in Japan after 1587. As far as the Middle Kingdom is concerned, the Jesuits arrived in China in the 1580s, gaining access to the imperial court in 1601. The mendicant orders, including the Franciscans, entered the empire slightly later, in the first half of the seventeenth century. Both the Jesuit and the Franciscan orders produced an extensive body of missionary documents, which comprise vast collections of letters, *relationes* (reports on the state of the mission), chronicles,

[13] The Jesuit methodology of accommodation does seem to have a hint of secrecy in the case of missions in Protestant countries. According to the instructions of the Jesuit Robert Persons, it was necessary to conceal the true identities and change the names of the missionaries, in order to avoid suspicion: Tutino, 'Jesuit Accommodation, Dissimulation, Mental Reservation', 220. As Tutino puts it (ibid. 225): 'Where is the boundary that separates blending in from faking it?' But this concealment of one's true identity (and faking something which is not) would be, naturally, impossible in the overseas missions, where the outer appearance of European servants of God immediately gave away their radical alterity.

[14] It is a matter of constant scholarly discussion whether the *accommodatio* (especially in China) implied a doctrinal shift, an adaptation of the Christian credo to the spiritual and religious sensibilities of the local population, and whether it brought about the perils of 'unlawful' syncretism and doctrinal contamination, a sort of 'syncretic hybrid'. 'It was a complex and multilayered entity in which the global was in constant tension with the local and the everlasting and atemporal truth of Catholic theology was both opposed to and in conversation with the "tropical" religious, devotional, and cultural contexts in a continuously dialectic process that rendered the global Catholic identity diverse, textured, porous, precarious, and discontinuous.' Tutino, 'Jesuit Accommodation, Dissimulation, Mental Reservation', 219.

and a complementary body of treatises on problems of moral theology, and confessional and pastoral practice. These exist, together with the reworkings of these original accounts, in contemporary European anthologies and *historiae* on the progression of the mission. All these documents must be read and contextualized with the utmost caution, since they often became vehicles of doctrinal edification and religious propaganda. Nevertheless, I would argue that, despite their ideological bias and chronological spread across the whole seventeenth century, a 'transversal reading' in search of dissimulation and hypocrisy is legitimate, because all these sources share the common experience of evangelization carried out in perilous, often hostile, and always challenging circumstances. Moreover, despite this very extensive *corpus*, testimonies of dissimulation are surprisingly few, and they can be classified into three different groups, all of which are related to missionary practice: first, the physical concealment of the missionary in hiding (*missionarius occlusus*); second, the dissimulation of faith; and third, the smuggling of faith. There is one fundamental difference between these thematic strands: while the *missionarius occlusus* deals with simple physical concealment, the dissimulation and smuggling of faith exemplify key theological questions relating to the enactment of the Christian credo in the challenging circumstances of the mission.

Let us return initially to the conceptual breadth of dissimulation. Some scholars have suggested that the polysemy of this term can be dichotomized into covering up the truth (*suppressio veri*) or, alternatively, stating or insinuating untruth (*suggestio falsi*). This dichotomy corresponds to the early modern distinction between dissimulation and simulation,[15] as set forth by the Italian writer Torquato Accetto, author of one of the most influential early modern treatises on dissimulation:[16] 'Si simula quello che non è, si dissimula quello ch'è' ('we simulate that which is not, we dissimulate that which is').[17] The analysis in this article will focus on the *suppressio veri* (the suppression or concealment of truth) which, in the framework of missionary activity, is epitomized in the biblical verse which forms the title of this paper, *prudentes sicut serpentes* ('wise as

[15] See Rubio, 'Di/simulación y fronteras religiosas en la temprana modernidad', 42.

[16] On Accetto, see Snyder, *Dissimulation and the Culture of Secrecy in Early Modern Europe*, 59–67.

[17] Torquato Accetto, *Della dissimulazione onesta*, ed. Salvatore Silvano Nigro (Turin, 1997), 78. My translation.

serpents'), as cited in 1679 by the Franciscan Francisco Péris (1635–1701), one of the most active missionaries in China, especially in the Canton province in the 1670s. In a letter to his Father provincial, Fernando de la Concepción, Péris informed his superior about the advancement of the Franciscan mission in his province (Canton) and commented on the request of his brethren in Fokien (now the province of Fujian) for more missionaries. Warning against this, Péris explained that 'this is no time for simplicity and fervour; on the contrary, we have to proceed with utmost tact and prudence: *be ye therefore wise as serpents, quia omnia tempus habent*'.[18] Later in his letter, Péris exhorted that the arrival of new missionaries in China should be 'without noise, without any annoyance [*sin ruido, sin disgusto, y sin mucha nota*], and without attracting excessive notice, because in these times, much prudence and wisdom is needed.'[19]

This approach, related to the *suppresio veri* in that it implies 'not stating the whole truth', is also at work in the case of Ferdinand Verbiest (1623–88), one of the key figures of the Jesuit Apostolate in China during the seventeenth century. In one of his letters to Europe and to his fellow missionaries in China, Verbiest warns against the oath of obedience towards the Vicars Apostolic of the *Congregatio de Propaganda Fide* (Congregation for the Propagation of the Faith, CPF), which had been ordered by the decree of 29 January 1680, especially if the oath was to be delivered in written form by the missionaries. Even if done in secret, Verbiest cautions, the Chinese emperor would surely learn about it: firstly, because native clergy and catechists would have to swear it in Chinese; secondly, because servants and others in the missionaries' households would learn about it; and thirdly, because of potential Chinese apostatizing priests.[20] That would undoubtedly lead to the destruction of the mission and to widespread persecution, because the emperor

[18] Lorenzo Pérez, OFM, 'Cartas y relaciones de las misiones de China', *Archivo Ibero-americano* 8 (1917), 390–486, at 444. The first reference is to Matt. 10: 16: 'I am sending you out like sheep surrounded by wolves, so be wise as serpents and innocent as doves'. The second is to Eccles. 3: 1: 'For everything there is an appointed time, and an appropriate time for every activity on earth' [NET]. Emphasis in Péris's original.

[19] Ibid. 446.

[20] Verbiest to Gregorio López (in Canton), 15 January 1683, in Noël Golvers, ed., *Letters of a Peking Jesuit: The Correspondence of Ferdinand Verbiest, SJ (1623–1688)* (Leuven, 2017), 464 (no. 54). The same argument is subsequently developed in a letter from Verbiest to the cardinals of the CPF, 25 January 1684, in ibid. 545.

would learn that the pope does not require the Chinese emperor's licence in promulgating and practising the Christian religion.[21]

It is therefore absolutely necessary, insists Verbiest, to dissimulate the spiritual and legal authority of the pope and the fact that he does not respect the Chinese emperor's power over spiritual matters within the Chinese empire.[22] The Jesuits, Verbiest asserts, proceed always with the utmost care and caution, and 'we do not reveal to the Chinese (to the Mandarins and much less to the Emperor) even the fact that we have a father provincial.'[23] In sum, in relation to the power structures of the order and of the whole church, Verbiest recommends absolute dissimulation in the form of *suppressio veri*: to avoid disclosing the true state of affairs as much as possible. While writing this epistle, he asserts, the Vice Provincial Fr Dominicus Gabiani 'remains hidden in his cell … so that the members of the imperial family and the servants, who often visit us, know nothing about him; and in this way we avoid any inquiries.'[24]

Casuistry of Dissimulation and Deceit

Missionarius occlusus

This strategy of absolute secretiveness is the most discernible facet of dissimulation at work in the body of early modern Jesuit missionary documents from China and Japan, but it is by no means exclusive to the Society of Jesus. All the orders had to deal with the imperative of *missionarius occlusus*, the missionary who, for safety reasons, was obliged to remain hidden,[25] often physically 'hidden in his cell', as

[21] Verbiest to the cardinals of the CPF, 25 January 1684, in Golvers, ed., *Letters of a Peking Jesuit,* 545.

[22] Golvers, ed., *Letters of a Peking*, 447.

[23] Ibid. 469. All translations of Latin primary sources are mine.

[24] 'Manet ita occlusus in cubiculo … ut familiares et domestici Regis, qui omni momento solent nos adire, nil sciant de illo: et hoc facimus ad evitandas multas interrogationes': ibid. 469.

[25] In the context of Japanese mission, the condition of the *missionarius occlusus* even received a Japanese term. Ehalt, 'Theology in the Dark', 255, comments: 'numerous Christians helped hide missionaries during the persecution, a condition which European and Japanese alike referred to as *hissoku* (*fisocu* in Jesuit documents), i.e., "to be hiding, or enclosed, secluded, not going public"'. Ehalt further describes the fascinating phenomenon of a Japanese 'underground church' established after the persecutions at the end of the sixteenth and beginning of the seventeenth centuries, and the role of Christian brotherhoods (charitable confraternities following the model of the Portuguese

seen in Verbiest's letter.[26] This approach is further exemplified in the decision to dress so as to disguise the religious habit,[27] a common strategy mentioned in many accounts from Japan after the harsh persecution of Christians at the end of the sixteenth century and in the first decades of the seventeenth. One of the reports on the persecution of Christians in Japan during the 1630s recounts that the Franciscans Francisco de Santa María and Bartholomé Lauret, together with some of their servants, were unable to hide from their pursuers even at night (which is the 'disguise of the sinners'), so in the end had to 'withdraw to the mountains, under the cover of the forests and scrubland.'[28] We learn also that 'the fathers are never free from danger in Japan', and that the local Christian church is 'in grief and despair', since its ministers 'have no home, no place to stay; they are obliged to wander from house to house under the cover of the night, crossing deserts without ever feeling safe ... almost never can they celebrate the Mass in peace'.[29]

In this and similar cases of *missionarius occlusus*, the prudent *suppressio veri* entails the concealment of the missionary's true identity, habit and appearance, or the act of physical hiding. Jerónimo de Jesus was appointed the superior of the convent in Osaka in 1596, but his arrival was delayed and he was thus saved from being imprisoned with the other Franciscans, Jesuits and Japanese neophytes who were to be martyred as the 'Twenty-Six Martyrs of Japan' in 1597.

Misericórdias and native Buddhist lay organizations) that provided shelters for the hidden missionaries: ibid. 255.

[26] Another example from Verbiest's letters: Father Manuel Laurifice remained hidden in his cubicle for more than one month, 'and the emperor learns nothing about him. We have to hide our own brethren with so much caution ...': Golvers, ed., *Letters of a Peking Jesuit*, 633.

[27] For more information on missionary habit and dressing customs, also in relation to the accommodation practices, see above n. 10. For the study of this topic in the context of missions in Muslim territories, see Hugues Didier, 'Entre el disfraz y el martirio. Los viajeros jesuitas en el Asia musulmana (siglos XVI y XVII)', *ISIMU. Revista sobre Oriente Próximo y Egipto en la antigüedad* 6 (2006), 77–87. Didier points out that many Jesuits travelling in Muslim countries in Asia in the early modern period would of necessity wear Muslim clothes. He explores, with more detail, the case of Francisco de Georgis (1595), whose martyrdom was related to his confession of faith and also to his dress.

[28] Diego Aduarte, *Relacion de la persecucion que tubo la iglesia en el Japon en dos años, es a saber, desde el 1626 hasta el 1628. Singularmente à cerca de seys religiosos de la orden predicadores, es à saber, dos sacerdotes españoles y quatro legos Iapones* (Barcelona, 1669), fol. 14^{v}.

[29] Aduarte, *Relacion de la persecucion*, fol. 23^{r}.

Jerónimo de Jesus camouflaged his habit 'under Japanese dress' and remained hidden in the house of a native Christian. He narrates the misery and torments of such an existence in his letters. 'I could not possibly describe', he writes to his 'dearest brother', Juan de Garrovillas, on 20 December 1598,

> my going underground in caverns and finally in a sugar cane plantation, whose chill penetrated me in such a manner that I was close to death for a month and a half. I cannot possibly describe how I listened to the public announcement that whoever gave me food [*limosna*] or whoever attended mass was to be proscribed.[30]

There is great anxiety and tension in this testimony, but there is no conflict implied in the dissimulation and hiding, born, as they were, out of necessity.

Dissimulation of Faith

In certain contexts, however, the *suppressio veri* did entail a deeper confrontation between inner convictions and their outer manifestation, for example, when neophytes were forced to dissimulate their newly acquired faith. The European chronicle of the Jesuit mission in South Asia, based on the missionaries' regular reports and annual letters, the *Historia y anal relacion de las cosas que hizieron los padres de la Compañia de Iesvs por las partes de Oriente y otras en la propagacion del Santo Euangelio los años passados de 607 y 608* (*History and Annual Relation of Things Accomplished by the Fathers of the Society of Jesus in the Orient .... in the Years 1607 and 1608*) quotes a letter, presumably written by a Japanese woman, in which she laments being forced to conceal her 'newly acquired piety from the people of my household', since she cannot 'embrace *the things of salvation* with complete freedom of the heart'. Consequently, she prays at midnight and very early in the morning: 'I make the sign of the Cross and I pray before the others can see me'.[31]

[30] Lorenzo Pérez, OFM, 'Fr. Jerónimo de Jesus. Restaurador de las misiones del Japón. Sus cartas y relaciones', *Archivum Franciscanum Historicum* 16 (1923), 507–44, at 517.

[31] Christóbal Suárez de Figueroa, *Historia y anal relacion de las cosas que hizieron los padres de la Compañia de Iesvs por las partes de Oriente y otras en la propagacion del Santo Euangelio los años passados de 607 y 608* (Madrid, 1614), 308. Emphasis added.

The concealment or dissimulation of one's faith, as it appears here, is a complex theological problem related to the *confessio fidei,* the act of (public) declaration of faith. The intricate casuistry of the *confessio fidei* was developed in the body of European moral theology in the framework of expositions on the first precept of the Decalogue ('You shall have no other gods before me'; NET).[32] It is not possible to explore this topic in detail in this article, but it is apparent that in the South Asian missions, the act of *confessio fidei* very often took on features that clearly show the profound implications of dissimulation in the particular context of the missions.

The list of sixty-one *quaesita* (controversial issues, from the point of view of pastoral or confessional practice, whose resolution was to be made by church authorities) collected from the missionaries in Japan and analyzed by a group of Jesuit elders of the province of Japan gathered at the *Colégio da Madre de Deus* in Macau on 8 July 1620, includes several queries concerning the legitimacy of the efforts of Japanese neophytes to hide their faith by simulating being non-Christians. One of the doubts refers to the 'custom of hanging an *ofuda,* a slip of paper or a tablet placed at the entrance of a house that could indicate, among other things, that its residents were affiliated to a Buddhist temple or a Shintō shrine'.[33] The Japanese missionaries were doubtful about the legitimacy of this practice: were the Christians actually allowed to hang *ofuda* in their houses? In their resolution, the Jesuits judged the use of the *ofuda* to be a public denial of faith, and therefore illicit, but it might also have been perceived otherwise, in accordance with the casuistry of the *simulatio* of alien faith (*simulare alienam fidem*) which, according to some church authorities, could be tolerated in certain circumstances because it did not mean denying the faith of Christ internally (*interna voluntate*) but only externally (*externis signis*).[34]

[32] The theological authority is Thomas Aquinas, *Summa Theologica*, II–II. q. 147, 'De simulatione et hypocrisi'. For the casuistry of the *confessio fidei* in the particular context of the overseas missions, see Ehalt, 'Theology in the Dark', 251 n. 10, where he lists scholastic summas and treatises on moral doctrine that were most relevant for the missionary work.

[33] Ehalt, 'Theology in the Dark', 264.

[34] See, for instance, Martinus Becanus, *R. P. Martini Becani Societatis Iesu Theologi Manuale Controversiarum Huius Temporis* (Monasteri Westphaliae, 1624), 677. The discussion is included in ch. 2, 'An liceat negare fidem Christi, ad vitandam mortem' ['Whether it is allowed to deny faith in Christ in order to avoid death'], and ch. 3, 'An

This precept is related to the doctrine of *humanae aures* ('human ears') which allows for external dissimulation if the heart remains true. This principle was famously formulated by Pope Gregory the Great (d. 604) who, in his commentary on Job 35: 2, asserts:

> The ears of men judge our words as they sound outwardly, but the divine judgment hears them as they are uttered from within. Among men the heart is judged by the words; with God the works are judged by the heart.[35]

In sum, the confession of the faith was a highly controversial issue in contemporary theological debate, and its casuistry became even more complex in the challenging circumstances of overseas missions.

The Strategy of Smuggling the Faith

There is yet another relevant and specific aspect of dissimulation in early modern missionary documents from China and Japan, one which is not acknowledged in the body of moral theology and which does not appear, as far as I am aware, in any early modern guidelines on evangelization.

The chronicle on the Jesuit mission in South Asia quoted above, *Historia y anal relacion de las cosas*, describes an exorcism performed on a pagan Japanese woman in Meaco (present-day Kyoto), to whom a Christian physician was called. When the doctor arrived, he grew suspicious and he 'acknowledged the illness through its effects', meaning that he interpreted the illness as an action of the devil; consequently, he placed, secretly (*dissimuladamente*), an *agnus* (a pendant or medallion, showing the Agnus Dei) under the head of the bed. The possessed (or the devil inside her) 'acknowledged the virtue of the *agnus*, and she became very agitated, making loud noises'. The people around the bed realized what was happening and placed the *agnus* directly on the woman's body; the devil departed, leaving her quiet and in peace.[36]

aliquando liceat tacere aut dissimulare fidem Christi' ['Is it ever allowed to silence or conceal faith in Christ?'], 673–7.

[35] Gregory the Great, *Moralia* 26.10, online at: <http://monumenta.ch/latein/text.php?tabelle=Gregorius_Magnus&rumpfid=Gregorius%20Magnus,%20Moralia%20in%20Iob,%2026,%20%20%2010&level=4&domain=&lang=0&links=&inframe=1&hide_apparatus=1>, accessed 10 June 2022.

[36] Suárez de Figueroa, *Historia y anal relacion de las cosas*, 307.

A similar testimony, which concerns the imperative of secrecy in the missionary practice and – importantly – depicts the transition from an initial disguise towards subsequent disclosure, can be found in one of the reports from the province of Canton, written in 1695 by the Franciscan and Provincial Commissary Jaime Tarín. In it, Tarín mentions the practice of 'disguising/concealing the [religious] habit of the missionaries when proclaiming the Gospel'. He explains that this practice was initially introduced by the Jesuits, but that the Franciscans had deliberately chosen to maintain it and therefore wear Chinese dress until 'the time has come to lift the veil' (*hasta que sea tiempo oportuno para correr el velo*).[37]

The report does not elaborate further on this act of disclosure, but analogous testimonies provide indications of what it might have meant. In a letter written in Spanish and Latin in Beijing in 1684 (some ten years before the Franciscan report) and addressed to the Dominican José Duque in Manila, the Jesuit Ferdinand Verbiest provides recommendations to a group of Dominican missionaries who are to be sent to China. He asserts that they should be very careful when relating to the Chinese authorities. Drawing on his favourite metaphor which depicted mission as a perilous journey through rough seas, he here employs the image of a sea journey to emphasize the need to 'steer according to the directions of experienced pilots', that is, to adhere to the Jesuit approach. Claiming that 'the extraordinary and indiscreet fervour is of no use here in China', he recommends that missionaries must manage their missions ('gobernar la cristiandad'; literally 'govern their Christendoms') 'peacefully, in secret, and without making much noise'.[38] In this way, he claims, mission will gradually take hold, until such time as China discovers, 'to its own surprise, that it has become completely Christian' (*mirabitur se totam Christianam esse*).[39]

This must have been a vital strategy for Verbiest, since he repeated the same argument, almost verbatim, in another letter written the same year to the cardinals of the Congregation of the Propaganda Fide. In this second letter, he describes the 'silent and secret Christianization' that the Jesuits have been carrying out with the

[37] Lorenzo Pérez, OFM, 'Origen de las misiones franciscanas en la provincial de Kwang-Tung (China). Conclusión', *Archivo Ibero-americano* 8 (1917), 237–96, at 276.
[38] Golvers, ed., *Letters of a Peking Jesuit*, 559.
[39] Ibid. 559.

utmost caution for over a century. In his opinion, this strategy of initial concealment, eventually followed by an unexpected disclosure, was the only possible policy in the Middle Kingdom. Verbiest compares it to the approach of the Muslims, whose numbers, he says, 'have been progressively growing in the Chinese empire, so that now the authorities could not expel them without causing huge tumults and revolts'. In the same way, he writes, '*ipsa Sina tandem mirabitur se totam Christianam esse*' ('China itself, to its own surprise, will discover that it has become completely Christian').[40] The same idea of China discovering, with surprise, that it has become Christian was used by Verbiest in a third letter, addressed to Louis de Cicé, Missionary Apostolic: *miretur se totum paene insensibiliter esse Christianum* ('[China] would find itself, with surprise, Christian'). Here, Verbiest describes the process as *paene insensibiliter*, that is, 'almost imperceptible'.[41]

This is arguably the most remarkable aspect of dissimulation in early modern missionary documents. The clandestine approach perceives evangelization as a sort of 'smuggling the faith': introducing it in a furtive and covert way and behind the backs of the Chinese. Some scholars might associate this attitude with the accommodation method frequently associated with the Jesuits, and described as 'Jesuit willingness to accommodate themselves and their message to different audiences'.[42] However, it is also related to those strategies which have been described by modern historians as the 'apostolate through books',[43] or the 'apostolate through sciences and arts', or also the

[40] 'Atque eiusmodi cautela missionarii nostri Sinenses semper usi, Religionem Christianam iam per centum et amplius annos in vasto hoc gentis tam politicae imperio sustentarunt, cum interim a multis aliis Orientis regnis saepius fuerit in exilium expulsa, et a multis adhuc exulet. Et siquidem Emin(entiis) V(est)ris visum fuerit ut eadem cautela pergamus, tunc sacra Religio alterius et alterius saeculi iubilaeum intro hoc imperium celebrare poterit, *et ipsa Sina tandem mirabitur se totam Christianam esse*, vel certe Christianorum in illa numerus paulatim adeo excrescet, ut ipsa etiam invidia externam armorum vim contra illas adhibere vereatur; sicut nimirum cum Mahometanis modo contingit, qui iam a pluribus saeculis ita paulatim intra hoc Regnum invaluerunt, ut ipsiusmet Regni potentia de illis expellendis sine sui perturbatione et tumultus periculo consilium inire non possit': Golvers, ed., *Letters of a Peking Jesuit*, 547. Italics added.

[41] Ibid. 778.

[42] Andrés I. Prieto, 'The Perils of Accommodation: Jesuit Missionary Strategies in the Early Modern World', *Journal of Jesuit Studies* 4 (2017), 395–414, at 395.

[43] See Ad Dudink and Nicolas Standaert, 'Apostolate through Books', in Nicolas Standaert, ed., *Handbook of Christianity in China*, 1: *635–1800* (Leiden, 2001), 600–31.

'apostolate through gifts',[44] also typical of the Jesuits, which exploited the interest of the mandarins, and sometimes even of the emperor, in music, European mechanical tools such as clocks, or in astronomy, and in the European sciences more generally,[45] in order to promote evangelization. The assumption was that their knowledge of these disciplines would grant missionaries access to these highly-ranked officers and scholars, and indeed to the imperial court in general.[46] However, the strategy of the 'apostolate through earthly interests' was not conceived in the same, quasi-secretive ways as the approaches described by Verbiest. Rather, it was perceived as a necessary concession to Chinese tastes, and was often experienced as a heavy burden by the missionaries, who found that these earthly matters occupied too much time and did not allow enough space for spiritual matters. 'Smuggling the faith', in contrast, should be understood as a completely undisclosed, secret programme of mission, which seems to have been conceived specifically for China, precisely due to the empire's traditional secrecy and hermetic attitude.

Here we return to the phrase *prudentes sicut serpents*,[47] as used by the Franciscan Péris in 1679. According to the Gospel of Matthew, Christ's words, 'Be ye therefore wise as serpents', addressed to the apostles charged with spreading the faith, were followed by a further simile, 'and harmless as doves' (Matthew 10: 16): 'Behold, I am

[44] See, for instance, Qinghe Xiao [肖清和]: 'Apostolate through Gifts: Social-net and Accommodation of Catholicism in China during Late Ming and Early Qing Dynasties' ['礼物与明末清初天主教的适应策略'], *Dongyue Tribune* [东岳论丛] 3 (2013), 81–94.

[45] Ferdinand Verbiest was himself a skillful astronomer.

[46] The Jesuits were by no means the only order that would recommend the strategy of 'apostolate-through-earthly-matters'. The Franciscan Blas García writes in his autobiography about his relations with the local governor or king, and his attempts to introduce the Christian faith to him. Importantly, Blas García and his companions were granted access to the king because they were able to repair his European watches: 'I strived for *fitting in him* the knowledge of true God and of his holy law [*Yo procuraya encaxarle el conocimiento del verdadero Dios y su santa ley*], and on various occasions, I exposed it completely to him. However, even though the prince "would assert that he believed in what I was saying", he did not try to become Christian, because he knew he would have to abandon his concubines and the unjust interest he was obtaining from his vassals.' Lorenzo Pérez, OFM, 'Origen de las misiones franciscanas en la provincial de Kwang-Tung (China)', *Archivo Ibero-americano* 7 (1917), 203–354, at 230.

[47] It is worth noting that this text was refuted by Calvin as a justification for dissimulation and the duplicity of heart and language of the spiritualists, libertines and the Nicodemites. See Zagorin, 'The Historical Significance of Lying and Dissimulation', 894.

sending you out like sheep surrounded by wolves, so be wise as serpents and innocent as doves' [NET].

It should be noted that Thomas Aquinas refers to this instruction in his *Commentary on Saint Matthew's Gospel*,[48] when elaborating on the polarity between serpentine wisdom and dove-like *simplicitas* (simplicity, frankness, openness), which he associates with sincerity, both in the heart and in the mouth. Péris, on the other hand, did not contrast the prudent serpent with the dove, but characterized the need to be 'as serpents' with a reference to Ecclesiastes 3:1: *quia omnia tempus habent* ('because everything has its time').[49] In replacing the reference to the dove with this temporal qualifier, Péris therefore avoids the tension inherent in the Gospel of Matthew, namely the problem of deceit and the duplicity of the heart and of the mouth, which was the focus of Aquinas's exegesis.

By arguing that no more missionaries should be sent to China at the moment, because 'this is no time for simplicity [*simplicidad*] and fervour; on the contrary, we have to proceed with the utmost tact and prudence',[50] Péris called into question the *simplicitas* required by Christ in spreading the faith.[51] He rejects the idea that missionaries in China can take a frank and undisguised approach, instead giving priority to the highly pragmatic notion of the 'proper time which is yet to come', because there is 'time for every purpose under heaven'.[52]

For Péris, it seems that the pace of evangelization, at least in the challenging environments of the Japanese and Chinese missions, was a question of God's appropriate time and God's favourable moments and, more importantly, of the due measure that achieves the aim. In his argument, the concurrence of prudence and simplicity, inherent in Jesus's parable and in Aquinas's commentary,

48 Thomas Aquinas, *Corpus Thomisticum. Sancti Thomae de Aquino Super Evangelium S. Matthaei lectura*, ed. Roberto Busa (Turin, 1951), caput 10, lectio 2, online at: <https://www.corpusthomisticum.org/cml0619.html#87357>, accessed 12 June 2022.

49 Eccles. 3: 1: 'Omnia tempus habent, et suis spatiis transeunt universa sub caelo' ('For everything there is an appointed time, and an appropriate time for every activity on earth' [NET]. Pérez, 'Cartas y relaciones de las misiones de China', 444.

50 Ibid.

51 I cannot delve here into the intriguing relationships between deceit, duplicity of heart and language, and the shadowy side of dissimulation, which are implicit in this seemingly straightforward reference to serpents and doves. In a future article, I intend to explore this particular exegesis of the parable, along with the slippery space of two-facedness, and hypocrisy and trickery in missionary practice.

52 Pérez, 'Cartas y relaciones de las misiones de China', 444.

disappears, because the arduous circumstances of the mission required the simplicity of the doves to be left behind in order to adopt the prudence of the serpents. In missionary contexts, in sum, distinctive forms of concealment and smuggling of the faith exemplify the nature of dissimulation in religious practice, and particularly the tension between, on the one hand, the expectation that inner faith should manifest itself outwardly, and, on the other, the necessary concessions of outward faith in complex circumstances.

Conclusion

Various forms of dissimulation can be found in the context of Christian evangelization in late sixteenth- and seventeenth-century China and Japan. These reflect the specific circumstances of the local culture, which demanded secrecy and hiding. In this sense, the strategy of concealment seems to respond to the pragmatical requirements of the mission. However, this article has shown that 'smuggling the faith' might also be related to the slippery notion of two-facedness, and to the duplicity of heart and language, condemned by Thomas Aquinas. There is here a blurring of the distinction between *suppressio veri* and *suggestio falsi*, which undoubtedly deserves to be explored further, especially in relation to early modern strategies of evangelization. It has profound implications for the very idea of conversion and the profession of faith in the context of the Apostolate.

Unlike theological doctrine, which builds upon a complex casuistry regarding dissimulation in the *confessio fidei*, missionaries in their daily practice do not seem to have emphasized conversion as an act of individual consciousness, but rather to have seen it as a state of grace which should be achieved by any means. In other words, while official theological discourse might perceive dissimulation as a potential threat to the inner experience of faith, missionary practice, at least in the contexts described in this article, seems to have acknowledged deceit as an inevitable reaction to demanding circumstances. From this point of view, to see 'smuggling the faith' as morally questionable would seem to entail an anachronistic projection of our own spiritual and moral dilemmas onto these missionary documents. Modern scholarship on the history of Christianity in Asia, and particularly the early modern missions in China and Japan, needs to bear in mind the disparity between doctrinal discourse and missionary practice.

Early modern missionaries in China and Japan did not experience 'managing their mission in secret' ('que los missionaries goviernen su Christianidad … como a las escondidas', according to Verbiest)[53] as ethically ambivalent. Their attitude was pragmatic, not in the sense of 'the end justifies the means', but rather because of their deep belief that they were bringing the grace of faith to the gentiles. For these missionaries, 'smuggling the faith' did not represent a moral conflict, or a confrontation between authenticity and dishonesty, because it was done for the sake and salvation of the souls of the infidels. The early modern missions in China and Japan reveal not only the ambiguous and intricate nature of dissimulation, but also the dilemmas associated with it, especially in religious settings and in matters of faith.

[53] Golvers, ed., *Letters of a Peking Jesuit*, 559.

Hypocrisy, 'Prudence', 'Conscience' in Administration: The Congregation of Bishops and Regulars in Seventeenth-Century Italy

Simone Maghenzani*

University of Cambridge

The article argues that the post-Tridentine papacy was more focused on maintaining its own centrality than on implementing the reforms established by the Council of Trent. It shows that the Roman Curia often undermined its own bishops and interfered with their efforts to reform their dioceses. This practice – which might be perceived as hypocritical by us and was viewed as such by some contemporary commentators – was seen as justified by the baroque political virtue of 'prudence', and the idea of bishops being the conscience keepers of their dioceses. The article, in pondering the theme of hypocrisy, explores the work of the Sacred Congregation of Bishops and Regulars, which was responsible for overseeing the episcopate and religious orders. It uses previously unnoticed sources from the Bodleian Library in Oxford to show how the Congregation operated and how it perceived its role in defending the rights of the church and its clergy.

Introduction

'I would like to present the hypothesis,' wrote the German church historian Günther Wassilowsky, 'that the post-Tridentine papacy was more interested in the permanent assertion of its own decision-making powers and the symbolic representation of papal sovereignty than in the realisation of Tridentine reform.' 'I would like to make the case,' he argued, 'that the post-Tridentine papacy massively violated

* My thanks go to Miles Pattenden and Joan Redmond for reading a draft of this article, and to the Librarian at Girton College, Cambridge, Jenny Blackhurst, for her practical help. Girton College, University of Cambridge, Huntingdon Road, Girton, Cambridgeshire, CB3 0JG. E-mail: sm955@cam.ac.uk.

Studies in Church History 60 (2024), 216–237
doi: 10.1017/stc.2024.8

the order that was in fact created by the Tridentinum.'[1] It would be hard to disagree with these statements. The empowerment of Roman Catholic bishops to reform their dioceses pastorally is one of the most celebrated outcomes of the Council of Trent (1545–63), almost a term of reference of Counter-Reformation scholarship.[2] Many studies have nevertheless shown that to achieve such reform often meant going through a real struggle with Rome. In seventeenth-century Italy, the ability to improve diocesan discipline very often did not align with the actual instructions bishops received from the Curia, the Holy See's administrative centre.[3]

During the entirety of the Counter-Reformation, as much of the recent historiography has illustrated, the Roman Curia often undermined its own Italian bishops via the work of its congregations, the apostolic visitations of the dioceses, and the offices of the nuncios (who not only discharged the function of ambassadors, but also led their own tribunals).[4] On the ground, and almost on an everyday basis, aristocrats, clerics and common people tried to escape from the jurisdiction of their bishops. Clergy, especially when accused of wrongdoing, tried any possible expedient route to undermine episcopal decisions. In this, they repeatedly found a powerful ally in Rome.

The aim of this article is to consider the practice of the Curia in weakening diocesan reforms. Most importantly, I want to investigate the mindset of one of its institutions that was *de facto* at the heart of the unravelling of the local projects of episcopal reform, the Sacred Congregation of Bishops and Regulars, which, from the late sixteenth

[1] Günther Wassilowsky, 'The Myths of the Council of Trent and the Construction of Catholic Confessional Culture', in Violet Soen and Wim François, eds, *The Council of Trent: Reform and Controversy in Europe and Beyond (1545–1700)*, 3 vols (Göttingen, 2018), 1: 91, 82–3.

[2] See, for instance, Ronnie Po-chia Hsia, *The World of Catholic Renewal (1540–1770)*, 2nd edn (Cambridge, 2005; first publ. 1998); John W. O'Malley, *Trent and all That: Renaming Catholicism in the Early Modern Era* (Cambridge, MA, 2000).

[3] Celeste McNamara, *The Bishop's Burden: Reforming the Catholic Church in Early Modern Italy* (Washington, 2020); Thérèse Peeters, *Trust in the Catholic Reformation: Genoa 1594–1664* (Leiden, 2022); Thomas B. Deutcher, *Punishment and Penance: Two Phases in the Bishop's Tribunal of Novara* (Toronto, 2013).

[4] Massimo Firpo, *Riforma cattolica e concilio di Trento. Storia o mito storiografico?* (Rome, 2022); Elena Bonora, *Giudicare i vescovi. La definizione dei poteri nella Chiesa postridentina* (Rome and Bari, 2007); Michele Mancino and Giovanni Romeo, *Clero criminale. L'onore della Chiesa e i delitti degli ecclesiastici nell'Italia della Controriforma* (Rome and Bari, 2013).

century, was the Roman dicastery with oversight of the episcopate and religious orders, and of controversies among clergy.

This article will demonstrate that the Curia did not perceive as hypocritical the distance that occurred between the theory established at Trent and the outcome of many of its decisions. On the contrary, this article argues that the Congregation of Bishops and Regulars emphasized two ideas as justifications for its actions: the political virtue of 'prudence', so typical of seventeenth-century politics; and the idea of the bishop as the 'keeper of the conscience' of his diocese, and therefore the need for the prelate in question, in extreme circumstances, to obey a superior order of priorities and principles, sometimes even going against the letter of ecclesiastical law. The split between the narratives of reform and moral conformity of the clergy coming out of Trent's decrees, and the practice of 'negotiated justice', in which the Congregation was often embroiled, is palpable. At the heart of the Congregation's purpose was the defence, at all times, of the rights of the church and of its clerks in holy orders.

To our eyes, as well as in the eyes of some contemporary critics, hypocrisy was a key aspect of the Congregation's modus operandi. Hypocrisy is of course a polyhedric concept: it can belong to our interpretation, as well as appearing in accusations formulated at the time. It can be a contested concept. To some extent, hypocrisy as we understand it was framed in the age of the baroque as a form of political deception: it belonged to the virtues of statesmanship. But how else should the fact that, as we will see, almost none of the bishops in charge of the Congregations of Bishops and Regulars actually had any pastoral experience be interpreted? How should the fact that the ultimate authority in charge of local episcopal reforms and discipline consistently lay in the hands of absentee bishops be judged, if not as hypocritical?

When we look at the self-protective instincts of the ecclesiastical hierarchy, we can undoubtedly find elements of continuity, as well as discontinuity, throughout the history of the church. The preoccupation with scandal, and its avoidance, has through the centuries influenced the development of clerical discipline. It has also been deeply intertwined with Christian attitudes towards gender and sexuality. Extensive scholarship has paid attention to such themes, both in terms of historical research and of Christian ethics, as well as part of current political and ecclesiastical debates. This includes the work of Dyan Elliott, Francesco Benigno, Vincenzo Lavenia, Thomas

P. Doyle, Jean Bartunek and many others.[5] This article is more specifically concerned with investigating the new institutional mentalities of 'cover-up' that developed within the Roman Curia during the Counter-Reformation.

This article will explore material from five volumes of records (previously unnoticed by scholars) of the Congregation of Bishops and Regulars dating from the period 1604–7, currently held at the Bodleian Library in Oxford.[6] Most of these are copy letter books, with correspondence between officials of the Congregation and Italian dioceses, priests and ecclesiastical institutions. These show some of the day-to-day actions of the Congregation, their interest in pursuing certain cases, or the lack thereof. With the entire correspondence for a year at our disposal, we can see the routine nature of the work of the Congregation, what it cared about and how it thought. Antonio Menniti Ippolito has done something similar with the so-called *Positiones Episcoporum*, the official reports and complaints by the bishops to the Congregation in Rome, for the year 1664.[7] Our sources bring us to a much earlier period, and an even less organized and more indiscriminate operating of the Congregation at the moment when the initial post-conciliar willingness to reform was fading away.[8]

[5] Dyan Elliott, *The Corrupter of Boys: Sodomy, Scandal, and the Medieval Clergy* (Philadelphia, PA, 2020); Francesco Benigno and Vincenzo Lavenia, *Peccato o crimine. La Chiesa di fronte alla pedofilia* (Rome and Bari, 2021); Thomas P. Doyle, A. W. R. Sipe and Patrick J. Wall, *Sex, Priests and Secret Codes: The Catholic Church 2,000-Year Paper Trail of Sexual Abuse* (Horley, 2016); Jean M. Bartunek, Mary Ann Hinsdale and James F. Keenan, eds, *Church Ethics and Its Organisational Context: Learning from the Sex Abuse Scandal in the Catholic Church* (London, 2005).

[6] The Bodleian Library purchased these records from an Oxford antiquarian dealer in the mid-1980s. Prior to that date, we can only make the hypothesis that these papers were among those brought from Rome to Paris during the Napoleonic occupation (1809–14) and that, in 1815, rather than being sent back to Rome or destroyed, they passed into private hands.

[7] Antonio Menniti Ippolito, *1664. Un anno della Chiesa universale. Saggio sull'italianità del papato* (Rome, 2011), 87–94.

[8] Some of the administrative changes of the Congregation, compared to an earlier period, are described in Menniti Ippolito's *1664*. As with much of the Curia, a more substantial reorganization of the Congregation's operations would come in 1693, with the reforms of Pope Innocent XI: see Silvano Giordano, 'Uomini e dinamiche di Curia durante il papato di Innocenzo XI', in Richard Bösel et al., eds, *Innocenzo XI Odescalchi. Papa, politico, committente* (Rome, 2014), 41–56.

If we look at those sources most used in the historiography of Counter-Reformation pastoral reform – acts of synods, conciliar doctrinal documents, reports of visits *ad limina* (the compulsory quinquennial trip to Rome by diocesan ordinaries), apostolic visitations, letters to and from the Congregation of the Council – we might be justified in thinking that a transformation of the discipline of the clergy and an end to clerical abuses was actually taking place in the sixteenth and seventeenth centuries. But the Congregation of the Council was mostly tasked with (re)interpreting the legal corpus of Trent, as well as with encouraging the celebration of (often neglected) diocesan synods, checking pastoral reports and organizing episcopal visits to the Holy See. Except for oversight on the matter of forced vocations, it dealt with very few disciplinary cases.[9] In drawing instead on the documents of the Congregation of the Bishops and Regulars (and we could probably say something similar for the Camera Apostolica and the Tribunal of the Apostolic Signatura), the gap between the lofty ideals of Tridentine reform and the practical compromises of its everyday reality hit home quite quickly.[10]

It is not my intention to deny the centrality and creativity of Counter-Reformation bishops, especially outside of Europe and in missionary contexts. As Simon Ditchfield has rightly articulated, 'de-centering Trent' has to be a priority in the current historiography on the Counter-Reformation.[11] In addition, national contexts were hugely different, from France to Spain, to the Holy Roman

[9] Anne Jacobson Schutte, *By Force and Fear: Taking and Breaking Monastic Vows in Early Modern Europe* (London and Ithaca, NY, 2011). On the Congregation of the Council, see Federica Meloni, 'La Sacrée Congrégation du Concile et l'inteprétation de la réforme tridentine', in Soen and Wiem, eds, *The Council of Trent*, 1: 371–96, at 387; Christian Wiesner, *Tridentinisches Papsttum und Trienter Residenzpflicht. Römische Konzilsrezeption zwischen Kurienzantralismus und Seelsorgsreform (1563–1680)* (Stuttgart, 2022). See also Menniti Ippolito, *1664*, 23–5. On local synods, see Pietro Caiazza, *Tra stato e papato. Concilii provinciali postridentini (1564–1648)* (Rome, 1992).

[10] Maria Grazia Pastura Ruggiero, *La reverenda Camera Apostolica e i suoi archivi* (Rome, 1984); Christopher Weber, 'Il referendariato di ambedue le Segnature. Una forma speciale del 'servizio pubblico' della Corte di Roma e dello Stato pontificio', in Armand Jamme and Olivier Poncet, eds, *Offices et papauté (XIVe–XVIIe siècle). Charges, hommes, destins* (Rome, 2013), 565–86; Mario Rosa, *La Curia romana nell'età moderna. Istituzioni, cultura, carriere* (Rome, 2013).

[11] Simon Ditchfield, 'De-centering Trent: How "Tridentine" Was the Making of the First World Religion?', in Soen and François, eds, *The Council of Trent*, 3: 185–208, at 192.

Empire.[12] Even within Italy, the nature of episcopal appointments, their jurisdiction and the pressure put on them by secular authorities, differed significantly between the papal states and the Kingdom of Naples, and those localities where the secular state was more involved (or tried to be) in the administration of ecclesiastical justice, such as the Duchy of Milan, the Duchy of Savoy and the Republic of Venice.[13] Further, as it has been amply demonstrated, when we look at the Italian episcopate, periodization also matters: it is undeniable that there was an early push for reform by some bishops in the immediate aftermath of the Council.[14] Nevertheless, such efforts soon weakened, and by the early seventeenth century, Rome was not that keen to oversee the implementation of sweeping reforms (and would not be until at least the 'second wave' of reforms in the 1670s and 1690s, or even until those of Benedict XIV in the eighteenth century).[15]

It is my contention that the documents examined here offer an insight into Rome's thinking about church discipline and local ecclesiastical justice. What emerges is a world of political dissimulation, cunning political manoeuvring, legal escamotages and, sometimes, outright hypocrisy.

The Congregation of Bishops and Regulars

The Sacra Congregatio negotiis et consultationibus Episcoporum et Regularium praeposita traced its origins to the curial reforms of Pius V (1566–72), Gregory XIII (who in 1576 created a Congregation of

[12] Joseph Bergin, *The Making of the French Episcopate, 1589–1661* (New Haven, CT, 1996); Christian Hermann, *L'Église d'Espagne sous le patronage royal (1476–1834)* (Madrid, 1988).

[13] Federico Chabod, *Lo Stato e la vita religiosa a Milano nell'epoca di Carlo V* (Turin, 1971); Achille Erba, *La Chiesa sabauda tra Cinque e Seicento. Ortodossia tridentina, gallicanesimo savoiardo e assolutismo ducale (1580–1630)* (Rome, 1979); Paolo Prodi, 'Chiesa e società', in Gaetano Cozzi and Paolo Prodi, eds, *Storia di Venezia. Dalle origini alla caduta della Serenissima*, 14 vols (Rome, 1995), 6: 305–39.

[14] Mario Rosa, 'La Chiesa meridionale nell'età della Controriforma', in Giorgio Chittolini and Giovanni Miccoli, eds, *Storia d'Italia Einaudi. Annali 9* (Turin, 1986), 295–346, at 299. Rosa clearly shows that by the 1580s a settlement was reached between Naples and the Roman Catholic Church, allowing several traditional practices to continue.

[15] Firpo, *Riforma cattolica*; Bösel et al., eds, *Innocenzo XI Odescalchi*; Maria Teresa Fattori, *Benedetto XIV e Trento. Tradurre il concilio nel Settecento* (Stuttgart, 2015).

Bishops) and, most importantly, Sixtus V (who famously reformed the Curia via his bull *Immensa Aeterni Dei* in 1588).[16] The joint oversight of bishops and regulars by one congregation was achieved only in 1601 under Clement VIII. A few decades later, Urban VIII made clear that the Congregation's remit was essentially 'universal', with the only limitation that it could not (re)interpret Trent's canons. From the Congregation of Bishops and Regulars in 1622 stemmed the Congregation of *Propaganda Fide*, as well as the Congregation of Ecclesiastical Immunity in 1626.[17] We should not think of congregations as being like modern cabinet ministries: the boundaries of responsibility were porous, and the outcome of a request often depended on who was approached in Rome. The congregations received reports on all sorts of questions, but mostly accusations concerning bishops, priests and the regular orders, as well as complaints of bishops to Rome. The key issues were: matters of benefices, patronage and patrimony; clerical concubinage (a terrain disputed, of course, with the Inquisition); diocesan and parish vacancies, especially when not everything went smoothly; questions concerning rites, especially how much it was right to charge for certain services; disputes among clergy and local authorities, between regular and secular clerics, and between bishops and monasteries; conflicts of jurisdiction among tribunals, especially between the tribunal of the bishop, that of the nuncio, and the Holy Office; and finally the issue of the 'dowries' of young aristocratic women who joined the regular life.

When we look at the actual archive of the Congregation in Rome – a very extensive one, preserved in the Apostolic Archive – the reality seems less grand. According to the statistics compiled by Antonio Menniti Ippolito, ninety-eight per cent of the sources pertain to

[16] Antonio Menniti Ippolito, 'Sacra Congregazione dei Vescovi e Regolari', *Associazione Italiana dei Professori dei Storia della Chiesa*, online at: <https://www.storiadellachiesa.it/glossary/congregazione-dei-vescovi-e-regolari-e-la-chiesa-in-italia>, accessed 8 January 2024; Giovanni Romeo, 'La Congregazione dei Vescovi e Regolari e i visitatori apostolici nell'Italia post-tridentina: un primo bilancio', in Maurizio Sangalli, ed., *Per il Cinquecento religioso italiano. Clero, cultura e società* (Rome, 2003), 607–14; Maria Teresa Fattori, *Clemente VIII e il Sacro Collegio, 1592–1605. Meccanismi istitutionali e accentramento di governo* (Stuttgart, 2004), 173–8.

[17] Massimo Carlo Giannini, 'La Congregazione dell'Immunità ecclesiastica. Per una storia dell'istituzione e dei suoi componenti (1623–1700)', *Archivium Historiae Pontificiae* 53 (2019), 301–26.

Italy. Of these, eighty per cent refer to southern Italy.[18] The main exception is some correspondence with the Iberian peninsula. Simon Ditchfield is correct in articulating some caution in inferring from this that the early modern papacy – as Menniti Ippolito argued – could be seen less as a universal monarchy (the classic argument put forward by Paolo Prodi),[19] and more as a commonwealth of national churches.[20] Of course, it would be possible to argue that there was quite a difference between the representation the papacy gave of itself and the everyday (and very Italian) life of the Curia. Maria Antonietta Visceglia has found the right balance in describing the self-understanding of the papacy at the turn of the seventeenth century, showing the presence both of strong Italian dynamics and of globalizing forces and narratives.[21] In sum, we would be too quick in reducing the preoccupation of much of the Curia to Italy. Nevertheless, it is quite clear, in this instance, that the focus of interest of the Congregation was often local and Italian, deeply intertwined with specific cultural, political and social dynamics, in which the Italian cardinals and bishops of the Curia were personally embedded.

Investigating the administrative workings of the early modern Roman Curia can often feel like entering into a thick forest.[22] The forest turns into an impenetrable jungle when we move onto the ground of church life. Trying to make sense of rights and privileges, feudal entitlements and ecclesiastical liberties, forms of patronage and local traditions, can become bewildering, and can make any attempt at systematization and generalization almost impossible.[23] Michele Mancino and Irene Fosi, for example, have shown the many conflicts

[18] Menniti Ippolito, *1664*, 87–152.

[19] Paolo Prodi, *Il sovrano pontefice: un corpo e due anime. La monarchia papale nella prima età moderna,* 2nd edn (Bologna, 2006; first publ. 1982).

[20] Ditchfield, 'De-centering Trent', 192. See also, idem, '"In Sarpi's shadow": Coping with Trent the Italian way', in *Studi in memoria di Cesare Mozzarelli*, 2 vols (Milan, 2008), 2: 1585–606.

[21] Maria Antonietta Visceglia, 'The International Policy of the Papacy: Critical Approaches to the Concepts of Universalism and Italianità, Peace and War', in eadem, ed., *Papato e politica internazionale nella prima età moderna* (Rome, 2013), 17–62.

[22] Niccolò Del Re, *La Curia romana. Lineamenti storico-giuridici*, 4th edn (Vatican City, 1998; first publ. 1952), 369–72.

[23] Claudio Donati, 'Vescovi e diocesi d'Italia dall'età post-tridentina alla caduta dell'antico regime', in Mario Rosa, ed., *Clero e società nell'Italia moderna* (Rome and Bari, 1992), 321–89. See also Gaetano Greco, 'Fra disciplina e sacerdozio. Il clero secolare nella società italiana dal Cinquecento al Settecento', in ibid. 45–113.

of jurisdiction among the several branches of ecclesiastical penal justice.[24] When we move to the matter of benefices, the complications can appear endless: in early modern Italy, these benefices could be major or minor, they could be chaplaincies *sine cura* (without care of souls), curacies, canonries, or be constituted by the simple right to officiate. One could be the holder of a *provostura* or *prepositura nullius*, a type of benefice free from episcopal oversight – and the language would often change according to regional habits. Patronages could be ecclesial (that is, owned by religious orders, bishops or monasteries) or secular, and in turn these could be split among those kept by individual families, those which were elective, and those belonging to secular institutions.[25] Even the best-intentioned bishop had to negotiate a constant set of limitations to his authority and see many doors slammed in his face: a constant reminder that he had no right to trespass. If much of this was typical throughout early modern Europe, the Italian south was for many reasons the apex of this complex world: the Kingdom of Naples had the highest number of dioceses (131) of any country in Christendom, which were often extremely small and with very limited financial resources.[26] Its clergy was therefore very often poor and highly dependent on local economic and social networks, not least because of the common presence of *ricettizie* churches, temporal associations of self-organized and property-owning priests. Clerical literacy was rather limited (it would take up to the eighteenth century for the establishment of diocesan seminaries in some localities); the number of ecclesiastical properties was enormous and deeply intertwined with the power of local feudal and urban aristocracy; monasteries and churches could be quite isolated, and it could take years for illegal practices to become noticed by superiors.[27] All this was the cause of endless conflicts and

[24] Michele Mancino, 'La giustizia penale ecclesiastica nel primo Seicento: linee di tendenza', *Studi Storici* 51 (2010), 1003–33; Irene Fosi, *La giustizia del papa. Sudditi e tribunali in età moderna* (Rome and Bari, 2007).

[25] On the matter of the *jus patronatus*, see Gaetano Greco, 'I giuspatronati laicali in età moderna', in Chittolini and Miccoli, eds, *Storia d'Italia*, 9: 531–72. For the patronage of bishoprics, see Mario Spedicato, *Il mercato della mitra. Episcopato regio e privilegio dell'alternativa nel Regno di Napoli in età spagnola, 1529–1714* (Bari, 1996). See also Simone Maghenzani, 'Giuspatronati laicali e benefici ecclesiastici. Ripartendo dal protestantesimo', *Rivista Storica Italiana* 133 (2021), 783–824.

[26] Rosa, 'La chiesa meridionale'.

[27] Enrico Stumpo, 'Il consolidamento della grande proprietà ecclesiastica nell'età della Controriforma', in Chittolini and Miccoli, eds, *Storia d'Italia*, 9: 264–89; Giovanni

of numerous reports to the Curia in Rome, which was frequently asked to intervene by those who wanted to keep their bishop at bay.

The Congregation of Bishops and Regulars shows us a world of clerical privileges and of resistance to reform, an opposition evenly shared between local clergy and parts of the Curia in Rome. Hypocrisy was essential to this reality. It appeared in the form of immunities and cover-ups of corruption accusations, but most importantly in protecting clerical power and entitlement above the rights of lay victims of all sorts of abuses. Protecting the status and public honour of the clergy – even sometimes defending the indefensible – was at the heart of the Congregation's operation. But what was the reasoning behind all this?

Cardinal Giovan Battista de Luca – the great ecclesiastical lawyer of the mid-seventeenth century – offered a good insight into the mindset of those who governed the Bishops and Regulars.[28] 'The Congregation', he wrote:

> is used to proceed reasonably as an ecclesiastical prince, with the rules of prudence, not deviating of course from the *sensus*, that is, from the reasons of the sacred canons and the councils, but also with those news and information that are perhaps best kept secret, as the nature of these matters require, many of which concern supporting the dignity of bishops, the reputation of orders, and that of monasteries, and therefore it is better not to show these in public ... as it is necessary to govern them with pious ecclesiastical politics.[29]

Prudence, *sensus ecclesiae*, dignity, reputation: these are four terms that remind us of the forms and expressions of politics in the age of the baroque. They are four pillars of the politics of dissimulation

---

Brancaccio, 'La geografia ecclesiastica', in Giuseppe Galasso and Rosario Romeo, eds, *Storia del Mezzogiorno* (Rome, 1994), 235–76; Firpo, *Riforma Cattolica*, 172–3.

28 Agostino Lauro, *Il cardinale Giovanni Battista de Luca. Diritto e riforma dello Stato della Chiesa* (Naples, 1991).

29 'Ragionevolmente alle volte suol camminare da principe ecclesiastico, con le regole prudenziali, non devianti però dal senso, ovvero dalla ragione de' sacri canoni e de' concilii, e con le notizie e informazioni anche occulte, così richiedendo la qualità de' negozi, molti de' quali, o per sostenere la dignità episcopale, o la riputazione delle religioni, o de' monasteri, non conviene di mettere in pubblico ..., sicché comple di governarli con una pia ecclesiastica politica' : Giovan Battista de Luca, *Il Dottor volgare ovvero il compendio di tutta la legge civile, canonica, feudale e municipale* (Rome, 1673), 4: 514. See also Menniti Ippolito, *1664*, 26.

that were so typical of this era (and perhaps are typical of outright hypocrisy too). To some extent, this was clearly the legitimization of outright Machiavellian behaviour. Indeed, to some extent too, De Luca was simply rationalizing, a posteriori, the practice of the Congregation. This was an explanation, also, that Rome had to think with the 'mind of the Church', keeping its reputation as its highest priority, and that, at all costs.

Keeping the Conscience of the Church

In the spring of 1604, the Congregation wrote to the office of the archbishop of Naples, asking to exert pressure on the archpriest (the dean) of the cathedral, that he should not reprimand and discipline one of the canons, known for going around with a knife with which he intimidated people.[30] The canon was apparently a 'well connected' man, and some of the city greats would be upset if he were to be punished, despite his behaviour.[31] On 27 July, the Congregation wrote again to the see of Naples regarding accusations of sexual impropriety against one of the priests: they objected that 'he is known to us as a good man, and honourable priest', and recommended that the authorities close the inquiry.[32]

These exchanges are a good example of the Congregation's practices. Several letters from the Congregation of Bishops and Regulars engage with Trent's decisions, formulating exceptions to the new rules concerning discipline and oversight. Trent had established a new disciplinary system, but, in response to emergencies, for reasons of 'prudence', or in needing to keep scandals from coming out, the old procedure of managing affairs was often still invoked. The preferred method of solving an issue was the extrajudicial one. Often a letter would be sent from the Congregation, presenting the way out: it was rare that Rome would indicate that a petition had to be heard by a court, and even more rarely, by a local one. Occasionally, the Congregation of the Council would be consulted on a point of

30 These letters reached Naples during the vacancy that had arisen with the death of the archbishop, Cardinal Alfonso Gesualdo, in February 1603; he was replaced only in 1605 by Cardinal Ottavio Acquaviva d'Aragona. The *sede vacante* might help to explain the rather peremptory tone used by the Congregation.

31 Oxford, Bodl., MS Ital. c. 82–86, now in MS Cons. Res. c. 44, vol. 1, fol. 58^{r}.

32 Ibid., fol. 69^{r}.

doctrine or principle, but mostly the Congregation took its own decisions directly. From time to time, a case was entrusted to a cardinal of the Congregation, who would have to come up with a solution, and would have oversight of the outcome.[33] Sometimes, the Congregation simply wanted to exercise what was, essentially, a moderating effect. When the bishop of Alatri (Lazio), Michelangelo Brancavalerio, became the object of a complaint from his community concerning his brother who had been lending money at high interest, beating people up and issuing threats, the Congregation encouraged the bishop to try to calm down his sibling and stop him from misbehaving (instead of exiling him, as demanded by the petitioners).[34] The general picture is of a Congregation that was constantly concerned about the defence of the rights and privileges of the church and the clergy, even on matters as trivial as asserting the right to choose the preacher for the Lenten cycle.[35]

Priests were not always defended. A clear situation in which a priest would face the punishment of the Congregation was if he himself had decided to avail of secular justice. On 14 October 1604, for example, the Congregation wrote to the bishop of Senigallia (Marche), Antaldo degli Antaldi, about a priest causing 'discord among the people', because he had decided to turn to a secular tribunal – instead of an ecclesiastical one – to defend some of his privileges. This would potentially destabilize the recognition of ecclesiastical immunities, and so was to be brought to an end, and the priest punished for unintentionally undermining the church.[36] The only eventuality in which the Congregation was not reluctant to involve secular justice was in cases of sexual violence of priests against nuns: in such situations, the Congregation generally favoured the hanging of the priest, mostly privately, but occasionally in public. Sometimes, there was no better outcome for the victim: in extreme cases, nuns (especially those who had become pregnant and either given birth to children or undergone an abortion) were enclosed in

[33] Gaetano Moroni, *Dizionario di erudizione storico-ecclesiastica*, 109 vols (Venice, 1840–78), 16: 278.

[34] Rome, Vatican City, Apostolic Vatican Archive, Congr. Vescovi e Regolari, *Registra Episcoporum*, 109, c. 50^{r-v}.

[35] Stanislao da Campagnola, 'La predicazione quaresimale. Gestione, evoluzione, tipologie', in idem, *La predicazione in Italia dopo il Concilio di Trento tra Cinquecento e Settecento* (Rome, 1994), 243–80.

[36] Bodl., MS Ital. c. 82–86, now in MS Cons. Res. c. 44, vol. 1, fol. 221^{r}.

their cells for the remainder of their lives, with the doors bricked up.[37]

Matters of privileges and benefices constantly appear in these Oxford documents: the Congregation for the Ecclesiastical Immunity was, at this stage, yet to be founded. The case of the bishop of Gravina (Puglia), Girolamo De Mari, who had also acted for a while as the apostolic administrator of the diocese of Matera, and who refused – once an episcopal vicar had been dispatched to Matera – to give up the income of several pensions imposed on benefices by him, is indicative of much of the correspondence.[38] Often the Congregation wrote in support of the local bishop against some monastery or stubborn parish priest who was unwilling to submit to the will of the ordinary. Sometimes, the pettiness was extraordinary. The bishop of Vicenza (in theory, the absentee Cardinal Giovanni Dolfin, but in all probability the auxiliary bishop Raffaele Inviziati) had no success in resolving a dispute between a nunnery and a parish priest on the matter of who should possess the lock and keys of a church (and thus the right to open up and close the building). In the end, only Rome could resolve the dispute.[39] Whilst on financial issues the Congregation usually took the side of the bishop, on disciplinary matters the Congregation often undermined the decisions of the ordinary, frequently restoring priests to their previous roles, regardless of their suspensions or excommunications.[40] The Congregation was always adamant in defending clergy from any secular inquiry, or from any dispute with local authorities. Occasionally, the technique was a bureaucratic one: constantly asking for additional information, for further discussion, or for a re-examination of the jurisdiction's rights, before any decision should be taken.[41] The practice of undermining the local bishop became quite evident. In 1600, as part of his attempts to limit the success of those who opposed pastoral reforms in the Kingdom of Naples, Clement VIII had to explain to the Congregation that 'from now onwards we should proceed with more calm with bishops, and not trust so easily the reports of the complainants.'[42] His plea went unheard.

[37] Mancino and Romeo, *Clero Criminale*, 182.
[38] Bodl., MS Cons. Res. c. 44, vol. 1, fol. 166$^{r–v}$.
[39] Ibid., vol. 2, fol. 105^{r}.
[40] Ibid., vol. 1, fol. 429^{v}.
[41] Ibid., vol. 2, fol. 272^{r}.
[42] Quoted in Fattori, *Clemente VIII*, 178 n. 97.

Several cases in these files concerned some of the more isolated dioceses of the Italian south. The lack of clergy able to say mass was always given as a reason (or an excuse?) for priests previously accused of wrongdoing or suspended, to be moved or redeployed. Close to Easter of 1607, the Congregation did not hesitate to announce to the southern Italian dioceses: 'We judge right that – among those who had incurred excommunication or had been suspended – some will be given the faculty to absolve in foro conscientiae [i.e. in confession] as the timing requires it because of the imminence of the Holy Days.'[43] Scarcity of priests was also the reason behind the solution offered in the following strange case. The bishop of Marsico (Basilicata) had initially refused to absolve a priest who had entered a marriage, but had also recently become a widower, arguing that this was a case reserved for the pope. The issue was serious because the priest had married in church after having been ordained. In the end, the general agreement was for an absolution, because the diocese was in desperate need of clerics, and after all the poor chap was indeed a good man.[44]

Despite the lack of available priests, in many parts of Italy – and especially in Calabria – there was a plethora of men ordained only in minor orders. They often did not have a benefice to support themselves and frequently ended up leading the life of brigands, yet they still routinely asked for exemptions from the secular courts. Criminality was a common way of life in these circumstances, and cases of homicide were frequent. A group of minor clergy had even managed to 'run a brothel' out of the church of Magisano, in the diocese of Catanzaro (Calabria), in order to make ends meet. The bishop's frustration could not be greater: it was like fighting against a hydra, with new heads constantly reappearing despite his actions.[45] He was not alone. The bishop of Montepeloso (Basilicata), Lucio Maranta, complained to the Congregation that the local 'bosses' among the clergy were making his life hell, although he had inflicted on them 'ten trials' (the most significant case concerned sexual

[43] 'Di quelli i quali per il passato fussero incorsi in scomunica o sospensione si giudica bene [che si] dia l'autorità ad alcuni che possano assolvere et abilitare *in foro conscientiae* tanto più che l'opportunità del tempo lo richiede per la vicinanza dei giorni santi.' Bodl., MS Ital. c. 82–86, now in MS Cons. Res. c. 44, vol. 3, fol. 271^{r}. Italics mine.

[44] Apostolic Vatican Archive, Congr. Vescovi e Regolari, *Registra Episcoporum*, 109, c. 143^{v}.

[45] Menniti Ippolito, *1664*, 129.

intercourse with a virgin, fornication with married women and usury). The Congregation did not take the side of poor Maranta, instead referring the case to a neighbouring bishop who quickly proved to be more friendly to the accused.[46] In a story well illustrated by Massimo Firpo, some bishops decided to give up: according to Cornelio Musso, bishop of Bitonto (Puglia), his flock was 'undisciplined and undisciplinable', and he was lost in a nest of vipers of 'pretentions of patronages of churches and monasteries'. In the end, he decided to ask Rome to be allowed 'to leave this Egypt': a bishopric was just a way 'to lose time, stuff, and scholarship'.[47]

In the more sordid stories, it is often clear that the incriminated clergy were aware that Rome could offer them a helping hand in getting out of trouble. Invoking a conflict of jurisdiction was one possible way out. Several priests, for example, had been found sleeping or living with young boys or girls (a four-year-old girl, in the case of Larino's priest). Bishops often denounced these situations to Rome: in the words of the contemporary ordinary of Pozzuoli (Campania), Jerónimo Bernardo de Quirós, several priests were guilty of 'the most indecent actions in respect of their habit and clerical honesty.'[48] Rarely were they dismissed or put on trial: more often, they were simply moved to another parish or diocese.[49] When a priest who had raped his own daughter in a church building in the diocese of Ferentino was put in jail (in the same room as the victim!), he did not hesitate to call on Rome on procedural grounds, to free him both from the episcopal tribunal and from the secular one, claiming the immunity provided by the building. When the archpriest of the *nullius* church of San Pietro di Scafati (a peculiar) was found to have killed a man during a wild boar hunt, a conflict between the bishop of Nola, Francesco Gonzaga (whose diocese surrounded San Pietro's Church) and the archbishop of Brindisi, Francesco de Estrada (where the crime had been committed) ensued. Despite having been jailed by Nola's ordinary, the archpriest claimed, in Rome, that only the nuncio's court in Naples could judge him and, of

[46] Mancino and Romeo, *Clero criminale*, 127.

[47] 'Di perdere il tempo, la robba et gli studi': Firpo, *Riforma cattolica*, 181.

[48] Pasquale Lopez, *Ischia e Pozzuoli. Due diocesi nell'età della Controriforma* (Naples, 1991), 256.

[49] For a discussion of clerical paedophilia, see, in particular, Mancino and Romeo, *Clero criminale*.

course, from there he could appeal once again to Rome.[50] When a clerk in holy orders had intercourse with a woman in Rimini, intending to impede her marriage to one of his cousins, the father of the victim insisted that a secular and not an ecclesiastical court punish the priest, so that an exemplary condemnation could be inflicted. However, Rome was keen to protect the clerical status of the culprit and denied the request.[51]

Of course, Rome could also offer sensible legal remedies, especially in cases in which the penalty inflicted by bishops and their vicars had been objectively too harsh, or people had experienced too much cruelty in torture. The aristocratic condition of some clergy could also allow some sort of protection. Maintaining good relationships with the local aristocracy was a constant pressure on bishops from the Congregation, especially when examining issues such as the dowry expected from a noblewoman who was due to enter the conventual life, as in the case of Caterina Orsini.[52]

Reinstating priests subject to episcopal discipline, avoiding scandals and mitigating punishments was at the core of the practice of the Congregation.[53] But what was the mentality underpinning this process? What was the justification offered by Rome? A letter in the Oxford papers presents the clear mindset with which – according to the Congregation – the bishop should approach all disciplinary matters. The 'heart of any ecclesiastical policy', the Secretary of the Congregation wrote, 'is to avoid a scandal breaking out'.[54] This is not a surprising sentence, given what we have seen so far, but in this instance the secretary elaborated this idea: the bishop was the 'keeper of the conscience of the church', and he had to act with that responsibility in mind.

'Keeper of the conscience' was not a casual expression employed by the secretary. Indeed, I would like to maintain that it was, in fact, a 'legal cryptotype', elegantly employed by a well-trained lawyer.[55] In medieval legal thought, 'conscience' was the faculty of applying moral reasoning to individual cases. Such morality was objective,

[50] Menniti Ippolito, *1664*, 137.
[51] Ibid. 141.
[52] Bodl., MS Ital. c. 82–86, now in MS Cons. Res. c. 44, vol. 2, fol. 260^{r}.
[53] Ibid., fol. 153^{r}.
[54] Ibid., vol. 3, fol. 33^{v}.
[55] See Rodolfo Sacco, 'Legal Formants: A Dynamic Approach to Comparative Law', *The American Journal of Comparative Law* 39 (1991), 1–34.

according to Thomist natural law. Most importantly, it was commonly believed that – although positive law could only stem from natural law – in exceptional instances, such conscience could even disregard the law.[56] Much of the discussion within the *jus commune* on the nature of judicial *arbitrium* (discretion) – at least since Gratian's *Decretum* – saw the conscience as something to employ with restraint, as it was opposed to the *allegata et probata* (that is, the required proof) in trial. Significantly, the conscience was believed to be 'private' and could also correspond to a 'special judicial knowledge' reserved to the judge.[57]

Furthermore, the employment of the 'conscience' was a function proper to the exercise of the *episcopé*. The bishop, once again, was not left complete discretion in judging according to his 'conscience': this was not an arbitrary decision, but obedience to a higher principle of sovereignty and authority, and to a moral concern which demanded a sort of primacy. Nowhere was this more visible than in medieval English law, when a bishop at court was named as the 'keeper of the King's conscience' (a role soon subsumed into the office of Lord Chancellor). Albeit not in such an obvious form, elements of a 'prerogative court' that kept the monarch's conscience also existed in some of the procedures employed by the imperial Reichskammergericht, in the French Parlement of Paris, and in the Grand Conseil of Malines of the dukes of Burgundy.[58] Despite using the expression 'keeper of the conscience', the Congregation might not have developed a full theory on the matter. This is why I believe it could be helpful to talk of a 'legal cryptotype' (that is, 'a non-verbalized legal formant'), although further research is needed to see the extent of its use.[59] However, in Rome's parlance, the meaning of 'keeper of the conscience' was shifting in comparison to secular thought. The secretary was not imagining a separate, parallel jurisdiction, a 'remedy' to the system (as, for example, the English Court of Chancery). For Rome, the 'conscience' was a real ordering principle, which enabled the achievement of the ultimate aim: avoiding a

[56] Mike McNair, 'Equity and Conscience', *Oxford Journal of Legal Studies* 4 (2007), 659–81, at 662. See also Stefania Tutino, *Uncertainty in Post-Reformation Catholicism: A History of Probabilism* (Oxford and New York, 2018).
[57] Thomas A. Green, *Verdict According to Conscience* (Chicago, 1985).
[58] Heinrich Brunner, *Grundzüge der deutschen Rechgeshichte* (Münich, 1930); Albert Matthieu, *Hitoire du Grand Conseil de Malines* (Bruxelles, 1874).
[59] Sacco, 'Legal Formants'.

scandal. The bishop's calling as 'keeper of the conscience' of his diocese was the conceptual framework that legitimized an entire system of episcopal judicial administration, for which the church, not unsurprisingly at this juncture, adopted the language of the state. The fundamental concern for the bishop's conscience was that of the defence of the honour of his church. In the idea of being the 'keeper of the conscience' of the whole episcopate, the Congregation further found its own intellectual justification for disregarding rules and decisions which, by then, and in the aftermath of the Council of Trent, it should have been bound to. Tridentine reform was not the goal: protecting the hierarchical church and its reputation was. What to us can only appear as a justification for the hypocritical covering up of the misdeeds of the clergy, and an arbitrary way to administer justice, was instead endorsed as the ultimate service to a higher moral imperative.

'Prudence in all matters'

During the Counter-Reformation, the choice of the Roman Catholic Church to protect the clergy and its own institutions above other interests – in some respect, an instinct common to most human organizations – expanded for at least two reasons. First, in the aftermath of the Council of Trent, the reaffirmation of clericalism became obvious, as well as the repositioning of the hierarchy as the exclusive mediator between the divine and the faithful. This, of course, carried with it all sorts of gatekeeping issues, but also resulted in the recommendation to victims of abuses that they entrust themselves to an authority that, statutorily, was perceived as 'good'. Secondly, the Counter-Reformation church was deeply influenced by the nature of baroque politics and political thought, in which seventeenth-century Italian ecclesiastical elites were truly embedded.[60] This was an age in which terms such as 'novelty' and 'change' were perceived as negatives, and in which the idea of 'reason of state' was making its way into public discourse. It was the role of the prince to be 'prudent

[60] Rosario Villari, *Politica barocca. Inquietudini, mutamento e prudenza* (Rome and Bari, 2010); idem, *Elogio della dissimulazione. La lotta politica nel Seicento* (Rome and Bari, 2003; first publ. 1987); José Antonio Maravall, *Culture of the Baroque: Analysis of a Historical Structure* (Manchester, 1986).

as a serpent' (occasionally forgetting the other bit about being as 'harmless as a dove').[61] Hypocrisy, as we might perceive such behaviour today, was understood as the virtue of prudence. With their prudential and deceptive manners, many protagonists of the Roman Curia appear to us, even if this was not all that they were, as politicians of the baroque age.

A look at the profiles of the personnel at the top of the Congregation of Bishops and Regulars might help us further our understanding of the Congregation's mental *habitus*. Throughout the early seventeenth century (1598–1621), the Congregation had as its prefect Cardinal Benedetto Giustiniani, mostly remembered today for the extraordinary art collection which he patronized with his brother, the marquis Vincenzo.[62] Giustiniani came from a distinguished family of Genoese aristocrats and bankers, and during his career, he spent much of his time concerned with Rome's finances, as well as the administration of the papal state. He became a cardinal at just thirty-two, having previously been the treasurer of the Camera Apostolica; he was a 'prince of the church' for sixteen years before accepting ordination as bishop as well (despite being deputized to oversee bishops). In the end, the pope would express the opinion of many when he praised Giustiniani's 'industry and prudence' in managing the affairs of the church.[63] Under the Cardinal Prefect, each Congregation had a secretary of episcopal rank. The Secretary of the Congregation at the start of the seventeenth century was the Bolognese lawyer Girolamo Agucchi, the architect of the implementation of Clement VIII's reform of the Congregation. A man of the Curia and sometime referendary (solicitor) of both tribunals of the Signatura, Agucchi was described as 'an eminently dexterous man, circumspect, born to do business'.[64] He in turn would become cardinal in 1604, and be replaced as secretary by Monsignor Berlingero Gessi. Gessi, too, was a lawyer from Bologna, and knew well the machinery of the administration of diocesan ecclesiastical justice,

[61] Robert Bireley, *The Counter-Reformation Prince: Anti-Machiavellism or Catholic Statecraft in Early Modern Europe* (Chapel Hill, NC, and London, 1990).

[62] Simona Feci and Luca Bortolotti, 'Giustiniani, Benedetto', *Dizionario Biografico degli Italiani* 57 (2001), online at: <https://www.treccani.it/enciclopedia/benedetto-giustiniani_%28Dizionario-Biografico%29/>, accessed 8 January 2024.

[63] Apostolic Vatican Archive, Segreteria di Stato, Bologna, 184, c. 42.

[64] 'Uomo insignemente destro, avveduto, e nato per maneggiare affari': Lorenzo Cardella, *Memorie storiche de' Cardinali di Santa Romana Chiesa* (Rome, 1793), 109.

having served as vicar general of the archbishop of Bologna, Gabriele Paleotti, then in both Signaturae, and latterly as vicegerent to the cardinal vicar of Rome, Camillo Borghese, before finally joining the Congregation.[65] There is no doubt that he was Borghese's man: when Borghese became Pope Paul V in 1605, Gessi's career took off further. He was appointed absentee bishop of Rimini whilst being posted to the role for which he is today mostly known to scholars: as nuncio to the Republic of Venice (1607–18) during the difficult years following the Venetian Interdict (1606–7), which had seen the total breakdown of relations between the papacy and the Serenissima. When describing Gessi, the words chosen by his contemporaries were once again 'dexterous and prudent.'[66]

None of these men were theologians or Tridentine reformers. They were bishops, but only by virtue of office, and sometimes even reluctantly so, with no pastoral experience whatsoever. They were shrewd officials and politicians, learned and experienced in matters of finance, canon law, patronage, jurisdiction and benefices. At their core was the sense of the dignity of their office and of the church, and the centrality of the papacy in ecclesiastical life. Their aim was – no matter what – the 'prudent' protection of the interests of the clergy or, even more so, that of the papacy (and the two did not always coincide). Their prudence was not the Ciceronian *prudentia*, the moral attribute much loved by the humanists.[67] Of course, prudence was a charged word in the Thomist tradition, where it was understood as the ability to adapt broad principles to individual situations. But 'prudence' was here a key part of the seventeenth-century political imagination: a political virtue. 'Prudence' was what was needed, as the over-reaching of the secular state could pose a risk to Rome and its clergy. This was not a theoretical possibility: it was before everyone's eyes *c.*1605. By then, the cardinals of the Curia stood firmly with Robert Bellarmine in his strong polemic against Paolo

[65] Paolo Prodi, *Il cardinale Gabriele Paleotti, 1522–1597* (Bologna, 2022).

[66] Simona Feci, 'Gessi, Berlingero', *Dizionario Biografico degli Italiani* 53 (2000), online at: <https://www.treccani.it/enciclopedia/berlingero-gessi_%28Dizionario-Biografico%29/>, accessed 8 January 2024. See also Birgit Emich, *Bürokratie und Nepotismus unter Paul V (1605–1621)* (Stuttgart, 2011).

[67] See, for example, Brendan Cook, '*Prudentia* in More's *Utopia*: The Ethics of Foresight', *Renaissance and Reformation* 36 (2013), 31–68.

Sarpi and the idea of the primacy of the Venetian Republic over the clergy.[68] The interdict, and the 'Venetian overreach', had caused a real shift in Rome. According to the Curia, defending the honour of the church meant standing along clear battle lines: lines which, at the time, passed through the Venetian lagoon.

Somewhat ironically, Bellarmine's theology, and that of other flag-bearers of Counter-Reformation militancy, had not always been a favourite of the curial eminences. When just a few years earlier, in the autumn of 1600, Bellarmine had reprimanded Pope Clement VIII over the nature of episcopal appointments with the essay *De Officio Primario Summi Pontificis*, much of the Curia's ranks had closed behind the pope.[69] According to Bellarmine, too many bishops did not have the pastoral qualities required for the office; too many still 'failed to reside in their dioceses, thereby explicitly contradicting the dictates of the Council of Trent that established that bishops had to reside in their dioceses praecepto divino, by divine precept (this almost forty years since the end of the Council).'[70] The finger was quickly pointed at people such as Agucchi and Gessi. Pope Clement did not hesitate to push back, ultimately sending the theologian away from Rome to the see of Capua (Campania).[71] Bellarmine pointed to the theory, but the practice was more complicated. 'Those things can be indeed said, but, when we come to practice, we stumble over many difficulties,' the pope objected.[72] As Stefania Tutino has demonstrated, Bellarmine's intended purpose in all this was, in fact, to strengthen the authority of the pope over secular rulers in appointing bishops, and to mitigate against an excessive episcopal autonomy. But it also reveals the ongoing messy state of episcopal affairs throughout much of Italy. This was something that even the same Clement VIII had been aware of, given his fight to reform the behaviour of cardinals, and his consciousness of their wealth, double-dealings and hypocrisies.[73]

68 Robert Bellarmine, *Risposta di Card. Bellarmino a il trattato di sette theologi di Venetia sopra l'interdetto della santità di nostro signore di Papa Paolo Quinto* (Rome, 1606).

69 Robert Bellarmine, *De officio primario Summi pontifices*, now in *Actuarium bellarminianum*, ed. Xavier Marie Le Bachelet (Paris, 1913), 513–18.

70 Stefania Tutino, *Empire of Souls: Robert Bellarmine and the Christian Commonwealth* (Oxford, 2010), 261–92.

71 Fattori, *Clemente VIII*, 214–39.

72 Tutino, *Empire of Souls*, 261–92.

73 Fattori, *Clemente VIII*, 315–25.

Scholarship has sometimes seen the *De Officio* as an out-dated document, and has maintained that Tridentine reform (as in the case of the Bolognese Paleotti) was already happening.[74] The documents of the Congregation of Bishops and Regular leave a very different impression of the reality on the ground. The issues were such that, in 1634, Pope Urban VIII ended up promulgating the apostolic constitution, *Sancta Synodus Tridentina*, feeling the need to reaffirm the obligation for bishops to reside in their dioceses. The problem was such that the following year a separate Congregation was created, with both judicial and executive powers to impose such residence.[75] However, at the start of the seventeenth century, Rome was only too aware of a hiatus between theory and practice, between theology and the political management of ecclesiastical affairs. In that gulf, 'prudence' was the statesmanlike virtue to employ in the discretion afforded to the episcopal conscience. The gap between what the church claimed to be doing, and what it ended up doing, especially in many of the southern Italian dioceses, might appear to us as hypocritical. But to quote once again Cardinal de Luca: the Congregation of Bishops and Regulars moved 'like a prince, not like a judge'. And indeed, a prudent baroque prince it was, concerned, above all, with the preservation of its 'estate'. It was a prudent prince, in charge of many hypocritical judges.

[74] As argued in Prodi, *Paleotti*.

[75] 'Congregazione della residenza dei vescovi', in Del Re, *Lineamenti*, 378–9.

'See sincerity sparkle in thy practice': Antidotes to Hypocrisy in British Print Sermons, 1640–95

Anna Pravdica*
University of Warwick

Seventeenth-century British preachers persistently defined hypocrisy in contrast to its divine antidote: sincerity. This article looks at four such case studies from across the 'puritan'-'Anglican' divide, analysing the sermons of the Independent Nicholas Lockyer, the Presbyterian Christopher Love, the Church of England clergyman James Oldfield, and the archbishop of Canterbury John Tillotson. It considers to what extent Protestant instruction on sincerity and hypocrisy shifted according to religious affiliation and socio-political context, arguing that although these sermons possessed considerable continuities in their theological underpinnings, they also exhibited divergences in focus and instruction that are sometimes, but not always, predictable along denominational lines. These differences held weighty implications for the individual receiving spiritual guidance on how to forswear hypocrisy and live a truly sincere life, particularly throughout the period of instability and contention that marked Britain from the Civil Wars to the Glorious Revolution.

In a sermon first printed in 1640, the Independent minister Nicolas Lockyer preached that 'NO grace, how glorious soever in the eye of man, goes for good weight in the eye of God, without sincerity.'[1] Over a decade later, the Presbyterian martyr Christopher Love assured his readers: 'If you have sincerity in you, the Lord accounts

* I would like to thank Dr Naomi Pullin, Professor Mark Knights and Professor Kate Loveman for their continual guidance and support in the writing of this article, as well as Professor Beat Kümin, Dr John West and Dr Michèle Plott for their similarly invaluable feedback on earlier drafts. I am also grateful to my funding body, AHRC-Midlands4Cities, for making this research possible. E-mail: anna.pravdica@warwick.ac.uk.

[1] Nicholas Lockyer, *A Divine Discovery of Sincerity According to Its Proper and Peculiar Nature* (London, 1640), 1.

Studies in Church History 60 (2024), 238–263
doi: 10.1017/stc.2024.9

of you as if you had attained perfection.'[2] These ideas remained in fashion after the Restoration. First at the pulpit after the Great Fire of London in 1666, and again in print a year before the Glorious Revolution, the provincial clergyman James Oldfield asserted: 'sincerity is the highest pitch that a Christian is able to attain unto in this life'.[3] Finally in the 1690s, the archbishop of Canterbury John Tillotson maintained that 'sincerity is the very heart and substance of Religion'.[4]

Regardless of differences in time, place and belief, these preachers positioned sincerity as the antidote to hypocrisy in all its forms. Yet they also continually addressed how difficult it was to define and identify sincerity, and all agreed that they lived in an especially hypocritical and deceitful age. With immortal souls on the line, the stakes were high: the specifics of what these preachers were telling their audiences about sincerity's nature and its real-life applications in opposition to hypocrisy mattered greatly. By reading these sermons alongside one another, one can tease out to what extent Protestant instruction on sincerity and hypocrisy shifted according to religious affiliation and socio-political context. I argue that although these sermons exhibited considerable continuities in their theological underpinnings, they also bear out divergences in focus and instruction that are sometimes, though not always, predictable along denominational lines. These differences held weighty implications for the individuals receiving spiritual guidance on how to forswear hypocrisy and live a truly sincere life, particularly throughout the period of instability and contention that marked Britain from the Civil Wars and Commonwealth, to the years following the Restoration and Glorious Revolution.

In a useful summary of sincerity's conceptualization in early modern England, Scott L. Newstok writes that 'sincerity was posed as the antithesis to hypocrisy, "flattering and fauning," or "deceitfull" speech'.[5] He and others have considered the prevalence of Protestant ideas about sincerity in opposition to hypocrisy, defining the

[2] Christopher Love, 'The True Israelite', in idem, *The Mortified Christian Shewing the Nature, Signes, Necessity, and Difficulty of True Mortification* (London, 1654), 29.

[3] James Oldfield, *Sincerity, Or, the Upright Mans Walk to Heaven* (London, 1687), 12.

[4] John Tillotson, *Of Sincerity and Constancy in the Faith and Profession of the True Religion* (London, 1695), 4.

[5] Scott L. Newstok, '"Here Lies": Sincerity and Insincerity in Early Modern Epitaphs Onstage', *Christianity & Literature* 67 (2017), 50–68, at 50.

Reformed sincere ideal as the 'rigorous alignment' between 'internal feelings and external expression'.[6] This characterization is undoubtedly broadly true, but scholars have applied it interchangeably to groups identified as Protestant, Calvinist or – perhaps most often – puritan, seldom exploring points of divergence between or within these categories, or amongst particular sects and ministers. This critical tendency to treat doctrines of sincerity under a broad umbrella covering either Protestantism, Calvinism or puritanism can be useful in determining overarching theological belief on these topics. However, it can also lead to the overlooking of more nuanced differences, particularly when groupings such as 'Protestant' and 'puritan' are either collapsed or conflated.

For instance, Lockyer's *A Divine Discovery of Sincerity* (1640) has been used as a representative example of puritan belief on sincerity as contrasted with hypocrisy.[7] This makes sense, as Lockyer was a prominent Parliamentarian and puritan figure during the seventeenth century. However, if we consider him alongside another 'young Puritaine' such as Love, it becomes apparent that their differing religious beliefs, political orientations and preaching contexts greatly influenced their guidance on how to counteract hypocrisy and practice sincerity.[8] Nonetheless, it is important not to downplay their similarities or fully reject the concept of puritan 'brands' of sincerity and hypocrisy. In his work on puritan rhetoric about sincerity, David Parry has demonstrated how 'puritan' can still be a useful categorization for those preaching in the tradition of practical divinity.[9] I follow this approach in part, recognizing that individuals like Lockyer and Love adhered to a broad set of puritan beliefs and practices, while stressing the significance of acknowledging their theological and

[6] Ibid. 51. See also Jonas Barish, *The Antitheatrical Prejudice* (Berkeley and Los Angeles, CA, 1985); Jennifer Clement, 'The Art of Feeling in Seventeenth-Century English Sermons', *English Studies* 98 (2017), 675–88; Charles Lindholm, 'The Rise of Expressive Authenticity', *Anthropological Quarterly* 86 (2013), 361–95; Ana Schwartz, *Unmoored: The Search for Sincerity in Colonial America* (Chapel Hill, NC, 2023); Lionel Trilling, *Sincerity and Authenticity* (Cambridge, MA, 1972).

[7] Newstok, 'Sincerity', 50–1.

[8] Elliot Vernon, 'Love, Christopher (1618–1651), clergyman', *ODNB*, online edn (2004), at: <https://doi.org/10.1093/ref:odnb/17038>, accessed 13 January 2024.

[9] David Parry, '"A Divine Kind of Rhetoric": Rhetorical Strategy and Spirit-Wrought Sincerity in English Puritan Writing', *Christianity & Literature* 67 (2017), 113–38. See also Alec Ryrie, *Being Protestant in Reformation England* (Oxford, 2013), 6–9.

political differences as men on opposite sides of the Civil War-era Independent-Presbyterian divide.[10]

These differences were also affected by social contexts, from audience to time and place, and were not limited solely to puritan preachers. Historians have largely overlooked non-puritan or non-Calvinist Protestants' theological treatments of sincerity and hypocrisy post-1640, and I attempt to bridge this gap by considering Oldfield and Tillotson. I have selected these four preachers due to their range of belief and experience, offering two 'puritan' and two 'Anglican' perspectives at times when these classifications were theoretically aligned with 'establishment' theology. In turn, I seek to interrogate these classifications with an eye to commonality, as well as divergence. Not only are these four ministers' works representative examples of the extent to which print sermons discussed sincerity and hypocrisy throughout the period, but they were amongst a small number that explicitly signposted their attention to sincerity in their titles, intentionally advertising their practical guidance on what was an increasingly significant religious ideal during the latter half of the seventeenth century. This can be seen, for example, in one 1654 collected edition of Love's sermons, which included 'Sincerity in Opposition to Hypocrisie' in its title (Figure 1).[11] My aim in analysing these case studies is twofold: first, to explore their similarities and differences by situating these doctrines of sincerity and hypocrisy in their wider religious and socio-political cultural contexts; and second, to discover what practical instruction about sincerity and hypocrisy these sermons dispensed to their audiences.

'*Personall*, *domesticall*, *sociall*, or *nationall*': Sincerity and Hypocrisy in Context

Scholars have highlighted preoccupations with hypocrisy and deceit in early modern society, demonstrating how the religious dimension of this debate was inextricably intertwined with social, cultural and

10 See Tim Cooper, 'Congregationalists', in John Coffey, ed., *The Oxford History of Protestant Dissenting Traditions,* 1: *The Post-Reformation Era, 1559–1689* (Oxford, 2020), 88–111.

11 Christopher Love, *The True Doctrine of Mortification: and Sincerity in Opposition to Hypocrisie* (London, 1654). For sincerity and hypocrisy in manuscript sermons, see David Parry's article in this volume: 'The Problems of Performing Piety in some Exeter Dissenting Sermons *c.*1660–1745'.

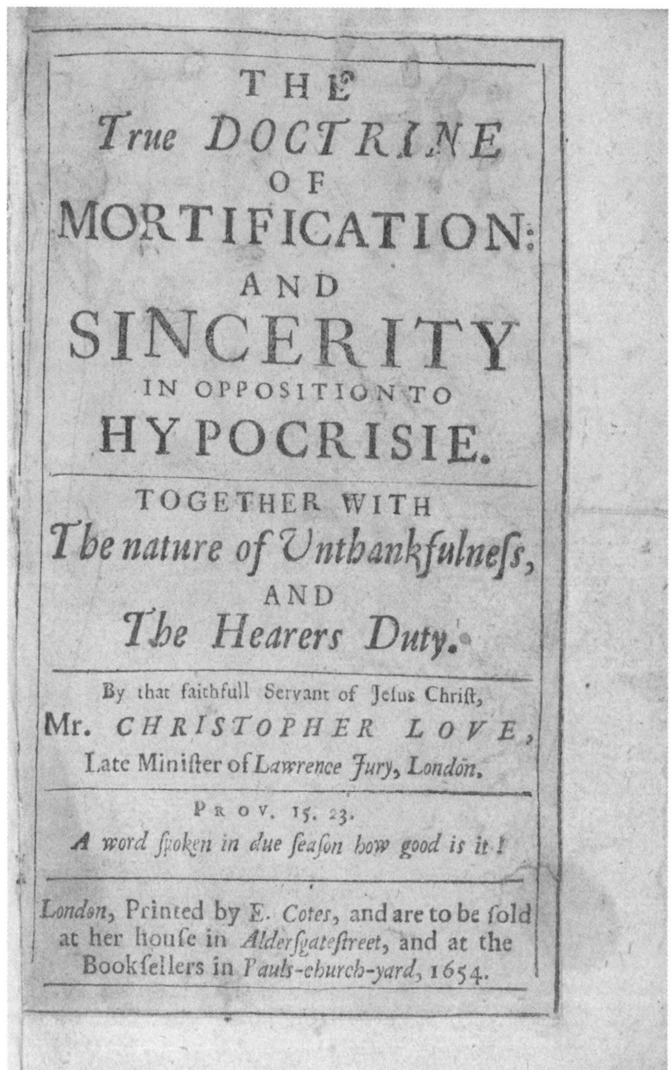

THE
True DOCTRINE
OF
MORTIFICATION:
AND
SINCERITY
IN OPPOSITION TO
HYPOCRISIE.

TOGETHER WITH
The nature of Unthankfulneſs,
AND
The Hearers Duty.

By that faithfull Servant of Jeſus Chriſt,
Mr. *CHRISTOPHER LOVE,*
Late Miniſter of *Lawrence Jury, London.*

PROV. 15. 23.
A word ſpoken in due ſeaſon how good is it!

London, Printed by E. *Cotes,* and are to be ſold at her houſe in *Alderſgateſtreet,* and at the Bookſellers in *Pauls-church-yard,* 1654.

Figure 1. Title page of one edition of the sermon collection that included Love's preaching on sincerity and hypocrisy, 1654. Reproduced by permission of Llyfrgell Genedlaethol Cymru / National Library of Wales.

political issues. Hypocrisy, or the absence of sincerity, is often at the forefront of these studies, as scholars have convincingly argued that anxieties surrounding hypocrisy were heightened during the seventeenth and eighteenth centuries due to contemporary cultural developments and conflicts in religious and political life.[12] Indeed, Carys Brown notes that 'the charge of hypocrisy was flung from all sides', while Mark Knights has discussed the often partisan nature of such accusations.[13] One reason for its increased polemical usage was the widespread backlash against the stereotype of the zealous puritan who justified his fanaticism as sincerity while accusing his opponents of hypocrisy. Lawrence Klein and others have linked this idea to the late seventeenth-century rise of politeness, as '[s]ociability and manners in religion were urged as alternatives to enthusiasm and fanaticism'.[14] More recently, Brown has argued that many saw politeness as 'a means to promote truth and virtue as well as social ease', a view that 'could be used to interpret the supposed ill-manners of Dissenters as symptomatic of hypocrisy'.[15] But there was another side to this coin, since polite social ceremony could all too easily bleed into hypocrisy. Endorsements of hypocrisy might masquerade as defences of politeness and civility, an anxiety that became increasingly prevalent at the turn of the eighteenth century.[16] The passage of the Toleration Act in 1689 did little to ameliorate these concerns, obfuscating as it did previously clear-cut delineations between conformity and nonconformity, friendship and enmity, hypocrisy and sincerity.[17]

[12] See, for instance, Carys Brown, *Friends, Neighbours, Sinners: Religious Difference and English Society, 1689–1750* (Cambridge, 2022), 120; Tobias Hug, *Impostures in Early Modern England: Representations and Perceptions of Fraudulent Identities* (Manchester, 2013), 1–11; Mark Knights, *The Devil in Disguise: Deception, Delusion, and Fanaticism in the Early English Enlightenment* (Oxford, 2011), 7; Kate Loveman, *Reading Fictions, 1660–1740: Deception in English Literary and Political Culture* (Aldershot, 2008), 3.

[13] Brown, *Friends, Neighbours, Sinners*, 121; Mark Knights, 'Occasional Conformity and the Representation of Dissent: Hypocrisy, Sincerity, Moderation, and Zeal', *PH* 24 (2005), 41–57.

[14] Lawrence Klein, 'Politeness and the Interpretation of the British Eighteenth Century', *HistJ* 45 (2002), 869–98, at 889.

[15] Brown, *Friends, Neighbours, Sinners*, 112. See also Peter Lake, 'Anti-Puritanism: The Structure of a Prejudice', in Kenneth Fincham and Peter Lake, eds, *Religious Politics in Post-Reformation England* (Woodbridge, 2006), 80–97.

[16] See, for example, Knights, *Devil in Disguise*, 163–4; Soile Ylivuori, *Women and Politeness in Eighteenth-Century England: Bodies, Identities, and Power* (New York, 2018), 67–101.

[17] See Brown, *Friends, Neighbours, Sinners*, 2–3; Knights, *Devil in Disguise*, 98–9.

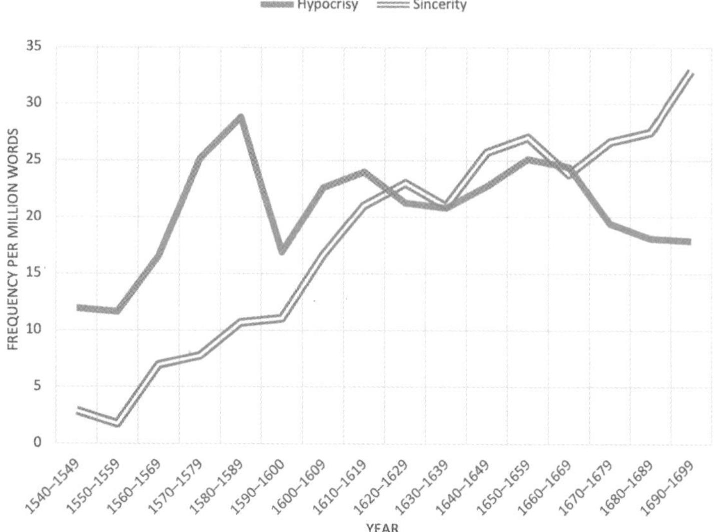

Figure 2. Frequency of 'sincerity' and 'hypocrisy' proportional to total print output, 1540–1699.

This heightened preoccupation with hypocrisy is borne out by the frequency with which the word itself appeared in print over the course of the sixteenth and seventeenth centuries (Figure 2).[18] This data also visualizes the marked and rapid rise of 'sincerity' during this period. Although 'hypocrisy' appeared in the English language earlier, 'sincerity' became increasingly prominent as the early modern era progressed. This trend is still more pronounced in print sermons, with 'sincerity' being used in nearly half of all texts in this genre throughout the early modern period (Figure 3). As Figure 2 shows, the frequency with which 'sincerity' appeared in print came to equal, and eventually overtake, that of 'hypocrisy' during the

[18] The Text Creation Partnership (TCP) has transcribed over 44,000 pre-1700 texts, all of which have been uploaded to the CQPweb database, online at: <https://cqpweb.lancs.ac.uk/>, accessed 13 January 2024. CQPweb can determine a term's 'frequency' proportional to total print output in a timeframe or genre, considering fluctuations in quantity. See Andrew Hardie, 'CQPweb: Combining Power, Flexibility and Usability in a Corpus Analysis Tool', *International Journal of Corpus Linguistics* 17 (2012), 380–409. Figures 2 and 3 visualize results for 's[i,y]ncerit[y,ie]' and 'h[i,y]pocris[y,ie]'.

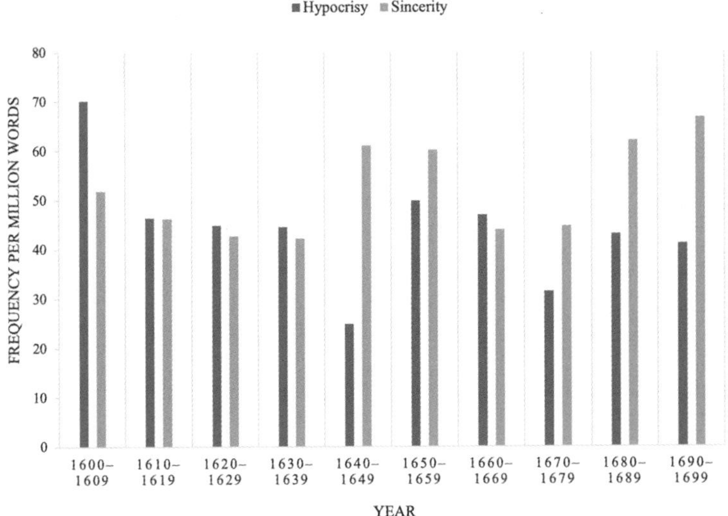

Figure 3. Frequency of 'sincerity' and 'hypocrisy' in print sermons, 1600–99.

seventeenth century. These data indicate the necessity of looking at seventeenth-century hypocrisy through the lens of sincerity, particularly in religious texts, such as the sermons considered here, which understood hypocrisy as a diabolical corruption that could only be rooted out by the divine ideal of sincerity. Furthermore, the broader cultural picture painted by Figure 2 underscores the importance of considering the socio-political contexts that surrounded religious instruction on how not to be a hypocrite, an issue these sermons approached via the controversial question of what it meant to be truly sincere.

The first of the four ministers considered here, Nicholas Lockyer (1611–85), was an Independent and an ardent Cromwellian to his death. After the Restoration, he refused to conform, was ejected from the ministry, and spent the rest of his life as a dissenting, incendiary preacher.[19] He first printed his *Divine Discovery of Sincerity* in 1640, a collection of four sequential sermons. It enjoyed success, with

[19] Elliot Vernon, 'Lockyer, Nicholas (1611–1685), Independent minister', *ODNB*, online edn (2004), at: <https://doi.org/10.1093/ref:odnb/16914>, accessed 13 January 2024.

reprints in 1643, 1644, 1645 and 1649. It is regrettably unclear when and where Lockyer first preached these sermons, but it was possibly in one of the university environments he inhabited during the 1630s.[20] In these sermons, Lockyer preached that there were 'special times and occasions' during which individuals needed to 'declare' their sincerity to counteract hypocrisy: these were '*personall, domesticall, sociall,* or *nationall*'.[21] Lockyer's national example was particularly telling. He argued there were appropriate times to disobey monarchs and that this was one of the finest possible demonstrations of godly sincerity, citing the biblical precedent of Moses and Pharaoh.[22] With sentiments like these, it follows that Lockyer 'counselled that patience and obedience to God's word was the key to parliamentarian success' during the Civil Wars, '[opposing] a quick settlement for the sake of an ungodly peace'.[23] That Lockyer was an unambiguous supporter of the regicide and republic is all the more significant when considering the fact that his sermons were republished in 1649, the year of Charles I's execution, and noting Lockyer's appointment as one of Oliver Cromwell's chaplains.[24]

In contrast, the Welsh Presbyterian Christopher Love (1618–51) was one of 'the most virulent critics of the new republic', and his involvement in a plot to restore the monarchy resulted in his execution in 1651.[25] Elliot Vernon argues that Love was representative of a segment of fiery, usually younger Presbyterians who moved from intense Parliamentarian support at the start of the Civil Wars, to monarchical plotting by the end, a shift brought about by the controversy surrounding Pride's Purge (1648) and the regicide.[26] Love's activities from 1649 to 1651 were overtly subversive: he was amongst those Presbyterians the government warned against 'medling with state-matters in their sermons', and he opposed Parliament's 'Engagement' (1649), which demanded declarations of loyalty to

[20] Vernon recounts that Lockyer 'matriculated from the notoriously Puritan college of New Inn Hall, Oxford, on 4 November 1631 and graduated BA on 14 May 1633. Migrating to Emmanuel College, Cambridge, where his BA was incorporated in 1635, he proceeded MA in 1636. In June 1654 he returned to Oxford to take his BTh'. Ibid.

[21] Lockyer, *Divine Discovery*, 181. Emphasis original.

[22] Ibid. 191–2.

[23] Vernon, 'Lockyer'.

[24] Ibid.

[25] Elliot Vernon, *London Presbyterians and the British Revolutions, 1638–64* (Manchester, 2021), 221. For an in-depth study on Love, see ibid. 220–36.

[26] Ibid. 10.

the Commonwealth.[27] The two consecutive sermons that made up Love's *Discovery of Sincerity* were twice printed in posthumous collections in 1654 – part of a successful campaign by his friends and widow to cement his memory as a Presbyterian martyr – and it seems likely that he originally preached them during the 1640s at one of the parish churches in London where he ministered.[28] Though free of any explicit polemic, Love's teachings on sincerity and hypocrisy applied to what had been a very political life. In his final moments on the scaffold, he gave a widely admired speech in which he expressed his certainty that he would soon be with God. Crucially, he found comfort in the fact that he had never become a hypocrite by '[dealing] falsely in his Covenant', proving himself sincere to the end.[29]

Of the ministers discussed here, the Restoration-era clergyman James Oldfield (*fl.* 1655–81) was the most obscure.[30] In the only reference I have found to Oldfield in the scholarly literature, David Stoker groups him with an assortment of Presbyterian writers whose work was printed by the nonconformist Norwich publisher Edward Giles.[31] While Oldfield does appear to have subscribed to a Calvinist worldview, which could have extended to Presbyterian leanings or sympathies, he was, for all intents and purposes, one of the 'conciliatory or friendly' Church of England clergy that, as Stoker notes, also featured in Giles's publication output.[32] From 1661 until his death twenty years later, Oldfield was the rector of Stratton St Michael, a small parish about ten miles outside

[27] Quoted in ibid. 221–3.

[28] Vernon, 'Love'. The *Discovery of Sincerity* title is taken from the sermon collection entitled *The Mortified Christian* (1654), the edition quoted throughout this essay; the same sermons were printed in the 1654 *True Doctrine of Mortification* edition pictured in Figure 1, but I quote *The Mortified Christian* edition throughout this article as its text is more complete and features fewer typographical errors.

[29] Quoted in Vernon, *London Presbyterians*, 230.

[30] See 'James Oldfeild' (CCEd Person ID 53788), *The Clergy of the Church of England Database 1540–1835*, online at: <http://www.theclergydatabase.org.uk/>, accessed 13 January 2024. The name was spelled 'Oldfeild' in some records (hence the clergy database spelling), but in his own sermon publications it is spelled 'Oldfield', the form that is used in this article.

[31] David Stoker, 'Norwich "Publishing" in the Seventeenth Century', in John Hinks and Catherine Armstrong, eds, *Printing Places: Locations of Book Production and Distribution since 1500* (London, 2005), 31–46.

[32] Ibid. See also John D. Ramsbottom, 'Presbyterians and "Partial Conformity" in the Restoration Church of England', *JEH* 43 (1992), 249–70.

Norwich, a city which boasted a particularly fervent culture of dissent.[33] Much to Oldfield's chagrin, this nonconformist bent did not confine itself to the city limits, and his sermons are littered with references to religious strife in his community. He frequently came into conflict with local nonconformists who were hostile towards his presence, viewing him first and foremost as a conforming clergyman. Oldfield's tone often reads as long-suffering exasperation, but his sermons were undeniably intent on smoothing over any interpersonal disputes brought on by religious difference. He chose to preach on sincerity as the antidote to hypocrisy precisely because of the ongoing strife in his parish, and England as a whole. It was in late 1666 that he originally preached his sermons, in the shadow of the Plague and the Great Fire. Contemporaries interpreted these catastrophes as signs of God's wrath and, for Oldfield, they were evidence of how important it was to tend to the sincerity of one's own soul, rather than fanatically combatting the hypocrisy of others. When his sermons were posthumously published over twenty years later on the eve of the Glorious Revolution, Oldfield's promotion of a civil, tolerant form of sincerity remained a socially, politically and religiously relevant rejection of sectarian conflict in the spiritual battle against hypocrisy.

The archbishop of Canterbury John Tillotson (1630–94) dealt with similar issues to Oldfield, albeit on a far more prominent stage as London's 'most celebrated preacher'.[34] Tillotson's was a position of latitudinarian tolerance, and Ralph Stevens has shown how he was at the forefront of a moderate contingent that sought 'to revise the liturgy in pursuit of Protestant unity' prior to the Toleration Act.[35] The religious and socio-political strife that marked the Restoration period greatly informed this stance, compounded by the intolerant, reactionary and conspiratorialist atmosphere that char-

[33] Ibid.

[34] Ralph Stevens, *Protestant Pluralism: The Reception of the Toleration Act, 1689–1720* (London, 2018), 15.

[35] Ibid. See also Isabel Rivers, 'Tillotson, John (1630–1694), archbishop of Canterbury', *ODNB*, online edn (2004), at: <https://doi.org/10.1093/ref:odnb/27449>, accessed 13 January 2024; Julius J. Kim, 'Archbishop John Tillotson and the Seventeenth-Century Latitudinarian Defense of Christianity, Part I', *Torch Trinity Journal* 11 (2008), 130–46; idem, 'Archbishop John Tillotson and the Seventeenth-Century Latitudinarian Defense of Christianity, Part II', *Torch Trinity Journal* 12 (2009), 127–48.

acterized the 1670s and 1680s.[36] So, too, did the memory of the Civil Wars and Commonwealth, still fresh in the cultural imagination and effective in provoking calls for moderation in opposition to zeal.[37] After 1689, toleration brought about further dilemmas, as nonconformists' newfound legal rights introduced an uncertain social order. How could conformists practice tolerance without being hypocritical? How could conscientious dissenters practice civility while staying sincere to their own beliefs?[38] It was in this cultural climate that Tillotson preached his *Of Sincerity Towards God and Man* at Kingston (London) in 1694. It was the last sermon he gave before his death, and his publishers promoted it as such in a larger 1695 collection. Tellingly, it was preoccupied with how to avoid causing offence without being a hypocrite. Coupled with this concern, however, was Tillotson's discussion of the inherent conflict between sincerity and politeness. Though Tillotson felt dissenting zealots such as Lockyer had pushed sincerity too far in the past, he also feared that late seventeenth-century English society was overcorrecting, veering into a different, but equally pernicious form of widespread hypocrisy. While tensions between sincerity, politeness, hypocrisy and toleration had been relevant throughout the seventeenth century, they were given new meaning in Tillotson's England.

Contemporaries viewed sincerity and hypocrisy as theological concepts applicable to nearly every aspect of real-world experience, from the consequential to the everyday. Yet the problem was that such a notion might be put into practice in a huge variety of ways. Considering this, it should perhaps be unsurprising that, throughout these sermons, we find the recurring idea that the most common and insidious form of hypocrisy was the self-deluding kind.[39] As will be seen from the discussion of Lockyer and Love's sermons in the following section, this idea was inextricably intertwined with the ambiguous nature of conscience, but it was also born of the very subjective interpretations that abstract concepts such as sincerity and hypocrisy could invite. Overall, core theological understandings of sincerity and hypocrisy did not change hugely across these sermons. Rather, the

[36] See, for instance, John Spurr, *The Restoration Church of England, 1646–1689* (New Haven, CT, 1991).
[37] Knights, 'Occasional Conformity', 47–9.
[38] Brown, *Friends, Neighbours, Sinners*, 11–13.
[39] Clement, 'Art of Feeling', 680.

differing social, political, cultural and religious backgrounds of the preachers navigating these ideas were what changed. As a result, practical understandings about the nature of hypocrisy and how sincerity should be employed as its antidote shifted. With this contextual awareness, we can better explore the practical implications of these shared beliefs and their divergent applications.

Two Puritans Define Religious Sincerity during the Civil Wars and Commonwealth

Lockyer and Love both emphasized concepts such as conscience and scriptural knowledge as central to sincerity, but they also exhibited differences. The most important of these differences was this: for Love, sincerity could exist on a spectrum, improved by education, but not negated by ignorance. For Lockyer, however, sincerity operated in a binary fashion: you either had it or you did not. Lockyer divided sincerity into two types: 'godly' or 'theological' sincerity, and 'moral' sincerity. Moral sincerity was the incorrect sort, for it was 'close hypocrisie', making the morally sincere man 'but an out-side holy man'.[40] In Lockyer's sermons, moral sincerity was equivalent to hypocrisy, an external, 'counterfeit' performance not indicative of true godly sincerity, which was '*a speciall work of God upon the soule of man, making him laborious, to walke according to Gods Will*'.[41]

Godly sincerity was unique. It necessitated prayer as it did not occur naturally, in accordance with the Calvinist understanding of the heart as inherently dishonest due to original sin.[42] Capable of cleansing the deceitful heart, godly sincerity made 'a man see a transcendant worth in the will of God; and worth begets love … and love begets labour, to attaine the thing beloved'.[43] A truly sincere soul was thus capable of comprehending God's supreme perfection; this comprehension inspired love, which in turn incentivized the continual labour necessary to retain that love. Lockyer continually highlighted the emotional benefits of godly sincerity, insisting that the joy and

[40] Lockyer, *Divine Discovery*, 12–13.
[41] Ibid. 13. Emphasis original.
[42] Ibid. 14. See also Clement, 'Art of Feeling', 678.
[43] Lockyer, *Divine Discovery*, 16–17.

spiritual bliss it inspired made the required labour worthwhile, offering comfort to the godly in times of trouble and persecution.[44]

But sincerity remained hard work. Lockyer hammered this point home, reminding his audience that labour was required '*alwaies*'.[45] Hypocrisy was never fully 'extirpated', and one had to 'grub up' these 'rootes of bitternesse' regularly.[46] He admitted that '[s]trong trials may make a sincere heart give backe for a time', but argued that 'they never prevaile, to make a sincere heart give off his labour to obey God'.[47] Lockyer spoke at length of how much self-reflection was necessary to be assured of godly sincerity, and this was at the heart of what made it a potentially anxiety-inducing subject.[48] Conscience, Lockyer claimed, was the most crucial tool in this self-examination, the key to living a life free from sin for the right reasons and avoiding mere 'moral' sincerity or hypocrisy. One had to understand God's will by understanding God's word (i.e., Scripture), thus awakening conscience and enabling it to function properly.[49] Unlike sincerity, conscience was a natural, inborn tool. It could be used to identify the true state of the heart and soul, and forsake iniquity.[50] Yet this, too, was difficult. Conscience, Lockyer admitted, was 'better felt then defined'.[51] It was supposed to be the solution to sincerity's evasive unwieldiness, yet Lockyer recognized that theologians did not agree on its exact nature or definition.[52] Despite this, he insisted that conscience was necessary to the attainment of godly sincerity, and although he stressed the high level of spiritual understanding required to activate conscience and uproot hypocrisy, he did not design his sermons to provide that extensive education.[53]

If we can identify the key points of significance for Lockyer as sincerity's intensely inward nature, dependent upon the mechanisms of conscience, then how did this compare with Love's understanding?

44 Ibid. 111–76.
45 Ibid. 18. Emphasis original.
46 Ibid. 61.
47 Ibid. 20.
48 See, for instance, Clement, 'Art of Feeling', 676–80; Lindholm, 'Expressive Authenticity', 366–7.
49 Lockyer, *Divine Discovery*, 77.
50 On the Protestant conscience, see W. B. Patterson, *William Perkins and the Making of a Protestant England* (Oxford, 2014), 90–113.
51 Lockyer, *Divine Discovery*, 69.
52 Ibid. 70.
53 Ibid. 76–8.

Love spoke about the absence of 'guile' or 'hypocrisie', and the inward, heart-based nature of sincerity in similar terms to Lockyer. However, he clarified that sincerity did not necessarily equate to a lack of ignorance. Love insisted that one could be well-intentioned but sinful, and therefore free from hypocrisy but ignorant.[54] This proposition would have been problematic for Lockyer, whose understanding of conscience meant that ignorance and sincerity were in direct opposition. Love also felt that ignorance was a problem, saying: 'If you are ignorant, and yet do not desire and labor after knowledg, this is inconsistent with sincerity'.[55] Love, though, qualified this in a way Lockyer never did:

> You that are sincere … do not conclude against your selves, that because you have some ignorance, therefore you have no truth and sincerity in you … I beseech you that you would not pass hard censures upon your own Souls; do not say, you have no truth in your hearts, because you have little understanding in your heads.[56]

Lockyer's sermon was devoid of this more lenient, flexible attitude. Though Lockyer had encouraged constant self-improvement and self-reflection, he was only ever hostile towards the limits arising from ignorance. Ignorance and sincerity were mutually exclusive for Lockyer, due to the 'understanding' fundamental to a functioning conscience. Even such understanding was limited, Lockyer warned: '*We know but in part,* though God *know all things;* and knowing but in part, conscience yet can doe his office but in part'.[57]

One can imagine the anxiety this uncertainty might inspire.[58] Conscience was difficult to define, required extensive learning and was impossible to be sure of until the day of judgment. There existed the very real possibility that one's efforts would not prove enough. Love acknowledged this concern in his comforting entreaties to his audience not to 'conclude against' themselves or 'pass hard censure' on their souls. Love was able to offer this comfort because he did not place sincerity and ignorance in absolute opposition, quite possibly because his Presbyterian brand of Calvinism was not as rigid as

[54] Love, 'True Israelite', 7–14.
[55] Ibid. 10.
[56] Ibid. 13.
[57] Lockyer, *Divine Discovery*, 84. Emphasis original.
[58] For Calvinist despair, see, for example, Ryrie, *Being Protestant*, 27–48.

Lockyer's Independent position. Love preached that 'sincerity of heart is consistent, not onely with ignorance in the minde, but also with many infirmities in the practice'.[59] Love's reference to 'infirmities in the practice' was important, since those who had little theological learning were unlikely to have ideally functioning consciences. As long as such people were well-intentioned, vigilant against hypocrisy and determined to learn, Love was ever indulgent: 'Know, for your Comfort, all you true … men without guile, that the Lord looks upon you as perfect men and women'.[60]

None of this is to say that these sermons did not possess profound similarities, or to suggest that theological tenets such as conscience were significant for Lockyer, but insignificant for Love. Love also spoke incessantly of conscience, and he especially disapproved of those who only forsook iniquity because their consciences 'accused' them. Such people were textbook hypocrites who would return to their sinful ways once conscience fell silent again.[61] Lockyer shared this notion, but Love's concern for educating the 'ignorant' resulted in a different approach. Vernon notes that Love required his parishioners to be 'conversant with the fundamentals of Reformed Christianity before they attended holy communion', a policy in line with 'the presbyterians' insistence that communicants should be able to examine their consciences'.[62] In Love's view, it was the responsibility of church government to educate parishioners towards these ends.[63]

Lockyer had other priorities. As an Independent, he was not interested in the Presbyterians' uniformly educated national church. His sermons were preoccupied with different issues, such as the 'trialls' faced by the theologically sincere. This, too, can be understood in light of the backlash Congregationalists faced as they established themselves during the tumultuous 1640s.[64] Although Lockyer was

[59] Love, 'True Israelite', 13.
[60] Ibid. 29.
[61] Ibid. 23.
[62] Vernon, 'Love'.
[63] Ibid.
[64] Lockyer, *Divine Discovery*, 111–63. See also Joel Halcomb, 'Godly Order and the Trumpet of Defiance: The Politics of Congregational Church Life during the English Revolution', in Michael Davies, Anne Dunan-Page and Joel Halcomb, eds, *Church Life: Pastors, Congregations, and the Experience of Dissent in Seventeenth-Century England* (Oxford, 2019), 25–44.

not representative of some broad category of 'Independents' any more than Love was of Presbyterianism, teasing out these differences helps nuance our understanding of puritan conceptualizations of sincerity and hypocrisy in seventeenth-century England. It also demonstrates how different audiences would have been receiving different practical guidance regarding sincerity and hypocrisy, depending on whose sermons they heard or read. As such, the potential influence of these sermons' disparate understandings and treatments of sincerity and hypocrisy should not be underestimated.

Plain Country Sincerity: Audience, Time and Place

Who, then, was hearing these ideas, and how did these listeners influence what preachers emphasized about sincerity and hypocrisy? This question is crucial to Oldfield's later sermons, which focused on educating lay audiences practically about sin in order to help them on the path towards sincerity. Accordingly, Oldfield's work proves especially useful in thinking about how listeners and congregations shaped homiletic communications of sincerity and hypocrisy. As Arnold Hunt reminds us: 'Sermons were not preached in a vacuum, and to treat them simply as literary artefacts, without considering the time and place of delivery and the persons to whom they were addressed, is to miss much of their significance'.[65] Indeed, religious ideas about sincerity and hypocrisy were communicated to very different audiences, from learned urban listeners to provincial congregations.

Oldfield's overarching ideas about sincerity aligned with those established by Lockyer and Love. He declared sincerity the ultimate Christian grace and instructed his flock: 'your Consciences witness with you, your simplicity of heart and sincerity towards God'.[66] Perhaps most importantly, he addressed the problem that many individuals were hypocrites without themselves realizing it.[67] Oldfield warned: 'if you live in sin and your consciences smite you not, do not rejoyce, all such rejoycing is vain.'[68] Once again, we encounter the problem of the silent conscience. Lockyer and Love had insisted

[65] Arnold Hunt, *The Art of Hearing: English Preachers and Their Audiences, 1590–1640* (Cambridge, 2010), 292.
[66] Oldfield, *Sincerity*, 205.
[67] Ibid. 54–5.
[68] Ibid. 205.

that a thorough understanding of God's word was the solution, and scriptural understanding was certainly crucial for Oldfield too. But like Love, he differed from Lockyer in his approach to the ignorant. Of all the preachers discussed in this article, Oldfield spent the most time attempting to define iniquity for his provincial congregation: '[T]his is the nearest way to sincerity,' he preached, 'for a man to keep himself from his Iniquity.'[69]

The first part of Oldfield's sermon was a lengthy, often repetitive lecture on sin. We can identify it with what Ian Green calls 'plain country divinity', 'a suitably plain expression of a body of doctrine that was strong on moral exhortation … that even "the simplest and rudest people" could grasp'.[70] This categorization sheds some light on Oldfield's treatment of conscience, which he implied was sometimes too unreliable to rely upon. He pushed this idea further than Lockyer or Love, for whom conscience worked effectively with enough learning. Oldfield never rejected this approach to conscience, as he, too, prized its theological consequence. Yet the fact remained that it was a tricky concept to explain. Congregants might struggle with the prospect of grappling with such an intangible construct in what must have felt like a fruitless effort to detect some equally elusive inward sincerity. Or, worse still, they might wrongly think themselves sincere, simply because their consciences were silent.[71]

Recognising this, Oldfield focused on doing the work of activating his parishioners' consciences. It was better to familiarize oneself with the nature of sin, he insisted, to consult Scripture and receive liturgical instruction, to denounce hypocrisy for the *right* reasons, and consequently live a sincere, upright life inspired by Christ's sacrificial love. This, he assured his congregants, was the path to sincerity, the 'Upright Man's *Walk to Heaven*', and it was a walk which did not retain the looming unknowability as seen with Lockyer.[72] Lockyer had warned that it was impossible to be certain about one's own sincerity until conscience gave its full report in the afterlife. This doubt fell by the wayside with Oldfield, who insisted that

[69] Ibid. 12.
[70] Ian Green, 'Preaching in the Parishes', in Hugh Adlington, Peter McCullough and Emma Rhatigan, eds, *The Oxford Handbook of the Early Modern Sermon* (Oxford, 2012), 138–54, at 139.
[71] Oldfield, *Sincerity*, 204–5.
[72] Ibid., title page. Emphasis original.

scriptural education and repudiation of sin would get the job done. Towards the end of his sermon, he told his congregants, in a characteristically no-nonsense fashion, that he was going to review some points on iniquity 'as plainly and as practically' as he could. 'So', he said, 'if after all this you still retain your own Iniquities and go to Hell, you shall thank your selves for it.'[73]

Oldfield understood this more concrete, less theoretical guidance to be of greater use to his congregation, and therefore more likely to have an actual impact on their behaviour and the fate of their immortal souls. Oldfield reflected on this when he considered the role of the preacher and his duty to his congregation:

> General Preaching is as good as no Preaching at all; Ministers must not only tell People of sin, but of their sins. Should a Physician come to a sick man, and discourse learnedly before him of the nature and causes of sickness in general, and not tell him what is his disease and sickness, and tell him what means he must use against it, this would do him no good … He is not to be accounted for a good Preacher, that can make a quaint Sermon or a Learned discourse; but if we would do good by our Preaching, we must tell every one of his own Iniquities; *we must not Preach against the sins of the Court in the Country, nor against the sins of the Country at Court; we must not set men against other mens sins, but every man against his own sins.*[74]

Oldfield's denouncement of 'General Preaching' was a frank acknowledgment of the preacher's need to adapt to his audience if he hoped to make opaque concepts, such as sincerity and hypocrisy, useful to non-theologians. This assertion was in the long-established tradition of practical divinity.[75] Oldfield unambiguously situated himself in the camp of 'plain style', rather than 'metaphysical', preaching, an adherence common to all four preachers discussed in this article, despite their differences.[76]

A consideration of liturgical context illuminates the differences in practical instruction on sincerity and hypocrisy found in these sermons. Genuine theological difference was undoubtedly significant,

[73] Ibid. 289.
[74] Ibid. 50–1. Emphasis mine.
[75] See Michael P. Winship, 'Weak Christians, Backsliders, and Carnal Gospelers: Assurance of Salvation and the Pastoral Origins of Puritan Practical Divinity in the 1580s', *ChH* 70 (2001), 462–81.
[76] Green, 'Preaching', 151–2.

but the question of audience was critical. Unfortunately, it is also frequently elusive. Unlike Oldfield, who was preaching in his parish church, we cannot be certain of Lockyer's and Love's original audiences. While it is possible that Lockyer might have brushed aside practicalities such as lecturing on sin because of the more elite context in which he potentially preached his sermons, this is speculative.[77] Nevertheless, something can be said about the nature of these works as print publications. Lockyer's published collection included only his sincerity sermons, which he dedicated to his genteel aunt, Lady Bridget Lyddell, in what reads like a traditional letter to a patron.[78] In contrast, Love's sermons on sincerity were sandwiched between a series of sermons on the mortification of sin, and a final work devoted to the question of how to listen to sermons properly. Love's publishers positively construed the broad usefulness of these 'old', 'common', 'plain Doctrines', claiming they had intentionally collected and arranged the sermons for this reason.[79] Readers were consequently provided with ten sermons on the mortification of sin before they came to Love's material on sincerity, furnishing them with the extensive education on iniquity that Oldfield had also offered his congregation. With what is known of Love's ministerial style, he probably preached them in a similar manner originally, and Love and Oldfield were undeniably alike in their efforts to educate the ignorant amongst their flocks. Though Oldfield's sermons offer particularly valuable insight into what religious guidance non-elite, rural people heard regarding sincerity and hypocrisy, he was not alone in considering the importance of audience when preaching about these theologically weighty topics.

Sincerity's Limits: Hypocrisy vs Social Harmony

What was the relationship between sincerity, hypocrisy and social life in these sermons? Audiences clearly influenced the focus, style and dogma of such texts, but what did this mean for the actual practice of sincerity and hypocrisy? Did preachers acknowledge real-world limits to the religious idealization of sincerity and demonization of hypocrisy? These questions were all relevant to Oldfield, for whom

[77] Lockyer's movements *c.*1635 to 1640 are unclear: see Vernon, 'Lockyer'.
[78] Lockyer, *Divine Discovery*, front matter.
[79] Love, 'True Israelite', front matter.

the issue of how to navigate living in a religiously diverse community was a very real one. Was it possible to be tolerant of beliefs and behaviours one opposed without being hypocritical? While Oldfield never posed this question explicitly, it permeated his sermons. Although, in one instance, he maligned some 'lately turned' Quakers who had said 'they got no good by hearing of me,' he also said that even if the church were comprised of each and every heretical sect, 'I am persuaded we should all agree in this, that every man ought to keep himself from his own Iniquity.'[80] In another instance, he preached:

> Hell is the place that God hath prepared on purpose for Hypocrites, and all those (be they what they will of this or that opinion of this or that Sect, Conformists or Nonconformists) that have not kept themselves from their own Iniquities, this great sin are but Hypocrites in the sight of God.[81]

As far as Oldfield was concerned, it was the battle against sin that mattered most, suggesting that nonconformists could be truly sincere, so long as they properly combated iniquity and hypocrisy within their own souls. How, then, did he want his congregants to conduct themselves amongst those with whom they disagreed? Certainly not combatively: ''Tis our selves we must judge and censure … but we must not go abroad … 'tis dangerous medling'.[82] Likewise, he continually railed against any individuals more concerned with the behaviour of others than their own:

> [Y]ou wonder at your neighbours that they are no better, why, wonder at your selves that you are no better; you say all the good that comes by Sermons is practise, why then if you would get good by hearing Sermons follow your own directions. Do not give away all your counsel to others and take none your selves.[83]

For Oldfield, hypocrisy lay not in failing to declare one's sincerity in opposition to others, but in sectarian belligerence that relished in pointing fingers, yet failed to address insincerity in one's own heart. In his pursuit of social harmony, Oldfield demonstrated an inclination towards moderation and civility that was absent from Lockyer's sermons and inconsistent in Love's.

[80] Ibid. 283, 282.
[81] Ibid. 42.
[82] Ibid.
[83] Ibid. 290–1.

Back in the 1640s, Lockyer had argued that a truly sincere heart served as a model for others, claiming that the theologically sincere were beholden to declare themselves in opposition to hypocrisy in themselves, their family, their community, and the state. He was evidently unconcerned about the interpersonal strife this might cause or the divisions it could sow on a larger scale.[84] Love similarly stressed the importance of the individual's behaviour in relation to others, claiming the sincere man was 'the same man in all companies … If he be in bad company, he will shew a dislike of their ways, and labor to make them better; if in good company, he will commend and approve of their doings.'[85] Such a prospect was not exactly conducive to polite conduct or civil discourse. Yet Love's further reflections on the sincere individual's external behaviour distanced his doctrine from Lockyer's and, in the process, complicated his own teachings. He preached:

> A man without guile discovers his sincerity in his carriage amongst men, in that he orders his conversation so, as not to give offence to any man where he lives, neither to the *Jew* or *Gentile,* or to the Church of God … those that are sincere, it is their continual endevour to walk without offence to any.[86]

Lockyer was not particularly worried about the possibility of causing offence; on the contrary, he encouraged it when righteously done. While Love agreed that the sincere individual should serve as a model for others and 'shew a dislike' for the ways of 'bad company,' this was at odds with the more civil bent of his rhetoric and belief. Love associated polite concepts like '[walking] without offence' *with* sincerity, instead of making them mutually exclusive.

This brings us to John Tillotson in 1695. Though his basic theological understanding of sincerity and hypocrisy did not differ from Lockyer, Love or Oldfield in any obvious way, he was the least concerned with the theological trappings of these concepts. The tangled web of sincerity, conscience and iniquity that we see in earlier sermons has all but disappeared; in its place, we find a consideration of sincerity's everyday applications in contexts of social interaction. Tillotson preached: 'we must not so fix our eye upon Heaven, as to

[84] Lockyer, *Divine Discovery*, 181.
[85] Love, 'True Israelite', 26–7.
[86] Ibid. 28. Emphasis original.

forget that we walk upon the Earth, and to neglect the ordering of our steps and Conversation among Men'.[87] He continually prized inoffensive behaviour, promoting a moderate, tolerant civility over what he called 'A fierce … ill governed … ignorant and injudicious Zeal for the Honour of God,' which 'hath made many Men do many unreasonable, immoral and impious things'.[88] He argued that the real hypocrites were those who used religion as an excuse to be:

> very unpeaceable … as if their profession of Godliness did exempt them from the care and practice of Christian Vertues … as if it were the priviledge of great Devotion, to give a license to Men to be … sower and morose, supercilious and censorious in their behaviour towards others.[89]

One can assume it was the likes of Lockyer to whom Tillotson referred in his allusion to the archetype of the zealous, hypocritical puritan. The 'Moral Duties' Lockyer had all but equated with hypocrisy were, for Tillotson, 'Christian Vertues', evidence of truly 'sincere Piety.'[90]

But how could one avoid causing offence without being a hypocrite? Tillotson advised: 'Not that we are obliged to tell every Man all our mind, but we are never to declare any thing contrary to it'.[91] He encouraged a delicate balance which effectively resolved the conflict between sincerity and civility present in Love's sermon, but which one suspects would not have been satisfying to that earlier preacher, and would certainly have been odious to the more rigid Lockyer. Tillotson's prudent instruction never to express insincere sentiments but to keep some thoughts to oneself set him apart from these puritan ministers. Yet there was not as great a distance between Tillotson and Love as one might expect. The Presbyterian Love had opposed toleration on the grounds that it 'would encourage religious libertinism and lead to social turbulence', but, crucially, this stance was in pursuit of the 'peace, union, and brotherly love' he envisioned in the national church.[92] This can be linked to Tillotson's own pursuit of unity in his support for the 'comprehension' of nonconformists into the Church of England prior to the Glorious

[87] Tillotson, *Of Sincerity*, 11.
[88] Ibid. 13.
[89] Ibid. 10–12.
[90] Ibid. 11, 9.
[91] Ibid. 16.
[92] Quoted in Vernon, 'Love'.

Revolution.[93] Alternatively, the Independent Lockyer would have supported some form of tolerance, but Congregationalist ideas about toleration were complicated and not always compatible with social harmony.[94] Toleration, civility and politeness were not necessarily congruous values, nor were the roles sincerity and hypocrisy played in their dynamic constant. Furthermore, despite any visions of religious unity that the later archbishop of Canterbury might have shared with Presbyterians such as Love, Tillotson was a very different minister and, by 1695, he was preaching in a very different context. Presiding over a now officially divided country in terms of religion in the wake of the Toleration Act's authorization of Protestant religious diversity, it is evident that Tillotson attempted to bring cohesion to ideals such as toleration, politeness and sincerity in his final work.

Moreover, Tillotson's belief in civility and social harmony did not prevent him from acknowledging and condemning the hypocrisies of polite society for the remainder of his sermon. He argued that overly performative incarnations of social ceremony were a threat to godly sincerity and that the pursuit of inoffensiveness could go too far, morphing into 'Dissimulation'. This was 'contrary to Sincerity, because it consists in a vain shew of what we are not'.[95] What Tillotson saw as prevalent displays of ostentatious social ceremony were, he argued, no better than ungodly hypocrisy. Worse still, he complained, was the fact that:

> falsehood, and fraud, and perfidiousness, and infinite little Crafts and arts of deceit, which Men practise upon one another in their ordinary conversation … are look'd upon by many, as signs of great depth and shrewdness, admirable instruments of business, and necessary means for the compassing our own ends and designs.[96]

There is copious evidence of Tillotson's influence on those who felt similarly distressed by the hypocritical direction society was taking at the turn of the century. Indeed, the famously successful early eighteenth-century periodical the *Spectator* quoted this Tillotson sermon three times from 1711 to 1714, in issues discussing the dearth of

93 See Kim, 'Tillotson, Part II', 128–34; Rivers, 'Tillotson'.
94 See Cooper, 'Congregationalists', 101–2; Halcomb, 'Godly Order', 27–8.
95 Tillotson, *Of Sincerity*, 18.
96 Ibid.

candid and honest behaviour in fashionable society, a fact which should be unsurprising to anyone familiar with the *Spectator*'s frequent ridicule of ostentatious, hypocritical social conduct.[97] Personal examples exist as well, such as the prolific diarist Sarah, Lady Cowper, who copied the passage from Tillotson quoted above into her commonplace book nearly word for word in 1711.[98] This sermon was one of Tillotson's numerous best-sellers throughout the eighteenth century and, thanks to periodicals like the *Spectator*, held particular cultural influence. Its success was not solely due to contemporaries' desire to receive spiritual instruction from the most famous preacher of the seventeenth century; rather, it was also because many, looking at the world around them, felt they recognized the truth in Tillotson's claims. This perception would only intensify in both religious and socio-political spheres going into the eighteenth century, as newly prominent issues such as occasional conformity took centre stage.[99]

Conclusion: Paradigms of Sincerity and Hypocrisy?

Towards the end of his sermon, Tillotson claimed hypocrisy was both contemporaneously ascendant and pervasive in English society:

> Amongst too many other Instances of the great corruption and degeneracy of the Age wherein we live, the great and general want of sincerity in Conversation is none of the least; the World is grown so full of Dissimulation and Complement, that Mens words are hardly any signification of their thoughts … *The old English plainness and sincerity … is in a great measure lost amongst us.*[100]

Lockyer, Love and Oldfield would have all agreed with him on this point. It was clear to each of these preachers that the world was 'full of Dissimulation', and it is implausible that any of them would have claimed Tillotson's ideal period of 'old *English* plainness and sincerity' had occurred either thirty, forty or fifty years earlier.[101] Questions of sincerity and hypocrisy were as relevant in the 1690s as they had

97 Christina Lupton, 'Sincere Performances: Franklin, Tillotson, and Steele on the Plain Style', *Eighteenth-Century Studies* 40 (2007), 177–92, at 181.
98 Knights, *Devil in Disguise*, 163.
99 See, for instance, Knights, 'Occasional Conformity', 47.
100 Tillotson, *Of Sincerity*, 23. Emphasis mine.
101 Emphasis in the original.

been in the earlier decades of the Restoration era, or during the Commonwealth and Civil War periods. Yet while their relevance was constant, their socio-political significance and cultural conceptualization was not. Like Lockyer, Love and Oldfield before him, Tillotson's sermon shows that homiletic communications of sincerity and hypocrisy shifted according to these societal contexts, rather than being congruous expressions of theological doctrine. These shifts were, to some extent, denominationally explicable, but they were also underpinned by social, political and cultural factors that were intertwined with religious belief, yet not solely beholden to it.

In this article, I have identified both similarities and differences between these sermons, paying needed attention to conceptions of sincerity and hypocrisy across the 'puritan'-'Anglican' divide. I have also sought to demonstrate the merit in considering dynamics within these groupings, as well as the significance of audience, approaches which could be extended to other sects mired in debates about sincerity and hypocrisy, such as Quakers and Baptists. These methods would assist in determining to what extent there were 'puritan' and 'Anglican', or 'Calvinist' and 'Arminian' brands of sincerity and hypocrisy after 1640. Peter Lake has warned that 'the contemporary binary opposition between puritanism and what has since become known as Anglicanism … or of that between Calvinism and Arminianism … leads us not so much through as into … circularities and anachronisms'.[102] By staying attuned to the potential pitfalls of these paradigms, we can gain better awareness of both continuity and divergence. Sometimes, differences and subtleties reared their heads in surprising places; at others, commonalities and complexities popped up in similarly unexpected spots. We should expect and welcome these messy inconsistencies with ideas as perennially important, yet conceptually abstract and malleable, as sincerity and hypocrisy. Matthew J. Smith and Caleb D. Spencer acknowledge this in their work on sincerity's literary history, noting that 'with respect to its Christian roots, the idea of sincerity has long been a discourse of struggle.'[103] The same was naturally true for hypocrisy, which time and again proved itself inseparable from its divine antidote, sincerity, throughout the revolutionary second half of the seventeenth century.

102 Peter Lake, 'Anti-Puritanism', 90.

103 Matthew J. Smith and Caleb D. Spencer, 'Preface', *Christianity & Literature* 67 (2017), 3–7, at 6–7.

Providence and Puritan Deceit: John Davenport's Forgery Revisited

Christy Wang*

The University of Tokyo

Many scholars have told the story of how John Davenport (bap. 1597, d. 1670), a prominent Congregationalist minister in New England, was fatally discredited as a fraudster when a letter he had forged was exposed in 1669. However, no one has analyzed how this extraordinary scandal fits into the larger narrative of puritan providentialism and its disenchantment. Focusing on the manipulation of providential language, this article shows that intra-Congregationalist conflicts over church polity could often be more political than theological. God-talk, or 'providential pragmatism', empowered New Englanders to navigate the ecclesiological ambiguities inherent in the Congregational system in a way that most benefited themselves. Davenport's scandal, precisely because it was the most blatant form of such pragmatism, offers a case study of a pattern of self-contradiction and double standard already observable in similar cases of schisms over church membership and infant baptism in late seventeenth-century New England.

On 24 September 1667, John Davenport, the seventy-year-old pastor of the New Haven church, received an invitation from the First Church in Boston to become their new teaching officer.[1] In order to secure the offer from the First Church, once led by the famous John Cotton from 1633 to 1652, Davenport repeatedly lied to the First Church by asserting that New Haven had agreed to release him from office, so that he was free to go to Boston. In reality, New Haven refused to let him go and, according to New England's mainstream Congregationalist practice, which Davenport had tirelessly advocated for decades, he was covenantally bound to New Haven until his church dismissed him. The established procedure and expectation were that the New Haven church would send a

* E-mail: wang.yi.jye@gmail.com.

[1] Richard D. Pierce, ed., *The Records of the First Church of Boston, 1630–1868*, 3 vols, Publications of the Colonial Society of Massachusetts 39–41 (Boston, MA, 1961), 1: 62.

Studies in Church History 60 (2024), 264–289 Published by Cambridge University Press on behalf of the Ecclesiastical History Society.
doi: 10.1017/stc.2024.11

formal dismissal letter to the First Church before Davenport could be called to office elsewhere.

In order to be installed successfully in Boston, Davenport; his son, John Jr; James Penn, Davenport's most loyal supporter and the ruling elder in the First Church; and James Allen, another candidate for ordination to the First Church, together decided to change significantly the content of a letter the New Haven church had sent them.[2] The original letter had explicitly refused to dismiss Davenport, but the forgery made it sound like the direct opposite. However, rumours that Davenport had never actually been dismissed by New Haven continued to spread after his ordination in Boston, and they eventually led to the full exposure of his fraudulent dealing. The First Church congregation finally realized that they had been deceived by their leaders, Penn, Davenport and Allen. After extensive debates and even conflict with neighbouring churches and leaders, who rose together to publicly condemn Davenport and his close associates, the First Church decided to retain Davenport and endorse his claim that his Boston ordination had been providential.

Several scholars have presented an overview of this scandal, most notably Francis Bremer, who helpfully delineates the fierce debates over church polity that paved the way to the divisions over Davenport's appointment to the First Church of Boston.[3]

[2] It was common practice in New England for ministers to be ordained, not simply installed, as they began to pastor a congregation, regardless of whether they had been ordained before. This was based on key ecclesiological differences between Congregationalism on the one side, and Presbyterianism and Episcopalianism on the other. Congregationalists questioned the existence of a visible catholic or universal Church and instead saw individual congregations as the most fundamental representation of the Church. They believed that a minister's office was derived from congregational assent and was therefore ultimately bound up with individual churches. See Geoffrey F. Nuttall, *Visible Saints: The Congregational Way, 1640–1660* (Oxford, 1957), 88–91; David Hall, *The Faithful Shepherd: A History of the New England Ministry in the Seventeenth Century* (Chapel Hill, NC, 1972), 102–3; Francis Bremer, *Lay Empowerment and the Development of Puritanism* (Basingstoke, 2015), 96–7. As Davenport, the protagonist of this case study, argued, ministers were 'limited to the Church': 'take away the relation [between the congregation and its officer], the office (and so the work) ceaseth.' John Davenport, *An Answer of the Elders of the Several Churches in New England unto Nine Positions Sent Over to Them* (London, 1643), 66.

[3] Francis Bremer, *Building a New Jerusalem: John Davenport, a Puritan in Three Worlds* (New Haven, CT, 2012), 254–350; James F. Cooper, *Tenacious of their Liberties: The Congregationalists in Colonial Massachusetts* (New York, 1999), 88–114; Janice Knight, *Orthodoxies in Massachusetts: Rereading American Puritanism* (Cambridge, MA, 1994),

However, Bremer's account, like the majority of those on which it draws, narrates the scandal without demonstrating how it illuminates the ways in which New England Congregationalists navigated competing orthodoxies and practices. This article argues that this controversy is of much greater significance, because it shows that intra-Congregationalist conflicts over church polity in the localities, centring on the Half-Way Covenant – a measure to expand church membership – could often be more political than theological.[4] Divine ends might justify some rather less than creditable means. By focusing on a case of forgery, this study goes beyond current scholarly attention on the theological diversity within New England Congregationalism to explore the discrepancies between belief and practice. How theologically and morally flexible could puritans be in order to win the cut-throat battle for New England orthodoxy? The answer is very.

By the second half of the seventeenth century, New Englanders had discovered, to their disappointment, that their Congregationalist ideals could not be neatly implemented. Escalating conflict over church membership and restrictions on infant baptism created even more uncertainties about how a church should be governed. Should a congregation abide by the advice of a council? Should church elders impose the will of the majority upon the dissenting minority if the latter were significant in number? Was a formal dismissal absolutely necessary whenever a minister or layperson left a church for another? This article argues that, time after time, puritans could adopt a providentialist rhetoric to get the answers they wanted. God-talk, or 'providential

189–97; Michael G. Hall, *The Last American Puritan: The Life of Increase Mather, 1639–1723* (Middletown, CT, 1988), 55–60, 78–82.

4 'Half-Way Covenant' was originally a term of disparagement, coined only in the mid-eighteenth century. It refers to the practice, endorsed by the Boston synod of 1662, of allowing baptized adults to present their children for baptism, regardless of whether or not the parents were fully covenanted members of the church. Since the term 'Half-Way Covenant' is widely used in current scholarship, this article applies it when discussing that practice. See Robert G. Pope, *The Half-Way Covenant: Church Membership in Puritan New England* (Princeton, NJ, 1969), 7–8; Katharine Gerbner, 'Beyond the "Halfway Covenant": Church Membership, Extended Baptism, and Outreach in Cambridge, Massachusetts, 1656–1667', *The New England Quarterly* 85 (2012), 281–301, at 286–7; Michael P. Winship, *Hot Protestants: A History of Puritanism in England and America* (New Haven, CT, 2018), 192.

pragmatism', empowered many Congregationalists to navigate the ecclesiological ambiguity in a way that most benefited themselves. By situating Davenport's forgery within the larger, regional crisis over the Half-Way Covenant, this article offers an illuminating example of a pattern of self-contradiction and double standard already observable in similar cases of schisms over church polity, precisely because it was the most blatant form of such pragmatism. This case study also demonstrates that puritans were well aware that hypocrisy existed among them and were inclined to believe that God's providence exposed sins with a vengeance. Providentialism proved a double-edged sword, sometimes perpetuating abuses of power through politicized interpretations of God's will, and at other times challenging such abuse and restraining puritans from a purely pragmatic, self-serving use of the doctrine of providence.

There exist ample scholarly discussions of puritan providentialism, characterized by an 'existential terror' and obsession with hypocrisy as a prevalent sin.[5] Alexandra Walsham speaks of a paradoxical hybrid of confidence and fear among the self-titled godly. Puritans found comfort in their own status as the elect and yet constantly dreaded God's displeasure, understanding that both could be observed from God's providential interactions with creation.[6] Andrew Dorsey, in his analysis of the fear of divine wrath among New England Congregationalists, emphasizes the centrality of hypocrisy as a notion in puritans' incessant questioning of their own faith and godliness: 'how do I know I'm not a hypocrite?'[7] Ethan Shagan likewise notes the 'plague of subjective atheism and hypocrisy' experienced by Calvinists as a consequence of their predestinarian doctrine.[8]

[5] Ethan Shagan, *The Birth of Modern Belief: Faith and Judgment from the Middle Ages to the Enlightenment* (Princeton, NJ, 2019), 140.

[6] Alexandra Walsham, *Providence in Early Modern England* (Oxford, 1999), 19. Walsham also draws attention to Robert T. Kendall's similar observation in his analysis of puritans' 'experimental predestinarianism' in his *Calvin and English Calvinism to 1649* (Oxford, 1979), 79–138. Other early discussions of puritan providentialism include Perry Miller, *The New England Mind: The Seventeenth Century* (Cambridge, MA, 1954); Peter Lake, *Moderate Puritans and the Elizabethan Church* (Cambridge, 1982), 116–68; and Barbara Donagan's many writings, such as 'Providence, Chance and Explanation: Some Paradoxical Aspects of Puritan Views of Causation', *JRH* 11 (1981), 385–403.

[7] Andrew Dorsey, 'A Rhetoric of American Experience: Thomas Shepard's Cambridge Confessions and the Discourse of Spiritual Hypocrisy', *Early American Literature* 49 (2014), 629–62, at 633.

[8] Shagan, *The Birth of Modern Belief*, 140.

Scholars have also uncovered internal tensions and contradictions within the puritan rhetoric of piety and providence. Alexandra Walsham, for instance, points out puritans' ability to justify both good and evil as God's blessings and signs of their spiritual superiority as the godly. This way of thinking fed on a heightened sense of God's active involvement in believers' lives, winning puritans notoriety for hypocrisy.[9] David Hall likewise suggests that puritans could utilize providential language, such as the use of wonder stories, for political gain.[10] This article builds on the work of these (and other) scholars to delineate a particular form of spiritual abuse within puritanism. Puritan providentialism, with its accompanying language of godly waiting and submission, a clean conscience, and divine sovereignty, could be weaponized to deceive the public, suppress opposition and pursue private profit. This distinctively puritan hypocrisy was especially useful to ecclesiastical authorities who were most familiar with providentialist tropes and most empowered to take advantage of them to sustain their dominance over ecclesiastical affairs. While a full investigation of puritan providentialism and deceit exceeds the scope of this article, this case study serves as an initial step of inquiry, demonstrating how puritan colonists maximized this 'providential pragmatism' in the area of ecclesiological ambiguity.

Davenport against Hypocrisy

It was clear from the very beginning, when John Davenport received the invitation from the First Church in Boston to be their new teaching officer, that the New Haven minister and his congregants were of different minds. Two weeks after he received the invitation, on 8 October 1667, Davenport wrote to the First Church to express his 'strong inclynation' to accept the call.[11] The minister highlighted his own 'nothingness' and 'unworthiness', but in reality, he was desperate to leave New Haven for the flagship church in New England.[12] Both Davenport and the First Church in Boston were aware that this

[9] Walsham, *Providence in Early Modern England*, 17.

[10] David Hall, *Worlds of Wonder, Days of Judgment: Popular Religious Belief in Early New England* (New York, 1989), 71–116.

[11] John Davenport to the First Church Boston, 8 October 1667, in *Letters of John Davenport, Puritan Divine*, ed. Isabel M. Calder (New Haven, CT, 1937), 270.

[12] Ibid.

invitation marked a crucial attempt at a robust comeback of the old way – in their eyes, the only biblical way – of Congregationalism. For many in the First Church, one of their previous pastors John Norton (d. 1663) had already damaged his own reputation when he promoted reconciliation with the crown as early as 1661, and failed to secure sufficient economic liberty in the negotiations with London in 1662.[13] They also shared Davenport's suspicions of 'Presbyterian' leanings among many New England ministers, including Norton and John Wilson, their recently deceased minister, both of whom had been staunch advocates for a more inclusive church membership and infant baptism.[14] The overwhelming support for what later became known as the Half-Way Covenant aroused the fears of many, including civil and clerical leaders in New Haven, as well as the majority of the Boston First Church, that New England was turning away from its 'first love'.[15] For them, the church should be a covenanted community of visible saints, and neither a mixture of believers and the visibly relapsed, nor a parish system in which every child, regardless of their parents' faith, was baptized and brought up within a national, all-inclusive church.

The dispute over church membership revealed a common anxiety about hypocrisy among puritans on both sides of the Atlantic. The English Presbyterian luminary William Gouge argued against the religious Independents at the Westminster Assembly that since individual congregations, while being 'a company that professe[d] the truth', could 'all be hypocrites', particular churches must not be the holder of the keys, that is, the ultimate authority over discipline and doctrine.[16] Among the Congregationalists, even those who advocated the strictest terms of church membership, such as Davenport, admitted that churches were inevitably a mixture of true believers and hypocrites.

[13] Stephen Foster, *The Long Argument: English Puritanism and the Shaping of New England Culture, 1570–1700* (Chapel Hill, NC, 1991), 196–202; Winship, *Hot Protestants*, 190–2; Francis Bremer, 'Norton, John (1606–1663)', *ODNB*, online edn (2004), at: <https://doi.org/10.1093/ref:odnb/20348>, accessed 15 February 2023.

[14] Winship, *Hot Protestants*, 189; Bremer, *Lay Empowerment and the Development of Puritanism*, 166.

[15] Charles J. Hoadly, ed., *Records of the Colony or Jurisdiction of New Haven, from May, 1653, to the Union. Together with New Haven Code of 1656* (Hartford, CT, 1858), 196–8.

[16] William Gouge, *The Minutes and Papers of the Westminster Assembly, 1643–1652*, ed. Chad Van Dixhoorn, 5 vols (Oxford, 2012), 5: 234.

Even so, congregations must ensure their visible godliness, as Davenport insisted.[17]

In fact, active cultivation of visible godliness and rigorous assessment of candidates for church membership were the most dominant themes in Davenport's sermons throughout the 1650s. As minister in New Haven, he repeatedly emphasized that, besides public confession of faith, there must be a proper examination of whether these self-proclaimed believers were actually hypocrites, who 'had the forme of … [godliness] & yet visibly denie[d] the power of it'.[18] With the increasingly mainstream practice of a broadened church membership in mind, Davenport reminded his flock in November 1656 of the 'stewardly fidelity' (a concept borrowed from John Cotton) required of them to ensure the 'honour & wellfare of gods house'.[19] Again, Davenport stressed that this prerequisite 'profession of faith & obedience' for membership was never based on 'judgm[en]t of infallibility' but that of 'charitable discretion'.[20]

When the Massachusetts Bay Colony and the Connecticut Colony endorsed the expansion of infant baptism to the children of baptized, but unconverted, parents in a council in 1657, New Haven officially became a minority in its adherence to the stricter practice. The Boston synod of 1662 further confirmed the mainstream status of the Half-Way Covenant. In October 1662, New Haven received yet another blow: the restored Stuart monarch, Charles II, had

[17] Boston, MA, The Congregational Library & Archives, MS 5374, John Davenport Sermon Book, 1649–52, 347 (15 August 1652). Other Congregational leaders shared this observation: John Cotton, *Of the Holinesse of Church-Members* (London, 1650), 27; Thomas Hooker, *A Survey of the Summe of Church-Discipline* (London, 1648), 28.

[18] The Congregational Library & Archives, MS 5374, John Davenport Sermon Book, 1649–1652, 344, 345, 347 (15 August 1652). Davenport quoted Cotton and Hooker verbatim at times in these notes, and here he was citing Hooker, *Survey*, 32. There is ample secondary literature on admission tests or spiritual assessment as a way for Congregationalists to keep out hypocrites: see, for example, Paul Miller, *The New England Mind: From Colony to Province* (Cambridge, MA, 1967), 568–81; Sarah Rivett, *The Science of the Soul in Colonial New England* (Chapel Hill, NC, 2011), 31–2, 36–7, 61–2.

[19] New Haven, CT, Yale University, Beinecke Rare Book and Manuscript Library, GEN MSS 202, John Davenport Sermons and Writings, 1615–1658, 'Sermons Preached at New Haven, 1656–1658', 71–2 (9 November 1656); John Cotton, *Holinesse*, 107 (mispaginated as 95).

[20] Beinecke Rare Book and Manuscript Library, GEN MSS 202, John Davenport Sermons and Writings, 1615–1658, 'Sermons Preached at New Haven, 1656–1658', 68 (9 November 1656).

granted Connecticut a new charter that incorporated the entire New Haven Colony. In Davenport's eyes, Connecticut was a nearby, rival colony in worrying spiritual decline, whose leadership and churches were deeply divided over church membership and embroiled in disputes over synodical authority. Samuel Stone's Hartford church and John Warham's Windsor church had long advocated for the Half-Way Covenant, whereas churches in Wethersfield and New London were divided on this question.[21] Despite repeated objections raised by New Haven authorities, Connecticut immediately initiated the merger, incorporating New Haven towns into their structures. On 13 December 1664, the nearly bankrupt New Haven Colony finally voted to confirm its submission to Connecticut.[22] Davenport considered this a fatal blow to the ongoing campaign for his version of the 'New England Way', proclaiming 'Christ's interest in New Haven Colony as miserably lost'.[23] It was in this context of acute disillusionment that the co-founder of the New Haven Colony received the invitation from Boston in 1667.

Davenport, a Hypocrite?

Davenport might have regarded moving to Boston as a way to further his influence as the champion of stricter church membership that could better fend off hypocrites. Many in Boston had nevertheless been wary of his potential move to the First Church, even before an invitation was offered, and would repeatedly question the true motives behind his relocation. The First Church congregation had been bitterly divided over many issues, including the treatment of sectarian Protestants and the Half-Way Covenant. Besides Elder James Penn, Davenport enjoyed support from the majority of the church, many of whom desired greater toleration for Baptists and Quakers. These included Edward Hutchinson, whose mother Anne

[21] Paul R. Lucas, 'Presbyterianism Comes to Connecticut: The Toleration Act of 1669', *Journal of Presbyterian History* 50 (1972), 129–47; idem, *Valley of Discord: Church and Society along the Connecticut River, 1636–1725* (Hanover, NH, 1976), 73–86. John Warham would abandon the Half-Way Covenant in 1664, which further divided the Windsor First Church: ibid. 78–9.

[22] Bremer, *Davenport*, 301; Isabel M. Calder, *The New Haven Colony*, Yale Historical Publications Miscellany 28 (New Haven, CT, 1934), 249–53.

[23] Davenport, as quoted by Edward E. Atwater, *History of the Colony of New Haven to its Absorption into Connecticut* (Meriden, CT, 1902), 527.

Hutchinson had played a central role in the Antinomian Controversy of 1636–8, and John Leverett, major-general of the Massachusetts militia and future governor of the Bay Colony (1673–9). Other firm supporters of Davenport included Anthony Stoddard, Thomas Clark, Thomas Grubb, and the delegates sent to extend the invitation to New Haven, Edward Tying, James Oliver and Richard Cooke.[24] In opposition were John Hull, merchant and diarist, Hezekiah Usher, one of the earliest New England booksellers, and others in the congregation such as Edward Rainsford, Robert Walker, Theodore Atkinson and William Salter, who had been in favour of the expansion of church membership and therefore opposed the appointment of Davenport as John Wilson's successor.[25]

While Davenport considered himself an advocate for the most biblical polity that could effectively prevent churches from the infiltration of hypocrites, he himself had never been free from accusations of hypocrisy. As early as 1624, while still a curate of St Lawrence Old Jewry in London, the twenty-seven-year-old Davenport had declared his 'hearty detestation' of the 'hypocrisy' of being a puritan, which he carefully defined as 'one, that secretly encourageth men in opposition to the present government'.[26] Having been labelled 'puritanically affected', the young preacher ran into problems with his appointment as vicar of St Stephen's, Coleman Street, in London

[24] Bremer, *Davenport*, 317–18. Hutchinson, Oliver and Grubb were among those who petitioned the General Court to release imprisoned Baptists in November 1668. While Leverett did not sign the petition, he refused to issue an arrest warrant in the same year and was praised by Baptists for his tolerance: E. Brooks Holifield, 'On Toleration in Massachusetts', *ChH* 38 (1969), 188–200, at 92–3. When the General Court legislated that Quakers should be banished 'upon paine of death' in October 1658, future supporters of Davenport, such as Hutchinson and Clark, dissented from the majority of the court, resisting the heavy-handed approach promoted by their former church leaders Norton and Wilson: John Norton, *The Heart of N-England Rent at the Blasphemies of the Present Generation* (Cambridge, MA, 1659), 48–9; Bremer, *Davenport*, 317; Nathaniel B. Shurtleff, ed., *Records of the Governor and Company of the Massachusetts Bay in New England*, 5 vols (Boston, MA, 1853–4), 4/1: 346. For Davenport's own disapproval of the imposition of death penalties upon Quaker missionaries, such as Mary Dyer, see Davenport to John Winthrop Jr, 6 December 1659, in *Letters*, 147–8.

[25] Bremer, *Davenport*, 317; idem, 'The New England Way Reconsidered: An Exploration of Church Polity and the Governance of the Region's Churches', in Elliot Vernon and Hunter Powell, eds, *Church Polity and Politics in the British Atlantic World, c.1635–66* (Manchester, 2020), 155–73, at 169.

[26] London, TNA (PRO), SP 14/173, fol. 50^r, John Davenport to Sir Edward Conway, Secretary of State, 13 October 1624.

in 1624, and was eager to assert his loyalty before the bishop of London, George Montaigne.[27] Davenport emphasized that he had consistently preached obedience to governments both 'ecclesiastical and civill' and eventually secured the incumbency.[28] Accusations of hypocrisy came from godly allies as well. After fleeing London for Amsterdam in 1633, Davenport complained about the 'persecucion of the Tongue', especially from those who 'profess[ed] religion in an higher strayne then some others', clearly referring to his conformable friends.[29] Accusations raised against the now nonconformist minister included abandonment of his London congregation and misappropriation of funds raised for the Feoffees for Impropriations.[30] With noticeable bitterness, Davenport stressed in a letter to his patron Lady Mary Vere that his departure from London was purely a matter of conscience: 'I did conforme with as much inward peace … but [now] my light [is] different.'[31]

After a period of relative peace, free from Laudian surveillance across the Atlantic, challenges to Davenport's assertions of his own piety and political loyalty resurfaced upon the restoration of the Stuart monarchy. Under Davenport's leadership, New Haven gained notoriety for being a deeply disaffected colony. Not only was New Haven the last among the New England colonies to celebrate the reinstituted Crown and proclaim the king, but it systematically sheltered two regicides, Edward Whalley and William Goffe.[32] Reports of disloyalty travelled far and fast, and Davenport, together with other New Haven authorities such as Governor William Leete, felt compelled to explain themselves to London, with varying degrees of sincerity.

[27] Ibid.

[28] Ibid.

[29] John Davenport to Lady Mary Vere, 1633, in *Letters*, 38–9.

[30] The Feoffees for Impropriations was an organization established in 1625, and Davenport was one of the clerical feoffees. They solicited funds to buy impropriations and advowsons with the aim of appointing puritan-leaning ministers to strategic places throughout the kingdom, 'especially in Cities, and Market Towns', clearly targeted in order to build up godly sympathies in places that sent MPs to the House of Commons: Samuel Clarke, *A Collection of the Lives of Ten Eminent Divines* (London, 1662), 111.

[31] John Davenport to Lady Mary Vere, 1633, in *Letters*, 39.

[32] A recent and thorough account of Whalley and Goffe's flight to America is Matthew Jenkinson, *Charles I's Killers in America: The Lives & Afterlives of Edward Whalley & William Goffe* (Oxford, 2019). See also Bremer, *Davenport*, 286; Christopher Durston, *Cromwell's Major-Generals: Godly Government during the English Revolution* (Manchester, 2001), 235–6.

While Leete asked for Richard Baxter's intercession before the court, Davenport's similar request went to Sir William Morice, secretary of state and a former Presbyterian, through Sir Thomas Temple.[33] The New Haven minister's account of how Whalley and Goffe had escaped the search in the colony was deliberately vague. Completely omitting his reception of the regicides into his own home, Davenport depicted a story of miraculous, unpreventable escape by divine intervention that demanded acceptance: 'I believe if his ma[jes]tie Rightly Understood the Curcumstances [*sic*] of this Event he would not be displeased with our majestrates, but to acquiesce in the Providence of the most high.'[34]

An anonymous informer, well aware of Davenport's track record of problems with the Caroline regime, and taking advantage of the brewing animosity between Davenport and supporters of the Half-Way Covenant in Boston, accused the minister of seditious preaching.[35] Richard Nicolls, governor of New York and a committed Royalist who already had his eye on Davenport, started a renewed investigation of these claims in the months leading up to the First Church's official decision to approach Davenport. The minister's long-time friend and governor of Connecticut, John Winthrop Jr, came to his defence. In a letter to Nicolls in July 1667, Winthrop questioned the character of the informer, who must have 'not heard him [Davenport] preach a sermon since Noahs Flood'.[36] In reality, Winthrop protested, with not-too-subtle sarcasm, Davenport merely preached 'the true way of worship, or Christs government in the church against the popish, Antichristian, Roman Hierarchy'.[37] Nicolls could do little to disrupt Davenport's plans. To defend the polity that he believed could best keep hypocrites away, and also to promote himself, Davenport would go to

[33] TNA (PRO), Colonial State Papers, CO 1/15, nos 80, 81, Sir Thomas Temple to Secretary of State William Morice, 20 August 1661. Jenkinson seems to portray Temple as simply another Royalist authority who distrusted Davenport and genuinely desired to capture the regicides, but Temple would become a hearty supporter of Davenport's ministry and a regular attendee at the First Church of Boston, where Davenport became pastor. Davenport's protection of the regicides and preaching in support of them is discussed in Jenkinson, *Charles I's Killers in America,* 52.

[34] John Davenport to Thomas Temple, 19 August 1661, in *Letters*, 193.

[35] Boston, MA, Massachusetts Historical Society, Winthrop Family Papers, John Winthrop Jr to Richard Nicolls, 15 July 1667.

[36] Ibid.

[37] Ibid.

extraordinary lengths to secure the most prestigious ministerial position in New England, even if it meant that he would have to violate the principle of congregational covenanting he had relentlessly defended.

Providentially Freed from Congregational Covenanting

As the first step of the ordination process in New England, a congregation seeking a new church officer had to debate among themselves and discern whether it was the will of God to elect the particular preacher they had in mind.[38] In a typically puritan manner, this was the question that everyone in Boston and New Haven dutifully asked: did God want Davenport to be the new pastor of the First Church in Boston? It seemed that Davenport had the answer before everyone else in New Haven, being so overwhelmed by the 'clearnes[s] and strength of the call of Christ' that he had no choice but to accept the invitation.[39] However, both New Haven and a minority party in the First Church were unconvinced. In fact, as Davenport reported in another letter to Boston, 'the strong opposition of above 40 Brethren' among the First Church members alerted his own flock in New Haven that the invitation might not be God's will, since Davenport's transition to Boston could cause a 'breaking' of both churches.[40] Remarkably, disregarding these concerns and the principle of congregational assent, which he had so consistently preached, Davenport reasserted his plan to relocate to Boston 'for a further triall for to finde out the minde of God'.[41] Little did New Haven know that their pastor would never come back.

While New Haven and the minority party in the First Church struggled to accept what Davenport presented as 'the call of Christ', the majority party in Boston was already claiming that it was God who had directed them to Davenport. In the letter of invitation, Elder Penn described how the First Church was

[38] For a concise description of the process of ordination among New England Congregationalist churches, see Ralph F. Young, 'Breathing the "Free Aire of the New World": The Influence of the New England Way on the Gathering of Congregational Churches in Old England, 1640–1660', *The New England Quarterly* 83 (2010), 5–46, at 13–14.

[39] John Davenport to the First Church Boston, 8 October 1667, in *Letters*, 269–70.

[40] John Davenport to the First Church Boston, 28 October 1667, in *Letters*, 271.

[41] Ibid.

'providentially led' to seek Davenport as their new pastor, who was also 'providentially loosened' from any commitment to New Haven.[42] Davenport had told an extraordinary story to Elder Penn indeed: during the preliminary discussions, even before the official invitation was sent, Davenport had already alluded to a 'free pass', an agreement between himself and the New Haven church 'in our first begin[n]ing for my being at liberty to follow the call of God'.[43] In essence, the Congregationalist Davenport was arguing that, although he had been championing a vision of the Church as a gathering of visible saints, built upon covenant-making and governed through congregational assent, without which none could become a member, access the sacraments or leave for another church, he himself had not been bound by the same rule.

Davenport's free pass theory was unusual and irregular in seventeenth-century New England, where covenanted members could not easily break from their church without the consent of the majority of the congregation. When obtaining unanimous support was the ideal, leaving without an official dismissal not only left one vulnerable to accusations of being a schismatic, but could create further ecclesiastical rejections from other churches. Even in the case of serious schisms, disaffected members of a congregation would not simply depart for another church, but would still hope to secure proper release, even if it turned out to be a long, torturous or even futile process.[44] Clergy were expected to abide by the same rule. When the Massachusetts General Court voted to appoint John Norton as one of the colony agents to London in 1662, they engaged in an extensive negotiation with the First Church to seek permission for the minister's temporary absence.[45] Church records further suggest that, by 2

[42] Hamilton Andrews Hill, *History of the Old South Church (Third Church) Boston: 1669–1884*, 2 vols (Boston, MA, 1890), 1: 14–15.

[43] Davenport to the First Church Boston, 28 October 1667, in *Letters*, 272.

[44] In both the First Church controversy over Davenport's appointment and an earlier schism in Hartford over the selection of Michael Wigglesworth as minister in the late 1650s, the dissenting minority underwent a painful process of requesting a dismissal to no avail: see, below pp. 278–9, 283–5.

[45] Thomas Hutchinson, *The Hutchinson Papers*, ed. Henry William Whitmore and Williams S. Appleton, 2 vols (Albany, NY, 1865), 2: 65–7. During the negotiation, Massachusetts magistrates were even composing letters to other churches, asking them to provide 'neighbourly assistance' to the First Church if Norton were to be sent away. These letters were never sent because the First Church wanted to make their own arrangements.

May 1668, the time of Davenport's relocation to Boston, the First Church had witnessed generations of lay and clerical members admitted and dismissed to other churches, all on the basis of consent from both the sending and receiving congregations.[46] While on rare occasions, the lack of formal dismissals was tolerated, especially when the departure was blessed by a council, it was extraordinary for a minister in New England to deny outright his obligation to obtain a formal release before leaving his flock, let alone to fake such a confirmation of release.

Davenport's theory of a free pass seemed to satisfy no one except those already in support of his relocation to Boston. The minority party in the First Church rejected Davenport's purported liberty and questioned the motives behind his claim: '[Davenport] looketh at himself as free from the Church but by what doth appeare hath not bin dismissed from them, whose temptation may hereby be heightned to dessert [*sic*] his flock without any cause.'[47] Not only was the concept of a free pass unheard of, but the fact that Davenport continued to seek a formal dismissal from New Haven must have weakened the force of his argument. To make things worse, Nicholas Street, New Haven's other minister and now spokesman, told Penn outright that the whole New Haven congregation unanimously rejected Davenport's claimed liberty. While seeing 'no cause nor call of God' to dismiss Davenport, Street nevertheless conceded: '[S]uch is our tender respect to him that we have soe declared ourselves to his satisfaction as we hope; As he is able for to give you a more full answer not only of his owne minde but of our also in this weighty matter.'[48]

Here is Street's implicit rebuke of Davenport's wilfulness, rather than a real desire to let Davenport speak for New Haven. Fully aware of a significant faction of dissenters at the First Church of Boston, Street knew perfectly well that if his carefully worded letter were read out, Davenport would never be installed. Street's motives were however unclear: either Davenport's old friend genuinely wanted the minister to remain in New Haven, or Street was refusing

[46] See *Records of the First Church of Boston, 1630–1868*, 1: 15–62.

[47] 'Humble Request of the Dissenting Brethren', 30 September 1667, in Hill, *History of the Old South Church*, 1: 16.

[48] 'The Church of New Haven Letter in Answer to the Brethrens Letter Returned by Captain Clarke', 28 October 1667, in Hill, *History of the Old South Church*, 1: 20.

to release the man who had abandoned his own flock. Caught in a terrible impasse, Davenport soon realized that he could only break free by deceit. In the event, Street's letter was withheld by Penn, who seemed to have been determined to bring Davenport to Boston regardless of New Haven's opinion on the matter. On 2 May 1668, Davenport arrived in Boston, as promised. John Hull, one of the dissenters in Boston, recorded that a 'great shower of extraordinary drops of rain fell' as the Davenport family entered the town, perhaps interpreting the downpour as a sign of divine displeasure.[49]

Conscience against Conscience

Davenport's arrival in Boston marked the rapid escalation of conflict between the minister's supporters and his opponents, with providentialist language being used indiscriminately by both groups. As this internal dispute among the First Church congregants grew into a regional affair, it became clear that this high-profile puritan infighting had always been about something much greater than the appointment of a pastor: the schism was between two clashing visions of church polity among New England Congregationalists. Similar conflicts had plagued other churches. Hartford minister Samuel Stone promoted an expanded church membership and a more inclusive infant baptism. He asserted a heightened clerical authority over his own congregation by blocking the selection of Michael Wigglesworth, a young Harvard graduate who had grown up in New Haven, as his colleague after Thomas Hooker died in 1647.[50] However, the minority faction of the Hartford church, including the ruling elder William Goodwin, saw Stone's behaviour as an infringement of the congregation's authority to elect its own ministers. Leaders from neighbouring New Haven, including Davenport and

[49] John Hull, 'John Hull's Diary of Public Occurrences', *Archaeologia Americana: Transactions and Collections of the American Antiquarian Society* 3 (1857), 109–318, at 227; Bremer, *Davenport*, 326. For John Hull's career, theological position, relationship with the First Church, Boston, and interpretation of divine providence, see Mark Valeri, *Heavenly Merchandise: How Religion Shaped Commerce in Puritan America* (Princeton, NJ, 2010), 74–110. For Valeri's discussion of Hull's close attention to everyday events, often natural phenomena like storms or cold winters, as signs of God's providence, see ibid. 91–2, 105.

[50] For a detailed account of the Hartford controversy, see Bremer, *Davenport*, 258–67.

Governor Theophilus Eaton, affirmed the dissenters' concerns. Stone, on the other hand, found sympathy and support among ministers in the Bay Colony who shared his views on church membership, such as John Norton. This local dispute escalated into an extraordinary scandal that involved clergy and magistrates from many colonies, with two councils that reached diametrically opposed verdicts. The controversy ended with Stone's triumph after the Hartford church granted a series of his requests, including submission to the minister's teaching 'as inferiors hearken to their superiors'.[51]

Another similar, but largely neglected, case was the conflict between Nathaniel Clap (1668/9–1745), minister of the Newport church, and his congregation in 1728. Clap was notoriously strict on the administration of communion and had alienated a significant number of the Newport church by withholding the Lord's Supper from them for around four years. Tensions escalated into open controversy when Clap and his followers refused to appoint a younger and more moderate preacher, John Adams, as Clap's colleague. After arbitration that involved ministers from six other churches, the congregation eventually split into two.[52]

The subsequent controversy surrounding Davenport's dealings with the First Church demonstrated the same recurring themes in New England ecclesiastical politics: ambiguities in church polity – whether it be the boundary of church membership, clerical power in relation to the congregation, or synodical authority – and, in order to navigate these ambiguities, discernment of God's will and providence, as well as the politicization thereof. Puritans followed a series of steps when they ventured into the realm of spiritual discernment.[53] They were to maintain an attitude of godly passivity and subject their conscience to constant scrutiny in order to perceive God's providential ways and obey his will with a pure heart. When they witnessed sin and evil, they must decide whether to right the wrong that might have been providentially exposed, or accept the consequences

[51] Samuel Stone to the church of Hartford, 2 August 1657, in *Collections of the Connecticut Historical Society*, ed. James Hammond Trumbull, 31 vols (Hartford, CT, 1870), 2: 75.

[52] *Records of the First Church of Boston, 1630–1868*, 1: 239–40. For a more detailed analysis of the Newport scandal, see Benjamin Franklin V, *The Other John Adams, 1705–1740* (Madison, NJ, 2003), 27–52.

[53] See Barbara Donagan, 'Godly Choice: Puritan Decision-Making in Seventeenth-Century England', *HThR* 76 (1983), 307–34.

of sin as part of God's sovereign plan to bring good out of evil. A genuine adherence to this way of thinking could create intense anxiety, and yet many could also adopt this language of discernment and providence to repackage questionable behaviour with a pietistic appearance.[54]

In 1675, Ezekiel Fogg, a skinner imprisoned in Boston for failing to honour a bond, told the Court of Assistants that he needed to petition for freedom to attend Sunday services, as a godly response to having been cursed the previous night by John Gifford, his creditor and adversary.[55] In order for him to 'Experience whilst men Curse God blesse', Fogg boldly suggested that magistrates with a Christian conscience should not deny his request to participate freely in public worship.[56] Given Fogg's notoriety as a fraudster, it was no surprise that the court denied his request. With casual references to providence, empty words could also be dressed up as credible promises. One such example might be John Dinely, a Boston shipmaster, who guaranteed Cornelius Steenwyck, mayor of New York City, in 1668 that he would pay off his debt if God granted him a safe return from Barbados. Dinely allegedly never repaid Steenwyck, despite arriving back safely.[57]

Davenport was a master of this providential pragmatism. His status as a highly respected Congregationalist leader, theological proficiency, and access to the pulpit ensured that he could effectively broadcast his rhetoric. On his arrival in Boston, the preacher embarked on a series of sermons. Picking up the theme of being 'purely passive' that he had begun to speak of before leaving New Haven, he again stressed his posture of discernment and self-examination against those who questioned the nature of his relocation.[58] In

[54] Ibid. 311–12; Walsham, *Providence in Early Modern England*, 17–19.

[55] Samuel E. Morison, ed., *Records of the Suffolk County Court, 1671–1680*, 2 vols, Publications of the Colonial Society of Massachusetts 29–30 (Boston, MA, 1933), 1: 546–7, 2: 656–8. Fogg's parents, Ralph, also a skinner, and Susanna, migrated from London to New England in 1633 but returned to England in 1652. Ezekiel Fogg was 'citizen and skinner of London' by 1673, but was spending extensive time in Boston in the 1670s: Susan Hardman Moore, *Abandoning America: Life-Stories from Early New England* (Woodbridge, 2013), 111–12; George Francis Dow, ed., *Records and Files of the Quarterly Courts of Essex County, Massachusetts*, 9 vols (Salem, MA, 1911–75), 6: 82.

[56] Dow, ed., *Records and Files of the Quarterly Courts of Essex County, Massachusetts*, 2: 657.

[57] Ibid. 1: 169.

[58] Davenport to the First Church Boston, 28 October 1667, in *Letters*, 271.

one of the sermons he preached in Cambridge in the Bay Colony during this time, Davenport focused on Acts 24: 16: 'And herein doe I exercise my selfe to have alwayes a conscience void of offence toward God, and toward men.'[59] Davenport taught that 'men should not set their wills above the way of their own understanding'; indeed, speaking directly about himself, the preacher declared: 'nor doe I exercise myself in Things to[o] high for mee.'[60] This was precisely what Davenport was doing, however, and his self-deprecation and language of godly submission must have seemed insincere to those who had doubts about his release from New Haven.

Not only did Davenport affirm his honesty before God from the pulpit, but he also condemned his opponents as self-seekers. Before moving to Boston, he had already warned the First Church dissenters in writing against 'strife and vaine glory'.[61] Seeing that dissenters had persisted in opposition, Davenport decided to challenge them in person on a lecture day on 16 July 1668. According to one of the dissenters, Joshua Scottow, Davenport rebuked them for jeopardizing the unity of the church 'in the presence of a great part of the Countrey' and declared: 'Satan hath a great hand in it.'[62] On 10 August 1668, the church voted to call Davenport to office. Since Davenport, now elected, had to be admitted into the First Church before being formally ordained, the congregation sent yet another letter to New Haven to ask for written confirmation that they had indeed released their former pastor.[63]

Based on what Nicholas Street had written the previous year, it is hard to imagine that Penn and Davenport would be hoping for a

[59] Here I cite the 1611 King James Version, which the notetaker seemed to use, although, in the sermon notes, the quoted verse appeared to be incomplete and mixed with other scriptural texts, such as Ps. 90: 12. See Cambridge, MA, Harvard University, Houghton Library, MS Am 2356, First Church (Cambridge, MA) Sermon Papers, 1665–1837, 'Notes on Sermons Preached in Cambridge, Feb 1667 to Jul 1668', 281.

[60] Bremer, *Davenport*, 327–8; Harvard University, Houghton Library, MS Am 2356, First Church (Cambridge, Mass.) Sermon Papers, 1665–1837, 'Notes on Sermons Preached in Cambridge, Feb 1667 to Jul 1668', 287 (mispaginated as 288).

[61] Davenport to the First Church Boston, 28 October 1667, in *Letters*, 273.

[62] For Davenport's prayer, recorded by Joshua Scottow, see Hill, *History of the Old South Church*, 1: 24.

[63] The established Congregationalist practice was that, after securing an agreement among themselves over the appointment of a candidate as church officer, the congregation would vote to elect the person, admit the elected candidate into their church and, finally, proceed to the formal ordination service: Young, 'Breathing the "Free Aire of the New World"', 13–14.

positive response. A few weeks later, another clear denial of a dismissal arrived. Just as Davenport had resorted to the notion of a clean conscience accountable only to God (and, clearly, not to the congregation), Street declared that New Haven simply could not provide proof of a dismissal that had never existed: 'we can better beare that [human censure] than God's displeasure by wronging of our consciences.'[64] Two months later, Street sent an even longer letter after repeated demands from both Penn and Davenport. Laid out in the most cold and flawless manner, Street's condemnation should have been devastating to Davenport:

> A man can not have the essentials … of a Church officer put upon him in your Church that is not first a member of your Church soe that your hands are tied up by your own act, It is not for us to dismiss to the Church of Boston one that is all ready called to be a teaching officer to your Church at Boston … but that which doth most strike with us is matter of conscience though yourselves and our Reverend Pastor are fully satisfied in these motions yet the church of Newhaven is not soe.[65]

Determined to set the seal on Davenport's installation, Elder Penn and James Allen, another minister called to office along with Davenport, decided to draw up an abbreviated version of this letter that only highlighted New Haven's recognition of Davenport's departure as if it indicated a willing dismissal.[66] The Davenports were intimately involved, with John Jr personally transcribing the edited letter.[67] After Davenport's admission to the First Church on 1 November 1668, the ordination service was finally held on 9 December, thus finalizing the installation of Davenport as a church officer of the First Church. According to Scottow, Davenport again publicly cited divine endorsement at his own ordination service: 'An outward call could not satisfy mee, if I had not an inward call,' and indeed Christ had 'cleare[d] his will … to the full satisfaction of my

[64] 'Copy of a Concealed Letter', New Haven to the First Church Boston, 28 August 1668, in Hill, *History of the Old South Church*, 1: 30.

[65] 'The Suppressed Letter', New Haven to the First Church Boston, 12 October 1668, in Hill, *History of the Old South Church*, 1: 34.

[66] For a comparison between the edited letter and the actual letter, see Hill, *History of the Old South Church*, 1: 33–6.

[67] Scottow's account in Hill, *History of the Old South Church*, 1: 33.

conscience'.[68] While Scottow painted a very negative picture of Davenport from the perspective of a dissenter, John Davenport Jr, anxious to whitewash his father's behaviour, described the 'general satisfaction' among the First Church congregants with his father in a letter to John Winthrop Jr.[69] Completely silent about his own deceit, Davenport Jr reported 'the passage of divine providence' on the ordination day: 'the season being moderate, & congregacon [*sic*] was full.'[70]

Providence and Communal Accountability: The Wider Story

From the beginning, the neighbouring churches closely watched the schism unfold and were keen to intervene. Elder Penn first initiated an arbitration as early as August 1668, when he called for a council to consult other churches on the question of whether the dissenters should be censured. While congregational autonomy was a guiding principle in church government, conciliar arbitration was a common and respectable way of mediating conflicts in New England. It could be viewed as careful, collective discernment among seasoned ministers who could suggest a course of action most pleasing to God. However, for Penn and Davenport, this council proved a miscalculation that yielded room for dissenters to solicit support. On 6 August 1668, representatives from Dorchester, Dedham, Roxbury and Cambridge in the Massachusetts Bay Colony gathered to hear both sides of the case. Most delegates were advocates of the Half-Way Covenant, including Richard Mather, Daniel Gookin and John Elliot. Richard Mather's son, Increase Mather of the Second Church, Boston, who had long stood with Davenport against the broadening of church membership, did not attend.[71] The representatives from these neighbouring churches saw nothing punishable in the dissenters' protest. Instead, the council believed that it was a matter of 'mutual grievances' and

[68] Ibid. 41.

[69] Massachusetts Historical Society, Winthrop Family Papers, John Davenport Jr to John Winthrop Jr, 12 December 1668. Bremer cites this letter as 10 December 1668, possibly because Davenport Jr recorded the date as '12.10.68', but 10 signified the tenth month under the old style of dating, hence giving the date 12 December: cf. Bremer, *Davenport*, 333 n. 73.

[70] Ibid.

[71] See, for example, Increase Mather's preface to John Davenport, *Another Essay for Investigation of the Truth* (Cambridge, MA, 1663).

advised that dissenters be amicably dismissed to form their own church. The dissenting brethren lauded the verdict as the 'dispensation of Divine Providence', whereas the First Church decided to ignore the advice of the council they themselves had called.[72]

An uncontested ordination service in December 1668 did not put an end to the speculations about Davenport's departure from New Haven, nor did it frustrate the dissenters' incessant request for a dismissal from the First Church. In a church meeting on 6 January 1669, Richard Trewsdale, one of the deacons, complained that he had heard of a letter from New Haven that had not been read to the congregation.[73] Another dissenter, Thomas Savage, accused Davenport of leaving New Haven 'for worldly ends'.[74] The minority party finally secured another council on 13 April 1669. Under the leadership of Richard Mather, the neighbouring churches intervened for the second time to mediate between the First Church and its disaffected members. Fully aware of what this second council intended to do, First Church elders refused to recognize the assembly as 'an orderly Councill' and declined to attend.[75] Davenport Jr indignantly recalled that the council was held 'contra[ry] to the express mind of the church', disregarding his own father's contravention of the will of the New Haven church by leaving his old flock without their consent.[76]

In order to seek an in-person conversation with Davenport's party, the council delegates visited the First Church on 14 April 1669. However, the church door was locked against them. The delegates waited for so long that one of the dissenters, Peter Oliver, had to bring chairs for them to sit at the door.[77] On 16 April, the council reconfirmed the advice of the first council that the dissenters should be dismissed, adding that they were free to form their own church

[72] The council also indicated that given the number of residents, Boston could use a third church anyway. See Scottow's account in Hill, *History of the Old South Church*, 1: 25–6, 28.

[73] See ibid. 1: 42.

[74] Ibid. 1: 63.

[75] John Davenport and James Penn to the messengers of the churches, 13 April 1669, in Hill, *History of the Old South Church*, 1: 60.

[76] Massachusetts Historical Society, Winthrop Family Papers, John Davenport Jr to John Winthrop Jr, 16 April 1669.

[77] Scottow's account in Hill, *History of the Old South Church*, 1: 60. Davenport Jr also recorded the attempt by Mather and other representatives' to enter the First Church to speak to the First Church leaders in: Massachusetts Historical Society, Winthrop Family Papers, John Davenport Jr to Winthrop Jr, 16 April 1669.

even if they could not obtain a dismissal. Davenport's party reacted by condemning the dissenters as schismatics and banning them from communion.[78] On 12 May, the Third Church of Boston was formally established, despite lacking unanimous support from Massachusetts' magistrates, among whom were First Church members, including Governor Richard Bellingham, John Leverett and Edward Tying.[79]

Rumours about Davenport's dismissal were finally confirmed when Nicholas Street visited Boston in June 1669, and it was more generally realized that there were significant discrepancies between what Street had written and what had been read out to the church. On 17 June 1669, a church meeting was called to respond to these serious charges, which had become impossible to ignore. Davenport agreed to present Street's first letter, written after he had been called to office, and sent his son to fetch it, but when John Jr returned, he claimed that he could no longer find the letter. When Penn declared that whatever was evil in the matter would be his full responsibility, Davenport retorted that he saw 'no appearance of evill' at all.[80]

When Street's second letter, which had been forged into a fake dismissal, was read in its entirety to the congregation, many who had once passionately supported Davenport became 'sorely troubled' that 'a reall injury' had been done to both the First Church and neighbouring churches.[81] Davenport remained unrepentant, insisting that the extract was not a forgery because only 'some superfluities and such things as did not properly belong to it' had been left out.[82] However, he was anxious to emphasize that he had very little to do with it, again adopting the language of quiet submission to God: 'I neither disswaded from reading the extract nor perswaded to the reading of

[78] Scottow's account in Hill, *History of the Old South Church*, 1: 76.

[79] Bremer, *Davenport*, 338. Bremer noted that Thomas Thatcher prayed 'that this infant church might live to condemn its condemners', but the person who offered the prayer on this occasion was in fact John Oxenbridge, who would succeed Davenport as pastor of the First Church after the latter's death in 1670. See Scottow's account in Hill, *History of the Old South Church*, 1: 80. The citation Bremer provides is Davenport Jr's letter to John Winthrop Jr, in which Davenport Jr spoke of Thatcher's sermon on 22 December 1669 that marked the completion of the new church building: Hill, *History of the Old South Church*, 1: 139; Massachusetts Historical Society, Winthrop Family Papers, John Davenport Jr to John Winthrop Jr, 24 December 1669.

[80] Scottow's account in Hill, *History of the Old South Church*, 1: 82.

[81] Ibid. 82.

[82] Ibid.

the Originall script in publique, leaving events to God.'[83] Many congregants were obviously torn, since Davenport's defence was hardly convincing. A Mr Search begged the congregation to stop pressing the elders for an explanation, 'for Jacob got the blessing in a wrong way'.[84] In an extraordinary manner, Davenport went along with the comparison, complaining that his church had 'searched for haltings, with more eagernes[s] than Laban did Jacobs stuff for his Idolls'.[85] While many believed that they had indeed been deceived, the church finally affirmed their support for the elders, endorsing the conclusion that the ordination of Davenport was the result of divine providence.

Davenport did not find such favour among the neighbouring churches. On 15 July 1669, seventeen ministers who had formed a council to address the controversy issued a public condemnation of the three First Church leaders – Davenport, Penn and Allen – for their 'fraudulent dealing' and 'the great and publique scandall of unfaithfullnes and falshood'.[86] While the seventeen condemned all three elders, they singled out Davenport because he did the most to 'justify the fact and himself as having no hand in the writing'.[87] This time, Increase Mather's name appeared among the signatories. Davenport's old friend and fellow opponent of the Half-Way Covenant, whose father Richard Mather had died only eight days after the disgraceful humiliation of being refused entry into Davenport's church, had now joined others to condemn him.[88] Increase Mather was not the only one struck by the timing of his father's death. A leading dissenter, John Hull, contrasted Richard Mather's death, which he saw as God's providential reception of the minister into eternal glory and vindication, with the humiliating rejection he had endured at the hands of Davenport's party: 'The church of Boston would not let him [Richard Mather] into the

[83] Ibid. 83.
[84] Ibid. 82.
[85] Ibid. 82.
[86] Ibid. 84.
[87] Ibid. 88.
[88] Richard Mather had been struggling with poor health for years, and was particularly troubled by kidney stones. On 16 April 1669, two days after he and other delegates were denied entry into the First Church, he started to suffer from the 'a totall stoppage' of urine. He was brought to Increase Mather's house in Boston that evening and returned to Dorchester the next morning: see Increase Mather, *The Life and Death of that Reverend Man of God, Mr. Richard Mather, Teacher of the Church in Dorchester in New-England* (Cambridge, MA, 1670), 26.

doors … but the Lord soon opened his way into the church triumphant.'[89] It is clear that, for Hull, God was very much on the dissenters' side.

Davenport died on 15 March 1670, only eight months after the scandal broke out.[90] After his death, the First Church leadership would remain opposed to the Half-Way Covenant, and those who shared his ideals of church polity would continue to rely on his writings. One notable exception was Increase Mather, who not only joined others in condemning his old friend, but would soon change his mind about synodical power and the Half-Way Covenant.[91] Richard Mather's death amid the Boston controversy and the revelation of Davenport's forgery were decisive in Increase's change of alliance. Possibly burdened with guilt and regret, Increase recalled his father's last words, in which Richard Mather reaffirmed the Half-Way Covenant: '*I have thought that persons might have Right to Baptism, and yet not to the Lords Supper; and I see no cause to alter my judgement as to that particular.*'[92] Here, Increase undoubtedly intended to narrate a reconciliation between father and son, as well as to account for his own theological transformation. In 1671, Increase wrote *The First Principles of New-England*, his first public endorsement of the Half-Way Covenant against 'the *Antisynodalian Brethren*'.[93]

Besides Increase's high-profile change of opinion as a prominent minister, there were others who keenly searched for God's will in this torturous schism and voiced their concerns that real judgment would come if New Englanders continued to politicize providence. Shortly after Davenport died, freemen from Hadley and Northampton, opponents of the Half-Way Covenant, petitioned the Massachusetts General Court in May 1670 for a public enquiry

89 Hull, 'Diary', 229.

90 Davenport Jr recounted his father's death in detail in a letter to Winthrop Jr: Massachusetts Historical Society, Winthrop Family Papers, John Davenport Jr to Winthrop Jr, 28 March 1670. Winthrop Jr would later report it to Nicolls, the Royalist who had once inquired about Davenport's preaching: Massachusetts Historical Society, Winthrop Family Papers, John Winthrop Jr to Richard Nicolls, 24 September 1670.

91 Mather, *Life*, 27; Hall, *The Last American Puritan*, 80–1, 140–1.

92 Mather, *Life*, 27. Italics original.

93 Increase Mather, *The First Principles of New-England* (Cambridge, MA, 1675), preface, unpaginated. Italics original. The preface was dated May 1671, but the work was not published until 1675.

into the cause of God's 'departure' from the country.[94] The House of Deputies responded by pointing out many signs of divine wrath, including the deaths of many preachers (no doubt Davenport and Richard Mather came to mind), plagues of caterpillars and grasshoppers, and the appearance of comets.[95] As to the proposed causes, 'innovations threatening the ruin of the Congregational way' and the founding of the Third Church in Boston were the most contentious.[96] These highly polemical charges rekindled debates among Massachusetts magistrates, deputies, and other lay and clerical leaders, and sparked the outpouring of competing interpretations of God's providence from within the General Court. Francis Willoughby, deputy governor of Massachusetts, who was then ill and confined at home, lamented the whole episode as a 'pretended enquiry into the Cause of Gods anger' and urged his colleagues to cease the infighting before they further provoked God's displeasure.[97]

Conclusion

This episode formed an ignominious end to the career of an otherwise esteemed pastor. The Boston controversy that plagued the final years of Davenport's life tells us that seventeenth-century New Englanders were not oblivious to hypocrisies among themselves. In fact, they saw Christian society as a place where saints and hypocrites cohabited, and evaluated themselves and others through the same lens of spiritual dichotomy. Sometimes, puritans' self-scrutiny was a genuine introspection to root out any hint of hypocrisy in order not to become full-fledged unregenerate hypocrites. And yet, there were other times when the rhetoric of providence and discernment was purely a tactic to hide, justify or even glorify questionable motives. Such 'providential pragmatism' could go so far as to affirm God's use of unworthy sinners to accomplish his goals in order to gloss over the most distasteful cases of hypocrisy.

The increasingly obvious ecclesiological ambiguity and accompanying conflicts prompted many colonists to anxiously search for

94 Sylvester Judd, *History of Hadley, Including the Early History of Hatfield, South Hadley, Amherst and Granby, Massachusetts* (Northampton, MA, 1863), 85–6.
95 Hill, *History of the Old South Church*, 1: 97.
96 Judd, *History of Hadley*, 86.
97 Hill, *History of the Old South Church*, 1: 105.

remedies so as to secure New England's providential status before God. However, competing proposals and interpretations about God's will only threatened further the once rosy image of a unified, godly 'city upon a hill'. Contradictions and thinly veiled agendas in providentialist narratives, coupled with the spread of natural philosophers' scientific findings, set New England on an even speedier course of disenchantment after Davenport's generation died, especially among the learned elite.[98] Even enthusiasts such as Increase Mather became selective in their reception of wonder stories and stressed the unpredictability of God's providential ways: 'One providence seems to look this way, another providence seems to look that way, quite contrary one to another … . [T]he works of God sometimes seem to run counter with his word: so that there is dark and amazing intricacie in the ways of providence.'[99]

The First Church scandal was an early sign of such disenchantment and, as David Hall observes, of a consequent discrepancy between elite and popular culture.[100] Taking advantage of the still pervasive belief in providence, Davenport packaged his lies as divine truths and, along with other elders of the First Church, reinforced control over their congregation even after the forgery was exposed. Quite possibly, for some of Davenport's supporters, the language of providence was not entirely a smokescreen for political plays, but, as they were moved to reconcile with their pastor, they were genuinely inclined to believe that Davenport was their Jacob, and the blessing and honour that he had obtained by deceit were blessing and honour providentially bestowed by God after all. From this perspective, one might say that providence, regardless of whether it was merely a social construct or not, did favour Davenport in the end.

[98] Hall, *Worlds of Wonder*, 106–8.

[99] Ibid. 94; Increase Mather, *The Doctrine of Divine Providence Opened and Applyed* (Boston, MA, 1684), 43.

[100] This discrepancy was not always obvious since seventeenth-century New Englanders enjoyed high literacy and religious proficiency: Hall, *Worlds of Wonder*, 21–70, esp. 21–43.

'A Herd of snivelling, grinning Hypocrites': Religious Hypocrisy in Restoration Drama

David Fletcher*

University of Warwick

This article explores the various manifestations of religious hypocrisy to be found in new plays written in England between 1660 and 1720. It shows how the dramatists used hypocrisy both as a polemical weapon at times of religious conflict, and as an engaging form of theatricality. Exploring hypocrisy through drama is apposite as many of the key characteristics of hypocrisy – masks, role-playing, disguise and dissimulation – have been features of the theatre since ancient Greek times. The post-Restoration dramatists created worlds of masquerade for their hypocritical characters to inhabit, while the plays themselves offer examples of unself-conscious casuists, disreputable clerics, predatory monsters, and those who dissimulate religious beliefs, or have none at all.

The restoration of the episcopal Church of England in 1660 led to decades of religious turmoil as the various denominations grappled with the new religious settlement. A climate of religious conflict and uncertainty was generated by a number of factors throughout this period: attempts by the regime to enforce uniformity on a pluralistic religious society; intense anti-Catholicism in the wake of the Popish Plot of 1678; and the growing debate concerning the issue of toleration. As groups and individuals searched for polemical weapons, one prominent feature of these debates was the recourse to accusations of hypocrisy. Most religious groups were accused of being false Christians; papists were assumed to be hiding everywhere in masquerade; nonconformists were seen as dissemblers seeking to avoid penal laws through occasional conformity; and many conformists were seen as papists in disguise. In 1673, the playwright William Wycherley described the period as a 'masquerading age'.[1]

* E-mail: David.Fletcher.1@warwick.ac.uk.

[1] William Wycherley, *The gentleman dancing-master* (London, 1673), 10.

Studies in Church History 60 (2024), 290–311
doi: 10.1017/stc.2024.12

One of the most distinctive features of the changing cultural landscape after 1660 was the reopening of the theatres, closed since 1642, a reawakening that generated a rich repertoire of new plays. This article will show that these plays provide prominent examples of how hypocrisy could be weaponized during periods of religious conflict. Mark Knights has observed that hypocrisy often involves 'an inner (often sinister) self that was being disguised, one that could be revealed, unmasked, and exposed'.[2] Disguise and the mask are key features of hypocrisy, and they are also, of course, theatrical concepts. At a fundamental level, all actors disguise themselves in their characters, but many plays take this a step further when the characters themselves adopt disguises, usually with the intention of deceiving others. The stage, therefore, offers an excellent medium for engaging with the theme of hypocrisy. After all, the etymology of the word hypocrite includes the Greek word for an actor on the stage, ὑποκριτής ('the acting of a part on the stage, feigning, pretence').[3] In *The Folly of Priestcraft* (1690), the earliest extant printed text to include the word 'priestcraft' in its title, the heroine Leucasia draws the parallel between hypocrisy and acting: 'Of all the Men by God and Nature curs'd, / Surely the fawning Hypocrite is worst. / To his compar'd, the Player's Life is ease; / He always Acts—They only when they please'.[4] The concept of the hypocrite as actor offers theatre audiences a multi-layered way of exploring how performance and disguise can conceal or reveal.

The figure of the stereotypical religious hypocrite appears in many of the plays examined here. This is usually a cleric and, therefore, a man; there is disreputable behaviour, often a mix of lasciviousness, drunkenness, avarice and gluttony; and there is usually some element of dissimulation, deception or disguise. There are, of course, variations to these tropes, including hypocritical members of the laity, and some fascinating female characters. These tropes are used in similar ways against characters of all religious denominations, including the Church of England. The preponderance of clerics in this article reflects a potent strain of anticlericalism in this period. Indeed, this

[2] Mark Knights, *The Devil in Disguise: Deception, Delusion, and Fanaticism in the Early English Enlightenment* (Oxford, 2011), 7.

[3] 'Hypocrite, noun', *OED*, online at: <www.oed.com>, accessed 20 December 2023.

[4] Anon., *The converts, or, The folly of priest-craft* (London, 1690), 9 [hereafter: *The folly of priest-craft*].

sense of anticlericalism is driven home by the absence (in these plays) of positive or benign clerics. Even the names of the clerics are highly distinctive and are often used to denigrate: such names include Smerk, Doublechin, Wordy, Bull, Littlesense, Turbulent, Shittle, Wolf, Soaker, Tickletext, Sneake, Quibble, Humdrum, Dunce, Thummum, Pricknote, Noddy, Dogsears, Stiffrump, and Snuffle.[5] These clerical characters probably amused many in the theatre audiences. 'Did your Lordship ever perceive that the Gentry were ever better pleas'd with a Play, than when the poor Parson was jeer'd?', asks a character in the anonymous 1690 pamphlet play *The Folly of Priestcraft*.[6] The Restoration dramatists did not, of course, invent the trope of the religious hypocrite. The plays of the previous century offer many famous examples, including Malvolio in Shakespeare's *Twelfth Night* (1601), Tribulation in Ben Jonson's *The Alchemist* (1610), Zeal-of-the-Land Busy, 'a notable hypocritical Vermine', in Jonson's *Bartholomew Fair* (1614), and Stupido, 'that plodding puritane, That artless ass, and that earth-creeping dolt', in the anonymous *The Pilgrimage to Parnassus* (1597–1601).[7]

Scholars have, however, warned against treating hypocrisy as a one-dimensional term. David Runciman emphasizes the importance of distinguishing between different kinds of hypocritical behaviour: 'deliberate and inadvertent, personal and collective, self-deceptions and other-directed deceptions'.[8] Similarly, Brian Walsh offers a differentiation between what he calls self-conscious and unselfconscious hypocrisy in his examination of puritans on the Shakespearean stage. We will see examples of what he describes as 'predatory monsters', as

[5] Abraham Cowley, *The Cutter of Coleman Street* (London, 1663); Thomas Shadwell, *The humorists* (London, 1671); Edward Howard, *The man of Newmarket* (London, 1678); Thomas Rawlins, *Tunbridge Wells* (London, 1678); Aphra Behn, *The feign'd curtizans* (London, 1679); Thomas Shadwell, *The Lancashire witches* (London, 1682); Thomas Jevon, *The devil of a wife, or, A comical transformation* (London, 1686); Aphra Behn, *The widdow Ranter* (London, 1690); Thomas Durfey, *Love for money* (London, 1691); Thomas Durfey, *The marriage-hater match'd* (London, 1692); Peter Anthony Motteux, *Love's a jest* (London, 1696); John Vanbrugh, *The relapse* (London, 1697); John Gay, *The wife of Bath* (London, 1713); Christopher Bullock, *The cobler of Preston* (London, 1716); Colley Cibber, *The non-juror* (London, 1718); Archibald Pitcairn, *The Assembly* (Edinburgh, 1752).

[6] Anon., *The folly of priest-craft*, 16.

[7] Ben Jonson, *Bartholmew fayre* (London, 1640; first publ. 1614), 6; Anon., *The pilgrimage to Parnassus* (London, 1649; first publ. 1597), 14.

[8] David Runciman, *Political Hypocrisy: The Mask of Power, from Hobbes to Orwell and Beyond*, rev. edn (Princeton, NJ, 2018; first publ. 2008), 11.

well as the type of character whom he sees as 'more psychologically complex and identifiably human figures hobbled by … self-delusion'.[9] Lucia Nigri has also explored hypocritical characters in plays from the late sixteenth and early seventeenth century, concluding that their complexity and dynamism make them both entertaining and thought-provoking.[10] Kristen Poole argues that, in contrast to the image of the abstemious puritan, we must not lose sight of the representation in early modern literature of the 'drunken, gluttonous, and lascivious puritan'.[11] This article will show that the analysis of these scholars is also relevant to many religious characters in the plays of the Restoration period.

The characters under attack in these plays are not restricted to puritans and dissenters, but range across the denominational spectrum. For example, as we will see below, Poole's 'puritan Bellygod' finds its most explicit Restoration equivalent in the Roman Catholic Fr Dominic.[12] Peter Lake has argued that anti-popery and anti-puritanism were polemically ambiguous and 'could be bent to a range of often widely divergent political and polemical ends'.[13] This use of polemical ambiguity can most obviously be seen in adaptations of one play, Molière's *Tartuffe*, first performed at Versailles in 1664. Scholars have identified a range of plays that are obvious versions of *Tartuffe* or have been influenced by it.[14] Roseann Runte includes a table of over twenty plays in the seventeenth and eighteenth centuries which have been 'usually cited as bearing some

[9] Brian Walsh, *Unsettled Toleration: Religious Difference on the Shakespearean Stage* (Oxford, 2016), 46.

[10] Lucia Nigri, 'Religious Hypocrisy in Performance: Roman Catholicism and the London Stage', in eadem and Naya Tsentourou, eds, *Forms of Hypocrisy in Early Modern England* (New York, 2017), 57–71, at 70.

[11] Kristen Poole, *Radical Religion from Shakespeare to Milton* (Cambridge, 2000), 12.

[12] Ibid. 45.

[13] Peter Lake, 'Anti-Popery: The Structure of Prejudice', in Richard Cust and Ann Hughes, eds, *Conflict in Early Stuart England: Studies in Religion and Politics, 1603–1642* (London, 1989), 72–106, at 79; idem, 'Anti-Puritanism: The Structure of a Prejudice', in Kenneth Fincham and Peter Lake, eds, *Religious Politics in Post-Reformation England: Essays in Honour of Nicholas Tyacke* (Woodbridge, 2006), 80–97, at 94–5.

[14] Roseann Runte, 'Cross-Cultural Influences: Versions of "Tartuffe" in Eighteenth-Century France and Restoration England', *Romance Notes* 36 (1996), 265–76; Noel Peacock, 'Molière Nationalised: Tartuffe on the British Stage from the Restoration to the Present Day', in David Bradby and Andrew Calder, eds, *The Cambridge Companion to Molière* (Cambridge, 2006), 177–88.

resemblance' to *Tartuffe*.[15] The relevance of these versions to this article relates to the shifting religious denomination of the title character. The earliest English translation of the play was Thomas Shadwell's *The Hypocrite* (1669), but this is sadly lost to us.[16] The first version to share Molière's title appeared in 1670, and its author, Matthew Medbourne, gave it a subtitle of 'or the French Puritan'.[17] As the subtitle suggests, Medbourne portrays his Tartuffe in the tradition of the hypocritical puritans of the early Restoration satires. When the playwrights turned their fire on Roman Catholics in the wake of the Glorious Revolution, Crowne wrote a version of Molière's play called *The English Frier* (1690). The target changes again in *The Non-Juror* (1717) by Colley Cibber, in which Tartuffe becomes a nonjuror (although this character turns out to be a Roman Catholic in disguise). This denominational flexibility shows that portrayals of hypocrisy were weaponized in plays against the perceived enemies of the moment, whether puritans, Roman Catholics, dissenters, nonjurors, or even some conformists. In addition, the dramatists' use of polemical ambiguity sometimes added another dimension to their anti-clerical attacks. By using established tropes of anti-Catholicism or anti-puritanism, audiences could be shown a disreputable cleric, not only as a representative of his own denomination, but also as a representative of the entire class of clerical hypocrites. As the late seventeenth-century anti-theatrical critic Jeremy Collier observed, the playwrights 'attack Religion under every Form, and pursue the Priesthood through all the Subdivisions of Opinion. Neither Jews nor Heathens, Turks nor Christians, Rome nor Geneva, Church nor Conventicle, can escape them.'[18]

As similar tropes are used whichever group is under attack in these plays, this article will not use a denominational analysis, but will offer four alternative categories for exploration. The first takes up Walsh's idea of the unselfconscious hypocrite. In Restoration drama, this usually manifests itself in the form of casuistry, as we watch characters struggle to find justifications for their actions which are contrary to religious norms. The second category includes those characters who

[15] Runte, 'Cross-Cultural Influences', 275.

[16] Ibid. 266.

[17] Peacock, 'Molière Nationalised', 177–8.

[18] Jeremy Collier, *A short view of the immorality, and profaneness of the English stage together with the sense of antiquity upon this argument* (London, 1698), 110–1.

profess religious adherence, but whose disreputable behaviour – licentiousness, gluttony, drunkenness, and other forms of excess – contravenes the expectations of their religion. Michael D. Bailey has described accusations of this kind of behaviour against religious opponents as 'a standard component in Christian moralists' rhetorical tool-kit'.[19] This category will be limited to modes of behaviour of a personal kind that do not seriously harm others. The harmful kind, Walsh's predatory monsters, make up the third category. These will be defined as those whose hypocritical behaviour usually involves deception that is used for the acquisition of power or wealth, irrespective of the potential damage caused to others. Finally (and fourthly), there is religious dissimulation: those characters who pretend to adhere to one faith while inwardly believing in another, or to disguise the absence of any faith at all. Miriam Eliav-Feldon and Tamar Herzig see the entire early modern period as a 'heyday of religious dissimulation and of the authorities' preoccupation with unmasking it', and Andrew Hadfield argues that early modern life in England had come to be characterized by a culture of lying. Hadfield also sees literature as 'often a testing ground for ideas about lying', using Shakespeare's *Othello* as a case study to explore the complex ways in which dissimulation can be represented, including equivocation, which he argues lies at the heart of the play.[20] The plays examined in this article reveal some of the political reasons for dissimulation, together with examples of dissimulation for more personal reasons. In some cases, we will see how the dramatists create a metaphorical world of masquerade for their characters to inhabit.

Before examining the plays, it is worth highlighting some interesting gender issues that will emerge. Attitudes to the participation of women in the world of the theatre eased after the Restoration. Women started appearing on stage and, although the number of female dramatists in the period was small (only ten are recorded, which is just over five per cent of the total), some of them were now able to make a living from writing for the stage. The only one of these women who engaged with hypocrisy was Aphra Behn, and

[19] Michael D. Bailey, 'Superstition and Dissimulation: Discerning False Religion in the Fifteenth Century', in Miriam Eliav-Feldon and Tamar Herzig, eds, *Dissimulation and Deceit in Early Modern Europe* (London, 2015), 9–26, at 13.

[20] Ibid. 3; Andrew Hadfield, *Lying in Early Modern English Culture: From the Oath of Supremacy to the Oath of Allegiance* (Oxford, 2017), 4, 30, 304.

we will see that she adopted a nuanced approach by offering the audience, as well as the usual clerical male hypocrites, some lay female hypocrites, one of whom outclasses the men. Most of the characters examined in this article, however, are male, in plays written by men. Every cleric in the period was male, but it is interesting to note that the fiercest criticism can be seen in *The Female Prelate* (1680), where Elkanah Settle seized this rare opportunity to add misogyny to his anticlericalism and anti-Catholicism.

Casuistry

Navigating the complex religious pathways of the late Stuart age could be very challenging, particularly for those with tender consciences, and casuistic arguments were often used to find a solution, or at least a compromise. Casuistry has been primarily associated with Jesuitical reasoning, but some historians have also identified an important strain of casuistry in puritan and nonconformist writing.[21] Although casuistry had been a prominent feature of moral reasoning for a century, it had become subject to attack in some quarters, most notably from the French religious philosopher Blaise Pascal in his *Provincial Letters* in 1656/7. As Barbara Warnick has observed, casuistry had allowed so many caveats and exclusions that it was felt by many that 'the force of moral law was thoroughly dissipated'.[22] This was particularly pertinent in issues relating to oaths. This negative attitude to casuistry can be seen in some of the early anti-puritan satires of the period.[23] The character Lockwhite in *The Rump* (1660) argues that 'He that will live in this world, must be endowed with these three rare Qualities; Dissimulation, Equivocation, and Mental reservation'.[24] In *The Cutter of Coleman Street* (1661), two lovers

[21] Keith Thomas, 'Cases of Conscience in Seventeenth-Century England', in John Morrill, Paul Slack and Daniel Woolf, eds, *Public Duty and Private Conscience in Seventeenth-Century England: Essays Presented to G. E. Aylmer* (Oxford, 1993), 29–56, at 43; Edward Vallance, 'Oaths, Casuistry, and Equivocation: Anglican Responses to the Engagement Controveſsy', *HistJ* 44 (2001), 59–77.

[22] Barbara Warnick, '*The Abuse of Casuistry: A History of Moral Reasoning*, by Albert R. Jonsen and Stephen Toulmin', *Philosophy and Rhetoric* 24 (1991), 76–80, at 78.

[23] Susan Staves sees 'villainous puritans invariably justifying the most transparent perjuries with Jesuitical casuistry': Susan Staves, *Players' Scepters: Fictions of Authority in the Restoration* (Lincoln, 1979), 192, 203.

[24] John Tatham, *The Rump* (London, 1660), 8–9.

(who have sworn to their parents that they will not speak to each other) solve their problem by hatching a plan 'to save their Oathes like cunning Casuists' by marrying in the dark and in silence.[25] The cleric in this play – the 'fuddling little Deacon' Soaker – is satirized for his behaviour and his acceptance of casuistry. He is usually to be found in the buttery, and he agrees to marry the silent lovers in the dark and says they should give their consent by using 'reverences and giving of hands', rather than breaking their oath by speaking to each other.

Criticism of casuistry reaches its apogee in John Wilson's *The Cheats* (1663), in which the nonconformist minister Scruple sells his religious adherence to the highest bidder; the winners are a group of dissenters and not the Church of England. In the play, Scruple often calls on casuistry to support his disreputable arguments and flawed behaviour. When calling for a 'great tankard', he argues that 'The Casuists, speak comfortably in this point—A man may eat, and drink abundantly, without any necessity, but merely for his pleasure'.[26] He also shows disrespect for marriage when he calls on the casuists to justify adultery:

> If a Woman, great with Child, long for another man, besides her Husband, and this Husband will not give consent; In this case we say, (and so we generally agree) that she may follow her natural inclination; Provided alwayes, she have no intention of sin, but only to satisfie her longing.

and abortion:

> If a young woman, of a godly Parentage, do fall into a holy Fornication (not out of Lust, but Love) and thereupon prove with Child; In such case we say, That it may be lawful to procure Abortion, provided alwayes, it be not done, with an intention of Murder, but only to save Life, or Reputation.[27]

Scruple's most egregious display of casuistry relates to the question faced by all clergy at the time: whether to conform, or not, to the restored Church of England following the 1662 Act of Uniformity. The act had been enforced just a few months before

25 Abraham Cowley, *The Cutter of Coleman Street* (London, 1663), 31.
26 John Wilson, *The cheats* (London, 1664), 15.
27 Ibid. 23.

the play was first performed, making this a very topical issue. The act plunged many clergy into a crisis of conscience that led to the ejection of over a thousand of them from their livings, some of whom suffered considerable distress. Despite the misery experienced by these ejected clergy, many conformists took an unsympathetic view. They saw struggles of conscience as nothing but a mask that would lead to what Thomas Ashenden would later call 'a monstrous medley of mischiefs'.[28] Although there is extensive primary material relating to the act, *The Cheats* is the only play of the period that engages with it.

In the play, when Scruple is offered a £300 living if he will conform, we watch him alone on stage as he calls on casuistry, equivocation and every other possible methodology to help him to justify his conformity and his abandonment of his 'brethren'. He also tries to negotiate his way around the issue of oaths. The monologue is long, rambling and highly entertaining, and Scruple reaches the climax of the speech with a rapturous conclusion:

> I have found an Expedient (and yet not mine, but our Brethrens still) The Swearer is not bound to the meaning of the Prescriber of the Oath, or his own meaning—How then?—Sweetly:—To the reality of the thing sworn:—I think the hair is split:—But who shall be Judge of that?—Of that hereafter:—In the mean time— Here is 300 l. a year, and a goodly house upon't:—I will Conform, Reform, Transform, Perform, Deform, Inform, any Form: —Form—Form— 'Tis but one syllable, and has no very ill sound—It may be swallowed.[29]

The word 'form' becomes the central image in this virtuoso display of formlessness. Having made this enormous effort to arrive at the decision to conform, he is then offered more money to stay with his nonconformist brethren, which he accepts.

Another casuistic cleric can be found in John Dryden's *The Spanish Fryar* (1680), written at the height of the Popish Plot. Dryden's portrayal of the Roman Catholic Fr Dominic is a vividly drawn character assassination. Dominic's drunkenness and avarice are clear from his first appearance when he imbibes several drinks in swift succession and accepts a bribe from Lorenzo to deliver a letter to the object of Lorenzo's love, Elvira. Dominic is her confessor and is the only man her jealous husband Gomez will allow into her

[28] Thomas Ashenden, *No Penalty, No Peace* (London, 1682), 19.
[29] Wilson, *The cheats*, 73.

presence. Once he is with her, he takes on the role of what Collier described as 'a pimp for Lorenzo'.[30] Like Scruple in *The Cheats*, Dominic uses casuistic arguments that undermine the sacrament of marriage. He tells Elvira that a marriage vow 'is a very solemn thing: and 'tis good to keep it: —but, notwithstanding, it may be broken, upon some occasions.' He asks her whether she has 'striven with all [her] might against this frailty?' She says she has, and he absolves her by saying that 'when we have done our utmost, it extenuates the Sin.'[31] This sense of 'when all else fails' is emphasized later when Dominic tells her that 'when the Spiritual means have been apply'd, and fails: in that case, the Carnal may be us'd.'[32]

The next scene that features Dominic highlights the perceived connection between hypocrisy, costume and disguise. Dominic sees another friar in the street, only to discover that it is Lorenzo in disguise, 'my noble Colonel in Metamorphosis'. Lorenzo has decided to try to get access to Elvira dressed as a friar. For him, the similarity between his disguise and Dominic's normal attire is not just about their dress. Lorenzo emphasizes Dominic's hypocrisy by observing that 'my holiness, like yours, is meer out-side'. What is a temporary costume for Lorenzo is a fundamental and hypocritical disguise for Dominic. Lorenzo also generalizes the hypocrisy of clerical dress, 'a Habit that in all Ages has been friendly to Fornication'.[33] Lorenzo asks Dominic to go with him to Elvira. In a soliloquy before they arrive, Elvira declares that her conscience is not troubled by her impending adultery because Dominic 'has given it a Dose of Church Opium, to lull it.'[34]

These plays have shown us lay and clerical characters twisting and turning along narrow moral pathways to arrive at the answers they need to justify their hypocrisy. As Scruple proclaims, 'I think the hair is split.'[35]

Disreputable Behaviour

In the plays, we see very few sober, moderate, slim, honest and chaste clerics: Fr Dominic also provides an example of the disreputable hypocritical cleric and the 'Bellygod'. In the first scene of *The Spanish*

[30] Collier, *A short view*, 98.
[31] John Dryden, *The Spanish fryar* (London, 1681), 26.
[32] Ibid. 27.
[33] Ibid. 29.
[34] Ibid. 30; this anticipates Marx's famous quote about religion.
[35] Wilson, *The cheats*, 73.

Fryar, we hear a description of Dominic before he appears, and even before his name is mentioned. In this speech by Colonel Pedro, Dryden weaves together anti-Catholic comments with the wider anti-clerical tropes of gluttony and lechery:

> I met a reverend, fat, old, gouty Fryar;
> With a Paunch swoln so high, his double Chin
> Might rest upon't: A true Son of the Church;
> Fresh colour'd, and well thriven on his Trade,
> Come puffing with his greazy bald-pate Quire,
> And fumbling o'er his Beads, in such an Agony,
> He told 'em false for fear: About his Neck
> There hung a Wench; the Labell of his Function;
> Whom he shook off, 'faith, methought, unkindly.[36]

Hypocritical Roman Catholics were not the only targets for dramatists, and clerics of the Church of England did not escape criticism. In Wycherley's *The Gentleman Dancing-Master* (1673), Don Diego, an old rich Spanish merchant, portrays the clergy as sexually untrustworthy. He says that 'we are bold enough in trusting them with our Souls, I'le never trust 'em with the body of my Daughter', whom he keeps locked up at home.[37] This parental concern can also be seen in Durfey's *The Marriage-Hater Match'd* (1692). Lady Bumsiddle says of her niece: 'if she were my Daughter, I had as lieve trust her with a Dragoon as a Parson'.[38] In *The Squire of Alsatia* (1688), Thomas Shadwell portrays the parson as hypocritical and gluttonous: 'tappes'd in some Ale-house, Bawdy-house, or Brandy shop … . He's a brave swinging Orthodox'.[39] And in John Vanbrugh's *The Relapse* (1697), Chaplain Bull is accused of many faults:

> For as Chaplains now go, 'tis probable he eats three pound of Beef to the reading of one Chapter—This gives him Carnal desires, he wants Money, Preferment, Wine, a Whore; therefore we must Invite him to Supper, give him fat Capons, Sack and Sugar, a Purse of Gold, and a plump Sister.[40]

[36] Dryden, *The Spanish fryar*, 3.
[37] Wycherley, *The gentleman dancing-master*, 22.
[38] Durfey, *The marriage-hater match'd*, 12.
[39] Thomas Shadwell, *The squire of Alsatia* (London, 1688), 72.
[40] Vanbrugh, *The relapse*, 89.

Nonconformists were also subjected to attack. In Thomas Jevon's *The Devil of a Wife* (1686), Lady Lovemore's chaplain Noddy is described as 'A Hypocritical Phanatick Parson, loves to eat and cant'.[41] His gluttony is prodigious: he orders two chickens, some bacon and a pie, together with 'a Bottle of Sack, a Bottle of Ale and a Bottle of March Beer' just to get him through till supper time.[42]

Aphra Behn was similarly adept at turning her barbed pen towards the nonconformists. The wife of *Sir Patient Fancy* (1678) describes his religious friends as 'a Herd of snivelling grinning Hypocrites that call themselves the teaching Saints, who under pretence of securing me to the number of their Flock, do so sneer upon me, pat my Breasts and cry, fy, fy upon this fashion of tempting Nakedness'. Once again, we see polemical ambiguity at work as the conforming Lady Fancy is herself portrayed as a dissembling cheat who accuses religious hypocrites of pretence.[43] In *The Roundheads* (1681), the hypocrisy and lasciviousness of the puritan cleric Gogle is clear from his first appearance. Within moments of being left alone on stage with Lady Desborough, he is fondling her breasts. When she rejects his advances, he defends himself by explaining that many 'Ladies of high Degree in the Commonwealth' take up the opportunity offered by clerics of sexual encounters without risk of public exposure.[44] In *The Feigned Curtizans* (1679), the character Timothy Tickletext describes himself as 'principal holder forth of the Covent Garden Conventicle, Chaplain of Buffoon-Hall in the County of Kent'. At his first appearance, we see him preening himself for the ladies. In contrast to the plays in which lovers disguise themselves as clerics, Tickletext adopts an antithetical disguise when he sets off 'wenching'. He sees his clerical habit as a restriction and, once it is cast off and he is 'disguised' as a member of the laity, he is free to follow his sexual urges. He takes hypocrisy and dissembling to a new level: 'Certo 'tis a wonderfull pleasure to deceive the World'.[45] This image of the hypocrite relishing his deception is also a key factor in the next category.

These portrayals of clerics and other religious adherents present such bad examples of how to behave that their hypocrisy undermines

[41] Thomas Jevon, *The Devil of a Wife* (London, 1686), 'The Actors Names', unpaginated.
[42] Ibid. 5.
[43] Aphra Behn, *Sir Patient Fancy* (London, 1678), 14–15.
[44] Aphra Behn, *The Roundheads* (London, 1682), 30.
[45] Aphra Behn, *The Feign'd Curtizans* (London, 1679), 34.

the doctrines of their religious groups, and perhaps of religion in general.

Predatory Monsters

Some plays offer a more sinister manifestation of hypocrisy, with religious characters manipulating others for their personal gain, whether political or financial. We have already seen how the hypocrisy of the puritan cleric Gogle in *The Roundheads* reveals itself in licentiousness, but hypocrisy goes deeper in this play. In the wake of the Tory backlash after the Popish Plot, dramatists sought to link the Whigs with the puritans of the republican period by returning to the style of the early Restoration anti-puritan satires. Behn went a step further by adapting John Tatham's *The Rump* (1660), using some of Tatham's text. In this play, the leading puritans of the republican leadership after the death of Cromwell take pride in their ability to dissimulate and equivocate, which is so effective that they can 'outdo the Jesuits'.[46] General Lambert boasts to his wife that he believes he has secured the highest office through bribery, promises of preferment, and 'Hypocrisie and Pretence of Religion'.[47] Later in the play, when Lord Desborough says he has lost the ability to dissimulate, Gogle says he has lost a great virtue and pleads: 'let us not lose the Cause for Dissimulation and Hypocrisie, those two main Engines that have carry'd on the great Work'.[48]

The issue of polemical ambiguity can be seen in John Crowne's two-part *The Destruction of Jerusalem by Titus Vespasian* (1677). Although the plays are set during the Romans' destruction of the city of Jerusalem and its Temple in 70 CE, one of the major subplots is the violent division between two groups of Jews: the establishment Sanhedrin and the dissenting Pharisees. At a time when nonconformists were under attack in the campaign for religious uniformity, Crowne reflects the conflict between the Church of England and the nonconformists. In the epilogue to Part I, Crowne draws a clear parallel between the Pharisees and the nonconformists with the line 'Fanaticks are but Jews uncircumciz'd'.[49] The leader of the

[46] Aphra Behn, *The Roundheads* (London, 1682), 8.
[47] Ibid. 11.
[48] Ibid. 35.
[49] John Crowne, *The destruction of Jerusalem by Titus Vespasian* (London, 1677), part 1, 56.

rebellious Pharisees is John, described in the list of characters as 'A dissembling Pharisaick Jew'.[50] Despite his speeches and his plotting against the Sanhedrin, it is clear to the audience that he is a hypocrite. His real intention is his own advancement and, in an aside in Part I, he admits that 'One more Religious Lye, the Mitre's mine'.[51] In Part II, one stage direction says that John is wearing 'Pontifical Vestments'.[52] Linking an object of aversion with Roman Catholicism was a common trope of the period and conformists frequently sought to undermine dissent by linking it with Roman Catholicism. In *The Roundheads*, Lady Desborough calls Gogle 'the very Pope of Presbytery', and in an early Restoration play, *The Pragmatical Jesuit New-Leavened* (1665?) by Richard Carpenter, the character Aristotle calls two other characters a 'Puritanical Jesuit' and a 'Jesuitical Puritan', and accuses them of being 'both Enthusiasm'd with a singular spirit'.[53] This idea of a commonality of beliefs is articulated by Durfey in the preface to his play *The Royalist* (1682): 'I am sure your Papist and Phanatick have an entire Union and agree to a hair'.[54]

Crowne turned his fire directly on Roman Catholicism in *The English Frier* (1690), his version of Molière's *Tartuffe*, and the first new anti-Catholic play after the Glorious Revolution. *The English Frier* appears to be set during the reign of the Roman Catholic James II. Fr Finicall is the title character of the play and is a model of hypocrisy and deception. As with the other examples in this category, Finicall seeks to manipulate others for his own gain, but his attitude strikes wider and brings the integrity of the entire Roman Catholic faith into question. He admits that the stories told by priests in this world can never be tested until after death: 'My trade is a fine easy gainful cheat, / How easy 'tis, Saintship to counterfeit; / And pleasing fables to invent and spread; / And fools ne're find the cheat, till they are dead'.[55] The trope that Roman Catholics are not true Christians is amplified in the play when Lady Pinch-gut's servants describe her as 'a damn'd Papistical Heathen. She's a Papist,

[50] Ibid., 'The NAMES of the PERSONS in both Plays', unpaginated.

[51] Ibid. 37.

[52] Crowne, *The destruction of Jerusalem* (London, 1677), part 2, 27.

[53] Behn, *The Roundheads*, 29; Richard Carpenter, *The pragmatical Jesuit new-leven'd* (London, 1665), 34.

[54] Thomas Durfey, *The Royalist* (London, 1682), preface.

[55] John Crowne, *The English frier* (London, 1690), 41.

Sir, but no Christian'. They also describe her priests as irreligious – 'cunning Knaves; they have more Wit than to trouble themselves with Religion' – and avaricious – 'They'll have Religion for you, if you'll pay for't'.[56] Finicall embodies this avarice as he is attempting to cheat Sir Thomas Credulous of his estate. But Sir Thomas is aware of the plan and, in his plot to expose Finicall, he dissimulates a religious conversion and says he will 'pretend I am a Convert, and sick and dying', a deceptive deathbed conversion that is put to good use.[57]

Lord Wiseman's description of Fr Finicall adds licentiousness to the charge-sheet – 'the lov'd, slick, wash'd, clean, comb'd, curl'd shock o' the Ladies … 'tis thought he lyes between their Sheets' – and, in a later scene, we are shown clear evidence of this as he attempts to seduce Pansy, Lady Credulous's woman.[58] His justification for 'carnal Communion' with Pansy leads him to confess the hypocrisy and deception not just of himself, but of the entire Roman Catholic Church. His argument is that the ends justify the means and 'our frauds holy being for holy ends'. He talks of the 'holy Stratagem o' Priests … thereby religiously to deceive the world' and 'we Priests are forc'd to appear in many shapes'. He uses the metaphor of performance to show how their outward show conceals their frauds: 'And though like the Bearers o' my Lord-Mayors Pageant, we may have many a secret foul step, we must keep our Pageant pure, for that is seen, we are hid'.[59] There is a contrast here with *The Spanish Fryar*. In that play, Dominic uses casuistry to justify his statements and actions, but Finicall paints an explicit self-portrait of hypocrisy and irreligion. He is not, however, above using casuistry himself. He justifies cheating 'Lord Stately, and other Protestant fools' as a way of saving their souls: 'so we make 'em do some good; and are false to them, but sincere to our calling of Priesthood'.[60] This idea that deception is a job requirement for a priest substantiates the hypocrisy of the stage cleric.

[56] Ibid. 9.
[57] Ibid. 26.
[58] Ibid. 13.
[59] Ibid. 50–1.
[60] Ibid. 51.

The idea of the predatory monster reaches its apotheosis in *The Female Prelate* (1680), Settle's version of the legendary ninth-century female pope. The audience learns that, before the play even begins, Joanna was already an adulteress, a murderer and a dissembler. As the play progresses, we see her resort to blatant lying, intense lasciviousness and increasing violence. She has no redeeming features, and this character deserves to join the panoply of great stage dissembling anti-heroes, such as Iago, Richard III and Tartuffe. It is also a play rich with deception, with the elevation to the papacy of a woman disguised as a man and dissembling as a priest. Settle creates a world of masquerade for Joanna to inhabit. For example, the word 'false' appears eighteen times in the text; Amiran, a confidant of Joanna, spends the entire play disguising her gender as Joanna's page; and a double bed-trick is engineered to satisfy the lust of Joanna and her lover Lorenzo. The primary dissembler is, of course, Joanna herself. Her first disguise had been adopted years before the action of the play begins. She had been a lover of the old duke of Saxony and, when she was spurned, she decided to return to his court to seek her revenge. She chose to do this disguised as a Benedictine monk. 'Thus mask'd and Shrowded in his borrowed Russet', she became the duke's confessor and eventually murdered him.[61] She was able to maintain her disguise, both as a man and a cleric, even within the church, and 'Deceived the blinded world; for seven long years / My Arts and Sex concealed: nay, and to heighten / The miracle, I have lived an undiscovered Woman, / Bred amongst Priests, high fed, hot-blooded Priests … Yet I've defyed their keenest eyes to track me'. Lorenzo is full of admiration and describes her as 'my dear mask'd Divinity'.[62] When Joanna is chosen as pope, she is highly satisfied by her brilliant dissembling, asking: 'How dost thou like the Port our Greatness bears, / Do we not play the Royal Masquerader nobly?'[63] There is another level of dissembling in this play, which is that Joanna is not a true Roman Catholic and, as we will see below, probably not even a Christian.[64]

[61] Elkanah Settle, *The Female Prelate* (London, 1680), 27.

[62] Ibid. 5.

[63] Ibid. 25.

[64] Susan Owen argues that Joanna's religion is 'a fraud': Susan J. Owen, *Restoration Theatre and Crisis* (Oxford, 1996), 142.

These predatory monsters have no difficulty in exploiting others to advance their own positions. In many of these examples, this exploitation also requires a degree of dissimulation. It is to the theme of religious dissimulation that we now turn.

Religious Dissimulation

In a period when toleration was limited, religious dissimulation could be useful for maintaining a quiet life and, in some cases, as a means of self-preservation, particularly for Roman Catholics. The trope of the disguised Roman Catholic is explicit in the anonymous *The Excommunicated Prince* (1679), which is set in Georgia where Greek Orthodoxy is the established religion. The Jesuits look forward to the time when 'We need not then in these strange Shapes appear. / Wear others Looks, or speak in Character.'[65] They look back at many years of successful dissembling – 'These forty Years, unseen as Night, I've gone / Through snaky Ways; and more strange Shapes put on.'[66] They seek revenge against those who 'all our Cheats display; / Take off our Masks, and shew us to the Day.'[67] Some of the prince's friends see through the masquerade, but the prince does not. One of his friends is appalled at how the Jesuits pretend to be true to the Grecian church and use this as 'An holy Mask for their black Perjury! / Yet with such Paint they shadow the Deceit.'[68] As Roger L'Estrange's character Citt declared, 'your Papist in Masquerade, your Concealed Papist, these are all of 'em forty times worse than your Known, Jesuited, and Barefaced Papist.'[69]

In *The Roundheads,* Lady Desborough decides Gogle can be useful and turns to blackmail, promising that she will not report his lascivious hypocritical behaviour if he will rescue her lover from prison and bring him to her. We already know that Lady Desborough is a closet Royalist – her lover Freeman has told us that she feigns nonconformity – but she gives such an effective pretence of religion that her nonconformist husband believes she can be trusted with a Cavalier

[65] William Bedloe, *The excommunicated prince, or, The false relique a tragedy* (London, 1679), 9.

[66] Ibid. 10.

[67] Ibid. 22.

[68] Ibid. 26.

[69] Sir Roger L'Estrange, *Citt and Bumpkin, or, A learned discourse upon swearing and lying and other laudable qualities tending to a thorow reformation* (London, 1680), part 2, 6.

because she 'goes to a Conventicle twice a day, besides long Prayers and lowd Psalm-singing'.[70] Lady Desborough says to Gogle: 'for know, Sir, I am as great an Hypocrite as you, and know the Cheats of your Religion too; and since we know one another, 'tis like we shall be true.'[71]

Religious dissimulation can sometimes be hard work, and this can be seen in *The Cutter of Coleman Street* (1661). Colonel Jolly is a Royalist whose estates were sequestered, and he is also portrayed as a religious hypocrite. His neglect of religion is clear when he asks for a prayer book and his daughter, Aurelia, tells him that it is 'all mouldy, I must wipe it first.'[72] Jolly has two aims in the play. The first is to bring about the marriage of his ward in such a way that enables him to keep her substantial marriage portion. The second is to recover his sequestered estates by marrying the widow of the puritan who acquired them, 'Collonel Fear-the Lord-Barebottle, a Saint and a Sope-boyler'.[73] But the widow will only marry him if he converts to her religion. He dissembles conversion but finds it exhausting, 'a damn'd constraint and drudgery me-thinks, this Dissimulation'.[74]

The effort of dissimulation is also shown in *The Folly of Priestcraft*. Once again, hypocrisy and disguise are everywhere, as the dramatist creates another example of a world of masquerade. Almost every character dissembles at some point in the play and many of them do so in disguise. Even the 'hero' Turnabout is riddled with hypocrisy. At the start of the play, Turnabout is in love with Leucasia, but she is resisting him. He believes he will improve his chances if he becomes a Roman Catholic, but bewails that there is already too much conversion going on: 'this changing a Man's Religion is a meer drug, 'tis grown too common'.[75] As the play progresses, Leucasia starts to feel sorry for Turnabout and finds ways to rescue him from what she describes as the 'continual Drudgery of a whining Hypocrisy'.[76]

The epitome of this religious promiscuity can be seen in the title character in Thomas Durfey's *Sir Barnaby Whigg* (1681), who is

[70] Behn, *The Roundheads*, 18.
[71] Ibid. 31.
[72] Cowley, *The Cutter*, 23.
[73] Ibid. 5–6.
[74] Ibid. 32.
[75] Anon, *The folly of priest-craft*, 1.
[76] Ibid. 19.

described as willing to 'change his Opinion as easily as his Coat', another use of a clothing metaphor to describe a hypocrite.[77] It is money and power that drives him, and he admits that his soul is 'always in the heart of the City—in Lumbard street'.[78] He starts the play as a nonconformist and a member of the Church Militant but, when he hears a rumour that power is shifting towards the Church of England, he decides he will conform and impeach his 'quondam Brethren'.[79] The play was first performed in the autumn of 1681 when, in the wake of the discrediting of the Popish Plot, power was shifting towards the Tories and against the nonconformists. This change of coat is, however, only the first of Sir Barnaby's transformations. When he tells Wilding that he is now fixed in his conformity and 'I love Bishops with all my heart', Wilding decides to play a trick on him by getting his footman Swift to disguise himself as a Roman Catholic priest.[80] Swift persuades Sir Barnaby that a very wealthy widow is in love with him. Although she is the niece of the Grand Vizier, Swift says she is a devout Roman Catholic and causes Sir Barnaby serious discomfort by asking what his religion is. Sir Barnaby doesn't give a straight answer and so Swift says that only a 'honest, godly Roman Catholick' will win her. Sir Barnaby immediately declares that he has 'ever lov'd and honour'd' the Pope.[81] But yet another trap has been laid for him. A letter arrives from the widow's uncle, without whose consent she cannot marry, saying that any future husband must 'immediately turn Musselman'. Sir Barnaby promptly says he will 'turn Turk'. He shamelessly admits his religious promiscuity by adding that 'I'le turn Turk, man, Jew, Moor, Græcian, any thing: Pox on't, I'le not lose a Lady, and such a sum for the sake of any Religion under the Sun'.[82] He then adds that he will fight for the Turks in the forthcoming battle, whereupon Wilding and the Justice (who have been eavesdropping) emerge and Sir Barnaby is arrested for treason. The idea that such religious flexibility was not uncommon at the time is shown in a brief exchange after Sir Barnaby has been taken away. Wilding asks 'Was there ever

[77] Thomas Durfey, *Sir Barnaby Whigg* (London, 1681), 9.

[78] Ibid. 10. Lumbard Street (now Lombard Street) was in the financial centre of the City of London.

[79] Ibid. 30.

[80] Ibid. 41.

[81] Ibid. 49.

[82] Ibid. 50.

such a Rascal?' and his friend answers 'Yes, Thousands in their hearts'.[83]

Religious dissimulation could go further than concealing an inconvenient faith. It could also be used to conceal the absence of any faith at all. In *The Female Prelate,* an analysis of Joanna's religious position reveals an absence of religious commitment that borders on atheism. There is a mocking tone to the way she talks about the Roman Catholic faithful – 'poor little unambitious Church men' – and their beliefs – 'the airy Dreams of Faith, Religion, Piety'.[84] She is particularly scathing about those Roman Catholics who leave money to the church at the end of their lives: 'those / Dull pious dying fools, who in despair / To buy Eternity, make the Church their Heir.' She is, of course, very happy to pocket the cash 'which we in Lust consume'.[85] This highly derogatory attitude to the Roman Catholic Church and its followers does not mean she is entirely without belief. Although she hardly mentions God, there are a number of references to the devil. Before the new pope is elected, Joanna offers a Faustian pact to become pope: 'Bring me some God, or what else power beside, / Some kinder Devil, but toth' Roman Chair, / And I am thy Slave for ever.'[86] She clearly believes the pact is in place because, on two occasions later in the play, she calls on her 'Adored dear Devil' to save her from a dangerous situation.[87] Also, when confronted by the ghost of the old duke, she refers to him as 'This Messenger Of Hell'.[88] None of this would have been a surprise to Andrew Marvell who saw all Roman Catholic priests as adopting 'bold imposture … under the name of Christianity'.[89]

Another example of an atheist dissembling as a cleric can be found in Dryden's *Don Sebastian* (1689). The play is set in Islamic Barbary and the religious leader is the Mufti. When the emperor asks him to annul his marriage, the Mufti gets himself out of this tight spot by telling the emperor that, although the law forbids him to marry a Christian, there is no prohibition to his ravishing her. This

[83] Ibid. 51.
[84] Settle, *The Female Prelate*, 55.
[85] Ibid. 47.
[86] Ibid. 5.
[87] Ibid. 50, 69.
[88] Ibid. 50.
[89] Andrew Marvell, *An account of the growth of popery, and arbitrary government in England* (Amsterdam, 1677), 5.

willingness to bend the religious laws is only one aspect of the Mufti's hypocrisy. Early in the play he says that, although the law requires fasting and abstaining from alcohol, this should only apply to 'the Vulgar' and not to 'Kings and to their Guides', presumably including himself.[90] Feasting and fasting are used metaphorically by his wife to emphasize his hypocrisy: 'The Mufti wou'd feast himself upon other Women, and keep me fasting'.[91] When threatened with torture, he sets himself apart from the vulgar with his hypocrisy: 'we may preach Suffering to others, but alas, holy Flesh is too well pamper'd to endure Martyrdom'.[92] These are, however, minor infringements compared to his soliloquy in Act IV when he confesses not only his hypocrisy, but also his atheism. Religion is, to him, no more than a stepping stone to power: 'This 'tis to have a sound Head-piece; by this I have got to be chief of my Religion; that is, honestly speaking, to teach others what I neither know nor believe myself. For what's Mahomet to me, but that I get by him?'[93]

The hypocrisy of religious promiscuity has been clearly portrayed in these examples. The implication of this behaviour is that their religious commitment must be shallow. In some cases, we have seen a lack of any religious belief, usually concealed beneath a veneer of piety.

Conclusion

These portrayals of atheists masquerading as religious leaders cast doubt on the faith of the earlier examples of religious hypocrites. Through the contorted reasoning of the casuists, the scandalous behaviour of the reprobates, the deviousness of the predators, and the deceit of the dissimulators, the post-Restoration dramatists created an image of a world pervaded by religious hypocrisy. The use of these different forms of hypocrisy in the portrayals of religious characters across all the religious denominations shows that the trope of the religious hypocrite was not specific to puritans, dissenters or Roman Catholics, but had a much wider application. The remorselessness of these negative portrayals also raises the question of the

90 John Dryden, *Don Sebastian* (London, 1690), 6.
91 Ibid. 60.
92 Ibid. 96.
93 Ibid. 75–6.

attitude shown in the plays to religion in general. Dramatists could have included more examples of honest, decent religious characters to counterbalance the many negative portrayals, and this might have been expected if they themselves held religious beliefs and were not writing with the intention of undermining religion. Since they did not do this, it seems plausible that they did not care about the effect their works were having on religion in general. Their remorseless use of the religious hypocrite in their plays presents an impression of a society that goes beyond Wycherley's evocation of a masquerading age, and shows us instead a profoundly hypocritical one.

Laughing at Hypocrisy: *The Turncoats* (1711), Visual Culture and Dissent in Early Eighteenth-Century England

Adam Morton*
Newcastle University

This article considers The Turncoats *(1711), an anti-Dissent graphic satire published after the Tory victory in the 1710 General Election. The print ridiculed the hypocrisy of those Dissenters who abandoned their principles and conformed to the Church of England after that election, and pointed to the pervasiveness of religious hypocrisy in early eighteenth-century England more generally. This article contextualizes the print within the tense religious and political rivalries that developed after the 1688 Revolution and the trial of Henry Sacheverell.* The Turncoats' *ridicule resonated because it built on older traditions of stereotypes in anti-popery and anti-puritanism, which used mockery to attack those perceived to be hypocrites. Mockery is analyzed by considering how early modern culture understood laughter. It is argued that ridicule in* The Turncoats *expressed superiority over hypocrites by subjecting them to contempt and provided relief from anxieties about the prevalence of hypocrisy during the rage of parties.*

Ridicule in *The Turncoats* (1711) was an uneasy mixture of celebration and concern (Figure 1).[1] The print celebrated the Tory victory in the general election of autumn 1710 as a triumph of sincerity over hypocrisy. At the same time, it expressed concern that, despite that victory, hypocrisy continued to corrupt the Protestant interest.

* School of History, Classics, and Archaeology, Newcastle University, Newcastle-upon-Tyne NE1 7RU. E-mail: adam.morton@newcastle.ac.uk.

[1] Frederic Stephens and Dorothy M. George, eds, *Catalogue of Political and Personal Satires preserved in the Dept. of Prints and Drawings in the British Museum*, 11 vols (1870–1954), no. 1507 [hereafter: BM Satires]. Stephens dates the print to 1709. However, its publisher, William Pennock, advertised it in *The Evening Post*, 3–6 February 1711.

Studies in Church History 60 (2024), 312–339
doi: 10.1017/stc.2024.13

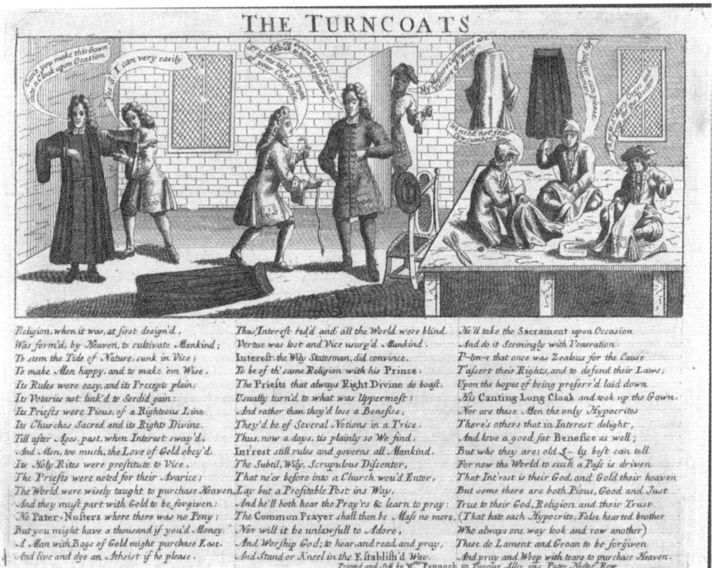

Figure 1. *The Turncoats* (1711). Reproduced by permission of The British Museum. Copyright of the Trustees of The British Museum.

A Tory victory was a victory for the high church party in England's established church over those which it felt threatened that church, namely those Dissenting Protestants and low churchmen who had advocated for Dissenters' place in English public life since their toleration after the 1688–9 Revolution. The fall of the Whig government in 1710 (and, with it, the low church interest) meant that Dissent would not be treated as leniently as it had been for the past twenty years, a change in fortunes that caused many ministers to conform to the established church that they had long claimed to be popish, seemingly putting preferment before principle. *The Turncoats* scoffed at the deftness of these conversions. It shows two ministers being measured in a tailor's shop, *turning their coats* from Dissenting cloaks to high church gowns, and exposing their hypocrisy in the process. 'Can't you make the gown into a cloak upon occasion?', the first minister asks his tailor, flaunting his intention to turn again in the future. 'Let my gown by lin'd with a cloak to turn at pleasure', demands the second, pointing at the cloak on the floor to indicate he will switch again when the situation suits. The hypocrisy is galling. But the tailors have the Dissenters' measure: 'Sir, let me take the length of your conscience'.

As we unpick the scene, mockery piles on top of mockery. The ministers are derided by their social inferiors. An apprentice looks in on the workshop purely to mock them, while on the right, three gossiping labourers jest that they 'need not fear cucumber time' (i.e. summer, normally a quiet season for tailors), because they will be busy sewing new gowns. Old jokes about hypocrites are picked, magpie-like, from the bricolage of popular culture and rearranged into a new conceit: 'My masters are vicars of Bray', chides the apprentice at the back of the scene, referring to the time-serving cleric of proverb, print and song, who saved his own skin by shifting with the times. 'My masters can please trimmers', replies one of the labourers, riffing on multiple definitions of 'trimming', combining the tailors (trimming clothes), Dissenters (trimming consciences) and 'Trimmer', a slur against clergy or politicians who changed parties out of self-interest.[2] Hypocrites 'trimmed' in the nautical sense, in which a ship's sails were adjusted to make best use of the wind. Turncoat clergy changed vestments to find their best 'trim' for gain.

There is, therefore, a lot of ridicule in *The Turncoats*. But to what end? What did all this laughter *do*? This print (and many others produced during 1709–11) was part of a tradition of polemic that used mockery to expose religious hypocrisy to aggressive, moral emotions: anger, contempt and shame. Such polemic dated from the Reformation. Protestants denigrated Roman Catholic doctrine and tradition as a gaudy mockery of Christian truth, deriding its miracles and scoffing at its saints to expose it as Antichrist, the arch-hypocrite.[3] This was a punishing, moral laughter which justified the Reformation by scorning what had gone before it.

There was much of this polemic in *The Turncoats*: Dissenting hypocrites were laughed to scorn. This is underscored by the politics of other graphic satires issued by *The Turncoats*' publisher, William Pennock, in 1710–11, which took a pro-Tory and -high church,

[2] 'Trimmer' was coined by George Saville, first marquess of Halifax, to celebrate the virtue of balance in politics in *The Character of a Trimmer* (London, 1682). It quickly became an insult.

[3] Adam Morton, 'Glaring at Antichrist: Anti-Papal Images in Early Modern England *c.*1530–1680' (PhD thesis, University of York, 2011), 71–185. See also Patrick Collinson, 'Ecclesiastical Vitriol: Religious Satire in the 1590s and the Invention of Puritanism', in John Guy, ed., *The Two Reigns of Elizabeth I* (Cambridge, 1995), 150–70.

and anti-Whig, -low church and -Dissent, stance.[4] It is argued below, however, that *The Turncoats* pushed at the conventional boundaries of party politics, decrying religious hypocrisy in general, alongside condemning Dissenting hypocrisy in particular.[5] Ridicule reflected acute concerns about the prevalence of hypocrisy in public life which was a crucial factor in the crisis of politics during the first age of party (*c.*1678–1714).[6] The public's growing political importance as voters, petitioners and readers was matched by growing worries about its ability to judge fairly in an era of rampant misrepresentation in which swollen volumes of partisan news used shams, cheats and frauds to distort truth to party ends. 'Hypocrisy is the profitable and consequently the reigning vice of the age', worried Richard Kingston, Jacobite turned informer, in 1709.[7] Its pervasiveness during the first decade of the eighteenth century provoked a moral panic that marked the collapse of trust in public life.[8]

During that crisis, mocking exposés of religious hypocrisy continued to express anger, contempt and shame as they had since the Reformation. But ridicule also did something else: it provided release from anxieties caused by the perception that hypocrisy was prevalent in public life. How laughter was understood in early modern culture is revealing on this score. One theory saw laughter as a mark of the malicious joy found in feeling superior to someone or something else: we laugh at what is contemptible. Another theory, found most commonly in medical writing, saw laughter as relieving, a physical release of tensions in mind and body caused by feelings of misery or melancholy. We see both superiority and relief in *The Turncoats*' mockery of hypocrisy. The print ridiculed the contemptible (Dissenters) to

[4] BM Satires, nos 1495, 1531, 1550 and 1570.

[5] Previous discussions of the print have noted that its targets were wider than Dissent alone: see Carys Brown, *Friends, Neighbours, Sinners: Religious Difference in English Society, 1689–1750* (Cambridge, 2022), 118; and Brian Cowan, ed., *The State Trial of Doctor Henry Sacheverell*, Parliamentary History Texts and Studies 6 (Chichester and Maldon, MA, 2012), 159.

[6] Mark Knights, *Representation and Misrepresentation in Later Stuart Britain* (Oxford, 2005), 3–11, 30–41, 223–72, 273–334. See also Kate Loveman, *Reading Fictions, 1660–1740: Deception in English Literary and Political Culture* (Aldershot, 2008), 19–46, 47–60, 85–108; and Rebecca Bullard, *The Politics of Disclosure, 1674–1725* (London, 2009), 1–26, 63–81, 183–9.

[7] Richard Kingston, *Apothegmata Curiosa* (London, 1709), 17.

[8] Mark Knights, 'Occasional Conformity and the Representation of Dissent: Hypocrisy, Sincerity, Moderation and Zeal', *PH* 24 (2005), 41–57.

celebrate the Tory-high church as morally superior; and it expressed horror that, despite that victory, hypocrisy was still a threat, for hypocrites were joining the church.

Dissent and Hypocrisy

The roots of the hostility to Dissent portrayed in *The Turncoats* lay in the fallout of the 1688 Revolution. The nature of the revolution meant that no group was safe from accusations of hypocrisy. The established church struggled to reconcile the removal of James II with the doctrines of passive obedience and non-resistance. For non-juring Anglicans – who refused to swear oaths of allegiance to William and Mary, because doing so violated those sworn to James – there was no reconciliation: 1688 was an affront to God and conscience.[9] That most Anglican clergy did take the oath was unsettling, because it smacked of interest trouncing principle and exposed an uncomfortable truth: hypocrisy was necessary for the new settlement to work. High churchmen accused their low church opponents of selling out the Church of England by supporting toleration and advocating for the place of Dissent within a comprehensive Protestant interest. High churchmen were in turn accused of hiding Jacobite sympathies under a pretended royalism; and Dissenters' sober dress and distain for socializing drew charges of hypocrisy, viewed as public displays of piety that masked the fanaticism that threatened England's church and state in the early eighteenth century as acutely as they had in the mid-seventeenth.[10] Most troubling, however, was the fact that religion had become a plaything of politics. Whigs and Tories were accused of adopting positions on religious matters to con the public and win votes. Mark Knights has shown that, by 1710, it was widely accepted that 'religious language was … used as a veneer covering private, sectional or group ends' and was 'deliberately chosen to hide

[9] Richard Sharp, '"Our Mother, the Church of England": Non-jurors, High Churchmen, and the Evidence of Subscription Lists', in Paul Klébor Monod, Murray Pittock and Daniel Szechi, eds, *Loyalty and Identity: Jacobites at Home and Abroad* (Basingstoke, 2010), 167–79; Robert D. Cornwall, 'Divine Right Monarchy: Henry Dodwell's Critique of the Reformation and Defence of the Nonjuror Bishops', *Anglican and Episcopal History* 68 (1999), 37–66.

[10] William Gibson, 'William Talbot and Church Parties, 1688–1730', *JEH* 58 (2007), 26–48.

nakedly political ambitions'.[11] Religious politics descended into the competitive unmasking of hypocrisy in which all sides decried their opponents' mendacity at all times. This caused a collapse in public trust in politics, provoking a moral panic about the decline of honesty and sincerity in English society. Where could the abuse of faith lead, but to apathy or atheism? As the author of *Moderation Truly Stated* (1704) noted, pretending in matters of faith 'gives religion the deepest wounds'.[12] No trust, no faith.

Much of this alarm can be traced to the religious settlement imposed by the Toleration Act of 1689. The act permitted all Trinitarian Protestant congregations who dissented from the established church to worship in their own meeting houses, jettisoning the ideal of uniformity that had been a cornerstone of the English Reformation.[13] Dissenters benefited significantly from this change. Presbyterians, Baptists, Quakers and other minority Protestant groups were no longer persecuted for practising their faith (as they had been from 1662). Their new freedom to worship was accompanied by formal recognition that they were part of England's Protestant interest, partners with the established church in the fight against popery.[14] Considering that 'puritans' had been joined with 'popery' as the twin terrors of that interest in conformist Protestant thought for over a century, this marked a substantial change in the public status of Dissent.

It was an embittered partnership, however. As Ralph Stevens has shown, the act did not end Anglican-Dissenter hostilities, but reframed them in the new context of the post-Revolution constitution.[15] Tensions reflected differing interpretations of the Toleration Act. For many Dissenters, the 1689 legislation had not gone far enough. It was merely a step towards full freedom, which could only be realized with the abolition of the penal code, a platform on which to agitate against the legal restrictions that continued to make their position in English society unequal. For many Anglicans, the

11 Knights, 'Occasional Conformity', 45.

12 Mary Astell, *Moderation Truly Stated* (London, 1704), 33–4.

13 Jonathan Israel, 'William III and Toleration', in Ole Peter Grell, Jonathan I. Israel and Nicholas Tyacke, eds, *From Persecution to Toleration: The Glorious Revolution in England* (Oxford, 1991), 129–70.

14 1 Will. & Mary c. 18.

15 Ralph Stevens, *Protestant Pluralism: The Reception of the Toleration Act, 1689–1720* (Woodbridge, 2018).

1689 Toleration was merely a temporary indulgence of Dissent, not an unbudgeable cornerstone of the constitution. High churchmen refused to accept the permanence of the new plural religious society, or the declining role of the established church in that society which followed on from it. They worked to restrain the scope of Dissenters' new religious freedoms in the period up to 1720, after which the declining political influence of their Tory allies left them with no feasible means of opposition.[16] Toleration created a religious marketplace, and the Dissenters' claiming their new place in public life caused the established church to fear the loss of parishioners at a local level, and the control of public life at a national one. The construction of new meeting houses, funerals of prominent parishioners, and the growing involvement of Dissenters in the provision of children's education became new flashpoints of old intolerances in an era of legalized religious difference.[17]

Occasional conformity was the most serious of those flashpoints. The political authority of the Church of England was protected by the 1688/9 constitutions, which barred Dissenters from holding political office by requiring all office-holders to prove that they had received communion in the established church.[18] Dissenters responded by practising occasional conformity, taking the Anglican sacrament once annually (while otherwise continuing to attend their meeting houses), thereby qualifying for political office via an unabashed act of public hypocrisy, receiving communion in a church that they had long held to be popish and persecutory, for naked political gain. They 'play[ed] bopeep with God Almighty', teased Daniel Defoe, for reasons of 'politick'.[19]

The debate about occasional conformity mapped onto existing divisions in England's fractious Protestant fraternity. Both the Whig politicians who steered the governments of William and Mary, and Anne, and the low churchmen who dominated the churches of their period, winked at occasional conformity as a means of promoting unity between Protestants, and extending the principle of toleration of the Revolution settlement.[20] This leniency

[16] Julian Hoppit, *A Land of Liberty? England 1689–1727* (Oxford, 2000), 35–6, 216–36.
[17] Brown, *Friends, Neighbours, Sinners*, 69–108, 151–230.
[18] This was required by the Test and Corporation Acts: 13 Cha. II St. 2. c. 1; 25 Cha. II c. 2; 30 Cha. II St. 2.
[19] Daniel Defoe, *An Enquiry into Occasional Conformity* (London, 1697), 11.
[20] Brent S. Sirota, 'The Occasional Conformity Controversy, Moderation, and the Anglican Critique of Modernity, 1700–14', *HistJ* 57 (2014), 81–105.

enraged high churchmen, who worried that allowing Dissenters into the political establishment gave them a platform from which to spread sedition and irreligion, and engaged in a bitter campaign to stop occasional conformity.[21] Three bills, submitted in the parliamentary sessions of 1702–3, 1703–4 and 1704–5, proposed punitive fines on office-holders who attended Dissenting meetings. Attempts to 'tack' the third bill onto the granting of a subsidy necessary to continue war with France provoked fury and pushed the Whig regime to the point of crisis.[22] The bills were defeated, but they underlined the extent to which concerns about Dissent and religious hypocrisy more generally destabilized English politics in the first decades of the eighteenth century.

Dissenting hypocrisy caused consternation because it played into long-standing stereotypes. Since the late sixteenth century, hypocrisy had been a major element of the anti-puritanism that now informed hostility to Dissent. 'Puritans' were popularly seen as irrational and seditious hypocrites, who hid their lust for power behind a pretend piety.[23] Those stereotypes had a long half-life in parishes across eighteenth-century England, and informed the 'graduated layers of religious exclusivity' which, as Carys Brown has shown, peppered everyday interactions between Protestant denominations in eighteenth-century England.[24] Yet hypocrisy took on new resonance after 1689, because of the emergence of polite, sober modes of speech, manners and behaviour as the guiding ideal of public life. Politeness rejected zeal in favour of moderation to limit the potential of religion to foment division.[25] Zealous or 'enthusiastic' displays of faith, such as the austere piety of many Dissenting congregations, were now

[21] Geoffrey Holmes, *British Politics in the Age of Anne* (London, 1967), 99–103.

[22] Clyve Jones, '"Too Wild to Succeed": The Occasional Conformity Bills and Attempts by the House of Lords to Outlaw the Tack in the Reign of Anne', *PH* 30 (2011), 414–27. An Occasional Conformity Act was passed in 1711 (10 Anne c. 6) following the Tory General Election result.

[23] Peter Lake, 'Anti-Puritanism: The Structure of a Prejudice', in Kenneth Fincham and Peter Lake, eds, *Religious Politics in Post-Reformation England: Essays in Honour of Nicholas Tyacke* (Woodbridge, 2006), 80–97; Adam Morton, 'Anti-Catholicism: Catholics, Protestants, and the "Popery" Problem', in Robert E. Scully and Angela Ellis, eds, *A Companion to Recusancy in Britain and Ireland: From Reformation to Emancipation* (Leiden, 2022), 410–48, at 433–8.

[24] Brown, *Friends, Neighbours, Sinners*, 230.

[25] Laurence Klein, 'Liberty, Manners, and Politeness in Early Eighteenth Century England', *HistJ* 32 (1989), 583–604.

deemed to be impolite, the foundation of the fanaticism which (in Anglican eyes) had caused the civil wars of the previous century. Politeness placed Dissenters in a bind. Conforming to the new mores led to suspicions of insincerity; rejecting them, to charges of hypocrisy and to accusations that these were pious performances that showed that Dissenters thought themselves to be 'better' Protestants than their Anglican brethren. Stereotypes drew connections between Dissenters' unfashionable dress and their outmoded zeal, presenting their clothing as a cloak for their sedition that proved they should not be tolerated.[26]

That Dissent had strong support within the Whig regimes of both William and Mary, and Anne, played into the Tory-high church 'Church in Danger' campaign that expressed fears that, since 1688, a conspiracy had been at work to undermine the established church. The campaign saw toleration, latitudinarianism and occasional conformity as corruptions of the constitution that provided platforms for religious heterodoxy and republican politics bent on undermining society.[27] Occasional conformity was about more than Dissent. It was totemic of broader tensions in the Revolution settlement about toleration and the place of the established church in the constitution. That some public figures were prepared to dissemble to gain power, and other political figures and parties were prepared to permit that dissembling, pointed to the decline of honesty, sincerity and piety in public life. This 'Church in Danger' platform was crucial to winning the Tory-high church party a landslide victory in the 1710 General Election.[28]

The Sacheverell Affair

Doctor Henry Sacheverell (1674–1724) was the unlikely architect of this Tory-turn in late Stuart politics. A 'Church in Danger' preacher and long-standing anti-Dissenter firebrand, Sacheverell was tried for high crimes and misdemeanours in February and March 1710, having indicted the Whig government in his 5 November sermon at St Paul's Cathedral, *The Perils of False Brethren*.[29] In that sermon,

[26] Brown, *Friends, Neighbours, Sinners*, 109–50.

[27] George Every, *The High Church Party, 1688–1718* (London, 1959), 105–47.

[28] Holmes, *British Politics*, 56–62, 97–106, 259–60.

[29] Geoffrey Holmes, *The Trial of Doctor Sacheverell* (London, 1973), 64–9. On Sacheverell, see also Alex W. Barber, *The Restraint of the Press in England, 1660–1715:*

Sacheverell proclaimed the established church to be corrupted by hypocrites, just like the church of Corinth described by St Paul. A conspiracy of Whigs, low churchmen and Dissenters had sought the undoing of Protestant England since 1688 by pursuing toleration, permitting latitude in doctrine and liturgy, and ignoring occasional conformity, thereby allowing heresy and sedition footholds in power. These false brethren, and the apostate Tories or high churchmen who did nothing to stop them, were hypocrites, pretend Protestants who put political interest over principle. What Sacheverell said was made doubly offensive by when he said it. Fifth of November sermons were a ritual set piece of Protestant memory, uniting parishes across England in collective thanksgiving for their nation's special place in providence. Preachers were expected to relate 5 November 1605 (the Gunpowder Plot) to 5 November 1688 (William of Orange's landing at Torbay) as a double deliverance from popery.[30] Sacheverell turned this celebration into mourning, damning the revolution as a seditious contravention of the church's doctrine (passive obedience and non-resistance), and the toleration as an act of schism.

At first, Sacheverell was laughed at, his sermon dismissed as having more spleen than substance. 'The roaring of this beast ought to give you no manner of disturb[ance]', affirmed Daniel Defoe, 'You ought to laugh at him, let him alone; he'll vent his gall, and then he'll be quiet'.[31] Defoe was wrong: ire proved to be catching. Sacheverell was a lightning rod for pent-up prejudice against Dissent. On 1 March 1710, riotous crowds of Sacheverell supporters sacked meeting houses, tearing one down in Lincoln's Inn Fields, brick by brick, before celebrating their iconoclasm with a giant bonfire of its gutted

The Communication of Sin (Woodbridge, 2022), esp. 183–203; Brian Cowan, 'Relitigating Revolution: Address, Progress, and Redress in the Long Summer of 1710', in idem and Scott Sowerby, eds, *The State Trials and the Politics of Justice in Late Stuart England* (Martlesham, 2021), 204–23; idem, ed., *State Trial of Dr Henry Sacheverell*; Mark Knights, *The Devil in Disguise: Deception, Delusion, and Fanaticism in the Early English Enlightenment* (Oxford, 2011), 142–92; and idem, ed., *Faction Displayed: Reconsidering the Impeachment of Dr Henry Sacheverell*, Parliamentary History Book Series 31 (Chichester and Maldon, MA, 2012).

[30] David Cressy, *Bonfires and Bells: National Memory and the Protestant Calendar in Elizabethan and Stuart England* (Stroud, 2004), esp. 67–92, 110–29, 141–55.

[31] Daniel Defoe, *A Review of the State of the British Nation* 6, 8 Dec 1709, 106. See also anon., *The Cherubin with a Flaming Sword* (London, 1709).

contents.[32] Sacheverell's popularity was a captivating blend of sympathy and infamy that ensured his trial generated more public interest than any since Charles I's in 1649. Christopher Wren employed fifty workmen to build the stands commissioned for the crowds expected in Westminster Hall, ripping out vendors' stalls to make the auditorium as large as possible, and there was a frenzied black-market competition for tickets.[33] News that Sacheverell would preach at St Saviour's, Southwark, after being released on bail, left that church packed to the rafters. Rumours in the pews that he was actually at Newington caused the panicked crowd to rush there instead. On the first day of the trial proceedings, Sacheverell was collected from his lodgings in Temple in a coach made largely of glass, a 'tawdry chariot' from which he was visible to the crowds who lined the streets daily to wave his cavalcade of eight coaches and 400 supporters on their path to Westminster, where they met crowds of ticket holders who had been gathering since 7 a.m., two hours before the court's doors would open, and five before the trial would begin.[34]

The trial was easily spun as proof that the conspiracy against the church of which Sacheverell spoke was real. He was found guilty, but the queen insisted on only a token punishment, a humiliation for the government that was greeted as a deliverance for the established church, and set in motion the downfall of the Whig regime. The Tories made full use of their new champion, trotting Sacheverell out as the prized prig of the 'Church in Danger' campaign to win seats across England in the general election that November.[35] In that election, and the campaign against Dissent that followed, he was a totem of sincerity besting hypocrisy. Sacheverell was briefly the most famous man in England, 'Huzza'd by the mob like a prize fighter' wherever he went.[36] Published on 25 November 1709, and selling over 100,000 copies by the following March, *The Perils of False Brethren* earned him an estimated readership of

[32] Geoffrey Holmes, 'The Sacheverell Riots: The Crowd and the Church in Early Eighteenth-Century London', *P&P* 72 (1976), 55–82.
[33] Holmes, *Sacheverell*, 117–18.
[34] Ibid. 120–2, 126–8.
[35] Ibid. 242–8.
[36] Alexander Cunningham, *The History of Great Britain from the Revolution of 1688 to the Accession of George I*, 2 vols (London, 1787), 2: 300.

250,000, equivalent to the entire electorate.[37] Sacheverell was painted by Thomas Gibson, a leading portrait artist of the period, and mezzotint reproductions of his image flooded London during the trial in February and March 1710, and were widely displayed in private homes and public spaces as a mark of support for Sacheverell and the church his supporters felt was on trial with him.[38] A generation later, his portrait still stood as an icon of popular Toryism. Hogarth sneered at it, pasting Sacheverell's face at Moll's bedside in plate 3 of the 'Harlot's Progress' to mock cheap veneers of respectability (Figure 2).[39]

Gilbert Burnet remembered the Sacheverell affair with astonishment as 'one of the most extraordinary transactions in my time'.[40] The most extraordinary aspect of the affair was its heat, which shocked contemporaries. Sacheverell entered the pulpit of St Paul's Cathedral with 'red overspread[ing] his face [and a] goggling wildness [in] his eyes … like a sybil to the mouth of her cave', before proceeding to preach on the fiery tip of fury.[41] 'I fancy he had bankrupt all the oyster-women, porters, watermen, coachmen and carmen in town to make up his collection', exclaimed one Whig, taken aback by the sermon's tone.[42] 'I could not have imagined if I had not actually heard it myself', said the Rev. John Bennett, that 'so much heat, passion, violence and scurrilous language, to say no worse of it, could have come from a Protestant pulpit'.[43] Sacheverell had many critics. Even high churchmen sympathetic to his cause were embarrassed that his attack on the church and government was guilty of the sins with which he charged the Dissenters: enthusiasm, sedition and zeal. Much of the polemic that emerged from the trial, and the Tory turn that followed, proved his equal in raillery.

Sacheverell soon changed tack. As Brian Cowan has demonstrated, during his speech in his own defence on 9 March 1710, Sacheverell

37 Holmes, *Sacheverell,* 74–5; Francis F. Madan and William A. Speck, eds, *A Critical Bibliography of Dr Henry Sacheverell* (Lawrence, KA, 1978), 19–23 (nos 57–74).

38 John Chaloner Smith, *British Mezzotinto Portraits*, 4 vols (London, 1883), 3: 1 and 4: 11.

39 BM Satires, no. 2061; Eirwen E. C. Nicholson, 'Sacheverell's Harlots: Non-Resistance on Paper and in Practice', *PH* 31 (2012), 69–79.

40 Gilbert Burnet, *History of His Own Time*, 6 vols (Oxford, 1833), 5: 434.

41 Thomas Hearne, *Remarks and Collections of Thomas Hearne*, ed. Charles E. Doble, 11 vols (Oxford, 1885–1907), 2: 229.

42 J. P., *The Priest turn'd poet* (London, 1709), dedication.

43 Hearne, *Remarks and Collections*, 2: 304–5, 317. See also William Bisset, *Remarks on Dr Sach-'s Sermon* (London, 1709), 2–7; George Ridpath, *The Peril of Being Zealously Affected, but not Well* (London, 1709), 6.

Figure 2. William Hogarth, *A Harlot's Progress* (1732), plate 3. Reproduced by permission of The British Museum. Copyright of the Trustees of The British Museum.

presented himself as a 'living martyr of the high church cause'.[44] Even his opponents thought that the sympathy his performance elicited was remarkable.[45] Sacheverell's temperate, humble speech won him victory in the court of public opinion. Printed copies ran through twenty editions in 1710 alone and shaped the representation of Sacheverell in the public sphere, coupling him with other Anglican martyrs, Archbishop William Laud and Charles I (whose portrait he was often pictured holding).[46] Cowan has shown that the speech also changed what was on trial. The Whig prosecution had been designed to defend the 1688 Revolution by condemning the high

[44] Brian Cowan, 'The Spin Doctor: Sacheverell's Trial Speech and Political Performance in a Divided Society', *PH* 31 (2012), 28–46, at 28.

[45] Cowan, ed., *State Trial*, 35–42; Burnet, *History of His Own Time*, 5: 440–5.

[46] *A Complete Collection of State Trials*, comp. Thomas B. Howell, 34 vols (London, 1809–28), 15: 364–78; *The Speech of Henry Sacheverell D.D. Upon his Impeachment at the Bar of the House of Lords, in Westminster Hall, March 7 1709/10* (London, 1710). For reprints, see Madan and Speck, eds, *A Critical Bibliography*, 72–7 (nos 248–67). For martyr portraits, see BM Satires, nos 1510, 1514, 1525 and 1545.

church principles that Sacheverell advocated so vehemently in his 5 November sermon: passive obedience and non-resistance. Styling himself as a martyr allowed Sacheverell to sidestep matters of controversy and present the trial as a partisan attack on the church: he was being persecuted for doing his duties as a minister, preaching the church's doctrine and rebuking sin.[47] Moderate language and pathetic oratory were essential to Sacheverell's studied performance of sincerity.

The crude logic of polemic dictated that if Sacheverell embodied sincerity, his opponents must embody hypocrisy. In the winter of 1710–11, Burnet was mocked as a hypocrite and so, with even less mercy, was the Whig cleric Benjamin Hoadly, who became Sacheverell's antithesis, the low church champion to the doctor's high. Dissenters were vilified with equal ferocity. The scathing tone of *The Preaching-Weathercock: A Paradox* (1712) by John Dunton, bookseller and founder of the Athenian Society, was typical.[48] Dunton attacked William Richardson, a former Presbyterian minister in Clerkenwell who had taken orders in the established church in 1711. Richardson's change of heart was public: he published the sermon delivered in his new parish of St Mary's, Whitechapel, in which he justified his conversion. It also brought him speedy preferment: within a year, he was chaplain to the earl of Londonderry. This did not make him popular. Nor did his telling his former brethren that there were no legitimate reasons for their Dissent from the established church, a choice he now labelled fanatical.[49] The gall of this was too much. Richardson became an embodiment of Dissenting hypocrisy, accused by Anglicans and Dissenters alike of converting for self-interest and gain. Even his own family condemned him.[50] Dunton had sharpened his hatchet:

> Another – VICAR OF BRAY – (or *Preaching Weathercock*) is *Turncoat Will* – For with the FANATICS, you are Demure and Saintish – with

[47] Howell, ed., *State Trials*, 15: 366–75.

[48] For a discussion of Dunton, see Stephen Parks, *John Dunton and the English Book Trade* (New York and London, 1976). In *The Bull-Baiting* (London, 1710), Dunton had lambasted Sacheverell, but happily admitted that the doctor was on the nose when it came to Dissent in *The Preaching Weathercock: A Paradox* (London, 1712), 25.

[49] William Richardson, *God's Call of His Ministers* (London, 1711), 1–5, 14–15, 23–6.

[50] See William Richardson, *The Serpents Head Bruised* (London, 1713), 1–7, 12–13, 15–18, 20–2, an account of Richardson's trial for immorality; and idem, *Episcopacy Vindicated* (London, 1712) and idem, *Malice Defeated* (London, 1712), 4–6, on the public disputes around it.

> HIGH CHURCH you can rail at Dissenters, and call 'em Schismaticks – with the TRIMMERS, you're moderate, and good Natur'd .... And with ALL PARTIES, you can *Conform, Transform, Reform, and turn to any Form* for the sake of a good Living.....a meer VICAR OF BRAY....with the infamous Character of being TURNCOAT....and your *High-flying Brother* [Sacheverell] tells you as much in that scandalous sermon he bellow'd out at St. *Pauls*....But assure your self that your Turning thus with every Wind, gains you neither Credit, not Profit, but makes a sort of *Preaching Jest*, or *Vicar of Bray*.[51]

Richardson was a turncoat, a trimmer and a Vicar of Bray: the very insults hurled at Dissenting converts in *The Turncoats*.

Vicars of Bray

The Turncoats' image, then, was an assortment of clichés. It asked its viewers to laugh at jokes they knew well and its ridicule was potent because it was direct. 'Trimmers', 'turncoats' and 'Vicars of Bray' were commonplaces, instantly familiar images that worked as insults because the associations of their mockery – deceit, insincerity, interest – were immediate. In the wake of the Sacheverell affair and the Tory-turn in politics that followed it, those associations had a new resonance. The alarmism of Sacheverell and the 'Church in Danger' campaign made commonplace images of hypocrisy more urgent.

Commonplace insults were remarkably changeable – they meant different things in different contexts. The Vicar of Bray is an instructive example. The vicar was a shorthand for a weathercock cleric whose principles turned with the prevailing wind. The proverb was recorded in Thomas Fuller's *The Worthies of England* (1662):

> The vivacious vicar [of Bray] living under King Henry VIII, King Edward VI, Queen Mary, and Queen Elizabeth, was first a papist, then a protestant, then a papist, then a protestant again. He had seen some martyrs burnt (two miles off) at Windsor and found this fire too hot for his tender temper.

[51] Dunton, *The Preaching Weathercock*, 25–7. Italics original.

> This vicar, being taxed by one for being a turncoat and an inconstant changeling, said 'not so, for I always kept my principle, which is this – to live and die the Vicar of Bray'.[52]

The tone here was merry, not mocking. Fuller teased clerical hypocrisy – he did not attack it. The proverb was circulated as a pleasantry in the period's compendiums. Its incongruous humour (an *a*-moral priest) was enjoyed as an absurdity in works like 'The Vicar of Bray: or, a Paradox in Praise of the Turncoat Clergy' in Alexander Brome's *Athenian Sport: Or two thousand paradoxes* (1707).[53] The time-serving vicar was the subject of a popular ballad. In it, he recalls that he was high church under Charles II, stout in support of the Royal Supremacy and divine right, before opposing both under James II, when 'The Church of Rome I found would fit / Full well my constitution. / And I had been a Jesuit, / But for the Revolution'. After 1688, he ditched James for William III: 'Old principles I did revoke, / Set conscience at a distance', embracing the Whigs until Anne became queen, 'The Church of England's Glory', and 'Another face of things was seen / And I became a Tory'. He was Whig again after 1714, happy to swear loyalty to the Hanoverians for as long as 'they can keep possession'. The ballad was a farce. Sixty years of religious history were collapsed into the hypocritical code of one cleric: interest over principle. The ballad's refrain jests over and over: 'And this is law, I will maintain / Unto my Dying Day, Sir. / That whatsoever king may reign / I will be the Vicar of Bray, Sir!'[54]

Other reuses of the Vicar of Bray were more aggressive. Between 1660 and 1720, 'Vicar of Bray' was used to insult clergy of all stripes. It exposed the hypocrisy of Nonconformists and moderate Anglicans who supported comprehension or toleration. In his Lord Mayor's sermon of 1682, John Evans sneered at ministers who turned with the times and made the Vicar of Bray 'the vicar of the day'.[55] A year later, *The Character of A Church-Trimmer* raged at hypocrites who loved

52 Thomas Fuller, *The History of the Worthies of England* (London, 1662), 82–3.

53 Alexander Brome, *Athenian Sport* (London, 1707), 400–1; anon., *Anglorum Speculum* (London, 1684), 22; Anon., *The Compleat Book of Knowledge* (London, 1698), 102.

54 Anon., *The Vicar of Bray* (London, 1714), single sheet. See also anon., *The Religious Turncoat: or, A Late Jacobite Turned Williamite* (London, 1693), single sheet.

55 John Evans, *Moderation Stated* (London, 1682), 41.

power, not their church, and backed campaigns for toleration out of political expediency. 'He resolves to be *somebody* (and not Vicar of *Bray* still)', using Whig politics to graduate to '*Beelzebub* or Prince of TRIMMERS, the *Devil* of a Saint, and the Monster of a Man, into the bargain; for he is *Two-fold* all over'.[56] After 1688, however, the insult was less specific to Nonconformity. The readiness of so many Anglicans to renounce their oaths to James II was condemned as unctuous hypocrisy in texts like *Hysteron Proteron. A Sermon lately Preached by the Vicar of Bray* (*c.*1690).[57] The hypocrisy of William Sherlock, who performed a spectacular volte-face in August 1690, taking oaths to William and Mary having previously been a vociferous nonjuror, was met with dismay: 'a right *Sherlockain* will live in every Air, side with every Government, and conform to all sorts of Revolutions [he is] a Harlot [who] resolves to be Vicar of *Bray*'.[58] *The State Proteus* (1690) unpicked Anglican justifications for taking the oaths as sophistry. 'All honest men' judged the oath 'a mean and unworthy Compliance … unbecoming of *Ecclesiastical Professours*', the preserve of 'such Vicars of Bray' who are 'well known to be a scandal to their function' as clergy. There are *some* truths in Christianity which are beyond qualification, the author noted. Passive obedience was one of them.[59]

The ire of these charges was a long way from Fuller's merry proverb. The Vicar of Bray was a stock joke, and stock jokes are pliable. As a shorthand for clerical hypocrisy, its connotations of self-interest over principle were stable. But its effect varied according to how it was used. The 'Vicar of Bray' could be proverbial, the gentle ribbing of a type in order to amuse (after Fuller); or personal, the charging of an individual or group of clergy with hypocrisy in order to condemn. The same joke was a source of mirth in one text, and of invective in the other. Laughing at hypocrisy meant something different in each register. Stock jokes such as 'trimmers' and 'Vicars of Bray' had a different resonance in the moral panic of 1709–11 because they were

[56] Heraclitus his Ghost, *The Character of A Church-Trimmer* (London, 1683), n.p.; J. R., *Religio Laici* (London, 1688), 8. Italics original.

[57] No copy of this text survives. It was listed as for sale in anon., *Happy be Lucky, A catalogue to be sold by Lottery* (London, 1690), 3.

[58] Anon., *Sherlockianus Delineatus* (London, 1690), 2. Italics original.

[59] Anon., *The State Proteus* (London, 1690), 4; Abednego Seller, *The History of Passive Obedience* (London, 1689), 190. Italics original.

charged with the hostility of anti-puritan stereotypes. Stereotypes reduce people to categories: the repetition of stock jokes, familiar images and commonplace language is the root of their power. In religious polemic, those categories were moral: Protestants were good or bad, loyal or disloyal.

The 'Church in Danger' campaign pivoted on a binary. Dissenters (and their low church/Whig advocates) were hypocrites, while the high church was sincere; Dissenters sought the ruin of Protestant England, while the high church hoped to protect it.[60] Those binaries fell into a familiar polemical pattern. The twin ideologies of post-Reformation England – anti-popery and anti-puritanism – were structured around contrary couplings of good and evil, defining 'true' Protestants against their anti-Christian others.[61] The 'Church in Danger' campaign was a continuation of anti-puritanism. Its presentation of the dangers of 'Dissenting' hypocrisy, fanaticism and zeal in the early eighteenth century echoed Restoration Anglicanism's condemnation of the danger of 'Nonconformist' hypocrisy, fanaticism and zeal, which in turn echoed conformist Protestant damning of 'puritan' hypocrisy, fanaticism and zeal as a danger to the Elizabethan and Jacobean state. In each case, a true Protestant 'us' defined itself by describing a false Protestant 'them', with mockery and stereotypes used as the means of demarcation. In reusing old jokes, *The Turncoats* dressed current concerns about the prominence of Dissent in the familiar clothes of the 'puritan' stereotype that stretched back to the 1580s, in what amounted to a crude historical logic: *they* have always been like *this*.[62] Old images expressed current fears with new potency.

Settling Scores

But not all the print's ridicule was so conventional or loud. *The Turncoat*'s verses were subtle and allusive, ridiculing hypocrisy

[60] See Sandra J. Sarkela, 'Moderation, Religion and Public Discourse: The Rhetoric of Occasional Conformity in England 1697–1711', *Rhetorica* 15 (1997), 53–79.

[61] Peter Lake, 'Anti-Popery: The Structure of a Prejudice', in idem and Ann Hughes, eds, *Conflict in Early Stuart England* (Harlow, 1989), 70–129.

[62] Adam Morton, 'Fighting Popery with Popery: Subverting Stereotypes and Contesting Anti-Catholicism in Late Seventeenth-Century England', in Koji Yamamoto, ed., *Stereotypes and Stereotyping in Early Modern England: Puritans, Papists and Projectors* (Manchester, 2022), 184–217.

more cuttingly than the blunt crudities of anti-puritan stereotypes. The verses extended the image's ridicule of the Dissenters by accusing them of priestcraft, the practice of fraud, deceit and superstition behind which clergy throughout history had supposedly hidden their sinister pursuit of wealth and power. These charges had been levelled at the established church since the 1690s, a decade in which, Burnet recalled, 'priestcraft grew to become another word in fashion' and 'it became a common topic of discourse to treat all mysteries in religion as the contrivances of priests, to bring the world into a blind submission to them'.[63] The critique was part of a broader intellectual culture that subjected religion to reason to strip away superstition, leaving a primitive faith with a minimal creed, a Christianity spare in mystery.[64] This was an extended attack on Anglican authority, and it fuelled the 'Church in Danger' panic that feared that toleration, freethought and Dissent threatened to undermine the Protestant interest.[65] Freethinkers criticized the Church of England's doctrine, questioned the legitimacy of its political power, and challenged the scriptural basis of its claim to be an heir of the early church. They argued that the bases of clerical authority – doctrine, ritual, ordination and episcopacy – were not inherent in Scripture, but were the fabrications of priests who had slowly corrupted Christianity over the previous millennium, inventing superstitions in the interests of power and gain, and persecuting and censoring those who challenged their monopoly on the sacred. In this, the Anglican church was a sibling of Rome. The charge of priestcraft extended the core tenets of anti-popery to assault the tyranny of all established churches, not just the papal church.[66] The continued dominance of the established church and its attempts to curtail the role of Dissenters in English politics and society despite the

[63] Burnet, *A History of His Own Time*, 4: 387. On priestcraft, see Mark Goldie, 'Priestcraft and the Birth of Whiggism', in Nicholas Phillipson and Quentin Skinner, eds, *Political Discourse in Early Modern Britain* (Cambridge, 1993), 209–31.

[64] Some view claims of 'reform' as masking atheism: see David Berman, *A History of Atheism in England: From Hobbes to Russell* (London, 1987), 1–11, 48–70, 71–92; and Margaret Jacob, *The Radical Enlightenment* (Winchester, MA, 1981), 58, 75–89, 215–56, 280–9.

[65] Hoppit, *A Land of Liberty?*, 223–36.

[66] John Aubrey, *Brief Lives*, ed. Andrew Clark, 2 vols (Oxford, 1989), 1: 358. These themes are considered in Adam Morton and Rachel Hammersley, eds, *Civil Religion in the Early Modern Anglophone World 1550–1700* (Woodbridge, 2024).

comprehensive vision of the Protestant interest outlined in the 1688–9 Revolution were the latest examples of priestcraft at work.

The Turncoats' verses turned these charges of priestcraft on their head. The recent conversions showed that it was the Dissenters and their allies, the false brethren in the low church, who were guilty of priestcraft, self-interested hypocrites who wore principles lightly to mask their hunger for gain. The print mocked the Dissenters with their own language, undermining that language in the process. This was ridicule that cut to the quick, settling scores built up over twenty years of hostility.

This inversion was not immediately apparent. The verses gulled readers, appearing to relay a conventional account of priestcraft's slow ruination of Christianity as described by radicals like Charles Blount, John Dennis and Matthew Tindal.[67] *Priestcraft Expos'd* (1691), for example, depicted all priests as con men who abused religion, muddying faith with mystery to cast the world under their authority.[68] *The Turncoats* aped the language of these histories of priestcraft. Religion was 'Form'd by Heaven, to cultivate Mankind'. Originally, it had been pure, 'Its Rules were easy, and its Precepts plain; | Its Voteries not link'd to Sordid gain', but was corrupted by priests 'when Interest sway'd, | And men, too much, the love of Gold obey'd', selling superstition and conning the laity to buy a place in heaven rather than living by faith. Hypocrisy was the root cause of priestly corruption. History showed that priests changed their principles with the prevailing wind, 'And rather than they'd lose a Benefice, | They'd be of Several Notions in a Trice', sullying religion with politics and interest.

This conspiracy was alive in the present: 'Thus, now a days, tis plainely so we find, | *Int'rest* still rules and governs all mankind'. But where accounts of priestcraft pointed to the established church (particularly its *jure divino* claims to authority), the print targeted Dissent:

> The Subtil, Wily, Scrupulous Dissenter,
> That ne'er before into a Church wou'd Enter,

[67] Charles Blount, *The Oracles of Reason* (London, 1693); John Dennis, *The Danger of Priestcraft* (London, 1702); Matthew Tindal, *An Essay Concerning the Power of the Magistrate* (London, 1697).
[68] Anon., *Priestcraft Expos'd* (London, 1691). See also Edmund Hickeringill, *The History of Priestcraft* (London, 1705).

Lay but a Profitable Post ins Way,
And he'll both hear the Prayers & learn to pray:
The *Common Prayer* shall then be, Masse no more,
Nor will it be unlawfull to Adore,
And worship God; to hear and read and pray,
And stand or kneel in the *Establish'd* way.[69]

Principles were abandoned for profit. When presented with a rich benefice, the Dissenters no longer saw the established church as popish, or the Book of Common Prayer as idolatrous. One (former) Dissenter was singled out:

P_lm_r that once was Zealous for his Cause
T'assert their Rights, and to defend their Laws;
Upon the hopes of being preferr'd laid down
His *Canting long Cloak* and took up the Gown.[70]

Samuel Palmer, the former Presbyterian minister at Gravel Lane, Southwark, had taken orders in the established church in 1709. Parker's conformity was shocking. During the occasional conformity debates of 1703–4, he had been a public champion of Dissent, an advocate of the Dissenting academies attacked by an Anglican hierarchy keen to portray them as seditious conventicles. Palmer's hypocrisy galled because of its self-interest. He was suspected of seeking preferment in the church because he felt undervalued by the Dissenting hierarchy.[71] *The Turncoats* held him up for shame: this was the sort of man who was infiltrating the established church.

The 'Anglican' conversions during the Tory-turn of 1710–11 exposed Dissenters as agents of the priestcraft they decried in others. By inverting the language of priestcraft, the verses underscored the sincerity of the high church party, alluding to Sacheverell in its praise for the few 'Pious, Good and Just' priests who were 'True to their

69 BM Satires, no. 1507. Emphasis original.

70 Ibid. Emphasis original.

71 Palmer championed the academies in two works: Samuel Palmer, *Defence of the Dissenters' Education in their Private Academies* (London, 1703) and idem, *A Vindication of the Learning, Loyalty, morals and most Christian behaviour of the dissenters towards the Church of England* (London, 1704). These responded to Samuel Wesley's *A Letter from a country divine to his friend in London* (London, 1703). William Gibson, *Samuel Welsey and the Crisis of Tory Piety, 1685–1720* (Oxford, 2021), 97–101.

God, Religion, and their Trust'. However, there was no absolute Anglican (sincere)/Dissenter (hypocrite) binary here. Mockery of Palmer bled into broader swathes of ridicule. Dissent was not uniquely crooked:

> Nor are these Men [Dissenters] the only Hypocrites
> There's others that in Interest delight,
> And love a good fat *Benefice* as well …
> For now the World to such a Pass is driven
> That Int'rest is their God, and Gold their heaven.[72]

These hypocrites, the verses implied, were the majority. This was an indictment of the low churchmen who had supported toleration, Dissent and (in the eyes of high churchmen) encouraged and cultivated the freethought that threatened the church. Such men had exposed their true natures in 1688, breaking their oaths to James II to maintain preferment in the established church: 'The *Priests* that always *Right Divine* do boast, | Usually turn'd to what was Uppermost.'[73] But the indictment of hypocrisy went further. Charles Leslie – Tory, nonjuror and ally of Sacheverell – was damned as an arch-hypocrite who 'best can tell' where gain could be found. Leslie had a two-decade track record of vehement opposition to Dissent and the ideological foundations of the post-revolutionary regime (and had engaged in heated polemical exchanges about occasional conformity and passive obedience). Why would a pro-Tory, anti-Dissent print mock a man who was both of those things? In 1710, Leslie's extreme views on the Hanoverian succession (Burnet described him as 'the violentest Jacobite in the nation') led him to sever ties with Sacheverell and the Tories. Outlawed, he fled in 1711 to the Jacobite court at Saint-Germain-en-Laye, just outside Paris, where he advocated for an invasion.[74] Leslie, the print mocked, had turned coat on his own country.

[72] BM Satires, no. 1507. Emphasis original.

[73] Ibid. Emphasis original.

[74] On the Hanoverian succession, see Charles Leslie, *The Good Old Cause, or, Lying in Truth* (London, 1710), written against Burnet. On Dissent, see Leslie's newspaper, *The Rehearsal* (1704–9) and his works *The Wolf-stript of his Shepherd's Clothing* (London, 1704) and *The New Association of those called Moderate Church Men* (London, 1702). On resistance, see his *Cassandra* (London, 1704) and *The Best Answer Ever Made* (London, 1709). Compare also Burnet, *History of His Own Times*, 5: 436; James

The tone of the ridicule here was uncertain. *The Turncoats* was unquestionably part of an anti-Dissent and pro-high church/Sacheverell polemic that celebrated the Tory ascendency of 1710–11. At the same time, the lampooning of hypocrites here was not straightforwardly the us/them of party politics. Because the cast of hypocrites ridiculed was broader than those party boundaries, the print conveyed the impression that religious hypocrisy was pervasive in late Stuart society. *The Turncoats* was ambiguous: it was hostile to Dissent, but not solidly in support of the established church; it celebrated the Tory-high church victory of 1710–11, but worried that the hypocrisy of self-interested, turncoat clergy of many stripes threatened Protestant England despite that victory. This ambiguity responded to fears about religious hypocrisy in the early eighteenth century.

Those fears centred on public figures routinely dissimulating in matters of faith and thereby turning religion into a plaything of party politics. As Knights has shown, accusations of religion being used to cloak self- or party-interest became a normal part of politics. Whig and Tory, and churchmen high and low, competed to define themselves as sincere and moderate by painting their opponents as zealous hypocrites. This competition reached its apogee during the occasional conformity debates. High churchmen accused Dissenters of hypocrisy, but were in turn accused of adopting religious positions for party interests. Hypocrites were now celebrated 'under the name of a Church-Man', claimed the *Naked Truth of Phanaticism Detected* (1705), the 'high' label being merely the 'specious pretence of the Church' to win 'places of trust and authority' and bring down the government.[75] *Faults on Both Sides* (1710) saw the occasional conformity bills as cynical Tory devices designed to 'disable' Dissenters from voting Whig in the elections.[76] This saturation of the public sphere with a promiscuous use of images of hypocrisy was unnerving: 'the claims and counter-claims of hypocrisy and sincerity around the Occasional Conformity Bills reflected a perception that interest rather

Macpherson, ed., *Original Papers: Containing the Secret History of Great Britain*, 2 vols (London, 1775), 2: 211–16.

[75] Gentleman of the Church of England, *The Naked Truth, or Phanaticism Detected* (London, 1705), 2–3.

[76] *A Fourth Collection of Scarce and Valuable Tracts, on the Most Interesting and Entertaining Subjects*, 4 vols (London, 1751), 3: 306.

than conscience prevailed' in religion and that this threatened the public good.[77] *The Turncoats'* ridicule responded to those anxieties.

Laughter

Ridicule expressed contempt: ridiculing someone or something was a public indictment of their worth. 'Affectation', claimed Henry Fielding in 1741, is 'the only source of the true Ridiculous'. Vanity and hypocrisy were the worst affectations. Hypocrisy was the more ridiculous of the two because the gap between the hypocrite's inner and outer lives was greater, and therefore more contemptible, the hypocrite 'endeavours to avoid Censure by concealing vices under an Appearance of their opposite Virtues'.[78] Ridicule exposed those vices, shaming the hypocrite by subjecting them to derisive laughter. Ridicule was potent because it diminished its object.[79] 'They which wittely can … use a nippyng taunte, shalbee able to abolishe a ryghte worthy man', noted Thomas Wilson, and 'no marvaile: for when ye iest is aptly applied, the hearers laugh immediately & who would gladly be laughed to scorn'.[80] The potency of ridicule was seen in satire, which its authors claimed could shame offenders into reforming their vices; in the rough justice with which communities humiliated the shrews, cuckolds and other transgressors of the patriarchal codes that bound them together;[81] and in the use of derogatory libels in popular politics, the unseemly rhymes with which ordinary people protested against authority.[82]

The potency of laughter disturbed early modern society. Caution was urged over who and what should be exposed to contempt. Laughing at religion itself (as opposed to its hypocritical practitioners)

[77] Knights, 'Occasional Conformity', 51.

[78] Henry Fielding, *Joseph Andrews* (London, 1741), ed. Martin C. Battestin (Oxford, 1967), preface, 7–8: quoted in Marcus Walsh, 'Against Hypocrisy and Dissent', in Paddy Bullard, ed., *The Oxford Handbook of Eighteenth-Century Satire* (Oxford, 2019), 39–55, at 39.

[79] Adam Morton, 'Laughter as a Polemical Act in Late Seventeenth-Century England', in Mark Knights and idem, eds, *The Power of Laughter and Satire in Early Modern Britain: Political and Religious Culture, 1500–1820* (Woodbridge, 2017), 107–32.

[80] Thomas Wilson, *The Arte of Rhetorique* (London, 1553), sigs 74^{v}–75^{r}.

[81] Martin Ingram, 'Ridings, Rough Music and "the Reform of Popular Culture" in Early Modern England', *P&P* 105 (1984), 79–113.

[82] Alastair Bellany, 'Railing Rhymes Revisited: Libels, Scandals, and early Stuart Politics', *History Compass* 5 (2007), 1136–79.

was condemned as a path to atheism.[83] Rough laughter was also concerning because it could undermine authority and cause enmity and division. Satirists drew distinctions between their refined ridicule and the hacking raillery of lowly, immoderate mockery that sat uncomfortably with polite ideals.[84] Those ideals did not blunt the appeal of impolite laughter, however, which was a cruel and ever-present feature of eighteenth-century popular culture, as Simon Dickie and Vic Gatrell have shown in detail.[85] Early modern people were unnerved by laughter because they were uncertain about whether its causes were benign or malign. Was it a mark of good fellowship or malice?[86] That uncertainty was reflected in the words they used to describe laughter, which conveyed both mirth and malice. Laughter could be a 'jesting' or a 'scoffing', 'bantering' or 'taunting'.

That uncertainty is present in modern theories of laughter, which fall into three categories: incongruity, superiority and relief.[87] Incongruity theories propose that we laugh when something surprises us. Laughter expresses delight at our expectations being subverted. Wordplay, innuendo and absurdities are obvious examples and were described as sources of mirth in Henry Peacham's *Garden of Eloquence* (1577).[88] Frances Hutchinson discussed laughter in terms of incongruity, presenting it as an expression of wonder at novelty.[89] Where incongruity theories see laughter as benevolent, a good-natured source of pleasure, superiority theories stress its roots in malice and aggression. This understanding, articulated most fully by Thomas Hobbes, claims that laughter expresses the 'sudden glory' we feel in perceiving ourselves superior to a person, action or object.

[83] John Tillotson, *Works* (London, 1696), 40.

[84] John Dryden, *The Satires of Decimus Junius Juevenalis … together with the satires of Aulus Persius Flaccus… to which is prefixed a discourse Concerning the Original and Progress of Satire* (London, 1693), i–lii.

[85] Simon Dickie, *Cruelty and Laughter: Forgotten Comic Literature and the Unsentimental Eighteenth Century* (London and Chicago, IL, 2011); Vic Gatrell, *City of Laughter: Sex and Satire in Eighteenth-Century London* (London, 2006), 110–292.

[86] I am indebted here to Lucy Rayfield, 'Rewriting Laughter in Early Modern Humour', in Daniel Derrin and Hannah Burrows, eds, *The Palgrave History of Humour, History, and Methodology* (London, 2021), 71–91.

[87] Mark Knights and Adam Morton, 'Introduction: Laughter and Satire in Early Modern Britain 1500–1800', in eidem, eds, *The Power of Laughter and Satire*, 1–26, at 2–10.

[88] Henry Peacham, *Garden of Eloquence* (London, 1577), 34.

[89] Frances Hutchinson, *Reflections upon Laughter, and Remarks upon the Fable of the Bees* (Glasgow, 1750), 5–13, 19–22.

It dates from ancient Greece and Rome.[90] Plato described laughter as a malicious joy taken in others' misfortunes; Aristotle noted that we laugh at what is contemptible; and Quintilian characterized it as derisive and capable of diminishing an opponent.[91] Laughter of this sort was used in sermons to convey the superiority of one religious faction over another, to level scorn at stereotypes in jestbooks and plays, and to bind communities together against perceived others.[92]

Relief theories present laughter as a release of pent-up mental and physical tensions. Laughter's reviving properties were widely noted in early modern Europe. In 1553, Wilson claimed that by laughing the mind 'be refreshed, and find some sweete delite'.[93] His views were echoed five years later in Nicholas Udall's claim that 'mirth prolongeth life, and causeth health'.[94] The medicinal nature of laughter was considered most thoroughly in Laurent Joubert's *Traité du ris* (1579), which provided many examples of the physical sensations of laughter as a cure for melancholy and a purgative for the body. These views were shared by other medical commentary on the subject.[95] That commentary saw laughter as a problematic phenomenon, a contrary expression of joy and misery. Timothy Bright's *Treatise of Melancholy* (1586) considered that contradiction head on in the chapter 'Why and how one weepeth for joy, and laugheth for grief'. The answer, Bright explained, lay in nature's fecundity. If the sun's heat can make wax soft but clay hard, why should sorrow not elicit tears and laughter?[96] For Joubert, because we laugh at what is ugly, laughter must ultimately relate to misery. Medical writing presented the physical effects of laughter as a reflex to tensions caused by the clash of joy and misery, shaking strains out of the mind and body.

Incongruity, superiority and relief are seen as competing theories weighed against each other to find the 'best' explanation of laughter.

[90] Thomas Hobbes, *Leviathan*, ed. Richard Tuck (Oxford, 1996), 91–111; Quentin Skinner, 'Hobbes and the Classical Theory of Laughter', in Tom Sorell and Luc Foisneau, eds, *Leviathan after 350 Years* (Oxford, 2004), 139–66.

[91] Plato, *Philebus*, transl. Justin Gosling (Oxford, 1975), 51; Aristotle, *Poetics*, chs 2 and 3; transl. Stephen Halliwell (Cambridge, MA, 1987), 33 and 36.

[92] Daniel Derrin, 'Self-Referring Deformities: Humour in Early Modern Sermon Literature', *Literature and Theology* 32 (2018), 255–69.

[93] Wilson, *Arte of Rhetorique*, sig. 75.

[94] Quoted in Rayfield, 'Revisiting Laughter', 80.

[95] Laurent Jourbert, *Traité du ris* (Paris, 1579), 16–17, 33, 125–34, 330–5; Rayfield, 'Rewriting Laughter', 81–4.

[96] Timothy Bright, *Treatise of Melancholy* (London, 1586), 14.

It is more useful to see them as complementary, with aspects of all three present in each instance of laughter. This rings true for ridicule: we laugh at being surprised by a witty conceit (incongruity) that expresses scorn at what is mocked (superiority), which in turn releases pent-up hostility towards that object (relief). We see this combination in *The Turncoats*. The print's ridiculous image is *incongruous* (conscience worn as lightly as clothes); its mockery was *superior* and directed anger and contempt at hypocrites (who were laughed to scorn); and by providing its viewers with an outlet for those hostile emotions, the laughter it elicited *relieved*. There were plenty of anxieties to relieve during 1709–11, when the pervasiveness of hypocrisy in public life had caused a collapse of trust in politics. *The Turncoats*' uncertain ridicule spoke to those fears, expressing joy that the Tory-high church had triumphed over the Dissenters and low churchmen it mocked, and anguish at the fact that the hypocrisy it exposed continued to threaten the church. That anguish is expressed by the only character in the print who does not jest. Horrified by the hypocrisy they witness in the tailor's shop, the labourer on the far right evokes Sacheverell in the hope he can save them: 'I'll go to St Mary Overy's and pray for the Doctor'.[97] The Tories had won, but the church was still in danger.

Conclusion

That prints like *The Turncoats* were ephemeral does not mean that they were unsophisticated. The satire's witty conceit told old jokes in new ways, using laughter as a weapon at a moment of political change. Its ridicule was both a product of and a response to a defining problem of that moment: hypocrisy. Ridicule appealed because it evoked moral emotions such as anger and contempt, deriding the worth of one group (Dissenters/low church) to assert the superiority of another (high church/Tories). It also unnerved. Exposing hypocrisy ultimately served to highlight its existence as a real and present danger to eighteenth-century society. It has been argued that much lay behind laughter. *The Turncoats* built on older traditions and stereotypes, twisting anti-popery, anti-puritanism and the language of priestcraft to the polemical purposes of the present. Familiarity

[97] BM Satires, no.1507. St. Mary's was Sacheverell's parish.

ensured that the thrust of the print's anti-Dissenter and pro-Sacheverell mockery was intelligible to even those with only a cursory grasp of politics, while asides to Leslie, Palmer and priestcraft appealed to the more informed, the knowing viewers who could appreciate the closeness of the mockery. Graphic satires did not simplify or reduce debates. They were not secondary sources of politics, synopses of opinion developed elsewhere in political discourse, but sophisticated pieces of political commentary in their own right.[98]

[98] I have made similar claims about prints made in an earlier period: see Adam Morton, 'Popery, Politics, and Play: Visual Culture in Succession Crisis England', *Seventeenth Century* 31 (2016), 411–49; and idem, 'Intensive Ephemera: *The Catholick Gamesters* and the Visual Culture of News in Restoration London', in Simon Davies and Puck Fletcher, eds, *News in Early Modern Europe: Currents and Connections* (Leiden, 2014), 115–40.

The Problems of Performing Piety in some Exeter Dissenting Sermons *c.*1660–1745

David Parry*

University of Exeter

This article explores the theme of hypocrisy in a multi-volume collection of hitherto unstudied manuscript sermons by Exeter Dissenting ministers from the Restoration to the mid-eighteenth century, held by the Devon and Exeter Institution. In these sermons, the theme of hypocrisy is addressed in a variety of senses and contexts, including the imposition by conformists of forms of worship not required by Scripture; the false accusations of hypocrisy made against Dissenters; the insincere performance of piety; the tendency of sinners to justify vice as virtue and virtue as vice; and the incompatibility of persecution with true New Testament Christianity. These sermons trace a move from Reformed orthodoxy towards rational Dissent, with a soteriology that increasingly makes moral performance a condition of final salvation. The possibility of insincere performance of piety and virtue by hypocrites may have created increased anxiety in a context in which soteriology and ethics were increasingly entangled.

Hypocrisy was a double-edged term for puritans and Protestant Dissenters from the sixteenth to the eighteenth centuries. While 'the hotter sort of Protestants'[1] were often suspected by their

* The research for this article was undertaken as part of the Leverhulme Trust-funded project 'Writing Religious Conflict and Community in Exeter, 1500–1750' (RPG-2020-404). I am grateful to the staff and volunteers of the Devon and Exeter Institution, especially Paul Auchterlonie (who first alerted me to the existence of these MSS), Sonia Llewellyn and Beth Howell. I am also grateful to James Honeyford, Robert Strivens, Kathleen Lynch, Anna Pravdica, Robert Wainwright and the anonymous readers for SCH for their helpful feedback. Department of English and Creative Writing, University of Exeter, Queen's Building, The Queen's Drive, Exeter, EX4 4QH. E-mail: d.parry@exeter.ac.uk.

[1] A phrase applied to puritans by Percival Wiburn, *A Checke or Reproofe of M. Howlet's Untimely Schreeching in her Majesties Eares* (London, 1581), fol. 15^{v}, popularized in modern scholarship through its citation by Patrick Collinson, *The Elizabethan Puritan Movement* (London, 1967; repr. Oxford, 1990), 27.

Studies in Church History 60 (2024), 340–362
doi: 10.1017/stc.2024.15

neighbours and opponents of a performative piety that hid moral failings and religious delusions – as evidenced by literary caricatures of puritan hypocrites, from Ben Jonson's Zeal-of-the-Land Busy to Samuel Butler's Hudibras – the hypocrite was also a category that generated anxiety within puritan and Dissenting circles.[2] Within the context of puritan and later Nonconformist practical divinity, the hypocrite was not simply one who pretended to moral virtue while lacking it in practice, but one who professed saving faith while, in fact, being devoid of it.

As literary scholars have noted, John Webster's revenge tragedy *The White Devil* (1612) – which involves the hypocritical performance of virtue by murderous Italians, including a cardinal who becomes pope – was performed less than a year before a Paul's Cross sermon entitled *The White Devil, or the Hypocrite Uncased* was preached by the Bedfordshire minister Thomas Adams in March 1613.[3] Adams, and probably Webster, borrowed the phrase 'the white devil' from Luther's commentary on Galatians, in which Luther remarks that 'This white Deuill which forceth men to commit spirituall sinnes, that they may sell them for righteousnes, is farre more daungerous then the blacke deuill, which onely enforceth them to commit fleshly sinnes which the world acknowledgeth to be sinnes.'[4] Luther's 'white devil' refers to a more subtle and more deadly form of hypocrisy than the scheming poisoners of Webster's play. The agents of the white devil, in the context of Luther's commentary, are on a human level 'religious, wise, and learned men' who are not guilty of 'those grosse vices which are against the second table'

[2] On accusations of puritan hypocrisy and the figure of the 'stage puritan', see, for instance, Patrick Collinson, 'Ecclesiastical Vitriol: Religious Satire in the 1590s and the Invention of Puritanism', in John Guy, ed., *The Reign of Elizabeth I: Court and Culture in the Last Decade* (Cambridge, 1995), 150–70; idem, 'Antipuritanism', in John Coffey and Paul C. H. Lim, eds, *The Cambridge Companion to Puritanism* (Cambridge, 2008), 19–33; Kristen Poole, *Radical Religion from Shakespeare to Milton: Figures of Nonconformity in Early Modern England* (Cambridge, 2000); Peter Lake with Michael Questier, *The Antichrist's Lewd Hat: Protestants, Papists and Players in Post-Reformation England* (New Haven, CT, 2002), esp. chs 13–15 (521–700).

[3] Thomas Adams, *The White Devil, or the Hypocrite Uncased: In a Sermon Preached at Pauls Crosse, March 7. 1612* [i.e. 1613] (London, 1613). See, for example, Emma Rhatigan, 'Reading the White Devil in Thomas Adams and John Webster', in Adrian Streete, ed., *Early Modern Drama and the Bible: Contexts and Readings, 1570–1625* (London, 2012), 176–94.

[4] Martin Luther, *A Commentarie of M. Doctor Martin Luther upon the Epistle of S. Paul to the Galathians* [*sic*] (London, 1575), 20–1. Adams cites Luther in *The White Devil*, 1–2.

of the Ten Commandments.[5] Rather, in seeking salvation through human works and penances, Luther sees these men as denying the righteousness of Christ, freely given through faith, thus denying salvation to themselves and their followers.

This radicalization by Luther of the notion of hypocrisy that sees even, and especially, those who strive to live righteously as potential hypocrites, anticipates the soteriological anxiety that came to surround the notion of hypocrisy, especially among the hotter sort of English Protestants known as puritans and their successors in post-Restoration Protestant Dissent. The emphasis of Dissenting piety on sincerity of heart, intensifying concerns articulated in the sixteenth-century Reformation, generated anxiety, since the heart can only be known by the outward signs of speech, behaviour and the outward forms of worship, all of which can be counterfeited.[6] As Matthew J. Smith notes in his introductory essay for a special issue of *Christianity and Literature* on the history of sincerity, 'Protestants often described the sincerity of contrition as un-searchably internal, but for this reason, and paradoxically, the purity of outwardly visible practice accumulated new importance as a testimony to that internal reality.'[7] The paradox that Smith attributes to early modern Protestants in general is arguably even more true of the hotter sort of Protestants and their Dissenting offspring. As I note in the same issue of *Christianity and Literature*: 'Such culturally pervasive early modern anxieties about the gap between inner reality and outward performance are reflected in Puritan attacks on the "hypocrite" – that is, the person who plays the part of a believer but is not truly so'.[8]

[5] Luther, *Galathians*, 20. For Luther and hypocrisy, see in this volume Charlotte Methuen, '"God really hated the hypocrites": Hypocrisy and Anti-clerical Rhetoric in the Early Lutheran Reformation'.

[6] On the opposition between sincerity and hypocrisy in both conformist and Nonconformist sermons in the mid- to late seventeenth century, see in this volume Anna Pravdica, '"See sincerity sparkle in thy practice": Antidotes to Hypocrisy in British Print Sermons, 1640–95'. On the sixteenth-century reformers' emphasis on sincerity as a concord between one's heart, words and actions, see, for instance, John Martin, 'Inventing Sincerity, Refashioning Prudence: The Discovery of the Individual in Renaissance Europe', *American Historical Review* 102 (1997), 1309–42, esp. 1329–33.

[7] Matthew J. Smith, 'w/Sincerity, Part I: The Drama of the Will from Augustine to Milton', *Christianity and Literature* 67 (2017), 8–33, at 18.

[8] David Parry, '"A Divine Kind of Rhetoric": Rhetorical Strategy and Spirit-Wrought Sincerity in English Puritan Writing', *Christianity and Literature* 67 (2017), 113–38, at

This article explores the treatment of the theme of hypocrisy in a series of manuscript sermons by Exeter Dissenting ministers held in the archives of the Devon and Exeter Institution (DEI) that I believe are as yet unstudied, as no reference to them appears in key secondary studies of Protestant Dissent in Exeter that I would otherwise expect to cite them.[9] The DEI has catalogued as one collection twenty-six volumes of manuscript material, in several hands and bound in a variety of physical formats, from short quarto and octavo to substantial folio volumes. The collection is made up predominantly of sermon texts, many written out in full, but some presented as notes under brief heads or in shorthand notation. The collection also includes handwritten religious material other than sermons per se, such as catechisms, topical and controversial religious treatises, and historical notes on Scripture, all of which merit further study. This article will focus on the sermons to be found in the first sixteen volumes of the collection (DEI MSS 143.1–16), all of which appear to be written in the same hand, which are bound in volumes of a uniform size (*c.*165 x 105 mm), and therefore show internal evidence of forming a cohesive collection prior to acquisition by the DEI. These sixteen volumes contain a total of 297 sermons across 7,617 pages, which take the form of full-length sermons written out in longhand rather than summary notes.

Although I have not identified the scribe, at least in the case of the two sermons attributed to James Peirce it is evident that the scribe is not the preacher, since the volume in which these sermons appear (DEI MSS 143.2) contains a sermon in the same hand referring to Peirce's death. It seems likely that the scribe is not the preacher of

114. See also Michael P. Winship, 'Weak Christians, Backsliders, and Carnal Gospelers: Assurance of Salvation and the Pastoral Origins of Puritan Practical Divinity in the 1580s', *ChH* 70 (2001), 462–81, at 474–6; Leif Dixon, *Practical Predestinarians in England,* c.*1590–1640* (Farnham, 2014), esp. 39, 130–8, 273–4, 322–7.

9 Key secondary studies of Dissent in Exeter and the Exeter Controversy in particular include Allan Brockett, *Nonconformity in Exeter 1650–1875* (Manchester, 1962); Fred J. Powicke, 'Arianism and the Exeter Assembly', *Transactions of the Congregational History Society* 7 (1916–18), 34–43; Roger Thomas, 'The Non-Subscription Controversy amongst Dissenters in 1719: The Salters' Hall Debate', *JEH* 4 (1953), 162–86; William Gibson, *Religion and the Enlightenment 1600–1800: Conflict and the Rise of Civic Humanism in Taunton* (Oxford and New York, 2007); Bracy V. Hill, 'The Language of Dissent: The Defense of Eighteenth-Century English Dissent in the Works and Sermons of James Peirce' (PhD thesis, Baylor University, 2011); and David L. Wykes, 'The 1719 Salters' Hall Debate: Its Significance for the History of Dissent', in Stephen Copson, ed., *Trinity, Creed and Confusion: The Salters' Hall Debates of 1719* (Oxford, 2020), 31–61.

any of the sermons, but a third party who transcribed the sermons either from oral delivery or from earlier manuscript sources.[10] I have not found certain evidence of the scribe's identity, but one intriguing clue is that the fifteenth volume is inscribed 'F. Hallett 1747' on the front free endpaper (the right-hand page facing the inside of the front cover board).[11] This name and date potentially correspond to Frances Hallett, widow of the minister Joseph Hallett III who preached some of these sermons. This may point towards a familial preservation of Exeter Dissenting heritage in transcribing these sermons, though it is also possible that Frances could be the volumes' owner, but not their scribe.

The majority of sermons in these sixteen volumes are undated and appear to represent weekly morning and evening Sunday services. A handful of dated sermons were clearly preached on special occasions, including public and private fast days, the birthday of George II, the anniversary of the Gunpowder Plot, and the deaths of local Dissenters. Most of these sermons focus on matters of everyday faith and practice, such as prayer and temperate living, but they also address topics as wide-ranging as arguments for the afterlife, the nature of angels, and providentialist readings of English history. In these sermons, hypocrisy is addressed in a variety of senses and contexts, including the imposition by conformists of forms of worship not required by Scripture; the false accusations of hypocrisy made against Dissenters; the insincere performance of piety, even by some professing Dissenters, who are thus judged by these sermons to be in fact hypocrites; the tendency of sinners to justify vice as virtue and virtue as vice; and the incompatibility of persecution with true New Testament Christianity.

In the early modern period, Exeter was a key centre for the hotter sort of Protestantism.[12] Following the Restoration, Exeter's puritan

[10] On the relationship between oral, manuscript and printed sermons in this period, see, for instance, Jennifer Farooq, *Preaching in Eighteenth-Century London* (Woodbridge, 2013), esp. 144–50. For excellent discussions of these dynamics more widely, compare, on an earlier period, Arnold Hunt, *The Art of Hearing: English Preachers and their Audiences, 1590–1640* (Cambridge, 2010), esp. 131–63, and, in relation to New England, Meredith Marie Neuman, *Jeremiah's Scribes: Creating Sermon Literature in Puritan New England* (Philadelphia, PA, 2013).

[11] Exeter, Devon and Exeter Institution [hereafter: DEI], MSS 143.15, front free endpaper.

[12] On Exeter's religious politics from the sixteenth century to the Restoration, see, for example, Brockett, *Nonconformity in Exeter*, 1–17 (ch. 1, 'Before the Restoration'); Mark Stoyle, *From Deliverance to Destruction: Rebellion and Civil War in an English City* (Exeter, 1996); and Bernard Capp, *England's Culture Wars: Puritan Reformation*

leanings led to the presence of a substantial population of Protestant Dissenters. A nationwide 1715 survey of Nonconformist congregations by the London Presbyterian minister, John Evans, identified three Presbyterian meetings in the city with a combined attendance of 2,250, as well as an Independent congregation with 400 hearers, a Baptist congregation of 300, and 120 French Protestants.[13] Exeter was also the usual location for the meetings of the United Brethren of Devon and Cornwell, often known as the Exeter Assembly, a voluntary association of Presbyterian and Independent ministers across the region that cooperated for mutual counsel, the subsidy of poorer congregations, and the training, licensing and discipline of ministers from 1690 to the mid-eighteenth century.

Within the sixteen volumes of manuscript sermons under consideration here, many of the sermons are unattributed, but those that are attributed are assigned to four preachers who hail from the dominant Presbyterian strand of Exeter Dissent: Robert Atkins (1628/9–85); 'the Revd. Mr. Joseph Hallett' (i.e. Joseph Hallett II, 1656–1722);[14] the 'late Reverend Mr. J: P:', identifiable as James Peirce (1674–1726); and 'the Reverend Mr Jos: Hallett, Junr.' (i.e. Joseph Hallett III, bap. 1691, d. 1744).[15] Robert Atkins was a member of the founding generation of post-Restoration Dissenting ministers, being ejected from a parish living at St John's Exeter in 1662, having previously been a parish minister in Essex and then a preacher to the Presbyterian congregation of East Peter's that occupied half of Exeter Cathedral in the Interregnum. Atkins retained the respect of many conformists, including the bishop of Exeter, John Gauden, who intervened to have Atkins released when imprisoned on charges of slander, although this did not preclude Atkins from incurring several fines for preaching to conventicles in his house.[16]

and Its Enemies in the Interregnum, 1649–1660 (Oxford, 2012), 240–56 (ch. 12, 'Exeter: Godly Rule in Action').

13 London, DWL, MS 38.4, cited in Brockett, *Nonconformity in Exeter*, 71. Exeter also had a Quaker population, not included in Evans's Survey, perhaps as the Friends lay outside the boundaries of orthodox Dissent. On the Exeter Friends, see Brockett, *Nonconformity in Exeter*, esp. 15–16, 52–4, 61–2, 72, 111–13, 115–16.

14 DEI, MSS 143.1, contents page.

15 DEI, MSS 143.2, contents page.

16 Stephen Wright, 'Atkins [Adkins], Robert (1628/9–1685), clergyman and ejected minister', *ODNB*, online edn (2004), at: <https://doi.org/10.1093/ref:odnb/166>, accessed 25 January 2024; Brockett, *Nonconformity in Exeter*, 12, 21–30, 35–7, 45–7.

The two Joseph Halletts in these notebooks need disambiguating, a challenge made all the more complicated by the fact that there were three Joseph Halletts across three generations, all of whom were Dissenting ministers in Exeter. The three Halletts are conveniently differentiated by historians with Roman numerals. Joseph Hallett I (bap. 1620, d. 1689) was a parish clergyman in Somerset prior to his ejection at the Restoration in 1660 and, after some time ministering to a conventicle in Dorset, was licensed as a Presbyterian preacher in Exeter in 1672. Hallett I eventually became the first minister of James's Meeting, the largest of Exeter's four Presbyterian meeting houses, built in 1687 and named in honour of James II's declaration of indulgence of that year.[17] Given that one of the sermons attributed to Joseph Hallett Jr in this collection is dated after the death of Joseph Hallett II, it appears that, in the context of these notebooks at least, 'the Revd. Mr. Joseph Hallett' refers to Joseph Hallett II (1656–1722), and 'the Reverend Mr Jos: Hallett, Junr.' refers not to Hallett II (as one might suppose), but to Joseph Hallett III (bap. 1691, d. 1744).[18]

While Robert Atkins was an orthodox Trinitarian Presbyterian, Joseph Halletts II and III, alongside James Peirce, were key players in a controversy that split the Nonconformist community, not only in Exeter, but across the nation; a controversy variously referred to as the Exeter Controversy or the Exeter Arian Controversy. Joseph Hallett II was his father's assistant at James's Meeting, continuing as assistant minister to his father's successor, George Trosse, and becoming pastor of the congregation on Trosse's death in 1713,

[17] On Joseph Hallett I, see Alexander Gordon, rev. Stephen Wright, 'Hallett, Joseph (bap. 1620, d. 1689), clergyman and ejected minister', *ODNB*, online edn (2004), at: <https://doi.org/10.1093/ref:odnb/12008>, accessed 25 January 2024; Brockett, *Nonconformity in Exeter*, esp. 30, 36–7, 40–2, 45–6, 56, 67.

[18] On Joseph Hallett II, see David L. Wykes, 'Hallett, Joseph (1656–1722), Presbyterian minister and tutor', *ODNB*, online edn (2004), at: <https://doi.org/10.1093/ref:odnb/12009>, accessed 25 January 2024; Brockett, *Nonconformity in Exeter*, esp. 48, 62, 67, 77, 79, 82, 87–9, 92–5, 97–8. On Joseph Hallett III, see David L. Wykes, 'Hallett [Hallet], Joseph (bap. 1691, d. 1744), Presbyterian minister and biblical scholar', *ODNB*, online edn (2004), at: <https://doi.org/10.1093/ref:odnb/12010>, accessed 25 January 2024; Brockett, *Nonconformity in Exeter*, esp. 71, 78, 94, 113–14; Arthur W. Wainwright, 'Locke's Influence on the Exegesis of Peirce, Hallett, and Benson', in Luisa Simonutti, ed., *Locke and Biblical Hermeneutics: Conscience and Scripture* (Cham, 2019), 189–205.

with James Peirce appointed as his assistant.[19] From around 1713, a group of students at the Exeter Academy – the first of three Dissenting academies in Exeter, educating both laity and candidates for the Dissenting ministry, of which Hallett II was principal – secretly discussed, and in some cases adopted, Arian views on the Trinity. The group included Hallett II's son Joseph Hallett III. After these views came into the open in November 1716, the ensuing controversy saw the Exeter Assembly, after consulting colleagues in London, require ministers to affirm their belief in the orthodox doctrine of the Trinity at their meeting of May 1719. Those who refused included Hallett II and Peirce, who had by then already been expelled from the congregation of which they were ministers. Indeed, the locks on James's meeting house were changed without warning in March 1719 so they were unable to enter. Hallett II and Peirce's followers erected a new meeting house, known as the Mint Meeting, in which they were able to continue ministering to a congregation of Arian Nonconformists, whose non-Trinitarian views technically placed them outside the legal scope of toleration. Joseph Hallett III in turn became Peirce's co-minister at the Mint Meeting on his father's death in 1722.

'Gaudy Ceremonies' vs 'Gospel Simplicity'

Given that three of the four named preachers in these notebooks were on the non-Trinitarian side of the Exeter Controversy, it is striking that only a minority of the sermons explicitly advocate a heterodox view of the Godhead.[20] Many of the sermons reflect the preaching

[19] On Peirce, see David L. Wykes, 'Peirce, James (1674–1726)', *ODNB*, online edn (2004), at: <https://doi.org/10.1093/ref:odnb/21782>, accessed 25 January 2024; Wainwright, 'Locke's Influence on the Exegesis of Peirce, Hallett, and Benson', 189–97, 204–5; and esp. Hill, 'The Language of Dissent'.

[20] The Trinitarian controversy is outside the primary focus of this article. Sermons by Joseph Hallett III in particular occasionally advocate directly a subordinationist Christology, in which the Son is a distinct being who is not equal to the Father and is not to be given equal worship (for example, see his sermon on John 15:9: DEI, MSS 143.3, 102–24). Robert Atkins's sermons predate the split, and he appears to be an orthodox Trinitarian. For instance, in speaking of the roles of the three persons of the Godhead in salvation, he teaches 'That the whole Trinity, Father, Son, and Holy Ghost, do joyntly concur in this great work, to destroy the works of the devil in us. According to that known Maxim, those works of God that do respect the Creature, they are the joynt works and operations of the whole Trinity': DEI, MSS 143.7, 169–70. Atkins here paraphrases the

styles, piety, practices and perspectives common to Dissenters as a whole. For example, these sermons consistently polemicize against the ceremonies of the established church not contained in Scripture and the imposition of religious conformity, while recognizing that some members and ministers of the established church are truly godly.[21]

In a sermon on the need for a broken and a contrite heart, Joseph Hallett II attacks the hypocrisy of formalist ritual performance, which he particularly associates with the ceremonies of the established church:

> So little do ritual performances, tho' instituted by God himself, please him, when they are mere formalities, which they are always, where the heart is unhumbled, is not broken with a sense of sin, and sorrow for it, and when the Life is Unreformed. Much less are guady [*sic*] Ceremonies of Mens Appointment, such as Crosses, and Bowings, and Cringes, and white Garments, and the like, pleasing to God; when the heart is haughty, and proud, and the Life full of cruelty, oppression, and Scandalous Revilings of others.[22]

Hallett II tells us here that a sincerely repentant heart, rather than only outward forms of worship, is required to be accepted by God. This is the case even with those 'ritual performances' instituted by God, in the context of referring to the Old Testament sacrificial system with which the psalmist compares the broken and contrite heart. Conformist ceremonial worship, however, since it is only of 'Mens Appointment', is even further from pleasing God, although even Dissenters can be mere formalists and hypocrites if their hearts are unhumbled.

In another sermon, Joseph Hallett II links the contrast between ceremony and simplicity in worship more explicitly to the divisions

---

patristic maxim *opera trinitatis ad extra indivisa sunt* ('the external works of the Trinity are indivisible').

[21] Thus, for instance, while lamenting the established church's failure to accept godly Dissenters as Christians on an equal footing, Joseph Hallett III extends this courtesy to godly members of the established church: 'And thus we lay our Communion open (not indeed to profane men, and Unbelievers, but) to all serious, and faithful Christians, how much soever they may differ from us in matters not relating to salvation': DEI, MSS 143.5, 438.

[22] DEI, MSS 143.1, 147.

between conformists and Dissenters. Speaking of offence that is 'taken, but not given',[23] he expounds:

> Thus some are offended with those of the Dissenting way among us, because they do not worship God in the parish Churches; as if there were some what of holiness in their Churches, and as if the place made their Services the better, and the more acceptable to God, and the more profitable to the people. They will not hear a serious profitable discourse in a Meeting-House; they are offended because of the place, as if a pious Discourse was the worse for the place. This is an offence taken, but not given. Thus some are apt to be offended at the worship of God, when it is not set off with a great deal of pomp and Pageantry; as if a gaudy worship was the most acceptable to God: and a worship with Gospel Simplicity was to be disregarded.[24]

In this sermon, Hallett II does not deny that holiness can be found in the parish churches, only that it is inevitably tied to the place. It is interesting to note that 'gaudy worship' continues to be a concern for Dissenters decades after the struggle between puritans and Laudians.

Yet the accusation of hypocrisy is a double-edged one in the intra-Protestant polemic between Dissenters and conformists. The preachers of these sermons address how one should deal with false accusations of hypocrisy, including those that are laid against Dissenters by conformists. While advising in general against Christians speaking too highly of their progress in virtue and godliness, Joseph Hallett III makes the concession that it is right to vindicate one's character against false accusations of hypocrisy where the honour of true religion is at stake. He argues that 'Your clear reputation is a mean of supporting the honour of God, and of Religion, which would suffer thro' your disgrace'.[25] Giving biblical examples of self-defence from Job and St Paul, Hallett III observes that:

> After these Examples, it is always allowable for you to speak in your own just and necessary defense. If you are accused as hypocrites, you may modestly declare that you are the sincere servants of God. If you are accused as unrighteous and ungenerous, you may modestly speak of

[23] Ibid. 269.
[24] Ibid. 270–1.
[25] DEI, MSS 143.5, 304.

> the instances of Justice which you have shewn, and of the liberal alms that your hands have bestow'd.[26]

The vindication of Dissenters from charges of hypocrisy is a necessary aspect of the vindication of the godliness of the Dissenting cause.

'A SUBTILE DEVIL': PARADIASTOLE AND DIABOLICAL DISSIMULATION

Yet the preachers of these Exeter Dissenting sermons also concede that there are indeed hypocrites among their hearers. The fact of professing godly faith and adhering to a Dissenting congregation does not guarantee sincere repentance, upright life or saving faith on the part of the professing Nonconformist. In a sermon focused specifically on the topic of hypocrisy, Joseph Hallett III warns that 'This Delight in Piety and Virtue may be counterfeited' since,

> It is the natural Temper of a corrupt Heart to deceive it self, and the World, with a vain shew; and by the help of a subtile Devil, it soon finds out many Inventions, which shall, at first sight, resemble Grace, and not be distinguish'd from it, without a strict Examination, and careful Comparison.[27]

What is especially anxiety-inducing here for Hallett III and his hearers is that the hypocritical 'corrupt Heart' is capable of deceiving not only the outside world, but also itself. The hypocrite may thus falsely believe himself or herself to be sincere, since the devil is 'subtile' enough to counterfeit even the effects of divine grace, a counterfeit that can be discerned, but only with difficulty, through the tools of 'strict Examination, and careful Comparison' advocated by Nonconformist practical divinity. The 'subtile Devil' here has resonances with Luther's 'white devil', bringing to mind a soteriological anxiety about the counterfeiting of inward faith, as well as the counterfeiting of outward actions.

In this sermon, Hallett III outlines both blatantly egregious forms of hypocrisy, characterized by clearly visible impiety and immorality in outward behaviour, and the more outwardly respectable, but in fact more spiritually deadly forms of hypocrisy, in which one might deceive others, and even oneself, by a show of piety and virtue while

[26] Ibid. 308.
[27] DEI, MSS 143.6, 339–40.

lacking true inward faith. He speaks of the Israelite king Jehu, who 'pretended a Zeal for the Lord' in cutting off Ahab's house and the priests and worshippers of Baal, but continues: 'Yet there was no sincerity in this. For still he took no heed to walk in the Law of the Lord God of Israel, with all his heart'.[28] Sincere faith requires a wholeheartedness, not merely outwardly zealous actions. Where Jehu counterfeited a godly zeal, Hallett III observes:

> In like manner every other Grace may be counterfeited. And no Marvel: since Satan has transform'd him self into an Angel of Light. 2 Cor.XI.14. Now, if the Devil, who is a complete sinner, can appear like an Angel of Perfection, how much more easy is it for a Man that is not so wholly abandon'd to Vice, to imitate in appearance, an imperfect Saint?[29]

Here natural virtue, the human goodness that derives from common grace but is insufficient for salvation, contributes towards hypocrisy rather than working against it, since it can give the appearance of the working of saving grace that is only present within the true saints of God. However, the distinction between the two is muddied by the fact that the obedience of the saints is never perfect in this life, and thus the sins of the saints, that may make them appear to be hypocrites, act as cover for those who are truly hypocrites in their lack of the grace they profess to possess.

Those who are carnal and thus lacking the Holy Spirit within them to sanctify them can perform the outward forms of godly exercises, including religious practices characteristic of the Nonconformist community:

> Tis very possible, for instance, that a carnal Mind, which is enmity to God, and can take no Pleasure in Communion with him, may yet pretend to his Acquaintance, that he rejoyces, when the Lord's Day is come, and that another Opportunity, for going into God's Presence.

[28] Ibid. 340.

[29] Ibid. 340–1. 2 Cor. 11: 14 regarding Satan transforming himself into an angel of light is quoted in another context by Joseph Hallett III in a sermon on angels: 'Another title given to the good angels is, Angels of Light, 2. Cor. XI. 14. And no marvel, for Satan himself is transformed into an Angel of Light: that is, he acts as if he were an Angel of Light': DEI, MSS 143.3, 389. On the use of this biblical text in doctrinal controversies of the patristic era, see in this volume Sophie Lunn-Rockliffe, 'The Devil as "Father of Lies": Ideas of Diabolical Deceit in the Donatist Controversy'.

> Tis possible such a one may, in the Church, manifest to those around him the outward and usual Tokens of Seriousness, and Pleasure, such as lifting up the hands and Eyes, and a calm attentive look, that shall seem to express an undisturb'd Mind: and yet all the while, he may be so far from delighting in Acts of Devotion, as to wish in his heart that the day were over, and he might return without fear of Men's censure, to the pursuit of a beloved World, and to the Gratification of his Carnal Lusts.[30]

This is a form of hypocrisy in which the performer of godly piety deceives his companions, but there is an even deeper and more insidious form of hypocrisy that Hallett III highlights: 'But there is another kind of Hypocrisy, which is more difficult to be discern'd, and therefore the more dangerous and fatal'.[31] In this form of hypocrisy, the hypocrite deceives even his own heart, feeling a subjective sense of pleasure in obeying some divinely ordained duties, but yet not truly, in St Paul's phrase, 'delight[ing] in the law of God after the inward man' (Rom. 7.22).[32] The self-deceived hypocrite may even feel religious emotion in response to the means of grace: 'A Man, who lives in a continued Course of fleshly Lusts, all the week, may, I believe, be really affected under a Sermon, or in the Prayers of the Church, yet this is mere hypocrisy after all.'[33] Hallett III elaborates that the one who sincerely rejoices in obedience to God 'has a heart that is pleased in every Duty, without Exception: so far, at least, as that his Pleasure prevails over his Reluctance; or, in other words, that his Delight in every Virtue is greater than his Aversion to it'.[34] It is not enough to take pleasure in obedience to God in some things: for instance, being fervent in prayer while oppressing the poor. Only the one who takes pleasure in all divinely ordained duties can be deemed to have sincere and saving faith. Hallett III's emphasis on the need for a searching self-examination owes much to the puritan practical divinity of the sixteenth and seventeenth centuries, but his emphasis on duty and the moral affections as the means of distinguishing sincerity from hypocrisy echoes perhaps more the

[30] DEI, MSS 143.6, 342–3.
[31] Ibid. 343.
[32] The possibility of self-deceiving hypocrites was also raised in this period across the Atlantic by Jonathan Edwards: see Ava Chamberlain, 'Self-Deception as a Theological Problem in Jonathan Edwards's *Treatise concerning Religious Affections*', *ChH* 63 (1994), 541–56.
[33] DEI, MSS 143.6, 343–4.
[34] Ibid. 344.

emphases of the moral philosophy and divinity of the long eighteenth century.[35]

The passage from 2 Corinthians 11 cited by Joseph Hallett III regarding Satan transforming himself into an angel of light is also cited by the sixteenth-century German rhetorician Johannes Susenbrotus in relation to the rhetorical figure of paradiastole, which excuses a vice by redescribing it as a virtue that it resembles (for instance, calling cowardice prudence or rashness, courage). Susenbrotus observes: 'we have an example of *paradiastole* when vices show themselves under the guise of virtue, and by this means even the Devil himself can be transfigured into an Angel of light.'[36] The paradiastolic dynamic is one that is invoked both in more secular early modern moral philosophy, and in puritan practical divinity, to explore the subtleties of vice and satanic temptation, and it is one that surfaces numerous times in these Exeter Dissenting sermons.[37]

In one of the seventeenth-century sermons by Robert Atkins, for instance, we read:

> And so some Covetous persons, they labour to justify their covetous practices, under the notion of honest thrift, and good husbandry. So some drunkards, they will Nick-name that sin of theirs, and say, it is but good fellowship, and boon-companions, what harm is there in it?[38]

The description of covetousness as good husbandry, and of gluttony and drunkenness as good fellowship, are textbook examples given by sixteenth-century Elizabethan rhetoricians, such as Thomas Wilson

[35] See, for instance, Isabel Rivers, *Reason, Grace and Sentiment: A Study of the Language of Religion and Ethics in England, 1660–1780*, 2 vols (Cambridge, 1991–2000); Louise Joy, *Eighteenth-Century Literary Affections* (Cham, 2020).

[36] Johannes Susenbrotus, *Epitome troporum ac schematum* (Zurich, 1540), 46, cited in Quentin Skinner, 'Paradiastole: Redescribing the Vices as Virtues', in Sylvia Adamson, Gavin Alexander and Katrin Ettenhuber, eds, *Renaissance Figures of Speech* (Cambridge, 2007), 149–64, at 160.

[37] Paradiastole has been explored extensively in relation to early modern ethics and political rhetoric in the work of Quentin Skinner: see, for example, Quentin Skinner, *Reason and Rhetoric in the Philosophy of Hobbes* (Cambridge, 1996), esp. 138–80 (ch. 4, 'The Techniques of Redescription'), and idem, 'Paradiastole'. On paradiastole in relation to puritan practical divinity, see David Parry, 'As an Angel of Light: Satanic Rhetoric in Early Modern Literature and Theology', in Gregor Thuswalder and Daniel Russ, eds, *The Hermeneutics of Hell: Devilish Visions and Visions of the Devil* (Cham, 2017), 47–71; idem, *The Rhetoric of Conversion in English Puritan Writing from Perkins to Milton* (London, 2022), 52–60, 132–4, 194–200, 225–42.

[38] DEI, MSS 143.7, 246.

and Henry Peacham,[39] as well as by religious writers of a puritan leaning, including William Perkins,[40] Arthur Dent, Lewis Bayly, Richard Bernard and John Bunyan.[41] Robert Atkins's characterization of hypocrisy thus participates in the traditions both of Renaissance humanist rhetoric and of godly practical divinity, traditions whose influence can be seen as ongoing in the sermons of the later preachers found in these notebooks, despite their departures from the Presbyterian orthodoxy of Atkins.

In keeping with Aristotelian ethics, in which virtues are the golden mean between two vices,[42] Atkins notes that sinners are often happy to hear vices denounced that are opposite to their own:

> I am persuaded, that a Covetous heart, doth love to hear a sharp and searching sermon against Prodigality. And on the other hand, The Prodigal, he is willing that the base sin of Covetousness, should be loaded with most approbrious language, and that jearring, and scorning, and contempt should be cast upon it. But this doth not hinder, but that the one, and the other, may regard iniquity in the heart.[43]

Sinners are happy to hear the vice that is opposite to theirs denounced as this gives cover to their paradiastolic disguising of their vice as virtue, but this does not show any genuine love of virtue for its own sake.

[39] Peacham defines paradiastole as 'when by a mannerly interpretation, we doe excuse our own vices, or other mens whom we doe defend, by calling them vertues, as when we call him that is craftye, wyse: a couetous man, a good husband: murder a manly deede: deepe dissimulation, singuler wisdome: pryde cleanlynesse: couetousnesse, a worldly or necessarye carefulnesse: whoredome, youthful delight & dalyance: Idolatry, pure religion: glotony and dronkennesse, good fellowship: cruelty seuerity. This fygure is used, when vices are excused.' Henry Peacham, *The Garden of Eloquence* (London, 1577), sig. N4^{v}.

[40] Among the errors of the common people listed by Perkins is 'That drinking and bezeling in the alehouse or tauerne is good fellowship, & shews a good kinde nature.' William Perkins, *The foundation of Christian religion, gathered into sixe principles* ([London?], 1591), sig. A2^{v}.

[41] Arthur Dent, *The Plaine Mans Path-way to Heauen* (London, 1601), 102; Lewis Bayly, *The Practise of Pietie Directing a Christian How to Walke That He May Please God*, 3rd edn (London, 1613; first publ. 1611), 253–4; Richard Bernard, *The Isle of Man: or, the Legall Proceeding in Man-shire against Sinne* (London, 1626), 31 (see 28–32 for a wider attack on redescribing vice as virtue); John Bunyan, *The Holy War* (1682), ed. Roger Sharrock and James F. Forrest (Oxford, 1980), 130. Christopher Hill notes that all these texts attack the redescription of 'covetousness' as 'good husbandry', but Hill does not use the specific term paradiastole for this rhetorical redescription: Christopher Hill, *A Turbulent, Seditious, and Factious People: John Bunyan and his Church 1628–1688* (Oxford, 1988), 161–6.

[42] See Aristotle, *Nicomachean Ethics*, 1106a–b.

[43] DEI, MSS 143.7, 278.

Another key biblical passage often cited in these sermons in relation to the paradiastolic redescription of virtue as vice and vice as virtue is Isaiah 5: 20: 'Woe unto them that call evil good, and good evil; that put darkness for light, and light for darkness; that put bitter for sweet, and sweet for bitter!' [AV].[44] For instance, a seventeenth-century sermon by Robert Atkins comments:

> The Prophet, or God by the prophet, denounced against such a wo, that call evil good, and good evil; that put darkness for light, and light for darkness. Intimating, that there be some in the world, that call good evil, and evil good, that put darkness for light, and light for darkness. Now, Sirs, they that do so, it is no wonder if they chuse that evil, which they fancy to be good; and reject that good, which they apprehend to be evil.[45]

The sinner who redefines good as evil, and vice versa, here seems not to be a conscious hypocrite, since he or she chooses evil under the appearance of the good (*sub specie boni*).[46]

However, the sinner retains culpability for his or her disordered understanding, according to Joseph Hallett III, who says of the 'wilful sinner':

> The eyes of his Understanding are so darken'd, that he cannot see his Danger, and discern the difference between moral good and evil: or else his understanding is so disturb'd, and disorder'd, as that he fancies evil to be good, and good to be evil; and walks on quietly toward Hell, while he foolishly thinks himself to be in the safe way to heaven.[47]

Elsewhere Hallett III warns that we 'cannot but expect his vengeance, if thro' our own Carelessness, and Prejudice, we call evil, Good, and Good, evil.'[48] The blurring of moral boundaries signified by the Isaiah text evidently remains an ongoing concern for Exeter

[44] On this verse in relation to Milton's Satan exclaiming 'Evil be thou my good', see Paul Stevens, 'The Pre-Secular Politics of *Paradise Lost*', in Louis Schwartz, ed., *The Cambridge Companion to Paradise Lost* (Cambridge, 2014), 94–108, at 105; Parry, *The Rhetoric of Conversion*, 239.

[45] DEI, MSS 143.7, 254–5.

[46] Atkins comments: 'That they which do regard iniquity, they do not regard it as a thing that is evil, under that notion, but they regard it as a thing that which to them hath the appearance of Good. There is no man that loves the sin, but he loves it, either as pleasant, or as one way or other profitable.' Ibid. 254.

[47] DEI, MSS 143.4, 65–6.

[48] Ibid. 431.

Dissenters across the decades from Atkins's to Hallett III's ministry, despite the theological shifts between them, while Hallett III's sinner who 'walks on quietly toward Hell, while he foolishly thinks himself to be in the safe way to heaven' appears to be a 'sincere hypocrite' of the kind that Ava Chamberlain identifies in Jonathan Edwards's thought.[49]

'One of the greatest and worst of sins': The Double Hypocrisy of Persecution

Another key focus for discussion of hypocrisy in these manuscript sermons relates to religious persecution, a topic in which both orthodox and rational Dissenters had a vested interest. There are two key ways in which persecution fosters hypocrisy, according to these sermons. One is that if individuals are coerced by force into adopting religious practices or professing religious beliefs to which they do not truly adhere in their hearts, they are compelled to be hypocrites. The other is that religious persecution is incompatible with New Testament Christianity, and so professing Christians who persecute others reveal their profession of Christianity to be false, and thus hypocritical.

The hypocrisy of persecution is at times described within the framework of paradiastolic redescription. For instance, Joseph Hallett III laments that 'In Popish Countries the greatest crimes, such as Idolatry and persecution are transubstantiated into virtues: and the highest virtues, such as Scriptural Worship, and Christian Charity, are condemn'd as the most heinous sins'.[50] His vehement sorrow still has room for the ingenious pun of 'transubstantiated into virtues', a striking phrase that has the ring of a verbatim transcription of Hallett III's words.[51] In another sermon, Hallett III notes that even 'most of those, who call themselves Protestants' have 'imitated the Persecuting Example of the Church of Rome' by oppressing religious minorities, 'and then the exercise of Moderation

[49] Chamberlain, 'Self-Deception as a Theological Problem', 543.
[50] DEI, MSS 143.4, 324.
[51] Hallett III precedes this observation with the comment that 'in a country, where Popery, and Persecution are established by Law … it is most reputable, in the Opinion of the Majority, for a man to be superstitious and a Persecuter. Then he will obtain a good report, as a man of piety, and zeal. While those, that will avoid these things, will be branded with the odious names of Hereticks, or Lukwarm Professors.' Ibid. 324.

toward them, is by the furious and persecuting spirits [called] impious Lukewarmness'.[52] In relation to the evil of persecution, he elsewhere remarks that 'We must not call evil good, and good evil. We must not delude the souls of Men.'[53]

In exploring these themes, Hallett III in particular moves beyond the self-interest of advocating liberty for Protestant Dissenters towards a more universal notion of religious freedom for all, including Roman Catholics and even Muslims.[54] These themes are highlighted, for instance, in a series of three sermons by Hallett III on the Gunpowder Plot, the first of which is headed 'Preached on the, 5th November. 1733'.[55] These sermons provide a distinctively Nonconformist interpretation of English history and shed light on the troubled triangulation of early modern English religious politics between the established Church of England, Protestant Dissenters and Roman Catholics. Hallett III makes the point that the statutory commemoration of 5 November is not binding on Dissenters, commenting:

> And tho' the Government has not commanded us to observe this day (for it speaks only to the establish'd Church) yet we cannot but think our selves more than ordinarily obliged to Celebrate this day with hearty thankfulness to God, since our worthy Predecessors the Dissenters were particularly level'd at by the common enemies of the Nation, and must have been the first that would have fallen a Prey to their teeth, if a merciful God had not broken the snare, and given us a Deliverance.[56]

Hallett III here argues that it is appropriate and even especially fitting for Dissenters to mark the occasion, since they would have been first in the firing line in the event of the triumph of popish tyranny. He blames the Gunpowder Plot on 'Our restless and implacable enemies, the Persecutors of the Church of Rome', who 'would first have

[52] Ibid. 122–3.
[53] DEI, MSS 143.5, 190.
[54] Hallett III's advocacy of liberty in the religious sphere for Roman Catholics and adherents of non-Christian religions within a Protestant state may be linked to the decreased political threat of popery with the establishment of the Hanoverian succession and the defeat of the Jacobites in 1719. (I am grateful to one of the readers for SCH for this suggestion.)
[55] DEI, MSS 143.3, 452. Punctuation original.
[56] Ibid. 459–60.

devour'd the Dissenters, and then the larger body of the nation'.[57] He thus aligns Dissenters with the wider English Protestant cause, while privileging Dissenters as the truest Protestants and thus the most at risk from the tyranny of popish persecution. Hallett III also sees the Glorious Revolution of 1688, which deposed the Roman Catholic James II and led to the 1689 Act of Toleration, as another providential deliverance serving the cause of the true gospel: 'Thus again, the good Providence of God interposed for our Deliverance from the dreadful Dangers of the two worst things in the world, Popery and Arbitrary Power.'[58]

However, although Hallett III's providential reading of English history aligns Dissenters with a broader national Protestant cause that includes the established church and sees political 'Popery' as a persecutory force to be resisted, he advocates a wider religious toleration that would include Roman Catholics, as well as Dissenters. In his second Gunpowder Plot sermon, Hallett III argues that although papists are in error, for instance in their belief in transubstantiation, they should be reasoned out of such errors, rather than coerced into renouncing them:

> If we can by argument convince the Understanding of a Papist, that this is a false doctrine, we shall do well. But if we threaten him with Persecution, unless he will deny this doctrine, we shall hereby tempt him to deny what he verily believes to be the Truth of God. That is, we should hereby tempt him to sin against his Conscience, and so to sin against God, and ruin his own soul.[59]

Even though the papist is wrong about transubstantiation, Hallett III argues, to force him into denying this doctrine insincerely would be to lead him 'to sin against his Conscience', which will incur more severe divine judgment than the erroneous belief itself. It is sin to violate one's conscience or to coerce another person into denying theirs, even if that conscience is misguided. Although this sermon does not use the language of 'hypocrisy' explicitly, its condemnation of speaking or acting contrary to one's conscience is implicitly a condemnation of the hypocritical outward performance of that which is contrary to one's inward convictions. This emphasis on the sin of

[57] Ibid. 456.
[58] Ibid. 459.
[59] Ibid. 471.

coercing conscience resonates with the concerns of the Exeter Controversy and the consequent Salters' Hall Controversy (1719) that splintered English Dissent. It has been rightly pointed out that the 'non-subscribers' were not all necessarily united by anti-Trinitarian doctrine, but rather by the principle that subscription ought not to be compelled to doctrinal formularies beyond the plain words of Scripture.[60]

Yet Hallett III's rejection of coercion in matters of religion extends beyond debates around the limits of acceptable divergence in doctrine within Protestant Dissent to a wider advocacy of toleration, even to those who profess religions outside of Christianity altogether. In another sermon, he states that 'Persecution is one of the greatest and worst of sins that men can possibly commit'[61] and that it is contrary to the spirit of New Testament Christianity:

> That I may make this appear to the greatest advantage, I shall put the case of a professed christian (for I cannot allow him to be a real one) persecuting a Mahometan, in order to induce him to renounce his trust in Mahomet, and to receive the blessed Jesus as the only and alsufficient Mediator.[62]

Hallett III remains an exclusivist with regard to religious truth, affirming: 'I make no doubt, but that the Mahometan is grossly mistaken',[63] but condemns persecution on the principle that religious coercion is always wrong. If the persecutor forces the 'Mahometan' to deny his belief without truly persuading him to change his inner convictions, he is compelled to become a hypocrite, which is displeasing to God, even though the doctrine he is coerced into confessing is true. At the same time, the persecutor is also a hypocrite: he is a 'professed Christian' but Hallett III 'cannot allow him to be a real one' since his profession is denied by his un-Christlike actions.

[60] Thomas, 'The Non-Subscription Controversy'; Wykes, 'The 1719 Salters' Hall Debate', esp. 39–47. Wykes asserts that the Salters' Hall debate 'was not about doctrine' (31), perhaps an overstatement, but also observes that 'the controversy at Exeter does seem to have been about the Trinity' (59).

[61] DEI, MSS 143.3, 230.

[62] Ibid. 230–1.

[63] Ibid. 231.

'There is something still for You to do': Moralist Soteriology and Performance Anxiety

Finally, and more briefly, I would like to consider how theological shifts in English Nonconformity (as in English Protestantism more broadly) over the period covered by these sermons generated increased anxiety over the possibility of hypocrisy in the quest for salvation. The transition from orthodox to rational Dissent in the Exeter Presbyterian community marked by these sermons is a subtle one. While departures from previous orthodoxy are clear in the small number of sermons that deny the equality of the Son with the Father, they are less clear with regard to soteriology, the crucial questions of how individuals are saved and how they can know that they are saved.

While Joseph Hallett III certainly departs from the classic Calvinistic understanding of the election of particular individuals to salvation, in favour of an assertion of God's predestination of 'the believing Gentiles in general',[64] what is more subtle is an apparent drift away from the Reformation's emphatic assertion of salvation by grace alone, through faith alone, towards an understanding of salvation that makes the final salvation of an individual depend at least in part on a life of sincere, though imperfect, obedience.[65] Hallett III comments: 'It is very true that sincere Repentance, and a holy Life are absolutely necessary to our Salvation',[66] and though the grace of God and the presence of the Spirit enable Christians to prevail against sin, Hallett III exhorts: 'There is something still for You to do. You must repent, believe, and to the utmost of your power sincerely obey the Gospel. And then he will give his help and blessing'.[67] Hallett III even teaches that 'God loves his rational creatures, according to the moral qualifications that he observes in them'[68] and that 'God will love you more, when you become more like him'.[69]

[64] DEI, MSS 143.5, 8.

[65] For similar debates in sixteenth-century continental and English Reformed traditions regarding whether the covenant of grace required ethical performance on the part of believers as in some sense a condition of final salvation, see Robert Wainwright, *Early Reformation Covenant Theology: English Reception of Swiss Reformed Thought, 1520–1555* (Phillipsburg, NJ, 2020), esp. 1–41, 146–221, 331–49.

[66] DEI, MSS 143.4, 225.

[67] Ibid. 228.

[68] DEI, MSS 143.5, 336.

[69] Ibid. 339.

For Hallett III, the gospel dispensation is still one of grace, in that God no longer requires the impossible standard of perfect obedience for salvation that the old covenant of the law of Moses required. He says that the new covenant 'has lower'd the Terms of Acceptance with God',[70] but that we are still required to do that which is within our power: 'We can do some thing towards our Salvation: But then what we can do would not prove sufficient and effectual, unless God did work in Us and with us.'[71]

This emphasis on the necessity of obedience as a ground of final salvation, and not only an evidence of it, correlates with what C. FitzSimons Allison termed 'the rise of moralism' (though Allison's survey ends in the later seventeenth century) and what Isabel Rivers has identified as a shift from 'the religion of grace' to 'the religion of reason' in both conformist and Nonconformist circles during the long eighteenth century.[72] Joseph Hallett III's Dissenting preaching is in line with what Mark Smith has described as the neo-Arminian soteriology of the eighteenth-century Church of England, which:

> agreed with the Reformed position that God justified sinners on the basis of the merits of Christ but contended that sinners had nevertheless to qualify for the benefits available under the new covenant by fulfilling their obligations – a sincere attempt, assisted by the grace of God, to obey the law of Christ – in other words, the practice of holiness and good works.[73]

On the Dissenting side, there are close parallels with the 'neonomianism' of Richard Baxter, who argued that, in the gospel, Christ has given a new law in which sincere through imperfect obedience is required for an individual's acquittal and final salvation at the Day of Judgment.[74] There are also close links with the soteriological

[70] DEI, MSS 143.4, 445.

[71] DEI, MSS 143.5, 117.

[72] C. FitzSimons Allison, *The Rise of Moralism: The Proclamation of the Gospel from Hooker to Baxter* (London and New York, 1966), esp. ix–xii, 117, 189–212; Rivers, *Reason, Grace, and Sentiment*, esp. 1: 25–163.

[73] Mark Smith, 'The Hanoverian Parish: Towards a New Agenda', *P&P* 216 (2012), 79–105, at 85.

[74] On Baxter's soteriology, see Hans Boersma, *A Hot Pepper Corn: Richard Baxter's Doctrine of Justification in its Seventeenth-Century Context of Controversy* (Zoetermeer, 1993; repr. Vancouver, 2003). On Baxter's influence on rational and orthodox Dissent into the eighteenth century, see, for instance, Robert Strivens, *Philip Doddridge and the Shaping of Evangelical Dissent* (London, 2015), 21–45.

thought of John Locke, who (as summarized by Diego Lucci) required 'the fundamentals of Christianity – that is, faith in Jesus the Messiah, repentance for sin, and obedience to the divine moral law – and the conscientious study of Scripture as necessary for salvation', but in *The Reasonableness of Christianity* (1695) states that under the new covenant law of Christ '*Faith is allowed* to supply the defect of full Obedience'.[75]

I suggest that this shift to a soteriological emphasis on the absolute necessity of sincere repentance and sincere obedience to attain final salvation places additional weight on the inward sincerity of the individual, and conversely generates increased anxiety regarding the possibility of a hypocrisy that performs the outward form of obedience to God, but without sincerity of heart. Hypocrisy and sincerity function as key terms, both in relation to ethical virtue and saving faith, in Protestant thought from the Reformation onwards, but the anxiety caused by the possibility of insincere performance of piety and virtue by hypocrites was intensified in a context in which soteriology and ethics were increasingly entangled.

[75] Diego Lucci, *John Locke's Christianity* (Cambridge, 2020), 77; John Locke, *The Reasonableness of Christianity, As Delivered in the Scriptures*, ed. John C. Higgins-Biddle (Oxford, 1999), 19, cited in Lucci, *John Locke's Christianity*, 93 (italics original). For links between Locke's biblical exegesis and that of Peirce and Hallett III, see Wainwright, 'Locke's Influence on the Exegesis of Peirce, Hallett, and Benson', 189–97, 204–5.

The Rev. John Stainsby and the 'diffusion of Gospel truth' in Early Nineteenth-Century Jamaica

Alice Kinghorn*
University of Gloucester

First dispatched to Jamaica in 1818 by The Conversion Society, the Rev. John Stainsby became a prominent figure on the island. This article examines his intense involvement in Anglican missionary affairs to reveal how dishonesties and concealment of belief were used to expand Anglican missions in the Caribbean. Firstly, this article examines two key sites of contention between missionaries and the plantocracy – Sunday markets and baptism – where Stainsby used deception to reconcile his religious duties and colonial law. Secondly, it considers the motivations and actions of The Conversion Society and the Church Missionary Society more generally, including the heavily censored material used for religious instruction. Finally, it examines Stainsby as an enslaver, and considers the religious justifications used to support enslavement by many resident Anglican clergymen in the early nineteenth century.

Introduction

In an account entitled *The West Indies in 1837,* Joseph Sturge and Thomas Harvey depicted an Anglican clergyman whom they considered to have atypical sympathies: 'one of those who has ever manifested a sympathy with the oppressed, and is consequently, together with other estimable clergymen of the establishment, deemed "worse than a Baptist".'[1] The subject of their account, the Rev. John Stainsby (1782–1854), held his position as an Anglican incumbent in Jamaica for over thirty years.[2] Working with enslaved

* E-mail: alicekinghorn@live.co.uk. Quotation in title from: Birmingham, CRL, CMS/B/OMS CW/079/3, Rev. John Stainsby to Rev. Josiah Pratt, 25 May 1824, St Thomas in the East, Jamaica.

[1] Joseph Sturge and Thomas Harvey, *The West Indies in 1837* (London, 1838), 236.

[2] Hope Maslerton Waddell, *Twenty-Nine Years in the West Indies and Central Africa* (London, 1863), 104. On account of his 'evangelical piety' and 'sympathy with the

Studies in Church History 60 (2024), 363–386
doi: 10.1017/stc.2024.14

people and witnessing their transition to apprenticeship and freedom, it was in Jamaica that Stainsby's 'sympathies' took root.[3] In view of this, Stainsby's listing in the *Legacies of British Slavery Database* is perhaps unexpected. Together with his wife, he is recorded as having received £646 18*s.* 1*d.* in compensation for the freeing of thirty-six enslaved people in 1836.[4] The entry observes this apparent contradiction, describing Stainsby's slave-ownership as 'striking' because 'he was renowned as prominent campaigner for the improvement in conditions of the enslaved and for their religious instruction'.[5]

This article argues an alternative view. It suggests that Stainsby's enslaver status was not antithetical to his dedication to religious instruction and conversion in the Caribbean. Rather, it demonstrates how 'sympathizing' Anglican missionaries in the Caribbean, such as Stainsby, had to abstain from the issue of emancipation in order to maintain good relations with the plantocracy and thus further their missionary calling. In doing so, it argues that such missionaries became an integral part of the British Government's movement, throughout the 1820s, for the amelioration of the conditions of enslaved people. This focused assessment of Stainsby's intense involvement in Anglican missionary affairs in Jamaica reveals how dishonesties and concealed beliefs advanced the expansion of Anglican missions in the Caribbean.

With the exception of Adam Thomas's assessment of a slander case – to which Stainsby and another missionary named Samuel Oughton were parties – Stainsby's influence in Jamaica has largely gone unobserved.[6] By contrast, Anglican missionary activity during the period of amelioration has seen a recent surge of interest, which has served to nuance and complicate current understandings of relationships between missionaries and enslaved people.[7] In *Agency of the*

oppressed,' Stainsby was described as having to endure 'much obloquy and persecution': Henry Richard, *Memoirs of Joseph Sturge* (London, 1865), 154.

[3] 'Sympathies' are attributed scare quotes due to the problematic attitudes which Anglican clergymen held in encouraging conversion and instruction.

[4] 'Rev. John Stainsby', *Legacies of British Slavery Database*, online at: <https://www.ucl.ac.uk/lbs/person/view/14414>, accessed 31 October 2022.

[5] Ibid.

[6] Adam Thomas, '"Outcasts from the world": Same-Sex Sexuality, Authority, and Belonging in Post-Emancipation Jamaica', *Slavery & Abolition* 40 (2019), 423–47.

[7] Christa Dierksheide, *Amelioration and Empire: Progress and Slavery in the Plantation Americas* (Charlottesville, VA, 2014); Trevor Burnard and Kit Candlin, 'Sir John

Enslaved, Daive Dunkley examined the baptisms and religious instruction of enslaved people under the established Church of England and its missionary agencies, including the Church Missionary Society (CMS). He argued that the creation of the missionary education system 'was an indication of the power of slave freedom'.[8] Dunkley considered how Anglican missionaries aligned with the plantocracy, and posited that enslaved people maintained agency and autonomy in missionary interactions.[9] Anglican clergy in the Anglophone Caribbean more widely have been approached mainly through the study of resident clergy and their relations with enslavers. In an evaluation of breaches of the social norms of slave society, Matthew Strickland explored the actions of William Marshall Harte, an Anglican clergyman in Barbados, who was fined for preaching material that might 'hinder the enslaver-enslaved power dynamic.'[10] Strickland situates arguments surrounding Harte's actions in the wider context of amelioration through religious instruction sought by the British government in the 1820s.[11] By considering how Stainsby traversed these complex and important enslaver-enslaved dynamics, this article builds on Strickland's analysis. It demonstrates that the complexities of amelioration resulted in tensions as

Gladstone and the Debate Over the Amelioration of Slavery in the British West Indies in the 1820s,' *JBS* 57 (2018), 760–82. Michael Taylor examines amelioration in the West India Interest's defence of slavery in: Michael Taylor, *The Interest: How the British Establishment Resisted the Abolition of Slavery* (London, 2020), 125–40.

[8] Daive Dunkley, *Agency of the Enslaved: Jamaica and the Culture of Freedom in the Atlantic World* (Lanham, MD, 2013), 10.

[9] Scholarship on the Church of England's pro-slavery actions focuses mainly on the Society for the Propagation of the Gospel in Foreign Parts (SPG), including Travis Glasson's review of the SPG's participation in slavery in North America and the Caribbean: see Travis Glasson, *Mastering Christianity: Missionary Anglicanism and Slavery in the Atlantic World* (New York, 2012), 199–232. On the 'planter-clergy nexus', see David Lambert, *White Creole Culture: Politics and Identity during the Age of Abolition* (Cambridge, 2005), 19. For early colonial development of the Church of England, see Katherine Gerbner, *Christian Slavery: Conversion and Race in the Protestant Atlantic World* (Philadelphia, PA, 2018).

[10] Matthew Blake Strickland, '"The Protection of Slaves and Other Property": An Anglican Minister, Criminal Charges, and White Planters' Fear of Emancipation in Barbados', *Journal of Caribbean History* 5 (2021), 151–75, at 151. For more biographical approaches to this topic, see Sue Thomas, 'William Dawes in Antigua', *Journal of Colonialism and Colonial History* 12 (2011), unpaginated, and Mary Turner, 'The Bishop of Jamaica and Slave Instruction', *JEH* 26 (1975), 363–78.

[11] Strickland, '"The Protection of Slaves"', 154–5.

missionaries deceived others about their beliefs to align with ameliorative, Christian incentives.

Anna Johnston has examined missionary texts more generally, arguing that they are propagandist in nature because they were written to 'ensure an on-going supply of donated funds'.[12] In their writings, missionaries enforced 'colonial visions' by emphasizing the notion of the 'heathen' to justify their conversion attempts.[13] This article draws on Johnston's analysis by examining missionary correspondence, whilst considering the motivations of the writer, alongside published education materials and colonial slave registers, to understand Stainsby's influence in nineteenth-century Jamaica. It firstly examines two key sites of contention between religious instruction and the planter class – Sunday markets and baptism – showing that Stainsby used deception to reconcile his religious duties and colonial law. It then considers the motivations and actions of The Conversion Society and the CMS more generally, discussing the material provided to missionaries to support their educational mission. Finally, it explores Stainsby's role as an enslaver. Through consideration of Stainsby's attitudes towards his own slave-ownership, it points to Stainsby's assimilation into the plantocracy. Overall, it argues that Stainsby engaged in acts of hypocrisy and suppression to avoid curtailing the growth of mission and, in so doing, perpetuated a form of pro-slavery Christianity that was used by himself and the societies who employed him.[14]

Ordination and Mission

John Stainsby was born in 1782 in Low Coniscliffe, County Durham. Little is known about his life prior to his ordination, although we can gather that he remained single until then.[15] He was ordained deacon on 17 May 1818 and priested on 30 August the same year, with a view to becoming a missionary for the

[12] See Anna Johnston, *Missionary Writing and Empire, 1800–1860* (Cambridge, 2003), 7–11.

[13] Ibid.

[14] Unlike the Society's first missionary, James Curtin, Stainsby's actions generally aligned with the Society's views.

[15] In 1818, Stainsby recorded that he had been advised to 'take a partner': see London, LPL, FP Howley 40, 265, Stainsby to the Bishop of London, 3 August 1818, Low Coniscliffe, County Durham.

Incorporated Society for the Conversion and Religious Instruction of the British West India Negro Slaves.[16] The Society was a rejuvenation of the Christian Faith Society, originally founded in 1691 from assets left by the natural philosopher Robert Boyle.[17] The charity experienced a partial suspension of income during the American War of Independence (1775–83), which encouraged its trustees to find an alternative use for the income flowing from Boyle's Brafferton estate in Yorkshire. The alternative which was found was The Conversion Society, which was reconstituted in 1794 under the presidency of the then bishop of London, Beilby Porteus, until his death in 1809. Samuel Hinds, the future bishop of Norwich, became its president in 1809, until his resignation in 1822.[18] The Society's first stationed missionary was the Rev. James Curtin, who remained the principal missionary in the Caribbean until Stainsby's arrival in Jamaica in 1818.[19]

Stainsby was evidently eager to start his new position, making an inquiry to the bishop of London, by now William Howley, as to when his mission for The Conversion Society would begin. In his letter, he wrote:

> As many weeks have passed over since my ordination, and as the time of my proposed departure from my native country across the Atlantic to communicate those blessings to our fellow subjects, the Negroes, which God's eternal son came down to this our World to reveal and work out for sinful man, I hope I may be pardoned the liberty I now take in writing to your Lordship to enquire if anything further has been settled respecting me by the 'Society for the Conversion of Negro slaves in the British West India Islands.' I rather expected to hear from Mr Porteus previous to this, but have not.[20]

[16] London, London Metropolitan Archives [hereafter: LMA], Diocese of London Act Book, MS 9532A/2, 130, 133–4; ibid., Curates Licences MS 10300/2, 27.

[17] See Herbert L. Ganter, 'Some Notes on the Charity of the Honourable Robert Boyle, Esq. of the City of London, Deceased', *William and Mary College Quarterly* 15 (1935), 207–28; 'Christian Faith Society - Borthwick Catalogue', online at: <https://borthcat.york.ac.uk/index.php/christian-faith-society>, accessed 31 October 2022.

[18] LPL, CFS F/1/ 1, Samuel Hinds to Thomas Porteus, 29 April 1822, Barbados.

[19] On James Curtin's role in The Conversion Society, see Alice Kinghorn and Hilary M. Carey, 'The History of James Curtin: Catholic Priest, Protestant Missionary, and Pariah of British Proslavery, 1765–1845', *Journal of Colonialism and Colonial History* 24 (2023), unpaginated; LPL, CFS F/1/ 3, Rev. James Curtin to Rev. D. Barrett, 4 September 1822, Antigua.

[20] LPL, FP Howley 40, 265–6, John Stainsby to the bishop of London, Charles Blomfield, 3 August 1818, Low Coniscliffe, County Durham. 'Porteus' refers to the

Stainsby did not have long to wait. On 20 October 1818, he was appointed by Howley as 'a missionary in the Island of Jamaica to which [he was] duly appointed by the Society for the Conversion and Religious Instruction and Education of the Negro Slaves in the British West India Islands.'[21] This was reported in the 1818 *Missionary Register,* which also noted that Stainsby was to be paid the yearly stipend 'allowed by the Society.'[22] His first appearance in the Society's payment books was in November 1818 when he was paid £50 for the 'expense of his passage and in advance and in part of his salary.'[23] He was then paid £100 annually in quarterly instalments until 1823, when his annual salary increased to £115.[24] On Stainsby's arrival in Jamaica, a 'resident' clergyman, the Rev. John McCammon Trew, wrote to The Conversion Society that Stainsby 'came too late for the curacy of this parish [St Thomas in the East],' but assured the Society that Stainsby would still be able to 'further the ends of conversion among the slaves'.[25] Crucially, from 1820, Stainsby also maintained a relationship with the Church Missionary Society (CMS), and eventually became secretary for its Jamaican auxiliary in 1829.[26] Stainsby's bilateral positioning within

nephew of Beilby Porteus, Thomas Porteus, who had an influential administerial role in The Conversion Society.

[21] LMA, Diocese of London Act Book, MS 9532A/2, 130, 133, 134.

[22] Church Missionary Society, *The Missionary Register for 1818 Containing the Principal Transactions of the Various Institutions for Propagating the Gospel with The Proceedings at Large of the Church Missionary Society* (London, 1818), 420.

[23] LMA, Curates Licences MS 10300/2, 27; Kew, TNA, C 110/88.

[24] TNA, C 110/88; LPL, FP Howley 2, 361, John McCammon Trew to The Conversion Society, 13 June 1823, St Thomas in the East, Jamaica.

[25] 'Resident' clergy refers to those permanently stationed in the Caribbean. LPL, FP Howley 2, 145, John McCammon Trew to The Conversion Society, 13 January 1819, St Thomas in the East, Jamaica.

[26] CRL, CMS/B/OMS CW/079/6a, Stainsby to Dandeson Coates, 16 March 1829, Papine Estate, Jamaica. Adam Thomas stated that Stainsby was a missionary for the Church Missionary Society: Thomas, '"Outcasts from the world"', 423. Whilst Stainsby did have a relationship with the CMS, it was The Conversion Society that originally paid for his missionary position. The new missionaries and their salaries are also mentioned in *The Christian Herald* (London, 1819), 300. On the foundation of the CMS, see Gareth Atkins, 'Wilberforce and His Milieux: The Worlds of Anglican Evangelicalism, *c.*1780–1830' (PhD thesis, University of Cambridge, 2009); and Elizabeth Elbourne, 'The Anglican Missionary Impulse,' in John Walsh, Colin Haydon and Stephen Taylor, eds, *Church of England,* c.*1689–*c.*1833: From Toleration to Tractarianism* (Cambridge, 1993), 247–64.

both The Conversion Society and the CMS was unique to him, with most missionaries retaining associations with either one or the other.[27] Stainsby ratified his affiliation with the CMS in 1824, when he wrote to its secretary, the Rev. Josiah Pratt, confirming his mission of the 'diffusion of the Gospel truth in these parts of the world.'[28] Stainsby's employment by The Conversion Society and association with the CMS made him a central Anglican missionary in Jamaica.

Sunday Markets and Baptism

Stainsby's colonial mission in Jamaica began during a period of intense political turmoil in Britain. In 1823, Britain's foreign secretary, George Canning, introduced a number of resolutions that called for the amelioration of enslavement in the West Indies. Abolitionists such as William Wilberforce and Thomas Buxton hoped these measures could lead to the emancipation of enslaved people in the colonies.[29] However, Canning carefully refrained from suggesting that amelioration could lead to emancipation. By balancing the 'well-being of the slaves themselves, with the safety of the colonies,' he kept the West India Interest's support, and encouraged MPs to vote for these resolutions and support their implementation.[30] Canning's resolutions included measures to advance 'civilisation' amongst enslaved populations, such as abolishing the use of the whip for females, protecting enslaved peoples' rights to own property, and removing certain restrictions on manumission.[31]

Underlying the arguments for amelioration were calls for religious instruction amongst enslaved populations as a means of fostering 'improvement'. As demonstrated by Dunkley and Strickland, the

[27] Stainsby reported to both societies. He was also close friends with the Rev. John McCammon Trew, whose frosty relationship with The Conversion Society resulted in the creation of the Jamaican Auxiliary of the Church Missionary Society.

[28] CRL CMS/B/OMS CW/079/3, Stainsby to Rev. Josiah Pratt, 25 May 1824, St Thomas in the East, Jamaica.

[29] HC Deb. (2nd series), 15 May 1823 (vol. 9, col. 273). These measures had been set out by The Society for the Mitigation and Gradual Abolition of Slavery Throughout the British Dominions.

[30] The West India Interest were bankers, merchants and MPs with interests in transatlantic slavery. They represented views of the plantocracy in Parliament. See Michael Taylor, *The Interest,* 63.

[31] HC Deb. (2nd series), 16 March 1824 (vol. 10, cols 1091–198).

belief that religious instruction and conversion to Christianity were necessary to the implementation of amelioration policies meant that Anglican missionary societies became central to the cause of amelioration.[32] Dunkley, Glasson and Gerbner have demonstrated that missionaries relied on the support of resident planters in the Caribbean for physical access to their plantations in order to carry out religious instruction.[33] These studies have also suggested that enslavers supported Anglican missionaries financially as a way to ensure control over the type of religious instruction given, although analysis of this financial support has received less attention.[34] As such, Anglican missionaries had to navigate their relations with planters, even when this challenged the missionaries' principles.

When sending missionaries to the Caribbean, both the CMS and The Conversion Society explicitly told their candidates not to embroil themselves in local political affairs. The Conversion Society's first pamphlet, issued in 1795 and entitled *Instructions for Missionaries to the West-India Islands*, specified that missionaries 'must be careful to give no offence either to the Governor, to the Legislature to the Planters, the Clergy, or any other class of persons on the island … not interfering in the commercial or political affairs of the island.'[35] The CMS had similar guidelines and attitudes.[36] However, this led to internal difficulties for missionaries, and one such challenge came when Stainsby openly confronted the custom of Sunday markets.

Sunday markets were an integral part of the informal economy in Jamaica. At these markets, enslaved people sold surplus crops from their provision grounds, such as potatoes, ackee, yams, plantains, beans, peas, guavas and other dried roots.[37] By the late eighteenth

[32] Strickland, '"The Protection of Slaves"', 154–5.

[33] On early access restrictions, see Gerbner, *Christian Slavery*, 30–1; Dunkley, *Agency of the Enslaved*, 121–5. On the SPG and planter hostility, see Glasson, *Mastering Christianity*, 97–9.

[34] Dunkley has examined the financial support provided by planters to the Jamaican Auxiliary of the Church Missionary Society: Dunkley, *Agency of the Enslaved*, 67. This article builds on Dunkley's analysis, by considering the financial support of The Conversion Society and the Church Missionary Society more generally.

[35] Philanthropic Society, *Instructions for Missionaries to the West-India Islands* (London, 1795), 3.

[36] CRL, CMS/B/OMS CW/079, Stainsby to Rev. Josiah Pratt, 1 February 1821, St Thomas in the East, Jamaica.

[37] Provision grounds were sections of land allocated to enslaved people for growing food provisions or keeping livestock. John McAleer, 'Alison Blyth and Slavery in Nineteenth-

century, Sunday markets in Kingston saw the participation of an estimated 10,000 enslaved people.[38] However, since these markets involved working on the Sabbath, Sunday markets became a site of contention. Glasson argues that, particularly in the early nineteenth century, new metropolitan campaigners and missionaries to the Caribbean failed to appreciate either the work schedule established on Caribbean plantations, or the fact that enslaved people wished to attend Sunday markets.[39] Missionaries from most denominations objected to markets, and John McAleer has argued that such objections were expected 'from the average missionary,' who would instead encourage enslaved people to attend church and school on Sundays.[40]

The plantocracy of Jamaica proved resistant. They encouraged enslaved people either to carry out additional labour or to attend Sunday markets to sell goods from their provision grounds, and appreciated the problems that would entail from a ban of markets.[41] Alison Charles Carmichael, a Scotswoman resident in Jamaica, considered Sunday markets a 'nuisance', but also viewed them as a custom 'which were it abolished other worse consequences might follow.'[42] Similarly, writing in 1825, the English geologist and enslaver Henry Thomas De La Beche observed:

> No slave can be compelled to labour in Jamaica on Sunday, but to restrain them from doing so on their own account, would be considered by them as an act of great tyranny, and the practice cannot be prevented until they have received some religious impression of its impropriety.[43]

This would eventually come to a head for Antiguans in March 1831. Following a ban placed on Sunday markets, enslaved people resisted:

Century Jamaica', in Hilary M. Carey, ed., *Empires of Religion* (Basingstoke, 2008), 199–221, at 213.

[38] Gad Heuman, *The Caribbean: A Brief History,* 2nd edn (London, 2014; first publ. 2006), 42.

[39] Glasson, *Mastering Christianity,* 157.

[40] McAleer, 'Alison Blyth and Slavery', 212.

[41] Marshall K. Woodville, 'Provision Ground and Plantation Labour in Four Winward Islands: Competition for Resources During Slavery', *Slavery & Abolition* 12 (1991), 48–67, at 49.

[42] Quoted in Beth Fowkes Tobin, '"And there raise yams": Slaves' Gardens in the Writings of West India Plantocrats', *Eighteenth-Century Life* 23 (1999), 164–73.

[43] Henry Thomas De La Beche, *Notes on the Present Condition of the Negroes in Jamaica* (London, 1825), 47.

firstly, by ignoring the ban and secondly, by stirring revolt across two parishes.[44] Indeed, as Carmichael demonstrates, throughout the 1820s, the plantocracy recognized the need for Sunday markets, particularly if they were not willing to offer enslaved people another day off other than Sundays.[45] This became a tense issue between the plantocracy and missionaries.

John Stainsby's main concern was the importance of religious instruction on the Sabbath.[46] Consequently, as early as 1820, Stainsby wrote to Josiah Pratt, Secretary of the CMS, observing that Sunday markets must end if a 'school for slaves [were to] succeed to any extent'.[47] Stainsby maintained that Sunday markets would be 'the ruin of all efforts'.[48] Writing again in 1824, together with the Rev. John Matthew Trew, Stainsby pleaded the need to 'abolish the bane of Colonial Improvement: Sunday markets.'[49] Such opinions resulted in severe criticism from the plantocracy, with a slander case against Stainsby forcing him to retract his beliefs and principles.

Indeed, in 1824, Stainsby was accused by one Captain Ferrier of being 'in the habit of telling the [slaves] when [he] met them on Sundays going to market with provisions – that they should not go on that day, but that their masters should give them another day for this purpose.'[50] It was suggested that Stainsby had angered the planter in question. The allegation caused 'great injury' to Stainsby, and he made fervent attempts to deny it: writing two letters to the captain renouncing the claim, and visiting the estate to 'explain the

[44] See David Barry Gaspar, 'Slavery, Amelioration, and Sunday Markets in Antigua, 1823–1831', *Slavery & Abolition* 9 (1988), 1–21.

[45] Mary Prince wrote on the internal conflict of attending Sunday markets without another day allocated in *The History of Mary Prince*, ed. Thomas Pringle, 3rd edn (London, 1831; first publ. 1831), 16.

[46] CRL, CMS/B/OMS CW/O79/7, Stainsby to Dandeson Coates, 31 July 1830, St John's, Jamaica; CRL, CMS/B/OMS CW/O79/8, Stainsby to Dandeson Coates, 10 June 1830, Manchester, Jamaica. Stainsby writes about the Sabbath on both occasions.

[47] CRL, CMS/B/OMS CW/079, Stainsby to Rev. Josiah Pratt, 1 February 1821, St Thomas in the East, Jamaica.

[48] CRL, CMS/B/OMS CW079/1, Stainsby to Rev. Josiah Pratt, 11 December 1820, St Thomas in the East, Jamaica.

[49] Church Missionary Society, *The Missionary Register for 1824 Containing the Principal Transactions of the Various Institutions for Propagating the Gospel with The Proceedings at Large of the Church Missionary Society* (London, 1824), 89.

[50] LPL, CFS/F/1,104, Stainsby to The Conversion Society, Jamaica, 9 July 1824, St Thomas in the East, Jamaica.

misunderstanding'. Stainsby reported back to The Conversion Society that the estate's overseer understood and believed Stainsby, calling it 'nonsense'.[51] Whilst the veracity of the allegation is unknown, should it be true, it suggests that Stainsby possessed a wider understanding of the Sunday market system, and an appreciation for how integral that system was to the enslaved economy.[52] At the same time, Stainsby's palpable desperation to clear his name by retracting the strong views about Sunday markets he had expressed in his correspondence demonstrates the genuine importance that Anglican missionaries and their societies placed on good relations with planters.

A similar situation transpired in relation to baptism law in Jamaica.[53] The baptism of enslaved people had long been a contentious issue, and Dunkley has established that it was central to the Church of England's aims, particularly following the decision of the Jamaica House of Assembly to embark on a general pursuit of the 'mass baptism' of enslaved people from 1797.[54] Stainsby took issue with this approach, writing to The Conversion Society in 1823 of his grave concern that Jamaican law encouraged the baptism of all enslaved people regardless of 'any course of religious instruction'.[55] Stainsby argued that an enslaved person would leave the church 'in the same state of ignorance as when he entered it'.[56] Similarly, Stainsby critiqued the clergy's motivations for converting enslaved people, reporting to the CMS that he had noticed a lack of 'pious clergymen' since moving to the parish, and claimed that '"I am waiting for promotion to a benefice" [seemed] to be the general

[51] Ibid.

[52] McAleer, 'Alison Blyth and Slavery', 214. This argument is informed by McAleer's analysis of Alison Blyth, who was critical of Sunday markets, but sympathized with enslaved people as 'poor creatures' who should be offered another market day.

[53] Dunkley notes this was significantly sooner than Canning's 1823 proposals. On the development of baptism laws in Jamaica, see Dunkley, *Agency of the Enslaved,* 121–6, Nicholas M. Beasley, 'Domestic Rituals: Marriage and Baptism in the British Plantation Colonies, 1650–1780', *Anglican and Episcopal History* 76 (2007), 327–57; and Travis Glasson '"Baptism doth not bestow Freedom": Missionary Anglicanism, Slavery and the Yorke-Talbot Opinion, 1701–30', *William and Mary Quarterly* 67 (2010), 279–318.

[54] Dunkley, *Agency of the Enslaved,* 121. For a general account of the Sunday market system, see Heuman, *The Caribbean,* 41–3.

[55] LPL, CFS/F/1, 46, Stainsby to Rev. Barrett, 29 October 1823, St Thomas in the East, Jamaica.

[56] Ibid.

sentiment, and not "I am striving more than they all to convert souls."'[57]

Yet despite his criticisms, Stainsby continued to baptize large numbers of enslaved people. The following year, in 1824, he baptized 242 enslaved people, twice as many as any other Anglican curate working for The Conversion Society in Jamaica.[58] Stainsby's apparent hypocrisy in criticizing 'inappropriate' baptism on the one hand, and carrying these out on the other, was reflected more widely. The Rev. Richard Bickell, another clergyman stationed in Jamaica admitted:

> I am almost ashamed to confess, that in Kingston, I myself baptised nearly 1000 in the space of six months, with little or no examination; for being only [a] curate, I considered that my refusal to admit them in their ignorant state would considerably lessen the rector's income, there being a fee of two shillings and six pence for every slave baptised.[59]

As Bickell suggests, the reason for 'mass baptism' was to some extent financial.[60] Throughout the 1820s, rectors' incomes were partly dependent on the number of baptisms they performed. In addition, Jamaican island law fined any clergyman five pounds if he refused to 'baptize any Negro or other Slave that presents himself,' regardless of 'suitability' for conversion.[61]

Alongside financial motivations, campaigns for mass baptism were underpinned by the belief that enslaved people were unchristian, and thus uncivilized. In *Civilising Subjects,* Catherine Hall argued that racial hierarchies were central to the missionary enterprise more generally, due to the view that African people needed salvation.[62] Both the CMS and The Conversion Society in the 1820s were central in providing 'evidence' of an association between Christianity and civility, justifying the amelioration mission. Descriptions of 'savagery'

[57] CRL, C/W/079/137, Stainsby to the Secretary, Josiah Pratt, 11 April 1823, St Thomas in the East, Jamaica.

[58] Church Missionary Society, *The Missionary Register for 1824,* 89.

[59] Richard Bickell, *The West Indies as They are: Or, A Real Picture of Slavery: But More Particularly as it Exists in the Island of Jamaica, In Three Parts, With Notes* (London, 1825), 91.

[60] On 'mass baptism', see Dunkley, *Agency of the Enslaved,* 121.

[61] *Miscellaneous Papers: Ionian Islands; Slaves in the Colonies, Session 27 January–10 June 1818,* Parliamentary Papers 1818, vol. 17, 178–9.

[62] Hall, *Civilising Subjects*, 97.

were commonplace in both the *Missionary Register* and in the annual reports of The Conversion Society.[63] Thus, a combination of financial, practical and racist beliefs contextualized the motivations of John Stainsby as a missionary. Although Stainsby held strong beliefs on both Sunday markets and the practice of baptism in Jamaica, he suppressed these to appease planters, to ensure personal financial stability, and to contribute to the 'successes' of the mission. Stainsby was keen to attest to his own contribution to the mission: for instance, after his implication in the Sunday market rumour, he wrote to assure the CMS that he was a 'simple member of the Gospel who has done much good.'[64]

Missionary Reliance on Planters

The motivations of Stainsby and the missionary societies in appeasing the plantocracy were predominantly financial, but also practical, in that missionaries could only gain physical access to enslaved people on plantations with the planters' goodwill.[65] Indeed, Strickland has demonstrated that enslavers held strict criteria on the missionaries they would allow access to plantations. William Marshall Harte, an Anglican clergyman in Barbados, was fined for preaching material that might 'hinder the enslaver-enslaved power dynamic,' by discussing topics that breached the social norms of the system of slavery.[66] Thus, missionaries could not have a viable religious mission to enslaved people without the consent of enslavers. This was exacerbated by Anglican missionaries' financial reliance on planters. Following Canning's resolutions, the Standing Committee of the West India Planters and Merchants of the City of London resolved that 'the extension of the means of Religious Instruction, is the best and surest foundation for the improvement of the civil as well

[63] In the 1826 Missionary Register, the word 'heathen' appears over one hundred times: *The Missionary Register for 1826 Containing the Principal Transactions of the Various Institutions for Propagating the Gospel: with The Proceedings at Large of the Church Missionary Society* (London, 1826).

[64] CRL, CMS/B/OMS CW079/4, Stainsby to Rev. Josiah Pratt, 13 June 1825, St Thomas in the East, Jamaica.

[65] HC Deb. (2nd series), 16 March 1824 (vol. 10, cols 1091–198).

[66] Matthew Blake Strickland, '"The Protection of Slaves and Other Property": An Anglican Minister, Criminal Charges, and White Planters' Fear of Emancipation in Barbados', *Journal of Caribbean History* 5 (2021), 151–75, at 154–5.

as the moral condition of the Negroes in the West India Colonies.'[67] The committee praised The Conversion Society 'for their exertions in engaging Clergymen of the Established Church, to cooperate with the Clergy of the Colonies in promoting the object of their Institution.'[68] Subsequently, the committee offered a contribution of £1,000 to the Society, accompanied by donations from associations in Liverpool and Glasgow of £100.[69] The Conversion Society sought to 'secure an immediate application of the contributions' – that is, use of this money – by increasing the number of its clergy.[70]

The Conversion Society stressed its need for the support of the plantocracy. The 1823 report recognized that 'where the right of the Master over the services of the Slave is absolute, it is next to impossible to attempt the work of conversion on the latter without the aid of the former.'[71] Moreover, the Society promoted itself at the Colonial Associations in London in order to collect subscriptions and donations.[72] This initiative was successful, and by 1824, the Society's governors included prominent planters such as Henry Goulburn, Henry William Martin Bart, George Hibbert and Charles Rose Ellis. Their support generated a sense of 'satisfaction' that the Society 'had the support of the highest rank in both Church and state; as well as by several of the most considerable of the West India Proprietors.'[73]

Moreover, an analysis of subscribers and donors to The Conversion Society in the 1824 annual report demonstrates that fundraising efforts in 1823 had targeted and successfully gained the support of those invested in slavery more widely. By cross-referencing annual subscribers and one-time donors to the Conversion Society with the *Legacies of British Slavery Database,* the strong involvement of these individuals in transatlantic enslavement is revealed. Half (108

[67] The Conversion Society, *Report of the Incorporated Society for the Conversion and Religious Instruction and Education of the Negroe Slaves in the British West India Islands, from July to December 1823* (London, 1824), 7.

[68] Ibid. 7.

[69] Katie Donington, *The Bonds of Family: Slavery, Commerce and Culture in the British Atlantic World* (Manchester, 2019), 140.

[70] The Conversion Society, *Report of the Incorporated Society,* 9.

[71] Ibid. 6.

[72] Ibid. 39.

[73] The Conversion Society, *Report of the Incorporated Society for the Conversion and Religious Instruction and Education of the Negro Slaves in the British West India Islands for the Year 1824* (London, 1825), 6.

out of 215) of all donors and subscribers had connections to transatlantic slavery. The majority of these were either merchants or enslavers (42/108 were West India merchants, and 84/108 were enslavers).[74] The Conversion Society thus saw a significant level of financial support from merchants, enslavers and those with other connections to transatlantic slavery. While donors could have faith that, as an Anglican society, it would not 'corrupt the minds' of enslaved people, the Society's reliance on donors' financial aid also incentivized it against acting in opposition to enslavers' interests, perpetuating its own form of a pro-slavery Christianity.[75]

Support from the plantocracy became similarly central to the CMS in Jamaica. In an attempt to increase and monitor religious instruction in the Caribbean, George Canning's proposals had resulted in the establishing of two bishoprics in the Anglophone Caribbean in 1824.[76] Christopher Lipscombe was appointed to Jamaica; William Hart Coleridge to Barbados.[77] The bishops were expected to coordinate the work of clergy and missionaries across the Caribbean in policies of religious education and, ultimately, to supervise them.[78] However, their introduction, and their attempts to exercise control over the type of religious instruction given, caused conflict with missionaries employed by both The Conversion Society and the CMS.[79] Olwyn Blouet has argued that, generally, 'Lipscombe was reluctant to promote slave education.'[80] This was because he was 'primarily concerned with the status of the

[74] The names of donors and subscribers are taken from The Conversion Society, *Report of the Incorporated Society for the Conversion and Religious Instruction of Negro Slaves, July to December 1823* (London, 1824), 63–76. The names were entered into the *Legacies of British Slavery Database.* Once a reference was found, the *type* of appearance in the database was noted (owner, joint-owner, tenant-for life, etc.) These categories are listed on the *Legacies of British Slavery* website, at: <https://www.ucl.ac.uk/lbs/>, accessed 27 October 2022. The author is grateful to Keith McClelland (UCL) for his assistance in designing the database to compile this information.

[75] HL Deb. (2nd series), 16 March 1824 (vol. 10, col. 10467).

[76] Auxiliaries were also founded in St Kitts and Nevis, but no subscription records remain: Turner, 'The Bishop of Jamaica', 366.

[77] Ibid.

[78] Olwyn. M. Blouet, 'Earning and Learning in the British West Indies: An Image of Freedom in the Pre-Emancipation Decade, 1823–1833', *HistJ* 34 (1991), 391–409, at 395.

[79] James Curtin, the first missionary for The Conversion Society, frequently complained of Lipscombe's abandonment of him: LPL, FP Howley 3, 1–24, 31–4.

[80] Blouet, 'Slavery and Freedom', 630.

Church.'[81] Emphasis was placed on building churches, and in 1826 he consecrated the first new church built in Jamaica since his arrival.[82] By 1831, there were forty-six churches in Jamaica and seven chapels.[83] The focus on church-building, rather than providing religious instruction directly, meant that Lipscombe had a difficult relationship with missionaries. For example, from 1823, curates sent by the CMS were instructed to avoid any involvement in internal political matters due to Lipscombe's aim of keeping missionaries 'in strict subordination to the established clergy'.[84] Lipscombe refused to license multiple CMS catechists, seeing them as a threat to his authority in the Caribbean.[85] Stainsby noticed this and reported that the CMS were 'at present in bad odour with the Government here.' This again was due to tensions between 'the committee and the bishop.'[86]

This conflict eventually resulted in the creation of an auxiliary committee of the CMS, known as the Jamaican Auxiliary for the Church Missionary Society (JCMS), of which Stainsby became secretary.[87] In a letter written in July 1828 to Dandeson Coates, Assistant Secretary of the CMS (1828–30), James Wildman, a wealthy enslaver, discussed the need for extra funds to support new catechists and assistants.[88] He wrote:

> That it would be a most beneficial arrangement if a 'Jamaica Fund' were formed by the Society and by its several auxiliaries in Great Britain as it is highly probable that besides persons who support the Church Missionary Society, many West Indians and those who do not enter into the views of the Society would readily contribute to the amelioration of the spiritual slavery of the negro.[89]

[81] Turner, 'The Bishop of Jamaica', 369.
[82] Ellis, *The Diocese of Jamaica,* 65.
[83] TNA, CO 137/270, Comparative View of the Ecclesiastical Establishment, 1 Jan. 1831.
[84] Turner, 'The Bishop of Jamaica', 374.
[85] Ibid.
[86] CRL, CMS/B/OMS CW/O79/7, Stainsby to Dandeson Coates, 31 July 1830, St John's, Jamaica.
[87] By 1827, Stainsby's salary had increased to £215 annually from The Conversion Society; however, this is the last recorded salary for him: York, BIA, CFS/6 1827.
[88] Dandeson Coates became secretary for the CMS in 1830. For more on the JCMS, see Dunkley, *Agency of the Enslaved,* 53–94.
[89] CRL, CMS/B/OMS/CW/091, James Beckford Wildman to Dandeson Coates, 18 July 1828.

To encourage donations from British auxiliaries to the 'Jamaica Fund' for the provision of ministers, schoolmasters and catechists, the Rev. John McCammon Trew produced a pamphlet entitled 'A Few Simple Facts for the Friends of the Negro.'[90] Printed in Bristol, it sought to convince the British public to donate to the Jamaican Auxiliary of CMS.[91] The pamphlet sought to tap into appeals for amelioration by highlighting the supposed 'domestic tranquillity' of enslaved people following the Society's implementation of religious education.[92] It endeavoured to show 'the practical benefits likely to result both to the Master and to the Slave from the dissemination of Christianity among the latter.'[93] This openly identified the main target audience of the pamphlet as enslavers. In its final paragraphs the pamphlet asked:

> Is it not a duty incumbent on every Christian, but more especially in every West Indian Proprietor, as well as on every individual who participates in the least degree in any temporal advantage resulting from the labour of the slave, to assist in bringing him into a state of salvation through the Gospel? Surely it is.[94]

In both fundraising attempts, the JCMS exploited desires for amelioration by promoting to proprietors the perceived 'practical and spiritual benefits' of religious instruction.[95] By 1829, of the twenty-six leading members of the JCMS, twenty-one were enslavers, including the president, James Wildman, and the vice-presidents, the Rev. John McCammon Trew, William Stirling, William Stothert, Arthur Foulks, Archibald Sterling and James Miller.[96] John Stainsby was a secretary for the auxiliary alongside William Taylor and Richard Quarrell. Hence, by the late 1820s, both The Conversion Society and the JCMS relied on the financial support of the plantocracy, and also on their support in terms of access to allow them to carry out their missions. Accordingly, missionaries such as Stainsby became

[90] Ibid.
[91] Church Missionary Society, *A Few Simple Facts for the Friends of the Negro* (Bristol, 1828).
[92] Ibid.
[93] Ibid.
[94] Ibid.
[95] *Proceedings of the Jamaica Auxiliary Church Missionary Society, 1828 & 1829, Containing the first Report of the Committee* (Kingston, Jamaica, 1830), 3–7.
[96] Ibid.

even more inclined to align themselves with the plantocracy's vision of a Christian slave-society.

Censored Missionary Material

Due to the missionary societies' reliance on support from the West India Interest, material used in the instruction of enslaved people was heavily censored. It consisted of Scripture redacted by Anglican missionary societies to render it 'suitable' for enslaved people's consumption and acceptable to enslavers. Clergy, catechists and teachers could only read or teach from books which the bishop of Jamaica had approved.[97] Stainsby frequently wrote to both the CMS and The Conversion Society requesting such approved books,[98] which included 'Child's First Books,' sermons and spelling books.[99] In a letter to the CMS in 1829, Stainsby reported that the bishop of Jamaica had granted CMS catechists the authority to 'read prayers according to the rubric of formal service,' while clergy could only teach from books given approval by the bishop which were 'authorized writings of the Church,' including, for example, William Marshall Harte's lectures.[100] Indeed, in 1830, Stainsby recommended to the CMS that, to correspond with the bishop of Jamaica's wishes, Robert Dallas's instruction on an estate in Spanish Town should be 'oral only', due to the fears associated with a literate enslaved population.[101] Similarly, the CMS provided a prayer 'to be used every morning on a plantation' by enslaved people, which they stated had been 'recommended by the Bishop.'[102] The prayer echoed sentiments of enslavers and overseers, including a criticism of 'precious time

[97] CRL, CMS/B/OMS CW079/6, Stainsby to Dandeson Coates, 16 May 1829, Papine Estate, Jamaica.

[98] CRL, CMS/B/OMS CW079/8, Stainsby to Dandeson Coates, 10 June 1830, Manchester, Jamaica.

[99] LPL, CFS/G/3, 74. This list also included 'Harte's Lectures'. In 1826, both Stainsby and Lipscombe had fifty copies of *Harte's Lectures* sent to them. They were written by William Marshall Harte, a clergyman stationed in Barbados, and first published in 1822. Harte eventually became embroiled in a controversy over the content of his preaching. See Strickland, 'The Protection of Slaves', 163–4.

[100] CRL, CMS/B/OMS, CW/079/6, Stainsby to Dandeson Coates, 16 March 1829, Papine Estate, Jamaica.

[101] CRL, CMS/B/OMS CW/O79/9, Stainsby to Dandeson Coates, 24 August 1830, St John's, Jamaica. Emphasis original.

[102] CRL, CW/011/2, Original papers, 1827.

misspent' and a focus on an 'all-seeing God'.[103] As articulated in this prayer, the motivations of Anglican missionary societies appeared synonymous with those of the planters.

The most provocative learning tool for the plantocracy, however, was the Bible. John Coffey has demonstrated planters' fears regarding literacy and freedom, that if enslaved people could read the Bible then passages that did not support enslavement and which upheld total equality could be learnt and understood.[104] As early as 1807, The Conversion Society fostered a resolution to this problem by commissioning 'The Slave Bible', a version which was designed to be used exclusively by missionaries to teach enslaved people about Christianity and to encourage conversion. Under the guidance of Beilby Porteus, the Bible was edited down for 'simplicity' and Porteus gathered select portions of Scripture which 'related to the duties of slaves towards their masters.'[105]

The Slave Bible eradicated crucial passages. This included Galatians 3: 28–9: 'There is neither bond nor free, there is neither male nor female: for ye are all one in Christ Jesus' [AV].[106] In this attempt to eliminate all verses that could potentially 'result in rebellion,' around ninety per cent of the Old Testament and fifty per cent of the New Testament was removed. Psalms from the Authorized Version of the Bible, which 'expressed hopes for God's delivery from oppression,' were absent. In the Old Testament, the Book of Exodus excluded the story of the Israelites' liberation from slavery in Egypt, but did include the delivery of the Ten Commandments.[107] The Slave Bible promoted an 'Exhortation to Obedience.'[108]

[103] Ibid.

[104] Kazim Bacchus, 'Education and Society Among the Non-whites in the West Indies Prior to Emancipation', *History of Education* 19 (1990), 85–104, at 95. Compare also John Coffey, '"A bad and dangerous book"? The Biblical Identity Politics of the Demerara Slave Rebellion', in Gareth Atkins, Shinjini Das and Brian H. Murray, eds, *Chosen Peoples: The Bible, Race and Empire in the Long Nineteenth Century* (Manchester, 2020), 29–54; and Inge Dornan, 'Conversion and Curriculum: Nonconformist Missionaries and the British and Foreign School Society in the British West Indies, Africa and India, 1800–50,' in Morwenna Ludlow, Charlotte Methuen and Andrew Spicer, eds, *Churches and Education*, SCH 55 (Cambridge, 2019), 410–25.

[105] The Conversion Society, *The Negro Bible – The Slave Bible – Select Parts of the Holy Bible for the Use of the Negro Slaves of the British West India Islands,* ed. Joseph Lumpkin (Blountsville, AL, 2019), vii.

[106] Ibid.

[107] Ibid. viii.

[108] Ashleigh Elser, 'Reformations in Reading: Short Bibles and the Aesthetics of Abridgement,' *Journal of Religion & Society* 18 (2019), 119–34, at 128.

According to Peter Cruchley, the Slave Bible represents The Conversion Society's attempt to 'save without changing.'[109] The text certainly represents a remarkable example of the Church of England's overt manipulation of Scripture to appease planters. This, alongside the material permitted and recommended by the CMS and The Conversion Society, ensured that they were appropriate for enslavers' model of religious instruction in the 1820s. By censoring material provided for use by enslaved people, and restricting literate instruction, missionaries bowed to planters' fears of a literate enslaved population.[110]

Stainsby as an Enslaver

It has been seen that Stainsby engaged in hypocrisy and dissimulation to appease the plantocracy and the Anglican missionary societies who employed him, and that he, to some extent, recognized his own insincerity. However, there was one aspect of Stainsby's life in which he would not have been considered insincere: his position as an enslaver. Anglican missionaries who owned enslaved people were not considered hypocritical by either residents or the church. Like at least thirty clergymen resident in the British Caribbean and another fifteen 'transatlantic' clergymen who spent time on both sides of the Atlantic, Stainsby was actively involved in buying and selling enslaved people.[111]

Stainsby became the owner of the enslaved people registered to him through his second marriage to Catherine King in 1821, who, since at least 1817, had been the registered owner of Somerset Hall in St Dorothy, Jamaica.[112] Somerset Hall had functioned in the eighteenth century as a sugar and rum estate, but by 1821 the estate was split into three parts, and King (and subsequently Stainsby) probably held livestock and a small number of provisions. The other two sections of Somerset Hall were owned by Catherine King's brother, Joseph King.[113]

[109] Peter Cruchley, 'Ecce Homo…? Beholding Mission's White Gaze', *Practical Theology* 15 (2022), 64–77.

[110] Bacchus, 'Education and Society', 88.

[111] Information from *Legacies of British Slavery Database*.

[112] TNA, Office of Registry of Colonial Slaves and Slave Compensation Commission, T 71/13; LPL, FP Howley 40, Stainsby to the bishop of London, Charles Blomfield, 3 August 1818, Low Coniscliffe, County Durham.

[113] John Smith, *Map of Jamaica* (London, 1844), David Rumsey Map Collection, online at: <https://www.davidrumsey.com/luna/servlet/detail/RUMSEY~8~1~2777~270050:

An examination of colonial slave registers for Jamaica during this period makes evident both the shift in ownership from Catherine King to Stainsby, and Stainsby's later management of enslaved people. In the 1817 and 1820 registers, at least seventeen enslaved people were registered to Catherine King.[114] After her marriage to Stainsby in 1821, Stainsby became their listed owner. Between 1821 and 1823, two men, two women and two children were purchased by Stainsby, and one child, named Kitty, was born on the estate.[115] The purchased enslaved people included a family, Elizabeth (listed as Bess) with her two children, four-year-old Richard and two-year-old Bob. The same year, another family owned by Stainsby, forty-six-year-old Jenny and her four daughters, were sold to an estate in St Thomas in the East.[116] Hence, in the period immediately following Stainsby's acquiring ownership of the estate, he carried out multiple sales and purchases.

Between 1823 and 1829, another two children were born into slavery on Stainsby's estate. Stainsby sold Richard (Elizabeth's child, now aged ten) and purchased two men, William, a sixty-year-old 'African', and Charles, a twenty-year-old creole.[117] Subsequently, from 1829 to 1832, Stainsby purchased a twenty-four-year-old man named Paul Peterson, a thirteen-year-old boy named Richard, and a nine-year-old boy named John Thomas from an estate in Manchester.[118] It is likely that thirteen-year-old Richard was the same child whom Stainsby had sold three years prior. In this period, Stainsby also purchased three young women: Sarah, Fanny and Margaret; Sarah subsequently gave birth to a son, Joseph Thomas.[119] By 1832, twenty-five enslaved people were registered to Stainsby.

Between 1832 and emancipation in 1834, Stainsby purchased another eleven enslaved people, meaning that on 14 March 1836,

Map-Of-Jamaica=>, accessed 31 October 2022; 'Somerset Hill', *Legacies of British Slavery Database*, online at: <https://www.ucl.ac.uk/lbs/estate/view/12679>, accessed 31 October 2022.

[114] TNA, Office of Registry of Colonial Slaves, T71/13, 48; T71/14, 126.

[115] TNA, Office of Registry of Colonial Slaves, T 71/15, 147.

[116] Ibid.

[117] TNA, Office of Registry of Colonial Slaves, T 71/16; T 71/17, 136.

[118] TNA, Office of Registry of Colonial Slaves, T 71/18, 386.

[119] Ibid.

he received £646 18*s*. 6*d*. in compensation for thirty-six enslaved people registered to the St Dorothy estate.[120] During this period, Stainsby also apprenticed men, women and children following 1834, including Jane Stainsby and Sophia Stainsby, both about thirteen-years-old, who were listed as Stainsby's apprentices in December 1837.[121] Due to the number of people he enslaved and the nature of the land, it is likely that Stainsby's enslaved people were 'domestics' who carried out domestic chores, such as laundry and cooking, and tended a small amount of livestock, which was relatively typical for members of the middling class such as Stainsby.[122]

Since Stainsby did not write about his slave-ownership in letters or correspondence, we do not know how much influence his wife Catherine continued to have. It is necessary to look to other sources to consider how Anglican missionaries justified slave-ownership. The primary justification was the perceived differences between physical and spiritual freedom. At the formation of The Conversion Society's Bermuda branch meeting in 1829, Archdeacon Aubrey Spencer spoke of the compatibility of Christianity and slavery. Spencer stated that 'of course' he was against slavery, but that the evil was too difficult to eradicate, and thus mitigation of conditions through amelioration was sufficient.[123] Indeed, Spencer noted that even if he could eradicate slavery in a breath, he 'would not' because of enslaved people's 'present state of mental degradation,' which meant that 'liberty would be to [an enslaved person], instead of a boon and a blessing, a burden and a curse.'[124] Religious instruction could free enslaved people spiritually, thus mitigating the need for physical emancipation.

[120] TNA, Office of Registry of Colonial Slaves and Slave Compensation Commission, T71/857. The names of the enslaved people purchased in this period are unknown.

[121] *Slave Trade: Copy of the Report of Hall Pringle and Alexander Campbell, Esquires, Associate Justices of the Peace, Relatives to Certain Atrocities of Slave Trades* (House of Commons Parliamentary Papers, Paper 157, 1839), 4.

[122] Somerset Hall was not listed as a 'pen' or 'plantation'. Georgia Fox outlines the differences between 'pens' and 'plantations' in Colonial Slave Registers in Georgia L. Fox, 'The Great House', in eadem, ed., *An Archaeology and History of a Caribbean Sugar Plantation on Antigua* (Gainesville, FL, 2020), 16–32, at 29.

[123] The Conversion Society, *Report of the Incorporated Society for The Conversion and Religious Instruction and Education of the Negro Slaves in the British West India Islands for the year 1829* (London, 1829), 81–2.

[124] Ibid.

Similarly, the CMS emphasized the importance of spiritual freedom over physical freedom. During the final years of colonial slavery, the Bath auxiliary of the CMS in Britain stated that 'we trust that God designs that the deliverance of their bodies from the bonds of slavery shall be the fore runner of a deliverance which is *far more important*, the rescue of their souls from the bondage of sin and the service of Satan.'[125] Hence, Stainsby and other slave-owning Anglican missionaries would not have seen themselves as hypocrites. Firstly, because the enslavement of domestic workers was typical for the middling population in Jamaica. Secondly, they were confident that they were providing 'spiritual freedom,' which was, in their belief, superior to physical freedom.

Conclusion

Stainsby was employed by, and in correspondence with, the CMS until it withdrew from Jamaica in 1849, and he remained in Jamaica until his death in 1854.[126] In Hanover parish church, a plaque is dedicated to his memory. The memorial tablet was funded by subscriptions of the congregation who 'treasured his memory and deplored his loss.'[127] Back in Britain, Stainsby's obituary in the *Staffordshire Sentinel* recorded that 'finding Jamaica groaning under the terrible system of slavery, he took a decided part in mixing with the oppressed [slaves], whose souls it was his object to seek and save.'[128] Indeed, Stainsby's most important objective was to convert and instruct enslaved people under the guidance of the two missionary societies by which he was employed. As such, he carefully navigated plantation society in Jamaica to avoid antagonizing enslavers and stifling the mission's growth and success, and it is for his 'soul saving' that Stainsby is remembered on both sides of the Atlantic.

By consistently working to appease the plantocracy alongside the objectives of the CMS and The Conversion Society, Stainsby's actions can be defined by hypocrisy and suppression. He was required

[125] Taunton, Somerset Archives, D/P/langp/2/9/2, Minutes of the Mid-Somerset Branch of the CMS. Emphasis original.

[126] CRL, CMS/B/OMS, CWO79/15-20.

[127] Chris Bodden, 'The Historic St Mary's', *The Jamaica Gleaner*, 28 September 2013, online at: <http://jamaica-gleaner.com/gleaner/20130928/lead/lead7.html>, accessed 31 October 2022.

[128] *Staffordshire Sentinel*, 28 January 1854, 5.

to use manipulated religious material designed to restrict notions of equality and freedom, with a view to diminishing the risk of uprisings and emancipation. This included the heavily edited Slave Bible, and texts specifically written to promote obedience and servitude. Similarly, he was expected to refrain from political opinion, even when this went against his own beliefs. He frequently baptized more enslaved people than any other cleric in Jamaica despite his reservations that enslaved people were not 'ready'. Yet an element of Stainsby's life which evaded any need for his deception and avoided any claim of hypocrisy at the time was his slave-ownership. His position as an enslaver aligned completely, both with the middling population of Jamaica, and with the expectations of the Church of England, and as such, he was never questioned nor challenged on it. Stainsby was just one of many clergymen and missionaries who bought and sold enslaved people in Jamaica and across the Caribbean. Such analysis opens up further avenues for research and historical understanding: into an aspect of the Church of England's involvement in transatlantic enslavement that went far beyond religious instruction, extending to a form of pro-slavery Christianity that was carefully navigated by missionaries in the early nineteenth century.

Dissimulation as an Editorial Strategy in the *Life of William Wilberforce*

Mark Smith*
University of Oxford

In 1838, Robert and Samuel Wilberforce published, in five volumes, The Life of William Wilberforce. *Although the subject of some contemporary controversy, this work, containing extensive quotations from his diaries, rapidly established itself as the principal source for subsequent biographical writings about Wilberforce and strongly influenced later interpretations. The production of a complete initial transcription of the diaries by the Wilberforce Diaries Project for the first time enables a systematic comparison between the* Life *and its principal source. This reveals a systematic attempt by his sons to minimize references to Wilberforce's participation in some aspects of Hanoverian sociability, his use of medication to deal with his worsening health, his close associations with and respect for Nonconformists and his own evangelical commitment and spirituality. As a consequence, the Wilberforce we know from the biography is as much a product of early Victorian myth-making as the Wilberforce of 1759–1833.*

In 1838, less than five years after the death of their father, Robert and Samuel Wilberforce[1] published, in five volumes, *The Life of William Wilberforce.*[2] While it was well received in many quarters,[3] the book would soon become the subject of controversy. Initially, this centred around Robert and Samuel's rather shabby treatment of the contribution of Thomas Clarkson to the campaigns for abolition and emancipation in general, and of his account of the abolition

* E-mail: mark.smith@history.ox.ac.uk.

[1] Robert (1802–57) and Samuel (1805–73) Wilberforce were both ordained in 1838 as Anglican clergymen who, in contrast to their father, were high churchmen and early followers of the Oxford Movement. In 1845, Samuel became bishop of Oxford and then, in 1869, bishop of Winchester, while Robert became a convert to Roman Catholicism in 1854. The most sympathetic portrayal of their religious development remains David Newsome, *The Parting of Friends* (London, 1966).

[2] Robert Isaac Wilberforce and Samuel Wilberforce, *The Life of William Wilberforce*, 5 vols (London, 1838) [hereafter: *Life*].

[3] For example, *The Edinburgh Review* 67/135 (1838), 142–80.

Studies in Church History 60 (2024), 387–407
doi: 10.1017/stc.2024.18

campaign in particular.[4] This feature was noticed in an early consideration of the book in the *Quarterly Review*[5] and elaborated in a book-length reply, *Strictures on the Life of Wilberforce*, by Clarkson himself with the support of Henry Brougham and Henry Crabb Robinson.[6] Although they were initially inclined to defend their position, Robert and Samuel gradually withdrew the most egregious material from subsequent editions of the *Life* and, in 1844, wrote to Clarkson with a formal apology.[7] A further and more limited controversy emerged with the publication, in 1854, of the autobiography of Wilberforce's friend, the Independent minister, William Jay, chief pastor at the Argyle Chapel in Bath.[8] This protested against the impression given in the *Life* that their acquaintance was slight and formal, contending that it was, instead, cordial, generous and warm, and Jay's editors provided evidence to support their claims in the form of a collection of letters between Jay and William and Barbara Wilberforce.[9] The Jay controversy suggested that the brothers might have been somewhat selective in approaching their father's friends for copies of correspondence, and convinced Christopher Tolley, who has produced the most comprehensive account of Robert and Samuel's biographical practice, that his sons found this aspect of Wilberforce's religious life 'hard to understand'.[10]

Thereafter, despite some contemporary reservations about the use made of their father's religious journal,[11] the *Life* became a received text and its extensive quotations have been the main quarry for subsequent treatments of Wilberforce and his career, even by those who also made use of the diaries, such as the biographies by Robin

[4] Thomas Clarkson, *The History of the Rise, Progress and Accomplishment of the Abolition of the African Slave Trade by the British Parliament* (London, 1808).

[5] *The Quarterly Review* 62/123 (1838), 214–85.

[6] Thomas Clarkson, Henry Brougham and Henry Crabbe Robinson, *Strictures on a Life of William Wilberforce by the Rev. W[.]* [sic.] *and the Rev. S. Wilberforce* (London, 1838). Brougham (1778–1868) was a leading lawyer and politician who had been prominent in the abolition campaign. Robinson (1775–1867) was a diarist and journalist.

[7] Christopher Tolley, *Domestic Biography: The Legacy of Evangelicalism in Four Nineteenth-Century Families* (Oxford, 1997), 166–8.

[8] William Jay, *The Autobiography of the Rev. William Jay*, ed. George Redford and John Angel James (London, 1854).

[9] Ibid. 300–27.

[10] Tolley, *Domestic Biography*, 172.

[11] For a discussion of these concerns, see ibid. 173–6.

Furneaux[12] and William Hague.[13] Indeed, Reginald Coupland, whose biography of Wilberforce was first published in 1923, with a second edition in 1945, reported, on comparing one of the family collections of Wilberforce manuscript diaries with the work of Robert and Samuel, that: 'practically every item of interest or importance had been quoted in the *Life*'.[14] It was not until 1961, with the appearance of Ford K. Brown's *Fathers of the Victorians*, that modern historiographical claims began to be made about Robert and Samuel's agenda in writing the *Life*. In particular, Brown argued that Wilberforce's more high church sons had sought to conceal their father's evangelicalism by a variety of means, including minimizing the use of the word in the *Life*, failing to point out the religious character of his associates, and using sleight of hand to disguise the evangelical content of Wilberforce's language.[15] According to Brown, this enterprise was facilitated by the likelihood that Wilberforce himself had, in later life, 'gone over to High Church'.[16] He supported this claim by what he regarded as evidence that the later Wilberforce displayed a disdain for Nonconformity and a growing fear of ecclesiastical irregularity.[17] Brown's proposals were immediately challenged by David Newsome, who, in a fifteen-page review in the *Historical Journal*, assailed virtually every aspect of the book, from its theme and content, to its repetitive prose style and lack of sympathy with its subject.[18] Particular ire, however, was reserved for Brown's treatment of Robert and Samuel's biography of their father. Newsome argued, on the basis of a thorough review of the extensive correspondence between Robert and Samuel while writing the *Life*, that the sons did not create their portrait of their father through ambiguity, deliberate distortion or suppression of material.[19] He did accept, though, that they had been 'less than candid' in their depiction of

[12] Robin Furneaux, *William Wilberforce* (London, 1974).

[13] William Hague, *William Wilberforce: The Life of the Great Anti-Slave Trade Campaigner* (London, 2008). For an exception, though focussing on Wilberforce's domestic and family life, rather than aiming at a comprehensive biography, see Anne Stott, *Wilberforce: Family and Friends* (Oxford, 2012).

[14] Reginald Coupland, *Wilberforce*, 2nd edn (London, 1945; first publ. 1923), 431.

[15] Ford K. Brown, *Fathers of the Victorians: The Age of Wilberforce* (Cambridge, 1961), 487–98.

[16] Ibid. 499.

[17] Ibid. 500–1.

[18] David Newsome, 'Fathers and Sons', *HistJ* 6 (1963), 295–310.

[19] Ibid. 301–2.

their father's relationship with William Jay.[20] He also noted that much of Brown's criticism of the sons' work could only be conjectural because he was not able to consult the original sources.[21] However, neither party to the dispute was able to cite the manuscript diary to demonstrate their position and the argument therefore subsided into a clash of opinion.[22]

The production of a draft transcription of the extant portions of Wilberforce's diary – an early fruit of the Wilberforce Diaries Project[23] – offers for the first time not just a means of adjudicating between the rival claims of Ford K. Brown and David Newsome, now some sixty years old, but also the opportunity for a more systematic comparison between the *Life* and the diaries which comprise its most fundamental source. In undertaking such a comparison, it becomes possible to examine Robert and Samuel's biographical method and to draw some conclusions about the multiple agendas revealed by the choices that they made as they handled their material. This article focusses on the treatment of three aspects of Wilberforce by his sons: his participation in everyday Hanoverian life, especially in matters relating to the body, on which his sons were notably reticent; his relationship with non-Anglicans, especially Protestant Dissenters, including his long-running friendship with William Jay; and the character of his personal religion, including the question of the persistence of his evangelical position and the nature of his spirituality.

[20] Ibid. 305.

[21] Ibid. 301.

[22] Brown's work was based exclusively on printed sources. Newsome had been given access to collections of Wilberforce papers for the research which led to the publication of *The Parting of Friends* in the mid-1960s, but (at least up to 1963) seems to have restricted himself largely to material concerning the sons, rather than their father. See Newsome, *Parting of Friends* (London, 1966), x–xi, 455–8.

[23] For details of the Wilberforce Diaries Project, which aims to produce the first scholarly edition of Wilberforce's surviving diaries and journals, see online at: https://wilberforcediariesproject.com/. Thanks are due to my editorial colleagues, in particular John Coffey and Anna Harrington, without which the analysis presented here would not have been possible. Diaries kept at the Bodleian Library are catalogued in a number of series and are cited following Bodleian document references b.2 and c.40 etc. The large volume kept at the Wilberforce House Museum in Hull has no catalogue reference and is cited by name. The folios in each volume are as numbered by Wilberforce. In the case of the Hull volume, he numbered each page separately in two sequences, the second differentiated from the first by the addition of a lower-case x. For ease of reading, quotations from the diaries expand many of Wilberforce's abbreviations; inserted letters are given in square brackets.

The social and political culture of Wilberforce's contemporaries was strongly marked by its relish for the pleasures of food and drink and, for the political classes in particular, the dining table was a key locus of connection, conversation and sociability. According to the architect Robert Adam, while the French retired immediately after dining and sought out other rooms for conversation,

> It is not so with us. Accustomed by habit or induced by the nature of our climate, we indulge more largely in the enjoyment of the bottle. Every person of rank here is either a membre [*sic*] of the legislation, or entitled by his condition to take part in the political arrangements of his country, and to enter with ardour into those discussions to which they give rise; these circumstances lead men to live more with one another and more detached from the society of the ladies. The eating rooms are considered as the apartments of conversation, in which we are to pass a great part of our time.[24]

Many of Wilberforce's political contemporaries and associates were notable drinkers on these occasions. According to Sir Gilbert Eliot, in a much-quoted passage:

> Fox drinks what I should call a great deal, though he is not reckoned to do so by his companions, Sheridan excessively, and Grey more than any of them. … Pitt, I am told, drinks as much as anybody, generally more than any of his company and that he is a pleasant convivial man at table.[25]

Wilberforce's popularity in company meant that he was a frequent guest at social gatherings as well as a key host, especially at supper parties in his strategically placed lodgings in Old Palace Yard, a short stroll from the Commons debating chamber.[26] In the *Life*,

[24] *The Works in Architecture of Robert and James Adam*, ed. Robert Oresko (London, 1975), 48.

[25] Gilbert Elliot, *Life and Letters of Sir Gilbert Elliot, First Earl of Minto*, ed. Emma Eleanor Elizabeth Hislop Elliot, 3 vols. (London, 1874), 1: 189.

[26] Wilberforce took these lodgings in 1786 and used them regularly for parliamentary entertaining, even after his marriage in 1797, until 1808, when he moved his family residence from Clapham to Kensington Gore. See 'Places', *The Wilberforce Diaries Project*, online at: <https://wilberforcediariesproject.com/places/#homes>, accessed 6 August 2023. Sociable dining at the House of Commons is discussed in Caroline Shenton, *The Day Parliament Burnt Down* (Oxford, 2012), 121–4.

the details of Wilberforce's dining habits are largely excluded and the sons are at pains to draw a contrast between Wilberforce and his contemporaries on this point. Thus, they comment on the rules he set himself for conduct at the table: 'He was not labouring to reduce intemperate habits within the limits of that self-indulgent propriety which contents the generality of men. From this point he started, but aiming at a higher standard, he sought to live a life of mortification in the midst of luxury.'[27]

This passage suggests a high moral purpose in Wilberforce's rules for temperance while dining, portraying him as a sort of reasonable ascetic. In the diary, however, the rules seem related primarily to Wilberforce's concern for his fragile health. He noted in July 1788, for example: 'Hitherto always meat Suppers & plentiful – Begin to suspect they or fermented liquor at Night disturb my Heart.'[28] Wilberforce had to tread a narrow line between temperance and abstemiousness, since he believed that too much austerity might also prove dangerous, concluding later in the same month that 'my health requires throughout an indulgent regimen'.[29] Nonetheless, given that Wilberforce, at least after his conversion, regarded his health as a gift from God to be carefully stewarded so that he could continue to be useful,[30] it would be misleading to attempt to draw too great a distinction between the physical and spiritual motivations for his attempts at temperance.

A single passage in Volume I of the *Life* indicated that, at times, Wilberforce struggled with his own rules.[31] This is an example of a common editorial method employed by Robert and Samuel of producing a distorted picture not by outright omission of a prominent feature of their father's life, but rather by minimizing it. In the eleven years between 1788 and 1799, for example, there are well over two hundred references in Wilberforce's diaries to his having broken his own rules for the table. In November 1788, for example, he lamented: 'All my Mens Rules sadly violated again & again.'[32] These frequent infractions were almost as frequently preceded and

[27] *Life*, 1: 197.

[28] Oxford, Bodl., MS Wilberforce b.2, fol. 6, Diary, 27 July 1788.

[29] Quoted in *Life*, 1: 181.

[30] See, for instance, Bodl., MS Wilberforce b.2, fol. 10^{v}, Diary, 6 Feb 1789.

[31] *Life*, 1: 197–8.

[32] Bodl., MS Wilberforce c.4, fol. 4, Diary, 19 November 1788. 'Mens' (an abbreviation of *mensa*) was Wilberforce's standard shorthand for matters to do with the table and is

followed by renewed resolutions to keep to his regime. In 1789, for example, he noted in successive diary entries:

> Receiv[e]d Sacrament & strong Sense of past Follies & Determination by divine Grace to amend – yet wasted time sadly rather exceded Mens &c & all this most unpardonable because Buxton Waters have been of great Service to me. I now hope to amend – Mens: Mod[erate] – & ferms – No Des[sert].[33]

Congenial company was, with many Hanoverians, the route to excess at table and Wilberforce was no exception.[34] Dessert seems to have been a particular weakness. Earlier in 1789, for example, he recorded: 'In spite of all my solemn Resolutions, yesterday at Dinner at Lord Chatham's I exceeded Mens in all ways, chiefly dessert sweets'.[35] The diary also frequently comments on excessive consumption, by Wilberforce's own standards, of fermented drink, probably beer taken with meals, but possibly also including wine. Thus, in February 1791, he noted: 'din[e]d Pitt before House Moderately, but at night quite exceded ferms.'[36] Often though, he overindulged in food and drink together, as in October 1792: 'I have been going on everyway ill, & the Effects of this bad frame have appear[e]d in my almost constant Mens: Excedings as usual both in ferms & otherwise'.[37] Much less frequent are references to overindulgence in spirits, probably brandy consumed after dinner.[38] He also berated himself for indulgence in tea and coffee, which he believed interfered with his sleep and impaired his usefulness.[39] Robert and Samuel showed a particular determination to exclude such material from the *Life*, not only

often to be found in the diary in conjunction with the abbreviation 'reg' or 'regs', representing *regula* or regulations.

33 Bodl., MS Wilberforce b.2, fol. 18, Diary, 4–5 October 1789. 'Ferms' was Wilberforce's standard shorthand for fermented liquor.

34 See, for instance, Bodl., MS Wilberforce b.2, fol. 24^r, Diary, 12 Feb 1791: 'Sykess & Smiths & Xtian dined with me - again I did not adhere strictly - unless I can keep my Mens: & other Resolves – I must now break off this living so much in Company.'

35 Bodl., MS Wilberforce c.4, fol. 4, Diary, 3 Jan 1789.

36 Bodl., MS Wilberforce b.2, fol. 24^r, Diary, 14 Feb. 1791.

37 Bodl., MS Wilberforce c.40, fol.48, Diary, 4 Oct 1792.

38 Bodl., MS Wilberforce b.2, fol. 11^v, Diary, 2 March 1789. Wilberforce occasionally used the shorthand term 'dis' to represent overconsumption by his own standards of spirits. See, for example, Bodl., MS Wilberforce c.41, fol. 105, Diary, 2 April 1797.

39 Bodl., MS Wilberforce b.2, fol. 16, Diary, 15 June 1789; ibid., fol. 17^r, Diary, 31 July 1789.

steering clear of passages in the diary which dwelt on Wilberforce's consumption of food and drink, but also silently omitting references to his dining habits in material that they did use. May 1789, for example, saw a climactic moment in Wilberforce's public career as he prepared to introduce his first abolition motion in a three-and-a-half-hour speech to the House of Commons. The diary recorded that Wilberforce exceeded his own dietary rules twice in the preceding five days, first at Pitt's house at Holwood, where he found himself incapacitated from discussing the detail of abolition with the Prime Minister, and the second on the day before his speech, probably at Matthew Montagu's in company with leading abolitionists William Burgh, John Clarkson and James Ramsay. The consequences were frankly noted in his diary: 'Very indiff[eren]t *from hav[in]g exceeded day before*: came to town sadly unfit for work but by Divine Grace enabled to make my Motion so as to give Satisfaction'.[40]

The same passage is accurately reproduced in the *Life*, but with the italicized words silently omitted, the sons clearly reluctant to show that their father had almost tripped himself up on such an important occasion.[41] However, none of Wilberforce's consumption of food and drink was in the least remarkable for his age and place in society. Indeed, in their analysis of the political day in London, Hannah Greig and Amanda Vickery have identified the period 1780–1820 as 'the zenith of elite hard drinking and fast living, the epitome of Georgian excess', noting that the succeeding Victorian political culture eschewed heavy drinking. Thus, to Victorian readers, weakness in this area had perhaps become less acceptable in respectable circles, and especially in a Christian hero.[42] It is not surprising, therefore, that Wilberforce's sons chose to minimize this aspect of their father's life.

Masculine sociability, lubricated by alcohol, inevitably produced a freer mode of conversation than that which the sons wished to present to their early Victorian readership. Omitted from the *Life,* therefore, are diary entries in which Wilberforce lamented his having given countenance to inappropriate conversation around the table. For instance, in March 1798 after a dinner with the Prime Minister, he

40 Bodl., MS Wilberforce b.2, fol. 13, Diary, 12 May 1789. Emphasis added.
41 *Life*, 1: 218.
42 Hannah Greig and Amanda Vickery, 'The Political Day in London *c.*1697–1834', *P&P* 252 (2021), 101–37, at 131.

noted: 'Conv[ersation] & Comp[an]y Reg[u]l[ation]s sadly neglected, laugh[e]d improp[e]rly at someth[in]g rather profane Pitt said'.[43] Similarly excluded from the *Life* were Wilberforce's own occasional lapses into acerbity. In Volume IV, for example, the sons quoted Wilberforce's diary as recording: 'Thorpe has published a pamphlet addressed to me'.[44] The diary, however, reveals a much more extreme reaction:

> that vile demon Thorpe (really He must be a Subject of Black Inspiration or rather which is perhaps the same thing a little Insane, which when it affects the moral principle produces an extreme Intensity of wickedness & malignity), has published a pamphlet addressed to me.[45]

This is not typical of Wilberforce and a number of factors clearly contributed to this outburst. Robert Thorpe had been Chief Justice of Sierra Leone and his pamphlet attacking the administration there must have seemed like an act of betrayal to Wilberforce, who was at the time both grieving the loss of his close friends Henry Thornton and John Bowdler, and also trying to secure a registration bill aimed at tightening up the 1807 Abolition Act.[46] It is unsurprising that the sons wished to conceal that their father was capable of extreme language, but their decision rendered Wilberforce a blander character than the one the diary reveals.

Many other regular features of Hanoverian life are similarly expunged from the published presentation of Wilberforce's experience, despite being the subject of extensive and even reflective comment in the diary. Readers of Volume I, for example, would find Wilberforce in December 1794 passing the night at his London lodgings in some discomfort. Robert and Samuel quoted his journal as recording: 'A disturbed night – full of ambition. How small things confound human pride! why not such small things God's agents as

[43] Bodl., MS Wilberforce c.41, fol. 117, Diary, 11 March 1798.

[44] *Life*, 4: 242.

[45] Bodl., MS Wilberforce c.39, fol. 28, Diary, 11 Feb. 1815.

[46] For Thorpe, see, for instance, Gareth Atkins, *Converting Britannia: Evangelicals and English Public Life, 1770–1840* (Woodbridge, 2019), 165–6. For the deaths of Thornton and Bowdler of tuberculosis on 16 January and 1 February 1815 respectively, see Stott, *Wilberforce*, 172–88. For the registration bill, see, for example, John Pollock, *Wilberforce* (Tring, 1977), 249–51.

much as locusts?'[47] Only when reading the diary, however, is it possible to identify the precise source of his discomfort: 'Flea Bitten full of ambition &c how small things confound human Pride why not fleas as much Gods Judgem[en]ts & agents as locusts; sad night.'[48] For most Hanoverians, especially for frequent travellers like Wilberforce, attack by fleas was a regular problem. Such occasions are frequent objects of comment for Wilberforce, especially when his rest was disturbed. There are no fewer than eighty-six explicit references in the extant diary volumes which provide a sort of geography of hazard. Wilberforce was bitten frequently on his continental tour in both France[49] and Italy,[50] while in Switzerland he alarmingly encountered 'immense fleas even bigger than Bees'.[51] Back in Britain, he was bitten all through the night in a Leicestershire inn,[52] but also in more salubrious conditions, such as when on holiday in Ryde,[53] or while taking the waters at Bath.[54] His sleep was similarly impaired when he stayed with the Gisbornes at Yoxall Lodge,[55] and at Sir Charles and Lady Middleton's house at Teston.[56]

Robert and Samuel Wilberforce were not alone in wishing to erase evidence both of occasional angularity and of the less salubrious features of Hanoverian life from their presentation of their subject. Anne Stott notes a similar process in the biography of Wilberforce's friend Hannah More, first published in 1834.[57] Some thirty years later, a correspondingly liberal use of the redactor's pencil was evident in Edward Austen Leigh's edition of the surviving correspondence of Jane Austen. In order to preserve the existing Austen myth, he erased all traces of acerbity and all references to fleas.[58] Presented for a Victorian audience, the 'Christian Senator', like 'Aunt Jane', could be neither biting nor bitten.

47 *Life*, 1: 69–70.
48 Bodl., MS Wilberforce c.34, fol. 41, Diary, 30 December 1794.
49 Bodl., MS Wilberforce Don, e.164, fol. 81, Diary, 18 July 1785.
50 Bodl., MS Wilberforce Don, e.164, fol. 80, Diary, 5 July 1785.
51 Bodl., MS Wilberforce Don, e.164, fol. 83, Diary, 2 August 1785.
52 Bodl., MS Wilberforce b.2, fol. 21, Diary, 17 July 1790.
53 Bodl., MS Wilberforce d.54, fol. 14, Diary, 8 October 1808.
54 See, for instance, Bodl., MS Wilberforce c.34, fol. 148, Diary, 15–21 January 1798; Bodl., MS Wilberforce c.41, fol. 115, Journal, 21 January 1798.
55 Bodl., MS Wilberforce b.2, fol. 21ʳ, Diary, 5 August 1790.
56 Bodl., MS Wilberforce c.34, fol. 33, Diary, 5–7 August 1794.
57 Anne Stott, *Hannah More* (Oxford, 2003), viii–ix.
58 Emily Auerbach, *Searching for Jane Austen* (Madison, WI, 2004), 7–11.

However, in eliminating such references, the sons also deprived their readers of an important insight into the spirituality of their subject. In a document written largely in a penitential mode, one of the most joyful passages in Wilberforce's spiritual journal relates to his encounter with, and deliverance from, the attentions of a flea:

> Sadly wander[in]g in fam[il]y prayer. But may the promise be fulfill'd in me 1 Cor 1: 30.[59] I wo[ul]d not be Superstitious but hav[in]g felt last night ab[ou]t. Bedtime, a Sort of glorying, rather, & then a flea in Bed convincing me of Weakness, & pray[ing] to God that by catch[in] g it my night might be no longer disturb[e]d & I be unfitted for [the] Service of this day. I caught it almost immed[iatel]y. A similar Instance happen'd lately. Rem[embe]r Locusts, Grasshoppers, Flies &c. made God's Instruments, & whatever really lowest convinces of weakness, &c drives to him – 1 Cor. 1: 30.[60]

Wilberforce's capacity to see spiritual significance, not only in large matters of politics and philanthropy, but in the everyday accidents of life is particularly well captured in this passage, as are the immediacy of his relationship with God and his commitment to careful scriptural (as well as spiritual) application of his experience. This is a rather different spirituality to that suggested by Robert and Samuel's focus on their father's rules for living, the subject of so much attention in the *Life*.[61]

The largest and most extensive feature of Wilberforce's regime eliminated from the *Life*, however, was any proportionate representation of the measures he took to manage his health. This was in a delicate and deteriorating condition almost continuously from the late 1780s, when it was briefly thought that he might die.[62] His principal resort, especially when dealing with acute intestinal pain, from this point until the end of his life, was to the medical use of opium. Robert and Samuel made one reference to Wilberforce's opium use in the first volume of the *Life* which was embedded in a carefully crafted apologetic passage located after a discussion of his health crisis:

[59] In the Authorized Version, 1 Cor 1: 30 reads: 'But of him are ye in Christ Jesus, who of God is made unto us wisdom, and righteousness, and sanctification, and redemption.'
[60] Bodl., MS Wilberforce c.41, fol. 123, Journal, 23 September 1798.
[61] See below p. 407.
[62] See, for instance, Furneaux, *Wilberforce*, 76–8.

> Beyond all calculation he was visibly gaining strength at Bath. His returning health was in great measure the effect of a proper use of opium, a remedy to which even Dr. Pitcairne's judgment could scarcely make him have recourse; yet it was to this medicine that he now owed his life, as well as the comparative vigour of his later years. So sparing was he always in its use that as a stimulant he never knew its power, and as a remedy for his specific weakness he had not to increase its quantity during the last twenty years he lived. 'If I take,' he would often say, 'but a single glass of wine, I can feel its effect, but I never know when I have taken my dose of opium by my feelings.'[63]

As with many other aspects of their father's embodied life, Robert and Samuel would probably have preferred to omit any reference to his use of this particular medicine altogether. However, his use of the drug was no secret and certainly sufficiently well-known for Thomas De Quincey to refer to him as an opium eater in his *Confessions* alongside a range of other public figures, including Wilberforce's friend and mentor, Isaac Milner.[64]

Robert and Samuel's approach to defusing this issue was certainly a successful one and seems to have strongly influenced subsequent biographers. Coupland, for example, described Wilberforce as 'taking minute doses of opium',[65] while Furneaux reproduced the sons' account virtually verbatim, while opining that: 'The greatest amount of opium ever taken by Wilberforce seems to be about six grains per day.'[66] Later biographers, such as John Pollock and William Hague, followed a similar line, though with a greater concern to justify Wilberforce's use of the drug.[67] When compared with the diary,

[63] *Life*, 1: 173–4.

[64] For the original reference, see *The London Magazine* 4 (1821), 294. De Quincey, by his own account, intended a full public identification, but the discretion of his publisher delayed this until 1856. Thomas De Quincey, 'Original Preface to the Confessions 1821', in *The Works of Thomas De Quincey*, 16 vols (Edinburgh, 1878), 1: v–vi. For Milner, see Kevin C. Knox, 'Milner, Isaac (1750–1820), natural philosopher and dean of Carlisle', *ODNB*, online edn (2004), at: <https://doi.org/10.1093/ref:odnb/18788>, accessed 13 May 2005. Despite the reference to medical opinion in the *Life*, it is not unlikely that Milner was key as a trusted advisor in introducing Wilberforce to opium and his own experience of intestinal pain (like being gnawed by rats, according to De Quincey) was very similar to that of Wilberforce, who in his diary described his stomach as being 'raked': Bodl., MS Wilberforce b.2, fol. 10b, Diary, 2 February 1789.

[65] Coupland, *Wilberforce*, 90.

[66] Furneaux, *Wilberforce*, 78–9.

[67] Pollock, *Wilberforce*, 78–81; Hague, *Wilberforce*, 161–2.

however, it is clear that the sons were adopting a strategy of dissimulation through minimization in order to protect their father's reputation. Wilberforce's management of his opium regime was a major sub-theme of his journaling and, in all probability, a component of his reasons for continuing it. He usually took opium in the form of pills kept in a box,[68] which seems to have enabled him to monitor his dosage carefully. His record provides clear evidence that his dose gradually increased from three or four grains each day in the 1790s,[69] to around nine grains a day in 1803,[70] twelve in 1810,[71] to fifteen in 1826.[72] The increased dose was almost certainly a response to habituation as well as to worsening health, but the diary certainly does not support his sons' claim that he was sparing in his use of the drug, nor their suggestion that Wilberforce had no need to increase his intake for the last twenty years of his life. This must have been very apparent to Robert and Samuel as they deployed the diary in their biography.[73] The claim that Wilberforce was a stranger to the effects of opium as a stimulant is also contradicted by William's journalling. On 10 March 1813, for example, he noted that he was 'more languid' because he had forgotten his opium;[74] three years later, while dining with the Stephens, he reported being 'so sleepy f[ro]m want of sleep & hav [in]g forgot Opium that I could not keep awake.'[75] Contrary to the contrast between the effects of wine and opium recalled by his sons, Wilberforce was constantly conscious of occasions when he had missed or mismanaged his usual dose.[76] Although it may have gradually undermined his health in other respects,[77] Wilberforce seems to have had a good relationship with his medical regime, and to have

[68] Bodl., MS Wilberforce d.55, fol. 280, Diary, 4 June 1824.

[69] Bodl., MS Wilberforce c.34, fol. 117, Diary, 12 June 1796.

[70] Bodl., MS Wilberforce c.36, fol. 10, Diary, 6–7 September 1803.

[71] Bodl., MS Wilberforce d.54, fol. 67, Diary, 4 August 1810.

[72] Bodl., MS Wilberforce d.55, fol. 305, Diary, 6 October 1826.

[73] If the phrase indicating that William had no need to increase his dose as a 'remedy for his specific weakness' was intended to provide cover for the sons' handiwork, it is unclear whether it was their deception or self-deception that was being camouflaged.

[74] Bodl., MS Wilberforce d.54, fol. 171, Diary, 10 March 1813.

[75] Hull, Wilberforce House Museum [hereafter: WHM], Wilberforce Journal, fol. 61, Diary, 19 August 1816.

[76] For example, WHM, Wilberforce Journal, 7, Diary, 6 March 1814; WHM, Wilberforce Journal, 44x, Diary, 6 May 1816.

[77] For a discussion of the long-term health effects of Wilberforce's opium use, see Pollock, *Wilberforce*, 81.

regarded opium as a blessing. He noted in 1798, 'Much medicine today, (how thankful sho[ul]d I be for it), has just set me up again'[78]; in 1821, he described opium in biblical terms as 'my daily bread'.[79] It is understandable that in their presentation of their father as a Christian hero, Robert and Samuel sought to avoid linking him with the controversy around the use of opium ensuing from the publication of De Quincey's work and, possibly, emerging concern about the China trade.[80] However, in so doing, they concealed an important consideration bearing on any appraisal of his life, whether public or private.

A similar story emerges when examining the presentation in the *Life* of Wilberforce's relationship with Methodists and Dissenters. As high church Anglicans, influenced by Tractarian emphases on apostolic succession as the foundation of valid ministry, Wilberforce's sons were generally unsympathetic to Nonconformity, especially in its more assertive phase in the later 1830s and 1840s.[81] However, Wilberforce's close friendships and collaborations with a wide range of Nonconformists, including Quakers and even Unitarians, were far too well known to be excluded altogether.[82] Nonetheless, as with his opium use, Robert and Samuel chose to deploy in their biographical writing a range of techniques, including apologia, minimization and occlusion, to prevent Wilberforce's non-Anglican friendships from appearing too prominent and to contextualize them in such a way as to suggest that his approach to Nonconformity hardened over time. The most prominent example of apologia appeared in Volume III of the *Life* which, commenting on his involvement in the formation of the Bible Society, noted:

> Mr Wilberforce saw no danger to the Church from the cooperation of Dissenters who at that time professed an affectionate regard for the

[78] Bodl., MS Wilberforce c.41, fol. 118, Journal, 1 April 1798.

[79] WHM, Wilberforce Journal, fol. 255, Diary, 26 November 1821.

[80] For such concerns, see, for instance, Robert Philip, *No Opium! Or Commerce and Christianity, working together for good in China; a letter to James Cropper, Esq of Liverpool* (London, 1835). James Cropper, the putative addressee of the pamphlet, was an abolitionist associated with Wilberforce in the African Institution and a leader of the later emancipation campaign.

[81] See, for example, Newsome, *Parting of Friends*, 234–5.

[82] Some of Wilberforce's Nonconformist connections are explored in John Coffey and Michael Morgan, 'William Wilberforce and English Dissent', *Journal of the United Reformed Church History Society* 11 (2022), 3–20.

> national establishment. Bishops Porteus and Barrington, who had supported his efforts for enforcing the King's proclamation, readily joined with him here; and by no other machinery could the result have been obtained. So great was the torpor of the Church, that all more strictly regular exertions had absolutely failed, and they who devised this powerful instrument of good, are hardly to be blamed, though they have with a holy daring called up a spirit too mighty for their absolute control.[83]

The British and Foreign Bible Society was the most significant of the voluntary religious organizations in which Anglicans and Nonconformists cooperated in the nineteenth century, and Wilberforce was inescapably prominent among its founders.[84] The Society, while attracting wide support (not least because Wilberforce's name lent it respectability), was nevertheless controversial from its inception because of its irregular nature.[85] Opposition from high churchmen was, if anything, hardening in the late 1830s under Tractarian influence.[86] The apologia, like that for Wilberforce's use of opium, is therefore carefully constructed. In this case, the dangerous association with Dissenters is neutralized by an emphasis on the respectability of Wilberforce's involvement, endorsed by episcopal support and its suitability for the times when the church was torpid, and Dissenters well disposed. The reader is left to supply the conclusion that Wilberforce would have acted differently in the late 1830s, when the church was more active and Dissenting hostility more evident.

The technique of minimization in the *Life* was applied to references to Dissenters in general, but especially to Wilberforce's connections with Dissenting ministers and to matters of religious practice. The editors of William Jay's autobiography were entirely correct to suggest that the half dozen references to Jay in Robert and Samuel's biography did not present an accurate reflection of the cordiality of a relationship that stretched over forty years. They were also right to suspect that Wilberforce's sons had chosen not to use the

[83] *Life*, 3: 91–2.

[84] Roger H. Martin, *Evangelicals United: Ecumenical Stirrings in Pre-Victorian Britain, 1795–1830* (London, 1983), 85–6.

[85] See, for instance, H. H. Norris, *A Practical Exposition of the Tendency and Proceedings of the British and Foreign Bible Society*, 2nd edn (London, 1814; first publ. 1813).

[86] Martin, *Evangelicals United*, 93.

material at hand to paint a fairer portrait. There are almost eighty separate references to William Jay in the extant manuscript diaries and journals, and additional references in the parts of their father's correspondence to which the sons had access when writing their biography.[87] Of the material at their disposal, they deployed in the biography only four excerpts from the diary, two of which might be regarded as positive in tone[88] and two negative.[89] This is a very different balance to that found in the diary, where, at most, five per cent of Wilberforce's comments on Jay might be considered critical or disobliging, while the general tone is highly favourable. In October 1797, for example, after a disappointing Anglican sermon in the morning, Wilberforce went in the evening to the Argyle Chapel and heard 'Jays excellent Sermon on Abijah A Good Thing in him tow[ar]ds God – much edified.'[90] There is nothing in the *Life* that reflects the friendship and intimacy between the two men and their families, expressed in occasions of mutual sociability, as faithfully depicted in the diary.[91] Robert and Samuel also were at considerable pains to disguise the spiritual kinship between the two friends. They omitted altogether the many positive comparisons made by their father between Jay's preaching and that of mainstream Anglicans, as in May 1791, when he heard: 'M[r]. Jay at his Chapel – very powerful & able – O how earnest does he seem compar[e]d with the formal Preachers of the Establish[e]d Church'.[92] Wilberforce also much appreciated Jay's published devotional works, reading them for himself and to other members of his family.[93] As late as March 1833, just four months before his death, he began re-reading Jay's memoir of the Dissenting minister Cornelius Winter.[94] None of this material found its way into the *Life*. Indeed, in their account of the year 1815, Robert and Samuel resorted to unacknowledged selective quotation to

[87] While the sons seem to have sought out correspondence from a number of their father's friends (see *Life*, 1: vii), they do not appear to have asked William Jay. Jay's correspondence with Wilberforce was subsequently published in his own autobiography. See *William Jay*, ed. Redford and James, 299–324.
[88] *Life*, 2: 234, 313.
[89] *Life*, 2: 240; 5: 258.
[90] Bodl., MS Wilberforce c.34, fol. 144, Diary, 8 October 1797.
[91] For example, Bodl., MS Wilberforce c.34, fols 134–5, Diary, 12 February 1797; Bodl., MS Wilberforce c.39, fol. 79, Diary, 8 December 1825.
[92] Bodl., MS Wilberforce b.2, fol. 25[v], Diary, 29 May 1791.
[93] For instance, Bodl., MS Wilberforce d.54, fol. 9, Diary, 31 August 1808.
[94] Bodl., MS Wilberforce c.38, fol. 91, Diary, 25 March 1833.

disguise the origin of a sermon Wilberforce had read to his family, citing the diary as saying: 'Read in the evening a sermon on the fig tree a cumberer of the ground to my family',[95] whereas the manuscript text begins the sentence with: 'Read a most strik[in]g Sermon [of] Jay's …'.[96] In the *Life*, the same paragraph noted Wilberforce's reading of Voltaire and Hume, together with Blair's Lectures and Scott's *Waverley*. Only William Jay, seemingly, was too dangerous to mention.

Perhaps most consequential of Robert and Samuel's misleading depictions of Wilberforce's relationship with Jay is the final reference to the Dissenting minister, which appears in Volume V of the *Life*. This quoted the diary as saying: '__ at Jay's, where I greatly wished to go, but thought it wrong'.[97] This is largely an accurate quotation, the omitted name being that of Robert and Samuel's sister Elizabeth.[98] But by including this material, they clearly wished to give the impression that their father had come to the position that it was wrong for him to attend a Dissenting place of worship. However, in order to create this illusion, they were forced to omit subsequent entries in the diary that recorded attendance at Jay's chapel by Wilberforce[99] and other members of his family.[100] An almost identical manoeuvre was undertaken with respect to Wilberforce's attendance at the chapel of the Baptist Robert Hall in Bristol.[101]

A close comparison between the *Life* and the diary also makes it clear that the sons regularly deployed unacknowledged selective quotation to disguise Wilberforce's friendly relationships with Nonconformists. It was not uncommon, for example, on occasions when a Dissenting minister was staying the night or had come for breakfast, for Wilberforce to invite the guest to lead his family's morning devotions,[102] but none of these occasions was represented in the biography. When citing a portion of the diary where their father had assigned the title 'Revd' to a Dissenting minister, Robert

95 *Life*, 4: 225.
96 Bodl., MS Wilberforce c.39, fol. 26, Diary, 1 January 1815.
97 *Life*, 5: 258.
98 Bodl., MS Wilberforce c.39, fol. 77, Diary, 23 Oct 1825.
99 For example, Bodl., MS Wilberforce c.39, fol. 78, Diary, 4 December 1825; Bodl., MS Wilberforce c.38, fol. 60, Diary, 23 Sept 1832.
100 For instance, Bodl., MS Wilberforce c.39, fol. 78, Diary, 27 November 1825.
101 *Life*, 5: 140; Bodl., MS Wilberforce c.39, fol. 86, Diary, 28 May 1826.
102 For example, WHM, Wilberforce Journal, fol. 6, Diary, 3 March 1814.

and Samuel removed the title,[103] and they were similarly willing silently to intervene to excise what they presumably regarded as over-enthusiastic comments about Wilberforce's Dissenting acquaintances. Thus, a diary entry for December 1811, 'Allen the Quaker, truly great & good Man din[e]d with us',[104] is rendered in the *Life* simply as: 'Allen the Quaker dined with us'.[105] To further their project of minimizing Wilberforce's Dissenting contacts, Robert and Samuel even resorted, on occasion, to doctoring lists of people he had invited to breakfast. Their biography, for example, noted on 3 January 1814: 'Very large party at Breakfast Mr Cardale & several others';[106] whereas the corresponding diary entry reads: 'Very large party at Br[ea]kf[as]t Mr Cardale Mr Attley dissent[in]g Min[ist]er & several others.'[107] Christopher Tolley has suggested that the sons found it hard to understand their father's friendships with Dissenters.[108] It seems more likely that they understood only too well that his commitment to what he called 'real Christianity' was far more important to him than denominational boundaries, but that they did not like it and were not prepared to advertise his particular form of catholicity, especially in the new circumstances of the late 1830s.

The character of Wilberforce's religion was necessarily a central feature of any endeavour to write his biography and, as probably the most famous lay evangelical of the period, it would have been remarkable if his sons had attempted to disguise this aspect of their father's life. Nonetheless they appear to have made strenuous attempts to avoid the term, reducing the almost fifty uses of 'evangelical' and its cognates in the extant diary to a handful in the *Life*, and eschewing Wilberforce's critical use of the word 'unevangelical' altogether. Sometimes, they proceeded by simple omission, perhaps understandably in the case of the diary entry for 28 December 1828: 'Hendon Church Morn[in]g Dear Rob[er]t preached on If Ye love them that love you what reward have you, do not even the Publicans so … I own I'm not at all satisfied with dear Rob[er]ts

[103] Bodl., MS Wilberforce c.35, fol. 30, Diary, 9 January 1802.
[104] Bodl., MS Wilberforce d.54, fol. 126, Diary, 28 December 1811.
[105] *Life*, 3: 566.
[106] *Life*, 4: 153.
[107] Bodl., MS Wilberforce d.54, fol. 183^v, Diary, 3 January 1814.
[108] Tolley, *Domestic Biography*, 172.

Sermon nothi[n]g Evangel[ica]l in it.'[109] They also made frequent use of unacknowledged selective quotation, conducting a series of surgical strikes against the word evangelical where it appeared in material they otherwise wished to include. Thus, an entry for May 1817 reads in the diary: 'Lambeth public day Sat next [to] B[isho]p of Ossory Fowler, who immed[iatel]y began talk[in]g on Catholic Quest[io]n on which had spoke yesterday, w[ith] great frankness & afterw[ar] ds on Evangel[ica]l Clergy indicating a Generous manly spirit & good understanding.'[110] The same passage appeared in the fourth volume of the *Life* as: 'Dined Lambeth, public day – sat next the Bishop of Ossory, who immediately began talking on Catholic Question, on which he had spoken yesterday, with great frankness, indicating a generous manly spirit and good understanding.'[111] This was a largely accurate quotation, save for the excision of the evangelical clergy.

However, Robert and Samuel also faced the problem that there were sections of the diary which they wished to quote in their biography which featured the unwelcome use of the word evangelical and its cognates in contexts where the terms could not simply be excised. To deal with these passages, the sons deployed an additional technique: unacknowledged substitution of an entirely different word. This often changed the meaning or emphasis of the original. Volume I of the *Life*, for example, contained an account of a Sunday morning in 1789: 'Went to Cripplegate church to hear Gregory the Bishop of London's protégé for the Asylum – elegant, serious, and devotional, but sadly *obscure* in his views.'[112] The diary, however, was much clearer about Wilberforce's reservations about the preacher: 'went to Cripplegate Church to hear Gregory, Bishop of London's Protegé for the Asylum: "Come unto me all ye that labor" &c – elegant & serious & Devotional but sadly *unevangelical* in his Views.'[113] Similarly, in 1811, when contemplating a potential contested election in Yorkshire, the *Life* has Wilberforce musing: 'But if there should be any contest, the Sidmouth and Methodist story would be circulated … and people hostile to religion, and suspecting all *religious persons* of hypocrisy, would believe it; and

109 Bodl., MS Wilberforce d.55, fol. 344, Diary, 28 December 1828. See also Bodl., MS Wilberforce c.39, fol. 45, Diary, Monday 26 August 1816.

110 WHM, Wilberforce Journal, fol. 73, Diary, 17 May 1817.

111 *Life*, 4: 323.

112 *Life*, 1: 201. Emphasis added.

113 Bodl., MS Wilberforce b.2, fol. 9, Diary, 18 January 1789. Emphasis added.

the credit of true religion might with my own be tarnished.'[114] However, the diary is much more specific:

> if there sho[ul]d be a contest & the Sidm[ou]th & Meth[odis]t story might very prob[abl]y stir one up if the Elect[io]n to take place (before its falsehood can be prov[e]d,) the story would be circulated … & people hostile to Relig[io]n & suspecting all *Evangel[ica]l people* of Hypocrisy would believe & the Credit of true Relig[io]n might with my own be tarnish[e]d[115]

Here the substitution of 'religious' for 'Evangelical' was particularly urgent because of Wilberforce's identification of the latter with 'true Religion'.

This particular form of misrepresentation of their source text was also deployed by Robert and Samuel more generally, but it was applied with particular precision to the removal of the word evangelical. Their evident determination in this endeavour is perhaps best explained by developments in the Church of England in the first third of the nineteenth century. During this period, the term 'evangelical' had become ever more firmly a label attached to a particular party within the Church of England,[116] and one from which Robert and Samuel stood apart. They would not have wished to burnish the reputation of the evangelical party by linking it clearly with their heroic portrait of their father; neither would they have wished to diminish his reputation by close association with a party from which they wished to distance themselves.

A final aspect of their father's religious life on which the sons sought to tread a careful line was its interior character. Wilberforce had been a warm advocate for the importance and validity of religious affections in his *Practical View* (1797),[117] and there was plenty of material in his diaries and journals to display their importance in his own spiritual life. This was material that Robert and Samuel wished to use to illustrate their father's warm and lively character.

[114] *Life*, 3: 356. Emphasis added.

[115] Bodl., MS Wilberforce d.54, fols 115–6, Diary, 24 August 1811. Emphasis added.

[116] For the hardening of church parties, see, for instance, John Walsh and Stephen Taylor, 'The Church and Anglicanism', in John Walsh, Colin Haydon and Stephen Taylor, eds, *The Church of England* c.*1689*–c.*1833* (Cambridge, 1993), 29–51.

[117] William Wilberforce, *A Practical View of the Prevailing Religious System of Professed Christians in the Higher and Middle Classes in this Country Contrasted with Real Christianity* (London, 1797), 54, 85–6, 136–7.

On the other hand, it was vital for the portrait they aimed to create that Wilberforce should not appear as an enthusiast, and that his brand of Christianity was indeed 'a religion for gentlemen'. The journal, even in its oft repeated self-critical commentary on Wilberforce's dead and cold spiritual state, gave evidence of his expectation that its true condition was warm and lively. The sons, however, chose to emphasize the rules-based aspects of Wilberforce's spiritual practice and to comment that his prescriptions displayed, 'not the heated tone of enthusiasm, but the sober reality of a reasonable faith.'[118] This underlay their minimization and occlusion of Wilberforce's connections to those notorious enthusiasts, the Dissenters and evangelicals.

Robert and Samuel's attempt to write a biography of their father as centred around his public life as a politician and philanthropist was largely successful. They were perspicuous in stressing the importance of his orientation towards domesticity in the midst of his political engagement and to the importance of his personal spirituality. They were, however, much less reliable, and often positively misleading, when it came to the details of his lived experience, the breadth of his spiritual horizons and the character of his spirituality. The careful and systematic misrepresentations to which they resorted were in part, no doubt, the product of both filial piety and their own theological partisanship. Perhaps most importantly, however, the posthumous portrait they created, reproduced in many a subsequent biography, both pious and scholarly, of a hero more than worthy of a pedestal, was not really the William Wilberforce of 1759–1833. He was rather the Wilberforce of 1838: reminted, like the coinage, for a new reign with evolving canons of respectability and new religious alignments. In this sense, Ford K. Brown had his generations the wrong way round. The Wilberforce we know was in many of his essentials not the father of the Victorians, but their son.

[118] *Life*, 1: 107.

Bishops, Brothels and Byron: Hypocrisy and the 1844 Brothel Suppression Bill

Emily Baylor*
University of Edinburgh

The House of Lords debate over the 1844 Brothel Suppression Bill was derailed by an accusation of hypocrisy. An opponent of the measure, Earl Fitzhardinge, shifted attention from legal reform to the notorious brothels operating on Church of England property, and argued that the dean and chapter of Westminster Abbey should be prosecuted were the bill to become law. In addition to offering an interesting case study of clerical hypocrisy in practice, the story of the failed 1844 Bill provides useful context for better-known sexual reform projects of the late nineteenth century. This article focuses on three major themes that animated the events of 1844: the power of distraction and delay; the role of elite male perspectives; and the complicated but critical role of Christianity in sexual reform.

Introduction

During debate over the bishop of Exeter's 1844 Brothel Suppression Bill, Earl Fitzhardinge told the House of Lords that the 'most notorious brothels in London' were run on property owned by the dean and chapter of Westminster Abbey.[1] The press gleefully seized on this accusation of hypocrisy, which was neatly summarized by Earl Fitzhardinge: given the Church of England's 'peculiar duties', it should have suppressed sexual vice on its own property 'before their Lordships were called upon to legislate.'[2] Ultimately, the bill failed and its major provision, the introduction of summary judgement for the closure of brothels, would not become law for another forty-one years.

* E-mail: ebaylor@ed.ac.uk

[1] HL Deb. (3rd series), 14 June 1844 (vol. 75, col. 886).

[2] Ibid.

Studies in Church History 60 (2024), 408–430
doi: 10.1017/stc.2024.17

The fact that the 1844 Brothel Suppression Bill was withdrawn only partially explains why the story of its collapse has been omitted from histories of sexual reform.[3] Although Victorian prostitution is a popular subject, academic study of it has typically focused on events after 1860 that generated significant public attention and energy, including the Contagious Diseases Acts of 1864, 1866 and 1869, the Jack the Ripper killings, and the activism related to social purity and white slavery. Some historians have even suggested that prostitution was not a serious social concern until the end of the 1850s, a claim that is undercut by the work of the reformers behind the 1844 Bill.[4] A final possible explanation is historians' heavy reliance on materials produced by reformers, who may have been reluctant to record embarrassing failures.[5]

Despite its relative obscurity, the story of the 1844 Brothel Suppression Bill is an interesting case study in clerical hypocrisy and provides useful context for later, more successful sexual reform efforts. In particular, the 1844 debate highlights the way distraction and delay inhibit reform, the importance of elite male perspectives in the nineteenth-century debate over the laws surrounding prostitution, and the complicated role Christianity played in Victorian sexual reform. Before these points can be explored, it is necessary to recount the history of the 1844 Bill and the way its reception was shaped by charges of clerical hypocrisy.

The 1844 Brothel Suppression Bill

The impetus for the 1844 Brothel Suppression Bill (formally titled 'A Bill for the More Effectual Suppression of Brothels, and Trading in Seduction and Prostitution') came from voluntary groups, particularly the fashionable Society for the Protection of Young Females

[3] One history of social purity movements mentions the 1844 Bill, but only to note that it was poorly received. Edward Bristow, *Vice and Vigilance: Purity Movements in Britain since 1700* (Dublin, 1977), 61.

[4] Keith Nield, *Prostitution and the Victorian Age: Debates on the Issue from 19th Century Critical Journals* (Westmead, 1973), 1.

[5] This may be the reason for the absence of the 1844 Bill from M. J. D. Roberts's analysis of one of the major groups that supported it, the Society for the Protection of Young Females and the Prevention of Juvenile Prostitution: M. J. D. Roberts, *Making English Morals: Voluntary Association and Moral Reform in England, 1787–1886* (Cambridge, 2004), 159–61.

and the Prevention of Juvenile Prostitution (hereafter: the Society). Founded in 1835 and connected to the London City Mission, the Society tried to end the prostitution of young women. Although the Society was created in direct response to the death of a Norfolk girl in a London brothel, it was also part of a larger trend of social stabilization efforts and rising class consciousness following the passage of the 1832 Reform Act and the 1834 Poor Law.[6] Despite its success in attracting patrons, the Society was not without opponents. For instance, after the founding of a Birmingham branch of the Society in 1840, some local gentlemen pledged to form their own organization to protect prostitution and to defend 'keepers of infamous houses in any actions which may be brough [*sic*] against them by the society for the protection of young females.'[7]

The Society's work fell into three categories: the closure of brothels, the punishment of procurers, and the reclamation of young girls who had been seduced or were seen as particularly vulnerable.[8] Despite some success, the Society quickly became frustrated with existing laws relating to prostitution and committed itself to reforming them.[9] Assured by the evangelical leader and future earl of Shaftesbury, Lord Ashley, that their cause was 'that of religion, piety and virtue,' the Society planned to bring the matter before Parliament in the late 1830s.[10] Joining forces with other voluntary groups, including the Society of the Lock Hospital and Asylum, the Guardian Society, the London Female Mission, and the Maritime Penitent Female Refuge, the Society petitioned Parliament to change a law commonly used to close disorderly houses, circulated relevant material to clergymen and Dissenting ministers, and made appeals in the press.[11] The presentation of the

[6] Bristow, *Vice and Vigilance*, 60; Roberts, *Making English Morals*, 143, 146–7.

[7] 'News', *Carlisle Journal*, 19 December 1840, 3.

[8] These goals were laid out by the Society's secretary, James B. Talbot, at a public meeting in 1838. 'Multiple News Items', *The Standard*, 8 November 1838, 3.

[9] 'Facts, Fancies, and Fictions', *The Champion*, 18 November 1838, 5; 'The Protection of Young Females', *Leamington Spa Courier*, 24 June 1843, 3; 'Prevention of Juvenile Prostitution', *The Times*, 8 November 1838, 3.

[10] 'The Protection of Young Females', *Leamington Spa Courier*, 24 June 1843, 3; see also 'The London Society for the Protection of Young Females', *Morning Post*, 7 April 1841, 4.

[11] 'Members of the Committee of the London Society for the Prevention of Juvenile Prostitution' (19 March 1838), in 'Seventeenth Report of the Select Committee', in *Reports of the Select Committee on Public Petitions 1833–1918* (London, 1838), 196. For an example circular, see 'London Society for the Protection of Young Females',

Brothel Suppression Bill in 1844, therefore, was the result of years of effort. In fact, the project predated the Society: The Guardian Society had pressed for similar changes in the decades before the Society's founding.[12]

As originally drafted, the 1844 Bill sought to strengthen the legal mechanism for prosecuting people who facilitated prostitution. The justification for more aggressive legal intervention was explained in the introduction to the first draft of the bill: the fact that existing laws were 'ineffectual' and rarely enforced emboldened those who profited most from the sex trade, and 'encouraged' them to use increasingly unethical means to draw women into prostitution.[13] The influence of extra-parliamentary reformers is clear in the first draft, which proposed sweeping changes that had no chance of becoming law. These unlikely measures included the seizure of buildings used as brothels, even if they were rented properties, and the punishment of anyone who facilitated or allowed their dependant to commit adultery or fornication, including husbands who allowed their wives to be unfaithful.[14] Although these measures were removed from the final version of the bill, they reveal reformers' understanding of sexual exploitation and hint at their political naivety. The provisions directed at family members, for example, were designed to address prostitution as a family business, including concerns that parents were complicit in the prostitution of their children, and that husbands were exploiting their wives. The proposed measures could have resulted in serious unintended consequences, however, such as the prosecution of a husband who tolerated his wife's infidelity, even if no money exchanged hands.

Yet the key element of the bill survived the amendment process: the replacement of the 1752 Disorderly Houses Act with a summary

Bristol Mercury, 26 June 1841, 6. For examples of appeals made in the press, see 'London Society for the Protection of Young Females', *Essex Standard*, 30 July 1841, 3 and 'To the Editor of the Times', *The Times*, 13 December 1838, 5.

12 Tony Henderson, *Disorderly Women in Eighteenth-Century London: Prostitution and Control in the Metropolis 1730–1830* (London, 2013), 101–2.

13 *A Bill intituled an Act for the More Effectual Suppression of Brothels, and Trading in Seduction and Prostitution*, 1844 (HL Bill 107, 1844).

14 Ibid.

judgement for the closure of brothels.[15] Passed in the wake of the violent brothel riots of 1749, the Disorderly Houses Act was the subject of considerable criticism by the 1840s.[16] Under the 1752 Act, any two ratepayers could report a disorderly house, including a brothel, to a constable who was required to investigate. If the investigation resulted in a prosecution, the ratepayers received financial compensation. The limitations of this scheme were well documented by the 1840s. In 1841, the *Yorkshire Gazette* memorably described the 1752 Act as 'an act so ingeniously contrived as to ensure the escape, rather than the punishment' of brothelkeepers.[17] The 1752 Act depended on the initiative and resources of ratepayers, who risked ridicule, retribution and financial loss if they reported the existence of a brothel.[18] Furthermore, prosecutions under the act were expensive enough to deter local authorities.[19] They also involved a significant delay between the opening of an investigation and an indictment. This sometimes allowed the accused to flee, or simply move a few doors down, before charges could be brought, which was especially problematic as, under the 1752 Act, each investigation was tied to a specific address.[20] The 'great point' of the 1844 Bill, therefore, was to create a more effective mechanism for closing brothels.

In committee, legislators pruned off the most improbable elements of the bill. The final version consisted of two major provisions.[21] The first introduced the use of summary judgement to convict people who owned brothels, worked in brothels or otherwise knowingly benefited from the sale of sex. Under the streamlined mechanism, charges could be brought against an individual, rather than the house itself, and the two ratepayers required by the 1752 Disorderly Houses Act were replaced by one credible witness. Upon hearing the testimony of the witness, two justices of the peace could summon the accused. If the accused failed to appear, a magistrate could either issue a warrant

[15] The full name of the 1752 Disorderly Houses Act is 'An Act for the Better Preventing Thefts and Robberies, and Regulating Places of Public Entertainment, and Punishment of Persons Keeping Disorderly Houses', 1752 (25 Geo. II, c. 36).

[16] Bristow, *Vice and Vigilance*, 54–5.

[17] 'Prostitution—Its Fearful Extent', *Yorkshire Gazette*, 14 August 1841, 3.

[18] Bristow, *Vice and Vigilance*, 54–5.

[19] Ibid.; Henderson, *Disorderly Women*, 158–61.

[20] Bristow, *Vice and Vigilance*, 54–5.

[21] *A Bill [as amended by the Select Committee] intituled an Act for the More Effectual Suppression of Bawdy Houses, and of Trading in Seduction and Prostitution*, 1844 (HL Bill 151, 1844).

for them, or hear the case in their absence. Upon conviction, offenders faced imprisonment for up to three months with or without hard labour for a first offence, up to six months for a second offence, and up to two years for each subsequent offence. By creating a clear and limited mechanism for appealing decisions, the bill targeted legal loopholes that brothelkeepers commonly employed. The second major element of the bill was the criminalization of procuration and solicitation on behalf of another person, both of which were to become misdemeanours punishable by up to two years with or without hard labour.

House of Lords Debate

In May 1884, the bill had an uneventful first reading. Emboldened by petitions of support, advocates assured their fellow legislators that the bill would not criminalize prostitution, which was described as 'a question rather of morals than of law.'[22] Instead, the bill sought to stop 'trading' in prostitution by punishing the procurers and brothelkeepers who financially benefited from the prostitution of others.[23] A month later, the second reading began in a similar fashion. The bill's sponsor, the bishop of Exeter, Henry Phillpotts, tried to impress upon the House the narrowness of the proposed legislation by expounding, in detail, on the types of sexual activity that would not be criminalized: the cohabitation of unmarried couples, prostitution and seduction.[24] This conciliatory tone distanced him from the sweeping changes that had been proposed in the first draft of the bill. By explicitly acknowledging that he was not advocating the legal prohibition of all illicit sex, he presented a case for a narrower reform that focused on the facilitators of prostitution.

In his description of the bill, the bishop of Exeter described how the prosecution of procurers and brothelkeepers could check two of the most offensive elements of the sex trade: fraud and coercion. Citing precedent dating back to the ancient world, the bishop insisted that his bill was nearly identical to one issued by the emperor Justinian in the sixth century. More imminently, he described the

[22] HL Deb. (3rd series), 17 May 1844 (vol. 74, cols 1232–4).
[23] Ibid.
[24] In this context, 'seduction' refers to a man enticing a woman to whom he is not married into sexual acts.

type of cases that could be prosecuted, should the bill become law, including the employment of procurers by West End brothels, the use of false advertisements to lure young women from the country with promises of respectable work, and the importation of unsuspecting girls from Ireland. Unsurprisingly, these practices matched recent cases brought by the Society, including its failed effort to prosecute Richard Barnett and his wife for procuring country girls, and the successful prosecution of Emma Stone, who had procured Mary Ann Favell, an eleven-year-old girl.[25] Despite Stone's conviction for removing a child from her parents without their permission, for which she received a year's imprisonment, the case highlighted the weakness of existing laws against brothels. When charges were brought against the keepers of the brothel where Stone and Favell had stayed for several nights, the keepers simply closed the house and fled.[26]

The bishop of Exeter's speech was the most detailed discussion the bill would receive as the next speaker, William Berkeley (1786–1857), the first Earl Fitzhardinge, permanently derailed the debate. After seconding the bill, presumably in bad faith, Fitzhardinge accused the dean and chapter of Westminster Abbey of owning the property that housed the most notorious brothels in London. In the area known as the Almonry, where alms from Westminster Abbey had historically been distributed, Fitzhardinge alleged that there were twenty-four disorderly houses, which put them 'in a proportion of two brothels to one prebend.'[27] This allegation, *The Times* reported, was followed by 'much laughter, which continued for some time.'[28] Although Fitzhardinge assured his fellow peers that he was discussing buildings 'with which he was not acquainted', he insisted that the information was open and notorious.[29] He claimed to have read about the matter more than two years previously in a local newspaper, and reported, falsely, that no church official had

[25] Richard Barnett is discussed in 'Magistrates' Meeting—Christopher Inn', *Bucks Herald*, 3 August 1839, 3. For Emma Stone and Mary Ann Favell, see 'Police Intelligence', *Reading Mercury*, 18 April 1840, 4; 'Surrey Sessions—Thursday, May 28', *Morning Post*, 29 May 1840, 7.

[26] 'Surrey Sessions—Thursday, May 28', *Morning Post*, 29 May 1840, 7.

[27] HL Deb. (3rd series), 14 June 1844 (vol. 75, col. 886).

[28] 'House Of Lords, Friday, June 15', *The Times*, 15 June 1844, 3.

[29] HL Deb. (3rd series), 14 June 1844 (vol. 75, col. 886).

denied the charges.[30] Indeed, he claimed to have 'been astonished that no contradiction had been given to it, because it showed rather an inconsistency of conduct on the part of the dean and chapter.'[31]

While the charge of hypocrisy was obvious, given the bill's proposal by a bishop, Fitzhardinge did not focus on the church's inconsistent response to prostitution. Rather, he turned his attention to another controversy: the dean's refusal to install a statute of Lord Byron, the work of the renowned sculptor Bertel Thorvaldsen, in Westminster Abbey's Poet's Corner, on the basis that Lord Byron had been not only heterodox, but of dubious sexual morality. The question of whether to house Lord Byron's body or his likeness in Westminster Abbey had caused a media frenzy in the 1820s, full of opportunities for humour and indignation.[32] By 1844, the controversy was well-worn; the statue had been languishing in a warehouse for ten years, homeless. Just two months before the debate over the 1844 Brothel Suppression Bill, *Punch* had revisited the issue by publishing a satirical letter in which the statue tried to persuade abbey officials that it was a financial asset.[33] During the second reading of the 1844 Bill, Fitzhardinge built on the theme of clerical greed, suggesting that there was one important difference between brothels – allegedly welcome on church property – and the statue: 'The statue would not pay any rent.'[34]

The bishop of Gloucester, James Henry Monk, who had been given a canonry at Westminster in 1830, tried to mitigate the damage. However, instead of redirecting the conversation to brothel suppression, he focused on Fitzhardinge's charges. Although the bishop of Gloucester admitted that there had been brothels on property owned by the dean and chapter of Westminster Abbey, he claimed that the dean and chapter had removed them, either by refusing to renew the leases of tenants who used property for immoral purposes,

[30] The charges had been contested by the dean and chapter's surveyor in 1843. Although he acknowledged the existence of brothels on church property, he questioned the numbers alleged and claimed that the dean and chapter were taking action to remove them 'where practical at a reasonable price': 'To the Editor of the Standard', *The Standard,* 18 January 1843, 3.

[31] HL Deb. (3rd series), 14 June 1844 (vol. 75, col. 886).

[32] 'With Most Especial Disgust', *The Age,* 5 October 1828, 2; 'Alas!', *The Satirist,* 26 August 1838, 4–5.

[33] 'The Statue of Byron', *Punch*, 11 May 1844, 17–18.

[34] HL Deb. (3rd series), 14 June 1844 (vol. 75, col. 887).

or by using the dean and chapter's own money – 'which the noble Earl supposed they were so fond of' – to buy out unsavoury lease holders.[35] Based on his personal inspection of the area, the bishop of Gloucester claimed that all of the bad houses on church property had been removed. While this information was incorrect – brothels continued to operate on church property – it was not contested in that day's debate.

Nonetheless, the damage was done. The discussion moved further and further away from the bill. Subsequent speakers made it clear that Fitzhardinge's mention of Byron's statue had struck a nerve. Remarkably, given the bill under discussion, Lord Henry Brougham claimed that there was not 'any one passage in the history of this country of late years so discreditable to our national taste, to our reason, and to our good sense, as the refusal to admit this statue.'[36] Another member argued that Shakespeare was more 'indecent' than Byron and yet his statue was allowed, while the earl of Lovelace, William King-Noel, Lord Byron's son-in-law, pointed out that the Abbey displayed a statue of the poet John Dryden 'who died a Catholic and an apostate.'[37] The fact that the bishop of Exeter tried to make peace by proposing a national gallery of statues indicates how far the debate had strayed. Indeed, the only substantive response to the content of the Brothel Suppression Bill came from the final speaker, the noted legal reformer, John, Lord Campbell, who struck an ominous note, reminding the House that there was 'a difference between sin and crime', and suggesting that efforts to suppress prostitution made vice worse.[38]

While the press paid little attention to the bill, they seized on the allegations against the dean and chapter of Westminster Abbey and the renewed fight over Byron's statue; the scandal even received some coverage in an Indian newspaper.[39] The Tory weekly, *The Age and Argus,* wrote scathingly that 'a stupid conversation took place in the House of Lords the other night, into which the names

[35] Ibid.

[36] HL Deb. (3rd series), 14 June 1844 (vol. 75, col. 888).

[37] HL Deb. (3rd series), 14 June 1844 (vol. 75, cols 890–1).

[38] Ibid.

[39] *The Bengal Catholic Expositor* reprinted some of the *Examiner*'s coverage and provided its own commentary: 'The Bishop's Zeal and A Chapter's Practice', *The Bengal Catholic Expositor*, 7 September 1844, 12–14; 'Immorality Tolerated More than Dissent', *The Bengal Catholic Expositor*, 5 October 1844, 11–12.

of Shakspere [*sic*], Thorwaldsen [*sic*], and Byron, were dragged, with no particular reason, and decidedly no particular result.'[40] Despite the 'hackneyed' subject, however, *The Age and Argus* could not resist enumerating the reasons why no one as immoral as Byron could have his likeness in the Abbey. Others pounced on the Church of England. The radical *Examiner* suggested that the bishop of Exeter was only interested in suppressing brothels so that clergymen would have less opportunity to frequent them, citing the recent scandalous case of the Rev. Herbert Marsh, who had admitted to having a child with a woman he had met at a brothel in the parish of St James, Westminster.[41] Some publications had more fun. *Punch* used the debate as evidence of the pointlessness of Parliament.[42] *The Satirist,* famed for controversy, anti-Tory sentiment, and its editor's propensity for blackmail, made good on its name, publishing 'Byron vs Brothels: A Pious and Poetical Address to the dean and chapter of Westminster.' The poem mixed rhymes and ridicule, driving home the idea of clerical hypocrisy:

> Oh! Dean and Chapter, Byron sang
> 'Don Juan,' it is true;
> But thus to shelter Juans and
> Their loves was left for you![43]

Media coverage was not just about exposing an embarrassing encounter among the nation's elite. As *The Satirist* quickly noted, the press had played a pivotal role in exposing the connection between brothels and the clergy. Radical publications had covered the existence of brothels on the dean and chapter's property three years before it

[40] 'Saturday, June 22, 1844', *Age and Argus,* 22 June 1844, 9.

[41] The Marsh case attracted significant media attention, which focused on clerical hypocrisy. The Rev. Herbert Charles Marsh was the rector of Barnack and the son of Herbert Marsh, bishop of Peterborough from 1819–39: 'A Bishop's Zeal and a Chapter's Practice', *Examiner,* 22 June 1844, 2–3; 'Prosecution of a French Strumpet', *Stamford Mercury,* 8 March 1844, 2; 'Disgraces to the Church', *The Era,* 17 March, 1844, 5. The parish of St James, Westminster, is now known as St James, Piccadilly.

[42] 'The "Business" of Parliament', *Punch,* 20 July 1844, 18.

[43] 'Bryon vs Brothels: A Pious and Poetical Address to the Dean and Chapter of Westminster', *The Satirist,* 7 July 1844, 3. For more on the editor and owner of *The Satirist,* Barnard Gregory, see G. C. Boase, rev. H. C. G. Matthew, 'Gregory, Barnard (1796–1852), newspaper proprietor', *ODNB,* online edn (2004), at: <https://doi.org/10.1093/ref:odnb/11455>, accessed 20 August 2023.

reached the House of Lords, and they were certainly Fitzhardinge's source. In addition to repeating the exact number of brothels per street that the press had reported in 1841, Fitzhardinge had even lifted his jokes – including 'two brothels to one prebend' – from these columns.[44] While *The Satirist* had previously juxtaposed the brothels on church property with the rejection of Byron's statue, much of the earlier criticism focused on yet another case of clerical hypocrisy.[45] In 1841, the dean and chapter of Westminster Abbey had been labelled a 'crew of reverend hypocrites' because of their selective use of prohibitory clauses in leases for church properties.[46] While the dean and chapter inserted clauses in their leases that ensured that their properties could not be used as Dissenting meeting houses or chapels, they did not insert clauses that prevented the use of those same properties as brothels or as receiving houses for stolen and smuggled goods.[47] The specific charge of hypocrisy had been different, but the case was built on the same logic: critics suggested that the failure to insert prohibitory clauses in leases to prevent sexual vice reflected the fact that brothelkeepers, unlike Dissenting chapels, were known to pay above average rent.

At the vote to send the bill to committee for amendments, Fitzhardinge renewed his attack on the dean and chapter of Westminster Abbey. During the intervening week, he had gathered evidence that disproved the bishop of Gloucester's claim that the problem of brothels on church property had been solved. His source was a vestry clerk, who had provided the names of functioning 'brothels within two minutes' walk' of the Westminster Abbey Chapter House.[48] Unsurprisingly, Fitzhardinge also introduced the question of prohibitory clauses in leases and demanded to know why the church did not regularly insert them against vice. Given the enduring nature of the problem, and the fact that the dean and chapter were

[44] 'Dean and Chapter Landlords', *Examiner*, 18 December 1841, 1–2.
[45] 'Clerical Immorality', *The Satirist*, 30 October 1842, 7.
[46] 'Ecclesiastical Brothels', *The Satirist*, 26 December 1841, 7.
[47] 'Clerical Immorality', *The Satirist*, 30 October 1842, 7.
[48] HL Deb. (3rd series), 24 June 1844 (vol. 75, col. 1257). Hansard censored the addresses of the brothels, noting simply that there were 'several' and that they were 'notorious.': HL Deb. (3rd series), 24 June 1844 (vol. 75, col. 1257). *The Times* did not use the same discretion. It named the houses as numbers 3–8 on the left side of Dean Street; numbers 2, 3 and 5–8 in Jeffery's Buildings; and numbers 14–15 in New Way Buildings: 'House of Lords, Monday, June 24', *The Times*, 25 June 1844, 2.

not using the available measures for repression, Fitzhardinge implied that the dean and chapter were as guilty as any brothelkeepers. Therefore, if Parliament passed the 1844 Bill, 'knowing that the Dean and Chapter had been breathing the air of prostitution, and sharing the very wages of public infamy', the authorities would need to bring charges against the dean and chapter of Westminster Abbey.[49]

Forced to amend his previous claims, the bishop of Gloucester insisted that the dean and chapter were in the process of closing brothels on their property but had simply not completed this task. The bishop offered the House a series of defences, the most troubling of which was the claim that, while the property involved seemed significant, it was 'in the lower parts of Westminster' and therefore had little value and few options for tenants.[50] While the dean and chapter might like to own property in more a respectable – and expensive – part of town, 'Berkeley-square for instance', they did not, and therefore could not afford to be picky. The comment – probably a thinly veiled barb at Fitzhardinge, who had been denied the title earl of Berkeley decades previously due to questions about his legitimacy – enraged *The Economist*, prompting a scathing analysis of the priorities of the established church:

> We are now informed as to the terms on which the Dean and Chapter of Westminster—so anxious to promote morality—would change their present tenants. They would do so if only they could get 'property in other parts of the town—in Berkeley Square, for instance;'—in short, if they could get MORE RENT. Such a cool confession of greed, intolerance, and connivance at vice is happily not often made, even by bishops. The masses are more disinterested, more pure, more full of true genuine religion, than those who presume to teach them, especially in those respects.[51]

Once again, the discussion in the House of Lords strayed from the bill. The bishop of Gloucester and Earl Fitzhardinge argued about the original source of the charges against the dean and chapter of Westminster Abbey: the bishop claimed they were printed in the controversial evangelical journal the *Patriot,* to which Fitzhardinge

[49] HL Deb. (3rd series), 24 June 1844 (vol. 75, col. 1258).
[50] HL Deb. (3rd series), 24 June 1844 (vol. 75, col. 1260).
[51] 'Clerical Zeal', *The Economist*, 29 June 1844, 4.

replied that 'I never saw the *Patriot* in my life.'[52] They debated whether or not the charges were the result of a bias against the established church, whether or not they had been contradicted by officials, and whether the entire attack was revenge for the prohibitory clauses against Dissenting meeting houses. Once again, the bill was not discussed.

Although the third reading still did not focus on the bill, it lacked the theatricality of the previous two debates. Lord Foley's opening comments sounded the bill's death knell. He insisted that there had not been sufficient inquiry and recycled old arguments for segregating brothels into poor neighbourhoods, namely that it prevented them from operating in wealthier ones.[53] The earl of Galloway tried to save the bill, mentioning the work that had gone into it, and the fact that further inquiry was unnecessary because everyone present admitted that brothels were rampant. The bill should pass, he thought, if the House really wanted to close brothels and protect young women. His words fell on deaf ears, and the bill was withdrawn pending further investigation.[54]

Afterlife of the Debate

The failure of the 1844 Bill did not mark the end of efforts to reform the laws surrounding vice. Shortly after the bill was withdrawn, James Beard Talbot, Secretary of the Society, published *The Miseries of Prostitution*, which was intended to provide the evidence that Lord Foley had claimed was needed, and other reformers expressed hope that the bill would be reintroduced the following session.[55] When it was not, voluntary groups kept pressing for change, and the bishop of Exeter and others continued to present petitions to Parliament demanding the suppression of the prostitution trade.[56] Progress nonetheless remained slow. Although a similar bill was proposed in

[52] HL Deb. (3rd series), 24 June 1844 (vol. 75, col. 1261). *The Patriot* was a weekly national newspaper that catered to evangelical Nonconformists, particularly Congregationalists and Baptists: J. Nicoll Cooper, 'Dissenters and Journalism: "The Patriot" in the 1830s', *Victorian Periodicals Review* 14 (1981), 58–66.

[53] HL Deb. (3rd series), 9 July 1844 (vol. 76, col. 535).

[54] HL Deb. (3rd series), 9 July 1844 (vol. 76, cols 535–9).

[55] 'Suppression of Brothels—A Meeting Took Place', *The Times*, 1 November 1844, 7.

[56] 'Parliamentary Intelligence' and 'House of Commons, Tuesday June 23', *The Times*, 24 June 1846, 2–3; 'Court Circular', *The Times*, 30 April 1858, 9.

the House of Commons in 1847, it was withdrawn at its second reading at the behest of Sir George Grey who felt that its provisions were of 'so sweeping a character that there was no knowing who might be subject to a penalty under them.'[57] Grey made it clear that his main objection was to the use of summary judgement for the closure of brothels, which he feared could hurt landlords. Unfortunately, there is no record of the debate at the first reading because Craven Berkeley, Earl Fitzhardinge's younger brother – who opposed the 1847 Bill because he thought it would 'only increase the evil it was intended to remedy' – requested and received clearance of the public galleries.[58] Once again, *The Satirist* used a sexual reform bill as an opportunity to reprint the charges against the dean and chapter of Westminster Abbey.[59]

Despite the lack of legal change, the Society continued its work. By 1859, it claimed to have rescued seven hundred girls under the age of fifteen from dangerous situations, and took responsibility for the closure of five hundred brothels, even without a change in the law.[60] Nevertheless, the Society struggled to obtain convictions for procuration and punishments for brothelkeepers.[61] Meanwhile, Westminster remained 'the most prominent prostitution area in the Metropolis' well into the twentieth century.[62] The association between church property in Westminster and brothels also persisted, and word of it spread as far as Beijing.[63] In the end, only one issue involved in the 1844 debate reached a quick resolution: Thorvaldsen's statue of Lord Byron found a home in the Library of Trinity College, Cambridge,

[57] 'London, Thursday, May 13, 1847', *The Times*, 13 May 1847, 4.

[58] 'House of Commons, Tuesday, March 30', *The Times*, 31 March 1847, 2; HC Deb. (3rd series), 30 March 1847 (vol. 91, cols 616–17). For Craven Berkeley's opposition to the 1847 Bill, see 'House of Commons, Tuesday March 16', *The Times*, 17 March 1847, 2; HC Deb. (3rd series), 23 June 1847 (vol. 93, col. 811).

[59] 'The Almonry and the Abbey', *The Satirist*, 11 April 1847, 4.

[60] 'London Society for the Protection of Young Females', *The Musical World*, 7 May 1859, 300.

[61] Examples include the failed prosecution of Matilda Mallet for the procuration of Ellen Messent ('Police Intelligence', *The Satirist*, 14 October 1848, 3) and the fact that Frances and Ellen James were initially let off with a warning when charged with keeping a brothel, and only punished when they committed a second offence ('A Hint to Brothelkeepers', *Bell's Life in London and Sporting Chronicle*, 17 February 1850, 7).

[62] Julia Laite, *Common Prostitutes and Ordinary Citizens: Commercial Sex in London, 1885–1960* (Basingstoke, 2012), 18.

[63] 'Mr. Parkin', *The Times*, 3 July 1956, 5; 'Combatting Vice', *The Times*, 6 July 1956, 9.

where it remains today.[64] Although the statue never gained a place in Westminster Abbey, another figure in the 1844 debate did. Twelve years after the failed Brothel Suppression Bill, the bishop of Gloucester, James Henry Monk, defender of the dean and chapter, was honoured with a burial in the Abbey's north aisle.

Wider Implications

Despite the lack of concrete change attributable to the 1844 scandal, the episode offers interesting insights into nineteenth-century sexual reform efforts. First, it hints at the significance of delay and distraction. Second, it points to the way that elite male perspectives influenced the laws surrounding prostitution in the nineteenth century. For this reason, it also provides a useful point of contrast to the later nineteenth century, when women and working-class men played a larger role in the public debate over the state's role in the regulation of sex. Finally, it illustrates Christianity's complicated role in nineteenth-century sexual reform.

The demise of the 1844 Bill helps explain why it took more than one hundred years to reform a law as unpopular as the 1752 Disorderly Houses Act. Although brothels on church property did not remain a central theme as the century progressed, they represent the powerful combination of distraction and delay that stymied reformers for decades. In 1844, brothels in Westminster did not transform Earl Fitzhardinge into an opponent of the bill; he already saw it as 'a piece of fantastical and absurd legislation.'[65] When he challenged the bill in the House of Lords, Fitzhardinge did not need to discuss substance: his attack on the dean and chapter of Westminster Abbey distracted the chamber. The dean and chapter's failure to remove brothels from their property was a useful pretext to deny the 1844 Bill a fair hearing, and to ensure that the work of voluntary societies was barely discussed.

[64] For more information on the statue, see Robert Beevers, 'Pretensions to Permanency: Thorvaldsen's Bust and Statue of Byron', *The Byron Journal* 23 (1995), 63–75.

[65] 'Imperial Parliament', *The Economist*, 29 June 1844, 5. As a member of a select committee, Fitzhardinge had tried unsuccessfully to kill the bill by insisting that there was insufficient evidence of abuse to legislate: 'House of Lords, Monday, June 24', *The Times*, 25 June 1844, 2.

The 1844 debate also illustrates how an elite male perspective influenced legislators' view of criminal law. The life and legislative activity of Earl Fitzhardinge, who in many ways personified self-serving privilege, provides a useful example. By 1844, Fitzhardinge, a notorious womanizer, had been involved in several sex scandals. Described by one commentator as the 'archetypal Regency buck', Fitzhardinge was ordered to pay damages for criminal conversation in 1821, and was intimately involved in the Foote-Hayne scandal, during which it became clear that he had kept Miss Foote, an actress, as his mistress and fathered two children by her.[66] Allegations of more serious sexual misconduct – abduction and rape – cast a pall over his elevation to the earldom in 1841, which was also attributed to corrupt electioneering.[67] In 1844, *The Satirist* had joked that the behaviour of the dean and chapter of Westminster Abbey 'must have been of a bad complexion to have shocked such a peer as Fitzhardinge.'[68] As an aristocratic rake, hunter and landowner, Fitzhardinge supported laws that benefitted him – for example, those that protected property owners – while obstructing the passage of those that did not – like sexual reform – by labelling them as inappropriate legislative interventions. This perspective is clear in the 1844 session. He vociferously supported the 1844 Night Poaching Prevention Act, denying that poachers were motivated by deprivation: he told his fellow peers that 'he never knew a person of good character that was convicted of poaching.'[69] This was a safe enough claim in a room full of landowners. Three days later, he implied that a close examination of sexual exploitation put everyone in that same room at risk. If a 'subject was fit for legislation', he warned, 'it was necessarily fit for examination. If they would look into a sewer, they must expect to find a certain scent; and he must say that he thought they had been rather too hasty in their

[66] Malcolm Hal, *Murders and Misdemeanours in Gloucestershire 1820–1829* (Stroud, 2009), 21–31; 'Miss Foote and Mr. Hayne', *Bell's Life in London and Sporting Chronicle*, 26 December 1824, 1–3. For his reputation as a womanizer, see 'Anticipatory Epitaphs', *The Satirist*, 6 August 1843, 2 and 'Our Enlightening Dictionary', *The Satirist*, 13 August 1843, 3.

[67] 'The Morning Herald and Earl Fitzhardinge', *Morning Chronicle*, 4 September 1841, 3; 'Earl Fitzhardinge and the Morning Herald', *Morning Chronicle,* 10 September 1841, 2; 'Earl Fitzhardinge', *Devizes and Wiltshire Gazette*, 16 September 1841, 4; 'The Whig Radical Peerages', *Westmorland Gazette,* 25 September 1841, 4.

[68] 'The Almonry and the Abbey', *The Satirist,* 11 April 1847, 4.

[69] 'Imperial Parliament', *Morning Post,* 11 July 1844, 3.

legislation.'[70] This threat could work against elite men, but it would not persuade the middle-class women who helped push through legal changes later in the century.

Indeed, the idea that brothel suppression was a threat to property owners was an important obstacle to reform throughout the nineteenth century. Brothel suppression raised the possibility that property owners could be made liable for the behaviour of tenants, a key concern in the 1847 debate. This point dovetails with the previous argument that the charges against the dean and chapter were introduced in the House of Lords debate as a diversion. Fitzhardinge's status as a libertine and a property owner makes it clear that he deployed radical critiques of the established church out of convenience; that is, as part of a broader strategy of distraction to prevent the passage of a law he opposed.

The history of the 1844 Bill also hints at the male establishment's persistent ambivalence toward prostitution. The fact that many within the elite believed prostitution to be a necessary evil is clear from Lord Foley's claim that the segregation of brothels into certain neighbourhoods prevented prostitution from spilling out into other areas. The logic of this argument paralleled another popular idea about vice: that prostitutes constituted a sexual safety valve that protected virtuous women from dangerous male attention. Both beliefs were built on the idea of male sexual appetite for extramarital sex as a fixed quantity that could be directed, but not suppressed. Later reformers did not share these assumptions. During the agitation against the Contagious Diseases Acts (1870–85), the famous activist Josephine Butler made clear that she and her allies were not simply trying to change laws that encouraged a trade in prostitution; they were trying 'to do away with harlotry' and usher in a great 'hour of redemption'.[71]

Once female reformers gained a strong public voice, older patterns, once clear in the 1844 debate, became less viable. The case of the Rev. Herbert Marsh, invoked by the *Examiner* after the second reading of the 1844 Bill, points to a broader pattern of protecting the church's interests at the expense of prostitute women. When the Marsh case was discussed in the House of Lords a few months before the

[70] HL Deb. (3rd series), 24 June 1844 (vol. 75, col. 1257).

[71] 'Plymouth and Devonport / Crowded Meetings—Great Victory of the Opponents of the Acts', *The Shield*, 20 June 1870, 2–3.

introduction of the Brothel Suppression Bill, the bishop of Peterborough, George Davys, admitted under pressure that his stated reason for refusing to discipline Marsh for his sexual indiscretion with a woman he met in a brothel – namely that Marsh's crimes had not been committed in his diocese – was not legally sound. The bishop's defence was telling: 'he had felt something like an unwillingness to proceed against a clergyman when he was accused by a person of ill-fame for an act committed four years ago.'[72] While the bishop insisted that he was deeply committed to church discipline, he had also been concerned for Marsh's 'aged and excellent mother' whose poor health meant that any anxiety to her could have been 'fatal.'[73] Indeed, she died later that year.[74]

At the second reading of the 1844 Bill, the bishop of Exeter's explanation for why procuring and brothel-keeping should be criminal offences, when other types of sexual behaviour equally prohibited by Christian teaching were not, focused myopically on the moral lives of women. According to the bishop, prostitution could not be criminalized because 'the God of Mercy' had created it as a punishment to 'terrify innocent females' into remaining chaste.[75] Because prostitution was divinely ordained, he claimed, any human attempt to interfere with it directly would be 'as wild a scheme in his view, as if the guilty Cities of the Plain had thought of issuing a law against the storm of fire and brimstone of God, or as if the Israelites in the Wilderness had thought of legislating against the Destroying Angel of the Lord, who slew them for giving themselves to Baal.'[76] The bishop did not comment on why God would choose to create this type of gender specific punishment, or indeed, whether men who used prostitutes could expect any punishment at all.

The bishop of Exeter's reasons for not proposing the criminalization of seduction, a crime generally associated with men, also focused on female guilt. While he insisted that 'of all the ministers of Satan, there was none so truly satanical as the seducer', he could not

[72] 'Postscript. London, Saturday Morning, March 16, 1844', *The Economist*, 16 March 1844, 12.
[73] Ibid.
[74] Robert K. Forrest, 'Marsh, Herbert (1757–1839), bishop of Peterborough and biblical critic', *ODNB*, online edn (2004), at: <https://doi.org/10.1093/ref:odnb/18111>, accessed 20 August 2023.
[75] HL Deb. (3rd series), 14 June 1844 (vol. 75, col. 878).
[76] HL Deb. (3rd series), 14 June 1844 (vol. 75, cols 878–9).

countenance the idea of victims being required to testify, both because of the supposed shame of the experience, as well as the spiritual danger it created.[77] The bishop argued that the act of testifying would inhibit a seduced woman's ability to repent by distracting her with the promise of 'vengeance' and by inviting her to make 'an excuse for her fall', instead of accepting responsibility for her acquiescence.[78] It was 'for her sake', the bishop claimed, that he 'should not dare to attempt to punish the seducer.'[79] It was a painfully convenient thing to say in a room full of powerful men.

Yet while parliamentary debate and press coverage were controlled by men in 1844, women were already taking an interest in sexual reform. Adelaide, the Queen Dowager, was a patroness of the Society, and in the late 1840s women began playing a growing role in extra-parliamentary efforts to change the law to better protect young women, as exemplified by a well-publicized 1846 'Address to the Queen from the Women of Great Britain and Ireland', which pressed for legal change.[80] This work is rarely mentioned in studies of Victorian prostitution and offers an interesting, and largely unexplored, context for important female sexual reform groups, like the Ladies National Association for the Repeal of the Contagious Diseases Acts.

Probably because of the widening electorate, later reformers spent less time assuring powerful men that their proposals did not criminalize the types of activity that a powerful man might enjoy, such as the frequenting of prostitutes or seduction. Indeed, many middle-class reformers active later in the century were hostile toward the upper classes and framed aristocratic licentiousness as the reason for legal reform. While this idea had currency among voluntary workers much earlier, the electoral landscape was not favourable until the last decades of the century. Yet even in the 1840s, reformers saw public opinion as a powerful potential check on elite privilege.[81] This hope would be validated in 1885, when 'The Maiden Tribute of Modern Babylon', journalist and editor W. T. Stead's notorious series of articles about prostitution in the *Pall Mall Gazette*, triggered public

[77] HL Deb. (3rd series), 14 June 1844 (vol. 75, col. 880).
[78] Ibid.
[79] Ibid.
[80] Roberts, *Making English Morals*, 161.
[81] 'Prostitution—Its Fearful Extent', *Yorkshire Gazette*, 14 August 1841, 3.

outrage that fuelled the passage of the 1885 Criminal Law Amendment Act, which, among other things, introduced summary judgement for the closure of brothels.

The 1844 debate also demonstrates the critical role that Christianity played in nineteenth-century sexual reform efforts. The bill only existed because of the efforts of voluntary societies that were the product of Christian, particularly evangelical, social concern. Christian charity would drive more than legal reform: it was also the inspiration for the penitentiary system and the creation of reformatories for the rehabilitation of prostitutes.[82] Yet the 1844 episode also demonstrates how Christian institutions could damage the cause of sexual reform. In an immediate sense, it suggests that hypocrisy damaged the Church of England's ability to defend the vulnerable. It is clear that ecclesiastical officials struggled to balance their financial interests with the sexual morality they espoused (or claimed to espouse). Furthermore, the Church of England's practice of using leases to discriminate against religious rivals illustrates how the protection of institutional power inhibited the church's ability to serve as an effective agent of sexual reform. According to some accounts, the radical press originally learned about the brothels in the Almonry from a handbill printed by Dissenters who were furious that they were not allowed to rent Church of England property.[83] While the Church of England could claim Dissenters' heterodoxy was a source of spiritual danger, the fact that stronger measures were taken against Dissenters than against brothelkeepers or receivers of stolen goods implied that Dissent was a greater moral danger than thievery and prostitution. Yet while privileges and discrimination put some Christians at cross purposes, the story of sexual reform would largely be one of ecumenical cooperation. Just as the Society was a site of interdenominational cooperation, major efforts later in the century, including the National Vigilance Association, would also unite Christians from different denominations.

More broadly, the involvement of bishops made the 1844 Bill an ideal target for the Church of England's detractors. Even before Earl Fitzhardinge derailed the second reading, the idea of a bishop proposing that the police enforce morality was used in the House of

[82] Paula Bartley, *Prostitution: Prevention and Reform in England, 1860–1914* (London, 1999), 25–7.

[83] 'A Bishop's Zeal and a Chapter's Practice', *Examiner*, 22 June 1844, 4.

Commons as evidence of the pointlessness of the ecclesiastical courts.[84] The charges against the dean and chapter of Westminster Abbey were simply too good an opportunity for the Church of England's opponents. By 1844, the brothels in Westminster had already been used to argue against a series of initiatives, including church expansion (it was recommended that the church 'extend' its attention to 'the brothels in the shadow of Westminster Abbey, and see whether there be room for improvement there'); the practice of sending establishment clergy to compete with Nonconformist missionaries in South Africa; and a bill to compel Dissenters to pay burial fees to the established church, whether or not they were buried in its consecrated ground.[85] The idea that the Church of England had a hypocritical relationship to prostitution also became a powerful strain in the debate over the Contagious Diseases Acts, a series of laws that many reformers understood as the de facto regulation of prostitution. Although there were not the same charges of corruption, Christian opponents of the acts were infuriated when many Church of England clergymen, including high-ranking members of the ecclesiastical hierarchy, supported the acts.[86]

On an individual level, the two bishops involved in the 1844 debate were liabilities. As a villain in radical circles and known controversialist, the bishop of Exeter may have made the bill a more attractive target, while the bishop of Gloucester's mercenary invocation of Berkeley Square seemed to confirm critics' suspicion that the Church of England's hierarchy was more concerned with profit than morality. As conservative high churchmen, both bishops were known for their commitment to aggressively defending the establishment, and this impulse clearly influenced their response to Fitzhardinge's allegations.[87] Indeed, the bishop of Gloucester only participated in

[84] 'House of Commons, Friday, May 31', *The Times*, 1 June 1844, 3–4.

[85] 'Clerical Immorality', *The Satirist*, 30 October 1842, 7.

[86] Many Anglican clergymen participated in the campaign to extend the acts, and resisted overtures from the repeal campaign. An early list of members of the largest extensionist organization contains the names of numerous clergymen, including the dean of Westminster, Arthur Penrhyn Stanley; the lord bishop of Down and Connor, Robert Knox; and the lord bishop of Worcester, Henry Philpott, who all served as vice presidents: *Report of the Sub-Committee of the Association for Promoting the Extension of 'The Contagious Diseases Act,' of 1866, to the Civil Population, with a List of its Members* (London, 1869). See also Paul McHugh, *Prostitution and Victorian Social Reform* (London, 2013), 188.

[87] Arthur Burns, 'Phillpotts, Henry (1778–1869), bishop of Exeter', *ODNB,* online edn (2004), at: <https://doi.org/10.1093/ref:odnb/22180>, accessed 20 August 2023;

the debate to protect the church. He did not comment on the substance of the 1844 Bill but focused exclusively on defending the dean and chapter of Westminster Abbey, objecting twice to the idea that Fitzhardinge had criticized a group 'entitled to respect and decency.'[88] In his haste to protect the dean and chapter's reputation, the bishop of Gloucester exaggerated the steps taken against brothels on church property. When he falsely guaranteed, on the strength of a personal inspection, that the dean and chapter had made the financial sacrifices necessary to remove all brothels from their properties, he gave Fitzhardinge a reason to reintroduce the issue with new evidence, undermining the more credible argument that it was difficult to evict tenants and keeping the issue alive in the press. No doubt the bishops were particularly sensitive given the context. In the late eighteenth and early nineteenth centuries, radicals and libertines exploited clerical sex scandals to forward their political agendas.[89] Nevertheless, the bishops' commitment to defending their fellow clergymen's decisions – from refusing the statue of Lord Byron to the eviction of tenants – distracted them from the 1844 Bill and weakened their ability to serve as advocates of sexual reform.

Conclusion

The failed 1844 Brothel Suppression Bill offers an interesting vantage point from which to view nineteenth-century sexual reform and draws attention to important themes in the Victorian debate about prostitution, including the roles of gender, class and religion. The 1844 Bill also points to a few questions for future study. First, it invites closer scrutiny of female participation in sexual reform efforts before the agitation against the Contagious Diseases Acts. A comparison of female participation before and after the acts could highlight ways in which these acts amplified female interest in sexual exploitation as a serious political concern. Second, the 1844 Bill raises interesting questions about the relationship between sexual reform and

Richard Smail, 'Monk, James Henry (1784–1856), bishop of Gloucester and Bristol and classical scholar', *ODNB,* online edn (2004), at: <https://doi.org/10.1093/ref:odnb/18956>, accessed 20 August 2023.

[88] HL Deb. (3rd series), 24 June 1844 (vol. 75, col. 1262).

[89] William Gibson and Joanne Begiato, *Sex and the Church in the Long Eighteenth Century* (London, 2019), 225–41, 278.

partisan politics. In 1844, the bill's advocates were Tory paternalists like the earl of Shaftesbury, the bishop of Exeter and the earl of Galloway, yet by the end of the century, sexual reform would be closely tied with the Liberal Party. While the evolution of the Liberal Party is well studied, it would be interesting to see how far ideological continuity was maintained when sexual reform crossed the floor.

As a final matter, the collapse of the 1844 Bill offers two insights into how charges of hypocrisy operate. The first has already been explored: the charge of hypocrisy is a powerful distraction that is particularly damaging to those who wish to set or change moral standards. The second is simpler: the charge of hypocrisy is dangerous because so many people find it funny. Charges of hypocrisy contain incongruity that many people find humorous and, as a result, can turn a debate about coerced prostitution into a joke. A few lines from 'Byron vs Brothels', addressed to the dean and chapter of Westminster Abbey, illustrate the point:

> Each kiss that thrills, each sigh that springs
> From passion's heaving breast,
> To you—in shillings, pounds and pence—
> Is pleasantly expressed!
> Your tariff is a code of love,
> Not printed, yet in *sheets*!
> A very pretty income-tax
> You levy upon *sweets!*
> …
> Brothels and priests! how curiously
> Those clashing names unite;
> The *spiritual* body mixed
> With *flesh* and its delight![90]

[90] 'Byron vs Brothels', *The Satirist*, 7 July 1844, 3. Italics original.

Cavalier South vs Puritan North? Hypocrisy and Identity in the American Civil War

Edward G. Manger*
Charleston, South Carolina

During the antebellum period and American Civil War, 'puritan' was a contested identity, fraught with layers of meaning and interpretation. Historians have charted the ways Southern intellectuals cast the differences between North and South as an outplaying of the old conflict between Cavalier and puritan. This article highlights the ways Southern ministers claimed the puritan identity for the South and accused the North of hypocrisy, for having fallen far from the theological ideals of their puritan forebears. Furthermore, Southern ministers noted the hypocrisy of Northern puritans for having escaped religious tyranny only to impose it upon those who did not conform to their form of Christianity; they had thus fallen into the very sin which they had decried. This came from Southern ministers whose attempt to appropriate the memory of puritanism as liberty-loving revealed their own hypocrisy in fighting for the 'liberty' to maintain a system of racial slavery.

By the beginning of the American Civil War (1861–5), white Southerners had grown accustomed to accusing Northerners of hypocrisy. They bemoaned Northern attacks on slavery that hypocritically ignored the material and economic benefits that those in the Northern states enjoyed as a result of the 'peculiar institution'.[1] They also bewailed the fact that Northern ministers hypocritically claimed to be orthodox Christians, whilst dabbling in theological speculation.[2] Throughout the antebellum period (*c.*1830–60), this

* 4932 Durrant Avenue, North Charleston, SC, 29405, USA. E-mail: egmanger@gmail.com.

[1] See, for instance, Benjamin Morgan Palmer, *Thanksgiving Sermon, Delivered at the First Presbyterian Church, New Orleans, on Thursday, December 29, 1860* (New York, 1861), 10–11.

[2] See, for example, John H. Bocock, 'Modern Theology, Taylor and Bledsoe', *Southern Presbyterian Review* 4 (1856), 492–512, at 494–5.

Studies in Church History 60 (2024), 431–452
doi: 10.1017/stc.2024.16

accusation of hypocrisy was used to undermine the moral position from which Northern abolitionists criticized slaveholders. The charge of hypocrisy therefore became a significant component of white Southern rhetorical attempts to associate abolitionism with corruption in morality, piety and politics. Northern hypocrisy was often attributed to New England's puritan origins, especially in the context of the American Civil War, when both sides attempted to explain the conflict with reference to history. This attempt manifested itself in the common representation of the conflict between the Confederacy and Union as a replaying of the English Civil War, with the roles assigned as puritan (Parliamentarian) North vs Cavalier South.[3] In this article, I argue that this picture was contested by many Southern ministers who, sympathizing with puritanism in general, saw the locus of the North's hypocrisy in its departure from puritanism, not in puritanism itself.

Prominent historians of the religious dimensions of the Civil War have overlooked the nuances of Southern clergy's use of puritanism – both the term itself and its theology – in their sermons and religious literature. For example, Harry Stout writes that 'Many [Southern] writers justified the righteousness of their cause by contrasting the evangelical Christianity of the revivals with the "Puritan" spirituality of the North.'[4] Similarly, George Rable has observed that the common comparison between the Confederate general, Stonewall Jackson, and Oliver Cromwell was: 'Ironic in light of the widely held notion of a yawning gulf between Southern Cavaliers and Northern Puritans.'[5] Such comments ignore the fact that many Southern ministers did not see this 'yawning gulf' as being between themselves and Northern puritans, but rather as being between puritanism and what the North had become. Drew Gilpin Faust comes closer to an accurate description of the South's position when she points out that the white Southern view of puritanism was not an unalloyed critique, but acknowledged elements of good in the puritan

[3] See, for instance, John Quitman Moore, 'The Belligerents', *De Bow's Review* 31 (1861), 69–77, at 72–5. See also A. Jeffrey, 'European Emigration and New England Puritanism', *Southern Literary Messenger* 37 (1863), 463–72, at 470–1.

[4] Harry S. Stout, *Upon the Altar of the Nation: A Moral History of the Civil War* (London, 2007), 333.

[5] George C. Rable, *God's Almost Chosen Peoples: A Religious History of the American Civil War* (Chapel Hill, NC, 2010), 138.

past.[6] However, it was specifically the Southern clergy who insisted upon a positive view of puritanism, in distinction to secular commentators. This shows that Southern ministers did not simply regurgitate the narratives they encountered in the surrounding culture, but attempted to insert their own voice, views and priorities into their constructions of the Civil War's meaning.[7] Furthermore, the regularity with which Southern ministers referred to the puritans and to the English parliamentary armies indicates that clergy used a historical identity to explain, understand and interpret the war as vociferously as James Byrd has recently demonstrated they used the Bible.[8]

In this article, I argue that many Southern ministers and churches rejected the Cavalier vs puritan framing of the Civil War and were instead intent on claiming themselves as the true heirs of the puritans, both in their quest for liberty and in the Christianity of their armies. This enabled Southern clergy to cast the North as nothing more than hypocrites who claimed to be the descendants of the puritans, but were in reality persecuting and warring against the true successors to puritan ideals. This helped Southern ministers maintain the intellectual independence from the North that Micheal Bernath has convincingly argued was a concern for Southerners in general.[9] Ministers did not need to concede that they had anything positive to learn from the North just because they praised puritanism. Instead, they appropriated various aspects of puritan history for the South to emphasize the North's degeneracy. In doing so, Southern ministers unintentionally gave the North an instant retort in a counter-charge of hypocrisy, as the South claimed to be fighting for liberty, freeing themselves from supposed religious oppression from Northern abolitionists, whilst denying liberty to their slaves. This underappreciated aspect of Southern religion and the Civil War displays the contradictions inherent in the puritan legacy, including the label of puritan itself.[10]

[6] Drew Gilpin Faust, *The Creation of Confederate Nationalism* (Baton Rouge, LA, 1995), 27.

[7] This was an important but overlooked point made by Anne Lovelace, *Southern Evangelicals and Social Order, 1800–1860* (Baton Rouge, LA, 1981), ix–x.

[8] James P. Byrd, *A Baptism of Fire and Blood: The Bible and the American Revolution* (Oxford, 2021).

[9] Michael T. Bernath, *The Struggle for Intellectual Independence in the Civil War South* (Chapel Hill, NC, 2010).

[10] John Coffey has written of puritanism's 'puzzling set of legacies': see John Coffey, 'Puritan Legacies', in idem and Paul Lim, eds, *Cambridge Companion to Puritanism* (Cambridge, 2008), 327–45, at 327. Although necessarily puzzling, Southerners' use of puritanism is contradictory and somewhat unexpected.

Indeed, 'white Southerners' use of the term varied greatly, from abuse to praise. As George Rable has shown, the South built up negative stereotypes, depictions and tropes about the North in their rhetorical attempts to demonize the 'Yankees', and part of this was in referring to them as puritans, a term that could be populated with any number of derisory attributes and which served as a catch-all insult to denote the negative differences of the North when compared to the South. However, Rable's examples are primarily drawn from secular sources.[11] My survey of printed Confederate sermons and religious newspapers shows that Southern Protestant clergy were not as quick to use puritan as a term of abuse.[12] Puritan identity was malleable: it could simultaneously be used negatively, as a straw man constructed from negative attributes ascribed to the settlers of New England; and positively, to describe religious orthodoxy and love of liberty when puritanism was considered as a broader movement. To harmonize all such uses of puritanism, that is, to see it as a blanket term of abuse or a positive claim to identity would therefore be to overlook the complexities that the term reveals within white Southern society during the antebellum period and the Civil War.

Cavalier South vs Puritan North

Sidney Ahlstrom has described the Southern Cavalier trope as central to a new kind of Southern nationalism emerging from the 1830s onward.[13] It was advanced enthusiastically by leading white intellectuals in the pages of the most influential Southern publications, while at the same time being reinforced by Northern depictions of the South as exotic and 'other', as James Cobb has shown.[14] William

[11] George C. Rable, *Damn Yankees! Demonization and Defiance in the Confederate South* (Baton Rouge, LA, 2015), 11–15.

[12] This is based on the reading of over one hundred sermons and addresses delivered by Southern clergy during the war, as well as extensive reading of multiple issues of fifteen separate Southern religious journals and newspapers in which references to 'puritans', 'puritanism', 'Cromwell' and 'Parliamentarians' are overwhelmingly positive, and negative references to the same are rare.

[13] Sidney E. Ahlstrom, *A Religious History of the American People* (New Haven, CT, 1972), 654.

[14] James C. Cobb, *Away Down South: A History of Southern Identity* (Oxford, 2005), 1, 4. For a good overview of Southern anti-puritanism, largely through the work of the prolific Southern intellectual George Fitzhugh, see Jan C. Dawson, 'The Puritan and the Cavalier: The South's Perception of Contrasting Traditions', *The Journal of Southern*

R. Taylor summed up the result, writing that, by 1860, most Americans believed that 'each section of the country ... possessed its own ethic, its own historical tradition and even, by common agreement, a distinctive racial heritage.'[15] According to this tradition, the Southern states, particularly Virginia and the Carolinas, had been settled in the seventeenth and early eighteenth centuries by Cavaliers and their descendants. These settlers had, through their character and innate virtues, bequeathed to their posterity respect for order, propriety and regulated liberty. At the same time, they were also seen as enjoying the leisurely pursuits of plantation life, based on those of the English country gentry. This identity developed in distinction to that of the North, which was depicted as having been settled by puritans, joyless, overbearing fanatics who hypocritically chastised and oppressed the liberty-loving Cavaliers of the South.[16]

Upon the outset of the war, this regional association with the Cavaliers took on new levels of importance and became an implement in the Confederate rhetorical arsenal with which to attack the North. No less an authority on the nature of the Confederacy than its president, Jefferson Davis, was able to say in his first speech after his inauguration (as reported by the *Richmond Dispatch*) that 'the Northern Roundheads "bred in the bogs and fens of Ireland and Northern England", could never dominate the Southern people, who were descendants of the bold and chivalrous Cavaliers of old.'[17]

History 44 (1978), 597–614. The role of the North in romanticizing the South through travel is also a theme of Susan Mary Grant's *North Over South: Northern Nationalism and American Identity in the Antebellum Era* (Lawrence, KA, 2000), 81–111.

[15] William R. Taylor, *Cavalier and Yankee: The Old South and American National Character* (New York, 1957), 15.

[16] The relative merits of, or problems with, this view of the settlement of the various states of America are not our concern. Instead, it suffices to say that these distinctions were widely held to be true and meaningful by Northern and Southern commentators and historians, and literature consumed in the antebellum period would have confirmed that belief. In the twentieth century, Clement Eaton was of the opinion that the Cavalier origin of the South was not entirely without basis: see Clement Eaton, *A History of the Old South* (New York, 1949), 69. David Hackett Fischer has seen as fundamentally important the streams of migration from England forming 'Folkways', the Southern iteration of this phenomenon being created in part by 'Distressed Cavaliers'. See David Hackett Fischer, *Albion's Seed: Four British Folkways in America* (Oxford, 1989), 213.

[17] Bertram Wyatt-Brown, *The Shaping of Southern Culture: Honor, Grace, and War* (Chapel Hill, NC, 2001), 180.

The animosity between Cavalier and puritan became commonplace as an explanatory framework for the war. A writer in the *Richmond Dispatch* put it this way: 'We never believed that slavery had as much to do with this war as personal resentment and vindictiveness, transmitted from generation to generation, smoldering embers of the old Cavalier and Puritan feuds, which never died out.' This author asserted, in no uncertain terms, that 'the descendants of those two classes in the North and the South would have gone to war, sooner or later, if such a thing as slavery never existed.'[18]

Such interpretations of the war were also racialized, as can be seen by the title of an 1861 piece in the *Southern Literary Messenger*: 'The true question: A contest for the supremacy of race, As between the Saxon Puritan of the North, and the Norman of the South.'[19] This further equation of Norman with Cavalier, and puritan with Saxon, enabled Southerners to conceive of the war as a struggle between disparate races. Drawing on contemporary racial theory, the author of this article argued that due to 'ethnological differences' those who populated the North had a national character which was 'incapable of self-government, and ever violating, when left alone, the established law of reciprocal justice towards others.'[20] Two months later, an article in *De Bow's Review* made a similar case, arguing that the 'radical and irreconcilable' differences between the Cavalier South and puritan North had inevitably led to the disruptions of the Civil War.[21] It also maintained that 'The Puritans … were in their hearts tyrants.'[22] A direct line was drawn between the puritans of the seventeenth century and the Northerners of the nineteenth, which established their equivalence 'in all [their] vices', not least in their hypocrisy.[23]

This narrative of the Cavalier South vs the puritan North played into the hands of Northern ministers, providing them with ample opportunity to use the charge of hypocrisy as an attack against the South. Northern ministers, especially those in the New England

[18] *Richmond Dispatch*, 14 September 1863.

[19] Anon., 'The True Question: A Contest for the Supremacy of Race, as Between the Saxon Puritan of the North, and the Norman of the South', *Southern Literary Messenger* 33 (1861), 19–27.

[20] Ibid. 21.

[21] Anon., 'The Puritan and the Cavalier; or, The Elements of American Colonial Society,' *De Bow's Review* 31 (1861), 209–52, at 209–10.

[22] Ibid. 210–11.

[23] Ibid. 223.

states, were becoming increasingly proud of their puritan heritage. They were only too happy to conceive of their struggle in the American Civil War as a continuation of the principles for which the puritans had struggled before them.[24] Part of this puritan rehabilitation project involved clearing their own name of the charge of hypocrisy and rejecting the idea that the puritans of New England had been intolerant. Instead, the history of puritanism was reframed to make the puritans responsible for the ideals of liberty which stood behind the Declaration of Independence (1776).[25] For a Northern preacher such as the popular and widely read Henry Ward Beecher, the quest for liberty was innate to the puritan character, the cause of the church and the cause of the Union. Indeed, Beecher claimed: 'I love every drop of Puritan blood the world ever saw, because … Puritan blood means blood touched with Christ's blood.'[26]

Truly Puritan South vs Formerly Puritan North

From the outset of the war, the Roman Catholic Church in the South adopted a clear anti-puritan stance, seeing New England religion as a form of ultra-Protestantism and the Cavalier ethos of the South as more conducive to Roman Catholicism.[27] When it came to the Protestant churches, however, those most likely to subscribe to this standard narrative of Cavalier South vs puritan North were Episcopalians. They enjoyed ecclesiastical descent from the Royalists, specifically from the Restoration establishment that had ejected the vast majority of puritans from the Church of England in 1662. It made sense, therefore, for Episcopal churchmen to ride the wave of Cavalier nostalgia. Consequently, the Episcopal Church experienced a high level of influence in the Confederacy, particularly over its

[24] For an interest in puritan history during New England's antebellum period, see Edwin Hall, *The Puritans and Their Principles* (New York, 1847). For an interesting example of the 'multidimensional discourse of faith, history, and nation in antebellum New England', see Lindsay Dicuirci, 'Reviving Puritan History: Evangelicalism, Antiquarianism, and Mather's *Magnalia* in Antebellum America', *Early American Literature* 45 (2010), 565–92, at 566.

[25] Stout, *Upon the Altar*, 391, citing an 1864 sermon by Lavalette Perrin.

[26] Henry Ward Beecher, *Discourses on Topics Suggested by the Times* (Boston, MA, 1863), 75.

[27] Rable, *God's Almost Chosen Peoples*, 136.

president Jefferson Davis, who worshiped at St John's Episcopal Church in Richmond (Virginia) and was baptized and confirmed an Episcopalian during the war.[28] However, the Episcopal Church did not speak with one voice, and even when Episcopalian clergy criticized puritanism, they usually attacked the form that puritanism had taken in New England, rather than puritanism itself.[29] This is a crucial distinction, which, when combined with the broad sympathy with evangelicalism found among many Southern Episcopalians, allowed the popular and prolific wartime orator and Episcopal bishop of Georgia, Stephen Elliott, to praise Cromwell and invoke the 'Anglo-Saxon race' and the 'bold commoners who brought the Stuarts to the proper knowledge of a people's rights.'[30] Elliott was in sympathy with the cause of puritanism during the English Civil War, and expected his congregation to resonate with his exhortation to emulate puritan Parliamentarians rather than Cavaliers by asserting their rights against a despotic North.

Sermons and religious journals produced in the South during the war show that many Southern Protestant clergy never accepted the central tenets of the Cavalier vs puritan, South vs North narrative, steeped as they were in the literature of evangelical Christian militarism, which valued the piety of (Southern) Christian soldiers over the supposed aristocratic virtues of the Cavaliers.[31] Instead, Southern

[28] For Jefferson Davis's religion, see William J. Cooper, *Jefferson Davis, American* (New York, 2000), 388.

[29] The *Richmond Dispatch* has been seen as a religious publication under Episcopal editorship which perpetuated the Cavalier vs puritan narrative of the war, and capitalized on its connection to 'old Virginia Anglicanism': Harry Stout and Christopher Grasso, 'Civil War, Religion and Communications: The Case of Richmond', in Randall Miller, Harry Stout and Charles Reagan Wilson, eds, *Religion and the American Civil War* (Oxford, 1998), 313–59, at 336–7. It appears from Stout and Grasso's article that the criticism of puritanism in this publication focuses on its Northern fanaticism leading to 'Mormonism', 'Spiritualism' and the Northern hubris of 'manifest destiny', rather than a critique of Cromwell, the Parliamentarians, or broader English puritanism.

[30] Stephen Elliot, *How to Renew our National Strength: A Sermon Preached in Christ Church, Savannah, on Friday, November 15th, 1861, Being the day of Humiliation, Fasting, and Prayer, Appointed by the President of the Confederate States* (Savannah, GA, 1861), 15; Stephen Elliott, *The Silver Trumpets of the Sanctuary: A Sermon Preached to the Pulaski Guards* (Savannah, GA, 1863), 8; Diana Hochstedt Butler, *Standing Against the Whirlwind: Evangelical Episcopalians in Nineteenth-Century America* (New York, 1995).

[31] Olive Anderson, 'The Growth of Christian Militarism in Mid-Victorian Britain', *EHR* 86 (1971), 46–72. Southern ministers often called upon the memory of Henry Havelock and Headley Vicars, two British officers who had not long before died in the Indian

ministers tended to apply the aesthetic of the Cavalier heritage to the South, but crucially, fused this with the religiosity and independence of the puritans. In this way, they could consider themselves orthodox heirs to the piety of the puritans, whilst maintaining the hierarchical and chivalrous notions of society that were central to the Southern way of life.[32] Furthermore, the use of the Norman vs Saxon trope, in contrast to commentary from secular sources, is virtually non-existent in the sermons and literature produced by Southern ministers during the war.[33] Instead, they were more than happy to revel in their perceived Saxon racial identity as the embodiment of Protestant orthodoxy and political liberty.[34] At the same time, Southern clergymen wished to retain the charge of hypocrisy against the North, leading them to find new ways to praise the puritans and claim that the North was hypocritical in assuming that label for themselves.[35] In doing so, they recast the Civil War as puritan South vs formerly puritan North.

The evangelical culture of the largest Protestant denominations in the South – Baptist, Methodist, Presbyterian and Episcopal – had long drawn upon puritan spiritual traditions, not least devotionally. Authors such as John Bunyan and Richard Baxter remained staples for Southern religious readers.[36] Furthermore, Presbyterians and Baptists could trace the histories of their denominations directly

---

Mutiny and Crimean War, respectively, and who were praised and repeatedly written about as Christian soldiers: see, for example, William J. Hodge *Sketch of Dabney Carr Harrison: Minister of the Gospel and Captain in the Army of the Confederate States of America* (Richmond, VA, 1861), 34.

[32] In this way, the same publication, *The Southwest Baptist,* could praise Cromwell and the piety of Baptists in his army, but also run a piece from the *Huntsville Democrat* which used the language of Southern Cavaliers to denote manliness, bravery and chivalry in praising the military exploits of the Confederate Army: 'Manassas', *South Western Baptist*, 24 October 1861, 1.

[33] I have been unable to find any reference to the Norman nature of the South in my survey of Confederate sermons and religious publications from the war.

[34] See, for instance, William A. Hall, *The Historic Significance of The Southern Revolution* (Petersburg, VA, 1864), 24, 37. Stephen Elliott self-identified as Anglo-Saxon, not Norman, and declares: 'The Anglo-Saxon race has never waited until the stroke of tyranny actually descended.' Elliott, *The Silver Trumpets,* 8.

[35] This is the clear implication of the arguments in favour of the puritans and the attempts to disassociate the North from the puritanism of William, Hall, Alexander Sinclair and Joseph Atkinson discussed below.

[36] Elizabeth Fox-Genovese and Eugene Genovese, *The Mind of the Master Class: History and Faith in the Southern Slaveholders' Worldview* (Cambridge, 2005), 327–8.

back to the events of the English Civil War. The October 1861 edition of the *South Western Baptist* pointed out to its readers: 'Many of Cromwell's ablest officers were Baptists, and so were many of his army.'[37] Presbyterians were also highly attuned to their historical connection to the events of the English Civil War. The Westminster Confession of Faith, so highly prized by old school Presbyterians of the South, had been composed by an assembly of puritan divines convened at the behest of Parliament in the 1640s. It is therefore unsurprising that ministers and theologians from these traditions were slow to endorse the Cavalier vs puritan narrative.[38]

Southern churches and ministers preferred to adapt the history of the English Civil War to draw their own parallels and push back against any denigration of puritans. The *Central Presbyterian* commented in November 1862: 'There are a few senseless scribblers in some of our political papers who are never weary of heaping indiscriminate abuse upon the old Puritans; a class of men of whom, with all their faults, the world was not worthy.'[39] The most striking example is offered by the Presbyterian William Hall, chaplain to the Washington Artillery, in a lecture given at least four separate times in Richmond and Petersburg (both Virginia). This lecture focused on the historical meaning of what Hall termed the 'current revolution'. In it, he repudiated 'The absurd idea that this unprecedented struggle … is a renewal of the strife between the Puritan and the Cavalier,'[40] and offered an overview of the constitutional and ecclesiastical conflicts involving the puritans, from the Reformation to the English Civil War. Hall argued that it had been the Parliamentarians, not the Cavaliers, who had fought for liberty and inherited rights in a way comparable to the South. He reminded his listeners: 'The Puritans included all the lovers of civil and religious liberty in that age', continuing: 'England is indebted to the Puritans for every principle of liberty.'[41] Hall admired the puritans of England not only for

[37] *South Western Baptist,* 24 October 1861, 2.

[38] See, for example, Thomas Smyth, 'The History, Character and Results of the Westminster Assembly of Divines: A Discourse in Commemoration of the Bi-centenary Anniversary of that Body', in *Complete Works of Rev. Thomas Smyth D.D.,* vol. 4, ed. John W. Flinn (Columbia SC, 1908), 385–434.

[39] *Central Presbyterian*, 27 November 1862, 1.

[40] William A. Hall, *The Historic Significance of The Southern Revolution* (Petersburg, VA, 1864), 24.

[41] Ibid. 27.

their role in fighting for liberty, but also for their religious qualities. In his narrative, the North had fallen away from the pure puritan faith that it may originally have had. Hall argued: 'Puritanism, properly so called, has no connection whatsoever, with this inhuman crusade upon the confederate states,' and presented the North as having 'Repudiated every principle of the Puritan faith,' particularly its 'Reverence for the Word of God.'[42]

Other ministers in the South also attempted to rehabilitate what they understood to be the original meaning of puritanism. Alexander Sinclair, Presbyterian minister of the church in Six Mile (South Carolina), declared: 'I have heard men in their ignorance attribute our national disorders to the influence of Puritan doctrines. Egregious error! The doctrines of the original Puritans were, and are, the doctrines of the Bible.'[43] Far from seeing a great gulf between puritanism and Southern Christianity, he insisted: 'They are the truths which, from Sabbath to Sabbath, are preached in all the Presbyterian pulpits of the South.' However, he ended his thought with an indictment: 'But the descendants of the Puritans have gone far astray from the creed of their forefathers.'[44] One of the South's most prominent theologians, Robert Louis Dabney, also echoed this sentiment. He believed that puritanism was a mighty movement of God that had trailed off and become cold, formal and, finally, apostate. The lesson for the South was explicit: Southerners should maintain a fervency of spirit in orthodox piety, in order to avoid the doctrinal slide experienced in the North.[45]

An article published in the *Southern Presbyterian Review* in 1863 also sought to defend the puritans while accusing their Northern descendants of hypocrisy. The author, the Rev. Joseph Atkinson, exclaimed: 'No intelligent person can fail to have perceived, no evangelical believer can fail to have deplored, the undiscriminating censure

[42] Ibid. 31.

[43] Alexander Sinclair, *A Thanksgiving Sermon, Preached in the Presbyterian Church at Six-Mile, Lancaster District, S.C., on Thursday, Sept. 18th, 1862* (Salisbury, NC, 1862), 40.

[44] Ibid.

[45] See Richmond, Union Presbyterian Seminary, William Smith Morton Library Archives, Robert Lewis Dabney Faculty Papers Collection, Dabney Army Sermons 001, online at: <https://cdm17236.contentdm.oclc.org/digital/collection/p17236coll4/id/0/rec/1>, accessed 12 January 2024. For Dabney's influence and position as a Southern theologian, see Thomas Cary Johnson, *The Life and Letters of Robert Lewis Dabney* (Richmond, VA, 1903) and Sean Michael Lewis, *Robert Lewis Dabney: A Southern Presbyterian Life* (Phillipsburg, NJ, 2005).

and scorn with which the Puritans have been stigmatized of late.'[46] He argued that the puritans had been responsible for championing the cause of Parliament during the English Civil War against the tyrannical king. However, Atkinson refused to identify the 'insane and inhumane crusade now instituted against the people of the Confederate states with the creed and character of the Puritans.' Rather, he insisted the South was 'contending this day for the very truths and doctrines … for which the Puritans contended in Great Britain.'[47] He provided a sympathetic account of the history of the puritans, restricting himself to no single period of puritanism, but drawing lessons from the entire movement, including puritan resistance to the ecclesiastical policies of Queen Elizabeth I. He concluded: 'In contending for the rightful supremacy of the word of God in opposition to the mandates of kings and the decrees of councils, the Puritans conferred a priceless boon on the human race.'[48] However, the North had not been able to maintain the traditional beliefs and character of this honourable heritage and was hypocritical in claiming to do so.[49]

These examples are representative of a larger tendency among Southern ministers to speak positively about puritanism and negatively about what the North had become. Many Southern ministers

[46] Joseph M. Atkinson, 'The Puritans', *Southern Presbyterian Review* 15 (1862), 230–55, at 234. Atkinson's article is a review of Samuel Hopkins, *The Puritans: or The Church, Court and Parliament of England, During the Reign of Edward the Sixth and Queen Elizabeth*, 3 vols (Boston, MA, 1859). Atkinson was scathing about Hopkins's work and much preferred Daniel Neal's classic text, *The History of the Puritans,* first published between 1732 and 1738. Neal's work has been seen as 'prefiguring nineteenth-century Whig conceptions of Puritan history' and casting the puritans as the true source of liberty and individualism. For this view, see Laird Okie, 'Daniel Neal and the "Puritan Revolution"', *ChH* 55 (1986), 456–67. This Whig view of puritan history was well received in New England, but also found reception in the South. Many Southern ministers were influenced by Thomas Babington Macaulay and saw the rehabilitation of puritanism as beginning with his essays on Milton and Hampden, 'The Letters and Speeches of Oliver Cromwell', *Southern Presbyterian Review* 1 (1847), 121–55, at 127.

[47] Atkinson, 'The Puritans', 235.

[48] Ibid. 242.

[49] The thrust of Atkinson's argument is that Southerners should not be critical of puritanism and should not associate puritanism with the North. However, the charge of Northern hypocrisy is implied throughout the argument in as much as Atkinson consistently regards contemporary Northerners, who claimed to be puritans themselves, as less than puritan. He praises the puritan settlers of New England, Edward Winslow, John Winthrop and John Endicott, but sees Northerners of his day as 'corrupt and degenerate descendants': Atkinson, 'The Puritans', 236.

were convinced that its orthodoxy and genuine piety on the one hand, and commitment to liberty on the other, made puritanism the most fitting comparison to the South. Taken in these terms, puritanism could be readily appropriated, even by Southern ministers who had little historical claim to be its literal descendants. Southern ministers had been worried about the trajectory of what they considered Northern infidelity for several decades before the war.[50] They were suspicious of the revivalist methods of the popular Northern preacher Charles Finney, concerned about the challenges to confessionalism represented by Yale professor and theologian Nathaniel Taylor and influential minister Lyman Beecher, and aghast at the rise of Unitarianism.[51] Yet above these concerns was the potent mix of fear and consternation felt at the anti-slavery and abolitionist rhetoric emanating from Northern pulpits.[52] The growing strength with which the anti-slavery message was proclaimed was met with an ever more febrile assertion of the biblical basis for the racial slavery of the Southern states.[53] In this context, attacks on slavery and appeals to its justification became a question of faithfulness to God's word; the separation of North and South was, as Mark Noll has called it, a theological crisis.[54] If Southerners saw themselves as faithful to orthodoxy, the preservers of true Protestantism and biblical Christianity, it was a simple move to equate themselves with the

[50] The growing alienation between Northern and Southern Christians due to the Southern association of orthodoxy with pro-slavery and widespread fear about anti-slavery attitudes to the Bible, is the focus of much scholarship on Southern religion in the antebellum period: see, for instance, Samuel Hill, *The North and South in Southern Religion* (Athens, GA, 1980), esp. 46–89 (ch. 2, 'Third Cousins Alienated'); and Mitchel Snay, *Gospel of Disunion: Religion and Separatism in the Antebellum South* (New York, 1993). Fears and suspicions were only heightened by denominational divisions in the Methodist, Baptist and Presbyterian churches. This is most extensively covered in C. C. Goen's classic *Broken Churches, Broken Nation: Denominational Schisms and the Coming of the Civil War* (Macon, GA, 1988).

[51] John Holmes Bocock, 'Taylor and Bledsoe', *Southern Presbyterian Review* 9 (1856), 492–512; Thomas Curtis, 'John The Baptist: The Unitarian Jesus', *Southern Presbyterian Review* 2 (1848), 250–69.

[52] See, for example, George Armstrong, *Politics and the Pulpit: A Discourse Preached at the Presbyterian Church, Norfolk, VA* (Richmond, VA, 1856), 37.

[53] The desperate exasperation of Southern defenders of slavery on the eve of the Civil War can be detected in an article by George Howe, professor at Columbia Theological Seminary in South Carolina, in response to the raid by John Brown on Harpers Ferry: George Howe, 'John Brown and the Progress of Abolition', *Southern Presbyterian Review* 12 (1860), 784–816.

[54] Mark Noll, *The Civil War as A Theological Crisis* (Chapel Hill, NC, 2006).

puritans of old. Evangelicals in the South had a vested interest in claiming a robust form of Protestantism that had little or no place for the high church sensibilities of Cavalier clergymen or the Erastian authoritarianism of the Caroline church. When they looked back to the history of the puritans, they experienced implicit sympathy with their cause and resonated with what they found to be similar issues facing the churches of their own day.

The second feature with which puritanism was associated in the minds of Southern ministers was the quest for liberty. This was an association which Northern ministers also made. However, liberty is a slippery concept, and the rival claimants to the liberty of puritanism proffered vastly divergent visions of who should enjoy its benefits. Southern appeals to puritanism and the memory of the puritans rested on the assumption that they were the ones escaping oppression and seeking liberty. For most Southern clergymen, their concept of history, if not entirely and systematically thought out, was influenced by a Whig interpretation that emphasized progress toward (white) liberty and the constitutional rule of law. This explains why a thinker such as the Episcopal minister James Warley Miles was able to affirm to the graduating class of the College of Charleston (South Carolina) in 1863: 'The whole history of England is that of the progress of constitutional liberty.'[55] Similarly, the Rev. O. S. Barton could tell his congregation in Warrenton (Virginia) that each nation 'has represented some leading idea, England's [was] constitutional liberty'; while the Rev. John Bailey Adger was able to write in the *Southern Presbyterian Review* of the 'Pure stream of the English doctrine of liberty.'[56] Along the path to constitutional liberty, there were understood to be distinct steps where clear and accepted progress had been made, one of which was the English Civil War, which had reduced the arbitrary power of the monarchy. The Rev. George Howe, also writing in the *Southern Presbyterian Review,* informed his readers that when it came to constitutional liberty, 'The English Puritans have done their share, the Hampdens and the Sidneys of the

[55] James W. Miles, *God in History: A Discourse Delivered Before the Graduating Class of the College of Charleston on Sunday Evening, March 29, 1863* (Charleston, SC, 1863), 18.
[56] O. S. Barton, *A Sermon Preached in St James Church Warrenton, VA., on the Fast Day June 13th, 1861* (Richmond, VA, 1861), 6; John D. Adger, 'Motley's Dutch Republic', *Southern Presbyterian Review* 15 (1862), 94–159, at 99.

days of Cromwell.'[57] Those Southern clergymen who embraced this view saw the Cavaliers as emblematic of arbitrary rule and of a seemingly less godly, certainly anti-Calvinistic, stance in matters of religion. In an editorial of 1861, the *Southern Episcopalian* cast the South in the position of the puritans and Parliamentarians, comparing the actions of the Northern states to the 'despotic phases of Charles I,' a comparison that was also made by one of the South's most prolific preachers, Benjamin Morgan Palmer.[58] In this respect, the startling hypocrisy of the Southern ministers was put on full display. Core to their accusation of hypocrisy against the North was that, as puritans, the Northerners had escaped discrimination and persecution only to use their newfound liberty to oppress others. Yet, in a grim irony, which appears to have entirely escaped them, Southern ministers were engaged in precisely that. They claimed to be fighting for liberty from Northern oppression, but did so expressly to preserve the enslavement of over four million human beings.

Southern Cromwellians

When identifying a historical precedent for the Confederate armies, there was no choice between puritan Roundheads and Cavalier Royalists: Southern ministers appealed to the memory of Cromwell and his parliamentary armies repeatedly throughout the war. They believed that the morality of an army determined its success, so appeals to the Cavaliers were of little value. In the armies of Cromwell, ministers found the perfect example of a pious and godly soldiery with which to demonstrate to their men that soldiering and piety could go hand in hand. Soldiers could make good on ministers' claims to be fighting for a cause comparable to the puritans by imitating the piety and reliance on God that had characterized the Parliamentarian armies. Earlier historians, such as James Silver, observed that Southerners made this comparison between Cromwell's army and their own forces, but did not explore the

[57] George Howe, 'The Scotch-Irish and their First Settlements on Tyger River and Other Neighboring Precincts in South Carolina', *Southern Presbyterian Review* 14 (1861), 472–501, at 497.

[58] 'Editorial', *Southern Episcopalian* 8 (1861),147–9, at 147; Timothy F. Riely, 'Benjamin M. Palmer: Secessionist become Nationalist', *Louisiana History* 18 (1977), 287–301, at 293.

meaning of this equivalence.[59] Elizabeth Fox-Genovese and Eugene Genovese come close to the heart of the matter when concluding that the Confederates viewed 'their army [as] rightful heir to Cromwell's bible-reading army.'[60] The Rev. Thomas V. Moore, for example, pronounced to his Southern congregation: 'I believe, that there has never been an army since the time of Cromwell, in which there was a more pervading sense of the power of God than our own.'[61] He concluded his oration by reiterating the fact that it was the piety of the parliamentary armies that had enabled them to achieve great victories, affirming: 'Did time permit, it would be easy to show that the religion which fits men for any duty … nerved the iron men of Cromwell to such deeds of daring prowess.'[62] The Rev. Charles Wesley Andrews agreed, pointing out to the soldiers of the Confederacy that it was prayerfulness and reliance on God that had 'made the armies of Cromwell the terror of all Europe.'[63]

Anecdotes retold from pulpits around the South recalled how Cromwell's men would pray before battle, carry their Bibles under their armour, or sing Psalms during an engagement. In a sermon preached to the infantry regiments in Georgia before the Union and Confederates clashed in battle, the Rev. John Jones told the assembled forces that reliance on Scripture had made Cromwell's armies formidable: 'They were never defeated! These men, with their leader, carried their bibles into their camps and studied them as they did their maps and charts. Their battle cry often was a word or verse of scripture.'[64] Jones emphasized that piety bred discipline: by imitating the parliamentary army, the Confederates could become like 'Cromwell's men' who were 'remarkable for their obedience.' Jones buttressed his argument with a story about the inspiration Cromwell's army had found in their use of Scripture: 'In the midst of the battle of

59 James Silver, *Confederate Moral and Church Propaganda* (Tuscaloosa, AL, 1957), 32.

60 Fox-Genovese and Genovese, *The Mind of the Master Class*, 686.

61 Thomas V. Moore, *God our Refuge and Strength in this War: A Discourse Before the Congregations of the First and Second Presbyterian Churches, on the Day of Humiliation, Fasting and Prayer, Appointed by President Davis, Friday, Nov. 15, 1861* (Richmond, VA, 1861), 13.

62 Ibid. 15.

63 Charles W. Andrews, *A Christian Address to the Confederate Soldiers* (Winchester, VA, 1861), 15.

64 John Jones, *The Southern Solders Duty: A Discourse Delivered to the Rome Light Guards, and Miller Rifles in the Presbyterian Church of Rome, GA., on Sabbath Morning, the 26th May 1861* (Rome, GA, 1861), 13.

Dunbar, wherein the enemy was flying, Cromwell called off his Ironsides, and they united in singing the 117th Psalm … then they dashed upon their foes, sweeping them like chaff before the whirlwind.'[65] Similarly, the Rev. John S. Harris, in his letters of encouragement and counsel to Confederate soldiers, urged them: 'See what Oliver Cromwell with his immortal Ironsides achieved! With a firm confidence that theirs was the cause of God and truth and righteousness.' Harris proposed Cromwell's army as an example for the Confederate army to follow: 'before they would engage in a battle they would commit themselves in prayer to the God of battles, and chanting an inspired Psalm, they would make that dashing charge which always brought defeat to the army of Charles.'[66]

In 1863, a reproduction of the Soldiers' Bible issued to parliamentary soldiers during the English Civil War was printed for the Confederate troops. A brief introduction explained the reasons for its issue and offered encouragement to the reader: 'Cromwell's Ironsides … fed their faith upon God's word, went into battle with psalm-singing and prayer; and fearing God only, were the best soldiers perhaps the world has ever seen.'[67] The *Richmond Christian Advocate* even claimed that 'the success of Cromwell's army commenced immediately on the publication of "The Soldier's Pocket Bible", and they never lost a battle.'[68] This artifact provided an opportunity for the individual soldier to actively participate in the piety that had made Cromwell's army holy. In so doing, they were to recreate the success of the past and become, in the words of the introduction to the *Pocket Bible*, the 'best soldiers the world [had] ever seen'. At about the same time, a copy of the same Bible was also printed and issued in the North, further exacerbating the South's feeling that the North was intent on acting hypocritically.[69]

Such radically opposed uses of the memory of the Roundheads demonstrate the malleability of the puritan legacy and the ways it could be used to shape both Northern and Southern identities. Opposing claims to the same historical legacy were then simply

[65] Ibid.

[66] John S. Harris, *The True Soldiers Spiritual Armor: Being a Series of Letters to the Volunteers of the Confederate States* (Columbia, SC, 1861), 13.

[67] *The Soldiers Pocket Bible: Issued for the Use of the Army of Oliver Cromwell* (Charleston, SC, and Raleigh, NC, 1861), 4.

[68] *Richmond Christian Advocate*, 31 July 1862, 1.

[69] Rable, *God's Almost Chosen Peoples*, 131.

rejected as further evidence of a hypocritical mind. The war between the states became a competition to prove which was the actual godly army, and which was acting on behalf of the forces of oppression. Kenyon Gradert has demonstrated the centrality of a recapturing of the puritan heritage for Northern abolitionists, drawing out how free blacks in particular reappropriated the spirit of puritanism for their own narratives. Black soldiers enlisting in the armed forces of the Union were encouraged to think of themselves as black Cromwellians.[70] In the diametrically opposite case, Southern ministers of various denominations were keen to cast the self-consciously white Confederate troops as the only true modern Cromwellians.

Southern ministers' uses of the parliamentary army's history were primarily religious, and clergy were first and foremost concerned with increasing the piety of Confederate soldiers, considering the armed forces as the most significant mission field on which the Southern churches were engaged.[71] It is not easy to assess what impact – if any – this rhetoric had on the troops or on the home front. However, widespread revivals in the Confederate army in the years 1863 and 1864, which seemed to develop in size and fervour in proportion to the defeats that were suffered, only served to heighten the idea that the Confederate army was a genuinely holy army akin to that of Cromwell.[72] Regardless of how soldiers and non-combatant Confederates experienced their ministers' rhetoric, it is clear from sermons and the religious press that the clergy intended to influence the religious life of the soldiers in particular, the nation more generally, and indeed to affect the outcome of the war.[73] Reid Mitchell has argued that the image of the Confederate army as deeply pious increased with time. When emphasizing the piety of the defeated Confederate forces became a priority for Southerners following the war, Cromwell's army was again the obvious comparison.[74] The

[70] Kenyon Gradert, *Puritan Spirits in the Abolitionist Imagination* (Chicago, IL, 2020), 151–74.

[71] Arnold W. Miller, *The Confederate Army and Navy Bible and Tract Depository: Ministering to the Spiritual Need of our Noble Defenders* (Richmond, VA, 1861), 1.

[72] Steven E. Woodworth, *While God is Marching on: The Religious World of Civil War Soldiers* (Lawrence, KA, 2001), 209–10.

[73] For a helpful discussion of the religious press in the Confederacy, see Kurt O. Brends, 'Wholesome Reading Purifies and Elevates the Man: The Religious Military Press in the Confederacy', in Miller, Stout and Wilson, eds, *Religion and the American Civil War*, 131–66.

[74] Reid Mitchell, 'Christian Soldiers? Perfecting the Confederacy', in Miller, Stout and Wilson, eds, *Religion and the American Civil War*, 297–312.

consistent use of examples from the parliamentary forces by Southern ministers during the war laid the foundation for this development.

With all the attention focused on recreating the piety and success of the Roundheads, it is no surprise that commentators and ministers on both sides were casting about for a modern-day Cromwell. Some secular observers in the South were happy to associate Cromwell with Lincoln, highlighting the fanaticism of his campaign against slavery, and to equate the Northern invasion of the South with Cromwell's actions in Ireland.[75] Others earnestly desired to find a Southern Cromwell to lead their Southern Cromwellians to victory. Such a figure was found in the person of General Thomas 'Stonewall' Jackson. John Eston Cooke, the novelist, published a short memoir of Jackson in 1863 in which he twice compared him to Cromwell.[76] William Pendleton, Episcopalian priest and Confederate general, commented in his diary after reading Carlyle's life of Cromwell: 'General Jackson is the exact counterpart of Oliver as Carlyle draws him.'[77] At the funeral oration of Stonewall Jackson, Dabney chose instead to liken him to Cromwell's cousin, the renowned martyr to the Parliamentarian cause, John Hampden.[78]

Part of the reason for the popularity of Cromwell during this period can be attributed to two publications by the British historian Thomas Carlyle.[79] The first, published in 1841, was Carlyle's influential *Of Heroes, Hero-Worship, and The Heroic in History*, in which he placed Cromwell alongside Napoleon in the category of 'Hero as King'. 1845 saw Carlyle further develop his rehabilitation of Cromwell with an edition of his letters and speeches.[80]

[75] *Charleston Mercury*, 3 January 1862, 2.

[76] John Eston Cooke, *The Life of Stonewall Jackson: From Official Papers, Contemporary Narratives, and Personal Acquaintance* (Richmond, VA, 1863), 25, 283.

[77] Susan P. Lee, *Memoirs of William Nelson Pendleton, D.D., rector of Latimer Parish, Lexington, Virginia; Brigadier-General c.s.a.; Chief of Artillery, Army of Northern Virginia* (Philadelphia, PA, 1893), 230.

[78] R[obert] L. Dabney, *True Courage: A Discourse Commemorative of Lieut. General Thomas J. Jackson* (Richmond, VA, 1863), 22.

[79] Carlyle received a mixed, but generally warm reception in the Southern states, where readers relished his attitudes to race and appreciated his refusal to adhere to any prevailing scheme or philosophy of which they disapproved: see Gerald M. Straka, 'The Spirit of Carlyle in the Old South', *The Historian* 20 (1957), 39–57; anon., 'Carlyle's Works' (review), *Southern Quarterly Review* 14 (1848), 77–101.

[80] Thomas Carlyle, *Of Heroes, Hero Worship and the Heroic in History* (London, 1841), 317–93: idem, *Oliver Cromwell's Letters and Speeches: With Elucidations, in Two Volumes* (New York, 1845).

This publication found a generally favourable audience in the Southern religious press. The widely read *Southern Presbyterian Review* printed a positive review of the book, which expressed satisfaction that Carlyle had given appropriate attention to Cromwell's religiosity and fervent piety. The author lamented that Americans would 'sigh' over those Cavaliers who 'retarded the cause of freedom and the progress of civilization'.[81] Cromwell's religiosity allowed Southerners more generally, and ministers in particular, to make the equation between Cromwell and Confederate General Stonewall Jackson. Robert. E. Lee, as well as Jefferson Davis, reflected other values of the Southern elite, such as civility and chivalry, but it was Jackson who embodied the piety, devotion and other-worldliness which, to many, seemed to pervade Cromwell's life and personality.[82] Jackson's eccentric and enigmatic character, combined with the impressive military results he achieved, received adulation and praise in his lifetime from Southerners who were deeply bereaved at his death.[83] For his Southern observers, his life was the distilled essence of fervent faith and the good within puritanism.

This project of seeking a modern-day Cromwell was spurred by the popularity of Carlyle's 'great man' theory of history, which Southern ministers were quick to Christianize. When looking for a hero to lead the Confederacy to what they expected to be their God-ordained victory, ministers could reframe Carlyle's ideas to reinsert God into the picture. As the Rev. Sinclair of Six Mile (South Carolina) expressed it: 'When God would maintain a nation he raises up in their behalf men whom he endows with qualities fitted for the emergency of the times … When he would correct the abuses of suppressed State, he raises a Cromwell.'[84] For Southern ministers, great men did affect the

[81] Anon., 'The Letters and Speeches of Oliver Cromwell' (review), *Southern Presbyterian Review* 1 (1847), 121–58, at 126.

[82] Cromwell was not, of course, a universally admired figure, and his reputation in the South was not always associated with such positive virtues. For a Southern example of Cromwell as a hypocrite, see anon., 'Bonaparte, Cromwell, and Washington', *De Bow's Review* 28 (1860), 139–54. For Cromwell's wider reputation and associations with hypocrisy throughout history, see Blair Worden, *Roundheaded Reputations: The English Civil War and the Passions of Posterity* (London, 2001) and David Runciman, *Political Hypocrisy: The Mask of Power, from Hobbes to Orwell and Beyond* (Princeton, NJ, 2010), 62–3, 195.

[83] Daniel W. Stowell, 'Stonewall Jackson and the Providence of God', in Miller, Stout and Wilson, eds, *Religion and the American Civil War*, 187–207.

[84] Sinclair, *A Thanksgiving Sermon*, 8.

outcome of history and could be responsible for the rise and fall of nations and peoples. However, this was only possible through the providence of God and under God's guiding hand: God brought these great men to the fore and worked in them and through them. Ministers were sure this was the case with Jackson, as it had been with Cromwell before him.

Conclusion: Cavalier, Puritan or both?

Hypocrisy was a crucial accusation in the South's attempt to undermine and delegitimize the North's war effort. It was a propaganda tool used to rally support and denigrate the enemy. It was broadly deployed in white Southern culture in applying the trope of Cavalier South vs puritan North. However, it was also used by Southern ministers who wanted to claim the puritan heritage for themselves. For Southern Protestant clergy, the history of puritanism could be used to evoke the fight for religious or political liberty and provide parallels to the cause of the Confederacy. Moreover, puritanism also supplied the ultimate example of godly soldering in the form of the parliamentary armies, which proved useful for instilling religiosity in the Confederate troops. However, in using the historical memory of puritanism in this way, Southern ministers overplayed their hand. They revealed their own deep-seated hypocrisy in claiming to stand in the line of defenders of religious and political liberty to use that liberty to defend and perpetuate racial slavery.

Following the fall of the Confederacy in April and May of 1865, the discussion of hypocrisy and puritanism became ever more embittered. In the immediate post-war, Robert Louis Dabney, the former Confederate chaplain and chief of staff to Stonewall Jackson, published his life of the fallen general. Dabney was happy to refer to Jackson as a 'gallant Cavalier' and rejected the comparison to Cromwell, asserting that Jackson 'had a moral and spiritual character so much more noble that they can not be named together.'[85] The following year, in his diatribe against the Union, *The Defense of Virginia,* Dabney returned to this trope, accusing the North of 'crimes of malignant slander and vituperation which their people are accustomed to launch at us from the vile hiding place of their

[85] R[obert] L. Dabney, *Life, and Campaigns of Lieut.-Gen. Thomas J. Jackson* (New York, 1866), 610, 114.

hypocritical Puritanism.'[86] In 1888, former Confederate army chaplain John Jones published his homage to the Confederate troops, *Christ in the Camp*, which proved a foundational work in the mythology of the lost cause and highly influential in enshrining the memory of the Southern soldier as truly Christian. Jones argued that the 'devout piety' of the Confederate soldiers surpassed that of the Roundheads, whose 'religious fanaticism' he contrasted with what he saw as the 'genuine religious tone' of Jackson's men.[87] This is a return to a rejection of puritan motifs. However, for many Southerners in these post-war years, the insistence on a heroically defeated Cavalier South persisted alongside wistful memories of the Cromwellian religiosity of the Confederate army.[88]

The use of puritanism in the South during the antebellum and Civil War era offers an example of the complex and contradictory nature of the legacy of the puritan movement, and highlights how this legacy could be used in parallel ways within one cultural region. In the Southern secular press and among intellectuals and commentators who were not ministers, 'puritan' was often used as a stand-in for hypocrisy. Yet a significant number of clergy and ministers equated puritanism with godliness, liberty and pious soldering. Puritan identity could also be claimed by both Northern and Southern ministers in ways which were profoundly contradictory, yet overlapping: both sides saw puritanism as exemplifying liberty and piety, and both sides sought to recreate the faith and success of Cromwell's army. The irony of the Cavalier rhetoric of Southern politicians, orators and commentators was that the Cavaliers had been on the losing side of the English Civil War. In defeat, the South would most accurately emulate the Royalists before them. In the end, for the defeated Southern Cavaliers, their ministers' attempts to recreate the puritan army of the English Civil War were revealed to be nothing more than futile and ultimately hypocritical.

86 Robert L. Dabney, *A Defense of Virginia [and through her of the South,] in Recent and Pending Contests Against the Sectional Party* (New York, 1867), 285.

87 John William Jones, *Christ in the Camp: Or Religion in Lee's Army* (Richmond, VA, 1888), 20, 540.

88 For Lee as the 'supreme Southern Cavalier', and Jackson as puritan, see Charles Regan Wilson, *Baptized in Blood: The Religion of the Lost Cause 1865–1920* (Athens, GA, 1980), 48–51.

Enjoying what comes naturally: The Church of England and Sexuality in the 1930s

Mark D. Chapman*

University of Oxford

This article begins by outlining the changing approach in Anglican attitudes to contraception at the Lambeth Conference of 1930, where birth control was permitted for married couples and sex separated from the possibility of procreation. The logical extension of this teaching, as was noted by Bishop Charles Gore, was that other forms of sexual pleasure, including homosexuality, which was increasingly seen as a 'natural' condition, might eventually be sanctioned by the church. Later in the 1930s, a series of letters by Robert Reid to Cosmo Gordon Lang, archbishop of Canterbury, shows the beginnings of a campaign for a change of policy. At the outbreak of the Second World War, the Anglican writer Kenneth Ingram published Sex-Morality Tomorrow, *which pressed for full homosexual equality and provoked calls to William Temple to suppress the book. 1940 proved an inopportune moment for reform of church teaching on homosexuality, which continues to elicit widespread controversy.*

This article seeks to show how the acceptance of contraception in the resolutions of the 1930 Lambeth Conference of the Bishops of the Anglican Communion revealed an increasing awareness among church leaders that sexual intercourse was both a 'natural' and enjoyable act in itself, even when divorced from the possibility of procreation. By drawing on hitherto unpublished archival sources, which have yet to be discussed in detail,[1] it goes on to show how the (albeit limited) acceptance of non-procreative sex proved significant for some

* Ripon College, Cuddesdon, Oxford, OX44 9EX. E-mail: mark.chapman@rcc.ac.uk.

[1] In *Socialism and Religion: Roads to Common Wealth* (Basingstoke, 2011), Vincent Geoghegan discussed Kenneth Ingram's political thought in relation to his reflections on sexual morality and homosexuality: see esp. 53–84. The correspondence at Lambeth Palace is briefly discussed at ibid. 80–2.

Studies in Church History 60 (2024), 453–476
doi: 10.1017/stc.2024.21

pioneers within the Church of England who sought to explain the 'naturalness' of homosexuality, as well as the moral acceptability of some forms of homosexual activity. For some, including Charles Gore, former bishop of Oxford and a leader of Anglo-Catholicism, permitting contraception could be seen as the thin end of the wedge. It could be seen as marking a sexual revolution in which other forms of non-procreative sexual activity might increasingly be condoned by the church. At the same time, a greater scientific emphasis on the 'naturalness' of homosexuality led some members of the Church of England, including a number of those discussed in this article, to accuse the church of hypocrisy and of an ostrich-like mentality in its discussions of same-sex attraction. While the Second World War temporarily halted discussions in the Church of England about homosexuality, these were quickly to re-emerge in the run-up to the 1957 Report of the Committee on Homosexual Offences and Prostitution chaired by Lord John Woolfenden.[2]

In May 1930, Dr Helena Wright (1887–1982)[3] published *The Sex Factor in Marriage* which proved to be a bestseller, going through five editions by 1956.[4] At the time, Wright was working as Chief Medical Officer at the North Kensington Women's Welfare Centre, where, between the wars, she became one of the key figures in promoting contraception. Perhaps surprisingly, Wright's comprehensive guide to marital sex, which advocates birth control, as well as mutual pleasure, begins with a lengthy quotation from a speech given by the (unmarried) archbishop of Canterbury, Cosmo Gordon Lang,

[2] See Graham Willett, 'The Church of England and the Origins of Homosexual Law Reform', *Journal of Religious History* 33 (2009), 418–34; Matthew Grimley, 'Law, Morality and Secularisation: The Church of England and the Wolfenden Report, 1954–57', *JEH* 60 (2009), 725–41; Hugh McLeod, 'Homosexual Law Reform, 1953–1967,' in Melanie Barber, Stephen Taylor and Gabriel Sewell, eds, *From the Reformation to the Permissive Society: A Miscellany in Celebration of the 400th Anniversary of Lambeth Palace Library* (Woodbridge, 2010), 657–78.

[3] On Wright, see Barbara Evans, *Freedom to Choose: The Life and Work of Dr Helena Wright, Pioneer of Contraception* (London, 1984); Lesley A. Hall, 'Wright [née Lowenfeld], Helena Rosa (1887–1982), family planning practitioner and sex therapist', *ODNB*, online edn (2004), at: <https://ezproxy-prd.bodleian.ox.ac.uk:2102/10.1093/ref:odnb/31859>, accessed 14 July 2022.

[4] Helena Wright, *The Sex Factor in Marriage: A Book for those who are about to be Married* (London, 1930). The book went through a number of editions, with the fifth and final edition appearing in 1956.

on 4 April 1930, a few months before the publication of her book, to the London Diocesan Council for Social Work. Lang had made the bold claim: 'We want to liberate the sex impulse from the impression that it is always to be surrounded by negative warnings and restraints, and to place it in its rightful place among the great creative and formative things'. It was crucial to discuss the subject since, he claimed,

> I would rather have all the risks which come from free discussion of sex than the great risks we run by a conspiracy of silence. … I notice how silence has given place to free discussion. In my judgment this is a great improvement. In the old days silence drove one of the necessarily natural instincts within. Nowadays people recognise sex as one of the great fundamental questions of human society, and all thoughtful Christians and citizens ought to take their part in discussing the great problems with which it deals.[5]

Lang was quite clear, however, that there should be 'no over-indulgence in the emotions and stimulus of sex without the withering of that life that God gave and Christ redeemed and His Holy Spirit could make so rich and full and joyous.'[6]

Wright was rather less judgemental: on contraception, she simply felt that it was a matter of conscience between couples, referring them to Michael Fielding's *Parenthood: Design or Accident?* (1928), which had appeared in the same series as her own book.[7] Emphasizing mutuality and pleasure, she devotes a significant amount of space to women's enjoyment and the importance of clitoral stimulation and the female orgasm,[8] as well as variety (and reversal) of sex roles and positions.[9] Alongside the physicality of much of its content, the book retains a strong spiritual dimension, Wright even claiming that 'the sex-relation is one of the sacraments of life':[10] 'Every happy marriage should be a living source of spiritual light, radiating warmth and love to all those who come within its circle'.[11]

[5] Cited in Wright, *The Sex Factor* (London, 1930), 8.
[6] *Church Times*, 11 April 1930, 473.
[7] Michael Fielding, *Parenthood: Design or Accident? A Manual of Birth Control with a Preface by H. G. Wells* (London, 1928).
[8] Wright, *The Sex Factor*, 70–4.
[9] Ibid. 76.
[10] Ibid. 29.
[11] Ibid. 97.

Despite her Polish-Jewish roots, Wright had been baptized into the Church of England and became a member of the Student Christian Movement. She had risen to such prominence in church circles that she was invited to address the Lambeth Conference in Westminster Hall on 15 August 1930 on behalf of the National Birth Control Council: 'I realised that, if not actually hostile, there was nothing to encourage the belief that the Anglican church was sympathetic to the birth control movement, but I thought I might as well try as I'd been asked to.'[12] Global Anglicanism had changed in its approach to birth control through the 1920s.[13] Opposition to contraception had been made clear at the Lambeth Conference of 1908 which had resolved that contraception 'was demoralising to character and hostile to national Welfare'.[14] Similarly, in 1920, despite lobbying from Marie Stopes (1880–1958) and other early campaigners for contraception,[15] the bishops issued 'an emphatic warning against the use of unnatural means for the avoidance of conception, together with the grave dangers – physical, moral and religious, thereby incurred, and against the evils with which the extension of such use threatens the race'. It was clear, they reaffirmed, that 'the governing considerations of Christian marriage are the procreation of children and self control.'[16]

By 1930, however, things had changed, in part through the influence of Helena Wright, who drew on her practice in Kensington in her address to the bishops. She later reflected:

> They seemed all to be white-haired, a mass of dear old gentlemen. One or two of them smiled when I told them they knew nothing about the people I was talking about, the women who had been my patients. These working-class mothers all had more children than they could

[12] Cited in Evans, *Freedom to Choose*, 139.

[13] See Laura M. Ramsay, '"The Relation of the Sexes": Towards a Christian View of Sex and Citizenship in Interwar Britain', *Contemporary British History* 34 (2020), 555–79.

[14] Resolution 41, in *Conference of Bishops of the Anglican Communion holden at Lambeth Palace, July 6 to August 5, 1908: Encyclical Letter from the Bishops, with the Resolutions and Reports* (London, 1908), 56. See also Peter Sedgwick, 'The Lambeth Conferences on Contraception, 1908–68', *Theology* 123 (2020), 96–103.

[15] Timothy Willem Jones, *Sexual Politics in the Church of England 1857–1957* (Oxford, 2013), 134–5, 140.

[16] Resolution 68, in *Conference of Bishops of the Anglican Communion, holden at Lambeth Palace, July 5 to August 7, 1920* (London, 1920), 44. See also Charlotte Methuen, 'The Lambeth Conference, Gender and Sexuality', *Theology* 123 (2020), 84–94.

> afford. … Each woman came in a state of wonderment. It was as if they had been told they could control the weather.
>
> I had no idea if the bishops would listen, but as I described the changes I had seen in these women, and as the pictures unfolded I saw their expressions getting more and more human, and the transformation of the corporate feeling. One or two would look up, and I realised, 'Yes, he's taken it in. He sees something new.'[17]

While it is impossible to gauge the effect of her speech, after considerable debate the bishops resolved to change the approach from earlier conferences. After a number of revisions, Resolution 15 passed with a large majority:

> Where there is a clearly felt moral obligation to limit or avoid parenthood, the method must be decided on Christian principles. The primary and obvious method is complete abstinence from intercourse … Nevertheless in those cases where there is such a clearly felt moral obligation to limit or avoid parenthood, and where there is a morally sound reason for avoiding complete abstinence, the Conference agrees that other methods may be used, provided that this is done in the light of the same Christian principles. The Conference records its strong condemnation of the use of any methods of conception-control from motives of selfishness, luxury, or mere convenience.[18]

Despite the less than enthusiastic tone, this meant that for the first time there was an explicit separation of sexual activity from procreation in the pronouncements of the Lambeth Conferences.

The idea of separating sex from procreation proved highly controversial, especially among Anglo-Catholics. Bishop Walter Carey of Bloemfontein (South Africa) left the Lambeth Conference in protest and others, including Bishop Mark Napier Trollope of Korea, absented themselves from the debate.[19] Much hung on whether 'artificial' birth control was interfering with what was natural for men and women, which included the possibility of procreation, a line that has been maintained vigorously by the official teaching of the Roman Catholic Church. Charles Gore was acutely aware of what he regarded

[17] Evans, *Freedom to Choose*, 140.

[18] Resolution 15, in *The Lambeth Conference 1930: Encyclical Letter from the Bishops, with Resolutions and Reports* (London, 1930), 43.

[19] J. G. Lockhart, *Cosmo Gordon Lang* (London, 1949), 350.

as the dangers represented by condoning non-procreative sex and placing increased emphasis on sexual pleasure. Where sexual activity was divorced from procreation and consequently contradicted what was 'natural', Gore held, it would not be difficult to regard it as leading to the permissibility of forms of sexual activity outside marriage that many regarded as immoral. In a pamphlet written for the League of National Life, established in 1926 to oppose the theory and practice of birth control and in response to the Lambeth Resolutions,[20] Gore felt that their 'effect will be disastrous' at 'arresting the tide of sensualism'. He went on: 'The Church has regarded Birth Prevention as sinful because, like other sensual practices commonly called unnatural, it is a deliberate enterprise taken in hand to separate absolutely the enjoyment of the sexual act from its natural issue.' There could, he claimed, be no departure from the absolute demands of the gospel, or 'second best'.[21] Similarly, in another pamphlet produced for the League of National Life, where he discussed attitudes to birth control in other countries, Gore wrote: 'every one who believes that Christ is really "the Way" for humanity must refuse to countenance, either in theory or practice, the truly and fundamentally unnatural, and in their general result licentious, proposals and practices of the falsely-called movement for "Birth Control." It is "the enemy".'[22] For Gore, it would seem, all forms of natural sexual activity had to be open to the possibility of procreation: what went against nature was regarded as immoral.

Earlier, in a submission to the Special Committee of the National Birth-Control Commission, Gore had been clear that contraception, as an interference with nature, might have unintended consequences for other so-called 'unnatural' vices, including homosexuality:

> There exists a great deal of what we used to call unnatural vice … Now, those who are in favour of that vice are, of course, very much interested in the movement which is called birth control, and they say to me, or to

[20] See Lesley A. Hall, 'Movements to Separate Sex and Reproduction', in Nick Hopwood, Rebecca Flemming and Lauren Kassell, eds, *Reproduction: Antiquity to the Present Day* (Cambridge, 2018), 427–41.

[21] Charles Gore, *Lambeth on Contraceptives* (London, 1930), online at Project Canterbury: <http://anglicanhistory.org/gore/contra1930.html>, accessed 22 March 2023.

[22] Charles Gore, *The Prevention of Conception, Commonly Called Birth Control* (London, n.d.), 32.

> others, who speak with horror of their practices and tendencies: "yes, but you cannot any longer call it unnatural; for now everybody allows birth control, which aims at separating the sexual act from its connection with the production of offspring. If that is admitted, how can you condemn our practice, which is, according to our instincts, natural?"[23]

It was clear to Gore that if the theory of 'inversion', as developed by the progressive sexologist Havelock Ellis (1859–1939), which saw same-sex desire as the natural state of a minority of people, was accepted, then the floodgates might be opened: 'if contraceptives are in any circumstances permissible for normal married people, we, for our part, do not see how any adequate answer can be given to those who desire a safeguard in unauthorised connections, or to those who practise the most degrading forms of sensual indulgence'.[24] Gore's logic was faultless: if the sphere of what was natural expanded, then eventually morality would have to be adjusted to compensate. Contraception could thus pave the way for further sexual reform and even justify what Gore called 'the philosophy of homosexuality'.[25]

While the issue of homosexuality had been raised at the 1930 Lambeth Conference in the context of a discussion on the grounds for divorce, with Bishop Herman Page of Michigan noting that 'sex perversion' was being recognized by psychologists as a type of insanity,[26] there was no further consideration of the topic. A medical approach to homosexuality was becoming more common among Christian ethicists, with Peter Green writing a textbook, *The Problem of Right Conduct* (1931), which advocated treating what he called the 'unnatural' vice 'as one of insanity – as we should treat a homicidal maniac, or a kleptomaniac'.[27] Nevertheless, while the idea that homosexuality might be understood as natural remained

[23] Charles Gore's evidence appears in the report: *The Ethics of Birth Control: Being the Report of the Special Committee Appointed by the National Council of Public Morals in Connection with the Investigations of the National Birth-Rate Commission* (London, 1925), 67–72, cited in Timothy Jones, 'The Stained Glass Closet: Celibacy and Homosexuality in the Church of England to 1955', *Journal of the History of Sexuality* 20 (2011), 132–52, at 143.

[24] Jones, 'The Stained Glass', 143.

[25] Ibid.

[26] Cited in ibid. 142.

[27] Peter Green, *The Problem of Right Conduct: A Text-Book of Christian Ethics* (London, 1931), 225.

the preserve of sexologists and a handful of psychologists,[28] behind the scenes Archbishop Lang was drawn into an extensive correspondence on the subject later in the 1930s. It will become clear that Gore's slippery slope argument was put to use by some with quite different aims.

Robert Reid and Archbishop Lang

In 1937, the *Daily Telegraph* reported that John Clark, a scenic artist, had been remanded on bail, charged with conspiring with Robert Reid (1898–1983),[29] alias Rudd, a schoolmaster of Taunton, to procure a youth to commit grave offences.[30] The following month, Clark was sentenced at the Old Bailey to three years' penal servitude and Reid, who was headmaster of King's College, Taunton, from 1933 to 1937 and one of the first doctors of philosophy of Oxford University,[31] was bound over and ordered to pay costs of 30 guineas, as well as to receive an operation and medical treatment at home. Reid, who had been in the Somerset Light Infantry in the First World War, had expanded numbers at King's College from seventy to two hundred. His defence offered medical evidence of a swollen thyroid gland as an explanation of his 'abnormality'. There was no evidence of any wrongdoing at the school. He was placed in the care of the Anglo-Catholic chaplain Mowbray O'Rorke, formerly bishop of Accra in the Gold Coast (Ghana) and Guardian of the Shrine at Walsingham.[32]

Reid wrote to Archbishop Lang in 1938 after hearing that a committee was to be convened to explore the 'homosexual problem', enclosing a summary of a book he intended to publish 'in the hope of obtaining some relief for the unfortunate class of people to which I

[28] See Timothy W. Jones, 'The Church of England and Modern Homosexuality', in Lucy Delap and Sue Morgan, eds, *Men, Masculinities and Religious Change in Twentieth-Century Britain* (Basingstoke, 2013), 197–217.
[29] See Hugh McLeod, 'Homosexual Law Reform, 1953–1967', in Barber, Taylor and Sewell, eds, *From the Reformation to the Permissive Society*, 657–78, at 659.
[30] *Daily Telegraph*, 2 March 1937, 11.
[31] His thesis explored 'Isomerism in Metallic Oxides' (1924). See *Oxford's First DPhil Students: The First 50 DPhil Students to graduate from Oxford, 1920–1924*, online at: <https://www.ox.ac.uk/sites/files/oxford/media_wysiwyg/TheFirst50DPhilScholars.pdf>, accessed 27 March 2023.
[32] *Daily Telegraph*, 14 April 1937, 9.

belong.' He wrote frankly: 'With all due respect I am sure that Your Grace has little conception of all the misery and crime consequent upon the brutal attitude of the law and society, an attitude to which the Church by its silence acquiesces.'[33] In his brief summary,[34] Reid distinguished three views about 'the invert': they were usually classified either as 'a criminal', as 'mentally unbalanced' or as 'a definite variation of the human species'. He was 'convinced of the truth of this [third] view … from personal experience, from knowledge of many homosexuals, and from the conclusions of the latest scientific investigators such as Hirschfeld', who estimated that 'from 2 to 4 per cent of all populations, animal and human are inverted, and that 80 or 90 per cent of men concerned are guilty of offences prescribed by the law.' Speaking of the 'Urgency of the Problem', he noted that at 'least 800,000 men are thus living in England in danger of arrest and punishment.'[35] He went on to suggest a solution:

> It is only by imagining themselves in such a position that heterosexual or normal people can realise the untold misery and suffering endured year after year, the direct cause of mental troubles, and not infrequently suicide and murder. Most blackmail cases have their origin in homosexual offences. It may be the right policy for such respectable newspapers as the 'Times' and 'Daily Telegraph' to suppress such news, but this course gives a wrong impression as to the causes of blackmail.[36]

Reid spoke of the mental instability that came from the criminalization of homosexual acts, which would be 'removed if they were given a proper and recognised place in society', suggesting that the evidence of criminologists, judges, police and to some extent priests, who 'came into contact with the more degraded and less virile section of homosexual people' should be 'disregarded' because of its partiality. Similarly, those who sought 'cures' were likely to be attempting the impossible. Reid offered a personal example: 'The writer, who was born with and retains entirely inverted sexual instincts, has also the hands of a woman. Is it suggested that a psychologist will give him a new pair?'[37] He felt the church's failure to discuss homosexuality

[33] London, LPL, Lang Papers 164, fol. 166, Robert Reid to Cosmo Gordon Lang, 27 May 1938.
[34] Ibid., fols 167–9.
[35] Ibid.
[36] Ibid.
[37] LPL, Lang Papers 164, fol. 267, Memorandum.

was deplorable. Pointing to the standard work on moral theology by Bishop K. E. Kirk of Oxford,[38] which did not even mention the subject, he noted: 'The Church has led and encouraged society in its policy of concealment. No information whatever is available'. Another book, *Sexual Problems of To-day* (1924), dismissed homosexuality in one line as 'too horrible to discuss'.[39] The church's 'attitude of the ostrich has only served to alienate honest lay homosexual people who try to work out a position for themselves'. The only official opinion that Reid had been able to extract was 'one prohibiting all homosexual thought and action as being wilful perversion of God given in-born instincts'.[40]

Reid felt such advice to be useless since it 'serves to discredit what the church may say in other directions', since 'all homosexuals know perfectly well that they never possessed these instincts'. 'The majority of Church of England priests', he went on, 'left without guidance, seem to adopt the explanation of insanity, at the same time insisting on absolute chastity'. In turn, he continued with bitter irony, they 'apparently approve, by their silence, of mental invalids being thrust into gaol on charges involving life sentences – a curious treatment for insanity'.[41] Finally, Reid goes on to discuss chastity, which he sees as marked by hypocrisy since often the priest, judge and those in other professions indulge in exactly the same actions for which others were imprisoned (as Reid had observed from close quarters). Such rank hypocrisy embittered less well-connected homosexuals to both church and state.

Reid wrote about his own discovery of a homosexual subculture after his conviction:

> On my conviction I received letters of sympathy from inverts all over the country. I followed up these contacts in nearly all cases and so obtained an introduction to that homosexual underworld, the existence of which I was unaware. Here in an atmosphere of bitter hostility to authority, both religious and civil, these unfortunate people obtain the understanding of fellowship which is otherwise denied them.[42]

[38] Kenneth Kirk, *Some Principles of Moral Theology and Their Application* (London, 1920).
[39] Mary Scharlieb, ed., *Sexual Problems of To-day* (London, [1924]), 7, 221.
[40] LPL, Lang Papers 164, fol. 268, Memorandum.
[41] Ibid.
[42] Ibid., fol. 269.

He went on to note that while chastity is undoubtedly a vocation for some, there is no sense in which it can be imposed on homosexuals. He asked the archbishop directly: if homosexuality was natural, then why was it that all homosexuals had to choose celibacy, even when they were not called to such a life? 'It may be that chastity is the answer but the Church will *never* obtain it by its present policy of almost criminal silence, but only by vigorous preaching, *open* recognition and reorganisation of the social life of inverts, and by backing its policy with reasons which will satisfy intellectual enquiry'.[43] He concluded with a simple question: 'Is there any hope that the evidence of those most concerned, the homosexuals themselves, will be considered?'[44]

In his brief response to Reid, Lang noted that he had read the letter and memorandum with interest and 'with no little sympathy'. He went on to write of his own experience:

> I am indeed only too painfully familiar with the problem … as I have constantly to deal with clergy, some of them otherwise of high character, who have given way to instincts about which you write. But (1) I have known many others in like position with yourself who have by strength of will or by the grace of God been able to restrain these tendencies and I cannot bring myself to think that the position of those for whom you speak is so tragic as you would represent. (2) For many reasons into which I cannot now enter I am not at present prepared to suggest that offences of this kind should be put in the same order as indulgence of sexual instincts with the other sex. My experience shows me that this might be attended with the greatest possible dangers. I can only say that if you publish your book I shall read it with the greatest possible care and consideration.[45]

Reid wrote back to Lang thanking him for his careful consideration. Although he would have liked to have had his points addressed, he did not wish to encroach further on the archbishop's time. He merely offered one comment to Lang's chaplain:

> May I say just this in answer to his suggestion that I painted too tragic a picture. I can conceive of no greater tragedy, from a material point of

[43] Ibid. Italics original.
[44] Ibid.
[45] LPL, Lang Papers 164, fol. 270, Lang to Reid, 9 June 1938.

> view, than that of a man ruined socially and financially, lying in prison, knowing that he may be sentenced *for life*. This happens at least every week and probably every day, and for 'offences' not concerned with force, exhibitionism, or young people. And the Church consents.[46]

Lang's chaplain, Alan Don, responded straightaway to say that the archbishop:

> asks me to make clear that when writing to you he had in mind not those who have been sentenced by the law, but rather those who are prone to the tendencies of which you speak. His Grace asks me to say this in order that you may not misunderstand what he said in his letter to you.[47]

There the matter rested: no committee was appointed before the war. Reid, who had set up home in Wells, would resurface in the 1950s as a more public campaigner for decriminalization.

Kenneth Ingram

Shortly afterwards, one prominent Christian figure made a public contribution to the discussion of homosexuality. In 1940, shortly after the outbreak of war, Kenneth Ingram (1882–1965) published *Sex-Morality Tomorrow* with Allen & Unwin, the publishers of nine of his many books. Ingram, who had trained as a barrister, had been a prominent Anglo-Catholic layman and socialist, but in the early 1920s had gradually come to adopt a more modernist position, which accompanied his increasingly progressive views on homosexuality.[48] Developing an interest in sexual ethics from the early 1920s, he wrote a short book, *An Outline of Sexual Morality*, in 1922, which adopted the current theory which, while regarding homosexuality as natural, had also tended to pathologize the condition.[49] All people, he wrote, were a mixture of homosexual and

[46] LPL, Lang Papers 164, fol. 271, Reid to Lang's Chaplain, Alan Don, 11 June 1938. Italics original.

[47] LPL, Lang Papers 164, fol. 274, Don to Reid, 15 June 1938.

[48] There does not appear to be evidence that Ingram was open about his sexuality, although there are many accounts of homoerotic emotions and an idealization of close male friendships, including (chaste) relationships between men and boys, scattered throughout his works of fiction. See Geoghegan, *Socialism and Religion*, esp. 53.

[49] Kenneth Ingram, *An Outline of Sexual Morality* (London, 1922); more generally, see Jones, *Sexual Politics*, 172. There is a brief discussion of Ingram in David Hilliard,

'normal', which proved immensely important for social life. The desire to love, however, could have immense benefit for the community: 'In the social sphere also, the place of this aspect of homosexuality is obvious. … it is no exaggeration to declare that few men can be successful in educational or philanthropic work unless they have some homogenic temperament in their nature.'[50]

However, while Ingram did not deny the importance of same-sex desire and championed the idea of 'homogenic' love, including for younger men and boys (a view not uncommon at the time), he was clear at this stage that even where such same-sex friendship was intimate, 'there can be no religious countenance for any physical sex-act outside the sacrament of matrimony'.[51] In the end, and drawing on what was then the prevailing psychological theory, Ingram felt the human race would return to its true nature as the 'bisexual species from which I believe it has come'.[52] In his next substantial contribution to the study of sexuality, *The Modern Attitude to the Sex Problem*, published in 1930,[53] Ingram offered little to surprise the reader, despite devoting more space to the theory of the intermediate sex, as outlined by the early advocate of sexual liberation, Edward Carpenter (1844–1929).[54]

By the time *Sex-Morality Tomorrow* appeared in 1940, however, Ingram's opinions had changed significantly. The fact that he was writing about the future was important: like many others, he was already thinking about post-war reconstruction. He was to play a prominent role in the Malvern Conference of 1941 and was active in Richard Acland's Common Wealth Party.[55] This allowed him greater opportunity to exercise his powers of imagination: 'any attempt to deal with the problems of sex-life must therefore take into account a radically altered society which may produce an outlook

'UnEnglish and Unmanly: Anglo-Catholicism and Homosexuality', *Victorian Studies* 25 (1982), 181–210, at 203–5.

[50] Ingram, *An Outline*, 72–3.

[51] Ibid. 72–3.

[52] Ibid. 75.

[53] Ingram, *The Modern Attitude to the Sex Problem* (London, 1930).

[54] Edward Carpenter, *The Intermediate Sex: A Study of Some Transitional Types of Men and Women* (London, 1908).

[55] Kenneth Ingram, *Sex-Morality Tomorrow* (London, 1940), 9–10. See also Geoghegan, *Socialism and Religion*, esp. 75–80.

on sex very different from that with which we are familiar'.[56] Ingram had come to see his earlier Anglo-Catholicism as a type of legalistic moralism and explored the idea that a loving relationship outside marriage – including between people of the same sex – could be preferable to a loveless relationship within marriage.[57] Homosexual practice appeared to be on the increase and was not simply restricted to the stereotypes of the 'effeminate male' or 'masculine female', but was also common 'among men of the virile military type'.[58] Although *Sex-Morality Tomorrow* was written before the outbreak of hostilities, the recognition that homosexuality was common among 'manly' men proved important after the war, especially in the highly public trials of Edward Montagu, Michael Pitt-Rivers and Peter Wildeblood in March 1954 for committing acts of indecency.[59]

Ingram felt that while homosexuality may be 'contrary to the intention of nature' to reproduce the species, it was nevertheless natural,[60] which meant that the 'sex-morality of the future' would need to adapt itself so that the homosexual can 'reveal his nature as freely as if he were to acknowledge that he were left-handed or colour-blind'.[61] Such an acknowledgement would allow reform of the archaic laws, with their potential for blackmail, and for homosexuals to lead a fulfilled life.[62] Homosexuality was thus 'a variety of sexual temperament which has its natural place and its part to play in human affairs'. Most homosexual relationships were based on love and should be allowed to flourish in the public, rather than simply in the private, sphere.[63] Since the 'architecture of human society … requires the existence of different types',[64] there was little, if anything, to regret in being

[56] Ingram, *Sex-Morality Tomorrow*, 11.
[57] Ibid. 17–19; 30–3.
[58] Ibid. 102.
[59] For a lengthy account of the trials, which were formative in homosexual law reform, see Patrick Higgins, *Heterosexual Dictatorship: Male Homosexuality in Postwar Britain* (London, 1996).
[60] Ingram, *Sex-Morality Tomorrow*, 103.
[61] Ibid. 105.
[62] Ibid. 107–8. Ingram notes the role of the recorder of London, Sir Ernest Wild (1869–1934), in provoking blackmail cases: see Matt Houlbrook '"The Man with the Powder Puff" in Inter-war London', *HistJ* 50 (2007), 145–71, esp. 154; Christopher Hilliard, 'The Literary Underground of 1920s London', *Social History* 33 (2008), 164–82, at 175.
[63] Ingram, *Sex-Morality Tomorrow*, 119.
[64] Ibid. 121.

homosexual.[65] While recognizing that some homosexuals gathered in 'queer' spaces, he felt that this was simply an act of solidarity that was provoked by their being 'the victims of universal odium'.[66] The future, however, should be different, because sex was not principally about procreation, but about what he called the 'love-relationship', which meant – and here Ingram makes the direct link that had been so feared by Charles Gore – that 'homosexuality can no more be condemned than … contraception'.[67]

In his final chapter on 'Bisexuality', Ingram outlined a future in which there would be an equalization in relationships so that men and women would be true partners and the 'love-experience' would not be conditioned solely by a sense of sex differentiation: 'when I fall in love, I fall in love with a person: the attachment is personal, not radically sexual'.[68] Although he continued to use the term 'bisexual' to describe this approach, he had departed from his earlier biological explanation, which saw human beings as a blend of the masculine and feminine.[69] He now saw homosexuality less as an identity that was based on a balance of supposed feminine and masculine characteristics, and more in terms of relationships defined by the object of desire.[70] They were to be validated by an equality between the parties and by what he called the 'love-motive':

> The more the love-motive is absent the less moral the sexual relationship, whether that relationship has received the sanction of marriage or not. … Here we reach the ultimate issue which must divide the sex-morality of tomorrow from the orthodox tradition … Can love under any circumstances be immoral? … if the love is mutual and the desire for consummation is mutual, on what moral principle, as distinct from legalistic regulations, can the sexual consummation be evil?[71]

[65] Ibid. 128–30.
[66] Ibid. 124. On queer space, see Dominic Janes, *Visions of Queer Martyrdom from John Henry Newman to Derek Jarman* (Chicago, IL, 2015), esp. 1–29.
[67] Ingram, *Sex-Morality Tomorrow*, 122.
[68] Ibid. 164.
[69] Ibid. 154–73.
[70] Ibid. 161. This transition in understanding homosexuality is an important aspect of Matt Houlbrook's discussion in *Queer London: Perils and Pleasures in the Sexual Metropolis, 1918–1957* (Chicago, IL, 2005), 140–3, esp. 163.
[71] Ingram, *Sex-Morality Tomorrow*, 172–3.

As he contemplated the future of sexual morality, so Ingram came to be an advocate of non-domination and equality in relationships, which for him implied a degree of sexual diversity and pluralism:

> the love-motive is the only legitimate basis on which a positive sexual morality is likely to be built. Wherever there is love, wherever the desire is genuinely mutual, there can be no immorality in sex. Whenever in such circumstances prohibitions are introduced, they are artificial regulations. Love is the test of sexual morality. Sex divorced from love, whether it occurs in a union which is officially designated as lawful marriage or not, belongs to an altogether lower level.[72]

In short, he concluded: 'love, and usually love of the most complete kind, is the substance of the vast majority of homosexual relationships, and where love is sincerely mutual it is immoral to devalue it'.[73] At the same time, however, and here he was to prove most controversial and least prescient, Ingram's sense of the morality of the future also led him to suggest that forms of pederasty 'can probably be countenanced'.[74] Ingram's general call for liberalization of homosexual relationships was obviously likely to provoke those who sought to limit sexual relations to those within a monogamous marriage.

Response

Ingram's book provoked a strong reaction, from members of the general public to leading figures in the Church of England. In 1942, Miss Lettice A. MacMunn (1872–1951) of St Leonards in East Sussex, an erstwhile suffragist and art teacher,[75] who had been director of Queen Anne's Studios, Chelsea,[76] wrote to William Temple, now archbishop of Canterbury, claiming that 'there was never a time more unpropitious for such pernicious stuff to set before our young people'. Noticing that Ingram had been invited to speak at Malvern, she felt that the archbishop might 'be able to influence him

[72] Ibid. 168.
[73] Ibid. 119.
[74] Ibid. 153.
[75] She advertised art classes for ladies in *The Hastings and St Leonards Observer*, 3 February 1917, 1.
[76] On MacMunn, see Elizabeth Baigent et al., 'Women Geographers at the University of Oxford', in eadem and André Reyes Novaes, eds, *Geographers: Biobibliographical Studies* 38 (2020), 45–136, at 63.

to withdraw' his book.[77] Temple responded, noting that Ingram had 'developed what seemed to me extremely unsound and dangerous views of this subject, but I am afraid I should have no influence whatever with him in any suggestion that the book should be withdrawn. I am writing to him but I do not expect to produce any effect'. At the same time, he went on to note that it would not be possible to prosecute the book with any success. With a degree of subtlety, he wrote that the book was:

> [a] serious discussion of important questions and we have never checked, and I think we should do more harm than good if we could succeed in checking, such expressions of opinion, but there is a high price to be paid for liberty and the degree [of liberty] contained in this book are [*sic*] part of this price. The best that can be said is that it is a clearer expression of what is now a prevailing attitude than has I think appeared, and so far it helps us to see what we have to meet and devise a statement of our own case accordingly. I have not the least doubt that Mr Ingram represents an extreme swing of the pendulum. Some swing was inevitable and in my judgment desirable, but as usual his has gone to another extreme, worse in itself though I think probably less dangerous in its effect than the Puritan extreme from which it is a reaction.[78]

Temple promised to respond to her again, should he receive a reply from Ingram which might be of interest to her.

Temple wrote to Ingram the following day. While noting that there was a 'good deal in *Sex-Morality Tomorrow* with which I sympathise and from which some good may result', he also made a direct request to Ingram which amounts to a very Anglican form of censorship. There was, he felt,

> a great deal that seems to me entirely pernicious in effect though I know not in intention and due to an intellectualist handling of the matter which involves ignoring some of the deepest factors. I am afraid I think that the main result of the book must be very great damage and because of our co-operation in certain ways in the past I am writing to ask whether you can consider withdrawing it. I should be very sorry to advertise a breach in the ranks of those eager for social progress on

[77] LPL, Temple Papers 30, fol. 85, Lettice MacMunn to Temple, 3 July 1942.
[78] LPL, Temple Papers 30, fol. 85, Temple to MacMunn, 4 July 1942.

> Christian lines by taking any step myself to make public my dissent from much of what you say, but I might be very easily driven to this because your being one of the Malvern speakers tends to make people associate what you say in some degree with myself. Will you consider this and let me know? I am quite aware that I am asking a very big thing.[79]

Ingram wrote back asking for some time to think over the archbishop's request, also noting that he would have to consult his publishers.

> When I wrote that book I was anxious mainly to be sincere and to state without any equivocation what I felt about that subject. From that angle I should not want to do anything which would imply that I had not the courage of my convictions. But I am certainly very anxious not to persist in any line which will embarrass my friends, and I fully appreciate what you say in that connexion. Also, I realise that it is very easy to be misunderstood and that on some points in that book I have been misunderstood.[80]

Temple had also forwarded a copy of Ingram's letter to Hugh Cecil (1869–1956), recently ennobled as Baron Quickswood, a former Conservative politician, prominent member of the Church Assembly and provost of Eton College, asking for his views. Cecil responded that while he could not say anything from the point of view of those supporting the Malvern movement, since he was not in sympathy, he did not feel that it was 'the "socialist" side of Ingram's mind that has led him into these lamentable errors'. He was 'not the enemy of the family, at any rate directly', but was instead 'the enemy of chastity'.[81] He went on to offer his assessment of the changes of the inter-war years before criticizing Ingram:

> This rejection of chastity, though not often pressed so far as Ingram presses it, has spread far and wide in varying degrees in the last 20 or 30 years. Christians have in all ages been accustomed to accept as a revealed and unquestionable dogma that every sexual act or relation, except lifelong marriage, is, in very different degrees, sinful, because unchaste. This has been corroborated by considerations of social welfare and, in some points, of health; but essentially it is a revealed dogma

[79] LPL, Temple Papers 30, fol. 84, Temple to Kenneth Ingram, 4 July 1942.
[80] LPL, Temple Papers 30, fol. 86, Ingram to Temple, 7 July 1942.
[81] LPL, Temple Papers 30, fol. 88, Baron Quickswood (Hugh Cecil) to Temple, 11 July 1942.

> as much as the Trinity or the Incarnation. When I was young no one disputed it; but in my life-time it has far and wide been ignored or even expressly renounced. Ingram, no doubt seeking the sincerity of which he speaks, has attempted to rationalise and to press to all logical conclusions, a conception of sexual relations which casts out chastity altogether, and indeed does not seem to recognise that such a thing exists.[82]

For Cecil, the main problem was the novelty of regarding love as the basis for human relationships: because Ingram 'as he says strove to be sincere', he 'therefore formulated as best he could a new theory of sexual relation which had nothing to do with the revealed dogma of chastity, of the existence of which he hardly seems to be conscious'. Consequently, as 'a person who sincerely rejects chastity', Ingram could 'scarcely be called a churchman'. Cecil went on to remind Temple that Bishop Hubert Burge of Oxford had 'refused the Duke of Marlborough the status of a communicant because his guilt of adultery put him outside what was meant by communicant'.[83] While admitting that this might not have been good law, he felt it was 'sound religion; and it seems to me that Ingram may similarly be said to be outside the church so long as he holds the opinion that the rule of Christian charity does not govern sexual relations'. Consequently, he felt, Ingram should not be given the opportunity of 'explaining himself or correcting misunderstandings; for, as I see his opinions, they are not merely wrong in one respect or another but are the total negation of the church's teaching about chastity'.[84] Cecil went on to make his recommendation to Temple:

> What should be the practical consequences is of course entirely for Your Grace to judge. It seems obvious that if you deal with the matter at all you should make it clear that you do hold the Christian doctrine of chastity and that you cannot recognise anyone as a faithful member of the church who does not. What degree of withdrawal or association with Ingram this might mean is of course quite beyond my power to judge. But I do not think the mere withdrawal of his book would do

[82] Ibid.

[83] This notorious case had partly been the cause of the dissolution of Marlborough's marriage to Consuelo Vanderbilt in 1921.

[84] LPL, Temple Papers 30, fol. 88, Quickswood to Temple, 11 July 1942.

> much good. The point is that he does really and sincerely reject Christian chastity.[85]

For Cecil, freedom of thought for Christians on matters of dogma, which included sexual relations, was simply not possible, at least in public.

Temple responded to Cecil, agreeing that 'he starts from a completely non-Christian principle. One's line of approach to him will rather vary according to whether he decides to withdraw the book or leave it on the market'. If Ingram withdrew the book, then he would try to 'get a talk with him about the whole subject and see whether I can make him understand the Christian position in the matter'. However, if 'he does not withdraw I shall have to tell him that I regard it as having put himself outside the pale'.[86] Temple also noted the practical difficulties of such a policy:

> The whole position in the Church of England about anything like excommunication is so confused that I do not think one could profitably embark upon that. I should tell him that in my own judgment, which I express not only personally but officially this book does inevitably place its author out of fellowship with the Church. But if he were to withdraw it that would be so far a submission to the judgment of the Church that I should not want to take that kind of step and it would give me some hope of getting him to see what is really involved.[87]

Cecil wrote back, suggesting that if the book were censured in convocation, it 'would only enormously increase its circulation, which would be a pity'. 'However,' he went on, 'I do think the Church ought to make some declaration on the whole question somehow. I am one of those who thought that the treatment of these subjects by the Lambeth Conference was a disaster'.[88] Here again, there is an explicit linking of the issue of contraception with the question of homosexuality. Temple replied to Cecil, outlining his decisions. If Ingram withdrew the book,

> I shall approach him as an obviously erring member of the Church of England and try to bring him to another mind. I shall at any rate try to

[85] Ibid.
[86] LPL, Temple Papers 30, fol. 89, Temple to Quickswood, 15 July 1942.
[87] Ibid.
[88] LPL, Temple Papers 30, fol. 90, Quickswood to Temple, 16 July 1942.

balance his present view with the contrary one by showing the immense weight of tradition as well as of moral sanity which is to be found in the Church's doctrine.[89]

However, 'if he does not withdraw the book, I should have to tell him that I regard the views which he expressed as quite incompatible with practising churchmanship.' All this, however, was to happen in private, since 'it would be a great mistake to do any of this publicly because [it would], as you say, just advertise the book'. He concluded: 'More particularly anything so rare and, to the lower type of Press man, so exciting as a condemnation by Convocation would only add to the sales.'[90]

In the event, Ingram wrote to Temple that he did not wish to withdraw the book since it might imply that he did not have the 'courage of my convictions'.[91] In addition,

it would in some respects let down the several correspondents who have written to me to say that they have found the book to be a help to them in their various problems: I have to think of them. Moreover, I doubt if a withdrawal of the book would really satisfy those critics who might approach you, unless the withdrawal were accompanied by a confession that I had changed my views.[92]

Instead, Ingram suggested that he would insert an explanation outlining the purpose of the book and the nature of love in all copies still in hand. He would also ensure that there would be no future edition (even though, because of the paper shortage caused by the war, this was unlikely). He went on: 'I hope that you may consider this to be a satisfactory course, but, if not, I shall quite understand and not resent in the least any condemnation of the book which you may feel obliged to make.'[93] He also observed that conditions had changed significantly since the book was written:

I am anxious to save you and any other of our friends any possible embarrassment, and I would gladly do anything to help in this way, short of any course which would involve me in insincerity. I would

89 LPL, Temple Papers 30, fol. 91, Quickswood to Temple, 20 July 1942.
90 LPL, Temple Papers 30, fol. 91, Temple to Quickswood, 20 July 1942.
91 LPL, Temple Papers 30, fol. 92, Ingram to Temple, 24 July 1942.
92 Ibid.
93 Ibid.

> add that I wrote and agreed to the publication of this book at the end of 1939, before Malvern was on the horizon. Had I foreseen these developments I might have hesitated to publish a book of so controversial a character concerning an issue which had no direct relevance to the much more important issues of religious-social reconstruction.[94]

In his reply to Temple, Ingram included a typescript of his proposed explanation: alongside addressing some specific points, he answered his critics by suggesting:

> Most of the critics whom I have provoked have failed, I suspect, to pay sufficient attention to the conclusion which is fundamental to my own standpoint, that (p. 173) 'the real problem for us to solve is the nature of love. We have to disentangle more effectively than we have as yet succeeded in doing pure love from the impulses for selfish satisfaction'. Far from approving, I should hold that, where real love is absent from a sex-relationship, sexual intercourse denotes a failure to achieve the moral standard which I have advocated.[95]

Responding to Ingram, Temple thanked him for the 'way in which you are trying to meet me', yet also noting that he was 'bound to say that the result from my standpoint is to leave matters very much where they were'.[96] He did not feel that the proposed preface really addressed the question of the abandonment of chastity, which, in Temple's view, remained the only option for Christian homosexuals:

> Whether you insert such a Preface as you have suggested to any new edition or reprint of your book you must yourself decide; but it would have to be for making clear your own position. It would not really affect the attitude which I, and still more passionately many more Church people, would feel obliged to take up. Fundamentally the trouble is that your book gives the impression of abandoning the Church's insistence upon the obligation of chastity. That involves a departure so great as to seem in my own mind quite incompatible with practising Churchmanship. I do not think there really can be any doubt that this is your contention. There are many passages in the book which tend that way and some are almost explicit in

[94] LPL, Temple Papers 30, fol. 92, Ingram to Temple, 24 July 1942.
[95] LPL, Temple papers 30, fol. 93, Ingram to Temple, included with letter of 24 July 1942.
[96] LPL, Temple Papers 30, fols 94–5, Temple to Ingram, 28 July 1942.

> repudiation of that obligation unless it is interpreted as only a general self-control and avoidance of sheer licentiousness. … I am very sorry that there seems no doubt about our having reached this complete divergence on this subject but I find it quite impossible to doubt that the point has been reached and that I am obliged therefore to put this matter before you as I have attempted in this letter.[97]

Conclusion

There the correspondence ended. Ingram's book was not withdrawn; he was not publicly censured; and no new preface was inserted. While Temple was clearly opposed to any further liberalization of sexual ethics, both he and Cecil were astute enough to realize that any publicity would have simply added to the sales of the book. Ingram too noted that such negative publicity about somebody associated with the Malvern Conference might prove a distraction from some of its more far-reaching programmes for social reconstruction. In the end, the book, which was the most radical statement about homosexuality from a British Christian thinker written between the wars, sank almost without trace,[98] and the publishers Allen & Unwin failed to recoup their investment.[99] Wartime circumstances, it would seem, meant that the book had little immediate effect. Nonetheless, the twin premises that sex could be practised purely for the pleasure of the couple, as implied by the condoning of contraception, and the idea that homosexuality was simply a natural and normal condition among a minority of people, led Ingram to redefine the nature of Christian relationships.

It took another seventy years or so for Ingram's ideas to be realized in English secular legislation, with equal marriage entering the statutes in 2013. However, while the Church of England came to play a prominent role in the reform of the legislation on homosexuality in the 1950s and 1960s, arguments about the 'naturalness' of homosexuality, and of the importance of distinguishing between what was

[97] Ibid.

[98] There seem to have been just two very short reviews of the book: Alec Craig's in the *Eugenics Review* 32 (1940), 91; and an anonymous review in the *Times Literary Supplement*, 12 October 1940, 523, which concluded dismissively that Ingram had nothing 'startlingly novel to contribute to the problem'.

[99] The business correspondence with Kenneth Ingram from Allen & Unwin on the publication of *Sex Morality Tomorrow* is included in the Allen & Unwin papers: Reading, Reading University Special Collections, Allen & Unwin Papers, AUC 89/15.

lawful and what was sinful, frequently set out on the path taken by Ingram, but they never reached the same conclusion. The Church of England's official teaching on marriage and sexuality did not change to accept the equality of mutually loving relationships, even if it increasingly adopted a more pastoral approach to homosexuals.[100] Indeed, through the 1970s and 1980s, the shape of the debate came to be dominated by arguments from Scripture, rather than from nature and from science, which led large numbers in the Church of England away from further liberalization. The legacy of Charles Gore, Hugh Cecil and many others, which regards celibacy as the only Christian option for sex outside heterosexual marriage, continues to affect significant quarters of the Church of England to the present day. At the same time, many others continue to level the charge of hypocrisy (as did Robert Reid in the 1930s) at a church that claims to recognize the importance of natural law and scientific knowledge, while failing to draw out their implications for sexual morality.

[100] See also in this volume, William Whyte, 'OutRage! Hypocrisy, Episcopacy and Homosexuality in 1990s England'.

Humanity Defined, Hypocrisy Defied: Sacralizing the Black Freedom Struggle, 1930–60

Dennis C. Dickerson*
Vanderbilt University

The white ecclesia in the United States either opposed or equivocated on the matter of the humanity of African Americans. The 1939 unification of majority white Methodist bodies, for example, structurally segregated black members into a separate Central Jurisdiction. This action mimicked practices in the broader body politic that crystallized in American society both de jure *and de facto systems of second-class citizenship for African Americans. This hypocrisy mobilized adherents of Gandhian non-violence and elicited from them tenets and tactics which energized moral methodologies that defeated a church and civic collusion that perpetrated black subordination. Interracial alliances derived from the ecclesia and parachurch organizations articulated non-violence as a moral precept that sacralized a grassroots civil rights movement. This initiative morally discredited the racial hypocrisy aimed at America's formerly enslaved and segregated population.*

Any observer of the religious landscape in the United States in the early decades of the twentieth century would have viewed the Christian churches, whether Methodist, Baptist or Presbyterian, as rigidly segregated by race and poisoned by the proposition that African Americans belonged to a scripturally and socially proscribed population. Such commentators hardly needed any racial reminders from the nineteenth century, when some Christians had sanctioned slavery on a biblical basis and others, while seemingly sympathetic to blacks, either tolerated slavery or recommended that black people fill pulpits and pews only within a segregated ecclesia. These patterns of black and white separation, which tracked and reinforced the same structures in larger society, assumed that African Americans were unfit either as preachers or as parishioners to occupy the same ecclesial

* E-mail: dennis.c.dickerson@vanderbilt.edu.

Studies in Church History 60 (2024), 477–510
doi: 10.1017/stc.2024.23

space as whites. The Methodist unification of 1939 egregiously illustrated how Christianity, across the white denominational spectrum, sacralized racial segregation and adopted it as an ecclesiastical tenet. African Americans and their allies, through Christian and interfaith resources, resisted a racial order in the United States built on black inequality. Resistance in the United States to the ecclesial consolidation of racial hierarchy mobilized transnational resources, mainly through the diffusion of Gandhian non-violence, to fight this American manifestation of caste.

In 1939, the Methodist Episcopal Church, the Methodist Episcopal Church, South, and the Methodist Protestant Church met in Kansas City (Missouri) at a 'Uniting Conference' to merge these majority white religious bodies. Far from representing an ecclesiastical achievement, one scholar, Morris L. Davis, viewed the merger as a 'further institutionalization of racism.'[1] Indeed, Davis argues, it was 'a severe setback and a lost chance for the new church to take a stand against the prevailing injustices of racist U.S. culture.'[2] A seemingly reinvented Methodism calcified segregation by compelling its black membership into a separate Central Jurisdiction, a synodical component that was racially rather than geographically constructed. To force black Methodists into a segregated, subordinate body, the all-black Central Jurisdiction was to affirm that Christianity's encounter with twentieth-century modernity required an official ecclesiastical accommodation to African American inequality.[3]

As plans unfolded for the Central Jurisdiction, one black Methodist said that this decision 'violates the principle of brotherhood dominant in the life and teachings of Jesus and embodied in the organized fellowship of Christian believers in the church.'[4] Davis observes that Methodist unification signified that 'whiteness emerged more concretely into American culture as the primary marker of the pinnacle of human progress [embodied] in American Christian Civilization.' Moreover, he pointed out, 'the Christian

[1] Morris L. Davis, *The Methodist Unification: Christianity and the Politics of Race in the Jim Crow Era* (New York, 2008), 1. See also Peter C. Murray, *Methodism and the Crucible of Race* (Columbia, SC, and London, 2004), 36–44.
[2] Davis, *Methodist Unification*, 1.
[3] Ibid. 131–2.
[4] James S. Thomas, *Methodism's Racial Dilemma: The Story of the Central Jurisdiction* (Nashville, TN, 1992), 43.

churches, in both North and South' extended their blessing to this racially tainted triumph of Methodist unification. As a result, 'in the church and in the rest of America, Christianity was nationalized and racialized.'[5]

Perhaps more poignantly, the African Methodist Episcopal (AME) Church, a venerable Wesleyan body established in 1816 and a serious institutional onlooker, reviled the Methodist unification. Bishop John A. Gregg, speaking for his colleagues in their episcopal address to the 1940 AME General Conference, emphasized that: 'we hold that any church or communion that would segregate its members or practice any form of denial or discrimination on account of race or color, is less than Christian.'[6] Because African Methodists affirmed the humanity of blacks and eschewed the racial hypocrisy of Wesleyan whites, Gregg declared: 'Freedom, Liberty, and Equality of opportunity for all, in both church and state, are the foundation upon which the AME Church was built [and] upon which foundation it stands today.'[7] In affirming the humanity of blacks, a precept that the founder of Methodism, John Wesley, had espoused in the eighteenth century, the AME Church, which had been launched during Wesley's lifetime, became America's oldest continuous Methodist body. This moved Bishop Gregg to note that the racial fissures within the mainly white Methodist denomination shown in their 1939 unification removed them from any possibility of safeguarding black rights. 'Since the Methodist bodies represented by white churchmen have merged forming a new organization,' Gregg asserted, 'the African Methodist Episcopal Church becomes the oldest Methodist communion in the United States.'[8] With others in the black ecclesia and with parareligious groups, they, rather than white churches, occupied the moral high ground in pro-black advocacy.[9]

Hence, the Methodist unification was a clarifying event that displayed a formal ecclesial embrace of racial hypocrisy by white churches and a determination to reinforce parallel societal structures that compelled black subordination. Though the Methodist Church,

[5] Davis, *The Methodist Unification*, 132.
[6] *The Episcopal Address, presented by Bishop John Andrew Gregg to the Thirty-First Quadrennial Session of the General Conference of the African Methodist Episcopal Church at Detroit, Michigan, May, 1940* (n.pl., 1940), 21.
[7] Ibid. 21.
[8] Ibid. 37.
[9] Ibid. 37.

like the southern branches of the Presbyterians and Baptists in the 1940s, acknowledged that racial discrimination was a scourge and urged better treatment of African Americans, its leadership recommended that no legislation be enacted to achieve black equality. The Fraternal Council of Negro Churches (FCC) had been formed in 1934 to rebuke such displays of compromised Christianity. The black church federation started because the Federal Council of Churches would not support a congressional initiative to outlaw lynching and to renounce the Ku Klux Klan. Though the Federal Council at its 1946 meeting denounced segregation, some wanted to remove Benjamin E. Mays, an officer, from the stage where President Harry Truman was scheduled to speak.[10]

A vigorous pushback from James Farmer and A. Philip Randolph in the immediate aftermath of this Christian apostasy, however, asserted the humanity of African Americans and put in place religiously imbued initiatives that aimed to upend the discourse and ecclesial influence of white Christian racism. A competing narrative developed by Farmer and Randolph, two black freedom advocates with deep roots in African American Methodism, challenged the racist meaning of Methodist unification and put it on the moral defensive. Farmer, the son and namesake of a Methodist Episcopal minister, matriculated at the School of Religion at Howard University where his father taught the Hebrew Bible. At the time of the unification, Farmer's anger over the new denomination's segregation decision caused him to refuse to be ordained in a Jim Crow church, and instead to resolve to work to 'destroy segregation.'[11] 'How was I to preach Christ in a church,' Farmer asked, 'whose structure gave him the lie?' This ecclesial system would contradict Jesus's gospel.[12] Farmer's view echoed a similar denunciation from a fellow member of the Central Jurisdiction, Mary McLeod Bethune, an appointee of President Franklin D. Roosevelt and the president of a black Florida college funded by the denomination. Bethune, a member of the all-black Stewart Memorial Church in Daytona Beach, declared that she did not

[10] Murray, *Methodism and the Crucible of Race*, 56–7; Mary R. Sawyer, 'The Fraternal Council of Negro Churches, 1934–1964', *ChH* 59 (1990), 51–64, at 52.

[11] James Farmer, *Lay Bare the Heart: An Autobiography of the Civil Rights Movement* (New York, 1985; repr. Fort Worth, TX, 1986, with new preface), 146. References are to the 1986 edition.

[12] Ibid. 143.

want African American youth in future decades to associate her with approving 'anything that looked like segregation.'[13]

Because Farmer believed that anti-black racism permeated the white ecclesia, he chose a seminary thesis topic that would allow him to explore the origin of this sinful reality. He admitted to 'brooding over these questions' that informed the segregationist posture of the Methodist Church, this erstwhile anti-slavery religious body, and how white Methodists' stance morphed into a sinful ambivalence toward the humanity of African Americans.[14] Hence Farmer, in his bachelor thesis at Howard University (which was supervised by Howard Thurman), entitled 'A Critical Analysis of the Historical Interrelationship Between Religion and Racism,' explored 'the functional role of religion regarding race' and how religion buttressed 'the secular social values' of white Christians.[15] He surmised that 'parts of Protestant and especially Calvinist thought and ethics' interacted with capitalism to exploit 'distant lands peopled by strange folk of darker hue.' Anglo-Saxon culture, he wrote, had developed 'racist doctrines' that formed the basis of both slavery and segregation.[16] Farmer's focus going forward was to 'destroy segregation' through an alternative moral methodology that lay 'in the use of the Gandhi technique' in a sphere which was much broader than a pastoral vocation within the structural boundaries of his church's Central Jurisdiction.[17]

For this reason, the Fellowship of Reconciliation (FOR), not the Methodist Church, became the vehicle of conscience through which Farmer would attack segregation. Notwithstanding FOR's pacifist objectives, Farmer and a cadre of like-minded and morally motivated activists believed that a component of the organization should focus on opposition to the violence of segregation. One of them, Joe Guinn, had like Farmer been involved in the Methodist student movement. Guinn and Farmer applied the moral armament of non-violent direct action to sit-ins to desegregate restaurants and transportation, using them as venues to test the effectiveness of the 'Gandhian technique.' To regularize this moral methodology, Farmer and a few others launched in 1942 the Congress of Racial

[13] Barbara Dianne Savage, *Your Spirits Walk Beside Us: The Politics of Black Religion* (Cambridge, MA, 2008), 129.
[14] Farmer, *Lay Bare the Heart*, 143.
[15] Ibid. 143, 145–6.
[16] Ibid. 145.
[17] Ibid. 146.

Equality (CORE) as a derivative organization of FOR. Archibald J. Carey, Jr, the activist pastor of Chicago's Woodlawn African Methodist Episcopal Church, whom Farmer described as their 'patron saint', nurtured the group and provided them with office space in the basement of the parish church. Farmer recalled that 'when CORE needed money above that which could be raised by passing a hat at membership meetings, Arch would take up a collection in his church'; he also allowed them to use the church's 'mimeograph machine' to facilitate communications for CORE.[18]

Farmer's protest against ecclesially endorsed segregation morphed into a nationally transformative insurgency that helped to energize the non-violence movement in the succeeding decades of the 1950s and 1960s. Concurrent with Farmer's sacrally informed initiatives was A. Philip Randolph's March on Washington Movement (MOWM). Randolph, like Carey, drew activist energy from a major tributary of the Wesleyan social holiness that had emerged in the independent African Methodist Episcopal Church. The denomination's long tradition of fighting slavery and segregation, and of sharing this impulse with black Methodists in a white dominated ecclesia, provided a formidable institutional basis from which to sustain the pro-black advocacy that Carey and Randolph pursued in the 1940s.[19]

Archibald J. Carey, Jr, the son and namesake of the AME bishop Archibald J. Carey, Sr, was visible as a black spokesman and cultivated the socially conscious reputation of his Woodlawn congregation. He was also an attorney, a Republican who was elected in 1947 as a Chicago alderman. In 1948, he challenged the city council to enact a proposed ordinance to ban discrimination in publicly aided housing. Though unsuccessful, this initiative and his crucial support of Farmer and CORE pulled Carey onto a vanguard of sacrally motivated insurgents whose ecclesial witness belied the practices of white Christians too timid to advocate for the full humanity of African Americans.[20]

[18] Ibid. 109, 147; compare also Dennis C. Dickerson, *A Liberated Past: Reflections on AME Church History* (Nashville, TN, 2003), 62.

[19] For an account of this period, see Farmer, *Lay Bare the Heart*, 185–291; compare also Dennis C. Dickerson, *The African Methodist Episcopal Church: A History* (New York and Cambridge, 2020), 24, 378–95.

[20] Dennis C. Dickerson, *African American Preachers and Politics: The Careys of Chicago* (Jackson, MS, 2010), 95–103.

A. Philip Randolph, president of the all-black Brotherhood of Sleeping Car Porters, was similarly significant as a practitioner of non-violence whose militancy drew from sacral sources. Despite a misleading reputation for agnosticism and even atheism, Randolph, a fierce critic of white Christian racism, fully embraced his AME heritage. According to Cynthia Taylor, one of his biographers, he identified with the insurgency of the AME founder, Richard Allen, whose "wrath against religious jimcrow … struck a blow for civil rights and first-class citizenship" for African Americans.[21] Allen's example in the late eighteenth and early nineteenth centuries, Taylor observes, 'served as a role model for [Randolph's] own lifework fighting for black civil rights.'[22] Though a generation older than Farmer, Randolph's Gandhian-inspired activism, centred in grassroots mass mobilization, infused fresh religious energy into the black freedom struggle immediately after the segregationist actions that emerged from the Methodist unification.

Farmer and Randolph contemplated a possible partnership in implementing a Gandhian program, based on non-violent civil disobedience and non-cooperation.[23] Randolph had already threatened President Roosevelt in 1941 with a mobilization of 10,000 blacks in his March on Washington Movement, which proposed to descend on the nation's capital to demand an end to racial discrimination in the burgeoning defence industries. In response, Roosevelt issued Executive Order 8802, which opened steel, auto, shipbuilding and other mass production facilities to African Americans; failure to comply would cause firms to forfeit lucrative federal contracts. A Fair Employment Practices Committee was established to enforce this presidential mandate.[24] In 1942, Randolph turned to Gandhi's moral methodology as a resource for MOWM. His familiarity with the history of black boycotts against racist vendors in transit, restaurants and retail outlets, and his recent observations of sit-down strikes and other examples of labour protest in the New Deal era to win union recognition from employers, informed his thinking about what strategies were available to advance black civil rights. The

[21] Cynthia Taylor, *A. Philip Randolph: The Religious Journey of an African American Labor Leader* (New York, 2006), 13, citing Randolph's lecture, 'African Methodism and the Negro in the Western World.'

[22] Taylor, *A. Philip Randolph*, 13.

[23] Ibid. 158–9, 162–6; see also Farmer, *Lay Bare the Heart*, 154–7.

[24] Taylor, *A. Philip Randolph*, 130–4.

integration of Gandhian non-violence into his repertoire of movement methods enhanced his deployment of civil disobedience by infusing this strategy with moral meaning.[25]

At that time, Randolph considered a partnership with Farmer and CORE to launch a multi-front, Gandhi-like campaign to resist violations of African American civil rights. As a FOR official, Farmer had begun in 1941 to ponder Gandhian non-violence. He internalized the Gandhian tenet that in encountering racist practices the protester 'must, as a matter of conscience, as well as strategy, withdraw from participation in racist practices'.[26] However, he had doubts about sharing this initiative with Randolph, owing in part to what he perceived as the lack of 'training and discipline' in non-violence within the black population. Farmer convinced Randolph, the more experienced activist, to heed these warnings, whilst still urging CORE chapters to cooperate with Randolph's March on Washington Movement.[27] Engagement with the moral methodology of Gandhian non-violence enlarged the religious sensibilities of both Farmer and Randolph. Farmer's 'brooding' over white ecclesial racism, on the one hand, and the unprecedented possibilities of Gandhian non-violence or satyagraha (meaning 'soul force') on the other, moulded him into more than what his father had envisaged for him as a minister in a segregated church. At the same time, Randolph, who was equally adept in his own creative deployment of moral methodologies, harnessed the March on Washington Movement (MOWM) to the operational proficiency of the African American ecclesia.

Randolph, notwithstanding Farmer's reservations about the immediate readiness of blacks for a mass disobedience campaign, maintained MOWM momentum in challenging racial segregation. In Chicago, the site of an active MOWM affiliate, a grassroots rally was planned in 1942 with Charles Wesley Burton, a black Congregational minister, as local chair.[28] Other clergy in the AME Church and sundry other congregations comprised Randolph's ecclesial infrastructure. Perhaps the most prominent among Randolph's supporters was Archibald J. Carey, Jr, who invited the MOWM

[25] Ibid. 158–9.
[26] Farmer, *Lay Bare the Heart*, 74–5.
[27] Ibid. 155–7.
[28] Taylor, *A. Philip Randolph*, 136–8.

leader to speak at Woodlawn Church.[29] Similarly, in St Louis, MOWM partnered with the Interdenominational Ministers Alliance that included support from leaders from the African Methodist Episcopal Zion, Colored Methodist Episcopal, Baptist and Presbyterian churches, as well as other religious leaders.[30]

Neither Farmer nor Randolph pursued the contemplative facets of Gandhian satyagraha nor their grounding in Hindu and Jainist principles. The spiritual armaments of Gandhi's Hinduism and the ahimsa doctrine of non-retaliation embedded in Jainism were at best secondary to the praxis that Gandhian non-violence offered. Nonetheless, the two activists, while anchored in the insurgent sensibilities of black Methodism, blended their religious heritage with the interfaith resources that undergirded the principles and practices of non-violence. The interreligious character of non-violence, though muted, took these activists beyond the ecclesial and discursive boundaries of white Christian reckonings with race. The mutually reinforcing critiques of black religion and Gandhian satyagraha against the racial ideology of white Christians energized the religious thrust of the non-violent movement in the United States, sacralizing their defence of black humanity and mobilizing grassroots African Americans in their fight for equality.

Nonetheless, historian Stephen Tuck argues that 'religious rethinking and skepticism of prevailing beliefs' characterized African American discourse about matters of faith in the interwar period. He testifies to a spirited discourse and deep conflicts about religious belief and unbelief within the civil rights movement, as well as the seeming lassitude of black churches toward the African American freedom struggle.[31] Notwithstanding this discursive component of black religious conversation, Tuck overlooks the innovative alignments between Gandhian satyagraha and the black ecclesia. Rather than a 'rethinking and skepticism of prevailing beliefs', this engagement with Gandhian non-violence signified a blending and enhancement of a revived black religious insurgency already embedded in the faith tradition of the militant wing of the African American

[29] Ibid. 169.
[30] Ibid. 147.
[31] Stephen Tuck, 'The Doubts of Their Fathers: The God Debate and the Conflict between African American Churches and Civil Rights Organizations between the World Wars,' *Journal of Southern History* 86 (2020), 625–78.

ecclesia. The interfaith interactions that tied together peace, pacifism and non-violence channelled into the African American religious community a fresh discourse about what moral methodologies were available to affirm the humanity of black people, to liberate them from societal subordination, and to construct parareligious assemblies that challenged the racial hypocrisy of white Christianity. Tuck's study focuses on the internecine squabbles between black pastors and parishioners and civil rights organizations.[32] This ignores broader reckonings with fresh precepts and praxis that Farmer, Randolph and others introduced into African American religious discourse and poured into an emergent non-violence movement in the United States.

The sacralization of non-violent discourse that Farmer and Randolph had already 'kicked into high gear' in the 1940s, had its genesis in the previous decade on two seminary campuses, namely Yale Divinity School and the School of Religion at Howard University. At Yale Divinity School, six black students matriculated and, in 1930, organized themselves into the Upsilon Theta Chi society.[33] Their aim lay in 'Service and Sacrifice for Christ' and in engagement with insurgent African American clergy involved in reinventing the black church. In cooperation with a white faculty adviser, Jerome Davis, professor of practical philanthropy at Yale and a pacifist, the black divinity students sponsored a conference on 'Whither the Negro Church?' which took place in 1931. These divinity students and a significant cadre of clergy believed an energized black ecclesia was needed to rebut the vacillating posture of white Christian churches, which either affirmed the humanity of African Americans or advocated an outright denial of their civil rights. The aim of their seminary training and organization was 'to produce a new type of leadership' whose purpose lay in 'the uplift of the Negro race and other oppressed peoples.'[34] The black seminarians also sought 'the creation of a new social order based upon the principles of Jesus.'[35] These sensibilities provided an easy segue into explorations of

[32] Ibid. 633.

[33] Jerome Davis, 'Foreword', in William H. Holloway, ed., *Whither the Negro Church? Seminar held at Yale Divinity School, New Haven, Conn., April 13–15, 1931* (New Haven, CT, 1932), 3.

[34] Ibid.

[35] Ibid.

Gandhian non-violence, a praxis of resistance and a moral methodology aimed at societal reconstruction.

The presenters, all 'cutting edge' commentators,[36] believed that black churches should be retrofitted to spur social insurgency,[37] and that they should be pungent critics of Caucasian Christians too embedded in racial privilege to oppose anti-black discrimination.[38] Nonetheless, a fault line developed in their discussions. Some expressed scepticism about Caucasian Christian credibility on black and white issues.[39] Others reported promising experiences with interracial clergy interactions.[40] A. Philip Randolph, whose later engagement with Gandhian methodology would shift the black struggle onto another plateau of activism, thought that 'the Negro Church needs an economic philosophy and program' that aimed 'to improve the living standard of its membership.'[41] Conference participants generally agreed that alliances with the labour movement and its confrontation with corporate hegemony would benefit proletarian parishioners who comprised the majority in black churches.[42] John M. Ellison, however, lamented that it was 'emotional pleasure' that drove African Americans to attend their churches. 'Perhaps the greatest questions of economics', he suggested, 'have not entered very largely in the mind of the masses and very lightly in the minds of a

[36] The presenters were recorded as John M. Ellison, Professor of Sociology and Ethics, Virginia State College (from 1941, first African American president of Virginia Union University); George Edmund Haynes, Secretary of the Department of Race Relations of the Federal Council of Churches; Benjamin E. Mays, Director of 'A Study of the Negro Church', Institute of Social and Religious Research; Henry Hugh Proctor, pastor of the Nazarine Congregational Church, Brooklyn; A. Philip Randolph, General Organizer and President of Sleeping Car Porters; Frank T. Wilson, Executive for Colored Student Work, YMCA National Committee; and Jerome Davis (the only white speaker). See Holloway, ed., *Whither the Negro Church?*, 4 (contents) and 48 (roster of delegates).

[37] See, for example, John M. Ellison, 'The Negro Church and Economic Relations—II', in Holloway, ed., *Whither the Negro Church?*, 11–13.

[38] See especially the discussion following the paper by Henry Hugh Proctor, 'The Negro Church', in Holloway, ed., *Whither the Negro Church?*, 33–6.

[39] See, for instance, George E. Haynes, 'The Negro Church and our Changing Social Order', in Holloway, ed., *Whither the Negro Church?*, 17–21, esp. at 18, and also the discussion following Haynes's paper in ibid. 21–3.

[40] Proctor, 'The Negro Church', 31–2.

[41] A. Philip Randolph, 'The Negro Church and Economic Relations—I', in Holloway, ed., *Whither the Negro Church?*, 5.

[42] See the discussions following the papers by Randolph and Ellison, in Holloway, ed., *Whither the Negro Church?*, 5–10 and 13–16.

great many church leaders.'[43] Frank T. Wilson and Benjamin E. Mays, who would later mobilize African American religious intellectuals toward an embrace of Gandhi, saw too few possibilities for partnership with white churches to encourage black resistance to Jim Crow. Wilson observed that white missionary education societies that funded black colleges 'tend to retard the development of free and creative personalities within Negro students.'[44] Mays frankly asserted that 'there are some Negro groups in the South who hardly want to hear a white southern man preach.'[45]

In the discussion with George E. Haynes, Secretary of the Department of Race Relations of the Federal Council of Churches, one black Yale seminarian, Edward G. Carroll, discussed with Haynes the importance of the Student Christian Movement (SCM). Although he was concerned that SCM was 'drawing the youth's attention away from the church,' Carroll insisted, the organization was also 'drawing it to religion and life,' meaning engagement with pressing racial and international issues that churches too often eschewed; it was also providing future leaders with a religious perspective.[46] SCM, through its affiliation with the World Student Christian Federation and in conjunction with the YMCA office of Frank T. Wilson, arranged in 1935 and 1936 for Carroll and others to travel to India and neighbouring countries in a Pilgrimage of Friendship. As they brooded over the subordinate status of African Americans, Carroll and others in the Upsilon Theta Chi society, together with their adviser, Jerome Davis, thought 'the Negro Church' required 'a more prophetic and fearless technique in making applicable the implications of the religion of Jesus in relation to our social order.'[47] Carroll's consciousness, however, was especially aroused as he and fellow black seminarians endorsed an insurgent view of 'the Negro Church' that Davis also articulated. The drafting committee for the conference resolutions, which included one Upsilon Theta

[43] Ellison, 'The Negro Church and Economic Relations—II', 11.

[44] Frank T. Wilson, 'The Negro Church and Education', in Holloway, ed., *Whither the Negro Church?*, 24–6, at 24.

[45] Benjamin E. Mays's contribution to the discussion following Wilson's paper, 'The Negro Church and Education', in Holloway, ed., *Whither the Negro Church?*, 27.

[46] Carroll's contribution to the discussion following Haynes's paper, in Holloway, ed., *Whither the Negro Church?*, 29–30.

[47] Jerome Davis, Harry W. Roberts and E. F. Goin, 'Resolutions', in Holloway, ed., *Whither the Negro Church?*, 45–7, at 47.

Chi member, wrote that 'every Negro church must discover and develop a type of leadership that would do for America and the Negro race what Gandhi had done for India and what Jesus has done for the world.'[48] Carroll and his fellow seminarians were challenged to explore whether the praxis of Gandhian non-violence, a moral methodology embedded in interfaith sensibilities, might be harnessed to an African American religious heritage of pro-black advocacy. Notwithstanding these daring declarations, Carroll, a Methodist, entered the ministry in a denomination that, after 1939, consigned him to a racially restricted parish in the newly concocted Central Jurisdiction.[49]

The discursive event that occurred at Yale Divinity School in 1931 paralleled a more substantial examination of Gandhian non-violence at the School of Religion at Howard University. This developing discourse, which extended through the 1930s and into the ensuing decade, included the university president and successive divinity deans and faculty. Like his counterparts at Yale, Mordecai W. Johnson, a Harvard trained Baptist minister and the first African American president of Howard University, linked Gandhi, a holy man, to the black struggle for freedom. In 1930, Johnson observed that the 'movement for the redemption of the Indian people, through the endurance of suffering' possessed spiritual and political relevance to African Americans.[50] To highlight this observation, Johnson 'celebrat[ed] Gandhi's example' at Howard's 1934 religious convocation.[51] Moreover, Johnson made strategic appointments of Benjamin E. Mays and William Stuart Nelson as deans of the School of Religion, and Howard Thurman as dean of Rankin Chapel, which not only shaped the training and formation of black clergy but also sustained Johnson's Gandhian advocacy.[52] Mays, for example, envisaged the seminary as a venue to educate what Randal M. Jelks has described as 'an insurgent Negro professional clergy'; that is, he saw 'a professionally trained Negro clergy as educated religious leaders and insurgent militants to defeat Jim Crow laws and

[48] Ibid.

[49] Ibid. 29, 47.

[50] Thomas John Edge, 'The Social Responsibility of the Administrator: Mordecai Wyatt Johnson and the Dilemma of Black Leadership, 1890–1976' (PhD thesis, University of Massachusetts Amherst, 2008), 251.

[51] Ibid. 252.

[52] Ibid.

customs.'[53] Additionally, in 1936, Mays travelled as part of a delegation to attend the World Conference of the YMCA in Mysore (India). The trip permitted him to spend time with Gandhi, who told him that non-violence 'must be practiced in absolute love and without hate.' Non-violence, Gandhi added, was a moral methodology that cares for 'the welfare of the opponent' as well as for that of the cause's adherents, according to interfaith mandates on non-retaliation.[54]

Similarly, Thurman headed a delegation in 1935 and 1936 to the Asian subcontinent that included his wife, Sue Bailey Thurman, and Edward G. Carroll, now a pastor, and Carroll's wife, Phenola. Their itinerary included stops in India on the Friendship Pilgrimage sponsored by the World Student Christian Federation. Gandhi granted the Thurmans an audience, in which the Indian leader enquired in depth about the African American predicament. Gandhi also declared that the global dissemination of non-violence would be delivered by way of the black freedom struggle.[55]

William Stuart Nelson, who succeeded Mays as dean of Howard University's School of Religion, spent nearly a year in India in 1946 and 1947 on a sabbatical fellowship sponsored by the American Friends Service Committee. His encounter with Gandhi coincided with the outbreak of interreligious violence between Hindus and Muslims vying for influence in a newly independent India. Disappointed that his erstwhile followers so easily resorted to violence, Gandhi confessed to Nelson that non-violence was an inner spiritual discipline rather than a strategy. 'It is only the strong who are capable of non-violence,' he told Nelson. Non-violence drew from 'the soldiering and discipline required by one whose only

[53] Randal M. Jelks, 'Benjamin Elijah Mays and the Creation of an Insurgent Negro Professional Clergy', *AME Church Review* 118/387 (2002), 32–8, at 32 and 35; compare also Dennis C. Dickerson, 'African American Religious Intellectuals and the Theological Foundations of the Civil Rights Movement, 1930–55', *ChH* 74 (2005), 217–35, at 224. For Mays's approach, see, for example, Benjamin E. Mays, 'Future Leadership of the Negro Church', in Holloway, ed., *Whither the Negro Church?*, 39–42, and compare the descriptions of Mays's time as dean of Howard University's School of Religion and as president of Morehouse School of Religion in Benjamin E. Mays, *Born to Rebel: An Autobiography* (New York, 1971; repr. Athens, GA, 1987 and 2003), 139–48, 234–40. References in this article are to the 1987 edition.

[54] Mays, *Born to Rebel*, 154–7, quotations at 156.

[55] Howard Thurman, *With Head and Heart: The Autobiography of Howard Thurman* (New York, 1979), 132.

weapon is love.'[56] These black religious intellectuals, in what they gleaned from Gandhi, incubated a discursive learning environment at Howard that readied seminary graduates for insurgent activism against Jim Crow. In various vocational spheres, those inspired by Johnson or taught by Mays, Thurman and Nelson led non-violent movements to end the dehumanization of African Americans. Moreover, this intergenerational transfer from professors to their students provided intellectual and organizational leadership to a wide range of grassroots civil rights initiatives.[57]

Johnson, Mays, Thurman and Nelson fully realized that reckoning with anti-black racism in the United States paralleled resistance against colonialism in India and that country's grappling with its own caste system, which was not unlike 'the hierarchies of color among African Americans', according to Nico Slate.[58] When Mays met Gandhi, he challenged the Indian leader on whether he would crusade against 'the hard, rigid lines that had developed among various castes in India,' especially the scourge of 'untouchability.'[59] Gerald Horne contrasted the transnational issue of caste as 'the bilateral relationship between an oppressed national minority in a budding superpower and the world's largest colony' that Great Britain exploited since the nineteenth century.[60] Daniel Immerwahr examined discourse about these parallels of caste and colony as 'Indianizing race in the United States.'[61] African American religious intellectuals deepened the discourse about caste and colony through their Gandhian encounters. In doing so, they tracked the parallel involvement of Methodist Episcopal Church missionary E. Stanley Jones, whose long residence in India led to his transnational engagements with non-violence through integrated ashrams and support for the nascent black civil rights movement.[62]

[56] William Stuart Nelson, 'The Gandhi I Knew', *Friend Intelligencer* 15 (1948), 282–3.

[57] Daniel B. Cornfield et al., 'The Making of a Movement: An Intergenerational Mobilization Model of the Nonviolent Nashville Civil Rights Movement', *Social Science History* 45 (2021), 469–94.

[58] Nico Slate, *Colored Cosmopolitanism: The Shared Struggle for Freedom in the United States and India* (Cambridge, MA, and London, 2012), 79.

[59] Mays, *Born to Rebel*, 156–7.

[60] Gerald Horne, *The End of Empires: African Americans and India* (Philadelphia, PA, 2008), 15.

[61] Daniel Immerwahr, 'Caste or Colony?: Indianizing Race in the United States', *Modern Intellectual History* 4 (2007), 275–301.

[62] David R. Swartz, 'Christ of the American Road: E. Stanley Jones, India, and Civil Rights', *Journal of American Studies* 51 (2017), 1117–38.

Concurrent with transnational discourse about caste and colonialism among African American religious intellectuals, trans-oceanic interactions between them and their counterparts abroad elicited their ecclesial and intellectual involvements. In 1948, for instance, Mays was present in Amsterdam for the launch of the World Council of Churches. During the assembly, he proposed the strengthening of a resolution about race to say that the WCC condemned racism and urged that churches should extinguish this ungodly ideology within their ranks.[63] African American Methodists, since their participation in the 1881 Oecumenical Methodist Conference in London, had engaged in discourse about race in transatlantic contexts and the racist record of white Methodists in their interactions with Wesleyan blacks. Bishop William J. Walls, of the African Methodist Episcopal Zion Church, declared that the 1951 World Methodist Conference in Oxford (England) had 'the most segregated programme' ever, with no African Americans programmed for addresses on major topics.[64] Also during this period, the African Methodist Episcopal Church reckoned with international issues pertaining to white settler colonialism in South Africa. In fear of a potentially insurgent African American bishop presiding in the jurisdiction, the apartheid government compelled the denomination in 1956 to elect an indigenous prelate to supervise the hundreds of churches, schools and clinics among the nation's disenfranchised coloured and black populations.[65]

Civil rights activists in the United States during the 1950s and 1960s drew inspiration and instruction from this earlier generation of African American religious intellectuals.[66] Their pedagogical texts, all published in the late 1940s, generated ideas about how religion could inform the black struggle for racial equality, and how the moral methodologies that lay in non-violence could aid in achieving this objective. Benjamin E. Mays's *Seeking to be Christian in Race Relations* (1946),[67] William Stuart Nelson's *The Christian Way in*

[63] Mays, *Born to Rebel*, 256–8.
[64] William J. Walls, *The African Methodist Episcopal Zion Church: Reality of the Black Church* (Charlotte, NC, 1974), 481.
[65] Dennis C. Dickerson, *The African Methodist Episcopal Church: A History* (New York and Cambridge, 2020), 489–91.
[66] See Dickerson, 'African American Religious Intellectuals', esp. 229, 233–5.
[67] Benjamin E. Mays, *Seeking to be Christian in Race Relations* (New York, 1946; repr. 1952, 1957 and 1964).

Race Relations (1948),[68] and Howard Thurman's *Jesus and the Disinherited* (1949)[69] all functioned as foundational primers for critiquing American racism and dismantling the societal structures that sustained this pernicious ideology.

Two influences, one historic and the other contemporary, shaped the works produced by these intellectuals. Mays, Nelson and Thurman, all black Baptist ministers, were heirs to a tradition of religious insurgency against slavery, segregation and other mechanisms that subordinated African Americans. From the inception of the 'peculiar institution' in the seventeenth century, until its destruction in the mid-nineteenth century, abolitionists, both white and black, invoked biblical authority to inveigh against the bondage and inhuman treatment of African Americans.[70] In the decades after the American Civil War (1861–5), especially as Jim Crow became concretized in the early decades of the twentieth century, black preachers and their allies persistently pursued various strategies to oppose oppressive racial practices and violence against African Americans, and to affirm their humanity and their right to civic equality. African American religious intellectuals of the 1930s and 1940s embraced this protest heritage and situated their texts in this tradition.

Moreover, the inspiring and impressive example of Gandhi and his anti-colonial resistance to British imperialism in India became powerfully instructive to Mays, Nelson and Thurman as they pondered activist strategies to upend Jim Crow in the American South.

Though these thinkers needed no instruction about the evil of racism and its impact, they lacked an effective praxis to bring about the demise of this hegemonic ideology. Gandhi, through the philosophy and practice of satyagraha, provided an answer. How could Gandhian non-violence, so successfully deployed against the British in India,

[68] William Stuart Nelson, ed., *The Christian Way in Race Relations* (New York, 1948).

[69] Howard Thurman, *Jesus and the Disinherited* (New York, 1949).

[70] See H. Shelton Smith, *In His Image, but … Racism in Southern Religion, 1780–1910* (Durham, NC, 1972); Drew Gilpin Faust, 'Evangelicalism and the Meaning of the Proslavery Argument: The Reverend Thornton Stringfellow of Virginia', *Virginia Magazine of History and Biography* 85 (1977), 3–17; Eugene D. Genovese and Elizabeth Fox-Genovese, 'The Religious Ideals of Southern Slave Society', *Georgia Historical Quarterly* 70 (1986), 1–16; idem, 'The Divine Sanction of Social Order: Religious Foundations of the Southern Slaveholders' World View', *Journal of the American Academy of Religion* 55 (1982), 211–34.

inform their understanding of Christianity and transform this religion into a potent force against segregation, the American version of apartheid?[71]

These African American religious intellectuals, because they were morally and intellectually stimulated after meeting Gandhi, engaged in a reinterpretation of his non-violent precepts and praxis and adapted them to the normative beliefs of Christianity. As agents of Gandhian diffusion to the United States, they were challenged by Gandhi's embrace of Jesus as a moral teacher and by the unrealized possibilities that lay in Christian opposition to colonial and racial hegemony. As a result of these interactions, Mays, Nelson and Thurman enculturated Gandhian non-violence by inserting it into an African American religious context and incorporating it into crucial texts that informed the ideas and strategies of the civil rights movement in the United States. As Scalmer puts it, in the course of 'the transnational career of Gandhism', it was several times 'reshaped' to fit another venue or struggle far-away from its Indian progenitor.[72]

In the process, Gandhism was Christianized and made palatable to African Americans anxious to overthrow the Jim Crow regime reigning within American society. Mays, Nelson and Thurman, in producing three seminal texts, contributed to the intellectual foundation of the modern civil rights movement. Mays was first among his colleagues with his 1946 publication, *Seeking to be Christian in Race Relations*. Faced with racism, those who wanted to eliminate its effects should explore, Mays believed, the ways in which Christianity can form 'the basis for good relations.'[73] In God's relationship to humankind, he was convinced, lay a basis for human interaction. Because of human dependence on the Creator, who embodies justice, mercy and love, all people can realize their equality with each other in the divine

[71] Apartheid was imposed in South Africa in 1948.

[72] Sean Scalmer, *Gandhi in the West: The Mahatma and the Rise of Radical Protest* (Cambridge, 2001), 5. An example of Gandhian diffusion into the African American context can be seen in Larry W. Isaac et al., '"Movement Schools" and Dialogical Diffusion of Nonviolent Praxis: Nashville Workshops in the Southern Civil Rights Movement', in Sharon Erikson Nepstad and Lester R. Kurtz, eds, *Nonviolent Conflict and Civil Resistance*, Research in Social Movements, Conflict and Change 34 (Bingley, 2012), 155–84.

[73] Mays, *Seeking to be Christian in Race Relations*, x. References in this article are to the 1957 edition.

order. Moreover, 'love of God and love of man [are] inseparable.'[74] These relationships are concretized in Jesus because 'he combined in his person, life and religion the perfect relationship between himself and God, and between himself and man.'[75] Mays argued for 'a god-man-centered religion' which recognizes that 'man's good relationship to God is definitely dependent upon and conditioned by man's good relationship to man.'[76]

Additionally, two sections in Mays's book showed the congruence between Christianity and Gandhi's Hindu-derived precepts and praxis.[77] Fundamental to Gandhian non-violence is ahimsa, a Sanskrit term which forbids harm to others, even one's enemies, because such assaults are also self-destructive. Mays cited Matthew 5: 43–5, the New Testament passage in which Jesus instructed his followers to 'love your enemy', arguing that God blesses all with the sunshine and rain, whether such persons are good or bad, everybody is blessed with God's beneficence.[78] Mays's work reflected Gandhian influence in asserting that Jesus as 'our guide for Christian living' requires action.[79] Belief mandates a response to evil. Mays declared: 'if we say we believe in justice for all people, irrespective of race, and proceed to segregate, deny the ballot to, deny jobs to, and discriminate educationally against certain groups in the population on the grounds of race, we do not really believe in justice.'[80] The 'true Christian,' he said, 'will always find ways to act', either individually or through collective actions to attain justice.[81]

In 1948, Nelson published a compelling collection of essays, *The Christian Way in Race Relations*. In this volume, 'the result of a co-operative enterprise' of the Institute of Religion sponsored by Howard University, Nelson, Mays, Thurman and ten other black religious intellectuals showed 'the central role … the Christian way of life should play in the solution of these problems' of race relations

[74] Ibid. 16 (chapter title).
[75] Ibid. 25–6.
[76] Ibid. 24 (chapter title) and 26.
[77] Mays mentions Gandhi specifically: ibid. 13–14, 80.
[78] Ibid. 27.
[79] Ibid. 72.
[80] Ibid. 76.
[81] Ibid. 77.

in American society.[82] Nelson saw urgency in efforts to demonstrate the relevance of religion to actions and strategies aimed at ending the second-class citizenship of blacks.[83] He worried that the paucity of trained black clergy signified 'the irrelevance which young Negro men [and, we would add, women – DD] feel religion bears to the major concerns of their lives.'[84] Hence, Christianity should be energized, especially in the sphere of race relations and shown to be an important force in changing the racial status quo.

Nelson and his colleagues developed a discursive atmosphere in African American ecclesial and academic circles that connected to succeeding cohorts of clergy activists. These black religious intellectuals, through their writings, lectures and sermons in innumerable church and campus settings, and through ongoing interactions with insurgents from the 1930s to the 1960s, introduced them to Gandhian non-violence and other moral methodologies through intergenerational transmissions. Because Nelson knew the power of Gandhi's religious commitments, he had mobilized colleagues to reflect on how Christianity in the black freedom struggle could harness the same moral methodologies that facilitated anti-colonial victories in India. George D. Kelsey suggested guidelines for morally based protest activities. 'When a Negro,' he noted, 'makes a needed appeal for justice or engages in action leading thereto, he ought to examine all his relationships and see if they are just from his side.'[85] Echoing Gandhi, Kelsey also said: 'the method of protest or restraint must be such as not to injure.'[86] The system that the opponent defends, and not the protector of that structure, should be the target. The protester 'must be sure that it is democracy which he seeks and not the substitution of one tyranny for another.'[87] Kelsey's latter point resonated with Mays, who affirmed in his contribution that 'Mahatma

[82] William Stuart Nelson, 'Preface', in idem, ed., *The Christian Way in Race Relations* (New York, 1948), vii–ix, at vii. Contributors included Frank T. Wilson and George Edmund Hayes, who had spoken at the 'Whither the Negro Church?' conference. One woman contributed: Marion Cuthbert, on 'The Role of the Young Women's Christian Association', in Nelson, ed., *The Christian Way in Race Relations*, 162–82.

[83] William Stuart Nelson, 'Critical Issues in America's Race Relations Today', in idem, ed., *The Christian Way in Race Relations*, 3–25, esp. 20–3.

[84] Nelson, 'Critical Issues in America's Race Relations Today', 20.

[85] George D. Kelsey, 'The Christian Way in Race Relations', in Nelson, ed., *The Christian Way in Race Relations*, 29–48, at 43.

[86] Ibid.

[87] Ibid.

Gandhi was eminently correct when he insisted that the Hindus must get rid of untouchability and make the relationship between the various castes of India just and humane if they were to be justified in their insistence that England cease oppressing them and give them complete autonomy.'[88] He challenged 'the Negro Christian' to 'rise above hate', and 'the white Christian' to 'order his life progressively in the light of truth.'[89] Frank T. Wilson, the YMCA official who had arranged the India trip on which Howard and Sue Bailey Thurman met with Gandhi, commended the student associations for their 'work on the raw edge of racial injustice.'[90] He stressed their initiatives 'to eliminate practices of segregation and discrimination on college campuses as well as in non-academic communities.'[91] They also fought against poll taxes and lynching, and supported a permanent Fair Employment Practices Committee to end job discrimination.[92] Wilson suggested that the organization should intensify initiatives to racially integrate on all levels of its own organization and 'provide educational leadership in the eradication of racial prejudice.'[93] Though moral suasion was one method that some contributors recommended to improve race relations, Harry V. Richardson strongly endorsed church leaders who proposed that ecclesial federations should activate social action committees to work against black subordination in a world 'at war with flagrant vicious un-Christian forces'.[94]

George E. Haynes went further than Wilson and Richardson. A veteran official in the National Urban League and in the Federal Council of Churches, Haynes understood better than most the limits of the institutional initiatives of white-led organizations in spearheading transformational change for African Americans. Though convinced that religion should influence social movements, he was supportive of new vehicles through which religious ideas could

88 Benjamin E. Mays, 'The Obligations of the Individual Christian', in Nelson, ed., *The Christian Way in Race Relations*, 209–25, at 217.

89 Ibid. 224.

90 Frank T. Wilson, 'The Role of the Young Men's Christian Association', in Nelson, ed., *The Christian Way in Race Relations*, 143–61, at 159.

91 Ibid.

92 Ibid.

93 Ibid. 160–1.

94 Harry V. Richardson, 'What Can the Church Do?', in Nelson, ed., *The Christian Way in Race Relations*, 111–27, at 125, 126–7.

operate. Nelson invited his contribution and commentary about how Gandhian non-violence was influencing a nascent U.S. civil rights movement.[95] Haynes noted that alongside educational programmes and policy decisions, such as refusing to hold meetings in segregated hotels, 'public protest and agitation through mass meetings, picketing, newspapers, the radio, and other means have also been a part or all of the activities of many organizations.'[96] These methods, known as 'direct action', while influenced by the tactics of labour unions and left wing groups, also drew from the example of Gandhian non-violence in India. Similarly, Randolph's MOWM borrowed from Gandhian techniques in mass grassroots mobilization and represented a 'nonviolent direct action' organization. Farmer's CORE was commended for 'developing disciplined, nonviolent action against the color line.'[97] Haynes's contribution to Nelson's volume thus tracked the diffusion of Gandhian non-violence into the African American context.

Thurman's *Jesus and the Disinherited*, released in 1949, had been some time in the making, having evolved out of previous intellectual encounters. The first was an article entitled 'Good News for the Underprivileged' that Thurman had originally published in 1932 and then delivered as a speech in 1935.[98] Then, while Thurman was in Ceylon, a Hindu asked him how African Americans could embrace Christianity when so many of its practitioners had been either slave traders or slave owners. Moreover, this Hindu asserted, Christian churches in the United States were racially segregated and included members who participated in the lynching of blacks.[99] Thurman, who had no immediate answer to this probing inquiry, was challenged by the question of what the teachings of Jesus have to say to 'the masses of men [and women who] live with their backs against the wall', who included 'the poor, the disinherited,

95 George Edmund Haynes, 'The Role of Social and Civic Organizations and Agencies', in Nelson, ed., *The Christian Way in Race Relations*, 183–205.

96 Ibid. 196–8, quotation at 198.

97 Ibid. 199. Although Haynes does not actually mention Gandhi here, the influence is clear.

98 Howard Thurman, 'Good News for the Underprivileged', in *The Papers of Howard Washington Thurman*, ed. Walter Earl Fluker, 5 vols (Columbia, SC, 2009–19), 1: 263–70, originally published in *Religion and Life* 4 (1935), 403–9. See also Howard Thurman, *Jesus and the Disinherited*, new edn (Boston, MA, 1996), xx, and Vincent Harding, 'Foreword', in ibid. vii–xviii, at ix–x.

99 Thurman, *Jesus and the Disinherited*, 3–5.

the dispossessed.'[100] Having already concluded that the religion of Jesus paid special attention to marginalized peoples, he began to think about how Christianity could speak to oppressed African Americans and others similarly situated despite its association with slavery, colonialism and other hegemonic systems. Thurman elaborated on this theme in a 1948 lecture at Samuel Huston College in Austin (Texas), and this presentation was published a year later as *Jesus and the Disinherited.*[101]

Thurman described Jesus in his historical context and noted characteristics that unmistakably linked him to the disadvantaged during his era and beyond. In examining him 'against the background of his own age and people,' Thurman aimed to explain that Jesus had much to say 'to those who stand … with their backs against the wall.'[102] Three attributes tied Jesus to the lower stratum of his society and to others in a similar circumstance elsewhere in time and place. Jesus's Jewishness was the first characteristic. 'It is impossible,' said Thurman, 'for Jesus to be understood outside the sense of community which Israel held with God.'[103] Christians, he added, have 'tended to overlook' Jesus's Jewish origins as 'he went about doing his Father's business', becoming the central figure within this new religion, Christianity.[104] That he was Jewish identifies him within a racial category that has often been despised and degraded, much like the African American group to which Thurman himself belonged. In this respect, Jesus was one of the disinherited.

Moreover, 'Jesus was a poor Jew.' Thurman declared: 'the economic predicament with which he was identified in birth placed him initially with the great mass of men on the earth', for 'the masses of the people are poor.'[105] Thurman suggested:

> if we dare take the position that in Jesus there was not at work some radical destiny, it would be safe to say that in his poverty he was more truly Son of man than he would have been if the incident of family or birth had made him a rich son of Israel.[106]

[100] Ibid. 3.
[101] Ibid. xx; Harding, 'Foreword', x–xi.
[102] Thurman, *Jesus and the Disinherited*, 11.
[103] Ibid. 5–6.
[104] Ibid. 6.
[105] Ibid. 7.
[106] Ibid.

Born in a barn, the son of a carpenter, he became a preacher of whom it was reported in Mark's Gospel that 'the common people heard him gladly' (Mark 12: 37) [AV]. These attributes unmistakably tied Jesus to the mass of poor humanity.

Finally, 'Jesus was a member of a minority group in the midst of a larger dominant and controlling group.'[107] Rome ruled Palestine and its territorial possessions included peoples whom it colonized, exploited and even mocked for their religion and culture. Jews, among the various subject groups within the Roman Empire, nurtured their own insurgents who sought ways to end Rome's colonial hegemony. Thurman concluded: 'it is utterly fantastic to assume that Jesus grew to manhood untouched by the surging currents of the common life that made up the climate of Palestine.'[108]

Echoes of Gandhi in India, as well as of Jesus in Palestine, resonated through Thurman's provocative prose. Thurman also tried to explain what moral methodology should be chosen to challenge colonial hegemony, while preserving the moral integrity of insurgents. Armed resistance was unacceptable because it was 'a tragic last resort.'[109] In the earlier article that preceded the book, 'Good News for the Underprivileged', Thurman recognized that acquiescing to the violence of oppressors through 'the exercise of love' allowed 'the exploiters of the weak to keep them submissive and subservient.'[110] Jesus proposed instead that 'The Kingdom of Heaven is in us.'[111] Alternative citizenship in a divine sphere protected the oppressed from 'the three hounds of hell that track the trail of the disinherited', namely 'fear, hypocrisy, and hatred.'[112] As a part of God's kingdom, the haunting spectres of these predators 'need have no dominion' in the lives of the disadvantaged.[113] The inner being of the disinherited would be safeguarded from the physical and spiritual violence that colonizers imposed upon their subjects. Thurman highlighted in both Jesus and Gandhi the sacredness of their spiritual selves and their determined efforts to shield the core attributes of their humanity from the assaults of Roman and British hegemony. To follow their

[107] Ibid. 8.
[108] Ibid.
[109] Ibid. 15.
[110] Thurman, 'Good News for the Underprivileged', 268–9.
[111] Thurman, *Jesus and the Disinherited*, 17.
[112] Ibid. 19.
[113] Ibid.

path, Thurman said, was 'to be simply, directly truthful, whatever may be the cost in life, limb or security'.[114]

The ideas in these works by Mays, Nelson and Thurman diffused into the strategies and rhetoric of civil rights activists throughout the 1950s and 1960s, and converted their efforts into a non-violent movement in America. Non-violent precepts and praxis drew from interfaith sources and inserted religion into the core of the black freedom struggle. In a 1956 address immediately after the successful bus boycott in Montgomery (Alabama), for example, Martin Luther King, Jr, said that non-violent practitioners attempt 'never to defeat or to humiliate the opponent.'[115] Instead, the objective is 'to win (their) friendship and (their) understanding' and thus to achieve 'reconciliation'.[116] King also emphasized that non-violence 'does not seek merely to avoid external physical violence, but it seeks to avoid internal violence of spirit.'[117] The writings of George Kelsey and Thurman especially resonated in these King passages about love for the defenders of racial subjugation and the necessity of protecting the moral integrity of the activists' inner being while they opposed hegemonic forces. James M. Lawson, Jr, conducted non-violent workshops in Nashville (Tennessee) in 1958 and 1959, in which he instructed students from Fisk University, Tennessee Agricultural and Industrial University, American Baptist College, and Meharry Medical College, all local black institutions, in the techniques of non-violence. Lawson introduced these students to Thurman's *The Growing Edge* (1956) as part of his workshop curriculum.[118] Both King and Lawson believed that Thurman's works helped in training the students of non-violence and imbuing them with spiritual and

[114] For Gandhi, see ibid. 59–60, quotation at 60.

[115] Martin Luther King, Jr, 'Non-Aggression Procedures to Interracial Harmony. Address Delivered at the American Baptist Assembly and American Home Mission Agencies Conference, 23 July 1956', in *The Papers of Martin Luther King, Jr*, 3: *Birth of a New Age, December 1955–December 1956*, ed. Clayborne Carson (Berkeley, CA, 1997), 321–8, at 326.

[116] Ibid.

[117] Ibid.

[118] See the bibliography in James M. Lawson, Jr, 'Nonviolence: A Relevant Power for Constructive Social Change', in Nashville, TN, Vanderbilt University, Jean and Alexander Heard Library, Special Collections, Fisk Institute (of) Race Folder, James M. Lawson, Jr, Papers, Box 38, FOR III, NV Workshops, 1958; compare also Peter Eisenstadt, *Against the Hounds of Hell: A Life of Howard Thurman* (Charlottesville, VA, 2021), 272.

strategic sensibilities to upend American apartheid. Indeed, King kept a copy of Thurman's *Jesus and the Disinherited* in his briefcase.[119] These works by Mays, Nelson and Thurman drew from Gandhi's philosophy and praxis of non-violence and provided an intellectual foundation for the United States civil rights movement. By integrating Gandhian satyagraha into their reading of Christianity, these African American religious intellectuals helped to develop 'a force more powerful' – or, as Martin Luther King, Jr, put it, 'a love that can change individuals. It can change nations. It can change conditions' – to destroy structures that supported Jim Crow in American society.[120] Gandhi's moral methodology, through a process of diffusion and intergenerational transfer, informed discourse among advocates of pacifism and non-violence. Interlocutors who engaged these tenets and tactics, in varying timetables, became settled adherents to these beliefs.[121]

African American religious intellectuals in this way provided a religious scaffolding for grassroots activists, who, through bus boycotts, sit-ins and other techniques of direct-action resistance, advanced the non-violent movement in the United States. Bus boycotts in Baton Rouge, Montgomery and Tallahassee spurred black Southern insurgency in the 1950s. The resistance to segregated public transportation became foundational to a wider militancy against Jim Crow.[122] The onslaught of bus boycotts against the transit structure of segregation owed their grounding to black churches. Though newly established organizations coordinated the bus boycotts, they relied on black congregations as venues for rallies and sources of funding.[123] Moreover, black clergy, protected by their status from financial and vocational intimidation by segregationist whites, provided independent leadership to their now mobilized communities.[124]

[119] Harding, 'Foreword', xii.

[120] King, 'Non-Aggression Procedures to Interracial Harmony', 327. For the (perhaps apocryphal) Gandhian phrase 'a force more powerful', see Peter Ackerman and Jack DuVall, *A Force More Powerful: A Century of Nonviolent Conflict* (New York, 2000), and David Cortright, *Peace: A History of Movements and Ideas* (Cambridge, 2008), 211–32 (ch. 10, 'A force more powerful').

[121] Isaac et al., 'Movement Schools', 156–8, 164–72.

[122] Aldon D. Morris, *The Origins of the Civil Rights Movement: Black Communities Organizing for Change* (New York, 1984), 17–25.

[123] Ibid. 21–5, 40–76.

[124] Ibid. 19–20, 73–6.

Though blacks in Baton Rouge (Louisiana) persuaded the city council in 1953 to permit seating on a first come first serve basis, white bus drivers resisted Ordinance 222 and staged a strike aimed at the company's overwhelmingly African American patrons. After the drivers gained support from the Louisiana attorney general in opposing the relaxing of segregation, the Rev. T. J. Jemison, the pastor of Mt Zion Baptist Church, called for a strike of patrons. With solid support exercised through the United Defense League, the six-day boycott achieved an agreement of no reserved seats for whites. That Jemison's congregation mobilized the financing of the boycott to pay protective personnel and to fund alternative transportation for bus riders showed that this non-violent initiative enjoyed the blessing of organized black Christianity.[125]

Similarly, in Montgomery (Alabama), starting in December 1955, a bus boycott ignited by segregationist policies against a black passenger, Rosa Parks, stirred black non-violent resistance. The Montgomery Improvement Association, just like Baton Rouge's United Defense League, mobilized a united African American population to withdraw patronage from the local bus company. The city's black churches were crucial as organizational and funding sites for the 381-day boycott which lasted into late 1956. Religious influence, both clerical and lay, spread a canopy of sacralization over this anti-racist movement. Martin Luther King, Jr, the newly arrived pastor at Dexter Avenue Baptist Church in Montgomery, became the spokesman for the year-long non-violent protest. His numerous addresses included clear articulations of Gandhian principles of love, non-retaliation and a fortified spiritual discipline that yielded courage and persistence. This Gandhian language reflected his reading about the Indian leader; he had also heard a lecture about Gandhi, who had inspired Mordecai W. Johnson. Mentorship from his Morehouse president, Benjamin E. Mays, and the writings of Howard Thurman, especially *Jesus and the Disinherited*, refined King's education in non-violence.[126]

Equally significant was the dignified defiance of Rosa Parks, whose refusal to move from the arbitrarily declared white section of the bus spurred the boycott. Her determined resistance, a product of dangerous activism in defending black women victimized by racialized

[125] Ibid. 17–25.

[126] For the Montgomery bus boycott, see ibid. 51–63; compare also Harvard Sitkoff, *King: Pilgrimage to the Mountaintop* (New York, 2008), 45–8.

sexual violence and pressing for black voting rights, also drew on deep religious convictions. Parks, a stewardess at Montgomery's St Paul AME Church, regularly assisted in preparing the monthly eucharist at this Wesleyan congregation. The scriptural holiness enacted through personal renewal at the communion table spilled over into a resulting impulse for social holiness that aimed at societal renewal, similar to the aims that the AME founder Richard Allen had pursued through African Methodism. Parks's activism derived from these religious tenets and converted her bus protest into a sacred onslaught against societal sin and hypocrisy.[127]

The bus boycott in Tallahassee (Florida) started in May 1956, when two female students from Florida Agricultural and Mechanical College defied segregation and refused to give up their seats to whites. Fellow students mobilized and refused to ride on the buses. Thereafter, the wider black community joined them in the boycott and two black clergy assumed leadership through the Inter-Civic Council (ICC). A Transportation Committee was formed which developed alternatives to patronizing the buses. As in Baton Rouge and Montgomery, black churches generated funding for expenses incurred by avoiding public transit. C. K. Steele, the president of the local branch of the National Association for the Advancement of Colored People (NAACP) and pastor of Bethel Missionary Baptist Church, served as the head of the ICC and led the effort that bankrupted the bus company. During the boycott, James Hudson, chaplain at Florida A&M University and president of the Interdenominational Ministerial Alliance, conducted sessions on non-violence.[128] According to Larry O. Rivers, one of Hudson's biographers, 'a "new social awakening"' revealed by the boycott showed the potential for religiously inspired non-violence 'to overcome racism, violence, and fear that perpetuated Jim Crow segregation in Florida's capital city.'[129]

Martin Luther King, Jr, moulded these black church-based local movements into a regional organization to penetrate the wall of segregation in the system's vulnerable venues. In 1957, the Southern

[127] Dennis C. Dickerson, *African Methodism and its Wesleyan Heritage: Reflections on AME Church History* (Nashville, TN, 2009), 176–84.

[128] For the Tallahassee bus boycott, see Morris, *Origins of the Civil Rights Movement*, 63–8.

[129] Larry O. Rivers, '"A New Social Awakening": James Hudson, Florida A. & M. University's Religious Life Program, and the 1956 Tallahassee Bus Boycott', *Florida Historical Quarterly* 95 (2017), 325–55, at 355.

Leadership Conference (SLC) on Transportation and Nonviolent Integration was formed in Atlanta. King, the president of the SLC, was joined by Jemison and Steele, the respective leaders of bus boycotts in Baton Rouge and Tallahassee, as officers in what then became the forerunner group to the Southern Christian Leadership Conference (SCLC). The SCLC, in affirming the humanity of African Americans and in defiance of segregationist hypocrisy, put the black church front and centre in the African American freedom struggle. Alden Morris has called the SCLC 'the decentralized political arm of the black church.'[130]

Though the SCLC was closely linked to African American churches, the newly formed group also reached into a sphere in which the NAACP was already engaged. That organization's legal program and legislative lobbying, its officials believed, required the endorsement and financial support of the black religious community. In 1946, the NAACP's church committee had become a fully-fledged Church Affairs Department under the leadership of Walter P. Offutt, Jr, a Baptist minister who had been involved in the desegregation of public libraries in Louisville (Kentucky). He thought that 'if the social justice program of the NAACP can be combined with the religious ideals of our churches … we shall have a power for freedom that cannot be ignored' and the black freedom struggle would have greater success.[131] At a time when Mays, Thurman and Nelson were publishing major works that buttressed what Offutt was articulating, this meant that the NAACP was in step with these African American religious intellectuals. Another inflection point for the department occurred in 1957, just as SCLC was being launched. Roy Wilkins, the NAACP executive secretary, recruited Edward J. Odom, Jr, an AME minister who was active in the NAACP, to head the Church Affairs Department.[132] Wilkins and Bishop Stephen Gill Spottswood of the AME Zion Church and newly elected to the

[130] Morris, *Origins of the Civil Rights Movement*, 77–99, quotation at 77 (in the chapter title: 'The SCLC: The Decentralized Political Arm of the Black Church').

[131] Quoted in Tuck, 'The Doubts of Their Fathers', 676.

[132] Roy Wilkins to Edward J. Odom, Jr, 2 April 1957, as cited in: Washington, DC, Library of Congress, NAACP Administrative File, 1956–65, Group III, Box A312, General Office File, Folder 5, Staff Adm, Odom, Edward J., 1957–65, 'Biographical Sketch – Reverend Edward J. Odom, Jr.'; Library of Congress, MSS, Group II, Bd. of Directors, Spottswood, Box A32, Adm. File, 'New Chief of the NAACP'; Library of Congress, Manuscript Division, Records of the NAACP.

NAACP national board of directors, were sceptical of King's call for black churches to affiliate with SCLC, saying that it was a federal court case, Browder vs Gayle (1956), which the NAACP had sponsored, that brought victory to the Montgomery bus boycott.[133] Despite intergroup tensions, Odom addressed the 1962 convention of King's organization in Birmingham (Alabama), saying that: 'the NAACP shares with SCLC a high regard for the role that organized religious groups play in the quest for Justice, Freedom, and equality of opportunity.'[134]

Wilkins, the son of an AME pastor, and Spottswood, who in 1961 would become chair of the National Board of the NAACP, were surely pleased that Odom's first order of business was a Churches for Freedom initiative aimed at generating religious support for the organization. In the late 1950s, the SCLC and the NAACP's Church Affairs Department embedded black religion into the effort to establish black citizenship and thus affirm blacks' humanity. In contrast, the white ecclesia, in some venues supportive, but in other spheres either indifferent or hostile, became marginal or irrelevant to movements to affirm the personhood of blacks and to abandon all hypocrisy about a fundamental Pauline tenet: God 'hath made of one blood all nations of men for to dwell on all the face of the earth' (Acts 17: 26) [AV].[135]

While the NAACP focused its Church Affairs Department on fundraising for black rights projects, the SCLC replicated its success in supporting other religiously based local movements elsewhere in the American South. Two black clergy from Nashville (Tennessee) attended the SCLC's founding meeting and returned home to establish the Nashville Christian Leadership Conference (NCLC). Kelly

[133] 'Rev. Walter Offutt Jr., 63, Dies: Human Rights Aide for State', *New York Times*, 8 October 1974; Roy Wilkins with Tom Mathews, *Standing Fast: The Autobiography of Roy Wilkins* (New York, 1982), 226–8, 269; Yvonne Ryan, *Roy Wilkins: The Quiet Revolutionary and the NAACP* (Lexington, KY, 2014), 58; Stephen Gill Spottswood, 'Freedom: The New Frontier', *AME Church Review* 78/209 (1961), 42–9, at 43, 46.

[134] Rev. Edward J. Odom, Jr, NAACP Church Secretary, 'Meeting [of the] Southern Christian Leadership Conference, Wednesday, September 26, 1962, Birmingham, Alabama': see Library of Congress, Records of the NAACP, Edward J. Odom, Jr, Group III, Box A 293.

[135] Richard R. Wright, Jr, *Encyclopaedia of African Methodism* (Philadelphia, PA, 1947), 297–8; 'Bishop Spottswood of NAACP Dies', *New York Times*, 3 December 1974; 'Along the N.A.A.C.P. Battlefront: 49th Annual Meeting', *The Crisis* 65/2 (1958), 106–13, at 113.

Miller Smith, pastor of First Baptist Church (Capitol Hill) and Andrew N. White, the executive secretary of the Department of Christian Education of the AME Church, were graduates of the School of Religion at Howard University. They had matriculated at different times in the early 1940s when the presence and pedagogy of Mays, Thurman and Nelson permeated the school's educational environment. In launching the NCLC in 1958, Smith and White joined with the newly arrived Vanderbilt University divinity student, James M. Lawson, Jr, in spearheading the Nashville movement.[136]

Lawson, a 'Jesus Follower' and a member of the pacifist Fellowship of Reconciliation (FOR), had been reared in an AME Zion congregation served by his father James M. Lawson, Sr, in Massillon (Ohio), and then in the Methodist Church's segregated Central Jurisdiction. Lawson's opposition to the Korean War (1950–3) and his refusal to submit to the United States military draft landed him in a federal prison. An early release permitted the Methodist Church to dispatch him to Nagpur (India) to teach and coach at Hislop College. He immersed himself in Gandhi's writings and was stirred by the news of the successful Montgomery bus boycott. After his return to the United States and matriculation at the School of Theology at Oberlin College, he met King in 1957 who was giving a lecture at the seminary. King urged Lawson to come South immediately to deploy his Gandhian expertise in the southern civil rights movement. As FOR's southern secretary, a position that he interspersed with his Vanderbilt studies, Lawson decided with Smith, White and the NCLC that students from Nashville's four institutions of higher education – American Baptist College, Fisk University, Meharry Medical College, and Tennessee Agricultural and Industrial University – should form the vanguard of a local non-violent movement. Lawson's NCLC non-violent workshops became the training venue for the planned action.[137]

Lawson, as serious a Gandhian non-violence theoretician and practitioner as King, probed even more deeply into this moral methodology as a religious tenet. In defining non-violence, Lawson declared:

[136] Dickerson, *African Methodism and its Wesleyan Heritage*, 185–8; Leila Meier, '"A Different Kind of Prophet": The Role of Kelly Miller Smith in the Nashville Civil Rights Movement, 1955–1960' (MA thesis, Vanderbilt University, 1991).

[137] Isaac et al., 'Movement Schools', 164–8; Dennis C. Dickerson, 'James M. Lawson, Jr.: Methodism, Nonviolence and the Civil Rights Movement', *Methodist History* 52 (2014), 168–86.

> Nonviolence is the aggressive, forgiving, patient, long-suffering Christ-like and Christ-commanded love or good-will for all human kind even in the face of tension, fear, hatred, or demonic evil. It is the readiness to absorb suffering. With forgiveness and courage rather than to inflict suffering on others. It is the desire to resist evil not by imitating the evil, but with good-will, with an effort to convert the evil-doer.[138]

While he viewed non-violence as biblically-based, Lawson, by now an ordained Methodist minister, acknowledged that it also reflected tenets from other world religions. He therefore considered non-violence to embody scriptural attributes authenticated through interfaith sources. 'Non-violence', he asserted, 'is first a way of life, a religious faith, steeped in the religious tradition of the world.'[139] Moreover, 'one can discover it explicitly in the doctrine of ahimsa (Hinduism), non-retaliation (Buddhism), [and the] doctrine of the Cross (Christianity). The spiritual giants of all ages concur in this concept.'[140] Lawson, like the previous and still-living generation of African American religious intellectuals who had encountered Gandhi, was foundationally Christian, but open to interfaith resources that reinforced his commitment to non-violence.

Students from Nashville's four black institutions of higher education were inspired and enthused by Lawson's workshops on non-violence. From 13 February until 10 May 1960, they sought to achieve the desegregation of downtown Nashville lunch counters. King described the Nashville movement as 'the best organized and the most disciplined in the Southland.'[141] Alumni and alumnae from the Lawson workshops seeded other Southern movements from the Freedom rides in 1961 to the Birmingham marches in 1963. Increasingly, Lawson insisted, as did his workshop student, John

[138] James M. Lawson, Jr, 'Non-Violence: A Relevant Power for Constructive Social Change', in Vanderbilt University, Jean and Alexander Heard Library, Special Collections, Fisk Institute [of] Race Folder, James M. Lawson, Jr, Papers, Box 38, FOR III, NV Workshops, 1958.

[139] Ibid.

[140] Ibid. See also Dennis C. Dickerson, 'William Stuart Nelson and the Interfaith Origins of the Civil Rights Movement', in R. Drew Smith, William Ackah and Antony G. Reddie, eds, *Churches, Blackness and Multiculturalism: Europe, Africa, and North America* (New York, 2014), 57–72.

[141] Martin Luther King, Address at Fisk University, 20 April 1960, as reported in *The Nashville Banner*, 21 April 1960, online at: <https://teva.contentdm.oclc.org/digital/collection/p15138coll18/id/973>, accessed 26 February 2024.

Lewis from American Baptist College, that their efforts should be understood as the non-violent movement in America. They could have added that their espousal of non-violence sacralized their initiatives in Nashville and elsewhere in the American South.[142]

The theologian and ethicist George D. Kelsey recognized and explored how legalized segregation in the American South and racial discrimination throughout American society derived from a counterfeit Christianity that posited that blacks were inferior to whites and that, as God's marred creation, they deserved neither rights nor recognition as full human beings. 'Since racism assumes some segments of humanity to be defective in essential being', Kelsey observed, 'and since for Christians all being is from the hand of God, racism alone among idolatries calls into question the divine creative action.'[143] Kelsey, who had been King's undergraduate professor at Morehouse College, also objected that 'racism is complete self-deification', which results in 'the worship of the creature instead of the Creator.'[144] This perverted and hypocritical religious system had corrupted Christianity; however, it was now encountering the alternative voices of black religious intellectuals and on-the-ground activists who challenged racist hypocrisy and affirmed the full humanity of African Americans. Mays, for example, asserted that 'no belief in God is adequate unless it is a belief in universal God, who is a God of justice, mercy and love. He cannot be a racial or national God. He cannot be a class God. He must be a God for all peoples.'[145] These declarations validated the humanity of all African Americans and exposed the hypocrisy of anti-black racism. Their engagement with Gandhian non-violence and their role in diffusing this moral methodology to the United States and grafting it to African American religious sensibilities enhanced and sacralized the black freedom struggle.

Mordecai W. Johnson had long been denouncing Caucasian Christian complicity with white racism in the United States in general and in the American South in particular. He noted that 'we have to distinguish between being a Christian and being religious. We don't have any experience with that distinction, because Christianity is of a

[142] Isaac et al., 'Movement Schools', 169–78; Dennis C. Dickerson, Telephone interview with James M. Lawson, Jr, 19 July 2020.

[143] George D. Kelsey, *Racism and the Christian Understanding of Man* (New York, 1965), 25.

[144] Ibid. 73.

[145] Mays, *Seeking to be Christian in Race Relations*, 7.

radical, universal ethic. It is founded upon the conviction of the sacred and inviolable worth of every human individual.'[146] Hence Johnson, at the 1957 Howard University commencement, in conferring an honorary degree upon Martin Luther King, Jr, commended his fellow Baptist minister, declaring: 'You have revitalized religion in America; you have given a weak and conforming Christian church a vision of a rising and going forth to become an instrument of redemptive social power.'[147] Johnson could have added to that roster other thinkers and activists whose religious convictions energized the nonviolent movement in America and sacralized the civil rights struggle in the United States.

[146] *Education For Freedom: The Leadership of Mordecai Wyatt Johnson, Howard University, 1926–1960* (Washington, DC, 1976), 37.
[147] Richard I. McKinney, *Mordecai: The Man and his Message. The Story of Mordecai Wyatt Johnson* (Washington, DC, 1997), 318.

Vocation, Hypocrisy and Secularization: Iris Murdoch and the Clergy of the Church of England

Peter Webster*
Chichester

This article examines the treatment of Anglican clergy in the novels of Iris Murdoch, setting this discussion in the context of Murdoch's own engagement with Christianity: one of sympathy without assent, yet with detailed knowledge of the secularizing theologies of the period. Clerical interventions in pastoral situations, politely tolerated in the earlier novels, are openly and robustly rejected in the later books. That pastoral care is, for Murdoch, vitiated by a desire for control, against which Murdoch set her ideal of self-emptying attention. Murdoch also dramatizes the loss of faith which forced, on some of the clergy, an inconsistency between outward speech and inner conviction. For some, the apparent hypocrisy is resolved by suicide or exile; for others, their vocation must continue as a witness to something absolute, even if they themselves can longer articulate its nature with any conviction. The Church remains necessary even if God himself is not.

Almost from its first emergence as an art form, the novel has provided a unique means by which the intricacies of human feeling and action have been dramatized and (subsequently) read and pondered by others. As a means of understanding the continuities and disjunctures between conscious belief, unconscious motivation and visible action, it provides a source for the historian that complements the diary or the memoir. The novel offers particularly rich material for the historian of hypocrisy since the very notion seems, in some way, to require a kind of narration; to conceive of an action or omission as hypocritical, we must be able to imagine and describe a better course of action.

Though born in Dublin, Iris Murdoch (1919–99) lived most of her life in England, publishing twenty-six novels, the first in 1954 and the last in 1995. For this longevity and volume alone, her career provides a case study in the changing treatment of particular themes in fiction. As well as this, Murdoch was perhaps unique among

* I am indebted to Jem Bloomfield and Miles Leeson for their comments on draft versions of this article. E-mail: peter@websterresearchconsulting.com.

Studies in Church History 60 (2024), 511–532 Published by Cambridge University Press on behalf of the Ecclesiastical History Society.
doi: 10.1017/stc.2024.20

novelists of her generation, and rare among novelists in general, in being a professional philosopher, with interests in matters of metaphysics and ethics that impinged directly on the concerns of the churches. As such, it is possible to read the fiction both on its own terms, and alongside her philosophy, both of which were in dialogue with the theology and philosophy of her time.[1] Murdoch's upbringing, and the spheres of acquaintance and friendship in which she continued to move, gave her work an undertow of religious concern: often faint but persistent nonetheless.[2] In her novels, the institutional churches are seldom shown to be anything but ridiculous or irrelevant, without purchase on the important issues in contemporary life. Yet many of Murdoch's characters who have ostensibly taken leave of the inherited faith of their class or family spend a good deal of their time discussing what is left.

As well as this, her novels are often peopled with characters from the monied, landed and professional parts of English society, and it was from these classes that the Anglican clergy were often drawn, and with whom they maintained a kind of social connection that was less common with clergy of other churches. Murdoch shows the reader a great many professionally Anglican characters: parish clergy; two of their bishops; the ordained headmaster of a public school; members of religious orders, as well as lay churchgoers. It was among these formers of opinion that much of the debate about the secularization of English society was conducted. As Murdoch's characters think and write and talk about the loss of faith and the difficulty of filling the hole where their God once was, the historian may overhear the reflections of one creative artist on the secularization of the society around her.

As well as this, Murdoch should be read as one of a generation of artists, some of whom had themselves lost faith, and some of whom had never possessed it, but who had all been formed within a class and culture that still took religious language and symbolism seriously.[3] Murdoch's own religious beliefs were complex, and are the subject

[1] On Murdoch's engagement with theology at large, see Paul Fiddes, *Iris Murdoch and the Others: A Writer in Dialogue with Theology* (London, 2021).

[2] Peter S. Hawkins, 'Iris Murdoch (1919–1999): Anglican Atheist', in Judith Maltby and Alison Shell, eds, *Anglican Women Novelists from Charlotte Bronte to P. D. James* (London, 2019), 161–73.

[3] See, for instance, the relationship between Benjamin Britten and Walter Hussey, Anglican patron of the arts: Peter Webster, *Church and Patronage in Twentieth-Century Britain: Walter Hussey and the Arts* (London, 2017), 60–1, 69–71.

of a considerable critical literature and, indeed, disagreement.[4] She was confirmed as an Anglican in 1934 while at Badminton School, but by the early 1950s described herself as 'more of a fellow-traveller than a Party member'.[5] Well before the beginning of her career as a novelist, she had firmly rejected the notion of a personal God and, with it, the Christological and soteriological apparatus of Christian theology. However, while Murdoch's philosophical writing is atheistic in character, rejecting the notion of God as active or purposeful, she held nonetheless to the reality of something beyond the physical world, which she understood in Platonic terms as 'the Good'.[6] The Good, though 'distant and apart', was nonetheless an 'active principle of truthful cognition and moral understanding in the soul' from which moral deliberation could stem.[7] However, all religious attempts to posit an externally-directed framework of purpose to human existence – to construct a consoling narrative to one's existence and ultimate destiny, from which to make sense of the contingent – was a false comfort.[8] It was necessary to be good, but good for nothing.

The particular interest of Murdoch for the religious historian, however, lies not so much in what she rejected, as what she tried to retain.[9] Her upbringing had given her a deep familiarity with religious

[4] See, for example, David Robjant, 'As a Buddhist Christian: the Misappropriation of Iris Murdoch', *Heythrop Journal* 52 (2011), 993–1008. See also Elizabeth Burns, 'Murdoch and Christianity', in Silvia Caprioglio Panizza and Mark Hopwood, eds, *The Murdochian Mind* (London, 2022), 382–93.

[5] Peter Conradi, *Iris Murdoch: A Life* (London, 2001), 64, 306.

[6] The early *locus classicus* for Murdoch's metaphysics is *The Sovereignty of Good* (London, 1970; repr. 2001). On Murdoch and Plato, see David Tracy, 'Iris Murdoch and the Many Faces of Platonism', in Maria Antonaccio and William Schweiker, eds, *Iris Murdoch and the Search for Human Goodness* (Chicago, IL, 1996), 54–75; Miles Leeson, *Iris Murdoch: Philosophical Novelist* (London, 2010), esp. 86–109. On Murdoch's understanding of God, see also Stephen Mulhall, '"All the world must be 'religious'": Iris Murdoch's Ontological Arguments', in Anne Rowe, ed., *Iris Murdoch: A Reassessment* (Basingstoke, 2007), 23–34; Andrew Gleeson, 'Iris Murdoch's Ontological Argument', in Nora Hämäläinen and Gillian Dooley, eds, *Reading Iris Murdoch's* Metaphysics as a Guide to Morals (Basingstoke, 2019), 195–208.

[7] Iris Murdoch, *Metaphysics as a Guide to Morals*, 2nd edn (London, 2003; first publ. 1992), 474.

[8] On the self-narration of the religious characters in *The Bell*, see Bran Nicol, 'The Curse of *The Bell*: The Ethics and Aesthetics of Narrative', in Rowe, ed., *Iris Murdoch: A Reassessment*, 100–11.

[9] The paragraphs that follow build upon the observations of Hawkins, 'Anglican Atheist', 161–3.

language and symbolism, and the regular practice of prayer and public worship, and the novels abound with descriptions of both. In the 1970s and 1980s, she spoke of having recovered a sympathy for religious belief which had been crowded out to a certain extent during her engagement with Marx as a younger woman.[10] She certainly continued to read widely in theology, and to attend services of the Church of England, though sporadically, while holding back from participating in the eucharist.[11] Despite the ultimately unresponsive nature of the Good, Murdoch nonetheless remained open to the notion of mystical experience and to the usefulness of something like prayer. More than once she alluded to a kind of welcome captivity to Christianity: 'in a sense one is never outside Christianity if one has been caught up in it', she told an interviewer in 1962, 'nor would I altogether want to be.'[12] As she suggested in a later interview, although she could not believe the supernatural aspects of Christianity, 'of course, I can't get away from Christ, who travels with me'.[13]

Murdoch remained convinced that, after the removal of God, to leave a vacuum would prove intolerable. A 1988 interview with the theatre director Jonathan Miller clearly showed this preoccupation, which permeates the novels. Murdoch had come to feel a need to fill the space with 'a kind of moral philosophy, or even neo-theology, which would explain very fundamental things about the human soul and the human being'; to be human involved 'a kind of change, a pilgrimage … from illusion to reality, and falsehood to truth, and evil to good'. Despite the contingency of human life in a purposeless universe, there remained a 'particular orientation which is unique and special and belongs to us and is part of us.'[14]

Despite this, Murdoch was not an advocate of some new para-ecclesial body or movement that might supersede the Church. Her background and disposition led her to think, if not quite with her whole mind, that the existing institution had to survive the loss of belief that she described in her novels. It was this that led

[10] Gillian Dooley, ed., *From a Tiny Corner in the House of Fiction: Conversations with Iris Murdoch* (Columbia, SC, 2003), 43, 211.
[11] Interview with Jonathan Miller (1988), in Dooley, ed., *Tiny Corner*, 215.
[12] Interview with Harold Hobson (1962), in Dooley, ed., *Tiny Corner*, 7.
[13] Interview with John Haffenden (1983), in Dooley, ed., *Tiny Corner*, 136.
[14] See Dooley, ed., *Tiny Corner*, 209–17; quotations at ibid. 211, 212, 213.

Murdoch to advocate positions which, while apparently quixotic, have a kind of coherence when considered together.

In 1979, Murdoch contributed to a special issue of the poetry journal *PN Review*, in opposition to the looming displacement (as it was thought) of the Book of Common Prayer by the Alternative Service Book of 1980. 'We live continually in and through words,' she argued: 'Memories of words, poetic and sacred, travel with us through life.' To lose access to the words of the Prayer Book and the Authorized Version would be, '*whether or not one believes in God*, a spiritual loss'. Believers and unbelievers alike would find it difficult to 'live by' the new words as they had by the old.[15] 'Absence of ritual from ordinary life also starves the imagination', she wrote in *Metaphysics as a Guide to Morals*, the published version of her 1983 Gifford lectures: 'institutions, schools, universities, even churches abandon it.' Yet 'the inner [being] needs the outer because, being incarnate, we need places and times, expressive gestures which release psychic energy and bring healing.'[16] Another such suggestion was that a kind of religious education might be preserved within families, where parents, who did not themselves believe in God, might instruct children *as if they did*. 'How could a child, starting from scratch,' Jonathan Miller asked Murdoch, 'be introduced to the virtues and the galvanising powers of Christianity while being told at the same time that the story is completely untrue?' Though Murdoch disputed the word 'untrue', her discomfort was evident.[17] Later scholars have noted the considerable sophistication involved in behaving as if there were a transcendent reality whilst believing there to be no such thing.[18] But that Murdoch was not alone is clear from the career of her near contemporary, the poet and critic C. H. Sisson (the editor of *PN Review*) who, despite his difficulties with the idea of a personal God, was a trenchant defender of the Book of Common Prayer and the importance of the national church.[19] As Miller suggested, such a balancing act could perhaps only be attempted by one of

[15] Untitled article, *PN Review* 6/5 (1979), 5; see also Dooley, ed., *Tiny Corner*, 213. Italics mine.

[16] Murdoch, *Metaphysics as a Guide to Morals*, 307.

[17] Dooley, ed., *Tiny Corner*, 217.

[18] Gillian Dooley, 'Introduction', in Dooley, ed., *Tiny Corner*, xvii–xxx, at xxii.

[19] Peter Webster, '"Poet of church and state": C. H. Sisson and the Church of England', in John Talbot and Victoria Moul, eds, *C. H. Sisson Reconsidered* (London, 2023), 159–82.

Murdoch's generation and background. For Murdoch, it was necessary that certain aspects of the national faith should persist, even if its central beliefs could no longer be conscientiously held.

It is in this context of knowledge and sympathy without assent, and of emotional investment in the continuing presence of the Church, that we should read Murdoch's engagement with the churches. What follows is an examination of several (though not all) of the Anglican clergy in Murdoch's fiction, in terms of their integrity (or otherwise) to both their vocation and their conscience. I shall examine characters who, while themselves untroubled by doubt and acting within the norms of their profession, nonetheless fail to live up to the exacting ethical standard that Murdoch sets. I also explore Murdoch's treatment of those clergy who can no longer assent to the doctrine of their own church, and the subtleties and evasions into which they are forced as a result.

The period of Murdoch's career was also one in which the social status of Anglican clergy was shifting.[20] Though the social composition of the clergy changed to a degree, the more significant disruption was of the conventions that surrounded their role in public and private life, and the response their interventions might receive. Though its effect in private is hard to document, the increased readiness in public to question authority figures of all kinds was made most visible in the so-called 'satire revolution' of the early Sixties.[21] As well as this, the professional competencies of the clergy were increasingly usurped by secular specialists, in health, education and pastoral care. This was in part the continuation of a longer-term growth of the state, but also due to the availability of a greater range of voices offering spiritual counsel of different kinds, and multiple agencies offering advice on more pragmatic matters of physical and mental health.[22] This article, then, also explores the attitudes among Murdoch's characters to the clergy of the Church of England as a whole: the degree to which their pastoral interventions were assumed as a matter of course, and how far

[20] Martyn Percy, 'Sociology and Anglicanism in the Twentieth Century', in Jeremy Morris, ed., *The Oxford History of Anglicanism*, 4: *Global Western Anglicanism, c.1910–Present* (Oxford, 2017), 137–59.

[21] On the portrayal of the clergy on film and television, see Nigel Yates, *Love Now, Pay Later? Sex and Religion in the Fifties and Sixties* (London, 2010), 44–5.

[22] Anthony Russell, *The Clerical Profession* (London, 1980), 278; Frank Prochaska, *Christianity and Social Service in Modern Britain: The Disinherited Spirit* (Oxford, 2006), 148–61.

the social glue that fixed the clergy in such circles retained its adhesive power. I leave aside, however, a detailed exposition of the theology these characters articulate, which has been explored by others.[23] My concern here is with the Anglican clergy as social actors, and with the interplay of belief, status and action. As a result, I set aside other characters through whom Murdoch explores the same issues of belief, but who are set in quite different networks of social relations and expectations: the Roman Catholic priests Brendan Craddock and Cato Forbes in *Henry and Cato*, the abbess in *The Bell*, and the former nun Anne Cavidge in *Nuns and Soldiers*.

This article, then, aims to contribute to the critical literature on Murdoch, but its primary motivation is historical. Though the novel often appears in historical writing as a primary source, it rarely forms part of the load-bearing structure of an argument. Why this should be is far from clear, but there is perhaps among historians a wariness of the novel as a source, an uncertainty as to how best to interpret it. To change the metaphor, the novel can be a kind of garnish to the main dish, an imparter of flavour. That the flavour is one that suits the dish is often taken for granted, but it is not quite clear how or why it should be so.[24] But in the case of novels that may be classed broadly as realist – or, at least, as not fantasy, science fiction or magical realism – there exists an unspoken contract between author and reader that a character must act in ways that are at least plausible in one of their age, gender, class, occupation and location. As such, historians may legitimately read these characters as having some meaningful correspondence with how their real-life counterparts were present to the mind of the author. Whether or not the author's sense is typical does not wholly vitiate the novel's usefulness. Once

[23] For Carel Fisher in *The Time of the Angels*, see Peter J. Conradi, *The Saint and the Artist: A Study of the Fiction of Iris Murdoch*, 3rd edn (London, 2001; first publ. 1986), 174–8; Hawkins, 'Anglican Atheist', 166–8; Fiddes, *Murdoch*, 49, 60; Miles Leeson, 'Morality in a World with God', in Alison Scott-Baumann and M. F. Simone Roberts, eds, *Iris Murdoch and the Moral Imagination* (Jefferson, NC, 2010), 221–36; A. S. Byatt, *Degrees of Freedom: The Early Novels of Iris Murdoch*, 2nd edn (London, 1994; first publ. 1965), 251–60; Gary Browning, *Why Iris Murdoch Matters* (London, 2018), 49–51; Hilda Spear, *Iris Murdoch*, 2nd edn (Basingstoke, 2006; first publ. 1995), 56–62. The other characters I examine have attracted less attention. On the bishop, and on Angus McAlister, see Fiddes, *Murdoch*, 26, 54–5, 65. See also Reginald Askew, 'The Occasional Clergyman', *Iris Murdoch Newsletter* 12 (1998), 7–9.

[24] See the contrasting approaches in Peter Clarke and Charlotte Methuen, eds, *The Church and Literature*, SCH 48 (Woodbridge, 2012).

published, the novel then becomes part of public discourse, a set of characters whom unknown readers are invited to identify with, admire, ridicule or condemn. As such, it itself becomes an object of historians' attention as part of the conversation within a community of readers about the right way in which to live. What follows is an essay in the interplay of fact and fiction on both these levels. It commits to no particular theory of the relationship between reality and representation. It is offered as a reconstruction of a set of relations between author, character, reader and the state of Anglicanism at a point in time that, though hard to theorize, merits attention.

One of Murdoch's characters illustrates the formal but ultimately insubstantial basis on which many of her characters interact with the parish clergy: Mr Enstone, in *An Accidental Man* (1971).[25] The scene is the deathbed of Alison Ledgard, around which are assembled her two adult daughters and others of the family. She seems to be saying one word over and over again, which sounds like 'priest'. Alison was brought up a Methodist, but has not been near a church for many years. Her daughter Charlotte is horrified at the idea of some Roman Catholic priest mumbling and sprinkling holy water, an offence to her mother's dignity. What about 'that nice man, the local parson chap', someone suggests. He had visited a few times, had he not? Mr Enstone is summoned, and in the meantime the family fumble for the fragments of a remembered religious death. There is a Bible in the room; perhaps someone should read from it? 'The Lord is my shepherd' comes to mind, but which number is it? At length, the psalm is found and, as it is read, even Charlotte is quieted by the words, that take charge, 'silencing all voices but their own, soothing the place into something ancient and formal and calm, making of it the temple of a mystery, the perennial mystery of what was about to be enacted.' The family retain enough in their memory to recognize something distinctive and significant in the words and their recitation.[26]

Mr Enstone's arrival breaks the spell, and he is asked to talk to Alison, though Charlotte thinks him a 'dolt [who] cannot speak of ultimate things'. He takes Alison's hand and speaks of the self and God: a way of leading a soul to conversion at the last which, we are to understand, he has followed many times. His speech is gentle

[25] Throughout this article, I adopt whichever form of address Murdoch uses: in this case, Mr Enstone; later, Fr Jacoby.

[26] Iris Murdoch, *An Accidental Man* (London, 1973), 44–9.

and orthodox, yet it jars in the scene that Murdoch has drawn; it is definite, assertive, when the words of the psalm were open. He is cut off in mid-flow by Alison, again repeating the word, which the family now decides is not 'priest', but something else. 'I'm so sorry, Mr Enstone ... I don't think she wanted a priest after all.' Perfectly politely, he is put back in a box.[27] We meet him only twice more in the novel, both times at parties. 'Won't somebody go and talk to Mr Enstone?', frets the hostess; 'I don't think people should invite clergymen,' says a guest.[28] There is still, in the early 1970s, a certain residual status accorded to the parish clergy in middle-class society. However, as the generation that Alison represents passes away, this thin social connection, forgetfully maintained as a matter of good manners, increasingly loses its force, and becomes merely an embarrassment.

In *Henry and Cato* (1976), the Roman Catholic priest Cato Forbes is told by one of his young charges that 'you're the only one who has ever cared for me, Father, you're the only one who can really *see* me at all.'[29] The notion of vision as the key to moral behaviour has become central to readings of Murdoch's ethics, as expressed both in her philosophical writing and in her novels.[30] Christian ethicists, working during and in the wake of the sweeping changes in the moral content of English law that were largely complete by 1969, had in hand a project of reconstruction.[31] What was the substance of a Christian morality that was now no longer the basis of secular law? Did it deal in deeds, or in intentions? Theologians influenced by the thought of Paul Tillich, notably John A. T. Robinson, bishop of Woolwich, tried to direct attention away from this or that specific act, and towards the primacy of love as a governing principle.[32] Murdoch's

[27] Ibid. 49–51.

[28] Ibid. 427.

[29] Iris Murdoch, *Henry and Cato* (London, 1977), 38. Italics original.

[30] See, *inter alia*, Maria Antonaccio, *Picturing the Human: The Moral Thought of Iris Murdoch* (Oxford, 2000), 3–24 and throughout; see also the several essays in Antonaccio and Schweiker, eds, *Iris Murdoch and the Search for Human Goodness*; other relevant collections of essay are Scott-Baumann and Roberts, eds, *Iris Murdoch and the Moral Imagination*; and Anne Rowe and Avril Horner, eds, *Iris Murdoch and Morality* (Basingstoke, 2010).

[31] On the legislative programme in general, see Peter Webster, *Archbishop Ramsey: The Shape of the Church* (Farnham, 2015), 65–90; Yates, *Love Now, Pay Later?*, 88–108.

[32] See the chapter on 'The New Morality' in John A. T. Robinson, *Honest to God* (London, 1963), 105–21.

conception of morality, despite its atheistic basis, tended in the same direction.[33] The only guide to right behaviour was the good of the other, and in order really to learn from them – really to see them – a kind of renunciation of self was necessary. In three of Murdoch's clerical characters we are shown a kind of hypocrisy, or at least a disconnection, between a correctness of doctrine on the one hand and, on the other, actions that, whilst ostensibly well-meant, were ultimately self-serving.

Like Mr Enstone, the reader first meets Douglas Swann (*An Unofficial Rose*, 1962) in connection with a death. It is the funeral of Fanny Peronett (of a similar age to Alison Ledgard), to whom Swann had been spiritual advisor to the last. Fanny's husband Hugh was relieved that it was not Swann who had presided at the funeral: 'words of such terrible weight are best not profaned by those whom one has caught out being, if not positively frail, at least certainly absurd.'[34] The reader is not told the details of this past transgression of boundaries, but it involves their daughter Ann. Some in the family bear Swann's regular presence about the house with a kind of gentle mockery; Ann's estranged husband Randall is more frank: 'must we have that bloody priest infesting the house all the time?', he asks.[35] Ann herself defends Swann, but is uneasy with his attention. Despite the domestic setting, Swann, in a smart dark suit and collar, has 'a professional air of slightly self-conscious benevolence' and a 'clinically compassionate stoop'.[36] Ann feels as if 'he did, even if unconsciously, want her to break down so that he could console her.' This reading of him is correct, we find: as Ann attempts to end a conversation, he detains her. Does she pray, he asks? At this, her tears come: 'there, my child, my child,' he murmurs, with 'a sense of achievement, as of one who has brought a difficult piece of navigation to a successful conclusion.'[37] By the end of the novel, Ann's unease has become an unspoken but firm rejection of Swann's authority. She had hitherto been 'zealous, serious, on the whole undoubting, but a little vague about

[33] On Murdoch's engagement with Tillich, see relevant references throughout Julia T. Meszaros, *Selfless Love and Human Flourishing in Paul Tillich and Iris Murdoch* (Oxford, 2016).

[34] Iris Murdoch, *An Unofficial Rose* (London, 1964), 14.

[35] Ibid. 53.

[36] Ibid. 51.

[37] Ibid. 110–11.

dogma', including on the Christian doctrine of marriage.[38] A request for a divorce is received; Swann believes he has convinced Ann of the indissolubility of her union, and that she will reject Randall's request. But he leaves the scene (and the novel) not knowing that his advice has only confirmed how impossible it would be for her to live so. Ann is now free, both from Randall and Swann: there had been 'a change in the structure of her world, as if the crystals were forming with a difference.'[39] Few novelists have captured so precisely the subtle erosion of the authority of the churches, one issue and one person at a time.

The same themes appear, albeit drawn more strongly, in *The Philosopher's Pupil* (1983), in the person of Fr Bernard Jacoby. Though troubled, Jacoby is neither a comic, nor a malevolent figure. When pressed by others, he intervenes to try and help George McCaffrey, the figure at the heart of the novel; in the final crisis, he acts on the side of mercy against a strict idea of justice. But he has his 'fans', a number of penitent and needy folk, often women, with whom there are intense pastoral relationships. He is aware of the feeling of power in such pastoral situations, and the temptation to dominate, and he knows that the McCaffreys distrust him accordingly. Not being part of his tiny flock, they view him with a mixture of faint interest and suspicion, a 'creepy priest' in whom they detect a desire to 'see the strong made weak and the lofty made low, and to make those thus afflicted his spiritual prey.'[40] George, in his final refusal to submit to Jacoby's ministrations, sees through it all: 'you grow fat on people's troubles, you grow fat and sleek and purr.'[41] The assumption of good faith and of ease of access to homes and to inner lives, integral to a certain image of the parish priest, which in *An Unofficial Rose* is in question, but not yet openly attacked, is now approaching its end.

Murdoch revisited the theme with Angus McAlister in *The Book and the Brotherhood* (1987), but this time made the point still more starkly. Fr McAlister 'specialised in desperate cases', and so when his country congregation is swelled by visitors, it is Tamar, a young woman secretly pregnant and in turmoil, that he immediately spots.

[38] Ibid. 225.
[39] Ibid. 228.
[40] Iris Murdoch, *The Philosopher's Pupil* (Harmondsworth, 1984), 50, 108.
[41] Ibid. 494.

Tamar's case is a particular delight to him, over which 'he might positively have been said to gloat.'[42] To the consternation of Rose, her confidant and hostess, McAlister intrudes where he had not been invited, involving himself with someone to whom he had not even been introduced. What cheek, Rose thinks: 'it's not his business! He'll upset her!'[43] Tamar's first reaction is to reject his intrusion, but as she makes to leave the church, he grasps her by the wrist and instructs her to kneel. As she does, the tears flow, he prays and she begins to tell him of her situation. The reader is left to decide whether this is a brilliantly intuitive pastoral intervention or an abuse of power, or both. Their relationship, as McAlister leads Tamar through baptism and confirmation, deserves a fuller exposition than can be accommodated here, but the imbalance of power is clear. McAlister clearly *sees* Tamar clearly (in Murdochian terms), or at least thinks he does, working hard at judging her needs and '[singing] both high and low' to meet them.[44] Yet at the same time, McAlister enjoys the process more than is comfortable for the reader to see, and Tamar too knows it. His careful staging of a confrontation with Tamar's mother Violet slips from his control, and in her fury and grief Violet voices the critique that was made of Jacoby: 'you loathsome hypocrite, I know your type, peering into people's lives and trying to control them, breaking up families, smashing things you don't understand!'[45] In the end, McAlister manages only to release Tamar not into selfless love, but into a new selfishness. His reaction is a kind of shrug of resignation, as he moves on to the next difficult case. Murdoch's critique of the pastoral clergy is the same in all three cases: of a well-intentioned, but often inept interference, prone always to self-consciousness, and often self-interest, and open to the charge of exploitativeness.

It is not difficult to produce examples of clergy in novels of other periods who are similarly held up against the standard of their own profession and found wanting, from Jane Austen's Mr Collins onwards. But the theological atmosphere in which Murdoch was writing, and with which she engaged, was quite distinct in its professed focus on the secular. 'Modern Man', recently come of age

[42] Iris Murdoch, *The Book and the Brotherhood* (London, 1987), 487.
[43] Ibid. 282.
[44] Ibid. 488.
[45] Ibid. 507.

(as it was sometimes said) had no time for – indeed, could make nothing of – the stuff of traditional doctrine, which had to be demythologized and restated in non-supernatural terms. The setting was as important as the doctrine, it was thought. Only a new practical religion of love and service, carried out not within the walls of the church but in the street or the workshop, could now reach those whom (it now seemed clear) the Church had lost. The bishop of Woolwich, John A. T. Robinson, in *The New Reformation?* (1965), emphasized not the network of parish 'settlements', but rather 'signs' of reformation such as the anti-apartheid stand of Trevor Huddleston or the Christian-led work of the Notting Hill Housing Trust in Murdoch's familiar west London.[46] In this reading, the churches needed to efface themselves, if not indeed to dissolve themselves completely, in order fully to go out into the world.

This vogue for 'religionless Christianity', or what Mark Chapman has called an 'English Bonhoefferism', was short-lived.[47] Nonetheless, it is clear that Murdoch was aware of it; her own library included a copy of *The New Reformation?* and it seems likely that she also read Robinson's *Honest to God* (1963), perhaps the classic text of English Bonhoefferism.[48] Murdoch's engagement with Bonhoeffer himself in her philosophical writing is very slight, but revealing of her attitude to what she later described as the 'mild tinkerings' of Robinson and others.[49] In *The Sovereignty of Good* (1970), Murdoch does not work out her position on the non-existence of God, but asserts it as one of her assumptions. As such, she continued, 'when Bonhoeffer says that God wants us to live as if there were no God, I suspect he is misusing words.' There is no God in the traditional sense, and 'the traditional sense is perhaps the only sense.'[50] While its implications for Christology were drastic, the project of demythologization at this point remained theistic in character. For Murdoch, however, the churches were only tinkering if they imagined that it were possible to recast their structures in a convincing way, while trying to cling to the objective extramental existence of God. Such a realist position was no longer tenable, in Murdoch's view: the task for the churches

[46] John A. T. Robinson, *The New Reformation?* (London, 1965), 103–4.

[47] Mark D. Chapman, 'Theology in the Public Arena: The Case of "South Bank religion"', in Jane Garnett et al., eds, *Redefining Christian Britain* (London, 2007), 92–105.

[48] Murdoch refers to *Honest to God* in her later *Metaphysics as a Guide to Morals*, 452.

[49] Ibid. 455.

[50] Murdoch, *Sovereignty of Good*, 77.

was to face the reality of the death of God, and to work out what might remain. Four of her clerical characters, from *The Time of the Angels* (1966) through to *The Book and the Brotherhood* (1987) dramatize the loss of faith and the dilemma that it presented to a clergyman in his office.

The Time of the Angels is played out in the rectory of a ruined church in a twilit east London wasteland, blanketed in snow and shrouded in fog. There are two Fisher brothers: Marcus and his elder brother Carel, the rector of St Eustace Watergate. Marcus has become concerned about Carel, living as a recluse in the rectory and refusing all callers. Marcus is writing a book, *Morality in a World without God*, which will 'rescue the idea of an Absolute in morals by showing it to be implied in the most unavoidable human activity of moral evaluation'.[51] No longer would either theological metaphor or crude existentialism be necessary in order for society to function. Despite his professed wish to start afresh, in the eyes of his friend Norah, Marcus is a Christian fellow-traveller. The sooner the West can pass through its current twilight of the gods, the better, she thinks. For Carel, there is simply no God, but the crisis is even deeper and more implacable than this. All philosophy and theology, theistic or otherwise, has been and remains a means of distracting attention from the senselessness of a universe of pure chance. Goodness is impossible, he believes, and Marcus's project futile: 'there is only power and the marvel of power, there is only chance and the terror of chance.'[52] Carel intends to stay just where he is, however, since '[i]f there is no God there is all the more need for a priest'. Marcus begins to object – surely it would be wrong to act so – but is cut short: 'if there is no one there no one is going to mind.'[53] Later, Marcus presses the point: 'you are going to go on with that farce, with all those things inside you?' This time Carel's reply is less sanguine: he will carry on, but (quoting the *Dies irae*), '*nil inultum remanebit*': nothing would remain unpunished; 'although there is no judge I shall be punished quite automatically out of the great power of the universe. … Meanwhile I endure in the place in which I am.'[54]

[51] Iris Murdoch, *The Time of the Angels* (Harmondsworth, 1968), 72.
[52] Ibid. 172.
[53] Ibid. 79.
[54] Ibid. 174–5. Italics original.

Though the reactions of most readers are lost, it is hard to imagine many Anglicans receiving the 'High Anglican Gothic' of *The Time of the Angels* as very typical of church life.[55] Carel, who within the sepulchral darkness of the rectory exercises the most baleful power over his housekeeper, his daughter and his niece, could have found few documented counterparts. There had long been clergy who had lost their faith; from time to time, there were scandalous examples of those who, like Fisher, fell short of the moral standards expected of them, and both had their representatives in fiction. However, the period from the early 1960s onwards was characterized by a certain sense of professional crisis among the clergy across the churches, alongside – and mutually constitutive of – the broader intellectual crisis that Murdoch dramatized. In the Church of England, there was an awareness that existing clergy were deployed inefficiently, and rewarded unevenly. Numbers of new vocations fell sharply, and there also seemed to be an increase in the number of those leaving. Murdoch may well have known that the philosopher Anthony Kenny had arrived in Oxford in 1963 as a new agnostic immediately after having left the Roman Catholic priesthood; Kenny certainly encountered her, most likely at some point in the mid- to late 1960s.[56] By 1970, in the words of Cardinal Heenan, 'the path which [Kenny] trod has now become a great high road', and the problem was not only among Roman Catholics:[57] a survey in 1973–4 found that around eleven per cent of men ordained in the Church of England between 1951 and 1965 were no longer working within the church, and nearly half of those had formally resigned their orders.[58] The mid-1960s also saw a very particular discussion about the status of the Thirty-Nine Articles, the central doctrinal statement of the Church of England, unrevised in four centuries, to which clergy were required to assent in a very public and precise way. This was thought to be a difficulty to an increasing number of ordinands.[59] A report of the church's doctrine commission

[55] The phrase of A. S. Byatt in *Degrees of Freedom*, 260.

[56] Conradi, *Murdoch*, 301; Anthony Kenny, *A Path from Rome: An Autobiography* (Oxford, 1986), 191–203; idem, *Brief Encounters: Notes from a Philosopher's Diary* (London, 2018), 175–7.

[57] Kenny, *Path from Rome*, 205.

[58] Russell, *Clerical Profession*, 265.

[59] Paul A. Welsby, *A History of the Church of England 1945–1980* (Oxford, 1984), 234–5, 143–6.

recommended in 1968 that the public element of that assent should end, and the form of words be adjusted. At some point, Murdoch acquired a copy of the report, and parts of it concerning the form of assent are marked in the margin.[60]

So although the reasons for the draining away of the numerical strength of the clergy were complex, their professional position was certainly in question in a new and particular way. In *The Time of the Angels*, Murdoch explores the reactions of others to Carel and his likely future. Concerned about Carel's state of mind, Norah and Marcus consult with his bishop. Murdoch does not name him, but the parallel is very clearly with John Robinson.[61] He is clean, with a boyish face, and seems to Marcus to be too young to be a bishop. (The description matches the photograph of Robinson on the cover of *The New Reformation?*; Robinson was forty-five when it appeared, having become bishop at forty.) Surely, Norah thinks, something must be done about a rector who has lost his faith, and perhaps his mind. 'I should certainly call Carel an *eccentric*', he replies, and the Church of England has been noted for those. Perhaps it would not do to cause too much of a fuss that might be difficult to manage; 'it'll all come out in the wash!'[62] But this will not do for Norah: is it no longer important what a clergyman believes? Frowning slightly at being put on the spot, the bishop replies: 'It is a time,' he says, 'when, as one might put it, mankind is growing up. … Much of the symbolism of theology … is, in this scientific age, simply a barrier to belief. Our symbolism must change.' As for Carel, the key is not his beliefs, but 'passion, Kierkegaard said, didn't he, passion. That's the necessary truth.'[63] (Rowan Williams has pointed out a certain cult of earnestness in the period; for at least some adherents of the so-called 'South Bank Religion', what one believed was not so important as the seriousness with which one believed it.[64]) Despite his confession of

[60] Archbishops' Commission on Christian Doctrine, *Subscription and Assent to the 39 Articles* (London, 1968). Murdoch's copy of this report first belonged to Scott Dunbar, then a graduate student in the philosophy of religion, with whom Murdoch became friends in 1967; Kingston, Kingston University Archives and Special Collections [hereafter: KUAL], Iris Murdoch Papers, IML296.

[61] On the similarity between Robinson's views and those of Murdoch's bishop in *Time of the Angels*, see Fiddes, *Murdoch*, 53–4, 55.

[62] Murdoch, *Time of the Angels*, 91. Italics original.

[63] Murdoch, *Time of the Angels*, 90–4.

[64] Rowan Williams, '*Honest to God* and the 1960s', in idem, *Anglican Identities* (London, 2004), 103–20, at 106.

atheism, the bishop regards Carel as 'a profoundly religious man'. Norah thinks the bishop is playing with fire; it would be better to state plainly that God did not exist. Marcus is disturbed. Despite not believing himself in the redeeming Christ or the Trinity, it was important that someone else did, and that 'all that business should go on in the old way'. Anticipating a later insight of Grace Davie, Marcus's religion had been enacted vicariously on his behalf, but now 'behind the scenes it was all being unobtrusively dismantled.'[65]

Between *The Time of the Angels* and *The Philosopher's Pupil* in 1983, much of the confidence of Robinsonian radicals that the Church of England could be saved by a kind of relocation in the secular world had evaporated. As Sam Brewitt-Taylor has shown, by the early 1970s, some clergy associated with religionless Christianity found themselves sufficiently frustrated to leave parochial ministry entirely. Robinson returned to academic life in 1969; one of his priests in Woolwich, Nick Stacey, worked first in the charity sector, and then in social services in local government.[66] Murdoch had, in the meantime, read a good deal of the most controversial modern theology, including *The Remaking of Christian Doctrine* (1974) by Maurice Wiles, and the notorious collection of essays edited by John Hick, *The Myth of God Incarnate* (1977), both of them radical statements of a non-incarnational Christology.[67] Reading them, she wrote, with mock surprise, 'I have discovered that I am a Christian', in that her understanding of Christ matched that of Wiles and Hick and colleagues.[68] Also in her library were works by Don Cupitt, who, while a contributor to *The Myth of God Incarnate*, was shortly to go further, and take a position of explicit theological non-realism. The earliest of the three books by Cupitt in Murdoch's library was *Taking Leave of God*, published in 1980, which marked his 'coming

[65] Murdoch, *Time of the Angels*, 95; Grace Davie, 'Vicarious Religion: A Response', *Journal of Contemporary Religion* 25 (2010), 261–6.

[66] Sam Brewitt-Taylor, 'Inspiration and Institution in 1960s Anglican Radicalism: The Cases of Nick Stacey and John Robinson', in Charlotte Methuen, Alec Ryrie and Andrew Spicer, eds, *Inspiration and Institution in Christian History,* SCH 57 (London, 2021), 318–40, at 334–7.

[67] Her copies, both of them heavily annotated, are at KUAL, Iris Murdoch Papers, IML59 and IML322.

[68] Murdoch to Scott Dunbar, 19 October 1977, in Avril Horner and Anne Rowe, eds, *Living on Paper: Letters from Iris Murdoch, 1934–1995* (London, 2015), 450–1.

out' as a non-realist.[69] Writing in 1989, from what he regarded as a kind of internal exile (as dean of Emmanuel College, Cambridge), Cupitt asked what courses of action were open to those who, without owning a loss of faith, could not subscribe to theological realism and the dogmatic structure of the Church's theology. Should they leave and join an 'entirely unorganized invisible church of heretics, artists, writers, humanitarians, lovers of spiritual freedom and of the poor'?[70] A kind of exile was probably the only honest course of action. Cupitt was also a reader of Murdoch;[71] her characters had, he thought, modelled just such a kind of modern contemplative, who left the Church behind to 'go out into the world and into solitary, anonymous reflection and service [as] a symbolic action, a way of bearing unofficial witness to the extremity of the times.'[72] In Bernard Jacoby and Angus McAlister, Murdoch explores two possible responses to Cupitt's question.

Fr Jacoby, in *The Philosopher's Pupil*, had once prayed freely, but now has ceased to believe in any personal God, even though the idea of Christ somehow persists. His prayer, although it contains forms of words that suggest a feeling of petition, is largely a free flow of thoughts, a kind of meditative practice that – to his parishioners – seems to be nothing more than a kind of disciplined breathing. In the set piece debate between Jacoby and Rozanov (the fearsome philosopher of the novel's title), in which they probe together the emptiness of a world without a God, it becomes difficult to distinguish the two voices, so alike are their positions, and so far from anything resembling orthodoxy. Yet Jacoby does retain some sense of priestly distinctiveness. Part of it is pastoral, as I have already shown, but Jacoby also holds onto some idea of the sacraments, even though they are not a symbol of a wider spiritual reality, but something more magical, shamanic, which he finds 'endlessly and thrillingly arcane.' 'I enact rites,' he says, and 'wait for people to summon me.'[73] This, it seems, is

[69] Murdoch's annotated copy is at KUAL, Iris Murdoch Papers, IML1105; Murdoch, *Metaphysics*, 452–5.
[70] Don Cupitt, *Radicals and the Future of the Church* (London, 1989), 118.
[71] On Cupitt's engagement with Murdoch, see Don Cupitt, 'Iris Murdoch: A Case of Star-Friendship', in Anne Rowe and Avril Horner, eds, *Iris Murdoch: Texts and Contexts* (Basingstoke, 2012), 11–16; Fiddes, *Murdoch*, 57–8.
[72] Don Cupitt, *Radicals and the Future of the Church* (London, 1989), 121.
[73] Murdoch, *Philosopher's Pupil*, 156, 190. On Murdoch and the magical nature of religious symbols and ritual, see Fiddes, *Murdoch*, 26–7.

enough for him. But Murdoch shows us the gap between Jacoby's public and private faces. Rozanov asks the question: is it not time that Jacoby left the priesthood? 'With your beliefs you must feel you are in a false position, living a lie. You must have taken vows. Aren't you breaking them?' He had assented to the Thirty-Nine Articles, but they were just 'old-fashioned realistic theism', in which they agree that Jacoby does not believe. How can he go on? Jacoby, discomfited, answers: 'I just can, that's all.'[74] But he is put on the spot by his flock, vulnerable people who rely on him, to whom he lies directly. The final crisis of the novel sees him abruptly resign and leave England for an abandoned chapel on the Greek coast, where he can work out his vocation of finding true religion in the absolute repudiation of even the idea of God.

Of all Murdoch's priests, Fr McAlister in *The Book and the Brotherhood* is arguably the most fully-drawn, and also the most ambiguous. The son of a clergyman, he, like Jacoby, once believed the language of his upbringing, which flows freely from him still: 'the high spiritual rhetoric of the Bible and of Cranmer's Prayer Book was more familiar to him than nursery rhymes.' But he too has ceased to believe either in God or a divine Christ. Some kind of mystical Christ remains, however, as does the 'magical power' that his ordination conferred on him, to 'save souls and raise the fallen.'[75] His sense of there being something to which to direct prayer is stronger than in Jacoby; his intention to help his difficult cases is genuine. His improvised rite in memory of Tamar's aborted child, conducted in private and wholly uncanonical, is to him a 'most holy farrago', and yet somehow it provides what is needed.[76] He also remains sure that the whole of existence could not simply be an accident: 'it was something absolute, and what is absolute cannot be an accident.' Without the 'endlessly rehearsed drama of Christ … there was nothing at all'; nothing could separate him from the love of Christ, even the vague kind of Christ in which he could believe.[77]

McAlister is, however, strongly reminded of the precariousness of his position by the rites of the church. He is separated from the crib at

[74] Ibid. 229–30.
[75] Murdoch, *Book and Brotherhood*, 488.
[76] Ibid. 493.
[77] Ibid. 539–40.

Christmas, that 'glowing radiant object … because he was a liar, because a line of falsity ran all the way through him and tainted what he did.'[78] At Easter too, he is troubled by the message he still had to convey, 'the terrible particularity, the empirical detail of his religion'.[79] How, he asks himself, can he affirm in speech things about God or Christ that he did not believe? 'I have to,' he answers. 'Why? In order to carry on with the life which I have chosen and which I love.'[80] Though McAlister prays and worships, and feels himself to be 'a vehicle of power and a grace which was given, not his own,' there was all the while a 'terrible truth' never clarified. During the eucharist, he enacts something, points towards business transacted between God and his flock, but no longer with him, 'in agony, with tears', which 'did him no credit. Rather the contrary.'[81] While Fr Jacoby is propelled out of his position by doubt, Fr McAlister, like Carel Fisher, endures because he must. For him, unlike Murdoch's other priests, his dilemma is not resolved for him by events; as the reader sees him for the last time, on he goes, with his next hard case. Despite the loss of God, for Murdoch, the Church must endure because it is necessary.

Iris Murdoch's treatment of her Anglican clergy can be read, then, as an extended meditation, over nearly thirty years, on the faults of the church as she knew it, and at the same time as an assertion of its enduring necessity. Her characters, drawn largely from the upper strata of English professional and landed society, maintain a kind of social connection with the clergy as part of the givenness of English life, though it becomes increasingly threadbare as her novels enter the 1980s. But despite that connection, the apparent presumption of the clergy in trying to intervene in pastoral situations, politely tolerated in 1962 and *An Unofficial Rose* is, by 1987 and *The Book and the Brotherhood,* openly and robustly rejected. The character of that pastoral care is, for Murdoch, vitiated by the intrusion of the 'fat, relentless ego' that for Murdoch threatens all human relationships, and by a desire for control, against which Murdoch always sets her ideal of self-emptying attention to the Other. Though

78 Ibid. 516.
79 Ibid. 539.
80 Ibid. 516.
81 Ibid. 540–1.

these men are apparently blameless when judged against conventional Christian moral standards, Murdoch's other characters point, both silently and out loud, to a subtle hypocrisy in them, a falseness of motive. Murdoch holds these clergy against the rule which she would advocate as the truly Christian standard and finds them wanting.

In the same characters, Murdoch also dramatizes the loss of Christian faith which was for her a settled reality, but which presented the working clergy with acute agonies of conscience and a daily disjuncture between outward speech and inner conviction, to which other characters draw attention. Some of these men remain in place simply because they can; others persevere because if there is no God and no objective standard of belief, it no longer matters, and the very notion of hypocrisy falls away. Others again remain, somehow loyal to a sense of vocation and to those whom they can, in their way, continue to help. Largely absent in these characters, however, is any appeal to the teaching authority of the Church that might head off the charge of hypocrisy; any sense that, even if they cannot themselves assent to certain doctrines, they nonetheless accept them as a datum, in submission to the weight of historic orthodoxy and in fidelity to the historic and present Body of Christ. These men are largely alone. As Rowan Williams has noted, for all her turning to the everyday – and the attachment to the idea of the Church that I have explored – there is little sense in Murdoch's fiction of the Church as a community, or of the importance of a 'shared life, social and ethical tradition and the disciplines of common experience and common challenge'.[82]

In the case of Carel Fisher, the dilemma is resolved only by suicide; for Bernard Jacoby, it is resolved by external events which jolt him out of place and into a kind of exile; for Angus McAlister it continues, in struggle and tears. The ministrations of the Church must continue as a witness to something absolute, even if McAlister himself cannot resolve its nature. For him, as for Murdoch, the Church remains necessary, even if God himself is not. With this quixotic proposition, Murdoch exemplifies a tension in her generation which had not arisen quite so acutely before, and which is now much less common, and inflected differently. Some Anglicans are still disposed to try to recover a necessary connection between established church, nation

[82] Rowan Williams, 'Writing Morally', in Hopwood and Panizza, eds, *Murdochian Mind*, 376–81, at 378.

and culture, and the value of the Prayer Book and historic ritual. However, such loyalties are now less something in which people are (in Murdoch's terms) 'caught up', but a matter of conscious choice.[83]

[83] On this, see Peter Webster, 'Poet of Church and State', 174–5.

OutRage! Hypocrisy, Episcopacy and Homosexuality in 1990s England

William Whyte*

St John's College, Oxford

The brief but bitter campaign to expose the hidden homosexuality of Anglican bishops in the mid-1990s was framed as a contest about hypocrisy, with bishops – whether suspected of homosexuality or not – condemned as hypocrites, and the Church of England as hypocritical. However, the activists behind this 'outing', and the media which covered the story with such enthusiasm, were similarly attacked for hypocrisy. A neglected moment in recent ecclesiastical history, it reveals the ongoing importance of hypocrisy in debates about the nature of faith and the authority of the church. Still more, it sheds light on how contemporary assumptions about authenticity both intensified the perceived importance of hypocrisy and increased the chances of being accused of acting hypocritically.

On Friday 30 August 1968, a thirty-two-year-old Anglican clergyman was arrested in a Hull public lavatory. A fortnight later, on 13 September, he pleaded guilty in the local magistrates' court to committing an act of gross indecency with another man, a Yorkshire farmer. He was given a twelve-month conditional discharge and ordered to pay a small amount in costs. A married, ambitious minister, already on his way up the hierarchy of the Church of England, he had been unwise in his choice of location. Like many port cities, Hull had a long history of prosecuting such offences.[1] He was also unlucky

* For inviting me to prepare this paper, I must express my sincere thanks to Catherine Cubitt. I am also extraordinarily grateful to Diarmaid MacCulloch, Charlotte Methuen, Sam Rutherford, George Severs and Zoë Waxman for their wisdom and good advice on earlier versions of this text. St John's College, Oxford, OX1 3JP, UK. E-mail: william.whyte@sjc.ox.ac.uk.

[1] Helen Smith, *Masculinity, Class, and Same-Sex Desire in Industrial England, 1895–1957* (New York and Basingstoke, 2015), 37.

Studies in Church History 60 (2024), 533–556
doi: 10.1017/stc.2024.19

in his timing. Although private homosexual acts had been decriminalized a year before, the very same legislation reinforced a prohibition on sex in public lavatories. In fact, convictions for just that increased quite significantly after 1967.[2]

And yet, if this criminal act was both ill-timed and ill-placed, the clergyman proved more fortunate in its immediate aftermath. With his conviction barely noticed by the wider community, he remained chaplain to Donald Coggan, archbishop of York. He would, indeed, be supported by the primate for the rest of his career, and go on to write Coggan's entry in the *Oxford Dictionary of National Biography*.[3] Despite his offence, he was appointed Chief Secretary to the Church Army in 1976, archdeacon of Rochester in 1984, bishop of Rochester in 1988, and then named bishop of Durham in 1994.[4] Such was the general amnesia about the event in Hull all those years before, that this latter preferment to the third most senior post in the Church of England was greeted by one newspaper with the headline: 'Durham's next bishop eschews controversy'. Following a contentious predecessor, who had provoked much criticism for his liberal theology and left-wing politics, his was evidently an appointment designed to calm nerves and soothe brows. It would be seen, observed one knowledgeable commentator, 'as putting a stop to the excitements previously generated' in the diocese.[5]

Quite quickly, it became apparent that this was a very poor piece of prophecy. Interviewed as part of the media announcement of his move, the bishop-elect was certainly careful to avoid saying anything likely to provoke dissent. 'Unlike his controversial predecessor

[2] Sexual Offences Act 1967 s.1 (2) (b). See also Kate Gleeson, 'Freudian Slips and Coteries of Vice: The Sexual Offences Act of 1967', *Parliamentary History* 27 (2008), 393–409, at 409; Jeffrey Weeks, *Coming Out: Homosexual Politics in Britain from the Nineteenth Century to the Present* (London, 1990), 176.

[3] Michael Turnbull, 'Coggan, (Frederick) Donald, Baron Coggan', *ODNB*, online edn (2004), at: <https://doi.org/10.1093/ref:odnb/74124>, accessed 18 December 2023. Coggan was President of the Church Army when Turnbull was appointed Chief Secretary. He also supported his publications. See Donald Lynch, *Chariots of the Gospel: The Centenary History of the Church Army* (Worthing, 1982), 125–34; Michael Turnbull, *God's Front Line* (London and Oxford, 1978), v–vi.

[4] *Church of England Newspaper*, 14 October 1994, 6.

[5] Andrew Brown, 'Durham's next Bishop eschews Controversy', *Independent*, 3 February 1994, online at: <https://www.independent.co.uk/news/uk/durham-s-next-bishop-eschews-controversy-michael-turnbull-believes-in-the-virgin-birth-and-in-hell-writes-andrew-brown-1391605.html>, accessed 18 December 2023.

Dr David Jenkins,' observed *The Times* in a front-page story, this avowed evangelical believed 'in the Virgin Birth, the Bodily Resurrection of Christ, and eternal damnation.'[6] He was, at the same time however, equally keen to dismiss any suggestion that he greatly differed from the previous incumbent. As the questions went on, noted the *Independent,* it became clear that 'The only substantial area on which he disagrees with Dr Jenkins appears to be the treatment of gay clergy. Dr Jenkins has protected men in his diocese against pressure from parishioners who disapproved of their boyfriends.' The future bishop of Durham, by contrast, when 'asked what his policy would be, replied that, "An admitted and open lifestyle is incompatible with full-time ministry."'[7] It was a statement that both outwardly conformed to the official teachings of the church and prudently avoided reference to any particular sexual act. In that sense, it was very cleverly crafted – perhaps in anticipation of any further questions about his past. It was, however, almost certainly a mistake to say even this much, because it invited investigation of the bishop's own experiences.

On Sunday 25 September 1994, a mere month before his enthronement was scheduled, the *News of the World* broke the long-dormant story of Bishop Michael Turnbull's conviction more than a quarter of a century before. The tabloid had a long-standing interest in such revelations about the outwardly respectable, whether schoolmaster, scoutmaster or church leader.[8] It was, of course, also a disclosure that drew on a still longer history of high-profile clerical scandal, from the Regency bishop of Clogher discovered in flagrante with a guardsman in 1822, to the disgraced rector of Stiffkey defrocked for immorality with 'loose women' in 1932.[9] But this particular exposé would prove more important than most, because

[6] *The Times*, 3 February 1994, 1.

[7] Brown, 'Durham's next Bishop eschews Controversy'.

[8] Adrian Bingham, *Family Newspapers? Sex, Private Life, and the British Popular Press, 1918–1978* (Oxford, 2009), 174.

[9] As such, it finds its place in the popular history by Matthew Parris, *The Great Unfrocked: 2000 Years of Church Scandal* (London, 1998), 174–6. See also Anne-Marie Kilday and David S. Nash, 'The Rector of Stiffkey: "The lower he sinks, the greater their crime": Clerical Scandal, Prurience, and the Archaeology of Reputation', in Anne-Marie Kilday and David S. Nash, eds, *Shame and Modernity in Britain: 1890 to the Present* (Basingstoke, 2017), 53–66.

it induced a deluge of further coverage, campaigning, protests and problems, and not just for the bishop himself.

The revelation that Michael Turnbull had committed a homosexual act and yet condemned homosexual activity was the prompt for a furious and genuinely international debate about sexuality and religion. It would encourage activists to name other bishops they believed to be gay. This disclosure, in turn, would lead to further fury at what the *Daily Telegraph* described as 'homosexual terrorism', and what one writer in the *Observer* dubbed 'homofascism'.[10] More sympathetic commentators remarked on the astonishing and sudden upsurge of interest in the subject. Given the number of clerics being identified as gay, wrote one, there soon would not 'be a single priest, vicar, canon or bishop left in hiding.'[11] The whole affair encouraged some, and terrified others, to think that the Church of England – and perhaps even the worldwide Anglican Communion – would soon radically change its views on sex and sexuality.[12]

Underlying this furore was a contest about hypocrisy. At the most basic level, many thought that Bishop Turnbull's 'opposition to gay clergy' was 'extremely hypocritical in view of his previous conviction.'[13] There was a wider sense, too, that the church as a whole was behaving hypocritically; that it was acting according to the principle that 'The 11th Commandment of the Anglican Church is, apparently, *Thou Shalt not be found out.*'[14] As the controversy burned more brightly and consumed still further people within its blaze, the charges of hypocrisy also became more widespread. Even many of those who supported gay rights were struck by the sight of campaigners apparently bullying bishops about their alleged homosexuality.[15] 'It's so palpably vengeful', observed the openly gay actor Simon Callow. The activists, declared Michael Cashman, himself a prominent spokesman for gay equality, had turned themselves into 'the

[10] *Daily Telegraph,* 1 December 1994; *Observer*, 4 December 1994.

[11] Terry Sanderson, 'De-frocks Tactics', *Gay Times* 196 (January 1995), 41–2, at 41.

[12] George Carey, *Know the Truth: A Memoir* (London, 2004), 306.

[13] Glenn Halton of OutRage!, quoted in Jon Gallagher, 'Pastoral Offender', *The Advocate*, 29 November 1994, 27–8, at 27.

[14] London, London School of Economics [hereafter: LSE], HCA/TATCHELL/1994/2, Peter Tatchell, Speech to the Durham Union, 21 October 1994. Italics original.

[15] Stephen Bates, *A Church at War: Anglicans and Homosexuality* (London, 2004), 101.

sex police of the gay world.'[16] This was, claimed journalists, simply 'hypocrisy' on their part.[17] That the press benefitted from this scandal, whilst also claiming to condemn it, appeared to reveal them as hypocrites too.[18] Hypocrisy, in this history, is and was everywhere. In that sense, re-examining what happened as a result of that event in Hull presents a good opportunity to think about the church and hypocrisy in 1990s Britain and beyond.

Surprisingly, this is not a story that has so far attracted much sustained attention. It is, in truth, largely overlooked in most accounts of the contemporary Church of England and ignored even in those that focus on the issue of homosexuality and Anglicanism.[19] Yet the scandal and its consequences generated a substantial quantity of material at the time, all of which testifies to its impact on those involved and on the wider community, whether Christian, gay, or both. The agitation, claimed one leading figure, had truly 'put the hypocrisy and homophobia of the Establishment at the centre of public debate.'[20] It was discussed widely in the press, on television, in meetings and synods, and in churches across the world. It also helped shape the campaigning tactics of both gay rights activists and evangelical Anglicans thereafter. Subsequent silence on the subject is consequently very revealing, highlighting the fact that this cause célèbre grew out of a very particular conjunction of events in the mid-1990s. Examining the case further can thus illuminate that moment as well as wider debates about the church and sex, the boundaries between the public and the private, and how accusations of hypocrisy were strategically mobilized for very different ends.

None of this was predictable. Even after the *News of the World* had revealed Bishop Turnbull's arrest, it seemed unlikely that much more

16 Terry Sanderson, 'Moral Cowardice and the Demon Tatchell', *Gay Times* 200 (May 1995), 57.

17 *Independent*, 4 December 1994.

18 Terry Sanderson, 'Closet Case Histories', *Gay Times* 198 (March 1995), 40–1.

19 'Outing' is briefly mentioned in Bates, *A Church at War*, 101, and Monica Furlong, *The CofE: The State It's In* (London, 2000), 142. It is absent from Andrew Brown and Linda Woodhead, *That Was the Church That Was: How the Church of England Lost the English People* (London, 2016); Stephen Hunt, 'The Lesbian and Gay Christian Movement in Britain: Mobilization and Opposition', *Journal of Religion and Society* 4 (2002), 1–14; William L. Sachs, *Homosexuality and the Crisis of Anglicanism* (Cambridge, 2009); idem, 'Sexuality and Anglicanism', in Jeremy Morris, ed., *The Oxford History of Anglicanism, 4: Global Western Anglicanism, c.1910–Present* (Oxford, 2017), 93–116.

20 Peter Tatchell, 'Outing', in *Pink Paper*, 21 April 1995.

would follow. Noting the story in his diary, one campaigning clergyman remarked on the unfairness of a church that was still condemning 'gay clergy with loving partners and forgiving blowjobs in lavatories'. He also noted the irony that, in the past, 'Michael, whom I have known since university, took a very hard line on homosexuality when I asked him to lunch at the Athenaeum.'[21] But the clerical diarist nonetheless evidently assumed that the storm would blow over. Nor was he alone. The evangelical *Church of England Newspaper* observed that 'most clergy appeared relatively unmoved' by the disclosure.[22] Reporting for a wider audience, the headline in *The Times* was simply: 'Bishop shrugs off indecency revelation.'[23]

Writing to the archbishop of Canterbury in 1991, campaigners rather dubiously claimed that 'There are approximately the same number of practising Christians in the United Kingdom as there are practising homosexuals. Both groups embrace the support of large numbers of clergy'.[24] The figures might have been speculative, but the claim was not wholly ill-founded and the importance of gay men and lesbians to the institution of the church was undeniable. There had always been gay clergy in the church: some open about their sexuality, and others less so. Estimates at the turn of the twenty-first century suggested that perhaps one in five clergy were gay.[25] There were also gay bishops. One, for instance, was universally addressed as Mildred by those in the know.[26] The central administration of the Church of England was also largely run in the 1970s and 1980s by Derek Pattinson, the Secretary General of the General Synod, who lived out his retirement with a male partner, a man who had publicly declared his own homosexuality during a meeting of synod.[27]

21 Johnson, *Diary of a Gay Priest,* 144.
22 *Church of England Newspaper*, 30 September 1994, 1.
23 *The Times,* 27 September 1994, 2.
24 London, Bishopsgate Institute, LGBTM 715, Outrage 1990–6, OutRage! to George Carey, 12 March 1991.
25 Timothy Willem Jones, *Sexual Politics in the Church of England, 1857–1957* (Oxford, 2012), 162–82; Bates, *A Church at War*, 7.
26 Johnson, *Diary of a Gay Priest*, 167.
27 Brian Hanson, 'Pattinson, Sir (William) Derek (1930–2006), church administrator and Church of England clergyman', *ODNB*, online edn (2010), at: <https://doi.org/10.1093/ref:odnb/97466>, accessed 18 December 2023; Andrew Brown, 'Questions over Churchman's Charity Trip', *Independent*, 4 December 1992.

There had also been occasions in which clergy who asserted that they were heterosexual nonetheless found themselves accused of homosexual offences. That Michael Turnbull was not alone in confronting such issues can be seen in a comparison with one of his brother bishops, Frederick Stephen Temple, who experienced something similar at about the same time as Turnbull. Freddy Temple was arrested, 'soliciting for immoral purposes', in a Portsmouth public convenience less than a month after Turnbull's apprehension in Hull. Successfully persuading a court that he had been engaged in an act not of criminality, but of profound empathy as he sought to understand the compulsions that led some men to seek sex in lavatories, Temple was found not guilty. To be sure, the episode almost certainly frustrated his ambitions of becoming bishop of Birmingham, but it did not prevent him being elevated to the episcopate as suffragan for Malmesbury five years later, in 1973.[28] Although Temple had risked public disgrace by insisting on a jury trial, rather than the more discrete option of the magistrates' court, no mention of his arrest ever made it into the press. He was able to be consecrated to the episcopate without a word of his previous history becoming more widely known.

One man had, of course, been found guilty and another judged innocent. Accepting the truth of the charge against him bought Michael Turnbull time and a degree of privacy in 1968, but left him more vulnerable when the truth later came out. Yet there was more going on than just the difference between one bishop accused of soliciting for immoral purposes, and another bishop convicted for gross indecency. Despite the fact that their arrests were widely known within the church – at least among the hierarchy – both had been able to cover up their embarrassments in the 1960s, 1970s and 1980s. Why, one might ask, did Turnbull's conviction become public knowledge in the 1990s? Why did it spark such storm? What had changed to make his case suddenly precipitate such a drama?

In some respects, the attention Turnbull drew was the product of the high-profile position that he had reached. The bishop of Durham was an important figure, and the role was one that had become more public under his predecessor. To some extent, too, Turnbull's episcopal embarrassment also resonated with a wider set of concerns about

[28] Christopher Dobb, *Freddy Temple: a Portrait* (Calne, 2006), 208–10.

'sleaze' at the top of British society in the 1990s.[29] His exposure was just one of what a well-informed contemporary described as an 'almost constant barrage of scandal stories' in the press.[30] In hindsight, indeed, *The Times*' headline announcing Turnbull's preferment would come to seem strikingly prescient. 'Jenkins' successor goes back to basics,' it proclaimed.[31] The echoes of Prime Minister John Major's disastrous campaign of the same name, which had unleashed a torrent of bad news about the sexual peccadillos of Conservative MPs, are hard to ignore, and proved ironic, to say the least.[32]

Most importantly, what had changed, and what made Turnbull's case seem so salient to so many people, was an increasingly impassioned debate about homosexuality within Anglicanism.[33] Some assumed that this new emphasis on sex and sexuality would simply emphasize a commitment to traditional values. At General Synod in 1987, John Taylor, the bishop of St Albans, argued that 'the Church would gain popularity by taking a firmer line against homosexuality.'[34] Many conservative evangelicals also seized on the issue as a way of challenging, confronting – and defeating – liberalism within the church.[35] Homosexuality was first discussed in any depth by the worldwide gathering of all Anglican bishops, the Lambeth Conference, in 1978.[36] In the years that followed, the subject would assume a truly global significance, with wealthy American conservatives funding those African Anglicans who condemned same-sex

[29] Terry Sanderson, *Mediawatch: The Treatment of Male and Female Homosexuals in the British Media* (London and New York, 1995), 95–7.
[30] Roger Mortimore, 'Public Perceptions of Sleaze in Britain', *Parliamentary Affairs* 48 (1995), 579–89, at 582; David Leigh and Ed Vulliamy, *Sleaze: The Corruption of Parliament* (London, 1997), 149–51.
[31] *The Times*, 3 February 1994, 1.
[32] David M. Farrell, Ian McAllister and Donley T. Studlar, 'Sex, Money and Politics: Sleaze and the Conservative Party in the 1997 Election', *British Elections & Parties Review* 8 (1998), 80–94.
[33] Although focused on the U.S. scene, James K. Wellman, Jr, 'Introduction: The Debate over Homosexual Ordination. Sub-Cultural Identity Theory in American Religious Organizations', *Review of Religious Research* 41 (1999), 184–206, offers some interesting insights.
[34] Jeffrey Weeks, *Sex, Politics, and Society: The Regulations of Sexuality Since 1800*, 3rd edn (London, 2012; first publ. 1981), 378.
[35] Brown and Woodhead, *That Was the Church That Was*, 49.
[36] But see in this volume, Mark D. Chapman, 'Enjoying what comes naturally: The Church of England and Sexuality in the 1930s', which points to a mention of this issue at least in 1930.

desire. Building up as a backdrop to all Bishop Turnbull's sufferings was preparation for the 1998 Lambeth Conference which would condemn homosexuality as 'incompatible with Scripture'.[37]

At the same time, there were growing calls from gay Christians and their allies for greater liberalization, and the Lambeth resolution of 1998 would also commit the church 'to listen to the experience of homosexual persons'. The advent of Queer theology and the development of campaigning organizations seeking to create more 'inclusive' churches offered a challenge to seemingly settled notions of sexuality and sin.[38] The result was a fevered debate about homosexuality, about the nature of the Church, about the authority of Scripture, and about individual Christian life. Tellingly, the news about Turnbull's conviction would prompt both conservative evangelicals and campaigners for gay rights within the church to call for his resignation. Equally revealing was the fact that both groups believed the story helped their cause. A society-wide development, it was one that swiftly acquired a particular importance for global Anglicanism, which had, until relatively recently, largely ignored the topic.

Giving form to this Anglican argument was a set of wider changes. The 1970s had been critical in shaping a gay identity, and the experiences of the 1980s – especially the AIDS crisis – had radicalized many who identified as gay.[39] Social attitudes were slow to shift: a poll in 1988 showed that over fifty per cent of those questioned were opposed to the legalization of homosexual relations.[40] At precisely the same time, however, the gay community was generating a series of increasingly successful lobbying groups. What the archbishop of Canterbury, George Carey, would in retrospect call 'The Challenge of Homosexuality' was becoming harder for the government, the churches and other authorities to ignore.[41]

This was also an inherently international movement. The largest and most prominent of the British organizations, Stonewall, was

[37] See, for instance, Resolution I.10.d, Lambeth 1998; Charlotte Methuen, 'The Lambeth Conference, Gender and Sexuality', *Theology* 123 (2020), 84–94, at 90.

[38] Sean Gill, *The Lesbian and Gay Christian Movement: Campaigning for Justice, Truth, and Love* (London and New York, 1998); Hunt, 'The Lesbian and Gay Christian Movement in Britain'.

[39] Chris Waters, 'The Homosexual as a Social Being in Britain, 1945–1968', in Brian Lewis, ed., *British Queer History: New Approaches and Perspectives* (Manchester and New York, 2013), 188–201, at 189; Weeks, *Coming Out*, 185.

[40] Weeks, *Sex, Politics, and Society*, 379.

[41] Carey, *Know the Truth*, 293–313.

established in 1989 and named after the riots in New York twenty years before that had sparked the gay liberation movement. Their more radical rivals, OutRage!, came together in 1990. OutRage! owed much to ACT-UP, the British faction of a global movement, and was closely modelled on the American campaigners Queer Nation.[42]

These groups differed in their methods and often disagreed. Stonewall sought to influence through high-level lobbying; OutRage! preferred protest and direct action. Yet both quite quickly began to focus much of their attention on one particular objective: the equalization of the age of consent. Although male homosexual acts in private had been decriminalized back in the 1960s, it had remained the case that such activity was illegal below the age of twenty-one, while heterosexual sex was permitted at sixteen. Huge efforts were made to achieve a change in the law, especially by Stonewall, who hoped to show that constructive engagement was more effective than the shock tactics of outfits like Outrage!.

It was rightly seen as a considerable setback to the movement – and to Stonewall in particular – when Parliament resolved on 21 February 1994 to reform, but not fully equalize the age of consent for male homosexual acts.[43] This was set instead at eighteen, two years above the legal age for heterosexual sex.[44] Sceptical of Stonewell's establishment credentials, doubtful of their likely success, and undoubtedly envious of their media profile, Outrage! was well prepared for this disappointment. Even before the vote, its members had agreed that, in the event that full equality was not achieved, they would 'announce a campaign of non-violent civil disobedience'.[45] They were also looking, as agreed at a meeting in June

[42] Kelly Kollman and Matthew Waites, 'United Kingdom: Changing Political Opportunity Structures, Policy Success, and Continuing Challenges for Lesbian, Gay, and Bisexual Movements', in Manon Tremblay, David Patternotte and Carol Johnson, eds, *The Lesbian and Gay Movement and the State: Comparative Insights into a Transformed Relationship* (Farnham, 2011), 181–96, at 186–9; Ian Lucas, *Outrage! An Oral History* (London and New York, 1998), 55–8, 63; Lucy Robinson, *Gay Men and the Left in Post-War Britain: How the Personal to Political* (Manchester 2008), 175–9.

[43] Lucas, *OutRage!*, 171–2; Robert Crampton, 'Inside Outing', *Sunday Times Magazine*, 20 May 1995, 135–8, at 136.

[44] Michael Brown, 'The Age of Consent: The Parliamentary Campaign in the UK to Lower the Age of Consent for Homosexual Acts', *Journal of Legislative Studies* 2 (1996), 1–7. There was no age of consent for female same sex relationships.

[45] Bishopsgate Institute, LGBTM 715, Outrage 1990–6, Minutes, 17 February 1994.

1994, to find ways to provide a 'counter-offensive to neutralize the Stonewall propaganda machine.'[46]

OutRage! were already pretty creative in their campaigns. They stripped off to protest against a ban on nude sunbathing in Hampstead Heath. They dressed up – sometimes in T-shirts adorned with provocative slogans, occasionally in drag – to disrupt events of which they disapproved. They were known for these 'zaps', as they were called, and frequently focused their ire on the establishment. In 1991, some members of OutRage!, calling themselves the Whores of Babylon, had resolved that one of their primary targets would be the Church of England, choosing it 'as the most prominent religious group in the UK.' To that end, they attempted to disrupt the enthronement of George Carey as archbishop of Canterbury just a few months later in April 1991, with a man dressed as the primate 'flaying a group of lesbians and gay men with a bull whip, then burning these martyrs at stakes.'[47]

The failure of the campaign to equalize the age of consent in 1994 gave renewed energy and impetus to this sort of protest. Inspired by developments in the United States, OutRage! wanted to force public figures to acknowledge their own, previously hidden, homosexuality. 'Outing', as it was called, was highly controversial. It was deeply disapproved of by more moderate organizations like Stonewall. It was guaranteed to attract attention, far more so than any zap.[48]

Once again, it turned out that Michael Turnbull was unlucky in his timing. OutRage! activists had planned to begin their campaign by 'outing' gay MPs, a beguiling target given that several known to be gay had voted against reforms to the age of consent. The revelations about the new bishop of Durham, however, seemed to provide the perfect opportunity to combine a zap with something even more assertive. His enthronement in October 1994 was consequently marked by a protest. Members of OutRage! wielded placards: 'From Glory Hole to Glory Be'; 'From Cottage to Cloister'; 'He Had Gay Sex But He Won't Allow Gay Clergy'. Peter Tatchell, a leading figure in the group, was described by a fellow member as

[46] Bishopsgate Institute, OUTRAGE/94, Minutes 1995[*sic*]–97, 23 June 1994.

[47] Bishopsgate Institute, OUTRAGE/28, CofE/George Carey, Methodists, 'Whores of Babylon', 3 March 1991; Lucas, *OutRage!*, 73, 75.

[48] Paul Reynolds, 'In Defence of Outing', in Paul Bagguley and Jeff Hearn, eds, *Transforming Politics: Power and Resistance* (London and New York, 1999), 260–76, at 263–4, 268–70; Robinson, *Gay Men and the Left*, 176.

'running towards the bishop like some sort of frightened rat.' He was rugby-tackled to the ground by the police, but not before he had been heard shouting: 'The bishop is a hypocrite. He condemns gay people but has gay sex.'[49] It was undeniably chaotic, but it was effective. Images of the zap found their way to the front pages of numerous newspapers and magazines.[50]

More momentous, though in some ways equally chaotic and certainly less widely noted, was something that had occurred the day before. At the University of Durham Union, a debate was staged on whether Bishop Turnbull should resign. His side won, and convincingly so. The Union affirmed its support of his position by 110 to 90, with 47 abstentions.[51] It turned out, however, to be a pyrrhic victory. In advance of the debate, Peter Tatchell had publicly announced that 'There are at least eight closeted homosexual bishops. Most of them are hypocrites.'[52] During the debate, another speaker named three of them. It was the first outing, as it were, for 'outing' in a British public forum.

The man who crossed this Rubicon was Sebastian Sandys. He had briefly been a Franciscan friar and then became a leading figure in the Sisters of Perpetual Indulgence: a group of gay men who dressed as nuns; who believed themselves, in fact, to be an international order of gay male nuns.[53] Sandys was, as such, usefully distant from those members of OutRage! who were still anxious about whether 'outing' was a sensible or even defensible tactic, but he was also not necessarily the ideal vehicle to convey authority. Moreover, his speech at the Durham Union was delivered too late to make the morning newspapers. Small wonder that this important event was less widely covered than the more ostensibly dramatic scenes outside Durham Cathedral the next day.[54]

49 LSE, HCA/TATCHELL, 1994/2; Reynolds, 'In Defence of Outing', 260; Lucas, *OutRage!*, 188–9.

50 LSE, HCA/TATCHELL/1994/2, contains copies of many. The relationship between press and campaigners will be among the themes discussed in George Severs, *Radical Acts: HIV/AIDS Activism in Late Twentieth-Century England* (London, 2024).

51 *Church of England Newspaper*, 28 October 1994, 1.

52 LSE, HCA/TATCHELL/1994/2, Press release, 17 October 1994.

53 Interview with Sebastian Sandys by Rebecca Odell, 19 October 2019, online at: <https://museum-collection.hackney.gov.uk/object-2018-56>, accessed 19 May 2022. See also Melissa M. Wilcox, *Queer Nation: Religion, Activism, and Serious Parody* (New York, 2018), esp. 2, 21.

54 Lucas, *OutRage!*, 188; Terry Sanderson, 'Vicars ruined as Rent Boys cruise the Street of Shame', *Gay Times* 195 (December 1994), 48–9.

Yet once 'outing' was out, everything changed. Peter Tatchell later observed that 'information about the closeted gay bishops came to us in torrents.'[55] In November 1994, both a press conference announcing the agenda for the forthcoming General Synod of the Church of England and the award of an honorary degree to Michael Turnbull enabled further pressure to be put on him and on the wider church. OutRage! protesters disrupted the press conference and picketed the degree ceremony. A placard at the latter read: 'Eight Gay Bishops! *Hypocrites!*'[56] An *Evening Standard* headline about the former simply reported: 'Shamed Rev under siege.'[57] The meeting of General Synod on 30 November provided further opportunities to draw attention to the issue. In a press release and on the picket line outside Church House in Westminster, OutRage! named no fewer than ten bishops – including Turnbull – whom it claimed were gay and hiding the fact.[58]

The effect of this disclosure was explosive and the media coverage extraordinary. Nor was the impact merely confined to the press. Although he denied there was any link between his decision and the OutRage! action, one of the ten bishops swiftly stepped down, retiring to a monastery at the age of fifty-nine.[59] Other bishops expressed a hitherto unsuspected interest in dialogue with the gay community. 'Following General Synod and the activities of OutRage!,' recorded a meeting of the Lesbian and Gay Christian Movement, 'the Standing Committee of Anglican Bishops would give consideration to the place of gay people in the Church.'[60] In March 1995, a retired bishop chose to come out voluntarily. 'The priesthood as a whole is a haven – no, an attraction for gay men,' he reflected.[61]

Not everyone was impressed by such developments. The novelist A. N. Wilson observed that, in his experience, 'most bishops would hardly register as sexual beings at all'.[62] Others were horrified to

55 Lucas, *OutRage!*, 190.
56 *Capital Gay*, 18 November 1994. Italics original.
57 *Evening Standard*, 16 November 1994.
58 Bishopsgate Institute, PTA/6, Peter Tatchell 1994, Press release, 30 November 1994.
59 Andrew Brown, 'Bishop in "Outing" Row retires to Monastery', *Independent*, 31 January 1995; *The Times*, 31 January 1995, 9.
60 LSE, HCA/LGCM/1/209/1, 10 January 1995.
61 Valerie Grove, 'I realised I loved him. I was in real turmoil', *The Times*, 10 March 1995, 16.
62 Bishopsgate Institute, OUTRAGE/41, Synod 1994, Press cutting.

witness what they thought was a move towards liberalization. sixty-four per cent of readers polled by the evangelical *Church of England Newspaper* in April 1995 agreed that the bishops were 'taking the Church in the direction of gay priests', with only twenty-five per cent believing the opposite was true.[63] Conservative figures seized on the contretemps as an opportunity to mobilize. One influential group announced that they planned to leave the Church of England unless it returned to what they saw as the traditional teaching on sexuality. 'We are talking peace, but preparing for war,' exclaimed a leading figure in the conservative pressure group Reform.[64] Large numbers of gay campaigners were ambivalent – if not hostile – about the whole affair, with many condemning OutRage!'s tactics and distancing themselves from any sort of 'outing' campaign whatsoever.[65] There were also splits within OutRage! itself. Although pleased that 'printed coverage of the action had been superb', one anxious member voiced his fear that 'the debate was going to move on to the politics of outing, rather than the issue of homosexuality in the church.'[66]

He was right to worry. Among those bishops who had been identified as gay by OutRage!, but not named in their list of ten announced at General Synod, was the bishop of London, David Hope. Nicknamed 'Ena the Terrible' when head of the Anglo-Catholic and famously gay-friendly seminary St Stephen's House in Oxford, Hope was known as a quiet supporter of gay priests. It was as such that Peter Tatchell hand-delivered a private letter to him on 30 December 1994. 'We believe that you are, or can be, a person of honesty and courage', Tatchell wrote. 'You have the potential to play a very special role, both morally and historically. It is our sincere hope that you will find the inner strength and conviction to realise the importance of *voluntarily* coming out as gay'.[67] Nothing happened for several months. Then, discovering that he was likely to become the focus of press interest, David Hope released the letter and made his own statement: 'I am not a sexually active person', he

[63] *Church of England Newspaper,* 13 April 1995, 1.
[64] *Church of England Newspaper*, 31 March 1995, 1.
[65] *Pink Paper,* 9 December 1994.
[66] Bishopsgate Institute, OUTRAGE/94, 1 December 1994.
[67] Bishopsgate Institute, PTA/6, 30 December 1994; *The Times*, 14 March 1995. Italics original.

declared. But nor was he gay: 'I am talking about being more ambiguous about my sexuality.'[68] Pictured on the front page of *The Times* 'clutching a radiantly golden cross', as one journalist put it, there was 'No doubt who was being cast as the martyr' in this story.[69]

David Hope's 'outing' was, in some respects, as ambiguous as his sexuality. He had not in fact been outed by OutRage! at all. It was the threat of the press, rather than the demands of the campaigners, that led to his disclosure.[70] What he disclosed was not homosexuality, but something else. For some in the gay press, this was evidence of his 'moral cowardice'. For the overwhelming majority of commentators, however, this apparent bullying was proof of just how unspeakable OutRage! had become.[71] Writing of Hope, the Executive Director of Stonewall – no less – called on *Times* readers to 'applaud his integrity and oppose the intimidation to which he has been subject.'[72]

In any event, the outing campaign was encountering other problems. Peter Tatchell promised to name two Roman Catholic bishops as gay, but no names ever emerged.[73] A list of MPs believed to be gay was drawn up, but then, fearing legal action, it was 'vetoed' and 'never issued'.[74] There were rumours that one Unionist MP had died of a heart attack after receiving a letter from OutRage!.[75] Tatchell, to be sure, claimed that 'Our plan has worked like a dream'.[76] OutRage! also continued to zap in all sorts of inventive ways.[77] Towards the end of 1995, David Jenkins, former bishop of Durham, emerged from retirement to defend 'outing'. 'Enforced hypocrisy', he said, 'especially within the Church is very worrying. If this action changes the symptoms of fear, it will have done a lot of good.'[78] But the truth was that David Hope's announcement ended this short-lived, if dramatic, campaign. For his part, Hope would soon be translated from London to become archbishop of York.

[68] *The Times*, 14 March 1995, 1.
[69] *Scotland on Sunday*, 19 March 1995.
[70] David Smith, 'Bishop of London, bounced out by the press, not by OutRage!', *Gay Times* 201 (June 1995), 26.
[71] Sanderson, 'Moral Cowardice', 57.
[72] *The Times*, 18 March 1995, 19.
[73] *Guardian*, 3 December 1994.
[74] LSE, HCA/TATCHELL/1995/9, 21 February 1995.
[75] Lucas, *OutRage!*, 199–201.
[76] *Pink Paper*, 21 April 1995; *LGCM Members Newsletter*, June 1995, 2–3.
[77] Lucas, *Outrage!*, 204–8.
[78] *Scotsman*, 3 November 1995.

The contrast between Hope, who spoke out, and Turnbull, who was outed, is in some respects a telling one. Hope took control of his story; Turnbull became the subject of other people's narratives. Hope went public, while Turnbull tried in vain to keep things private. The extent to which 'outing' was always about breaking down the barriers between the public and the private is undeniable. Writing 'In Defence of Outing' a few years after these events, one scholar described it in precisely those terms. 'Outing', he asserted, 'challenges the private/public divide … . It removes sexuality from the private'. Instead, 'sexuality becomes a subject of public discourse'.[79] In that sense, this whole episode bears out Lucy Robinson's contention that among the goals of the gay rights movement was to 'reconceptualize the relationship between the public and private', making 'the personal political'.[80]

Certainly, the countervailing desire to maintain strict boundaries helps explain the discomfort some commentators expressed about the whole affair. Initially, the *Church of England Newspaper* was unwilling even to name Turnbull's crime, describing it only as a 'public lavatory offence.'[81] To be sure, even this description assumed some knowledge of just what that might amount to. But it was revealing that, when asked, thirty-seven per cent of its readers disagreed with the proposition that there should be 'an open debate' on the issue of clerical homosexuality. Another reader wrote in, threatening to cancel his subscription because the newspaper was choosing to use the word 'gay'.[82] In an editorial about David Hope, *The Times* was equally clear – and entirely representative of the more mainstream press – in its condemnation of 'the pernicious assumption that sexuality is essentially a public matter'.[83]

Hope's open ambiguity posed two further questions: who was being outed and for what? He, for one, refused to accept that he was gay, but did admit he was not straightforwardly heterosexual. He asserted he was celibate, but recognized 'that there is a whole spectrum of experience out there'.[84] When asked how they knew that

[79] Reynolds, 'In Defence of Outing', 269.

[80] Lucy Robinson, 'The Bermondsey By-Election and Leftists Attitudes to Homosexuality', in Matthew McCormack, ed., *Public Men: Masculinity and Politics in Modern Britain* (Basingstoke, 2007), 165–86. See also Robinson, *Gay Men and the Left*, 154–64, 175–9.

[81] *Church of England Newspaper*, 30 September 1994, 1.

[82] *Church of England Newspaper*, 13 April 1995, 1 and 5 May 1995, 6.

[83] *The Times*, 14 March 1995, 5.

[84] *The Times*, 14 April 1995, 16.

Hope was gay, OutRage! activists were unable to provide any evidence; and, in any event, it was not at all clear what evidence could be produced definitively to substantiate someone's homosexuality. When asked whether it was 'actually more liberating' to accept the somewhat fluid definition of sexuality that Hope seemed to articulate, at least one member of OutRage! agreed, although he swiftly added that 'Leaders of society should give an example.'[85]

Something similar might have been said about Bishop Turnbull. With the possible exception of a curious – and ostensibly fictional – account of a young, ambitious, over-worked clergyman whose unhappy marriage was saved by Librium and the Church Army, he never gave any explanation for what happened in Hull to occasion his arrest.[86] When Turnbull wrote of 'an instinct we are ashamed of and try to keep under control', it was prayer rather than gay sex to which he referred.[87] Although convicted for a homosexual act, Bishop Turnbull denied being homosexual. Indeed, he asserted his heterosexuality, adducing as evidence the fact that he was married with three children.[88] For critics, this was simply further demonstration of his hypocrisy, but they struggled to prove that beyond reasonable doubt. At the Durham Union on the eve of the bishop's enthronement, Peter Tatchell sought to build up the case for the prosecution. '*How* is it possible for a man to get aroused with another man if he is *not* gay?' he asked. How, too, Tatchell wondered, would a straight man know how to find sex in a public lavatory? 'Only a *seasoned* gay man', he concluded, 'would know about the ins and outs of glory-holes.'[89]

Well, perhaps.[90] But Tatchell did not convince the majority of his audience that evening, and the difficulty of proving these charges conclusively was apparent in other people's comments too. Turnbull's

[85] Crampton, 'Inside Outing', 136. On the ongoing difficulty of overcoming binary distinctions, even within the gay rights movement, see Martha Robinson Rhodes, 'Bisexuality, Multiple-gender-attraction, and Gay Liberation Politics in the 1970s', *Twentieth Century British History* 32 (2021), 119–42.

[86] Turnbull, *God's Front Line*, 79–87. That the 'pace was unremitting' for Donald Coggan's chaplains is recognized in Margaret Pawley, *Donald Coggan, Servant of Christ* (London, 1987), 167.

[87] Michael Turnbull, *Learning to Pray* (London and Oxford, 1981), 2.

[88] *Church Times,* 30 September 1994, 1; *The Times*, 28 September 1994, 4.

[89] LSE, HCA/TATCHELL/1994/2, 21 October 1994. Italics original.

[90] Laud Humphreys, *Tearoom Trade: Impersonal Sex in Public Places* (New Brunswick, NJ, 2008), provides some evidence that might back up Tachell's inference. See also

defence, argued Richard Kirker, General Secretary of the Lesbian and Gay Christian Movement, was unconvincing: 'The fact he was married at the time, doesn't make him any more or less of a homosexual than he may be now.'[91] That was true. However, as his verbal confusion suggested, even Kirker seemed unclear whether the bishop should be seen as a homosexual at all.

This conceptual problem was made all the more intractable by the different ways in which sex, sexuality and personal identity were described. As I have argued elsewhere, there was a fundamental incompatibility between the ideas of gay rights activists and those of more conservative – and, especially, evangelical – Christians. Their disagreement was not just about the morality of homosexuality, but also about its definition.[92]

For conservatives, it was vitally important to distinguish between identity and behaviour. 'Nowhere does the Bible condemn homosexual orientation, homosexual feelings, or homosexual temptation', observed Nicky Gumbel, the driving force behind the evangelical Anglican Alpha course, in 1994. It was only 'homosexual practice', he went on, that was forbidden by the Christian faith.[93] For many gay people – whether Christian or not – such a distinction was anathema, however. Indeed, the process of 'coming out' was conceived of as one in which an individual achieved wholeness by bringing identity and practice together.[94] 'Coming out' as gay was, in that way, not unlike an evangelical conversion experience: 'a life-giving choice'; 'a reliving of Good Friday and Easter'; a decision 'to align oneself with the deeper reality and reject the everyday expectations of our world', as one preacher put it at the Lesbian and Gay Christian Movement annual meeting in 1994.[95] Stripped of its explicitly Christian trappings, this was the understanding of 'outing' that OutRage! advocated. Yet Bishop Turnbull was one of those who continued to

---

Paul Johnson, 'Ordinary Folk and Cottaging: Law, Morality, and Public Sex', *Journal of Law and Society* 34 (2007), 520–43, at 536.

91 *The Times*, 28 September 1994, 4.

92 William Whyte, 'Performance, Priesthood and Homosexuality', in Jane Garnett et al., *Redefining Christian Britain: Post-1945 Perspectives* (London, 2007), 84–91.

93 Nicky Gumbel, *Searching Issues* (Eastbourne, 1994), 79–84.

94 Richard Cleaver, *Know My Name: A Gay Liberation Theology* (Louisville, KY, 1995), viii, 32, 42; Weeks, *Coming Out*, 191.

95 LSE, HCA/LGCM/1/19/1, Bill Countryman, Address, 15 April 1994.

insist on a sharp distinction between an individual act and a personal identity. Hence, after all, his insistence that 'An admitted and open' gay lifestyle was 'incompatible with full-time ministry.'[96]

Was this hypocrisy? In many respects, it was something much more complex. Yet throughout the fevered few months of the 'outing' campaign, every complexity did tend to be reduced to an accusation of hypocrisy, and the roll call of hypocrites grew ever larger as a result. Within the church, it was not just those few bishops named by OutRage! who came to be condemned. The whole hierarchy was attacked for hypocrisy. Senior figures had known about Turnbull. They must also have known about other individuals. They preached a gospel of love, but punished loving homosexual partnerships.[97] 'Kiss, but don't tell,' was the 'approach adopted by a number of bishops,' as one writer put it.[98]

Increasingly, the attack from gay campaigners encompassed the church as a whole, as they argued that current practice compelled hypocrisy. 'Is it moral', asked Richard Kirker, of the Lesbian and Gay Christian Movement, 'to have a life in the closet when your professional duties involve upholding standards of honesty and integrity?'[99] 'Outing', claimed one of its originators, Sebastian Sandys, was 'the inevitable result of the Anglican inability to tell the truth.'[100] Not least of the ironies of this whole affair was the fact that their conservative opponents agreed completely; they just differed about the solution, preferring 'the re-imposition of clerical discipline' to the acceptance of homosexuality.[101]

It was not just the church that was beset by claims of hypocrisy. There was a widespread sense that the press was also playing a double game. The tabloids had a long and notorious history of 'outing' gay men.[102] Other, seemingly more respectable sources were far from blameless either. True, it was the *News of the World*'s revelations about Bishop Turnbull that sparked the whole furore. But it was the threat of exposure in the *Daily Telegraph* that prompted David

[96] Brown, 'Durham's next Bishop eschews Controversy'.
[97] LSE, HCA/TATCHELL/1995/9, John Jackson to George Carey, 3 January 1995.
[98] Gill, *The Lesbian and Gay Christian Movement*, 61.
[99] 'Better Blatant Than Latent?', *Movement* (Spring 1995), 8–9, at 8.
[100] Ibid.
[101] *Daily Telegraph*, 1 December 1994.
[102] Justin Bengry, 'Profit (F)Or the Public Good? Sensationalism, Homosexuality, and the Post-war Popular Press', *Media History* 20 (2014), 146–66, at 146–7, 152–4.

Hope to issue his statement.[103] Derek Rawcliffe, the one bishop who did choose to 'come out' as gay, even claimed to have been 'outed' by the *Church of England Newspaper* in 1993, although it is an index of his relative anonymity and the low readership of that particular publication that very few people appear to have noticed.[104] At the same time, for all this, there was a near-universal hostility from the press towards the campaign waged by OutRage!.[105] That the media 'outed', but at the same time condemned 'outing'; that some parts of it expressed horror at homosexuality and nonetheless profited from exposing homosexuals: all this looked somewhat hypocritical.[106] Even the left-leaning *Guardian* was complicit. It was both vociferous in its attacks on 'outing' and one of the very few papers to publish the names of the ten bishops who had been 'outed'.[107] 'Do I detect double-standards?', asked a columnist in the *Gay Times*.[108] Many people did.[109]

Still others discerned hypocrisy in the act of 'outing' itself. Here were gay campaigners seemingly victimizing other gay men. Here were activists who attacked the press, and yet were utterly dependent on them, for, as one well-informed and sympathetic journalist noted, 'without the aid of the mass media, outing would be almost totally ineffective.'[110] The figure of the OutRage! campaigner Peter Tatchell became totemic in that respect. He had come to public prominence as the Labour candidate in a notoriously nasty by-election in Bermondsey in 1983. Not least, his sexuality had been used against him both by political opponents and by the right-wing media.[111] Nonetheless, and despite the urging of the gay press,

[103] Smith, 'Bishop of London', 26.

[104] Derek Rawcliffe, 'A Gay Bishop's Experience', in Cristina Sumner, ed., *Reconsider: A Response to* Issues in Human Sexuality *and a Plea to the Church to Deal Boldly with Sexual Ethics* (London, 1995), 18–20, at 18. Rawcliffe, who had been bishop of Glasgow and Galloway in the Scottish Episcopal Church, was at that time in retirement honorary assistant bishop in the diocese of Ripon.

[105] Gill, *The Lesbian and Gay Christian Movement*, 101.

[106] Sanderson, *Mediawatch*, 86–212.

[107] *Guardian*, 2 December 1994.

[108] Sanderson, 'De-frocks Tactics', 41.

[109] See also 'Better Blatant Than Latent?', 8.

[110] Terry Sanderson, 'Outing: The Press Can, Gays, Can't', *Independent on Sunday*, 4 December 1994.

[111] Paul Bloomfield, 'Labour's Liberalism: Gay Rights and Video Nasties', in Jonathan Davis and Rohan McWilliams, eds, *Labour and the Left in the 1980s* (Manchester and New York, 2018), 69–89, at 73–4; Ivor Crewe and Anthony King, *SDP: The Birth*

Tatchell chose not to 'come out' publicly at the time.[112] 'In our hearts,' he wrote afterwards, 'most of us felt that to be open and honest about my sexuality was ideally the best policy. However, we were not in an ideal situation'.[113] The glaring contradiction between his decision to dissemble in 1983, and his insistence that anyone in public life was fair game for 'outing' just over a decade later, proved irresistible for his opponents. *The Sun* was only just a little bit ruder than the others in claiming that Tatchell had 'squealed like a stuck pig' when his own sexuality was revealed, but was now backing 'a spiteful campaign' to do just the same to others.[114] Nor was it only the right-wing media that saw Peter Tatchell in this way. Other gay rights campaigners were equally ambivalent about his record and its implications for his subsequent plans. They, too, dubbed him 'a hypocrite'.[115]

Writing as Bishop Hope's adroit media management drew the 'outing' campaign to its close, the conservative columnist Janet Daley cheerfully observed that 'hypocrisy has had a good week'. 'Single-handedly,' she went on, Peter Tatchell had 'rehabilitated it as a minor virtue – or, at least, as the most benign of vices.'[116] This was to go too far. But Daley was not wrong to suggest that, in some respects, any campaign based primarily on the accusation of hypocrisy was always vulnerable to failure. For her, this was because the English had never placed much value on directness and frank speech. There was, perhaps, something in that. Certainly, there was a long tradition of defining hypocrisy as a characteristic English trait.[117] Still more, the universality of the accusation rendered it less and less compelling. If everyone was a hypocrite, then no-one was. In

and Death of the Social Democratic Party (Oxford, 1995), 192; Jonathan Dollimore, *Sexual Dissidence* (Oxford, 1981), 234–7; Robinson, 'The Bermondsey By-Election', reprinted in eadem, *Gay Men and the Left*, 154–84.

112 Stephen Brooke, *Sexual Politics: Sexuality, Family Planning, and the British Left from the 1880s to the Present Day* (Oxford, 2011), 242; Robinson, 'The Bermondsey By-Election', 180.

113 Peter Tatchell, *The Battle for Bermondsey* (London, 1983), 63.

114 Sanderson, 'Outing'.

115 Robinson, 'The Bermondsey By-Election', 181.

116 Janet Daley, 'Oh Why can't the English Learn to Speak – Straightforwardly', *The Times*, 16 March 1995, 16.

117 Peter Mandler, *The English National Character: The History of an Idea from Edmund Burke to Tony Blair* (New Haven, CT, and London, 2006), 57, 190.

such a context, indeed, it could come to seem that hypocrisy hardly mattered; or, as Daley argued, it might even be better than 'full-frontal honesty', enabling 'you to treat people decently even when you feel no affection for them.'[118]

All this begs the question of why hypocrisy had become such a point of contention in the mid-1990s. To some degree, recourse to that register was almost inevitable. As we have seen, arguments about sexuality in the church necessarily raised issues about the relationship between the public and the private, the institution and the individual, the claims of authority and the imperatives of personal identity. These discussions inevitably drew on the language of hypocrisy and the tensions between being and seeming to be.[119] It was a tendency heightened by the fact that hypocrisy had always played such an important part in debates within and about the Church. The danger of hypocrisy had scriptural authority.[120] Many church people would also have been aware of the long-standing popular assumption that Christians were more, rather than less, likely to be hypocrites.[121]

In that respect, it is illuminating to compare the rhetoric employed by OutRage! when speaking about clergy and when attempting to 'out' politicians. The gravest accusation levelled at the church throughout the campaign was always that of hypocrisy. When communicating with MPs they believed to be gay, however, OutRage! avoided this term and focused instead on the language of 'honesty'.[122] It was a deliberate tactic from a group that always attempted 'to use the Church's own language and symbolism against itself.'[123] It was also an adroit move. 'This hypocrisy we've been accused of,' observed one 'senior figure' within the Church of England, 'we've got to take it very seriously.'[124]

More than that, Janet Daley was right to see this emphasis on hypocrisy as a by-product of something more particular and period-

118 Daley, 'Oh Why can't the English Learn to Speak'.

119 Reynolds, 'In Defence of Outing', 268.

120 Matt. 23: 15, 33, is especially damning, in every sense. Condemning hypocrisy, Jesus exclaims, 'You snakes, you brood of vipers! How can you escape being sentenced to hell?' [NRSV].

121 Sarah Williams, *Religious Belief and Popular Culture in Southwark, c.1880–1939* (Oxford, 1999), 113–15.

122 Bishopsgate Institute, PTA/7, Letter from 'Outrage!' to 'Nigel Shirtlifter', 27 January 1995.

123 Lucas, *Outrage!*, 75.

124 *Church of England Newspaper*, 11 November 1994, 1.

specific: what she termed an 'ethic' that owed its origins to the 1960s.[125] Both the gay rights movement and the development of much contemporary Christian thought had their origins in that decade and the emphasis on ideas about authenticity that it helped bring to birth.[126] As Bernice Martin was perhaps the first to observe, it was indeed in the 1960s that a revival of Romanticism brought about an 'expressive revolution': one that placed a premium on self-discovery and self-realization.[127] Living authentically – becoming truly one's real self – increasingly became understood as one of the chief goals of a good life.

This 'ethic of authenticity', as Charles Taylor has argued, did not mean abandoning collective identities; rather, it required the individual to choose the groups they would join and the identities they would assume with care.[128] 'Coming out involved a struggle for authenticity,' as Steven Seidman and Chet Meeks have observed.[129] So, for that matter, did the choice of religious life. Some, of course, chose both.[130] Indeed, no one in this story had a single identity. There was never only one way of being authentic, and there was always the possibility of being perceived as something rather less. The pursuit of authenticity, in other words, provoked many questions and provided few, if any, definitive answers.

Representing the conjuncture of long-standing anxieties within the church about hypocrisy, newer ideas about the moral imperative to be true to oneself, and a short-lived upsurge in gay liberationist activism,

[125] Daley, 'Oh Why can't the English Learn to Speak', 16.

[126] Garnett et al., *Redefining Christian Britain*, 12, 84–91. See also Sam Brewitt-Taylor, *Christian Radicalism in the Church of England and the Invention of the British Sixties, 1957–1970: The Hope of a World Transformed* (Oxford, 2018), 178–202.

[127] Bernice Martin, *Sociology of Contemporary Cultural Change* (Harmondsworth, 1981), 15, 184. The term was one she borrowed from Talcott Parsons: see Bryan S. Turner, 'Talcott Parsons's Sociology of Religion and the Expressive Revolution: The Problem of Western Individualism', *Journal of Classical Sociology* 5 (2005) 303–18.

[128] Charles Taylor, *The Ethics of Authenticity* (Cambridge, MA, and London, 1991), esp. 81–92.

[129] Steven Seidman and Chet Meeks, 'The Politics of Authenticity: Civic Individualism and the Cultural Roots of Gay Normalization', *Cultural Sociology* 5 (2011), 519–36, at 527. Although a U.S. study, the themes are recognizable from a British perspective.

[130] Andrew Yip, 'The Self as the Basis of Religious Faith: Spirituality of Gay, Lesbian, and Bisexual Christians', in Grace Davie, Linda Woodhead and Paul Heelas, eds, *Predicting Religion: Mainstream and Margins in the West* (London, 2003), 135–46. For an interesting Australian account, see Bronwyn Fielder and Douglas Ezzy, *Lesbian, Gay, Bisexual, and Transgender Christians: Queer Christians, Authentic Selves* (London, 2018), 2.

the 'outing' campaign was consequently forced to contend with an array of ambiguity and potential contradiction.[131] In that sense, Bishop Turnbull's experience in Hull in 1968 is a good image of this unresolved dilemma. Here was a seemingly ordinary man doing something unexpected in the city from where Philip Larkin watched the sexual revolution. Here was a single surprising act in a year of global upheaval and rebellion. Here was an unanswered mystery that perhaps even he could not quite explain himself.[132]

[131] Michael Lovelock, *Reality TV and Queer Identities* (London, 2019), 33–62. See also Seidman and Meeks, 'The Politics of Authenticity', 519–36.

[132] On the unspoken and the intersection of religion and queer history, see George Severs, 'Reticence and the Queer Past', *Oral History* 48 (2020), 45–56, esp. 50–1.

Corrigenda

CORRIGENDUM

Ministering to Body and Soul: Medical Missions and the Jewish Community in Nineteenth-Century London – CORRIGENDUM

Jemima Jarman

https://doi.org/10.1017/stc.2022.13 Published online by Cambridge University Press: 08 June 2022

The author apologises that upon publication the funding information for Consortium of the Arts and Humanities South East was not included and should have read:

Acknowledgments
This work was supported by the AHRC [AH/R012806/1]
The online version of this article has been updated

REFERENCE

Jarman, J. (2022). Ministering to Body and Soul: Medical Missions and the Jewish Community in Nineteenth-Century London. *Studies in Church History*, 58, 262–283. doi:10.1017/stc.2022.13

doi: 10.1017/stc.2022.24

CORRIGENDUM

Unbelief, the Senses and the Body in Nicholas Bownde's *The vnbeleefe of S. Thomas* (1608) – CORRIGENDUM

Patrick S. McGhee

DOI: https://doi.org/10.1017/stc.2015.15 Published online by Cambridge University Press: 16 June 2016

This article was updated after publication at the author's request in order to remove personal data

The online version of this article has been updated.

REFERENCE

McGhee, P. (2016). Unbelief, the Senses and the Body in Nicholas Bownde's The vnbeleefe of S. Thomas (1608). *Studies in Church History*, 52, 266-282. doi:10.1017/stc.2015.15

doi: 10.1017/stc.2023.1

CORRIGENDUM

Pain as a Spiritual Barometer of Health: A Sign of Divine Love, 1780–1850 – CORRIGENDUM

Angela Platt

DOI: https://doi.org/10.1017/stc.2022.10 Published online by Cambridge University Press: 08 June 2022

Upon publication of *Platt A, 2022*, the line on page 213 incorrectly lists the name Joseph instead of Jonathan

The correct line should read 'On 13 December 1842, Hannah Backhouse wrote a letter to Maria Fox lamenting the death of her beloved husband, Jonathan'

REFERENCE

Platt, A. (2022). Pain as a Spiritual Barometer of Health: A Sign of Divine Love, 1780–1850. *Studies in Church History*, 58, 196–216. doi:10.1017/stc.2022.10

Studies in Church History 60 (2024), 560
doi: 10.1017/stc.2024.27